DK

B

OF

S

A

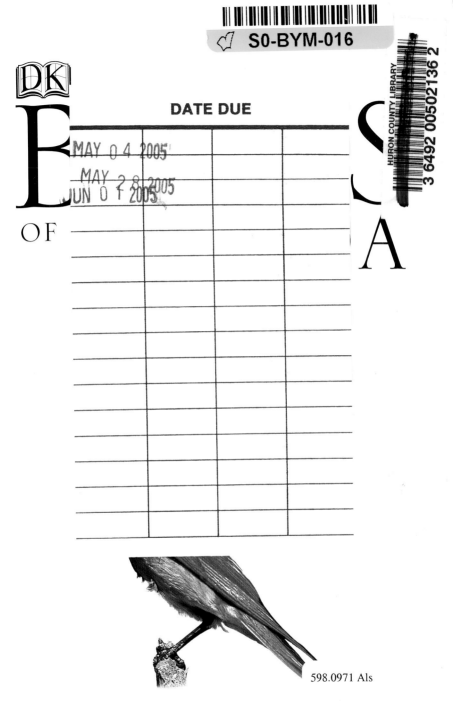

Alsop, F.
Birds of Canada field guide.

PRICE: $30.00 (3559/wi)

BIRDS
OF CANADA
FIELD GUIDE

Fred J. Alsop III

Editor-in-Chief Russell Greenberg, PhD

Editor, Canada Julia Roles
Senior Editor Jill Hamilton
Art Director Tina Vaughan
Production Heather Hughes, Luca Frassinetti

Original edition created by
Southern Lights Custom
Publishing

This edition produced by Dorling Kindersley India Limited
Managing Art Editor Aparna Sharma
DTP Designer Balwant Singh

Canadian Edition, 2005
Copyright 2001, 2002, 2004, 2005 Dorling Kindersley Limited

Dorling Kindersley is represented in Canada by
Tourmaline Editions Inc,
662 King Street West, Suite 304
Toronto, Ontario M5V 1M7

Library and Archives Canada Cataloguing in Publication

Alsop, Fred
Birds of Canada field guide / Fred Alsop III. -- Canadian ed.

Includes index.
ISBN 1-55363-046-7

1. Birds--Canada--Identification. I. Title.

QL685.A47 2005   598'.0971   C2004-906451-7

Color reproduction by Colourscan, Singapore.
Printed and bound in China by South China Printing Co. Ltd.

05 06 07 08 6 5 4 3 2 1

Discover more at
www.dk.com

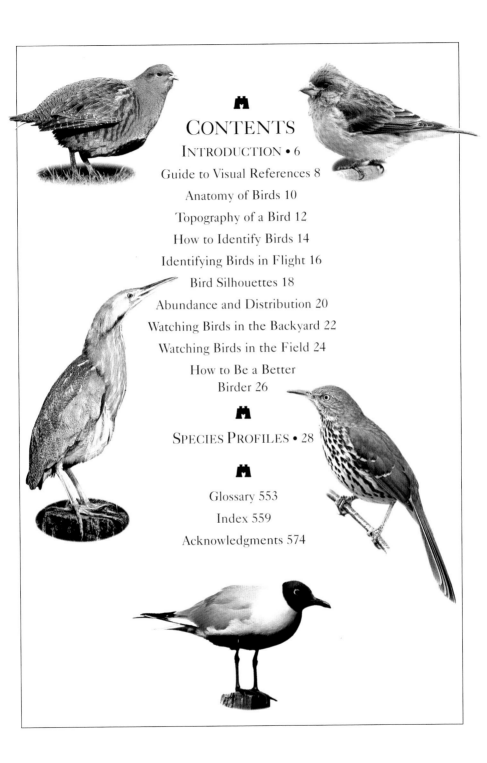

CONTENTS

INTRODUCTION

Written for the novice as well as the experienced birder, this book showcases in individual page profiles 524 species of birds that occur in Canada. These species can be found in a wide variety of habitats, including spectacular mountain ranges; extensive grasslands; deciduous, coniferous, and pine

The CANADA GOOSE can be found almost anywhere in North America at some point during the year.

forests; tundra; glaciers; and ice fields. Inhabiting this vast area are millions of individual birds.

Many birdwatchers practice their hobby close to their own backyards. They learn to recognize the species they see most often and occasionally identify a "new" species for the yard, perhaps even photograph the birds they see. Some are so keen that they travel throughout Canada identifying as many species as they can, often covering many kilometers on short notice to observe a newly discovered vagrant.

Not even the most ardent birder has seen all of the species that have been recorded in Canada. But that is part of the fun and challenge of birding. It holds something for all levels of interest, and the amateur birder stands as much chance as the professional of making a discovery that sheds important light on the field of ornithology.

FINDING YOUR BIRD

To find a bird, scan the pages of the book, or look up its scientific or common name in the index. The species are in taxonomic order, beginning with the non-passerines such as grebes, ducks, hawks, owls, doves, hummingbirds, and woodpeckers. They are followed by the passerines, the perching or songbirds. The species profiles will help you identify a bird as well as learn about its natural history.

RED-NECKED GREBE (non-passerine)
Birds that do not perch and sing are in the first part of this book.

TOWNSEND'S WARBLER (passerine)
Birds that do perch and sing are in the second part of this book.

Scientific family name •

Scientific name of species •

Average length from tip of bill to tip of tail •

Average length between tips of open wings •

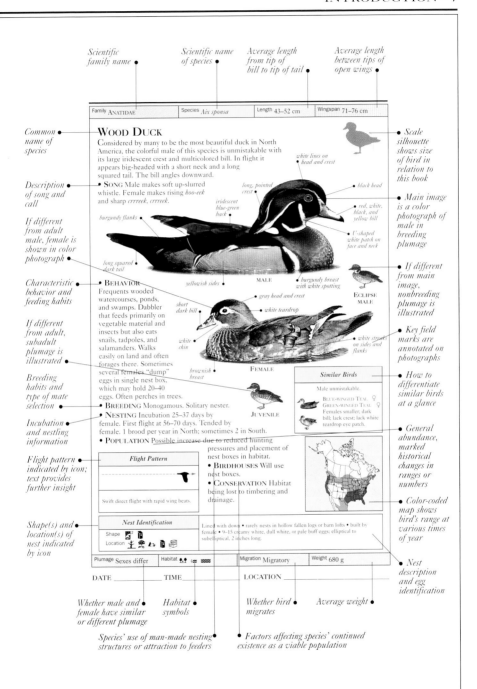

| Family ANATIDAE | Species *Aix sponsa* | Length 43–52 cm | Wingspan 71–76 cm |

Common • name of species

WOOD DUCK

Considered by many to be the most beautiful duck in North America, the colorful male of this species is unmistakable with its large iridescent crest and multicolored bill. In flight it appears big-headed with a short neck and a long squared tail. The bill angles downward.

Description • of song and call

• **SONG** Male makes soft up-slurred whistle. Female makes rising *hoo-eek* and sharp *crrreek, crrreek.*

If different from adult male, female is shown in color photograph •

Characteristic • behavior and feeding habits

If different from adult, subadult plumage is illustrated •

Breeding habits and type of mate selection •

Incubation • and nestling information

• **BEHAVIOR** Frequents wooded watercourses, ponds, and swamps. Dabbler that feeds primarily on vegetable material and insects but also eats snails, tadpoles, and salamanders. Walks easily on land and often forages there. Sometimes several females "dump" eggs in single nest box, which may hold 20–40 eggs. Often perches in trees.

• **BREEDING** Monogamous. Solitary nester.

• **NESTING** Incubation 25–37 days by female. First flight at 56–70 days. Tended by female. 1 brood per year in North; sometimes 2 in South.

• **POPULATION** Possible increase due to reduced hunting pressures and placement of nest boxes in habitat.

• **BIRDHOUSES** Will use nest boxes.

• **CONSERVATION** Habitat being lost to timbering and drainage.

Flight pattern • indicated by icon; text provides further insight

Shape(s) and • location(s) of nest indicated by icon

white lines on head and crest
long, pointed crest
iridescent blue-green back
burgundy flanks
long squared dark tail
yellowish sides
MALE

black head
red, white, black, and yellow bill
U-shaped white patch on face and neck
burgundy breast with white spotting

ECLIPSE MALE

gray head and crest
short dark bill
white teardrop
white chin
brownish breast
FEMALE
white streaks on sides and flanks

JUVENILE

Flight Pattern

Swift direct flight with rapid wing beats.

Nest Identification

Shape 🔺
Location 🌿🐚⚘🏠

Lined with down • rarely nests in hollow fallen logs or barn lofts • built by female • 9–15 creamy white, dull white, or pale buff eggs; elliptical to subelliptical, 2 inches long.

| Plumage Sexes differ | Habitat 🦆🌾〰️ | Migration Migratory | Weight 680 g |

DATE _____ TIME _____ LOCATION _____

Scale • silhouette shows size of bird in relation to this book

• Main image is a color photograph of male in breeding plumage

• If different from main image, nonbreeding plumage is illustrated

• Key field marks are annotated on photographs

Similar Birds

Male unmistakable.

BLUE-WINGED TEAL ♀
GREEN-WINGED TEAL ♀
Females smaller; dark bill; lack crest; lack white teardrop eye patch.

• How to differentiate similar birds at a glance

• General abundance, marked historical changes in ranges or numbers

• Color-coded map shows bird's range at various times of year

• Nest description and egg identification

Whether male and • female have similar or different plumage

Habitat • symbols

Whether bird • migrates

Average weight •

Species' use of man-made nesting• structures or attraction to feeders

• Factors affecting species' continued existence as a viable population

GUIDE TO VISUAL REFERENCES

PHOTOGRAPHS

Because users of this guide will be viewing these birds in backyards, woodlands, and other natural environments, realistic photographs are used as visual reference. Some rare and seldom-photographed species are illustrated. Unless otherwise noted, the primary image shows the male bird in breeding plumage. If the adult female has significantly different plumage from the male a second image depicts the female in breeding plumage. If field marks are not visible in a photograph they are described in the accompanying text.

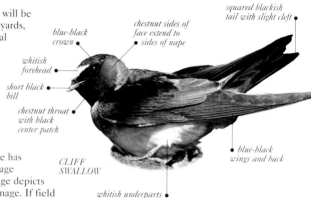

squared blackish tail with slight cleft

chestnut sides of face extend to sides of nape

blue-black crown

whitish forehead

short black bill

chestnut throat with black center patch

blue-black wings and back

CLIFF SWALLOW

whitish underparts with dusky gray-brown sides and flanks

ILLUSTRATIONS

Many birds also have other plumages, including the winter plumage, which are depicted in illustrations. The plumage of the immature if different from both adults also is illustrated. Some species have different color morphs, which are also illustrated.

LIGHT MORPH JUVENILE   **WINTER PLUMAGE**   **WHITE MORPH**

SIMILAR BIRDS

In many cases it can be difficult to distinguish between certain birds in the field. Thus species accounts feature a list of similar birds with accompanying text that identifies distinct features and behavior that clearly set them apart. Male and female symbols indicate the sex of the bird that could be mistaken for the species that is being profiled.

Similar Birds
CAVE SWALLOW Pale cinnamon-buff throat; cinnamon forehead; richer cinnamon-rust rump.

DISTRIBUTION MAP

Each species profile has a map showing where the bird is likely to be seen either all year long (permanent resident), in the breeding season (summer resident), or in the winter (winter resident). The maps depict only those parts of each species' range within North America and up to approximately 160 km offshore north of central Mexico to the northern borders of Canada.

 permanent resident   summer resident   winter resident

SCALE SILHOUETTES
These show the silhouette of the bird overlaid proportionally on a copy of this book.

NEST IDENTIFICATION
The Nest Identification box provides icons describing nest shape and location.

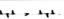

Flight Pattern	

Swift graceful flight alternating several deep, rapid wing beats with long elliptical glides with sharp sweeping upturns at the end. Soars on thermals and updrafts.

FLIGHT PATTERN
Each bird's flight pattern is shown in its species profile by an icon. For more information on flight patterns, see page 16.

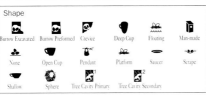

Nest Identification	Pellets of clay or mud, with lining of grasses, down, and feathers • usually under eaves of buildings or under dams or bridges; sometimes on ridges of canyons; rarely on trunk of conifer tree under overhanging branch • built by both sexes • 3–6 white, cream, or pinkish eggs, marked with browns; oval to long oval, 2.0 x 1.3 cm.
Shape	
Location	

Shape

Burrow Excavated	Burrow Preformed	Crevice	Deep Cup	Floating	Man-made
None	Open Cup	Pendant	Platform	Saucer	Scrape
Shallow	Sphere	Tree Cavity Primary	Tree Cavity Secondary		

Location

Bank	Building	Bridge	Cave	Chimney	Cliff	Conifer
Decidous	Floating	Grass	Gravel Roof	Hollow Log	Man-made	Pebbles
Reed/Cattails	Shrub	Snag	Bare Soil	Stump		

HABITAT

Habitat

At the bottom of each species account is a set of icons representing all the habitat types in the order in which the bird is found, from the most to the least likely.

forest: coniferous, broadleaf, temperate, or tropical

open forest; more space between the trees, tundra forest, semiopen areas

forest edge, oak and riparian

grassland with scattered trees (includes farmland, citrus groves, orchards)

bushes, shrubs, thickets and undergrowth; tropical lowland

areas of scrub vegetation, frequently with thorns

open landscapes: grassland, tundra, savanna, coastal ponds/sloughs – salt, brackish or freshwater, coastal marshes, coastal wetlands, salt marshes, prairie potholes

semidesert

desert

lakes, rivers and vicinity, sandspits, mudflats, ponds

upland streams and vicinity

open sea, low flat islands

rocky or sandy seashore, bay islands, coastal islands, shallow coastal habitats, coastal bays, coastal mangroves, tidal flats, sand spits, mudflats

freshwater marshes, swamps

rocky places or cliffs (both on the coast and inland)

mountains, wooded canyons

ANATOMY OF BIRDS

Birds are the most diverse terrestrial vertebrates with more than 9,800 extant species. Mammals are the only other homeothermic group with whom they share the planet. Yet, although mammal species number less than half that of birds, the mammals are much more varied in body shape and size. Mammals vary in form from primates to giraffes to armadillos, with specialists in running, hopping, flying, swimming, burrowing, digging, and climbing. Birds, however, all look like birds – with the same basic architecture, a body shape dictated by the demands of flight.

FEATHERS

Birds have three basic types of feathers: down, contour, and flight (wing and tail) feathers. Down feathers are next to the bird's skin for insulation. The contour is the most commonly recognized feather and the one that covers most of the bird's body. Typical contour feathers consist of a central shaft or quill and the flattened portion or vane. Contour feathers that extend beyond the wings and tail are the flight feathers.

DOWN

CONTOUR

FLIGHT
(WING AND TAIL)

BONES

In most species both the wings and the legs must be strong enough to transport the full weight of the bird, yet light enough to fly. Some bones have been fused and some bear internal struts. Ribs are overlapped for strength; others are hollowed, thinned, and reduced in numbers for lightness. In flying birds, and those flightless birds like penguins that use flipperlike forelimbs to "fly" under-water, the sternum, or breastbone, bears a thin knifelike keel to which the large flight muscles of the breast, the pectoral muscles, are attached.

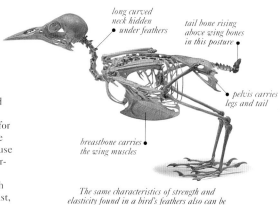

long curved neck hidden under feathers

tail bone rising above wing bones in this posture

pelvis carries legs and tail

breastbone carries the wing muscles

The same characteristics of strength and elasticity found in a bird's feathers also can be found in the anatomy of its skeleton.

BILLS

Birds' bills are composed of a horny sheath overlying a bony core. The entire lightweight structure has evolved in countless ways to the specialized needs of its owner, from seed-cracking to nectar probing and from fish-catching to fruit-picking. Birds also use their bills to build nests, preen, and court. Bills may change in size and/or color in breeding season.

The WHITE-FACED IBIS uses its decurved bill to probe for food such as crayfish in marshes.

The EVENING GROSBEAK uses its conical bill to crunch seeds.

The RUBY-THROATED HUMMINGBIRD uses its long needlelike bill to probe into flowers for nectar.

The RED CROSSBILL's bill features mandibles crossed at the tips that are ideal for digging the seeds out of pinecones.

LEGS AND FEET

The legs of birds are thin, strong, and springy, and in most species lack feathers on their distal parts where they are instead covered with scales. Muscles, which are concentrated on the portion of the leg nearest the body, control the extremities with a series of tendons. Toes generally number four with three forward and one opposable toe pointed backward, but some birds have only three. Toes are covered by scales and have claws at their tips which in birds of prey are enlarged into strong talons.

The AMERICAN ROBIN has a typical bird's foot: four toes with three forward and one back.

Some, like the HAIRY WOODPECKER, have two toes forward and two back.

The MALLARD has three webbed toes and one vestigial toe in back.

The DOUBLE-CRESTED CORMORANT has four webbed toes.

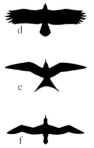

The BALD EAGLE has claws enlarged and elongated into talons.

WINGS AND TAILS

The shapes of wings and tails are an adaptation to where and how a bird flies. Look carefully at flight silhouettes: forest raptors (a) have rounded wings for living in dense vegetation; swallows (b) have narrow tapering wings. The tapering wings and narrow tail of a falcon (c) contrast with the broad splayed wings and broad tail of an eagle (d), which allow an eagle to soar. Terns (e) have long elegant wings; albatross wings (f) are very long, with an extended inner section for flying over water like a sailplane.

TOPOGRAPHY OF A BIRD

As you consult the species profiles in this book you will encounter a number of ornithological terms that describe the "landscape," or groups of feathers, of a bird's body. Learning these terms will help you use your field guide and, when you look at living birds, prompt you to see more detail with each sighting.

TIPS FOR THE FIELD

1. Start by looking at the bird's head. Note its bill and the markings on its face.
2. Get a feel for the bird's overall shape and size and note body markings.
3. Note shapes and markings of tail and wings.
4. Watch it fly and note markings visible in flight.

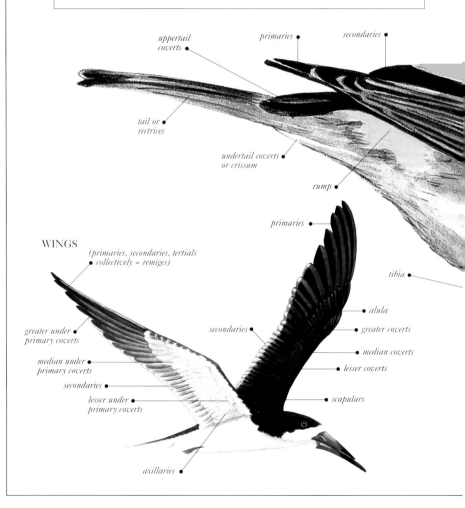

primaries

secondaries

uppertail coverts

tail or rectrices

undertail coverts or crissum

rump

primaries

WINGS
(primaries, secondaries, tertials collectively = remiges)

tibia

greater under primary coverts

median under primary coverts

secondaries

lesser under primary coverts

secondaries

alula

greater coverts

median coverts

lesser coverts

scapulars

axillaries

HEAD

lateral crown stripe

median crown stripe

supraloral area

supercilium (superciliary stripe)

lore

mustache

submustachial stripe

malar stripe

postocular stripe

ear patch (auricular)

crown

ear covert or auricular

nape

back

tertials

forehead

lore

upper mandible

lower mandible

chin

throat

side of neck

breast

scapulars

side

belly

tarsus or tibiotarsus

flank

HOW TO IDENTIFY BIRDS

Birds that come to backyard feeders often stay long enough for you to study them in detail, but not all birds are so cooperative and often a fleeting glimpse is all you get. Learn to get the best look you can under the conditions and to see the entire bird well. First impressions of a bird, especially a new species for you, will give you clues for comparing it with birds you already know. What you are looking for are field marks, those physical clues that include size, shape, color patterns, and behavior, and also the habitat the bird is in and the sounds it may make.

Learn to routinely and quickly look at the details of the head; markings on the body, wings, and tail; and the shapes of the bird's parts.

HEAD
Is the crown:

| striped | streaked | capped | crested |

Look for other markings on the face such as:

| superciliary stripes | eye lines | eye rings | spectacles |

| mustache marks | malar marks | ear patches | a mask through the eye |

BODY PLUMAGE
Are the underparts:

| plain and unmarked | streaked | spotted |

TAIL
Is the tail:

| forked | rounded | fan-shaped | wedge-shaped | pointed |

| notched | square | short | long |

MARKINGS
Does it have distinctive wing or tail markings such as:

| bars | bands | spots | contrasting colors |

BILL
Is the bill:

| cone-shaped | needlelike | hooked | decurved | spatulate | long or short |

SONG
Many expert birders rely on their ears as much as their eyes to identify birds. Any of the many cassette tapes, CDs, or videos can help you learn the songs, calls, and other sounds birds make.

BEHAVIOR
The behavior of the bird will also provide clues to its identity. Does it bob, wag, or pump its tail either up and down or back and forth? Note its flight pattern. Does it back down a tree or go headfirst?

IDENTIFYING BIRDS IN FLIGHT

How a bird flies – the speed of the wing stroke as well as the pattern – can often help you recognize a species.

Direct – steady flight with regular wing beats, along a constant line; typical of most species, including waterfowl, herons, doves, crows, shorebirds, and many songbirds.

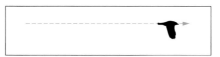

Dynamic soaring – glides over water "downhill" with the wind to its back and when close to the surface quickly turns 180 degrees back into the wind. There the bird is lifted back up to near the original height upon which it turns back and soars "downhill" again. Characteristic of many pelagic species, including albatrosses, shearwaters, and petrels.

Flap and glide – alternates a burst of several wing beats with a short or long level glide. Many birds of prey, both hawks and owls, use this flight pattern as do Black Vultures, ibis, and pelicans.

Flightless – many species living in environments free of predators have given up the energy-demanding activity of flight. The only flightless Canadian species, the Great Auk, was hunted to extinction in 1844.

Glide – wings are held fully or partially extended as the bird loses altitude. Many birds glide down to a landing, or from perch to perch. Hawks may glide from the top of one thermal to the bottom of the next in migration.

Hawking – flying up from the ground or down from an aerial perch to seize a flying insect and looping back down to the same or nearby perch. Characteristic of flycatchers and other small, active insect-eating birds such as warblers, the Cedar Waxwing, and several species of woodpeckers.

Hovering – rapid wingbeats while the bird remains suspended in one spot over the ground or water. Typical of hummingbirds, kingfishers, American Kestrel, Osprey, Rough-legged Hawk, and many small birds that hover briefly to glean food from vegetation.

Mothlike – an erratic, sometimes bouncy, slow flight seen in nightjars, a few storm-petrels, and in the display flights of some small birds.

Skims – the flight pattern in which the bird flies a steady course with its lower mandible cleaving the surface of still water as it feeds.

Static soaring – requires about a twentieth of the energy of flapping flight. Birds soar on rising heated columns of air, thermals, or on deflected currents and updrafts. Large hawks, eagles, vultures, storks, White Pelicans, and gulls soar this way.

Straight line formation – an energy-saving style of flight used by some larger birds such as cormorants, pelicans, ibis, some waterfowl, and others. Birds may fly one behind the other, or abreast as do some scoters and eiders.

Undulating – some small birds conserve energy by rising on one or more wing beats and then folding the wings to the body and swooping down to the next wing beat. Characteristic of woodpeckers, finches, and chickadees.

V formation – an energy-saving flight style used by some larger birds, including ducks, geese, cranes, and cormorants.

Zigzag – a pattern used by birds flushed from the ground as a way to elude predators. The Common Snipe and several species of quail are good examples.

BIRD SILHOUETTES

The first step in identifying a bird is to narrow down the possibilities to one or two families. Most species in a family share a unique combination of physical traits, such as the size and shape of the bill, that gives the family a distinctive silhouette. Some larger families are broken into subfamilies. For example, buteos and accipiters, both hawks in the family Accipitridae, have very different flight silhouettes. Identification becomes easier once you have learned the characteristic shape of each family and subfamily. The silhouettes shown here will help you place birds into their family groupings.

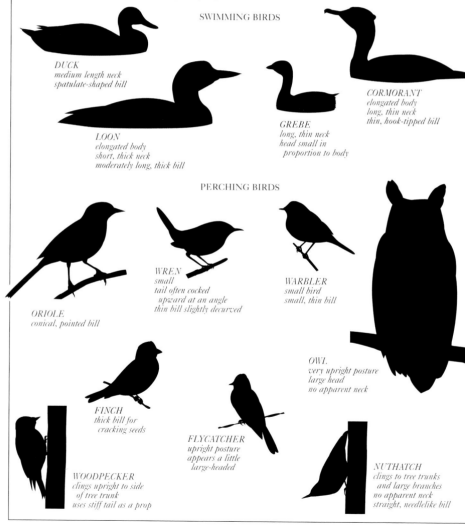

SWIMMING BIRDS

DUCK
medium length neck
spatulate-shaped bill

LOON
elongated body
short, thick neck
moderately long, thick bill

GREBE
long, thin neck
head small in
proportion to body

CORMORANT
elongated body
long, thin neck
thin, hook-tipped bill

PERCHING BIRDS

WREN
small
tail often cocked
upward at an angle
thin bill slightly decurved

WARBLER
small bird
small, thin bill

ORIOLE
conical, pointed bill

OWL
very upright posture
large head
no apparent neck

FINCH
thick bill for
cracking seeds

FLYCATCHER
upright posture
appears a little
large-headed

WOODPECKER
clings upright to side
of tree trunk
uses stiff tail as a prop

NUTHATCH
clings to tree trunks
and large branches
no apparent neck
straight, needlelike bill

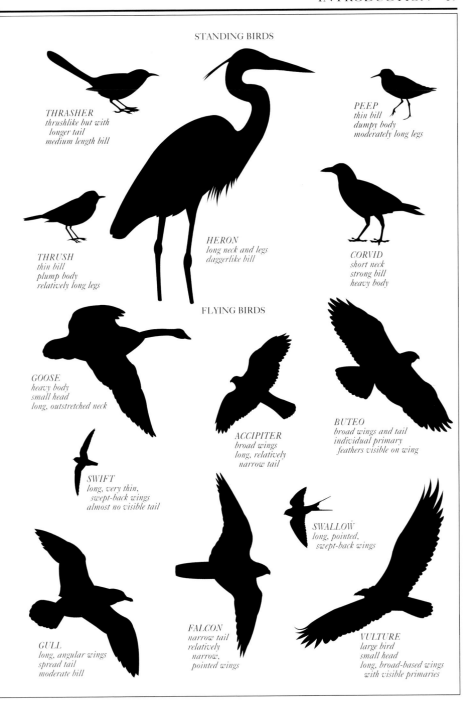

STANDING BIRDS

THRASHER
*thrushlike but with
longer tail
medium length bill*

PEEP
*thin bill
dumpy body
moderately long legs*

HERON
*long neck and legs
daggerlike bill*

THRUSH
*thin bill
plump body
relatively long legs*

CORVID
*short neck
strong bill
heavy body*

FLYING BIRDS

GOOSE
*heavy body
small head
long, outstretched neck*

ACCIPITER
*broad wings
long, relatively
narrow tail*

BUTEO
*broad wings and tail
individual primary
feathers visible on wing*

SWIFT
*long, very thin,
swept-back wings
almost no visible tail*

SWALLOW
*long, pointed,
swept-back wings*

GULL
*long, angular wings
spread tail
moderate bill*

FALCON
*narrow tail
relatively
narrow,
pointed wings*

VULTURE
*large bird
small head
long, broad-based wings
with visible primaries*

ABUNDANCE AND DISTRIBUTION

What does it mean when someone says a bird is "common" or that a species is "abundant" or "rare?" To appreciate a bird species' presence (or lack of it) in a given region you need to consider the factors of habitat, geographical range, and season of the year. Keep in mind that the distribution and abundance of birds, among the most mobile of the earth's creatures, are not static and the boundaries of populations often change. Birds are easily impacted by changes in climate and habitat brought about by natural or human causes, with seasonal migrations being the most obvious result. Thus knowing the seasonal occurrence of a bird is important in confirming its identification. The range maps in this guide are color-coded to provide you with this information. You can get even more specific information from local checklists, local bird books, websites, and local birders.

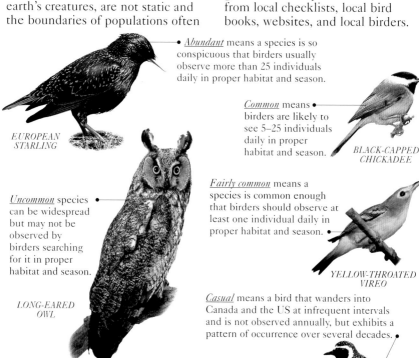

Abundant means a species is so conspicuous that birders usually observe more than 25 individuals daily in proper habitat and season.

EUROPEAN STARLING

Common means birders are likely to see 5–25 individuals daily in proper habitat and season.

BLACK-CAPPED CHICKADEE

Uncommon species can be widespread but may not be observed by birders searching for it in proper habitat and season.

LONG-EARED OWL

Fairly common means a species is common enough that birders should observe at least one individual daily in proper habitat and season.

YELLOW-THROATED VIREO

Casual means a bird that wanders into Canada and the US at infrequent intervals and is not observed annually, but exhibits a pattern of occurrence over several decades.

Rare can mean either the species is widely distributed outside Canada and the US but exists in low numbers here, or the entire population is small and local.

NORTHERN WHEATEAR

PACIFIC GOLDEN-PLOVER

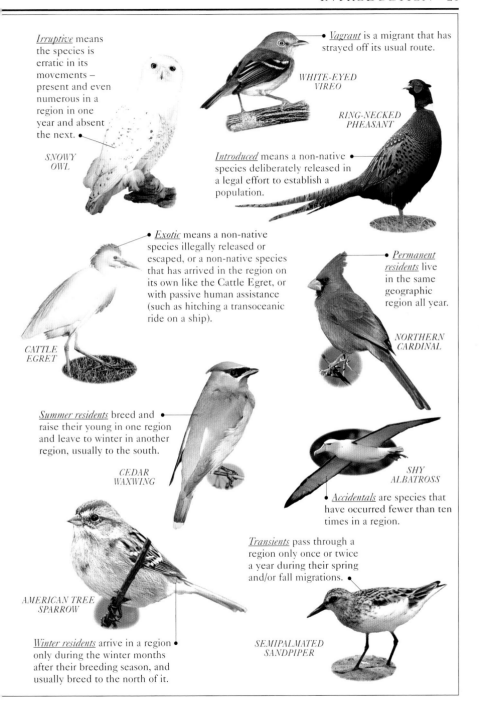

Irruptive means the species is erratic in its movements – present and even numerous in a region in one year and absent the next. •

SNOWY OWL

• *Vagrant* is a migrant that has strayed off its usual route.

WHITE-EYED VIREO

RING-NECKED PHEASANT

Introduced means a non-native • species deliberately released in a legal effort to establish a population.

• *Exotic* means a non-native species illegally released or escaped, or a non-native species that has arrived in the region on its own like the Cattle Egret, or with passive human assistance (such as hitching a transoceanic ride on a ship).

CATTLE EGRET

• *Permanent residents* live in the same geographic region all year.

NORTHERN CARDINAL

Summer residents breed and • raise their young in one region and leave to winter in another region, usually to the south.

CEDAR WAXWING

SHY ALBATROSS

Accidentals are species that have occurred fewer than ten times in a region.

Transients pass through a region only once or twice a year during their spring and/or fall migrations. •

AMERICAN TREE SPARROW

Winter residents arrive in a region • only during the winter months after their breeding season, and usually breed to the north of it.

SEMIPALMATED SANDPIPER

WATCHING BIRDS IN THE BACKYARD

If you provide suitable food, shelter, and water, birds will come to your backyard. If you offer a variety of these necessities you will attract a greater diversity of birds. Place your feeders, nesting boxes, and birdbaths where the birds will feel safe from people and animals and where you can see the birds as you go about your daily routine.

FOOD AND FEEDERS

Many people enjoy feeding birds year-round. Basic types of feeders include platform feeders, hopper feeders, tube feeders, ball feeders, window feeders, fruit feeders, nectar feeders, and suet feeders. Standard foods include black (oil) sunflower seed (the best single seed), striped sunflower seed, hulled sunflower (chips/hearts) seed, niger (called "thistle") seed, safflower seed, white proso millet seed, red millet seed, milo seed, corn (whole kernel, shelled, and cracked), peanuts, peanut butter, suet and suet mixes, fruits, and nectar.

HOUSE FINCHES and a NORTHERN CARDINAL find food and shelter.

AMERICAN GOLDFINCHES at a tube feeder

A female RED-BELLIED WOODPECKER finds suet in a wire cage feeder.

WATER

Birds need water as much as they need food. If you include even one dependable source of water in your yard you will attract a great variety of birds to drink, bathe, and cool off. If there is a running water or dripping water element even more species will come. There are many styles of water containers to choose from but the only requirement is: Maintain a stable supply of clean water in a shallow container no deeper than 8 cm.

NORTHERN CARDINAL at a traditional birdbath

"Hotel" for PURPLE MARTINS

Two types of nest boxes you can make yourself

SHELTER AND NEST BOXES

Planting trees, shrubs, and other vegetation not only provides food for birds but shelter and nesting places. Many species will use nest boxes. Others will use nesting shelves or ledges, and larger species will use raised nesting platforms. Nesting boxes can be made of wood, aluminum, or plastic; natural gourds are often used for martins and swallows.

Urban nest for MOURNING DOVES

WATCHING BIRDS IN THE FIELD

Very little gear is needed to watch birds, other than your own curiosity. Two indispensable items are a good pair of binoculars and a good field guide. Birding with experienced birders who know the area is also valuable in getting you off to a good start. It is a good idea to keep a small notebook handy. Later you may want to add a camera and telephoto lens; a spotting scope with tripod becomes a good investment for the more serious birder.

A long-lens camera and binoculars allow birders to photograph and see birds that might otherwise be missed.

BINOCULARS
Look for magnifying ranges from 7x to 10x power.

BINOCULARS
Look for magnifying ranges from 7x to 10x power. The outside diameter of the lenses that are farthest from your eyes (the objective lenses) should range from 35 mm to 50 mm. The power of magnification and the diameter of the objective lenses (the latter helps determine light-gathering ability) are combined and stamped on the binoculars as two numbers such as: 7 x 35, 7 x 50, or 8 x 42. Small compact binoculars such as 8 x 23 are lightweight and tempting to carry in the field, but the small size of the objective lenses limits the amount of light they can gather, making birdwatching under low light difficult.

BASIC PHOTOGRAPHY EQUIPMENT

The best camera body for bird photography is a 35 mm single lens reflex (SLR). This camera allows you to view the subject directly through the lens. Many birds move quickly so your camera should have a fast shutter speed of at least 1/500 sec or higher, and the films you use with natural light should have high exposure speeds in the range of 200–400 ISO (ASA). A telephoto lens will allow you to photograph a larger image; you will need one in the 300 mm to 500 mm range. A sturdy tripod is required for sharp exposures. Use blinds to conceal yourself from the bird and let you get much closer. Automobiles will work as long as you stay inside.

TRIPOD
To improve the sharpness
of your exposures

CAMERA
35 mm single lens reflex (SLR)

TELEPHOTO LENS
Look for a lens in the 300 mm to
500 mm range

A temporary moveable blind in the form of a simple tent can conceal birders enough to put wary birds at ease.

HOW TO BE A BETTER BIRDER

There are many ways to improve your birding skills and increase your enjoyment of birdwatching.

STUDY AT HOME
Time spent at home studying your field guide will make a big difference. Find local checklists of birds, or provincial and regional bird books, that provide even more specific information about the birds in your area. Listen to recordings of bird songs and calls.

Patience is one of a birder's most important skills.

IMPROVE YOUR FIELD SKILLS
Birds have keen color eyesight and hearing. They are frightened by sudden movements, loud noises, and bright clothing that does not "blend" with the background. Experienced birders move deliberately, stalking quietly. They converse in low tones and stand patiently.

Birds are curious and attracted to sounds. When you make "pishing" noises (forcing air out through clenched teeth as if saying "pish, pish, pish"), or "squeaking" (making a high-pitched squeak by sucking air through closely pursed lips, a sound that can be amplified by "kissing" the back of your hand) many birds' curiosity will be piqued and they will come closer. Often they produce alarm notes or assembly calls, causing even more birds to come out where you can see them.

KEEP A RECORD
Keeping good records of the birds you see will help you learn when seasonal species are present and how abundant they may be. There is still much science does not know about birds, particularly about behavior and abundance in some habitats, and the amateur birder can make valuable contributions. If you find a banded bird, call toll-free 1-800-327-2263, or write to Bird Banding Office, National Wildlife Research Centre, Canadian Wildlife Service, Hull, QC K1A 0H3.

PRACTICE BIRDING ETHICS

Birding is not without its responsibility to the welfare of the bird so practicing birding ethics when you are in the field helps species' survival and makes good sense. A birder's code of ethics rests on some of the following basic guidelines: your actions should not endanger birds or other wildlife; you should not harm the natural environment – leave only footprints; and you should always respect the rights of others, especially their rights to privacy and private property rights.

A female feeding baby BLUEBIRDS

The welfare of fledgling SCREECH-OWLS like these depends on birders who practice good ethics.

BIRD PROTECTION IN BREEDING SEASON

Remember that birds are sensitive to disturbance. Nothing should be done that will frighten them or alter the surroundings of their nest. Once frightened, they may abandon the nest, and this could set their breeding back a whole year.

RUBY-THROATED HUMMINGBIRD feeding her young

JOIN A CLUB

Each province has established bird clubs. Many local clubs are associated with provincial or regional ornithological societies that network activities, have regular meetings, and publish newsletters. You can locate your nearest bird clubs on the internet or though your provincial conservation or wildlife department, local library, or newspaper.

Birding organizations and initiatives exist on the national and international level as well as the local level. Some Canadian nationally operating organizations or programs are:
• Bird Studies Canada, PO Box 160, Port Rowan, ON N0E 1M0, Tel: (888) 448-BIRD.
• Ducks Unlimited Canada, PO Box 1160, Stonewall, MB R0C 2Z0, Tel: (800) 665-3825, Fax: (204) 467-9028.
• Partners in Flight, c/o Canadian Wildlife Service, Environment Canada, Ottawa, ON K1A 0H3, Fax: (819) 994-4445.

A few of the birding organizations active throughout North America are:
• American Birding Association, PO Box 6599, Colorado Springs, CO 80934, USA.
• National Audubon Society, 700 Broadway, New York, NY 10003, USA.
• Ornithological Societies of North America, 810 E. 10th St., Lawrence, KS 66044, USA.

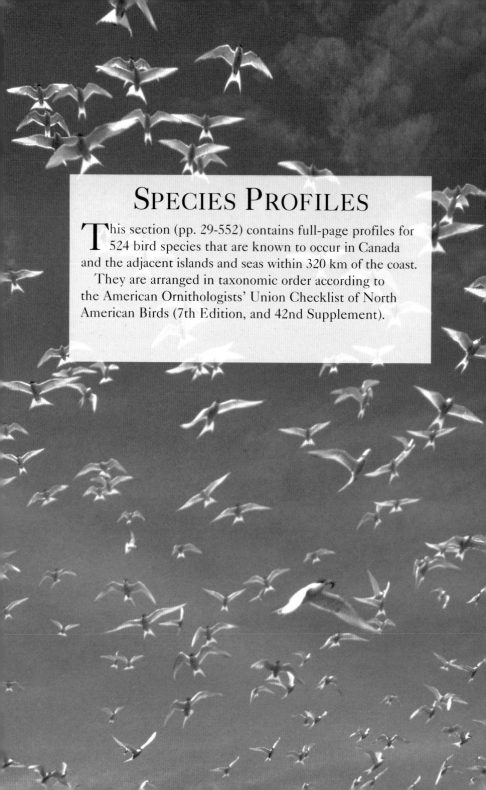

SPECIES PROFILES

This section (pp. 29-552) contains full-page profiles for 524 bird species that are known to occur in Canada and the adjacent islands and seas within 320 km of the coast.

They are arranged in taxonomic order according to the American Ornithologists' Union Checklist of North American Birds (7th Edition, and 42nd Supplement).

Family GAVIIDAE	Species *Gavia stellata*	Length 61–119 cm	Wingspan 107–114 cm

RED-THROATED LOON

This is the smallest loon and the only one without profuse white spotting on its upperparts in the breeding plumage. When the bird is on the water, its slender bill appears upturned and is often held pointed upward by the swimming bird. In juvenile and winter plumage both sexes have a gray crown and hindneck, dark gray back with many small white spots, pale upturned bill, and a white face, sides, foreneck, and underparts.

gray head and neck

dark slender upturned bill

medium gray back with small, indistinct spots

thin black stripes on hindneck

dull red patch on foreneck

- **SONG** Usually silent. On breeding ground, prolonged wails and gooselike *kwuk-kwuk-kwuk*.
- **BEHAVIOR** Flies with neck drooping. Only loon to leap directly into flight from water or land. Feeds primarily on fish, which it catches in dives down to 3 meters. Solitary except on wintering grounds and in migration, when hundreds may congregate in bays along the coast.
- **BREEDING** Usually a solitary nester. Sometimes forms loose colonies.
- **NESTING** Incubation 24–29 days by both sexes. Precocial young leave nest and take to water about 1 day after hatching, then fly at about 49–60 days. 1 brood per year.
- **POPULATION** Common to fairly common on breeding grounds; fairly common on coast in winter; casual to very uncommon inland in winter. Populations stable.
- **CONSERVATION** Vulnerable to loss of habitat due to development in high Arctic and to pollution, particularly oil spills, in wintering areas. Many drown in gill nets.

WINTER PLUMAGE

Similar Birds

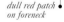

ARCTIC LOON
PACIFIC LOON
Breeding adults have dark throat; dark flanks; large white spots on back • in winter plumage, lack white spots on back; bill not upturned; dark gray of crown and hind neck contrast sharply with white face and foreneck. • Arctic Loon in the West only.

Flight Pattern
Direct flight with swift rapid wing beats.

Nest Identification	
Shape 〰 Location ▬ ✻✻✻	Moist depression or heap of damp vegetation mixed with mud • male sometimes constructs copulation platform away from nest • 1–3 olive-green to dark brown eggs, sometimes with blackish brown spots.

Plumage Sexes similar	Habitat 〰 〰	Migration Migratory	Weight 1.5 kg

DATE _____ TIME_____ LOCATION _____

| Family GAVIIDAE | Species *Gavia arctica* | Length 71 cm | Wingspan 114–125 cm |

ARCTIC LOON

This bird is very similar to the Pacific Loon, which was recently split from it as a separate species. When it's on the water, the white of its flanks is visible above the waterline. Winter birds have white throats without the "chin strap" mark shown by the Pacific Loon. Breeding adults have white underparts and flanks. Winter adults have gray-brown backs without spotting, a gray-brown crown and hindneck, and white cheeks, chin, foreneck, breast, and underparts.

medium gray head, nape, and hindneck

dark straight bill

black throat with green gloss at close range

bold black-and-white striping on side of neck and breast

WINTER PLUMAGE

black sides and back with rows of large white spots

- **SONG** During breeding season, a guttural *kquk-kquk-kquk-kquk*, often given in flight. Also various growls and croaks and a plaintive wail.
- **BEHAVIOR** A solitary bird. It is often found well inland on tundra, deep lakes, and in boreal forests. The Arctic Loon feeds primarily on fish, taken in dives to 14 meters; also feeds on mollusks and crustaceans.
- **BREEDING** Solitary nester.
- **NESTING** Incubation 28–30 days by both sexes. Semiprecocial young leave nest shortly after hatching, with first flight at 60–65 days. Both sexes feed. 1 brood per year.
- **POPULATION** Uncommon breeder in western Alaska; casual to uncommon in winter. Poorly known in Alaska; fairly common in Russia.

Similar Birds

PACIFIC LOON
Less white on flanks (rarely shows as patch); rounder head • in winter plumage chin strap separates chin from neck.

RED-THROATED LOON
In breeding plumage has reddish throat and upturned bill; lacks white spotting on back • in winter plumage lacks chin strap.

Flight Pattern
Direct flight with swift rapid wing beats.

Nest Identification	Varies from mere scrape or depression to mound of earth and plants • on ground or floating • 1–3 olive-green to dark brown eggs, with some black spots or blotches.
Shape ⚬ ⚬ Location ▬ ▬ ⸬ 〰	

| Plumage Sexes similar | Habitat 〰 〰 ___ | Migration Migratory | Weight 3.7 kg |

DATE _____ TIME _____ LOCATION _____

Family GAVIIDAE	Species *Gavia pacifica*	Length 66 cm	Wingspan 109–122 cm

PACIFIC LOON

Until recently this species was considered a race of the Arctic Loon, which it closely resembles. The Pacific Loon flies with its head and neck held straight. When swimming it holds its dark slender bill level. Winter adults have dark gray upperparts and a thin dark strap that reaches around the chin. Underparts are white year-round.

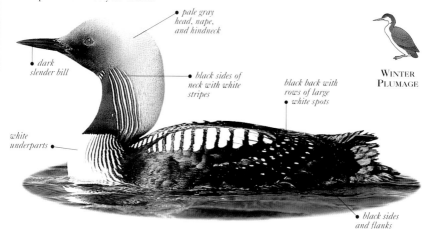

pale gray head, nape, and hindneck

dark slender bill

black sides of neck with white stripes

black back with rows of large white spots

WINTER PLUMAGE

white underparts

black sides and flanks

• **SONG** Generally silent. On breeding grounds, variety of guttural quacks and croaks, and a long drawn-out *ah-hah-awee*.

• **BEHAVIOR** Migrates in flocks, unlike other loons. Feeds primarily on fish but takes some crustaceans and mollusks. Nests on freshwater lakes and islands from tundra to boreal forests.

• **BREEDING** Solitary. Monogamous.

• **NESTING** Incubation 23–25 days by both sexes, but female does more. Precocial young leave nest shortly after hatching. First flight at 60–65 days. 1 brood per year.

• **POPULATION** Common to fairly common on tundra breeding grounds. During winter, uncommon on the West Coast, casual on the East Coast, and rare inland. Stable.

Similar Birds
ARCTIC LOON More white on flanks • breeding adults have dark chin • in winter lacks chin strap. • western range.
RED-THROATED LOON Breeding adults have red foreneck; lacks large white spots on back; bill is upturned.

• **CONSERVATION** Affected by encroachment of humans on breeding grounds. Vulnerable to the pollution of its wintering areas, including oil spills. Also vulnerable to drowning in gill nets.

Flight Pattern
Direct flight with rapid wing beats.

Nest Identification	
Shape ••• ⚬⚬ Location ▬ ⬩⬩⬩	Heap of vegetation pulled up around nest • edge of water on ground • built by both sexes • 1–3 brownish eggs with blackish brown spots.

Plumage Sexes similar	Habitat ≈≈ ▬ ≈≈	Migration Migratory	Weight 1.7 kg

DATE _____ TIME_____ LOCATION _____

Family GAVIIDAE	Species *Gavia immer*	Length 71–91 cm	Wingspan 127–147 cm

COMMON LOON

Frequenting quiet lakes and usually sleeping on the water, this large bird rarely comes on land except to nest. It must run at least 18 meters across water to gain enough momentum to fly. Loons require such pristine conditions to nest that their presence as a nesting bird is a good indicator of the wilderness condition of a lake and the frequency of human activity on it. Winter adults have gray or brown upperparts; an irregular or broken pattern on the head to the base of the eye and the sides of the neck; white underparts, chin, and foreneck; a blue-gray bill; and a white eye ring.

glossy black head with greenish sheen

red-brown eyes

stout, straight black bill

checkered black-and-white back

glossy black throat

broken white neck collar

white breast and belly

WINTER PLUMAGE

The Comon Loon is the provincial bird of Ontario.

• **SONG** Usually silent away from breeding areas. Different calls on breeding grounds: tremolo or "loon's laughter"; yodel, sounding like *yodel-ha-oo-oo*; wail; and talking *kwuk*.

• **BEHAVIOR** Rides low on water. Dives to 61 meters to catch fish. Eats freshwater and saltwater fish, crustaceans, amphipods, snails, leeches, frogs, salamanders, and aquatic insects. Eats larger prey on surface and smaller prey underwater. Can stay underwater up to 60 seconds. Loons migrate alone or in small groups.

• **BREEDING** Monogamous. Solitary nester on islands, always within 1 or 2 meters of water. May use same nest year after year.

• **NESTING** Incubation 26–31 days by both sexes, mostly by female. Precocial young leave nest soon after hatching; fed and raised by both sexes. First flight at 70–80 days. 1 brood per year.

• **POPULATION** Fairly common. Decrease in some breeding areas in southern parts of range.

Similar Birds

YELLOW-BILLED LOON Pale yellow bill in all plumages, with dusky base in winter; bill is larger and culmen is less curved • in winter has paler head and neck and brown patch over ear.

• **CONSERVATION** Prone to environmental loss due to human disturbance and reduced food supply resulting from acid rain. Some abandon nests due to human activity. Some breeding grounds protected by volunteers.

Flight Pattern
Rapid direct flight with strong wing beats. Head, neck, and legs extended and drooping slightly below midline of body give hunchbacked appearance.

Nest Identification	
Shape ⟿ Location ▬ ☵	Bed of stems, grasses, and twigs • floating in bog; or on ground, hidden in crevices or muskrat houses • built by both sexes • 1–3 olive-green to dark brown eggs usually scattered with dark brown spots; subelliptical to oval, 8.9 x 5.6 cm.

Plumage Sexes similar	Habitat ～～ ⟍	Migration Migratory	Weight 4.1 kg

DATE _____ TIME _____ LOCATION _____

Family GAVIIDAE	Species *Gavia adamsii*	Length 71–91 cm	Wingspan 137–152 cm

YELLOW-BILLED LOON

Once considered a weather prophet in Eskimo folklore, this loon is the largest of its species and has the northernmost range of any loon. Swimming with its head tilted slightly upward, this bird sometimes carries its young on its back. Winter plumage shows a tan crown with a white face and a dark ear patch.

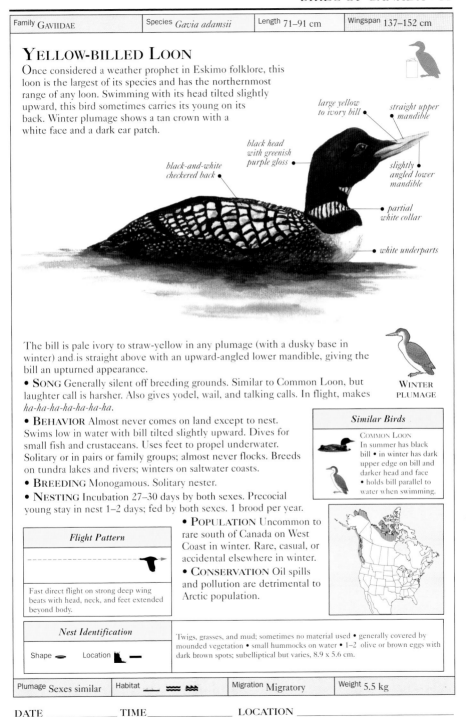

large yellow to ivory bill

straight upper mandible

black head with greenish purple gloss

slightly angled lower mandible

black-and-white checkered back

partial white collar

white underparts

The bill is pale ivory to straw-yellow in any plumage (with a dusky base in winter) and is straight above with an upward-angled lower mandible, giving the bill an upturned appearance.

WINTER PLUMAGE

• **SONG** Generally silent off breeding grounds. Similar to Common Loon, but laughter call is harsher. Also gives yodel, wail, and talking calls. In flight, makes *ha-ha-ha-ha-ha-ha-ha*.

• **BEHAVIOR** Almost never comes on land except to nest. Swims low in water with bill tilted slightly upward. Dives for small fish and crustaceans. Uses feet to propel underwater. Solitary or in pairs or family groups; almost never flocks. Breeds on tundra lakes and rivers; winters on saltwater coasts.

• **BREEDING** Monogamous. Solitary nester.

• **NESTING** Incubation 27–30 days by both sexes. Precocial young stay in nest 1–2 days; fed by both sexes. 1 brood per year.

Similar Birds
COMMON LOON In summer has black bill • in winter has dark upper edge on bill and darker head and face • holds bill parallel to water when swimming.

• **POPULATION** Uncommon to rare south of Canada on West Coast in winter. Rare, casual, or accidental elsewhere in winter.

• **CONSERVATION** Oil spills and pollution are detrimental to Arctic population.

Flight Pattern
Fast direct flight on strong deep wing beats with head, neck, and feet extended beyond body.

Nest Identification	
Shape ⬚ Location 🪺 ▬	Twigs, grasses, and mud; sometimes no material used • generally covered by mounded vegetation • small hummocks on water • 1–2 olive or brown eggs with dark brown spots; subelliptical but varies, 8.9 x 5.6 cm.

Plumage Sexes similar	Habitat ___ ≈≈ ≋	Migration Migratory	Weight 5.5 kg

DATE _____ TIME_____ LOCATION _____

Family PODICIPEDIDAE	Species *Podilymbus podiceps*	Length 30–38 cm	Wingspan 57 cm

PIED-BILLED GREBE

The most widespread and best-known grebe in North America sometimes hides from intruders by sinking until only its head shows above water or by diving like other members of the group. This stocky grebe has a large head and short thick bill that gives it a chickenlike profile, easily distinguishing it from other grebes, even at a distance. The bill is light-colored and has a black ring around it during the breeding season but lacks the ring in winter.

large head

dark eye

eye ring

brownish gray body

short neck

dark ring on short thick bill

WINTER PLUMAGE

• **SONG** Loud, cuckoolike call, *cuck, cuck, cuck, cow-cow-cow, cow-ah-cow-ah.*
• **BEHAVIOR** Forages by diving from the surface and swimming underwater, propelled by its feet. Feeds some on vegetation, but about half of the diet is made up of aquatic insects with the remainder split almost equally between small fish and crustaceans.
• **BREEDING** Monogamous. Solitary nester.
• **NESTING** Incubation 23–27 days by both sexes, but female does more. Young move from nest to adult's back less than an hour after hatching. Nest use stops in 24–42 days. First flight at 35–37 days. Young fed by both sexes. 1–2 broods per year.
• **POPULATION** Very common in range.
• **CONSERVATION** May be declining due to habitat loss.

Similar Birds

LEAST GREBE
Smaller with golden (not dark) eye; slender, dark bill; much more restricted North American range.

Flight Pattern

Direct flight with rapid wing beats.

Nest Identification

Shape ⌒⌒ Location ⑊⑊⑊

Platform of decaying vegetation • inconspicuously anchored to vegetation in open water among reeds or rushes • built by both sexes • 2–10 pale bluish white or nest-stained eggs; elliptical to subelliptical, 4.3 cm long.

Plumage Sexes similar	Habitat 〰〰 〰	Migration Some migrate	Weight 442 g

DATE _____ TIME_____ LOCATION _____

Family PODICIPEDIDAE	Species *Podiceps auritus*	Length 30–38 cm	Wingspan 61 cm

HORNED GREBE

The "horns" for which this bird is named are actually tufts of golden feathers above and behind the eyes, which are present only during the bird's breeding season. In summer the reddish neck of the Horned Grebe distinguishes it from the Eared Grebe, which shares much of the breeding range. The Horned Grebe's life is tied to water, breeding in freshwater habitats and often spending the winter both in freshwater and in saltwater.

• **SONG** This grebe gives an abrasive *keark, keark* or *yark, yark*. It also makes a repeated prattling sound followed by shrill screams.

black head

golden "horns"

reddish neck

dark straight bill

short tail

• **BEHAVIOR** The Horned Grebe eats as its primary diet mostly fish and some crustaceans as well as aquatic insects. Tamer than other grebes, it often allows a close approach by humans. Its nests are often built so that they are concealed poorly or not at all.

WINTER PLUMAGE

• **BREEDING** Monogamous. Most often a solitary nester; sometimes in loose colonies of 4–6 pairs.

• **NESTING** Incubation 22–25 days by both sexes. Precocial young fed by both sexes. First flight at 45–60 days. 1 brood per year, sometimes 2.

• **POPULATION** Common.

• **CONSERVATION** Declining apparently due to oil spills and habitat loss.

Similar Birds

EARED GREBE
More triangular head; has black neck in summer • dusky neck and black cheeks in winter.

WESTERN GREBE
CLARK'S GREBE
Black above and white below; much larger; much longer necks and bills.

Flight Pattern
Direct flight with rapid wing beats.

Nest Identification	
Shape 🐦 Location ⟱	Floating heap of wet plant material, including underwater plants, rotting vegetation, rubbish, and mud • often anchored to vegetation • 3–7 whitish to very pale green eggs, usually nest-stained; 4.3 cm long.

Plumage Sexes similar	Habitat 〰 〰 〰	Migration Migratory	Weight 454 g

DATE _____ TIME_____ LOCATION _____

Family PODICIPEDIDAE	Species *Podiceps grisegena*	Length 43–53 cm	Wingspan 76–81 cm

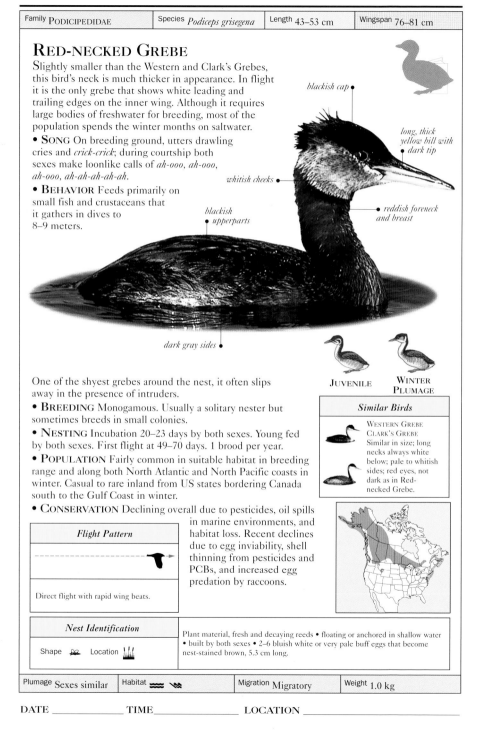

RED-NECKED GREBE

Slightly smaller than the Western and Clark's Grebes, this bird's neck is much thicker in appearance. In flight it is the only grebe that shows white leading and trailing edges on the inner wing. Although it requires large bodies of freshwater for breeding, most of the population spends the winter months on saltwater.

- **SONG** On breeding ground, utters drawling cries and *crick-crick*; during courtship both sexes make loonlike calls of *ah-ooo, ah-ooo, ah-ooo, ah-ah-ah-ah-ah*.
- **BEHAVIOR** Feeds primarily on small fish and crustaceans that it gathers in dives to 8–9 meters.

blackish cap

long, thick yellow bill with dark tip

whitish cheeks

reddish foreneck and breast

blackish upperparts

dark gray sides

JUVENILE   WINTER PLUMAGE

Similar Birds

WESTERN GREBE
CLARK'S GREBE
Similar in size; long necks always white below; pale to whitish sides; red eyes, not dark as in Red-necked Grebe.

One of the shyest grebes around the nest, it often slips away in the presence of intruders.

- **BREEDING** Monogamous. Usually a solitary nester but sometimes breeds in small colonies.
- **NESTING** Incubation 20–23 days by both sexes. Young fed by both sexes. First flight at 49–70 days. 1 brood per year.
- **POPULATION** Fairly common in suitable habitat in breeding range and along both North Atlantic and North Pacific coasts in winter. Casual to rare inland from US states bordering Canada south to the Gulf Coast in winter.
- **CONSERVATION** Declining overall due to pesticides, oil spills in marine environments, and habitat loss. Recent declines due to egg inviability, shell thinning from pesticides and PCBs, and increased egg predation by raccoons.

Flight Pattern

Direct flight with rapid wing beats.

Nest Identification

Shape   Location

Plant material, fresh and decaying reeds • floating or anchored in shallow water • built by both sexes • 2–6 bluish white or very pale buff eggs that become nest-stained brown, 5.3 cm long.

Plumage Sexes similar	Habitat	Migration Migratory	Weight 1.0 kg

DATE _____ TIME_____ LOCATION _____

| Family PODICIPEDIDAE | Species *Podiceps nigricollis* | Length 30–33 cm | Wingspan 57 cm |

EARED GREBE

The "ear" for which this bird is named is a wide golden tuft of feathers behind the eyes, present only in breeding plumage. It has a more triangular-shaped head than other grebes and is the only one that has a black neck during breeding season. The neck remains dusky gray in winter – a good field mark. The slender, dark bill appears slightly upturned.

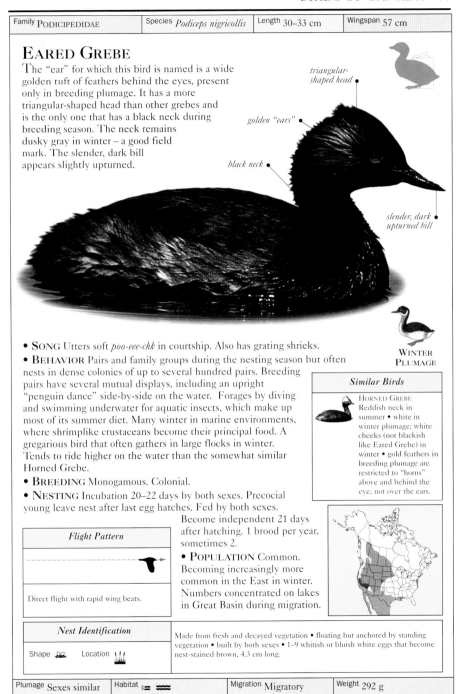

triangular-shaped head

golden "ears"

black neck

slender, dark upturned bill

WINTER PLUMAGE

- **SONG** Utters soft *poo-eee-chk* in courtship. Also has grating shrieks.
- **BEHAVIOR** Pairs and family groups during the nesting season but often nests in dense colonies of up to several hundred pairs. Breeding pairs have several mutual displays, including an upright "penguin dance" side-by-side on the water. Forages by diving and swimming underwater for aquatic insects, which make up most of its summer diet. Many winter in marine environments, where shrimplike crustaceans become their principal food. A gregarious bird that often gathers in large flocks in winter. Tends to ride higher on the water than the somewhat similar Horned Grebe.
- **BREEDING** Monogamous. Colonial.
- **NESTING** Incubation 20–22 days by both sexes. Precocial young leave nest after last egg hatches. Fed by both sexes. Become independent 21 days after hatching. 1 brood per year, sometimes 2.
- **POPULATION** Common. Becoming increasingly more common in the East in winter. Numbers concentrated on lakes in Great Basin during migration.

Similar Birds

HORNED GREBE
Reddish neck in summer • white in winter plumage; white cheeks (not blackish like Eared Grebe) in winter • gold feathers in breeding plumage are restricted to "horns" above and behind the eye, not over the ears.

Flight Pattern
Direct flight with rapid wing beats.

Nest Identification	
Shape	Location	Made from fresh and decayed vegetation • floating but anchored by standing vegetation • built by both sexes • 1–9 whitish or bluish white eggs that become nest-stained brown, 4.3 cm long.

| Plumage Sexes similar | Habitat | Migration Migratory | Weight 292 g |

Family PODICIPEDIDAE	Species *Aechmophorus occidentalis*	Length 56–74 cm	Wingspan 79–102 cm

WESTERN GREBE

Identical in shape and size to Clark's Grebe, the Western Grebe shares much of the same range. It has a long swanlike neck and a slender, greenish yellow bill. Like all other grebes, it has feet modified for swimming, and the toes are lobed, not webbed as in waterfowl. Fish make up most of its diet.

black of cap extends below eye

• **SONG** Bold *crick-kreek*. Grating, whistled *c-r-r-ee-er-r-r-ee*.

• **BEHAVIOR** Both Western and Clark's Grebes have a structure in the neck that allows rapid,

long, slender neck

dark back

long, slender, greenish yellow bill

grayish sides

spearlike thrusting of the bill. Like all other grebes, it practices the peculiar behavior of carrying newly hatched young snuggled in the feathers of its back as it swims, and even as it dives if disturbed by an intruder.

WINTER PLUMAGE

• **BREEDING** Monogamous. Colonial.

• **NESTING** Incubation 23–24 days by both sexes. Precocial young climb onto parents' backs within minutes of birth and leave nest soon after. Young fed by both sexes. First flight at 63–70 days. 1 brood per year.

• **POPULATION** Fairly common to common. Casual in East during fall migration and winter.

Similar Birds

CLARK'S GREBE
Almost identical in all plumages but paler with white face extending above eye; orange (not yellow-green) bill
• more similar head pattern in winter, when Western may have whiter lore and Clark's may have darker lore.

HORNED GREBE
In winter, plumage also black and white but much smaller; shorter neck; short, dark bill.

Flight Pattern

Direct flight with rapid wing beats.

• **CONSERVATION** From 1890s to 1906, thousands shot for feathers to make hats, coats, and capes. Oil spills and gill nets currently major causes of mortality. Vulnerable also to loss of habitat.

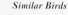

Nest Identification

Shape 〰 Location 〰

Made of plant material • floating or anchored to standing vegetation in shallow water • built by both sexes • 1–7 pale bluish white eggs that become nest-stained brown; subelliptical to long elliptical, some tending toward oval, 5.8 cm long.

Plumage Sexes similar	Habitat 〰 〰 〰	Migration Some migrate	Weight 1.5 kg

DATE _____ TIME _____ LOCATION _____

Family PODICIPEDIDAE	Species *Aechmophorus clarkii*	Length 66 cm	Wingspan 76-102 cm

CLARK'S GREBE

Until recently this bird was considered a pale morph of the Western Grebe, which it closely resembles in size, shape, behavior, habitat selection, and range. It differs in bill color and by having a white face above and below the eyes, topped by a black cap. The range is not well known.

• **SONG** Ascending *kree-eek*.

• **BEHAVIOR** Gregarious; often colonial during the breeding season; wintering mostly in large numbers along the Pacific Coast in salt water. Has structure in neck that allows rapid, spearlike thrusting of bill. Like other grebes, legs set far back under the body make walking on land slow and laborious but swimming

• *white face above and below eyes*

• *very short tail*

• *pale sides and flanks*

WINTER PLUMAGE

and diving easy. Courtship behavior much like Western Grebe, with water "dances" including pairs running across the surface with bodies vertical and necks thrust forward.

• **BREEDING** Monogamous. Colonial.

• **NESTING** Incubation 23–24 days by both sexes. Precocial young climb onto parents' backs within minutes of birth. First flight at 63–77 days. Young fed by both sexes. 1 brood per year.

• **POPULATION** Common to fairly common in number; accidental in the East.

• **CONSERVATION** Plume hunters once devastated populations. Oil spills and accidental drowing in gill nets are current major causes of mortality; also vulnerable to loss of habitat.

Similar Birds

WESTERN GREBE
Only other large, black-and-white grebe with a long neck; yellow-green bill instead of orange; black of cap extends down through eye.

Flight Pattern

Direct flight with rapid wing beats.

Nest Identification

Shape   Location

Made of floating detritus • in shallow water • built by both sexes • 1–6 bluish white eggs that become nest-stained brown, 5.8 cm long.

Plumage Sexes similar	Habitat	Migration Some migrate	Weight 1.5 kg

DATE _____ TIME_____ LOCATION _____

Family DIOMEDEIDAE	Species *Thalassarche chlororhynchos*	Length 71–81 cm	Wingspan 178–206 cm

YELLOW-NOSED ALBATROSS

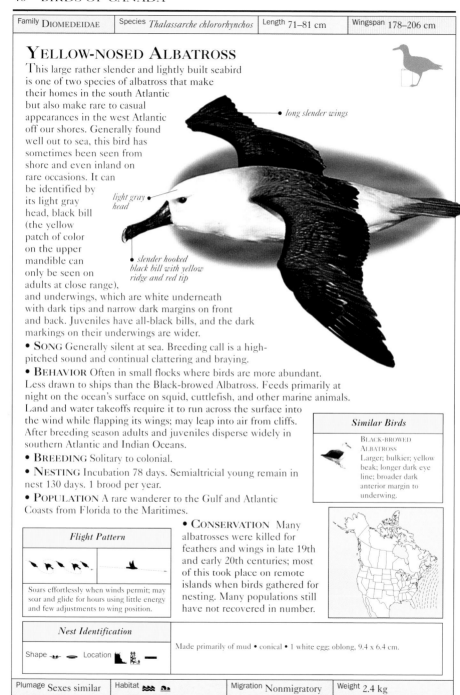

This large rather slender and lightly built seabird is one of two species of albatross that make their homes in the south Atlantic but also make rare to casual appearances in the west Atlantic off our shores. Generally found well out to sea, this bird has sometimes been seen from shore and even inland on rare occasions. It can be identified by its light gray head, black bill (the yellow patch of color on the upper mandible can only be seen on adults at close range), and underwings, which are white underneath with dark tips and narrow dark margins on front and back. Juveniles have all-black bills, and the dark markings on their underwings are wider.

long slender wings

light gray head

slender hooked black bill with yellow ridge and red tip

• **SONG** Generally silent at sea. Breeding call is a high-pitched sound and continual clattering and braying.

• **BEHAVIOR** Often in small flocks where birds are more abundant. Less drawn to ships than the Black-browed Albatross. Feeds primarily at night on the ocean's surface on squid, cuttlefish, and other marine animals. Land and water takeoffs require it to run across the surface into the wind while flapping its wings; may leap into air from cliffs. After breeding season adults and juveniles disperse widely in southern Atlantic and Indian Oceans.

• **BREEDING** Solitary to colonial.

• **NESTING** Incubation 78 days. Semialtricial young remain in nest 130 days. 1 brood per year.

• **POPULATION** A rare wanderer to the Gulf and Atlantic Coasts from Florida to the Maritimes.

• **CONSERVATION** Many albatrosses were killed for feathers and wings in late 19th and early 20th centuries; most of this took place on remote islands when birds gathered for nesting. Many populations still have not recovered in number.

Similar Birds

BLACK-BROWED ALBATROSS Larger; bulkier; yellow beak; longer dark eye line; broader dark anterior margin to underwing.

Flight Pattern

Soars effortlessly when winds permit; may soar and glide for hours using little energy and few adjustments to wing position.

Nest Identification

Shape ⤙ ⬭ Location ⬕ ⬔ ▬

Made primarily of mud • conical • 1 white egg; oblong, 9.4 x 6.4 cm.

Plumage Sexes similar	Habitat ≈≈ ⚓	Migration Nonmigratory	Weight 2.4 kg

DATE _____ TIME_____ LOCATION _____

Family DIOMEDEIDAE	Species *Thalassarche melanophris*	Length 81–94 cm	Wingspan 224–241 cm

BLACK-BROWED ALBATROSS

This albatross is a common bird on the open sea in the southern oceans, but only rarely crosses the Equator into the North Atlantic. The dark blackish back contrasting against the white head, neck, rump, and underparts recalls a very large Great Black-backed Gull, but the bird's black tail and stiff wing beats and glides on long narrow pointed wings

white head and neck

black eyebrow line

dark blackish back

large hooked yellow bill with reddish tip

black tail

white underparts

quickly identify this albatross. Juveniles have a darker bill and underwings, and a narrow grayish collar.

white rump

• **SONG** Loud braying from nest.

• **BEHAVIOR** Often follows ships. Settles on water to feed, making shallow dives from surface for food. Feeds on squid, cuttlefish, small fish, crustaceans, and garbage from ships. Like other albatrosses, it can spend extended periods at sea, where it drinks saltwater by removing excessive salts with salt glands in the tube nose. After breeding season adults and juveniles disperse widely in southern oceans primarily south of the Tropic of Capricorn.

• **BREEDING** Colonial.

• **NESTING** Incubation 64–79 days by both sexes. Semialtricial young stay in nest 4–5 months. First flight as early as 116 days. 1 brood per year.

• **POPULATION** Rare to casual in North American western Atlantic from North Carolina to Newfoundland. One of most abundant albatrosses in cold seas of the southern Atlantic.

Similar Birds

YELLOW-NOSED ALBATROSS
Black bill with yellow ridge on upper mandible; more extensive white on underwing with narrow dark borders; light gray head.

Flight Pattern

Soars effortlessly for long periods of time on stiff wings when there are winds; may circle, arc, and glide for long distances.

Nest Identification

Shape ◄━ ◄▬ Location

Mud and grass • grassy tufts on slopes or cliffs overlooking ocean • conical • 1 white egg with smattering of red spots at the base, 6.6 x 10.2 cm.

Plumage Sexes similar	Habitat ≈≈ ⌒⌒	Migration Nonmigratory	Weight Undetermined

DATE _____ TIME _____ LOCATION _____

Family DIOMEDEIDAE	Species *Phoebastria immutabilis*	Length 89 cm	Wingspan 198–208 cm

LAYSAN ALBATROSS

Although it breeds almost exclusively on a few
Hawaiian islands, this bird wanders to Alaskan
waters and the Pacific Coast, where it is the
only regularly occurring albatross with a dark
back and white head and underparts. The
largest seabirds, albatrosses have hooked
bills with tubular nostrils containing
salt glands that enable them
to drink seawater.

white head

*creamy pinkish
gray bill*

*dark brownish
black tail*

*dark brownish
black upper
wings and back*

*creamy pinkish
gray feet*

*white
uppertail coverts*

*white
underparts*

- **SONG** Series of sounds on breeding grounds includes *Eh-eh*,
Eh-eh-eh, a whine, a whinny, moans, inhalations, and a squeak.
- **BEHAVIOR** Performs elaborate courtship dance similar to that
of other albatrosses. Spends most of its life at sea, traveling to land
only to nest. Must either run into the wind to take off from water
or land, or jump into the air from a sea cliff like other albatrosses.
Feeds largely on squid taken from water surface at night.
- **BREEDING** Monogamous. Highly colonial.
- **NESTING** Incubation 65–66 days by both sexes. Altricial
young stay in nest 140–150 days. Fed by both sexes, who
alternate days of feeding and foraging. 1 brood per year.
- **POPULATION** Uncommon off Alaskan coast in spring and
summer; rare to casual off remainder of Pacific Coast. Total of
about 100,000 and expanding.
- **CONSERVATION** Populations on Midway Island growing because

Similar Birds
SHY ALBATROSS Accidental; larger; yellow-tipped, yellowish gray bill; more extensive white on rump and underwings.

of decreased human activity.
Thousands killed in 19th
century for millinery trade and
for feathers for pillows and
mattresses. Now thousands
killed annually by drift nets and
long-line fisheries.

Flight Pattern
Dynamic soaring and glides; stays aloft for hours with little flapping of wings.

Nest Identification	Shallow depression with built-up rim of leaves, twigs, and sand • on ground • building begun by female, finished by both sexes. 1 creamy-white egg, usually with brown spotting and a cap of reddish brown on the blunt end; ovate or elliptical ovate, 10.2 cm long.
Shape ⠀⠀ Location ▬ ⠀	

Plumage Sexes similar	Habitat ≋ ⠀	Migration Migratory	Weight 3.2 kg

DATE _____ TIME_____ LOCATION _____

| Family DIOMEDEIDAE | Species *Phoebastria nigripes* | Length 81 cm | Wingspan 178–203 cm |

BLACK-FOOTED ALBATROSS

The most frequently encountered albatross off the Pacific Coast of North America, the Black-footed Albatross appears as a large, mostly all-dark seabird soaring on long slender stiff wings. The bird is sooty brownish black with a dark bill, legs, and feet. Whitish uppertail coverts show in flight. Many birds have dark undertail coverts, although some show white ones.

• **SONG** Mostly silent at sea. Groans or squeals when in groups on land or at sea.

whitish ring around face at base of bill

uniformly dark plumage above and below

dark bill

white undertail coverts

• **BEHAVIOR** The Black-footed Albatross breeds primarily in and around the Hawaiian archipelago. This bird often follows ships at sea for hours, sometimes feeding on garbage thrown overboard. Its clumsy takeoffs and landings on nesting islands have contributed to its nickname of "gooney bird."

• **BREEDING** Monogamous with lifelong pairing. Colonial.

• **NESTING** Incubation 65–66 days by both sexes. Semialtricial young remain in nest 140–150 days. Young are fed by both sexes, with male and female alternating days of feeding their young and foraging.

• **POPULATION** Uncommon but regular. Numbers are stable.

• **CONSERVATION** Protected on nesting islands from the collection of eggs. It also is protected from the killing of chicks and adult birds.

Similar Birds

SHORT-TAILED ALBATROSS Accidental • older juveniles are dark showing some white in face; pink feet, legs, and bill.

Flight Pattern
Dynamic soaring. Glides for hours.

Nest Identification	
Shape 🐦 Location ▬ 🏝	Shallow scrape in sand in colonies • 1 creamy white egg.

| Plumage Sexes similar | Habitat 〰 🐚 | Migration Migratory | Weight 3.1 kg |

| Family DIOMEDEIDAE | Species *Phoebastria albatrus* | Length 84–94 cm | Wingspan 213–229 cm |

SHORT-TAILED ALBATROSS

The largest and only white-bodied albatross in the North Pacific, this rare bird was once hunted for its plumes until it became almost extinct in the late nineteenth century. In 1933 experts thought the last Short-tailed Albatross had been spotted. However, twenty years later a small nesting colony was located on a Japanese island, and today close to a thousand of these birds exist. The bird may exist in subadult plumages for more than a dozen years, showing differing amounts of white and blackish brown, but always with a white face and forehead and blackish brown nape that extends into a partial collar; in younger birds this brown nape may extend onto the crown.

heavy pink bill with light bluish tip

brownish black nape and crown

white face

white overall

• **SONG** Silent at sea. Voice on nesting grounds unrecorded.

dark primaries

• **BEHAVIOR** Highly pelagic, coming to land only to breed. Gregarious. Feeds mostly on squid and some fish and crustaceans. Eats at night when prey is more likely to be near surface. Rests on water and picks up food with bill. Sometimes makes shallow dive to grasp food. Does not follow ships.

dark band at tail tip

JUVENILE

• **BREEDING** Monogamous. Mates for life.

• **NESTING** Incubation 65–80 days by both sexes. Young semialtricial. Period of nesting stage unrecorded but known to be many months. 1 brood every 2 years.

• **POPULATION** Rare. Only a few recent records in late summer and autumn from waters off southern Alaska to California. Population in Japan slowly increased through last half of 20th century.

Similar Birds
BLACK-FOOTED ALBATROSS Similar to juvenile but has distinct white patch at base of bill; black bill; black legs and feet.

• **CONSERVATION** Protected by law on wildlife reservations in Leeward Islands, implemented by Theodore Roosevelt. Also protected in Japan by law on Torishima as a Natural National Monument.

Flight Pattern
Soars on wind for hours with wings set and bowed slightly downward. Alternates several deep wing beats with long glides.

Nest Identification	
Shape 〜 Location ▬	On sand or rocky soil • 1 white egg with reddish spots; oval or elliptical, 4.3–4.8 x 2.8 cm.

| Plumage Sexes similar | Habitat 〜〜 〜 | Migration Migratory | Weight Undetermined |

DATE _____ TIME_____ LOCATION _____

Family PROCELLARIIDAE	Species *Fulmarus glacialis*	Length 48 cm	Wingspan 107 cm

NORTHERN FULMAR

When threatened by an enemy or handled by a person, the Northern Fulmar discharges a foul-smelling oil from its stomach by spitting. This audacious bird follows fishing boats, often closely, to take advantage of refuse. The light morph is superficially gull-like in appearance, but its stiff-winged flight is like a shearwater's. It is mostly gray above with a white chest and belly; the dark color morph is gray overall. Fulmars are rarely seen from shore away from the breeding colonies, except during storms.

• **SONG** When feeding, makes chucking and grunting noises. During breeding season makes variety of guttural calls.

• **BEHAVIOR** Gregarious. Highly pelagic; may not come ashore until 3–4 years old. Grabs food with beak from just below surface and eats on the water. Sometimes makes shallow dives, using wings and feet for propulsion. Eats variety of fish, crustaceans, squid, marine worms, and carrion. Feeds alone, in pairs, or in flocks. Drinks seawater by sucking it up dove-fashion. In flight carries wings stiffly and wheels up in arcs over waves by taking advantage of winds.

• **BREEDING** Monogamous. Colonial.

• **NESTING** Incubation 52–53 days by both sexes. Semialtricial young fed by both sexes. First flight at 46–51 days. 1 brood per year.

• **POPULATION** Common; abundant in some places. In winter found at sea off both coasts.

short, rounded gray tail

pale wing patch at base of gray primaries

rounded, proportionally large white head

large raised nasal tubes

short heavy yellow bill with hooked tip

thick "bull" neck

DARK MORPH

Similar Birds

Light morph generally similar to gulls, which have a more slender neck; thinner bill without nasal tubes; deep, steady flapping wing beats (not stiff-winged)
• also generally similar to other shearwaters, which have more pointed wings; darker, thinner bill; most do not follow ships.

• **CONSERVATION** Population growth possibly supported by fishery wastes in North Sea. Humans, introduced predators, and avian predators take a toll, but humans are major predator for meat, eggs, and feathers.

Flight Pattern

Flap and glide flight on bowed wings with bursts of stiff wing beats alternating with periods of effortless banking and gliding.

Nest Identification

Shape   Location

Slight depression on ground • sometimes layered with pebbles • may be built by both sexes • 1 white or off-white egg, often nest-stained and occasionally marked with reddish brown; subelliptical, 7.4 cm long.

Plumage Sexes similar	Habitat	Migration Migratory	Weight 610 g

DATE _____ TIME _____ LOCATION _____

Family PROCELLARIIDAE	Species *Pterodroma inexpectata*	Length 33–36 cm	Wingspan 69–84 cm

MOTTLED PETREL

Also known as the Scaled Petrel, this medium-sized bird nests only on the islands surrounding New Zealand. It has a history of being a vagrant, so the possibility exists for it to make a rare appearance around the North Atlantic seaboard; however, North American birdwatchers are most likely to spot it off the southern coast of Alaska or well off the US West Coast. A solitary bird, it prefers the open sea and does not follow fishing boats. Seen from above, a dark bar across the back and the leading edge of the wings forms an M pattern.

distinct black bar on white underwing

dark gray overall with mottled gray and white markings

white face blends to dark gray crown

heavily marked black bill

white throat and midbreast

wedge-shaped tail

gray belly

fleshy legs and feet with distal webbing and black toes

- **SONG** Silent at sea. While breeding gives high-pitched repetitive rapid *ti-ti-ti*. Also a deep bugle-note, *goo-oo*.

- **BEHAVIOR** Like most petrels, eats small squid and some small fish. Solitary or in pairs away from breeding grounds. Displays high arcing flight typical of gadfly petrels, especially in windy conditions; at sea flight often is directional and very rapid.

- **BREEDING** Monogamous. Colonial.

- **NESTING** Incubation 54 days by both sexes. Young semialtricial; first flight is at about 90–105 days.

- **POPULATION** Uncommon off the southern coast of Alaska and Aleutian Islands; rare to casual well off US West Coast. Accidental in New York.

- **CONSERVATION** No concerns have been reported, although breeding range has been restricted by the loss of nesting burrows because of human intrusion as well as introduced predators.

Similar Birds

COOK'S PETREL
All-white underparts and underwing; outer tail feathers whiter.

BULLER'S SHEARWATER
White underparts; paler gray upperparts with black cap; black wing tips; diagonal bar on inner wing forms M pattern on back.

Flight Pattern

Dashing flight, alternating high soaring arcs and glides with rapid wing beats.

Nest Identification

Shape   Location

No nest material in burrow • atop small pile of grasses, in cliffs or rock crevices, or in caves, about 76–91cm deep • built by both sexes • 1 white egg; oval, 5.8 cm long.

Plumage Sexes similar	Habitat	Migration Migratory	Weight 315 g

Family PROCELLARIIDAE	Species *Pterodroma feae*	Length 36 cm	Wingspan 94 cm

FEA'S PETREL

Fea's Petrel and Zino's Petrel (*P. madeira*, a bird that breeds only on the island of Madeira) are so similar that it is extremely difficult to distinguish one from the other. Both are either threatened or endangered because of their small populations, so taking a specimen has not been appropriate. Without a specimen that would allow critical measurements to be taken in hand, it was not possible to certify which species had been seen off the mid-Atlantic Coast. However, recent photographs and field notes tend to indicate the petrel being observed is the Fea's. The combination of white underparts, a dark facial mask, a partial breast band, mostly dark underwings, grayish brown upperparts with a dark M pattern, and wings bent back at the wrist separate this gadfly petrel from others that appear off the East Coast.

dark mask around eyes

thick black bill

pale uppertail coverts and tail

gray tail

grayish brown upperparts

M marking across upperwings and lower back

• **SONG** Loud shrieking or softer twittering, heard only at night around nesting islands.
• **BEHAVIOR** Solitary off North and mid-Atlantic Coasts. Spends most of its time at sea. May rest on water. Often feeds in large flocks around nesting islands and in waters of Southern Hemisphere. Eats various small fish and squid. Occasionally follows ships. Flight alternates glides with rapid wing beats in a zigzag progression, sailing in high arcs in strong winds.
• **BREEDING** Monogamous. Colonial.
• **NESTING** Breeding biology poorly known. Incubation 48–54 days by both sexes. Young altricial; single hatchling fed by regurgitation by both sexes for 90–100 days, then abandoned. 1 brood per year.

Similar Birds

HERALD PETREL
Pale morph • ashy brown head and upperparts; ashy brown mantle with blackish brown primaries; dark M marking across upperwing; white underparts with dusky breast band; white-tipped blackish undertail coverts.

• **POPULATION** Rare in North America off coasts of North Carolina, Virginia, Nova Scotia; May through September.
• **CONSERVATION** Highly threatened species. Vulnerable to predation by rodents and cats on breeding islands.

Flight Pattern

Fluttery wing beats alternate with glides. High erratic soaring arcs become higher and more dashing as wind speeds increase.

Nest Identification

Shape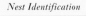

Location

Small amount of plant material • long horizontal burrow or space between rocks • built by both sexes • 1 white egg, flecked with reddish or violet at large end; short subelliptical to short oval, 5.6 x 4.2 cm.

Plumage Sexes similar	Habitat	Migration Migratory	Weight Undetermined

DATE _____ TIME_____ LOCATION _____

| Family PROCELLARIIDAE | Species *Calonectris diomedea* | Length 46–53 cm | Wingspan 112 cm |

CORY'S SHEARWATER

The largest shearwater found along the Atlantic Coast skims the surface of the ocean with slow wing beats and a buoyant flight similar to that of the albatross. When this bird is seen flying straight ahead, its wings show a distinctive downward bow from wrist to wing tip. The large pale bill as well as the way the brown upperparts blend gradually with the white underparts without producing a capped appearance is distinctive. Cory's is the only Atlantic shearwater that occasionally soars.

brownish gray • upperparts

narrow pale tips of uppertail coverts contrast • with dark tail

large pinkish • yellow bill with dusky tip

• white underparts

- **SONG** Generally silent except on breeding grounds.
- **BEHAVIOR** Gregarious, often forming flocks that number in the hundreds or thousands. Frequently follows predatory fish to feed on the bait fish they drive to the water's surface. Feeds at night on crustaceans and large squid it takes from the surface. Has a keen sense of smell.

• dusky trailing edge on underwing

• dusky primaries

Similar Birds

GREATER SHEARWATER Dark bill; distinct dark cap with white collar across nape; clear white rump band; smudge of dusky color on belly; clear contrast between dark upperparts and white underparts.

- **BREEDING** Monogamous. Colonial.
- **NESTING** Incubation 52–55 days by both sexes. Semialtricial young stay in nest about 90 days, although parents abandon young while still in nest. Young are fed by both sexes at night.
- **POPULATION** Numerous, but showing some decline.

Flight Pattern
Soars if wind is up, looping and circling on fixed wings. Or, deep wing beats with wings bowed downward in long low glide.

Nest Identification	
Shape ▨ ▨ ▨ Location ◣ 🪨	Both sexes work together to either dig a new burrow or clean out a previously used burrow • sometimes under a rock • no material added • 1 white egg; blunt oval or subelliptical, 7.1 cm long.

| Plumage Sexes similar | Habitat 〰〰 〰 | Migration Migratory | Weight 544 g |

DATE _____ TIME_____ LOCATION _____

Family PROCELLARIIDAE	Species *Puffinus creatopus*	Length 48 cm	Wingspan 109 cm

PINK-FOOTED SHEARWATER

Seen off the Pacific Coast near California and Oregon, this seabird returns every winter (its summer) to its breeding grounds near Chile. It spends most of its time at sea but because it prefers shallow continental shelf waters it can be seen from shore, often feeding with other types of shearwaters and boobies. The combination of the dark-tipped pinkish bill, white underparts with mottled whitish underwings, flight feathers bordered blackish brown, and gray-brown upperparts is diagnostic. The extent of the mottling on

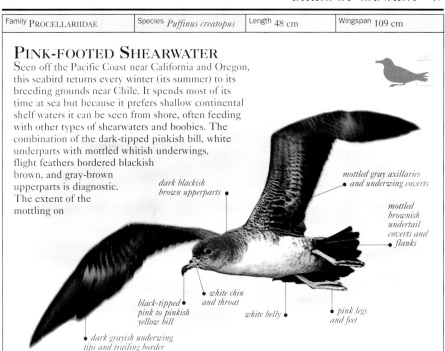

dark blackish brown upperparts

mottled gray axillaries and underwing coverts

mottled brownish undertail coverts and flanks

white chin and throat

black-tipped pink to pinkish yellow bill

white belly

pink legs and feet

dark grayish underwing tips and trailing border

this species' underwings and flanks is highly variable. In Pacific Coast waters this is the most common of the white-bellied shearwaters associated with large flocks of Sooty Shearwaters.

- **SONG** Silent except on breeding grounds, where voice has not been recorded.
- **BEHAVIOR** Highly pelagic. Solitary or gregarious. Feeds by plunging into water while flying to grab prey. Also dives or picks up food from surface. Diet consists of small fish, squid, and crustaceans. Rarely follows ships.
- **BREEDING** Monogamous. Colonial.
- **NESTING** Incubation 48–56 days by both sexes. Fed by both sexes. First flight at 89–95 days. 1 brood per year.
- **POPULATION** Common spring through fall off Pacific Coast; uncommon in Gulf of Alaska. Rare in winter.
- **CONSERVATION** Declining because of introduced predators on some islands where it nests.

Similar Birds

BLACK-VENTED SHEARWATER Smaller; black bill; dark capped appearance; darker upperparts; less mottling on underparts; dark undertail coverts; fast flutter-and-glide flight pattern.

Flight Pattern

Languid flight of slow wing beats with low glides; in strong winds swifter flight banking into high, broad arcs.

Nest Identification

Shape [icon] [icon]   Location ▰▰▰ ▬

Usually on a grassy island • burrow either freshly excavated or cleaned if used previously • 1 white egg; oval, 7.1 x 4.6 cm.

Plumage Sexes similar	Habitat ≈≈≈	Migration Migratory	Weight 726 g

DATE _____ TIME_____ LOCATION _____

Family PROCELLARIIDAE	Species *Puffinus carneipes*	Length 48–51 cm	Wingspan 99–109 cm

FLESH-FOOTED SHEARWATER

This large dark seabird spends more time near shore than most pelagic birds. Nesting on islands off New Zealand and Australia, stragglers make rare visits to North America and can be spotted off the Pacific Coast from Alaska to California. This adept diver often joins flocks of terns and gulls. In flight it appears brownish black with a creamy pink bill, legs, and feet. In good light the bases of the underwing primaries look silvery.

silvery to light brown bases of underwing primaries

dark brown overall

large creamy pink bill with dark tip

creamy pink legs and feet

• **SONG** Usually silent except on breeding grounds, where it makes a distinct mewing call. Also gives brief series of *gug gug gugs*, expanding to *ku koo ah*, which leads into shrieking.

• **BEHAVIOR** Gregarious. Feeds in open companies with other species but forms rafts at dusk off breeding grounds and when food is concentrated. Usually forages for food by diving from water's surface. Also feeds by skimming surface, extending pink feet to tread water between shallow belly flops. Eats fish and squid. Often follows fishing trawlers. Sometimes dives for bait on fishing lines.

• **BREEDING** Monogamous. Colonial.

• **NESTING** Incubation by both sexes, but period of time unknown. Young stay in nest 92 days. Fed by both sexes. First flight at 89–95 days. 1 brood per year.

Similar Birds

SOOTY SHEARWATER
Black bill; light underwings; blackish gray legs and feet; faster wing beats.

SHORT-TAILED SHEARWATER
Smaller; black bill; all dark, but sometimes with pale, often concentrated, underwing linings that form a panel; sometimes has whitish chin; blackish gray feet and legs.

• **POPULATION** Rare in summer and fall off the West Coast from California to Alaska.

• **CONSERVATION** Vulnerable to pollution of marine environment, oil spills, and introduction of predators at nesting colonies.

Flight Pattern

Slow flight with stiff-winged flapping and gliding near water surface. In higher flight soars and arcs, wheeling on stiff wings.

Nest Identification

Shape ⬛ Location 🪨 ▬

Scrape of vegetation in dry burrow lined with grass roots, feathers, and rush stems • at end of tunnel 1–2 m long • from near sea level to high on hills • 1 white egg, 7.4 x 4.6 cm.

Plumage Sexes similar	Habitat ≋	Migration Migratory	Weight 590 g

DATE _____ TIME_____ LOCATION _____

Family PROCELLARIIDAE	Species *Puffinus gravis*	Length 46–51 g	Wingspan 100–122 cm

GREATER SHEARWATER

This large powerful shearwater is fairly common off the Atlantic Coast of the US in spring migration where it remains well out to sea on its way to its south Atlantic breeding grounds. Party fishing boats and sports fishermen know this strong heavy-bodied bird well, for it often comes to their boats and may try to take the bait off their hooks as the lines are lowered to the bottom or retrieved close to the surface. The bird sometimes takes fish that are tossed back overboard. Although it appears gull-like at a distance, the bird is easily distinguished by its stiff straight wings. A dark brownish black cap extends beneath the eyes and is often separated from the brownish gray back by a white nape collar. A dusky smudge on its belly and pinkish legs and feet are visible from below when the bird is in flight.

U-shaped white band on uppertail coverts

black tail

dark cap extends below eye

hooked dark bill

white collar

white underparts

• **SONG** Noisy with catlike squalls when aggressively feeding around fishing trawlers.
• **BEHAVIOR** Attracted to boats and tame on water near them. Attends fishing boats where it competes for food in a hostile manner. Dives to 6–9 meters in pursuit of fish.
• **BREEDING** Monogamous. Colonial.
• **NESTING** Incubation by both sexes. First flight at 84 days. Semialtricial young fed by both sexes at night.
• **POPULATION** Total well over 5 million and seems to be increasing. From the Gulf of Maine northward it is common in the summer.
• **CONSERVATION** Many are killed by severe storms in North Atlantic; carcasses sometimes found on beaches.

Similar Birds

BLACK-CAPPED PETREL Smaller; different flight pattern; different under wing pattern; white forehead; larger white rump patch.

CORY'S SHEARWATER Pale bill; lacks distinctive cap, white nape collar, white U-shaped rump patch, and smudge on belly.

Flight Pattern

In strong winds soars in high arcs, often banking to change direction. Or, deep wing beats with a long glide near water.

Nest Identification

Shape | Location

Lined with grass • sharply angled • about 90 cm long • sometimes in crevice among rocks • 1 white egg.

Plumage Sexes similar	Habitat	Migration Migratory	Weight 862 g

Family PROCELLARIIDAE	Species *Puffinus bulleri*	Length 41 cm	Wingspan 97 cm

BULLER'S SHEARWATER

The blackish cap, primaries, and wedge-shaped tail of this shearwater contrast strongly with its gray upperparts and conspicuously white underparts. Also visible from below are the bird's pale yellowish to pink legs and feet. A wide black bar crosses the upper wing coverts, creating a W or M pattern across the wings and back. The striking pattern is unique in the Pacific to this shearwater, which was formerly called the New Zealand Shearwater. From late November to early April, these striking shearwaters are concentrated around their only known breeding place in the world, the Poor Knights Islands off the northern coast of New Zealand. After the breeding season they disperse widely as far north as Japan and the Gulf of Alaska.

W or M pattern on upperparts

long wedge-shaped black tail

black cap

hooked dark bill

white underparts

- **SONG** Largely silent.
- **BEHAVIOR** Lands on water to pick at small crustaceans and squid on surface or ducks head just beneath to snatch food. Extremely graceful in flight, with buoyant albatross-like flight close to water surface. In strong winds, flies in wide, swinging arcs.
- **BREEDING** Monogamous. Colonial.
- **NESTING** Incubation 51 days by both sexes. Semialtricial young stay in nest about 100 days. Fed at night through regurgitation by both sexes.
- **POPULATION** Feral pigs wiped out some island populations. Since pigs were eradicated in 1936 populations have rebounded. Current total about 2 million.

Similar Birds

Unmistakable. No other shearwater in the eastern Pacific has the striking W or M pattern on upperparts.

Flight Pattern

In strong winds soars, banks, and skims the surface, rarely beating wings. Or, deep, strong wing beats with long glides.

Nest Identification

Shape   Location

Leaves, twigs, and pebbles • on ground • up to 3 m long • built by both sexes • 1 white egg.

Plumage Sexes similar	Habitat 〰	Migration Migratory	Weight 862 g

DATE _____ TIME_____ LOCATION _____

Family PROCELLARIIDAE	Species *Puffinus griseus*	Length 46–51 cm	Wingspan 94–109 cm

SOOTY SHEARWATER

A common summer visitor off both the Atlantic and Pacific Coasts, this stocky short-necked sooty brown bird is probably the best-known shearwater in North American waters. It normally feeds well offshore, but during strong onshore winds hundreds of birds may be seen by observers from the shoreline. Look for the long slender dark wings with silvery gray underwing coverts. Some birds may have a white underwing lining. Legs and feet are blackish.

silvery gray underwing coverts

long slender dark wings

long dark bill

dark sooty brown plumage, darkest on tail and primaries

• **SONG** The Sooty Shearwater is silent except for noisy squeals when squabbling for food. Also makes inhaled and exhaled *koo-wah-koo-wah-koo-wah* when on breeding grounds.

• **BEHAVIOR** This bird often gathers in large flocks. Does not follow ships like some other seabirds, but is attracted to fishing trawlers. Flies with long glides on long narrow slightly swept-back wings. Sometimes makes short dives for fish, squid, and crustaceans. May plunge to dive on open wings from 1 to 3 meters above water.

• **BREEDING** Colonial. The Sooty Shearwater nests on various isolated islands in the southern oceans.

• **NESTING** Incubation 52–56 days by both sexes. Semialtricial young remain in nest for about 97 days. Adults usually leave at night. Young fed by both sexes at night.

• **POPULATION** The Sooty Shearwater is an abundant bird, with a total population of more than 10 million.

Similar Birds

SHORT-TAILED SHEARWATER Shorter bill; less contrasting grayer underwing linings often restricted to a panel on the median secondary coverts and extending slightly onto the inner median primary coverts; underwings may be dark overall, lacking pale panels • only in the West.

Flight Pattern

Strong direct flapping alternating with long glides.

Nest Identification

Shape | Location

Made of leaves and grass • up to 3 m long • built by both sexes • 1 white egg; elliptical, 4.8 x 7.6 cm.

Plumage Sexes similar	Habitat	Migration Migratory	Weight 816 g

DATE _____ TIME_____ LOCATION _____

| Family PROCELLARIIDAE | Species *Puffinus tenuirostris* | Length 41–43 cm | Wingspan 97–99 cm |

SHORT-TAILED SHEARWATER

Also known as the "muttonbird" in Tasmania and Australia, where millions nest, this bird and its young are often taken for their down and fat, and for food. Some have gray bars on the underwing coverts, and these birds especially resemble the Sooty Shearwater. Many appear all dark

short dark bill

dark sooty brown plumage over entire body

short, rounded dark tail

some have grayish barring under wing

blackish gray feet and legs

above and below, but some in molt have a pale chin and face, giving a capped appearance.

- **SONG** Wailing, crooning, and sobbing on breeding grounds. Usually silent at sea.
- **BEHAVIOR** Highly migratory, traveling great distances. Gregarious, often gathering in great numbers, with more than 60,000 per hour recorded to pass the coast of southern Australia. Sometimes follows boats. Feeds on fish and squid on water surface or in short swimming dives.
- **BREEDING** Colonial.
- **NESTING** Incubation 52–55 days by both sexes. Semialtricial young fed at night by both sexes through regurgitation. Young leave nest after abandonment at 82–108 days and fly shortly thereafter. 1 brood per year.
- **POPULATION** Stable and thriving. More than 20 million.
- **CONSERVATION** Not reported, but many young harvested on breeding grounds.

Similar Birds

SOOTY SHEARWATER
Larger; whiter, more contrasting wing linings; longer bill.

FLESH-FOOTED SHEARWATER
Larger; pink bill; pinkish gray legs and feet.

WEDGE-TAILED SHEARWATER
Dark morph has long tail; pinkish legs and feet.

Flight Pattern

Purposeful strong flaps followed by long glides; often soars for long periods, especially on brisk winds.

Nest Identification

Shape — Location

Lined with grasses • on ground on islands • built by both sexes • 1 white egg; elliptical, 4.7 x 7.1 cm.

| Plumage Sexes similar | Habitat | Migration Migratory | Weight 544 g |

DATE _____ TIME_____ LOCATION _____

Family PROCELLARIIDAE	Species *Puffinus puffinus*	Length 31–38 cm	Wingspan 84–89 cm

MANX SHEARWATER

From a distance in flight, this medium-sized shearwater appears simply black above and white below. The white undertail coverts extend almost to the tip of the short tail, and the underwing linings are white. Some rare East Atlantic races are not as white below. In all plumages note how the dark cap extends onto the face and auriculars below

black cap extends below eye

blackish upperparts

black hooked bill

white of chin and throat extends to side of head behind ear coverts

white undertail coverts

white underparts

pinkish gray feet and legs

the eye, bordered below and behind by a whitish crescent that extends from chin and throat to the side of the head behind the auriculars, or ear coverts. Manx Shearwaters seem to be increasing in numbers, with more birds being recorded on pelagic birding trips off the North Carolina coast.

• **SONG** Generally silent at sea.

• **BEHAVIOR** Gregarious. This shearwater is excellent on the wing with stiff rapid wing strokes followed by shearing glides low over the water. Banks from side to side, showing black upperparts first, then the snow-white underparts. Good swimmer; sometimes goes underwater for fish and squid. Adults may forage more than 965 km from nesting burrow, returning to it at night. Does not follow ships, but is attracted to smaller fishing boats and trawlers.

• **BREEDING** Monogamous. Colonial.

Similar Birds

AUDUBON'S SHEARWATER Similar but smaller; dark undertail coverts; different flight pattern with more rapid, fluttering wing beats.

BLACK-VENTED SHEARWATER In the West only • dark mottling on sides of face, neck, and breast; dusky to dark undertail coverts.

• **NESTING** Incubation 47–63 days by both sexes. Semialtricial young fed by both sexes. Parents abandon young at 60 days. Young leave nest 8–9 days later. 1 brood per year.

• **POPULATION** Apparently increasing off the East Coast.

Flight Pattern

Long glides interrupted by several rapid wing beats.

Nest Identification

Shape   Location

Lined with grass and leaves • on ground • on isolated islands • built by both sexes • 1 white egg; broad or blunt ovate or subelliptical, 6.0 x 4.1 cm.

Plumage Sexes similar	Habitat	Migration Migratory	Weight 454 g

DATE _____ TIME_____ LOCATION _____

Family PROCELLARIIDAE	Species *Puffinus opisthomelas*	Length 33–36 cm	Wingspan 76–89 cm

BLACK-VENTED SHEARWATER

Unlike most shearwaters, this bird sometimes can be seen from shore. It feeds relatively close to the coast and dives with its wings partially opened. Formerly considered a subspecies of the Manx Shearwater, it occasionally follows ships. In flight the white flanks extend around the sides of the rump, giving the appearance of a narrow white patch on each side of the uppertail – a good field mark. The upperwing is blackish brown, and the underwing is white with a black tip and narrow trailing edge. Legs and feet are blackish with purplish webbing.

- **SONG** Largely silent at sea.
- **BEHAVIOR** Swims well. Dives into water to feed; sometimes "flies" underwater, using wings to help it swim. Feeds no more than 16 km from the shore. Eats a variety of fish, crustaceans, and squid. Nocturnal around nesting colonies.

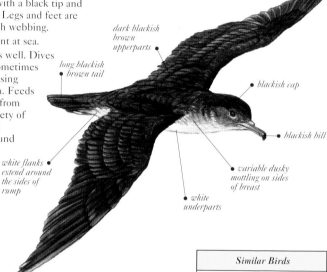

dark blackish brown upperparts

long blackish brown tail

blackish cap

blackish bill

white flanks extend around the sides of rump

variable dusky mottling on sides of breast

white underparts

- **NESTING** Incubation 51 days by both sexes. Semialtricial young fed by both sexes by regurgitation for about 60 days, then abandoned; young have "starving period" for 11–15 days. First flight at 70–75 days. 1 brood per year.
- **POPULATION** Fairly common and stable. Seen off of the California coast from August to May. Casual north to southwestern British Columbia.
- **CONSERVATION** Vulnerable to the introduction of predators on its breeding colony islands as well as to human disturbance.

Similar Birds

MANX SHEARWATER
Dark bill; dark blackish brown above with cap extending below eye; white below with white undertail coverts
• accidental.

Flight Pattern

Quick low flight with stiff short wing beats followed by a glide. Soars in bounding arcs in high-wind conditions.

Nest Identification

Shape ● ●   Location ▬ ▲

Lined with grass • sometimes in rocky ground from 2–2.5 m deep • built by both sexes • 1 white egg; elliptical, 5.1 x 3.3 cm.

Plumage Sexes similar	Habitat ≈≈ ⌇	Migration Nonmigratory	Weight 275 g

DATE _____ TIME_____ LOCATION _____

Family PROCELLARIIDAE	Species *Puffinus assimilis*	Length 25–28 cm	Wingspan 58–64 cm

LITTLE SHEARWATER

The smallest of the shearwaters, this bird has been spotted off the Atlantic Coast of North America only a few times. Unlike many seabirds, it often follows ships. Its small size, black-and-white or dark slaty-brown and white appearance (similar to that of the larger Manx Shearwater), white face, and stiff-winged fluttering flight are all distinctive. Under conditions of light winds, it flies with several quick shallow whirring wing beats, followed by short low glides. However, in higher winds it arcs and soars, wheeling, gliding, and sideslipping over waves and executing quick fluttering wing beats in the troughs.

short black bill

slaty brown to blue-black nape and cap

slaty brown to blue-black back

short tail

dark eye set in white face

extensively white underwing with narrow black margins and tip

white underparts and undertail coverts

slaty brown to blue-black on leading edge of wing, fading to lighter gray on trailing edge

- **SONG** Often silent at sea. Throaty, wheezy sounds; a rapid repetitive *kakakakakakaka-urrr.*
- **BEHAVIOR** Solitary; often in small flocks near breeding grounds. Swims and dives for food. Also picks food off surface of water, pattering with feet across water and with wings held above back like a large storm-petrel. Eats fish and squid. Usually feeds alone; sometimes in small flocks. Spends a lot of time on the water.
- **BREEDING** Monogamous. Colonial.
- **NESTING** Incubation 53 days by both sexes. Semialtricial young stay in nest 72 days; fed at night by both sexes. 1 brood per year.
- **POPULATION** Accidental off the Atlantic Coast.
- **CONSERVATION** Vulnerable to disturbance by humans; also predation at nesting colonies by introduced predators.

Similar Birds

AUDUBON'S SHEARWATER
Larger and chunkier; longer bill; dark undertail coverts; wider dark margins on underwings; less white on sides of neck and face; unmarked charcoal-gray wings.

MANX SHEARWATER
Larger, darker face; broader dark edge to underwings; different flight progression.

Flight Pattern
Flies low, fast, and straight with rapid flapping action and banking glides. In strong winds, arcing banks and glides.

Nest Identification	
Shape 🥚🥚🥚 Location 🏝️🪨	Burrow without lining • on ground under rock crevice or in bank • dug mostly by female • 1 white egg; elliptical, 4.8 x 3.3 cm.

Plumage Sexes similar	Habitat ≈≈≈	Migration Migratory	Weight 227 g

DATE _____ TIME_____ LOCATION _____

Family HYDROBATIDAE	Species *Oceanites oceanicus*	Length 15–19 cm	Wingspan 41–43 cm

WILSON'S STORM-PETREL

This is the storm-petrel that is most commonly seen off the Atlantic Coast, and it may be one of the most abundant birds in the world. It is the smallest storm-petrel seen off the Atlantic Coast. Few pelagic birds are easily identified from a rocking boat at sea, but this species can be identified by its short squared tail and feet extending beyond the tip of the

dark sooty brown plumage

dark bill

paler bar on upper surface of inner wings

squared to slightly rounded tail

broad U-shaped white band on rump extends to undertail coverts

dark legs

yellowish green webbing between toes

tail, its rather short rounded wings, and its large U-shaped white rump patch. These birds often come very close to boats, crisscrossing the wake of the boat and providing excellent views and easier confirmation of their identity.

• **SONG** Usually silent at sea, but makes noisy chattering sounds around nesting colonies.

• **BEHAVIOR** Generally flies close to water surface with purposeful shallow wing beats similar to those of a swallow or small tern. Frequently patters feet on water while holding wings above the body as it feeds on small marine organisms, often "dancing" on the surface and almost hovering in one place as the winds lift it kitelike a few inches off the surface of the water. Frequently follows ships and chum lines (slicks of fish oils); attends fishing boats and whales as it forages.

• **BREEDING** Colonial.

• **NESTING** Incubation 40–50 days by both sexes. Semialtricial young fed by both sexes. Young leave nest at 46–97 days.

• **POPULATION** Large and apparently stable.

Similar Birds

LEACH'S STORM-PETREL Larger; longer forked tail without feet protruding beyond tip; mothlike flight pattern.

BAND-RUMPED STORM-PETREL Larger; longer tail; flight pattern is with shallow wing beats followed by stiff-winged glides similar to those of a shearwater.

Flight Pattern
Direct flight with steady shallow wing beats.

Nest Identification	
Shape ⬛ Location ▬	No built nest • hides egg in hole or crevice • 1 white egg, usually with reddish brown spots on larger end.

Plumage Sexes similar	Habitat ≈≈ ⚓	Migration Migratory	Weight 31 g

DATE _____ TIME_____ LOCATION _____

Family HYDROBATIDAE	Species *Hydrobates pelagicus*	Length 14–15 cm	Wingspan 37–39 cm

EUROPEAN STORM-PETREL

Found primarily in the northern and eastern Atlantic and rarely reported in the waters off Nova Scotia, this gregarious bird is the smallest and most common of the storm-petrels in the waters off western Europe and throughout the Mediterranean. It has a weak batlike flight, fluttering low over the surface of the sea, and it often follows ships. Wintering at sea, strong offshore winds sometimes bring it close inshore off the British Isles. It appears small and dark in flight with a U-shaped white rump patch and narrow buff-gray bar on the upperwing. The broad white stripe on the underwing is diagnostic. It has black legs and feet. Juveniles resemble adults but have a more pronounced pale upperwing bar.

brownish black wings

white rump and uppertail coverts

dark brownish black overall

black bill

short blackish tail with rounded corners

sooty black underparts

- **SONG** In nesting colony, an ongoing churring song interspersed with *chikka* sounds, as if the bird were hiccoughing. Silent at sea.
- **BEHAVIOR** Solitary or in small groups or flocks. Feeds far offshore for small fishes and zooplankton containing mollusks and crustaceans. When feeding holds wings midway above back and patters on the surface with its feet. Follows ships for oils, animal fats, and scraps.
- **BREEDING** Monogamous. Colonial. Mates for life.
- **NESTING** Incubation 38–50 days by both sexes. Semialtricial young remain in nest 56–73 days, fed by both sexes through regurgitation. 1 brood per year.
- **POPULATION** Rare to casual vagrant off the North Atlantic Coast of the Maritimes.
- **CONSERVATION** Some colonies have declined due to the introduction of cats and other predators on nesting areas of offshore islands.

Similar Birds

WILSON'S STORM-PETREL
Larger; broader white band across rump; long legs; feet trail beyond tip of tail; yellow-webbed blackish feet; more direct and swallowlike flight.

LEACH'S STORM-PETREL
Larger in size; longer, more pointed wings; less white on rump; forked tail; erratic mothlike flight.

Flight Pattern

Weak, fluttering, rapid, almost continuous, batlike wing beats interspersed with short glides.

Nest Identification

Shape Location

No nest materials • preformed or excavated burrows, rabbit burrows, crevices in stone walls or between boulders, and cliffs • 60–90 cm deep • built by both sexes • 1 white egg, often speckled with reddish brown, concentrated at larger end; elliptical to subelliptical, 2.8 cm long.

Plumage Sexes similar	Habitat	Migration Migratory	Weight 26 g

DATE _____ TIME _____ LOCATION _____

Family HYDROBATIDAE	Species *Oceanodroma furcata*	Length 20–23 cm	Wingspan 46 cm

FORK-TAILED STORM-PETREL

As the only blue-gray storm-petrel in its range, this bird contrasts strongly with all its darker brownish black congeners. The forked tail appears long in flight. All tail feathers are narrowly tipped white, and a white outer web, the outermost vane of the outer tail feathers, borders its entire length. At a distance in bright sunlight, the bird appears almost white, so when sitting on the water it might be confused with a phalarope. It has pale bluish pearl-gray underparts, and its legs are dark in color. Juvenile plumage is similar to that of the adult. In Alaska these cold-water birds are commonly found near the shore, especially in fall, and near air holes after the water is covered with ice.

- **SONG** Song undescribed; faint squeaking when burrow is disturbed or bird removed and held in hand. Noisy only on breeding grounds.

- **BEHAVIOR** Primarily nocturnal. Flies low to the water, catching prey without alighting. Feeds on small fish and crustaceans. Gregarious. Often settles on water. When about to take flight from water, extends wings to allow breeze to lift the weight of its body. Nomadic and follows ships. Found on open sea during migration and in winter.

- **BREEDING** Monogamous. Colonial.

medium bluish gray upperparts

darker gray forehead

hooked dark bill

darker gray patch passes through eye and turns downward on ear

darker gray primaries

Flight Pattern

Flap-and-glide flight with rapid shallow wing beats and stiff-winged glide.

- **NESTING** Incubation 37–68 days by both sexes. Semialtricial young stay in nest 51–61 days. Fed by both sexes through regurgitation. 1 brood per year.
- **POPULATION** Common and considered stable.

Nest Identification

Shape Location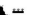

No lining • in soft soil on grassy slope or at base of cliff • built by both sexes • 1 dull white egg with wreath of dark purple with black spots, 3.3 cm long.

Plumage Sexes similar	Habitat ~~~ ___	Migration Migratory	Weight 54 g

DATE _____ TIME_____ LOCATION _____

Family HYDROBATIDAE	Species *Oceanodroma leucorhoa*	Length 20–23 cm	Wingspan 46–48 cm

LEACH'S STORM-PETREL

This slender long-winged storm-petrel can be seen off both coasts of North America. Some of the birds found off the Pacific Coast have dark rumps, rather than the more common and conspicuous white rump broken in the middle by a gray-brown stripe. Besides the rump, this bird's plumage is entirely dark brown. The tail is long and forked, but the fork is not always easily seen. It has short legs and feet that do not reach or protrude beyond the tip of its tail.

ATLANTIC

long narrow pointed wings

lighter grayish inner wing bar on upperwing

forked tail

dark brown plumage

PACIFIC

white rump patch broken by a gray-brown stripe

- **SONG** Short sharp ticking notes ending in a slurred trill.
- **BEHAVIOR** Strictly nocturnal on breeding grounds. Does not follow ships. Feeds on surface of water on small squid, crustaceans, and fish. Often feeds with wings held above horizontal while it patters on water surface. Its characteristic flight is slow, erratic, and mothlike, or similar to that of a nighthawk.
- **BREEDING** Monogamous and colonial.
- **NESTING** Incubation 38–46 days by both sexes. Semialtricial young remain in nest 63–70 days. Fed at night through regurgitation by both sexes. First flight at 63–70 days. 1 brood per year.
- **POPULATION** Slight decline, although total population is in the millions.
- **CONSERVATION** Some declines are showing on islands where humans have introduced predator species.

Similar Birds

WILSON'S STORM-PETREL Shorter, rounded wings; feet extend beyond squared, not forked, tail; has swallowlike flight pattern.

ASHY STORM-PETREL BLACK STORM-PETREL Both lack the erratic flight pattern • both range off Pacific Coast.

BAND-RUMPED STORM-PETREL Larger; shorter wider wings; conspicuous large white rump patch; stiff-winged glides and zigzag flight like a small shearwater • ranges off Atlantic Coast.

Flight Pattern
Bounding and erratic; mothlike with frequent changes of direction and speed.

Nest Identification	
Shape	Location	Lined with leaves and grass • under grass, rocks, or tree roots, or on bank • may be built by both sexes, although some literature states only the male digs burrow • 1 creamy white egg, often nest-stained and occasionally marked with reddish purple; subelliptical to oval, 3.3 cm long.

Plumage Sexes similar	Habitat	Migration Migratory	Weight 34 g

DATE _____ TIME_____ LOCATION _____

Family HYDROBATIDAE	Species *Oceanodroma castro*	Length 19–22 cm	Wingspan 42–46 cm

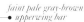

BAND-RUMPED STORM-PETREL

This tropical bird spends its time alone or in small groups at sea. It is seen in summer off the Atlantic Coast of North America. It seldom walks on the water. Often in the company of other storm-petrels, it can be separated from them by its flight pattern, which resembles that of a tiny shearwater. In flight the white rump patch is clear, and the black legs and feet do not project beyond the blackish tail, which in fresh adults has a slight notch.

faint pale gray-brown upperwing bar

sooty blackish brown overall

bold white band on rump and uppertail coverts

Juveniles resemble adults but paler greater coverts create a more distinct bar on the upperwing.

short stubby black bill

- **SONG** High-pitched squeak around nest. Silent at sea.
- **BEHAVIOR** Solitary, in pairs or small groups away from nests in nonbreeding season. Feeds at sea but does not follow ships. Eats crustaceans, small fishes, and other marine animals. Nocturnal around nesting burrow.
- **BREEDING** Monogamous. Colonial. Mates for life.
- **NESTING** Incubation 40–48 days by both sexes. Semialtricial young remain in nest 53–95 days, fed by both sexes through regurgitation. 1 brood per year.
- **POPULATION** Rare off North Atlantic; casual to uncommon in Gulf of Mexico; fairly common on mid-Atlantic Coast off North Carolina and Virginia. Storm-driven birds accidental inland.
- **CONSERVATION** Vulnerable to introduced predators in nesting areas and to pollution from oil spills.

Similar Birds

WILSON'S STORM-PETREL
Smaller in size; larger U-shaped white rump patch; longer black bill; yellow-webbed black feet project beyond squared tail; prominent diagonal secondary wing bar; more erratic and fluttery flight.

LEACH'S STORM-PETREL
Smaller; more distinct diagonal upperwing bar; longer more pointed wings; more deeply forked tail; ragged-edged white rump patch with central dividing line; bounding nighthawklike flight.

Flight Pattern
Buoyant zigzag with several rapid wing strokes followed by glide on horizontal or slightly downward-bowed wings.

Nest Identification	
Shape [icons] Location [icons]	No nest materials • burrows or crevices of rocky areas, 60–90 cm deep • dug by both sexes or cleaned out from previous year • 1 white egg; elliptical to subelliptical, 3.3 cm long.

Plumage Sexes similar	Habitat [icons]	Migration Migratory	Weight 45 g

DATE _____ TIME_____ LOCATION _____

Family PHAETHONTIDAE	Species *Phaethon lepturus*	Length 71–81 cm	Wingspan 89–97 cm

WHITE-TAILED TROPICBIRD

This bird nests in Bermuda, the Bahamas, and throughout the Caribbean. It is the smallest of the tropicbirds, and the one most likely to be spotted off North America's Atlantic Coast. It also is the only tropicbird with a long black bar on the upperwing coverts. The white tail streamers can be up to 41 cm long. Legs and feet are yellowish; toes have black webbing.

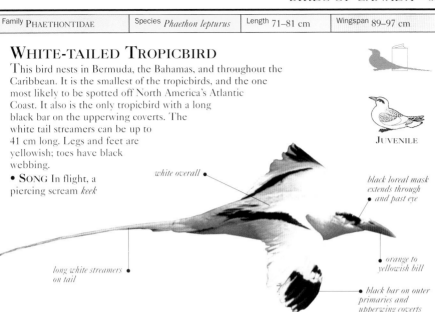

JUVENILE

• **SONG** In flight, a piercing scream *keek*

white overall

black loreal mask extends through and past eye

long white streamers on tail

orange to yellowish bill

black bar on outer primaries and upperwing coverts

or *keek*, often rapidly repeated. Call is a guttural squawk.

• **BEHAVIOR** Solitary or in noisy pairs or small groups. Ranges widely over oceans in nonbreeding season. Spots food from 15–31 meters above water, hovers, then makes direct dive. Eats small fish, crabs, and squid. Floats high in water with tail cocked upward. Attracted to ships, it may hover before landing in rigging. Comes farther inland than other tropicbirds.

• **BREEDING** Monogamous. Semicolonial.

• **NESTING** Incubation 40–42 days by both sexes, sometimes shorter period. Young altricial; first flight at 70–85 days; fed by both sexes. 1 brood per year.

• **POPULATION** Uncommon but regular in the Gulf Stream off North Carolina; rare and inconsistent on Dry Tortugas. Rare elsewhere on the Atlantic Coast to the Maritimes; one record in California.

• **BIRDHOUSES** Will nest in artificial in-ground chambers.

• **CONSERVATION** Vulnerable to introduced predators at nesting sites.

Similar Birds

RED-BILLED TROPICBIRD
Larger; mostly white crown; narrower black bars on upperparts; black eye stripe; black primaries and primary coverts; red bill
• juvenile has black eye stripe, usually meeting around nape; fine barring on upperparts; large black primary patch; yellow bill; lacks long streamers.

Flight Pattern

Buoyant graceful pigeonlike flight with fluttering wing strokes alternated with soaring glides; hovers briefly over prey or perch before dipping down to it.

Nest Identification

Shape

Location

No nest • on ground in ridges of cliffs, crevices, caves, or sheltered by grasses or bush • 1 whitish to pale buff egg, flecked with brownish and purple spots; ovoid, 5.8 x 4.1 cm.

Plumage Sexes similar	Habitat	Migration Migratory	Weight 434 g

DATE _____ TIME_____ LOCATION _____

| Family SULIDAE | Species *Sula leucogaster* | Length 66–74 cm | Wingspan 132–150 cm |

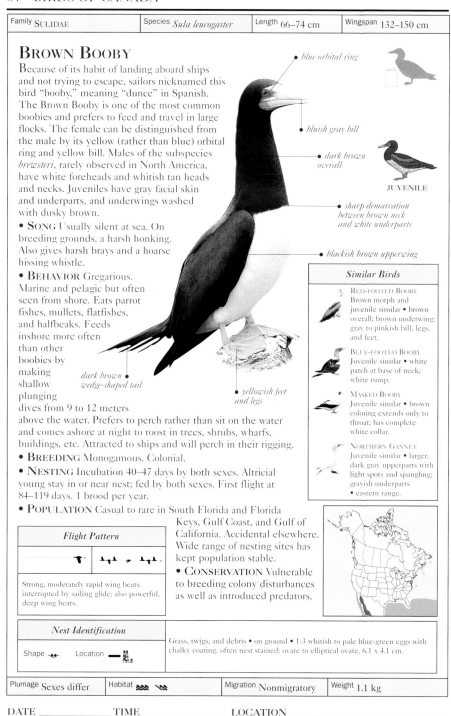

BROWN BOOBY

Because of its habit of landing aboard ships and not trying to escape, sailors nicknamed this bird "booby," meaning "dunce" in Spanish. The Brown Booby is one of the most common boobies and prefers to feed and travel in large flocks. The female can be distinguished from the male by its yellow (rather than blue) orbital ring and yellow bill. Males of the subspecies *brewsteri*, rarely observed in North America, have white foreheads and whitish tan heads and necks. Juveniles have gray facial skin and underparts, and underwings washed with dusky brown.

• **SONG** Usually silent at sea. On breeding grounds, a harsh honking. Also gives harsh brays and a hoarse hissing whistle.

• **BEHAVIOR** Gregarious. Marine and pelagic but often seen from shore. Eats parrot fishes, mullets, flatfishes, and halfbeaks. Feeds inshore more often than other boobies by making shallow plunging dives from 9 to 12 meters above the water. Prefers to perch rather than sit on the water and comes ashore at night to roost in trees, shrubs, wharfs, buildings, etc. Attracted to ships and will perch in their rigging.

• **BREEDING** Monogamous. Colonial.

• **NESTING** Incubation 40–47 days by both sexes. Altricial young stay in or near nest; fed by both sexes. First flight at 84–119 days. 1 brood per year.

• **POPULATION** Casual to rare in South Florida and Florida Keys, Gulf Coast, and Gulf of California. Accidental elsewhere. Wide range of nesting sites has kept population stable.

• **CONSERVATION** Vulnerable to breeding colony disturbances as well as introduced predators.

blue orbital ring

bluish gray bill

dark brown overall

JUVENILE

sharp demarcation between brown neck and white underparts

blackish brown upperwing

dark brown wedge-shaped tail

yellowish feet and legs

Similar Birds

RED-FOOTED BOOBY
Brown morph and juvenile similar • brown overall; brown underwing; gray to pinkish bill, legs, and feet.

BLUE-FOOTED BOOBY
Juvenile similar • white patch at base of neck; white rump.

MASKED BOOBY
Juvenile similar • brown coloring extends only to throat; has complete white collar.

NORTHERN GANNET
Juvenile similar • larger; dark gray upperparts with light spots and spangling; grayish underparts • eastern range.

Flight Pattern

Strong, moderately rapid wing beats interrupted by sailing glide; also powerful, deep wing beats.

Nest Identification

Shape — Location —

Grass, twigs, and debris • on ground • 1-3 whitish to pale blue-green eggs with chalky coating, often nest stained; ovate to elliptical ovate, 6.1 x 4.1 cm.

| Plumage Sexes differ | Habitat | Migration Nonmigratory | Weight 1.1 kg |

DATE _____ TIME_____ LOCATION _____

Family SULIDAE	Species *Morus bassanus*	Length 89–102 cm	Wingspan 165–180 cm

NORTHERN GANNET

Like a large white flying cross pointed at all ends – long pointed black-tipped wings, long pointed white tail, and long bill often pointed downward toward the water – this is the largest indigenous seabird of the North Atlantic. Gannets feed and travel in small flocks, but nest in huge dense colonies of five thousand or more birds. They stay at sea the first three years of life, then head for land only to breed. Juveniles have dark gray upperparts and heavily spotted, paler gray underparts, then become pied black, white, and gray as they progress into adult plumage. Males are larger than females.

creamy yellow to golden orange wash on head

long pale blue bill

black bare skin at base of bill

white overall

- **SONG** Silent at sea except when feeding. Clamorous honking and various low groans and clucks around nest.
- **BEHAVIOR** Gregarious. Dives underwater, as deep as 15 meters, plunging like an arrow from up to 31 meters high. Grabs fish and squid with bill. Roosts on water after feeding; sleeps in large rafts. Returns to nesting site annually; sites used for hundreds of years. Ranges primarily over continental shelf. Rarely pelagic over truly deep waters.

JUVENILE

dark gray legs and webbed feet

long black-tipped wings

long pointed white tail

- **BREEDING** Monogamous; mates for life. Colonial. Mated pairs perform complex "dance" at nest, similar to that of albatross, in which they face each other, wings slightly raised and opened, tail raised and spread. This is followed by a repeated series of bows, bills raised and waved in air, more bows, and feigned caressing of each other's breast.
- **NESTING** Incubation 42–44 days, by both sexes; male does more. Young stay in nest 95–107 days. Both parents feed by regurgitation. 1 brood per year.

Similar Birds

MASKED BOOBY
Yellow bill; black facial skin; black tail; solid black edging (all flight feathers) on wings.

RED-FOOTED BOOBY
White morph • smaller; white or black tail; all flight feathers and primary coverts are black; coral-red feet.

- **POPULATION** Common. Often seen from shore in migration and winter. Rare to casual on Great Lakes in fall.
- **CONSERVATION** Vulnerable to oil spills, human disturbance at nesting colonies.

Flight Pattern

Alternates rapid wing beats with short glides at frequent intervals. Soars to great heights. Glides low in strong winds.

Nest Identification

Shape   Location

Pile of seaweed and refuse • on ridges of cliff • 1 chalky light blue egg becoming nest stained; ovate to elliptical ovate; 7.6 x 4.6 cm.

Plumage Sexes similar	Habitat	Migration Migratory	Weight 2.9 kg

DATE _____ TIME_____ LOCATION _____

Family PELECANIDAE	Species *Pelecanus erythrorhynchos*	Length 152–160 cm	Wingspan 244–279 cm

AMERICAN WHITE PELICAN

One of the most distinctive birds in North America, this huge pelican, with its immense bill and vast wingspan, is one of the largest waterbirds. Making their summer home near inland lakes, breeding birds shed the upper mandible plate after the eggs are laid and show a dull grayish crown and nape. In flight the head is drawn back on the shoulders with the bill resting on the breast, and the black primaries and outer secondaries contrast sharply with the white plumage. Young have a dull grayish bill and a brownish wash on the head, neck, and upper wing coverts.

pale yellow crest

black wing tips and outer trailing edge of wing

graduated plates on upper mandible

oversized orange-salmon bill

short orange-red legs and feet

WINTER PLUMAGE

- **SONG** Mostly silent. On nesting grounds guttural croaks.
- **BEHAVIOR** Entire flock may work communally to catch fish by "herding" them into shallow water or an enclosed area, then scooping the fish out of the water with pouches that can hold over 11.5 liters of water. Eats fish of little or no commercial value.
- **BREEDING** Monogamous. Colonial.
- **NESTING** Incubation 29–36 days by both sexes. Young stay in nest 17–28 days; fed by both sexes. Gather in groups called pods after fledging and continue to be fed by adults. First flight at 9–10 weeks. 1 brood per year.
- **POPULATION** Fairly common to common. Breeds in western lakes; winters in southwest and Gulf Coast states. Casual wanderer in migration.
- **CONSERVATION** Some decrease due to habitat loss and pesticide poisoning; however, has increased since 1970s. Despite legal protection most deaths due to shooting.

Similar Birds

WOOD STORK Black trailing edge to wing (all flight feathers); black tail; dark head and bill; long legs trail beyond tail in flight.

BROWN PELICAN Gray-brown upperparts; dark wings; darker bill; plunge dives for fish while flying.

Flight Pattern

Strong slow deep wing beats. Soars high on thermals. Flies in straight line or V formation.

Nest Identification

Shape — Location —

Made of built-up dirt and rubbish • on flat ground • 1–2 dull or chalky white eggs; ovate to elongate-ovate with some nearly elliptical–oval, 8.9 x 5.6 cm.

Plumage Sexes similar	Habitat	Migration Migratory	Weight 7.0 kg

DATE _____ TIME_____ LOCATION _____

Family PHALACROCORACIDAE	Species *Phalacrocorax penicillatus*	Length 89 cm	Wingspan 124 cm

BRANDT'S CORMORANT

The black throat patch bordered by a buff-brown throat band quickly distinguish this cormorant during the nonbreeding season. In the shorter breeding season from March to July the gular patch becomes bright blue and fine white plumes adorn the head, neck, and scapular region. The nests of these highly colonial birds are built so close together that they almost touch. Flocks fly in long rows between feeding and roosting areas. Juveniles are dark smoky brown with a buff-brown breast.

pale buff band of feathers behind black throat patch

• *long neck*

• *black body*

• **SONG** Mostly silent, except at nest where it utters throaty croaks and low growling sounds.

• **BEHAVIOR** Gregarious. Feeds by diving for fish, crabs, and shrimp. Often forms dense floating flocks at sea over fishing areas. Flies in long lines to and from roosting areas to fishing grounds. Like other cormorants, when perched after fishing holds wings out to dry.

WINTER PLUMAGE

JUVENILE

• *short tail* • *black legs and webbed feet*

Similar Birds

PELAGIC CORMORANT
Smaller; dark red throat pouch and part of face; smaller, thinner bill; longer tail; large white patches on flanks.

DOUBLE-CRESTED CORMORANT
Longer, more pointed wings; yellow-orange throat patch • double tufts (white in western birds) evident in breeding season.

• **BREEDING** Monogamous. Colonial. Nests on sea cliffs and offshore rocky islands.

• **NESTING** Incubation 28–31 days by both sexes. Young are altricial and stay in nest 53–60 days. 1 brood per year.

• **POPULATION** Common. Uncommon to casual on Pacific Coast outside breeding range.

• **CONSERVATION** Vulnerable to oil spills and coastal pollution.

Flight Pattern
Strong direct flight with powerful rapid wing beats. Flocks fly in straight line formation.

Nest Identification	
Shape ⬬ Location	Made of moss, grasses, and seaweed • on rocky ground • male selects site and collects nesting material; built by both sexes • 3–6 bluish white eggs, long subelliptical, 6.1 x 3.8 cm.

Plumage Sexes similar	Habitat	Migration Nonmigratory	Weight 2.1 kg

DATE _____ TIME_____ LOCATION _____

Family PHALACROCORACIDAE	Species *Phalacrocorax auritus*	Length 81 cm	Wingspan 132 cm

DOUBLE-CRESTED CORMORANT

The most widespread cormorant in North America appears blackish overall from a distance, but may appear to have a green sheen in certain lighting. During breeding season it shows two small tufts of feathers; they are black in eastern birds, but larger and mostly white in western birds. Its wings are not completely waterproof, so upon leaving the water the bird often perches on exposed objects with its wings held out to catch the sun's rays and dry its feathers. This cormorant swims low in the water with its bill tilted slightly upward. In flight it has a distinct crook in its neck. Immature birds are brown with white face, foreneck, and breast.

bright orange-yellow facial skin

long pale hooked bill

bright orange-yellow gular skin

green sheen on neck, head, and underparts

brown upperparts with black scaling

blackish overall

JUVENILE

• **SONG** Deep guttural grunt.

• **BEHAVIOR** Gregarious. Dives for fish, crustaceans, and amphibians from surface. Excellent diver, using feet for propulsion. Able to stay at 1.5–7.5 meters below surface for 30–70 seconds.

black legs and feet

• **BREEDING** Monogamous. Colonial.

• **NESTING** Incubation 28–30 days by both sexes. Altricial young may leave nest at 21–28 days but may return to be fed by both sexes. First flight at 35–42 days. Independent at 63–70 days. 1 brood per year.

• **POPULATION** Common. Fluctuates because of persecution at nesting colonies, although increasing and expanding range, particularly in interior, in last 2 decades of the 20th century.

• **CONSERVATION** Often killed by fishermen who believe birds compete with them. Many populations hit hard, especially on California coast, in 1960s and 1970s by DDT, causing reproductive failures.

Similar Birds

NEOTROPIC CORMORANT Smaller; longer tail; posterior edge of gular skin often pointed with whitish border.

BRANDT'S CORMORANT Dark face; blue throat patch with buff border; shorter tail; flies with head and neck held straight • strictly coastal and pelagic western range.

GREAT CORMORANT Larger throat pouch bordered by white feathers; white cheeks and flank patches (breeding) • East Coast range.

Flight Pattern

Strong powerful direct flight. Sometimes soars briefly on thermals. Groups fly in straight line or V formation.

Nest Identification

Shape 〰 Location 🪹🌳🏞🪨—

In trees made of sticks and debris and lined with leafy twigs and grass • on rocks often made of seaweed and trash gathered at water's edge • near water • built by female • 2 nest-stained bluish white eggs; long subelliptical, 6.1 x 3.8 cm.

Plumage Sexes similar	Habitat 〰 🦢 🪨	Migration Migratory	Weight 1.8 kg

DATE _____ TIME_____ LOCATION _____

Family PHALACROCORACIDAE	Species *Phalacrocorax carbo*	Length 89–102 cm	Wingspan 160 cm

GREAT CORMORANT

heavy hooked bill

bright yellow throat pouch with large border of white feathers

blocklike head

JUVENILE

short tail

The largest North American cormorant is able to carry water in its throat pouch to pour over its chicks when they have been exposed to high temperatures. A proficient swimmer and diver, this bird has been found as deep as thirty meters below the surface. Its large size, large bill, pale yellow chin, and white throat patch distinguish it from the Double-crested Cormorant, the only other cormorant sharing its northern Atlantic range. In breeding season short white plumes appear on the side of the neck, and white patches are visible on its flanks while in flight. Juveniles have brown upperparts and a white belly.

• **SONG** Usually silent. Low throaty groans on breeding grounds.

• **BEHAVIOR** Excellent swimmer. Rides low in water, holding bill slightly angled above horizontal; uses webbed feet to swim. Dives for fish and crustaceans. When perched wet, holds wings in spread eagle position to dry.

• **BREEDING** Monogamous. Colonial. Breeds on cliffs or rocks.

• **NESTING** Incubation 28–31 days by both sexes. Altricial young stay in nest 50 days. Fed by both sexes. First flight is at 50 days. Fledged young may return to nest at night until they achieve independence in 30–40 more days. 1 brood per year.

• **POPULATION** Fairly common. Increased dramatically; range has spread southward. Thought to be limited by interactions with more numerous and well-established Double-crested Cormorant. Winters in small numbers from the Maritime Provinces south to South Carolina; rare farther south.

• **CONSERVATION** Vulnerable to disturbance at colonial nesting sites as well as the pollution of its marine environment.

Similar Birds

DOUBLE-CRESTED CORMORANT Smaller; orange throat patch; no flank patches • juveniles have slimmer bill, deep orange facial skin, pale breast and darker belly.

Flight Pattern

Strong direct flight with steady wing beats, but slow to reach full flight speed. Flies in V or straight line formation.

Nest Identification

Shape ⌣ Location 🪺 🪨 🗻 ━ 〰

Twigs, seaweed, and bits of refuse • lined with grasses and moss • on ground in moderately elevated area • built by both sexes • 3–5 pale blue-green eggs, often nest-stained; long oval, 6.6 cm long.

Plumage Sexes similar	Habitat 🦆 〰 ≋	Migration Migratory	Weight 2.3 kg

Family PHALACROCORACIDAE	Species *Phalacrocorax pelagicus*	Length 66–74 cm	Wingspan 102 cm

PELAGIC CORMORANT

The distinctive white patches on its flanks and short double crest during breeding season distinguish the Pelagic Cormorant from other Pacific Coast cormorants except for the Red-faced Cormorant in Alaska. Its small size and short neck are good additional field marks, and no other cormorant in its range has a slender black bill. Near the base of the bill is a blackish area of bare skin and reddish throat pouch. Slender white streaks appear on the bird's neck only when it is breeding. Juveniles are dark sooty brown.

dull red facial patch

small head

thin hooked blackish bill

reddish throat pouch

black with metallic green sheen in breeding plumage

long tail

white flank patches in breeding plumage

JUVENILE

- **SONG** Groans, croaks, or hisses.
- **BEHAVIOR** Not as gregarious as other cormorants, and frequently is sedentary. Often feeds by watching gulls, which attract the bird to schools of fish on which they are feeding. Diet consists of marine fish, crustaceans, and other invertebrates. Expert diver. Has been found in fishing nets as deep as 55 meters. Can leap directly into flight from water without running and flapping across surface like other cormorants. Returns to nesting site each year, preferring to add to its nest rather than build a new one.
- **BREEDING** Monogamous. Colonial.
- **NESTING** Incubation 26–37 days by both sexes. First short flight at 35–40 days. Altricial young leave nest at 45–55 days; continue to be fed by parents for a few weeks. 1 brood per year.

Similar Birds

RED-FACED CORMORANT Partly yellow bill; more extensive red in face extends onto forehead; bluish throat pouch.

DOUBLE-CRESTED CORMORANT Wider bill; yellow-orange throat patch; lacks white flank patches and red in face.

- **POPULATION** Stable.
- **CONSERVATION** Vulnerable to environmental pollution and drowning in commercial fishing nets.

Flight Pattern
Graceful direct flight with rapid wing beats. Flies in V formation.

Nest Identification	
Shape Location	Seaweed, grass, moss, debris, and twigs • may reach 1.5–2 m tall • on remote near-vertical cliffs facing water • built by both sexes • 3–5 chalky pale bluish eggs, 6.1 cm long.

Plumage Sexes similar	Habitat	Migration Nonmigratory	Weight 2.0 kg

DATE _____ TIME_____ LOCATION _____

Family FREGATIDAE	Species *Fregata magnificens*	Length 94–104 cm	Wingspan 208–239 cm

MAGNIFICENT FRIGATEBIRD

The male has a most striking courtship display when he inflates his throat sac into a huge brilliant red balloon. In flight it looks almost sinister with its black plumage, long thin crooked wings, and deeply forked tail often folded into a point. Juveniles are black without gloss and have a white head, neck, sides, breast, and belly. Even when not nesting, flocks of these birds often gather at their permanent roosts in treetops, or on high cliffs.

- **SONG** Clacks bill; nasal *kack* or *ka-ack*; soft chippering at nesting grounds. Silent at sea.
- **BEHAVIOR** Soars over sea to find food. Dives for prey and catches it in bill from surface. Eats fish, crustaceans, and jellyfish. Attacks other large seabirds in flight until they drop or disgorge their catch, which the frigatebird then catches in midair. Roosts communally and is gregarious.
- **BREEDING** Monogamous. Colonial.
- **NESTING** Incubation 40–50 days by both sexes. Fed by both sexes. First flight at 20–24 weeks. Young never left unguarded because other birds in colony may eat eggs and hatchlings. Most females do not breed every year.
- **POPULATION** Total difficult to monitor. Rare to casual on Salton Sea and along California coast to Washington. Breeds on Dry Tortugas off Florida Keys. Fairly common to casual along Gulf of Mexico, Florida coasts, and north to North Carolina. Rare straggler north to Maritimes and inland, especially after storms.
- **CONSERVATION** Frigatebirds are legally protected, but they are still killed in the nest by local people, who hunt at night with flashlights and clubs. Some years no young survive.

straight hooked gray bill

entirely black with purple gloss on back and head

bright red pouch usually shows as red patch on throat when not distended

MALE

JUVENILE

straight hooked gray bill

white breast and sides

FEMALE

black without gloss

long, narrow pointed wings

long deeply forked tail

Similar Birds

♂ GREAT FRIGATEBIRD Male has pale brownish alar bar; scalloped pale grayish axillars; green gloss on head and back • female has gray-white throat, breast, and upper belly; red orbital ring; broader black belly patch • juvenile has white head, neck, and breast; neck and head tinged with rust-brown.

Flight Pattern
Very high effortless soaring flight. Extremely graceful and buoyant in the air.

Nest Identification	
Shape 🐦 Location 🌿🌱🌳	Sticks, twigs, grass, and reeds • in mangroves, trees, or bushes, 60 cm–6 m above ground • built by female with materials gathered by male, which often steals from neighbors' nests • 1 white egg; rarely 2.

Plumage Sexes differ	Habitat 🪶	Migration Nonmigratory	Weight 1.3 kg

DATE _____ TIME_____ LOCATION _____

Family ARDEIDAE	Species *Botaurus lentiginosus*	Length 58 cm	Wingspan 107–127 cm

AMERICAN BITTERN

When it senses danger, the American Bittern hides by standing motionless with its bill pointed upward and its body tightly contracted. Thus it can be mistaken for a wooden stake in the marshes, saltwater and freshwater bogs, and wetland ponds it inhabits. The dark and light vertical streaks blend with shadows and highlights cast by surrounding vegetation, so the bird often goes unnoticed even from 1 to 2 meters away. In flight the somewhat pointed dark outer wings contrast sharply with the inner wings and body.

dark brown crown

pointed yellowish bill

white throat

streaked brown and buff upperparts

long black strip or patch on each side of neck

streaked brown and white underparts

pointed wings with contrasting dark tips

JUVENILE

• **SONG** *Oonk-a-lunk* or *punk-er-lunk*, often heard at dusk; it is one of the strangest sounds produced by any bird; sounds like someone driving a stake into the mud with a wooden mallet.

• **BEHAVIOR** Stands motionless, often hidden by marsh vegetation, on ground or in water to search for prey. Eats frogs, small eels, small fish, small snakes, salamanders, crayfish, small rodents, and water bugs.

• **BREEDING** May be polygamous. Solitary nester.

• **NESTING** Incubation 24–29 days by female. Young stay in nest 14 days. Fed by both parents. 1 brood per year.

• **POPULATION** Fairly common. Declining in the South from marshland drainage.

• **CONSERVATION** Protected by law. Wetland conservation is critical for this species.

Similar Birds

♂ **LEAST BITTERN** Much smaller; black crown and back; shows buff wing patches in flight.
♀

YELLOW-CROWNED NIGHT-HERON
BLACK-CROWNED NIGHT-HERON Juveniles have more heavily spotted upperparts; lack black mustache lines on face.

Flight Pattern

Strong direct flight with deep rapid wing beats.

Nest Identification

Shape   Location

Grasses, reeds, and cattails • lined with fine grasses • on dense marsh ground, dry ground above water, or mud in tall vegetation • built by female • 2–7 pale brown to olive-buff eggs, 4.8 cm long.

Plumage Sexes similar	Habitat	Migration Migratory	Weight 726 g

DATE _____ TIME_____ LOCATION _____

Family ARDEIDAE	Species *Ixobrychus exilis*	Length 28–36 cm	Wingspan 41–46 cm

LEAST BITTERN

This shy bird of the marshes is the smallest heron in North America. Because of the thick vegetation it frequents and its retiring nature, it often goes unnoticed and is probably more common than reported. Its small size and buff inner wing patches seen in flight quickly separate it from all other species. Adult females have a dark brown crown, back, and tail; juveniles are similar but more heavily streaked.

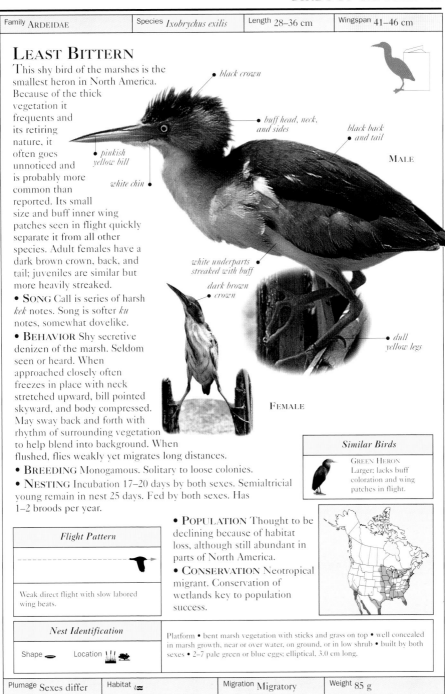

black crown

buff head, neck, and sides

black back and tail

MALE

pinkish yellow bill

white chin

white underparts streaked with buff

dark brown crown

dull yellow legs

FEMALE

• **SONG** Call is series of harsh *kek* notes. Song is softer *ku* notes, somewhat dovelike.

• **BEHAVIOR** Shy secretive denizen of the marsh. Seldom seen or heard. When approached closely often freezes in place with neck stretched upward, bill pointed skyward, and body compressed. May sway back and forth with rhythm of surrounding vegetation to help blend into background. When flushed, flies weakly yet migrates long distances.

• **BREEDING** Monogamous. Solitary to loose colonies.

• **NESTING** Incubation 17–20 days by both sexes. Semialtricial young remain in nest 25 days. Fed by both sexes. Has 1–2 broods per year.

Similar Birds

GREEN HERON
Larger; lacks buff coloration and wing patches in flight.

• **POPULATION** Thought to be declining because of habitat loss, although still abundant in parts of North America.

• **CONSERVATION** Neotropical migrant. Conservation of wetlands key to population success.

Flight Pattern
Weak direct flight with slow labored wing beats.

Nest Identification	
Shape ⬤ Location 🕯️🌿	Platform • bent marsh vegetation with sticks and grass on top • well concealed in marsh growth, near or over water, on ground, or in low shrub • built by both sexes • 2–7 pale green or blue eggs; elliptical, 3.0 cm long.

Plumage Sexes differ	Habitat 〰️	Migration Migratory	Weight 85 g

DATE _____ TIME_____ LOCATION _____

Family ARDEIDAE	Species *Ardea herodias*	Length 117–132 cm	Wingspan 196–208 cm

GREAT BLUE HERON

Often called "crane" or "blue crane" by locals, the Great Blue Heron is the largest, most widespread, and best-known heron in North America. Its size, long yellowish bill, and mostly bluish gray body readily distinguish it. In the breeding season several long black occipital plumes adorn the back of the crown. In south Florida a paler white-headed

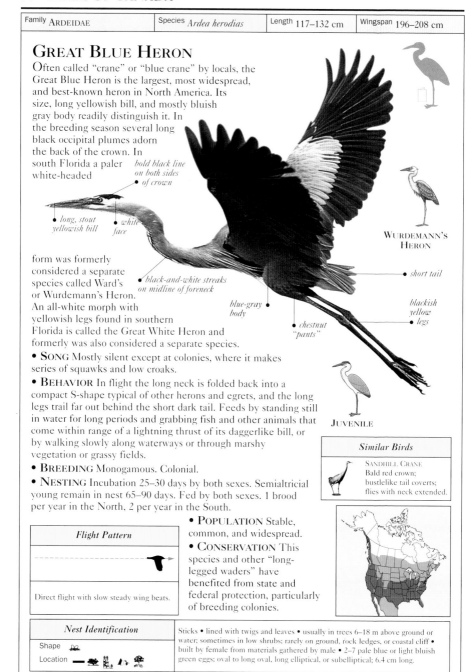

bold black line on both sides of crown

long, stout yellowish bill

white face

WURDEMANN'S HERON

short tail

black-and-white streaks on midline of foreneck

blue-gray body

chestnut "pants"

blackish yellow legs

form was formerly considered a separate species called Ward's or Wurdemann's Heron. An all-white morph with yellowish legs found in southern Florida is called the Great White Heron and formerly was also considered a separate species.

- **SONG** Mostly silent except at colonies, where it makes series of squawks and low croaks.

- **BEHAVIOR** In flight the long neck is folded back into a compact S-shape typical of other herons and egrets, and the long legs trail far out behind the short dark tail. Feeds by standing still in water for long periods and grabbing fish and other animals that come within range of a lightning thrust of its daggerlike bill, or by walking slowly along waterways or through marshy vegetation or grassy fields.

JUVENILE

- **BREEDING** Monogamous. Colonial.

- **NESTING** Incubation 25–30 days by both sexes. Semialtricial young remain in nest 65–90 days. Fed by both sexes. 1 brood per year in the North, 2 per year in the South.

- **POPULATION** Stable, common, and widespread.

- **CONSERVATION** This species and other "long-legged waders" have benefited from state and federal protection, particularly of breeding colonies.

Similar Birds

SANDHILL CRANE
Bald red crown; bustlelike tail coverts; flies with neck extended.

Flight Pattern

Direct flight with slow steady wing beats.

Nest Identification

Shape

Location

Sticks • lined with twigs and leaves • usually in trees 6–18 m above ground or water; sometimes in low shrubs; rarely on ground, rock ledges, or coastal cliff • built by female from materials gathered by male • 2–7 pale blue or light bluish green eggs; oval to long oval, long elliptical, or subelliptical; 6.4 cm long.

Plumage Sexes similar	Habitat	Migration Northern birds migrate	Weight 2.6 kg

Family ARDEIDAE	Species *Ardea alba*	Length 94–104 cm	Wingspan 140 cm

GREAT EGRET

The largest white egret found over most of its range can be distinguished from other white egrets and juvenile herons by its size, yellow bill, and black legs and feet. This tall, slender-necked bird develops long trains of lacy plumes on its back that extend beyond the tail when breeding, and its yellow bill appears more orange in color.

• **SONG** Bold throaty croaking or repeated *cuk, cuk*.

• **BEHAVIOR** Prefers to feed in open areas from salt marshes to freshwater habitats.

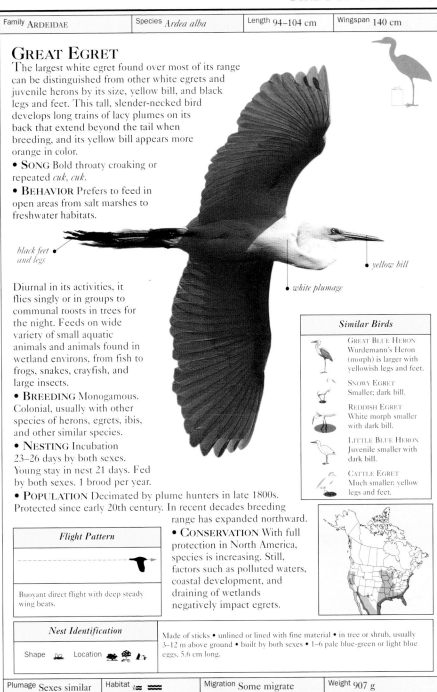

black feet and legs

yellow bill

white plumage

Diurnal in its activities, it flies singly or in groups to communal roosts in trees for the night. Feeds on wide variety of small aquatic animals and animals found in wetland environs, from fish to frogs, snakes, crayfish, and large insects.

• **BREEDING** Monogamous. Colonial, usually with other species of herons, egrets, ibis, and other similar species.

• **NESTING** Incubation 23–26 days by both sexes. Young stay in nest 21 days. Fed by both sexes. 1 brood per year.

• **POPULATION** Decimated by plume hunters in late 1800s. Protected since early 20th century. In recent decades breeding range has expanded northward.

• **CONSERVATION** With full protection in North America, species is increasing. Still, factors such as polluted waters, coastal development, and draining of wetlands negatively impact egrets.

Similar Birds

GREAT BLUE HERON Wurdemann's Heron (morph) is larger with yellowish legs and feet.

SNOWY EGRET Smaller; dark bill.

REDDISH EGRET White morph smaller with dark bill.

LITTLE BLUE HERON Juvenile smaller with dark bill.

CATTLE EGRET Much smaller; yellow legs and feet.

Flight Pattern

Buoyant direct flight with deep steady wing beats.

Nest Identification

Shape   Location

Made of sticks • unlined or lined with fine material • in tree or shrub, usually 3–12 m above ground • built by both sexes • 1–6 pale blue-green or light blue eggs, 5.6 cm long.

Plumage Sexes similar	Habitat	Migration Some migrate	Weight 907 g

DATE _____ TIME_____ LOCATION _____

Family ARDEIDAE	Species *Egretta garzetta*	Length 61 cm	Wingspan 91 cm

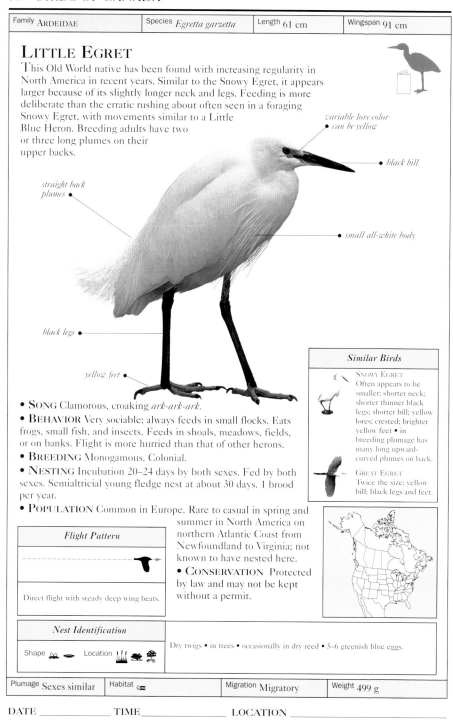

LITTLE EGRET

This Old World native has been found with increasing regularity in North America in recent years. Similar to the Snowy Egret, it appears larger because of its slightly longer neck and legs. Feeding is more deliberate than the erratic rushing about often seen in a foraging Snowy Egret, with movements similar to a Little Blue Heron. Breeding adults have two or three long plumes on their upper backs.

variable lore color can be yellow

black bill

straight back plumes

small all-white body

black legs

yellow feet

Similar Birds

SNOWY EGRET
Often appears to be smaller; shorter neck; shorter thinner black legs; shorter bill; yellow lores; crested; brighter yellow feet • in breeding plumage has many long upward-curved plumes on back.

GREAT EGRET
Twice the size; yellow bill; black legs and feet.

- **SONG** Clamorous, croaking *ark-ark-ark*.
- **BEHAVIOR** Very sociable; always feeds in small flocks. Eats frogs, small fish, and insects. Feeds in shoals, meadows, fields, or on banks. Flight is more hurried than that of other herons.
- **BREEDING** Monogamous. Colonial.
- **NESTING** Incubation 20–24 days by both sexes. Fed by both sexes. Semialtricial young fledge nest at about 30 days. 1 brood per year.
- **POPULATION** Common in Europe. Rare to casual in spring and summer in North America on northern Atlantic Coast from Newfoundland to Virginia; not known to have nested here.
- **CONSERVATION** Protected by law and may not be kept without a permit.

Flight Pattern
Direct flight with steady deep wing beats.

Nest Identification	
Shape ⬮ ⬯ Location 🌿🌳🌲	Dry twigs • in trees • occasionally in dry reed • 5–6 greenish blue eggs.

Plumage Sexes similar	Habitat 〰	Migration Migratory	Weight 499 g

DATE _____ TIME_____ LOCATION _____

Family ARDEIDAE	Species *Egretta thula*	Length 56–59 cm	Wingspan 97–114 cm

SNOWY EGRET

This is perhaps the most beautiful of all North American egrets and herons in its nuptial plumage, and the daintiest with or without it. This energetic medium-sized white egret has black legs and bright yellow "slippers." Slaughtered by the thousands for its soft, lacy breeding finery, it was the most persecuted of all egrets by plume hunters in the late 19th and early 20th centuries.

- **SONG** Generally silent. Vocalizations are harsh squawks.
- **BEHAVIOR** Most active heron when feeding. Rushes after prey in manner of Reddish Egret. Often sticks one foot forward in water and rapidly vibrates it to startle prey. Crustaceans, insects, and fish are important components of diet.
- **BREEDING** Monogamous. Colonial, often nests in mixed colonies with other herons and egrets.
- **NESTING** Incubation 20–24 days by both sexes. Semialtricial young stay in nest 30 days. Fed by both sexes. 1 brood per year.
- **POPULATION** Increasing. Range expanding northward.
- **CONSERVATION** Seemingly thriving today, but almost extirpated in the early 20th century by demand for its "cross aigrettes" for ladies' fashions.

yellow eyes

long, slender black bill

yellow lores

white plumage

WINTER PLUMAGE

Similar Birds

CATTLE EGRET Stockier; shorter neck; yellow bill and legs.

GREAT EGRET Much larger; yellow bill; black feet.

LITTLE BLUE HERON Juvenile has greenish legs; gray bill with black tip.

bright yellow feet

black legs

Flight Pattern
Buoyant direct flight with steady fast wing beats.

Nest Identification	
Shape Location	Sticks • lined with fine twigs and rushes • in short tree or shrub, 1.5–3 m high • sometimes on ground • built by both sexes • 2–6 pale blue-green eggs, 4.3 cm long.

Plumage Sexes similar	Habitat	Migration Migratory	Weight 371 g

DATE _____ TIME_____ LOCATION _____

Family ARDEIDAE	Species *Egretta caerulea*	Length 61–74 cm	Wingspan 102–104 cm

LITTLE BLUE HERON

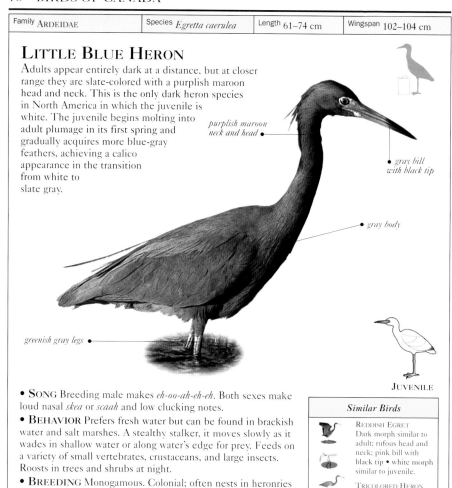

Adults appear entirely dark at a distance, but at closer range they are slate-colored with a purplish maroon head and neck. This is the only dark heron species in North America in which the juvenile is white. The juvenile begins molting into adult plumage in its first spring and gradually acquires more blue-gray feathers, achieving a calico appearance in the transition from white to slate gray.

purplish maroon neck and head

gray bill with black tip

gray body

greenish gray legs

JUVENILE

- **SONG** Breeding male makes *eh-oo-ah-eh-eh*. Both sexes make loud nasal *skea* or *scaah* and low clucking notes.
- **BEHAVIOR** Prefers fresh water but can be found in brackish water and salt marshes. A stealthy stalker, it moves slowly as it wades in shallow water or along water's edge for prey. Feeds on a variety of small vertebrates, crustaceans, and large insects. Roosts in trees and shrubs at night.
- **BREEDING** Monogamous. Colonial; often nests in heronries with other species.
- **NESTING** Incubation 20–24 days by both sexes. Semialtricial young stay in nest 42–49 days. Fed by both sexes. Has 1 brood per year.
- **POPULATION** Increasing and expanding.
- **CONSERVATION** Responding to protection of nesting colonies.

Similar Birds

REDDISH EGRET
Dark morph similar to adult; rufous head and neck; pink bill with black tip • white morph similar to juvenile.

TRICOLORED HERON
White underparts.

Flight Pattern

Direct flight with steady quick wing beats.

Nest Identification

Shape   Location

Sticks and twigs • unlined or lined with finer material • usually in tree or shrub, 1–5 m high • occasionally on ground • built by both sexes • 1–6 pale blue-green eggs; elliptical to subelliptical, 4.3 cm long.

Plumage Sexes similar	Habitat	Migration Migratory	Weight 366 g

DATE _____ TIME_____ LOCATION _____

Family ARDEIDAE	Species *Bubulcus ibis*	Length 48–53 cm	Wingspan 91–97 cm

CATTLE EGRET

This is the only small white egret with the combination of a yellow bill and yellow legs and feet. Breeding adults have patches of buff-orange on crown, nape, lower foreneck, and back. Nonbreeding adults and immature birds lack the buff-orange patches and have yellow bill, legs, and feet. A big-headed, thick-necked, short-legged egret of the Old World (originally found in Spain, Portugal, and Africa), it introduced itself to South America in the 1880s and to Florida by the early 1940s. From there it moved over most of the US and into southern Canada.

- **SONG** Various croaking sounds at breeding colonies; otherwise silent.

- **BEHAVIOR** Associates with cattle, horses, or other livestock in moist or dry pastures, where it feeds primarily on large insects disturbed by feeding livestock. Several birds may accompany a single cow, often riding on its back. Also follows tractors plowing fields to feed on the exposed insects and grubs. Largely diurnal, flying at dusk to communal roosts with other egrets, herons, and ibis to spend the night perched in trees or shrubs. They often form the nucleus of nesting colonies of other species of heron and egrets, and their presence may encourage the nesting of these birds in the heronries.

- **BREEDING** Monogamous. Colonial; often found in mixed breeding colonies with other species.

- **NESTING** Incubation 21–26 days by both sexes. Semialtricial young remain in nest about 45 days. Fed by both sexes. 1 brood per year.

- **POPULATION** North American population increasing.

- **CONSERVATION** Nesting colonies protected.

buff-orange patches on crown, nape, and back

yellowish orange bill

short thick neck

buff-orange patches on lower foreneck

white plumage

yellowish orange feet

short yellowish orange legs

JUVENILE

Similar Birds

SNOWY EGRET
Longer, more slender neck; black bill and legs.

LITTLE BLUE HERON
Juvenile is larger with longer, more slender neck; greenish gray legs and feet; black-tipped grayish bill.

GREAT EGRET
Larger; black legs and feet.

Flight Pattern

Direct flight with steady, rather rapid wing beats.

Nest Identification

Shape ___ Location ___

Sticks and reeds • lined with leafy green twigs • in tree or shrub • built by female from materials gathered by male • 1–9 pale blue or light bluish green eggs; subelliptical or elliptical, 4.8 cm long.

Plumage Sexes similar	Habitat	Migration Migratory	Weight 337 g

DATE _____ TIME _____ LOCATION _____

| Family ARDEIDAE | Species *Butorides virescens* | Length 46–56 cm | Wingspan 66 cm |

GREEN HERON

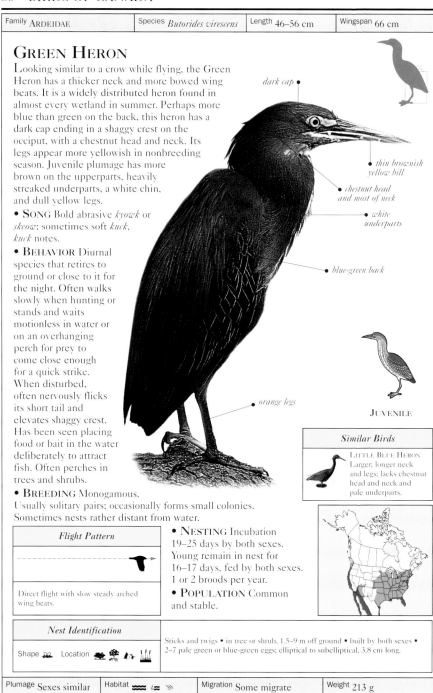

Looking similar to a crow while flying, the Green Heron has a thicker neck and more bowed wing beats. It is a widely distributed heron found in almost every wetland in summer. Perhaps more blue than green on the back, this heron has a dark cap ending in a shaggy crest on the occiput, with a chestnut head and neck. Its legs appear more yellowish in nonbreeding season. Juvenile plumage has more brown on the upperparts, heavily streaked underparts, a white chin, and dull yellow legs.

dark cap

thin brownish yellow bill

chestnut head and most of neck

white underparts

blue-green back

• **SONG** Bold abrasive *kyowk* or *skeow*; sometimes soft *kuck, kuck* notes.

• **BEHAVIOR** Diurnal species that retires to ground or close to it for the night. Often walks slowly when hunting or stands and waits motionless in water or on an overhanging perch for prey to come close enough for a quick strike. When disturbed, often nervously flicks its short tail and elevates shaggy crest. Has been seen placing food or bait in the water deliberately to attract fish. Often perches in trees and shrubs.

orange legs

JUVENILE

Similar Birds

LITTLE BLUE HERON
Larger; longer neck and legs; lacks chestnut head and neck and pale underparts.

• **BREEDING** Monogamous. Usually solitary pairs; occasionally forms small colonies. Sometimes nests rather distant from water.

Flight Pattern
Direct flight with slow steady arched wing beats.

• **NESTING** Incubation 19–25 days by both sexes. Young remain in nest for 16–17 days, fed by both sexes. 1 or 2 broods per year.

• **POPULATION** Common and stable.

Nest Identification	
Shape 🪹 Location 🌳🌿🌱🌾	Sticks and twigs • in tree or shrub, 1.5–9 m off ground • built by both sexes • 2–7 pale green or blue-green eggs; elliptical to subelliptical, 3.8 cm long.

| Plumage Sexes similar | Habitat 〰️ 〰️ 🌿 | Migration Some migrate | Weight 213 g |

DATE _____ TIME_____ LOCATION _____

Family ARDEIDAE	Species *Nycticorax nycticorax*	Length 64–71cm	Wingspan 112–114 cm

BLACK-CROWNED NIGHT-HERON

The scientific name of this bird means "Night Raven," and it refers to the nature of the bird, as does the common name of Night-Heron. A stocky bird with short legs and a thick, short neck, it prowls freshwater pools, marshes, and streams and coastal estuaries across much of North America. In flight the toes often protrude beyond the short tail. Juvenile plumage shows brown above with white spots and streaking, buff-brown below with dark brown spots and streaking. Juveniles have a yellowish bill with a dark tip and greenish yellow legs and feet.

- **SONG** Low, harsh *woe* and guttural *quock* or *quaik*.
- **BEHAVIOR** Primarily nocturnal. Roosts in trees by day and actively feeds at night. Some feed during daylight hours. Omnivorous, feeding on whatever is most handy. Diet ranges from fish to mollusks, small rodents, frogs, snakes, crustaceans, plant material, eggs, and young birds. Often stands very still in water for long periods of time, expertly grabbing fish that swim too close.
- **BREEDING** Monogamous. Colonial.
- **NESTING** Incubation 21–26 days by both sexes. Young stay in nest 28 days. Fed by both sexes. First flight at 42 days. After 49 days, may follow parents to foraging areas to beg and be fed. 1 brood per year.

black back

- *black cap and nape*
- *dark bill*
- *red eyes*
- *white face and underparts*
- *breeding adults have 2–3 long white plumes on back crown*
- *gray sides of neck, wings, and tail*
- *yellow legs and feet*

JUVENILE

Similar Birds

AMERICAN BITTERN
Similar to juvenile • thinner long yellowish bill; dark mustache stripes; lacks white spotting above.

YELLOW-CROWNED NIGHT-HERON
Similar to juvenile • more gray-brown with smaller white spots; thick dark bill; thinner neck; longer legs.

- **POPULATION** Overall stable or increasing.
- **CONSERVATION** Benefited from general protection by state, federal, and conservation agencies. Loss of wetland habitat affects food supply and reproduction.

Flight Pattern
Direct flight with slow steady wing beats.

Nest Identification	
Shape	Sticks, twigs, and reeds • lined with finer material • on or above ground as high as 46 m • built by female with materials gathered by male • 1–7 pale green or light bluish eggs; oval, 5.1 cm long.
Location	

Plumage Sexes similar	Habitat	Migration Migratory	Weight 862 g

DATE _____ TIME_____ LOCATION _____

Family ARDEIDAE	Species *Nyctanassa violacea*	Length 56–71 cm	Wingspan 107–112 cm

YELLOW-CROWNED NIGHT-HERON

At home in coastal mangroves, inland swamps, and riparian woodlands, this short-necked, stocky heron has a gray body and a large black head boldly marked with a white cheek patch and white crown with yellowish tints on the forehead. During breeding season adult males and females have long white occipital plumes on the back of the head. The long yellow legs protrude well beyond the short tail in flight.

long white occipital plumes

thick dark bill

large black head with yellowish white crown and white cheek patches

slender neck

- **SONG** Short *woe* or *wok*. Its *quak* is higher and less harsh than that given by the Black-crowned Night-Heron.

JUVENILE

- **BEHAVIOR** While mostly nocturnal, it is often active during the day. Exhibits strong preference for crustaceans, although it eats a variety of other aquatic organisms from fish to shellfish.

- **BREEDING** Monogamous. Solitary nester or forms small loose colonies. Also joins large nesting colonies with other herons and egrets, often chooses nesting site located on periphery of the colony.

long yellow legs

Similar Birds

BLACK-CROWNED NIGHT-HERON Black back; white head with black cap; short yellowish legs • juvenile has brown crown; brown upperparts with large white spots and streaks; whitish-tan underparts with brown streaking; short yellow-green legs and feet; yellowish bill with black tip.

- **NESTING** Incubation 21–25 days by both sexes. Semialtricial young remain in nest 25 days, fed by both sexes. Probably 1 brood per year.

- **POPULATION** Stable.

Flight Pattern
Direct flight with steady deep wing beats.

Nest Identification	
Shape Location	Sticks • lined with twigs or sometimes leaves • either on ground or in tree 9–12 m high • built by both sexes • 2–8 pale blue-green eggs; oval to long oval, 5.1 cm long.

Plumage Sexes similar	Habitat	Migration Migratory	Weight 726 g

Family THRESKIORNITHIDAE	Species *Plegadis falcinellus*	Length 48–66 cm	Wingspan 91–97 cm

GLOSSY IBIS

From a distance this large bird with a dark decurved bill appears dark overall in the freshwater or saltwater marshes it frequents, but closer observation reveals deep chestnut plumage glossed with metallic greens and purples. The species occurs widely in the Old World and evidence suggests that perhaps it introduced itself to North America in the 1800s. Its North American range may be limited due to its recent arrival on the continent, as well as competition with the already established White Ibis. Breeding plumaged birds show intense green patches in their wings, greenish legs with red joints, pale blue around the face and blue-gray facial skin in the loral region.

dark iris

metallic green and purple gloss on back, wings, head, and neck

dark gray lores bordered with pale blue

brownish black decurved bill

chestnut plumage

- **SONG** Guttural, grating croak, *ka-onk*.
- **BEHAVIOR** Gregarious. Flies in lines or groups, with individuals often changing position in the flock. In flight the head, neck, and legs are extended. Highly prone to wandering, thus turns up at great distances from breeding range, especially in spring. Uses long bill to probe for food, particularly crayfish and crabs in their holes. Also readily eats water snakes. Often feeds with other large wading birds, including the White Ibis. Flies to roost late in the day and frequently is seen roosting with other species of ibis, herons, and egrets.
- **BREEDING** Monogamous. Colonial; often nests in mixed colonies with other ibis, herons, and egrets.
- **NESTING** Incubation about 21 days, mostly by female. Semialtricial young remain in nest for about 28 days, fed by both sexes. 1 brood per year.
- **POPULATION** Common but local. Greatly increased and expanded during 20th century.

Similar Birds

WHITE-FACED IBIS
Reddish legs and lores bordered with white; white line around lore encircles eye; red iris.

WHITE IBIS
Juvenile • white underparts and rump.

Flight Pattern
Several shallow rapid wing beats followed by a short glide. Flies in straight line formation.

Nest Identification	
Shape Location	Platform of sticks and marsh plants with depression in center • occasionally lined with leaves • in shrubs or low trees; on the ground on islands • built by both sexes • 1–5 pale blue or green eggs, 5.1 cm long.

Plumage Sexes similar	Habitat	Migration Migratory	Weight Undetermined

DATE _____ TIME_____ LOCATION _____

Family THRESKIORNITHIDAE	Species *Plegadis chihi*	Length 51–66 cm	Wingspan 91–97 cm

WHITE-FACED IBIS

This bird is almost identical to the Glossy Ibis in all plumages; winter-plumaged birds and juveniles must be inspected closely to distinguish between the two species. The best field marks are leg and lore color (pinkish in winter and juvenile birds, red in breeding birds). In breeding plumage white feathers border the lores and extend behind the eye and under the chin. In summer and winter, adult White-faced Ibis has a red iris.

pink to red lores

dark chestnut and brownish olive plumage

white "face" ring of feathers outlines chin, lores, and eyes

decurved bill

bronze and green metallic glosses

reddish legs

- **SONG** Feeding call is a multisyllable *oink*. Also gives low-pitched *graa, graa, graa*.
- **BEHAVIOR** Gregarious. Flies in straight line formations. Feeds by probing with long bill, eating crayfish and other invertebrates, as well as frogs and fish. Usually frequents freshwater marshes, but coastal birds forage in salt marshes and include crabs in diet.
- **BREEDING** Monogamous. Colonial; often nests in mixed colonies with other ibis, herons, and egrets.
- **NESTING** Incubation 17–26 days by both sexes. Young stay in nest about 28 days. Fed by both sexes. 1 brood per year.
- **POPULATION** Uncommon to fairly common, but local. Local numbers fluctuate, but total North American population has increased since the 1970s. Range also has expanded eastward.
- **CONSERVATION** Serious concern in early 1970s, when reproduction failed in many colonies due to eggshell thinning from pesticides present in food chain.

Similar Birds

GLOSSY IBIS
Blue-gray lores; dark legs; dark eye.

Flight Pattern
Several shallow rapid wing beats followed by short glide. Flies in straight line formation.

Nest Identification	
Shape ● ᴅᴅ Location ⱴⱴⱴ ᴅᴅ	Bulrushes or other plant stems with depression in center • usually in thick marsh growth or short trees • built by both sexes • 2–5 pale blue-green to dark turquoise eggs; mostly elliptically ovate, some almost round; 5.1 cm long.

Plumage Sexes similar	Habitat ⱴⱴ ⱴⱴⱴ	Migration Most migrate	Weight 726 g

DATE _____ TIME _____ LOCATION _____

Family CICONIIDAE	Species *Mycteria americana*	Length 89–114 cm	Wingspan 165 cm

WOOD STORK

Numbers of the only stork that breeds in North America are much reduced from their former levels. This large bird of southern wetlands and swamps appears all white on the ground, except for its bare grayish "flinthead" and upper neck, blackish gray legs with pink feet, and black tail. In flight the trailing edge of the wings is black. Storks fly with legs and neck extended. Some wander northward after the breeding season in late summer and are irregularly recorded north to California, Tennessee, and Massachusetts; casually as far north as southern Canada. Many retreat to Florida in winter.

- **SONG** Usually silent. Adults clatter and snap bills during courtship and copulation. Adults also infrequently produce airy, low, rasping fizz or hiss reminiscent of Turkey Vulture.
- **BEHAVIOR** Walks or wades in shallow water up to its belly with head down when feeding. Reproductive cycles triggered by drying up of waterholes that concentrate fish in sufficient numbers for efficient feeding of young.
- **BREEDING** Monogamous. Colonial.
- **NESTING** Incubation 27–32 days by both sexes. Young stay in nest 55–60 days. Fed by both sexes. 1 brood per year likely.
- **POPULATION** Fairly common. Destruction of habitat and disruption of water flow through south Florida major causes of decline. Recently shifted range to South Carolina.
- **CONSERVATION** Endangered in US due to loss of breeding habitat.

• *bare gray head and upper neck*

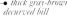
• *thick gray-brown decurved bill*

• *white body*

• *blackish gray legs*

JUVENILE

Similar Birds

GREAT EGRET Slender white neck; feathered head; yellow beak.

AMERICAN WHITE PELICAN Short legs do not trail behind white tail; much longer orange beak; shorter neck.

WHITE IBIS Smaller; entirely white except for red legs, feet, face, and decurved bill with black tip • in flight, body appears white with black wing tips; red features may look dark • flight pattern differs, with several rapid wing beats alternating with a glide.

Flight Pattern	
Alternates between strong flapping flight and gliding. Masterful at soaring, riding high on thermals.	

Nest Identification	
Shape ⌒ ⬯ Location 🪹	Large sticks • lined sparsely with fine materials and green leaves • 15–24 m above ground in large cypress trees standing in water • built by both sexes • 2–5 whitish eggs, elliptical to subelliptical, 6.9 cm long.

Plumage Sexes similar	Habitat 〰	Migration Nonmigratory	Weight 2.7 kg

Family CATHARTIDAE	Species *Cathartes aura*	Length 66–81 cm	Wingspan 173–183 cm

TURKEY VULTURE

Commonly known as a "buzzard," this bird ranges throughout the United States and into southern Canada and south to South America. It gets its name from the red skin on its head and dark body feathers that resemble a turkey. This carrion feeder is perhaps most often seen in flight, when its two-tone wings, black in front and silver-gray flight feathers behind, are most visible. Soaring birds hold their wings above their backs in a shallow V called a dihedral and rock from side to side as if unsteady in the air.

• **SONG** Usually silent. Makes hisses, grunts, or growls around food.

• **BEHAVIOR** Circles just above treetops and up to 61 meters high, searching for prey by smell and sight. Birds gather quickly after an animal dies. Feeds primarily on fresh or rotten carrion. Also eats roadkill (many become victims to autos themselves); stillborn livestock and afterbirth; and dead young of egrets, herons, ibis, and similar species, at heronries. Has been known to eat vegetables and even pumpkins if shortage of food. Master at soaring. Often roosts communally at night.

• **BREEDING** Monogamous.

• **NESTING** Incubation 38–41 days by both sexes. Semialtricial young stay in nest 66–88 days; both sexes feed by regurgitating. 1 brood per year.

• **POPULATION** Common. Very slight overall increase.

• **CONSERVATION** Remarkably resistant to most diseases, especially those likely to be present in carrion.

gray flight feathers

long slim tail

brown-edged dark upperwing coverts and upperparts

bare-skinned red head and dull red neck

semicircle of whitish to greenish warts below and in front of eyes

slightly hooked white bill

pale pinkish white legs

JUVENILE

Similar Birds

BLACK VULTURE
Very black, including head and stubby tail; longer whiter legs often protrude beyond tail in flight; white primaries under wing tip; flaps and glides more.

GOLDEN EAGLE
Much larger; looks heavier; shorter fan-shaped tail; larger feathered head; large strongly hooked yellow beak; flies with wings held in flat plane.

ZONE-TAILED HAWK
Black; feathered head; bold white tail bands; barred black flight feathers; yellow cere, legs, and feet.

Flight Pattern

Circles with wings in shallow V and rocks unsteadily; moderately slow steady wing beats when not soaring.

Nest Identification

Shape ♣

Location ▬ ⌂ ≈ ♣ ▦ ♠

Bare floors of caves, rock outcroppings, hollow trees, empty buildings, and rocks on cliffs • 1–3 white or cream eggs, often splashed with brown; subelliptical, long oval, or elliptical, 7.1 cm long.

Plumage Sexes similar	Habitat 🌳 ⌂ ♣ ✈ ⚘ ⚘	Migration Migratory	Weight 1.5 kg

DATE _____ TIME_____ LOCATION _____

Family ANATIDAE	Species *Anser brachyrhynchus*	Length 66 cm	Wingspan 33–43 cm

PINK-FOOTED GOOSE

This conspicuous short-necked, stubby-billed, pink-legged native of Greenland often feeds in flocks with birds of other species. During migration vagrants have made their way to the North American Atlantic Coast. In flight the blue-gray mantle and upperwing coverts contrast with the

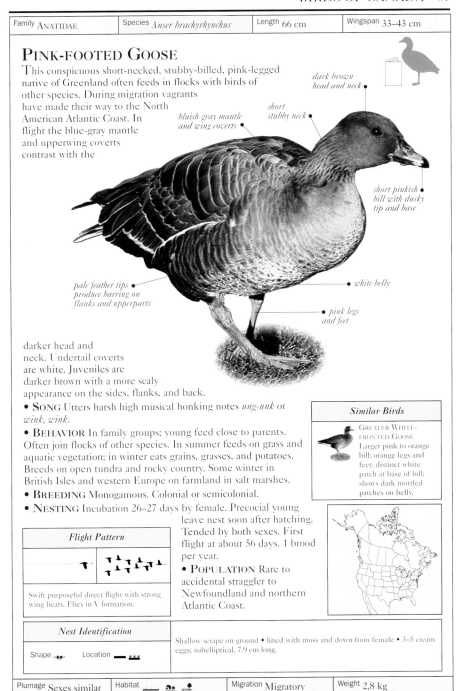

dark brown head and neck

short stubby neck

bluish gray mantle and wing coverts

short pinkish bill with dusky tip and base

pale feather tips produce barring on flanks and upperparts

white belly

pink legs and feet

darker head and neck. Undertail coverts are white. Juveniles are darker brown with a more scaly appearance on the sides, flanks, and back.

• **SONG** Utters harsh high musical honking notes *ung-unk* or *wink, wink.*

• **BEHAVIOR** In family groups; young feed close to parents. Often join flocks of other species. In summer feeds on grass and aquatic vegetation; in winter eats grains, grasses, and potatoes. Breeds on open tundra and rocky country. Some winter in British Isles and western Europe on farmland in salt marshes.

• **BREEDING** Monogamous. Colonial or semicolonial.

• **NESTING** Incubation 26–27 days by female. Precocial young leave nest soon after hatching. Tended by both sexes. First flight at about 56 days. 1 brood per year.

• **POPULATION** Rare to accidental straggler to Newfoundland and northern Atlantic Coast.

Similar Birds

GREATER WHITE-FRONTED GOOSE Larger pink to orange bill; orange legs and feet; distinct white patch at base of bill; shows dark mottled patches on belly.

Flight Pattern

Swift purposeful direct flight with strong wing beats. Flies in V formation.

Nest Identification

Shape • Location

Shallow scrape on ground • lined with moss and down from female • 3–5 cream eggs; subelliptical, 7.9 cm long.

Plumage Sexes similar	Habitat	Migration Migratory	Weight 2.8 kg

DATE _____ TIME _____ LOCATION _____

Family ANATIDAE	Species *Anser albifrons*	Length 66–86 cm	Wingspan 135–157 cm

GREATER WHITE-FRONTED GOOSE

This is the only North American goose with the combination of a white face at the base of the bill, dark barring on the belly, and orange-yellow legs and feet. In flight the blue-gray wing coverts contrast with the brown body and U-shaped rump patch, and the "specklebelly" is easily seen. Huge numbers winter on the eastern Great Plains. Individuals or small flocks, often mixed in with other species of geese, may show up

dark brownish gray head, neck, and upperparts

white on front of head and around base of bill extends to forehead

pink bill with white tip

brownish gray underparts with heavy dark mottling and barring

black tail

white undertail coverts

orange-yellow legs and feet

anywhere in eastern Canada or the northeastern US outside their normal range.

• **SONG** High-pitched laughing *kah-lah-aluek* and loud *wah-wah-wah*.

• **BEHAVIOR** Dabbles and walks well on land. Feeds on grasses, grain, aquatic plants, and insects. Favors freshwater pools, lakes, and marshes. In winter found in grasslands and agricultural fields. Flies high in V formations with clamorous "talking" among individuals in flock.

• **BREEDING** Monogamous.

Similar Birds

SNOW GOOSE
Juvenile dark morph has dark legs and bill; lacks white on face; lacks dark barring on underparts.

EMPEROR GOOSE
Juvenile has dark bill; lacks dark barring on belly • western range.

BEAN GOOSE
Black bill with yellow band near tip; gray-brown overall; darker brown on upperparts; orange feet and legs; whitish center to belly • western range.

• **NESTING** Incubation 22–28 days by female. Young precocial; first flight at 38–49 days. Tended by both sexes. 1 brood per year.

• **POPULATION** Common to fairly common. Midcontinent numbers increasing.

Flight Pattern

Steady direct flight with rapid wing beats. Flies in V formation.

Nest Identification

Shape ⬨ ⬬   Location ▬ ✦✦✦

Plant material and down • on ground near water in open, wet tundra • built by female • 3–6 buff, cream, pinkish white, or nest-stained eggs; elliptical to ovoid, 7.9 cm long.

Plumage Sexes similar	Habitat 🌿 ⚲ ≈≈	Migration Migratory	Weight 2.7 kg

DATE _____ TIME _____ LOCATION _____

Family ANATIDAE	Species *Chen canagica*	Length 66–76 cm	Wingspan 122–142 cm

EMPEROR GOOSE

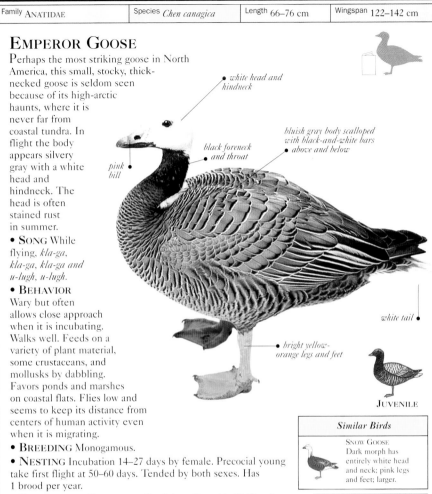

Perhaps the most striking goose in North America, this small, stocky, thick-necked goose is seldom seen because of its high-arctic haunts, where it is never far from coastal tundra. In flight the body appears silvery gray with a white head and hindneck. The head is often stained rust in summer.

white head and hindneck

bluish gray body scalloped with black-and-white bars above and below

black foreneck and throat

pink bill

- **SONG** While flying, *kla-ga, kla-ga, kla-ga and u-lugh, u-lugh.*

- **BEHAVIOR** Wary but often allows close approach when it is incubating. Walks well. Feeds on a variety of plant material, some crustaceans, and mollusks by dabbling. Favors ponds and marshes on coastal flats. Flies low and seems to keep its distance from centers of human activity even when it is migrating.

white tail

bright yellow-orange legs and feet

JUVENILE

- **BREEDING** Monogamous.

- **NESTING** Incubation 14–27 days by female. Precocial young take first flight at 50–60 days. Tended by both sexes. Has 1 brood per year.

- **POPULATION** Uncommon. Declining. Casual in California.

Similar Birds

SNOW GOOSE
Dark morph has entirely white head and neck; pink legs and feet; larger.

- **CONSERVATION** Eskimos once rounded up thousands in "goose drives" during postbreeding, the flightless molt period, then drove them into traps to be killed for food. Dramatic declines in 19th and 20th centuries.

Flight Pattern
Heavy direct flight with rapid wing beats.

Nest Identification	
Shape ⌒ ⬭ Location ▬ 🐦	Lined with grasses • on ground • built by female • 3–8 creamy white or variegated nest-stained eggs, 8.1 cm long.

Plumage Sexes similar	Habitat ≈ ▬ ⤳ ≈≈	Migration Migratory	Weight 2.7 kg

DATE _____ TIME_____ LOCATION _____

| Family ANATIDAE | Species *Chen caerulescens* | Length 64–79 cm | Wingspan 135–152 cm |

SNOW GOOSE

This species comprises two color morphs that, until the last quarter of the 20th century, were considered separate species: Snow Goose for the white morph and Blue Goose for the dark or blue morph. The plumage of the white morph is entirely white in adults except for black primary feathers. Blue morph adults have a white head and neck with a dusky gray-brown body and white tail coverts.

• SONG Shrill falsetto notes and occasional softened honking. High-pitched nasal barking continuously in chorus in flight.

• BEHAVIOR Flies in bunched flocks or in broad U formations. Dabbler that walks easily on land. Grazes on tender shoots, waste grain, and other vegetable matter. Color morphs tend to segregate on breeding grounds, but mixed partners sometimes do pair and nest.

• BREEDING Monogamous. Colonial; densities of up to 460 pairs per square km.

• NESTING Incubation 23–25 days by female. Precocial young leave nest soon after hatching, tended by both parents. First flight at 38–49 days. 1 brood per year.

• POPULATION Very common to abundant. Increasing overall, with blue morph increasing and white morph decreasing because of selection by predators on breeding grounds and hunters on wintering grounds.

• CONSERVATION Some management in certain areas of breeding range to prevent overpopulation and destruction of habitat by increased populations.

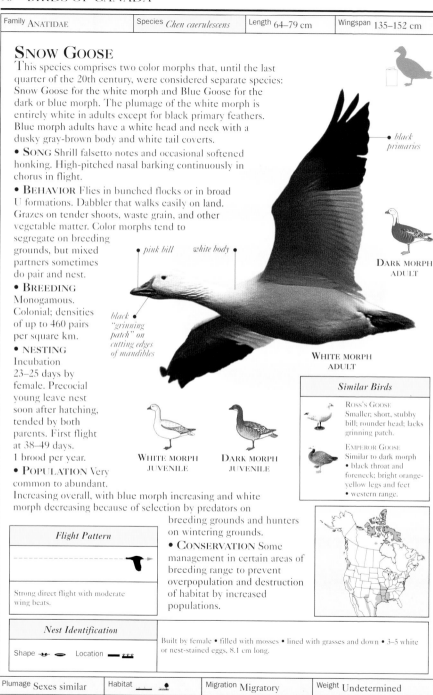

black primaries

DARK MORPH
ADULT

pink bill   *white body*

black "grinning patch" on cutting edges of mandibles

WHITE MORPH
ADULT

WHITE MORPH
JUVENILE

DARK MORPH
JUVENILE

Similar Birds

ROSS'S GOOSE
Smaller; short, stubby bill; rounder head; lacks grinning patch.

EMPEROR GOOSE
Similar to dark morph
• black throat and foreneck; bright orange-yellow legs and feet
• western range.

Flight Pattern

Strong direct flight with moderate wing beats.

Nest Identification

Shape ⬗ ⬭   Location ▬ ⋮⋮⋮

Built by female • filled with mosses • lined with grasses and down • 3–5 white or nest-stained eggs, 8.1 cm long.

| Plumage Sexes similar | Habitat ___ ⚘ | Migration Migratory | Weight Undetermined |

DATE _____ TIME_____ LOCATION _____

Family ANATIDAE	Species *Chen rossii*	Length 53–66 cm	Wingspan 119–137 cm

ROSS'S GOOSE

Often seen with the Snow Goose, North America's smallest goose is said to have a gentle expression. Like the Snow Goose, Ross's Goose has both a white morph and a very uncommon blue morph. It can be distinguished from the Snow Goose from a distance by its smaller size and shorter neck and at closer range by its stubby triangular bill, which lacks the "grinning patch." In flight it has faster wing beats than the Snow Goose.

round head

short neck

stubby, triangular, deep pinkish red bill with warty bluish base

black wing tips

snow-white body

WHITE MORPH

BLUE MORPH

• **SONG** Low throaty *kug* or weak *kek, kek* or *ke-gak, ke-gak*. Similar to call of smaller races of Canada Goose.
• **BEHAVIOR** Eats fresh grasses and grains. Often can be seen feeding with Snow Geese.
• **BREEDING** Monogamous. Colonial.
• **NESTING** Incubation 21–24 days by female. Precocial young are tended by both sexes. First flight at 40–45 days. Has 1 brood per year.
• **POPULATION** Rare to uncommon in migration and outside its wintering grounds in California, New Mexico, and the states along lower Mississippi River. Fairly common on breeding grounds.
• **CONSERVATION** Numbers were decimated by market hunting, especially in California, until it was regulated early in the 20th century. Populations increased in the last half of the 20th century.

Similar Birds

SNOW GOOSE Longer neck and bill; has "grinning patch" on cutting edge of bill; flatter head; rusty stains often visible on face in summer; slower wing beats.

Flight Pattern

Rapid direct flight with strong wing beats. Flies in V formation.

Nest Identification

Shape   Location

Soft grasses, moss, and twigs • lined with small amount of down • built by female • 4–5 white eggs; subelliptical, 7.4 x 4.8 cm.

Plumage Sexes similar	Habitat	Migration Migratory	Weight 1.7 kg

DATE _____ TIME_____ LOCATION _____

| Family ANATIDAE | Species *Branta canadensis* | Length 64–114 cm | Wingspan 191 cm |

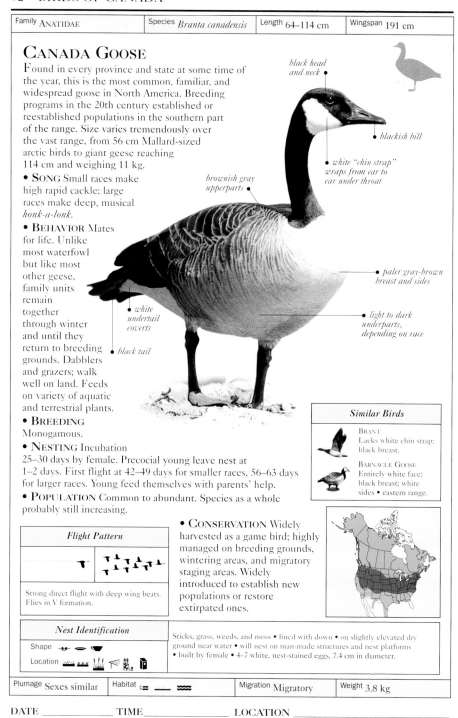

CANADA GOOSE

Found in every province and state at some time of the year, this is the most common, familiar, and widespread goose in North America. Breeding programs in the 20th century established or reestablished populations in the southern part of the range. Size varies tremendously over the vast range, from 56 cm Mallard-sized arctic birds to giant geese reaching 114 cm and weighing 11 kg.

black head and neck

blackish bill

white "chin strap" wraps from ear to ear under throat

brownish gray upperparts

paler gray-brown breast and sides

light to dark underparts, depending on race

• **SONG** Small races make high rapid cackle; large races make deep, musical *honk-a-lonk*.

• **BEHAVIOR** Mates for life. Unlike most waterfowl but like most other geese, family units remain together through winter and until they return to breeding grounds. Dabblers and grazers; walk well on land. Feeds on variety of aquatic and terrestrial plants.

white undertail coverts

black tail

• **BREEDING** Monogamous.

• **NESTING** Incubation 25–30 days by female. Precocial young leave nest at 1–2 days. First flight at 42–49 days for smaller races, 56–63 days for larger races. Young feed themselves with parents' help.

• **POPULATION** Common to abundant. Species as a whole probably still increasing.

Similar Birds

BRANT
Lacks white chin strap; black breast.

BARNACLE GOOSE
Entirely white face; black breast; white sides • eastern range.

• **CONSERVATION** Widely harvested as a game bird; highly managed on breeding grounds, wintering areas, and migratory staging areas. Widely introduced to establish new populations or restore extirpated ones.

Flight Pattern
Strong direct flight with deep wing beats. Flies in V formation.

Nest Identification	
Shape	Sticks, grass, weeds, and moss • lined with down • on slightly elevated dry ground near water • will nest on man-made structures and nest platforms • built by female • 4–7 white, nest-stained eggs, 7.4 cm in diameter.
Location	

| Plumage Sexes similar | Habitat | Migration Migratory | Weight 3.8 kg |

Family ANATIDAE	Species *Branta bernicla*	Length 56–66 cm	Wingspan 109–122 cm

BRANT

A tundra species most often seen wintering along sea coasts, this small short-necked goose is not much larger than a Mallard. The two races in North America differ in appearance. Both have dark brown backs, but whereas the western bird has a dark belly, the eastern form has a paler one and its white patches do not meet at the front of the neck. In both plumages the white rump is conspicuous in flight.

white scalloped patch on sides of upper neck

blackish bill

white rump, uppertail and undertail coverts

blackish legs and feet

black tail

black head, neck, and breast

dusky brown bars on sides and flanks

- **SONG** Call is throaty drawled *c-r-r-onk, crr-ronk.*
- **BEHAVIOR** Often flies low in ragged bunches with position of birds changing often and without appearance of a leader. Incubating birds sit tightly on nest and lie low with neck and head stretched flat, blending with surrounding tundra. Relatively tame. Feeds primarily on vegetable matter.
- **BREEDING** Monogamous. Mates for life. Forms loose colonies.
- **NESTING** Incubation 22–26 days by female. First flight at 40–50 days. Tended by both sexes.
- **POPULATION** Common and local. May be declining.
- **CONSERVATION** A die-off of eelgrass, a major source of food for the Brant, on the Atlantic Coast in the 1930s had serious impact on population. No long-term damage reported, because the Brant switched to another food source. Eelgrass made a partial recovery.

Similar Birds

CANADA GOOSE
Larger; longer neck; large white "chin strap;" pale brown breast.

BARNACLE GOOSE
Whitish face and sides
• eastern range.

Flight Pattern	

Heavy direct flight with strong wing beats. Flies in straight line formation.

Nest Identification	
Shape ⬦ ⬤ Location ▬ ▬▬ ✱✱	Shallow bowl of grass and other materials • heavily lined with down • on small island in tundra pond, usually 2–8 km from coast • built by female • 1–7 creamy white or buff eggs; subelliptical to elliptical, 7.4 cm in diameter.

Plumage Sexes similar	Habitat 〰 〰 ▬	Migration Migratory	Weight 1.4 kg

DATE _____ TIME_____ LOCATION _____

Family ANATIDAE	Species *Branta leucopsis*	Length 58–71 cm	Wingspan 132–142 cm

BARNACLE GOOSE

A stray from its breeding grounds in eastern Greenland to the north Atlantic Coast, this bird is kept by waterfowl fanciers, so birds observed inland are possible escapees. In flight birds show a U-shaped white rump patch and silvery underwing linings, and they are clamorous with hoarse barking terrier-like calls.

• **SONG** High piercing yelps. Frequently hisses when disturbed.

• **BEHAVIOR** Terrestrial species that grazes

white face, forehead, and chin

black lores

bluish gray back with narrow black-and-white bars

blackish bill

black breast and neck

black tail

scalloped pale gray sides, flanks, and belly

white underparts

blackish legs and feet

primarily near seacoasts and in pastures, grain fields, and meadows. Often places nests on inaccessible rock shelves on cliffs or on rocky pillars that are safe from many predators, which makes escape from nest difficult to impossible for young. Adults reported to transport young from nest to ground or water in their bills or on their backs.

Similar Birds

BRANT
CANADA GOOSE
Dark underwings, forehead, and on face; sides not white.

• **BREEDING** Monogamous. Scattered colonies.
• **NESTING** Incubation 24–25 days.
• **POPULATION** Casual to accidental; occasionally strays to North America from Greenland and Siberia.

Flight Pattern
Strong direct flight with steady wing beats. Flies in V formation.

Nest Identification	
Shape	Lined with feathers and down • in sand or on rock, often far from saltwater • 4–6 gray-white to yellowish eggs.
Location	

Plumage Sexes similar	Habitat	Migration Migratory	Weight 1.8 kg

DATE _____ TIME_____ LOCATION _____

Family ANATIDAE	Species *Cygnus olor*	Length 142–157 cm	Wingspan 213–244 cm

MUTE SWAN

naked black lores

Affluent residents and urban parks introduced this European swan to the environs of the Hudson River and Long Island through gardens, pools, and ponds. It has become established primarily along the north Atlantic Coast from southern New England to Virginia and secondarily around the Great Lakes (where there are now coordinated efforts to reduce its numbers). Adults, with their graceful S-curved necks, erected wing feathers, and black-knobbed orange bills, are unmistakable on the water.

white overall

orange bill with large black basal knob

long neck often held in S curve

- **SONG** Variety of hisses, barks, and snorts. Generally silent although not really "mute."

- **BEHAVIOR** Decorative and graceful on water but awkward on land. Feeds by thrusting its long neck down to collect aquatic plants from bottom or tips up. Aggressive in defense of territory, it attempts to drive away any large bird or animal (humans and dogs included). Prefers freshwater, salt marshes, and protected bays.

- **BREEDING** Monogamous. Forms long-term pair bonds. Pair defends large territory. Rarely nests in colonies.

- **NESTING** Incubation 35–38 days by both sexes, but female does more. Precocial young tended by both sexes but feed themselves. First flight at 100–155 days.

- **POPULATION** Introduced, naturalized, and locally common. Increasing by expansion from contiguous areas of release.

- **CONSERVATION** Exotic species; native of Eurasia. Efforts to systematically remove or reduce populations in some areas because of fear of competition with native species.

JUVENILE

Similar Birds

TUNDRA SWAN Winters in range of introduction • black bill without knob; naked yellow lores (not all birds); holds neck straight upright and bill parallel to water; does not elevate secondaries when swimming.

Flight Pattern

Direct flight with strong steady wing beats.

Nest Identification

Shape _____ Location _____

Plant material in mound • lined with down • on shoreline, small island, or mound built up in shallows • built by both sexes • 4–8 light gray or bluish green eggs; subelliptical, 11.4 cm long.

Plumage Sexes similar	Habitat	Migration Nonmigratory	Weight 11.8 kg

DATE _____ TIME_____ LOCATION _____

Family ANATIDAE	Species *Cygnus buccinator*	Length 147–183 cm	Wingspan 183–259 cm

TRUMPETER SWAN

The largest waterfowl in North America is also the largest swan in the world. The species was on the brink of extinction around 1900 due to egg and feather collection as well as the unlimited shooting of these birds. The population at that time is estimated to have been as low as a thousand individuals. Saving this species was one of the most notable conservation efforts of the 20th century.

- **SONG** Resonating honking notes; far-reaching deep rasping *ko-ho*. Often compared to old-fashioned *oo-ga* horns of vintage autos. Given frequently in flight and while swimming.
- **BEHAVIOR** Dabbler; plunges head and long neck deep into water to tear away aquatic plants from bottom; sometimes digs up tuberous roots with feet.

naked black lores taper into point at eye and form V at forehead

bill held parallel to water when swimming

pink line at base of bill forms "smile line"

long black bill slopes evenly into flattened forehead

neck held erect when swimming or walking

white overall

Defends large territory. Favors freshwater lakes, ponds, and rivers; sometimes retreats to coastal bays in winter.

- **BREEDING** Monogamous. Forms long-term pair bonds. Solitary nester.

JUVENILE

- **NESTING** Incubation 32–37 days, mostly by female. Precocial young tended by both sexes. First flight at 91–110 days. 1 brood per year.
- **POPULATION** Fairly common in breeding range. Numbers are low, perhaps 6,000 birds, but stable or increasing.
- **CONSERVATION** Some small local flocks stable, threatened, or extirpated because of changes in land use. Reintroduction into some former ranges still underway.

Similar Birds

TUNDRA SWAN Smaller; black lore tapers to point in front of eye and goes straight across forehead; yellow spot often present in front of eye; rounded head without flat slope of bill to forehead.

Flight Pattern
Strong direct flight with steady wing beats. Flights in either straight line or V formation.

Nest Identification	
Shape ⬤ ⬤ Location ▲▲▲ ◆◆	Low mound of plant material on floating platform • on top of muskrat and beaver lodges • made of bulrushes, reed grasses, and sedges • surrounded by water • built by both sexes • 2–13 cream, white, or nest-stained eggs; subelliptical to long elliptical, 11.2 cm long.

Plumage Sexes similar	Habitat 〜〜〜	Migration Migratory	Weight 11.4 kg

DATE _____ TIME_____ LOCATION _____

Family ANATIDAE	Species *Cygnus columbianus*	Length 119–147 cm	Wingspan 183–213 cm

TUNDRA SWAN

The most common and widespread swan in North America, this species breeds on arctic tundra and winters principally on the Atlantic and Pacific Coasts. Wintering concentrations on some coastal bays and lakes are spectacular in scope and activity. Swans are often associated with water; they are exceptionally fast swimmers. When flying they are large spectacular birds with long triangular wings, snow white to the tips of all flight feathers. The thin outstreached neck appears like a line more than half the length of the body, with a black point at the end.

• **SONG** Clamoring notes or yodeling; soft musical laughter, *wow-HOW-ow*, heavily accented on second syllable; repeated *who-who's*.

• **BEHAVIOR** Dabbler; plunges long neck and head beneath water to pick aquatic

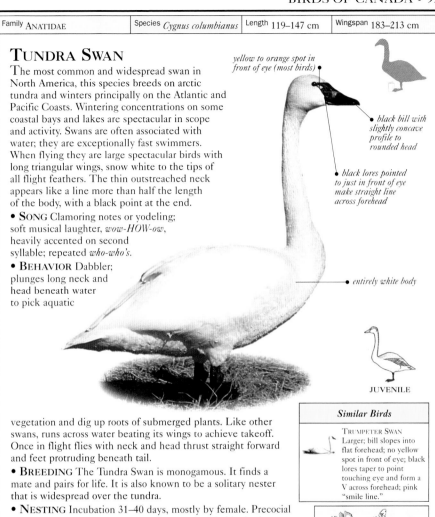

yellow to orange spot in front of eye (most birds)

black bill with slightly concave profile to rounded head

black lores pointed to just in front of eye make straight line across forehead

entirely white body

JUVENILE

vegetation and dig up roots of submerged plants. Like other swans, runs across water beating its wings to achieve takeoff. Once in flight flies with neck and head thrust straight forward and feet protruding beneath tail.

• **BREEDING** The Tundra Swan is monogamous. It finds a mate and pairs for life. It is also known to be a solitary nester that is widespread over the tundra.

• **NESTING** Incubation 31–40 days, mostly by female. Precocial young tended by both sexes. First flight at 60–70 days. 1 brood per year.

• **POPULATION** Common on breeding range. Common to rare on wintering range. Increasing.

Similar Birds

TRUMPETER SWAN Larger; bill slopes into flat forehead; no yellow spot in front of eye; black lores taper to point touching eye and form a V across forehead; pink "smile line."

Flight Pattern
T   ᴛᴬᵀᴬᵀ   ᵀᴬᵀᴬᵀᴬᵀ
Strong direct flight with steady wing beats. Flies in straight line or V formation.

Nest Identification	
Shape ⌒ � Location ▬ ✦✦✦	Low mound of plant material such as mosses, dried grasses, and sedges • near lake or other open water on ridge or island • built by both sexes, but male does more • 4–5 creamy white or nest-stained eggs; elliptically ovate, 10.7 cm long.

Plumage Sexes similar	Habitat ▬ ✿≈ ≈≈	Migration Migratory	Weight 7.1 kg

DATE _____ TIME_____ LOCATION _____

Family ANATIDAE	Species *Aix sponsa*	Length 43–51 cm	Wingspan 71–76 cm

WOOD DUCK

Considered by many to be the most beautiful duck in North America, the colorful male of this species is unmistakable with its large iridescent crest and multicolored bill. In flight it appears big-headed with a short neck and a long squared tail. The bill angles downward.

• **SONG** Male makes soft up-slurred whistle. Female makes rising *hoo-eek* and sharp *crrreek, crrreek.*

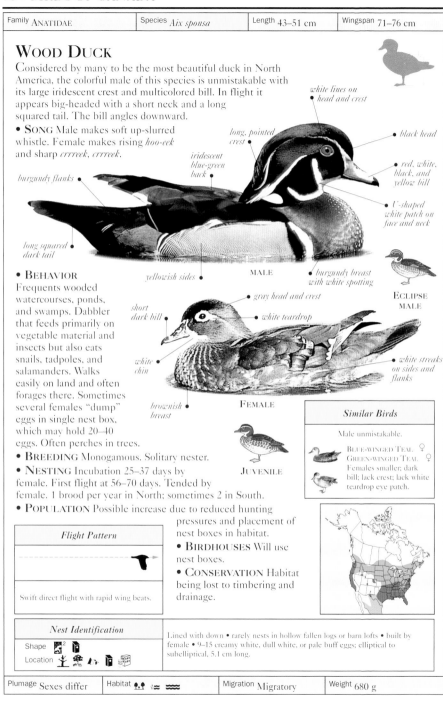

white lines on head and crest

long, pointed crest

iridescent blue-green back

burgundy flanks

long squared dark tail

yellowish sides

MALE

black head

red, white, black, and yellow bill

U-shaped white patch on face and neck

burgundy breast with white spotting

ECLIPSE MALE

gray head and crest

short dark bill

white teardrop

white chin

brownish breast

FEMALE

white streaks on sides and flanks

• **BEHAVIOR** Frequents wooded watercourses, ponds, and swamps. Dabbler that feeds primarily on vegetable material and insects but also eats snails, tadpoles, and salamanders. Walks easily on land and often forages there. Sometimes several females "dump" eggs in single nest box, which may hold 20–40 eggs. Often perches in trees.

• **BREEDING** Monogamous. Solitary nester.

• **NESTING** Incubation 25–37 days by female. First flight at 56–70 days. Tended by female. 1 brood per year in North; sometimes 2 in South.

• **POPULATION** Possible increase due to reduced hunting pressures and placement of nest boxes in habitat.

• **BIRDHOUSES** Will use nest boxes.

• **CONSERVATION** Habitat being lost to timbering and drainage.

JUVENILE

Similar Birds

Male unmistakable.

BLUE-WINGED TEAL ♀
GREEN-WINGED TEAL ♀
Females smaller; dark bill; lack crest; lack white teardrop eye patch.

Flight Pattern

Swift direct flight with rapid wing beats.

Nest Identification

Shape

Location

Lined with down • rarely nests in hollow fallen logs or barn lofts • built by female • 9–15 creamy white, dull white, or pale buff eggs; elliptical to subelliptical, 5.1 cm long.

Plumage Sexes differ	Habitat	Migration Migratory	Weight 680 g

DATE _____ TIME_____ LOCATION _____

Family ANATIDAE	Species *Anas strepera*	Length 46–58 cm	Wingspan 79–91 cm

GADWALL

The male Gadwall is the grayest dabbling duck. Its gray body contrasts with the black rear and blends into the brown back, neck, and head. In flight both sexes show a white speculum. On water or land the white secondaries often appear as a narrow white patch in the folded wing. The male has yellowish legs and feet.

• **SONG** Female makes series of loud quacks that fall in pitch, *kaaak, kaaak-kak-kak-kak*. Male makes single low quack and shrill whistling sound.

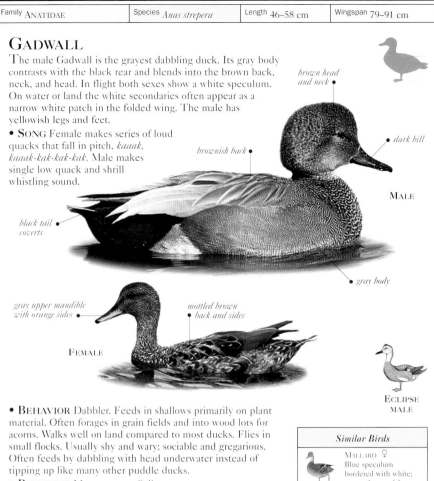

brown head and neck

dark bill

brownish back

MALE

black tail coverts

gray body

gray upper mandible with orange sides

mottled brown back and sides

FEMALE

ECLIPSE MALE

• **BEHAVIOR** Dabbler. Feeds in shallows primarily on plant material. Often forages in grain fields and into wood lots for acorns. Walks well on land compared to most ducks. Flies in small flocks. Usually shy and wary; sociable and gregarious. Often feeds by dabbling with head underwater instead of tipping up like many other puddle ducks.
• **BREEDING** Monogamous. Solitary nester.
• **NESTING** Incubation 24–27 days by female. Young precocial; first flight at about 48–56 days. Tended by female. 1 brood per year.
• **POPULATION** Uncommon. Increasing due to expansion of nesting habitat because of unusually wet conditions in breeding range in late 1990s.

Similar Birds

MALLARD ♀
Blue speculum bordered with white; orange legs and feet.

Flight Pattern	
Fast direct flight with rapid wing beats.	

Nest Identification	
Shape ⚬ ⚭ Location ▦ ⏏	Grasses and weeds • lined with down • near water or dry land, surrounded by dense weeds or grass • built by female • 7–15 white to dull cream eggs.

Plumage Sexes differ	Habitat 🌾 〰	Migration Migratory	Weight 1.0 kg

DATE _____ TIME_____ LOCATION _____

Family ANATIDAE	Species *Anas penelope*	Length 46–51 cm	Wingspan 76–81 cm

EURASIAN WIGEON

Although the Eurasian Wigeon is not known to nest on this continent, this dabbling duck has been a rare but regular visitor in winter on both coasts in North America for the last forty to fifty years. The adult female has a cinnamon-buff head in contrast to the male's reddish head. The female also has two morphs: rufous and gray. In flight it is best distinguished from the American Wigeon by its dusky axillars and underwing linings.

• **SONG** Male makes wild musical whistle, *whee-oo*, and short cheeping note. Female makes hoarse croak and sharp quack when alarmed.

• **BEHAVIOR** Highly gregarious after breeding season, often forming large flocks on the Eurasian wintering grounds. Dabbles in mud or tips up in shallow water to eat favorite foods: pond weeds, eelgrass, and other aquatic plants. Eats seeds but prefers leaves, stems, and buds. Also eats snails, beetles, and crickets. Walks well on land and often forages in fields and wooded lots some distance from water.

• **BREEDING** Monogamous. Semicolonial.

• **NESTING** Incubation 24–25 days by female. Precocial young leave nest shortly after hatching and find own food but still tended by female. First flight at 60–70 days.

• **POPULATION** Rare to uncommon visitor on both coasts but more common on the West Coast. Rare inland.

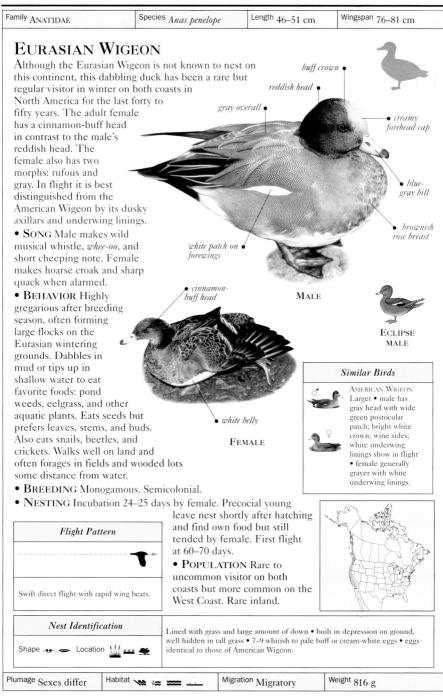

buff crown •

reddish head •

gray overall •

• creamy forehead cap

• blue-gray bill

• brownish rose breast

white patch on forewings •

• cinnamon-buff head

MALE

ECLIPSE MALE

white belly •

FEMALE

Similar Birds

AMERICAN WIGEON Larger • male has gray head with wide green postocular patch; bright white crown; wine sides; white underwing linings show in flight • female generally grayer with white underwing linings.

Flight Pattern

Swift direct flight with rapid wing beats.

Nest Identification

Shape ~~ ⬯ Location ⫲⫲ ⫶⫶ ⬥

Lined with grass and large amount of down • built in depression on ground, well hidden in tall grass • 7–9 whitish to pale buff or cream-white eggs • eggs identical to those of American Wigeon.

Plumage Sexes differ	Habitat	Migration Migratory	Weight 816 g

DATE _____ TIME_____ LOCATION _____

Family ANATIDAE	Species *Anas americana*	Length 46–58 cm	Wingspan 76–89 cm

AMERICAN WIGEON

This species is identified in flight by the bold white patches on its forewings, which are gray on females, and the white underwing linings. The male has a conspicuous white forehead and crown, leading hunters to nickname it "baldpate." Both males and females are more rusty brown on their breast and sides than other dabbling ducks. Legs and feet are gray. In flight females show a white belly and undertail coverts and a green speculum.

• **SONG** Throaty whistle, *whew, whew, whew.* Female makes weak guttural quack.

gray head with wide green postocular stripe

white forehead and crown

black-tipped blue-gray bill

MALE

black tail and undertail coverts

white of underparts extends onto flanks

reddish brown breast and sides

ECLIPSE MALE

• **BEHAVIOR** Dabbler. Flies in tight flocks that may twist and turn like those of teals. Eats plant material. Will graze on shore and in fields. Often feeds in shallow water with other duck species. Wary; takes flight quickly when it is disturbed.

gray bill with black tip

gray head and neck

brown back with rusty shoulders

rufous-brown breast, sides, and flanks

FEMALE

Similar Birds

EURASIAN WIGEON ♂ Rufous-brown head; creamy buff forehead and crown; gray sides and back • female shows dusky underwing linings in flight; gray-morph has brownish gray head, throat, and breast; rufous morph has rufous head, neck, throat, and breast.

• **BREEDING** Monogamous. Solitary. Nests on dry land, sometimes far from water; often on small islands.

• **NESTING** Incubation 22–25 days by female. Precocial young stay in nest 45–63 days. Fed by female. 1 brood per year.

• **POPULATION** Common and apparently stable. Breeding range expanding eastward in Canada and northeastern US. Increase has been due to wet conditions as well as increase in nesting sites.

• **CONSERVATION** No issues at present; carefully monitored and managed.

Flight Pattern
Swift direct flight with strong wing beats.

Nest Identification	
Shape ⚬ Location ⚬⚬⚬	Grasses and weeds lined with down • on dry land, sometimes on island • built by female • 6–12 white to creamy white eggs; elliptical, 5.3 cm in diameter.

Plumage Sexes differ	Habitat	Migration Migratory	Weight 771 g

| Family ANATIDAE | Species *Anas rubripes* | Length 48–61 cm | Wingspan 84–91 cm |

AMERICAN BLACK DUCK

The darkest dabbling duck on the water looks almost black at a distance, with a paler head and foreneck. In flight the white wing linings contrast boldly with the dark body and wings. The purplish blue speculum is bordered with black, and the posterior border often has a narrow white edge. It is as large as a Mallard. Into the 1940s this was the most abundant duck in eastern and central North America and was the most heavily hunted without noticable decline in numbers. Today it seems to be losing steadily to years of heavy hunting preasure and increasing displacement by Mallards.

greenish bill with black flecking

brownish black body

pale brownish gray head and foreneck

yellow bill

brownish black body

FEMALE

MALE

- **SONG** Typical female gives loud duck quack; male makes lower croak.
- **BEHAVIOR** Dabbler. Very alert and wary; one of the quickest ducks into the air when disturbed, thrusting upward energetically off water or land. Feeds in shallow water, taking mostly plant materials in winter and a variety of aquatic insects in summer.
- **BREEDING** Monogamous. Solitary nester. Sometimes hybridizes with Mallard.
- **NESTING** Incubation 23–33 days by female. Precocial young stay in nest 58–63 days. Fed by female. 1 brood per year.
- **POPULATION** Fairly common.
- **CONSERVATION** Management warranted due to decline in numbers, which may be caused by changes to its habitat and deforestation. Both of these circumstances seem to favor Mallards, which tend to replace Black Ducks where the two species coexist.

Similar Birds

MALLARD ♀
Female lacks contrast between head and body; paler brown; yellow-orange bill with blackish mottling; bright orange feet; metallic blue speculum bordered with a white front and back; white tail.

Flight Pattern

Swift direct flight with strong wing beats.

Nest Identification

Shape

Location

Shallow depression with plant material added • lined with down • on ground among clumps of dense vegetation • sometimes in raised situation, as on top of stump • built by female • 6–12 creamy white to greenish buff eggs.

| Plumage Sexes differ | Habitat | Migration Migratory | Weight 1.4 kg |

DATE _____ TIME _____ LOCATION _____

Family ANATIDAE	Species *Anas platyrhynchos*	Length 58 cm	Wingspan 76–102 cm

MALLARD

One of the best-known waterfowl in the world, the Mallard can be found almost anywhere shallow freshwater occurs. Some even reside in salt marshes and bays. The male is larger than the female. Many domesticated forms are entirely white with an orange bill, legs, and feet.

• **SONG** Female makes loud *quack-quack-quack, quack, quack-quack,* descending in scale. Male sounds double note and low reedy *kwek-kwek-kwek.*

• **BEHAVIOR** Generally found in shallow freshwater, where it dabbles primarily for plant food, also taking insects, mollusks, and crustaceans. Sometimes dives underwater. Walks well and often forages on shore in fields and woodlots. Leaps directly into flight from water. Frequently hybridizes.

• **BREEDING** Monogamous. Solitary nester.

• **NESTING** Incubation 26–30 days by female. Precocial young leave nest soon after hatching. 1 brood per year.

• **POPULATION** Common to abundant.

• **FEEDERS** Corn or grains. In city parks some are tame enough to be hand-fed by humans.

• **CONSERVATION** One of the ducks harvested in greatest numbers by waterfowl hunters. Prone to lead poisoning from ingesting spent lead shot with food from bottom ooze.

yellow bill
shiny green head
gray-brown back
metallic blue-violet speculum with white borders
white collar
2 curled-up black tail feathers
purple-chestnut breast
white sides and underparts
white tail
orange feet and legs

MALE

ECLIPSE MALE

orange and brown mottled bill
metallic blue-violet speculum with white borders
white tail
orange feet and legs

FEMALE

Similar Birds

Female resembles many other female ducks, but blue speculum bordered white is unique.

NORTHERN SHOVELER ♂ Long dark bill; white breast; chestnut sides.

COMMON MERGANSER ♂ Narrow red bill; puffy or crested head.

RED-BREASTED MERGANSER ♂ Narrow red bill; puffy or crested head.

Flight Pattern

Swift direct flight with strong wing beats.

Nest Identification

Shape

Location

Shallow pool of plant material gathered at the site, lined with down • may be more than 1.5 km from water, usually on ground among concealing vegetation • built by female • 5–14 greenish buff or grayish buff eggs, 5.8 cm long.

Plumage Sexes differ	Habitat	Migration Migratory	Weight 1.1 kg

DATE _____ TIME_____ LOCATION _____

Family ANATIDAE	Species *Anas discors*	Length 36–41 cm	Wingspan 58–79 cm

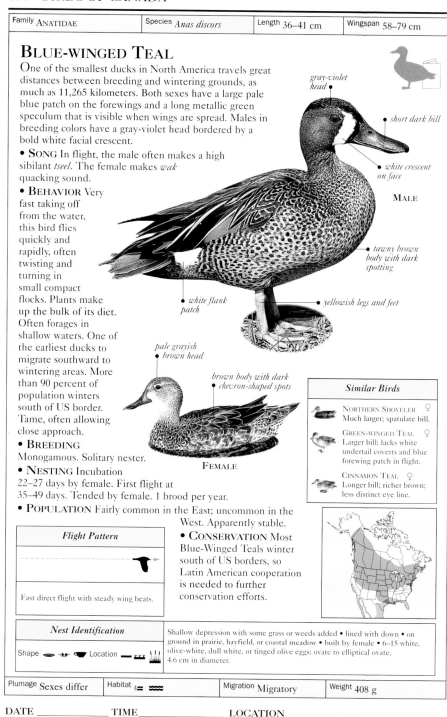

BLUE-WINGED TEAL

One of the smallest ducks in North America travels great distances between breeding and wintering grounds, as much as 11,265 kilometers. Both sexes have a large pale blue patch on the forewings and a long metallic green speculum that is visible when wings are spread. Males in breeding colors have a gray-violet head bordered by a bold white facial crescent.

- **SONG** In flight, the male often makes a high sibilant *tseel*. The female makes *wak* quacking sound.
- **BEHAVIOR** Very fast taking off from the water, this bird flies quickly and rapidly, often twisting and turning in small compact flocks. Plants make up the bulk of its diet. Often forages in shallow waters. One of the earliest ducks to migrate southward to wintering areas. More than 90 percent of population winters south of US border. Tame, often allowing close approach.
- **BREEDING** Monogamous. Solitary nester.
- **NESTING** Incubation 22–27 days by female. First flight at 35–49 days. Tended by female. 1 brood per year.
- **POPULATION** Fairly common in the East; uncommon in the West. Apparently stable.
- **CONSERVATION** Most Blue-Winged Teals winter south of US borders, so Latin American cooperation is needed to further conservation efforts.

gray-violet head

short dark bill

white crescent on face

MALE

tawny brown body with dark spotting

yellowish legs and feet

white flank patch

pale grayish brown head

brown body with dark chevron-shaped spots

FEMALE

Similar Birds

NORTHERN SHOVELER ♀
Much larger; spatulate bill.

GREEN-WINGED TEAL ♀
Larger bill; lacks white undertail coverts and blue forewing patch in flight.

CINNAMON TEAL ♀
Longer bill; richer brown; less distinct eye line.

Flight Pattern
Fast direct flight with steady wing beats.

Nest Identification	
Shape ⬩ Location	Shallow depression with some grass or weeds added • lined with down • on ground in prairie, hayfield, or coastal meadow • built by female • 6–15 white, olive-white, dull white, or tinged olive eggs; ovate to elliptical ovate, 4.6 cm in diameter.

Plumage Sexes differ	Habitat	Migration Migratory	Weight 408 g

DATE _____ TIME_____ LOCATION _____

Family ANATIDAE	Species *Anas cyanoptera*	Length 36–43 cm	Wingspan 61–76 cm

CINNAMON TEAL

The male, with its rich cinnamon hues, is one of the most recognizable ducks in western North America. The female's warm earth tones blend well with the cattails and reeds that surround its home. The Cinnamon Teal and the Ruddy Duck are the only waterfowl to breed in both North and South America. In flight the upper forewing features a large pale powder-blue patch and the speculum is metallic green with a white border. Juveniles and eclipse males resemble females.

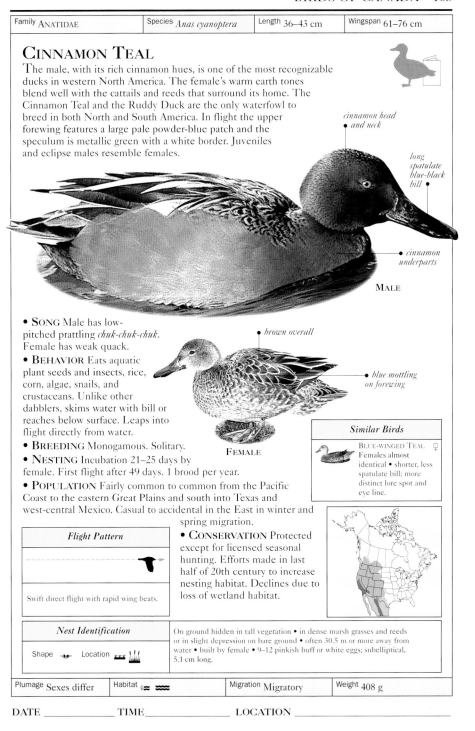

cinnamon head and neck

long spatulate blue-black bill

cinnamon underparts

MALE

- **SONG** Male has low-pitched prattling *chuk-chuk-chuk*. Female has weak quack.
- **BEHAVIOR** Eats aquatic plant seeds and insects, rice, corn, algae, snails, and crustaceans. Unlike other dabblers, skims water with bill or reaches below surface. Leaps into flight directly from water.
- **BREEDING** Monogamous. Solitary.
- **NESTING** Incubation 21–25 days by female. First flight after 49 days. 1 brood per year.
- **POPULATION** Fairly common to common from the Pacific Coast to the eastern Great Plains and south into Texas and west-central Mexico. Casual to accidental in the East in winter and spring migration.
- **CONSERVATION** Protected except for licensed seasonal hunting. Efforts made in last half of 20th century to increase nesting habitat. Declines due to loss of wetland habitat.

brown overall

blue mottling on forewing

FEMALE

Similar Birds

BLUE-WINGED TEAL ♀
Females almost identical • shorter, less spatulate bill; more distinct lore spot and eye line.

Flight Pattern

Swift direct flight with rapid wing beats.

Nest Identification

Shape   Location

On ground hidden in tall vegetation • in dense marsh grasses and reeds or in slight depression on bare ground • often 30.5 m or more away from water • built by female • 9–12 pinkish buff or white eggs; subelliptical, 5.1 cm long.

Plumage Sexes differ	Habitat	Migration Migratory	Weight 408 g

DATE _____ TIME_____ LOCATION _____

Family ANATIDAE	Species *Anas clypeata*	Length 43–51 cm	Wingspan 69–84 cm

NORTHERN SHOVELER

No duck in North America has a bigger bill. The large, spatulate bill is longer than the head, giving the bird a front heavy look. In flight both sexes show large powder-blue patches on the forewing and a metallic green speculum. Both males and females have bright orange legs and feet.

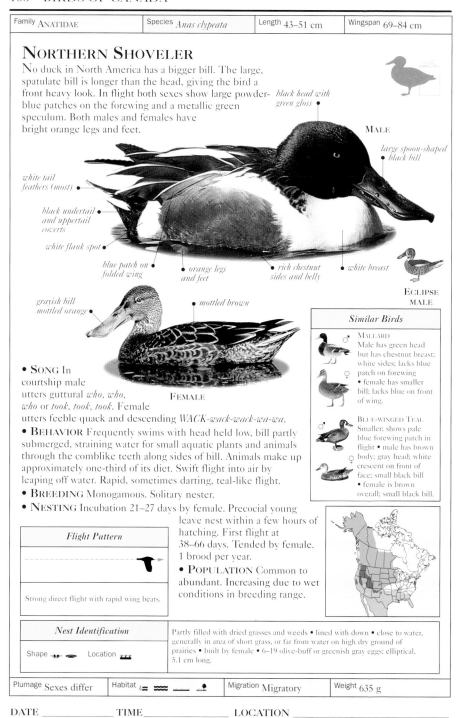

black head with green gloss

MALE

large spoon-shaped black bill

white tail feathers (most)

black undertail and uppertail coverts

white flank spot

blue patch on folded wing

orange legs and feet

rich chestnut sides and belly

white breast

ECLIPSE MALE

grayish bill mottled orange

mottled brown

• SONG In courtship male utters guttural *who, who, who* or *took, took, took*. Female utters feeble quack and descending *WACK-wack-wack-wa-wa*.

FEMALE

Similar Birds

MALLARD
Male has green head but has chestnut breast; white sides; lacks blue patch on forewing • female has smaller bill; lacks blue on front of wing.

BLUE-WINGED TEAL
Smaller; shows pale blue forewing patch in flight • male has brown body; gray head; white crescent on front of face; small black bill • female is brown overall; small black bill.

• BEHAVIOR Frequently swims with head held low, bill partly submerged, straining water for small aquatic plants and animals through the comblike teeth along sides of bill. Animals make up approximately one-third of its diet. Swift flight into air by leaping off water. Rapid, sometimes darting, teal-like flight.
• BREEDING Monogamous. Solitary nester.
• NESTING Incubation 21–27 days by female. Precocial young leave nest within a few hours of hatching. First flight at 38–66 days. Tended by female. 1 brood per year.
• POPULATION Common to abundant. Increasing due to wet conditions in breeding range.

Flight Pattern
Strong direct flight with rapid wing beats.

Nest Identification	
Shape ⚬ ⬭ Location ▮▮▮	Partly filled with dried grasses and weeds • lined with down • close to water, generally in area of short grass, or far from water on high dry ground of prairies • built by female • 6–19 olive-buff or greenish gray eggs; elliptical, 5.1 cm long.

Plumage Sexes differ	Habitat ⬚ ≋ ___ ⬩	Migration Migratory	Weight 635 g

DATE _____ TIME_____ LOCATION _____

Family ANATIDAE	Species *Anas acuta*	Length 53–74 cm	Wingspan 74–89 cm

NORTHERN PINTAIL

No other North American duck has the body shape of a pintail, either on the water or in the air. It holds its long slender neck erect and its long pointed tail at an upward angle on the water. In flight pintails are long and slender with a white trailing edge on the inner wing.

• SONG Female's low quacks more guttural than those of female Mallard. Male utters weak nasal *geeee* and double-noted whistle, *pruh* or *prripp*.

• BEHAVIOR Dabbling duck. Prefers shallows in freshwater, where it feeds primarily on vegetable material. Flocks of pintails have reputation of losing altitude rapidly, zigzagging in for a landing from considerable heights on wings that produce an audible "swish" and planing directly into a landing. Low-flying on breeding grounds, nesting individuals are sometimes killed by hitting utility wires and fences.

• BREEDING Monogamous. Solitary nester.

• NESTING Incubation 22–25 days by female. Young leave nest within a few hours of hatching. First flight at 36–57 days. Young tended by female but find own food. 1 brood per year.

• POPULATION Abundant in West; very common in East. Widespread and abundant, but some surveys show decline since 1960s.

• CONSERVATION As with other dabbling ducks, lead shot ingested from bottom ooze often leads to death.

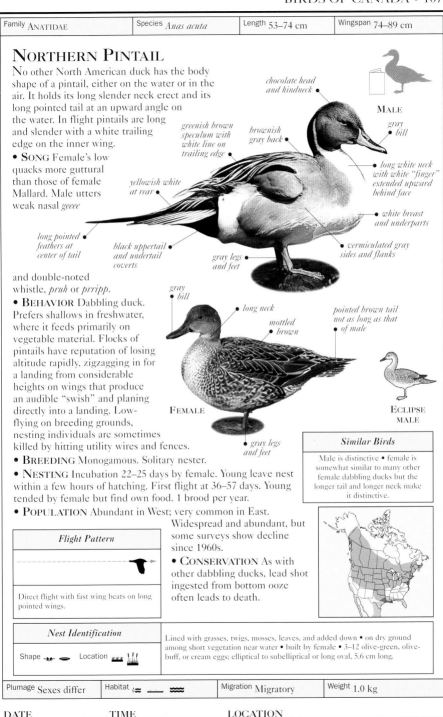

chocolate head and hindneck

MALE

greenish brown speculum with white line on trailing edge

brownish gray back

gray bill

long white neck with white "finger" extended upward behind face

white breast and underparts

yellowish white at rear

long pointed feathers at center of tail

black uppertail and undertail coverts

gray legs and feet

vermiculated gray sides and flanks

gray bill

long neck

mottled brown

pointed brown tail not as long as that of male

FEMALE

ECLIPSE MALE

gray legs and feet

Similar Birds

Male is distinctive • female is somewhat similar to many other female dabbling ducks but the longer tail and longer neck make it distinctive.

Flight Pattern

Direct flight with fast wing beats on long pointed wings.

Nest Identification

Shape ⚬⚬ ⚬ Location 🌱🌱 \|/

Lined with grasses, twigs, mosses, leaves, and added down • on dry ground among short vegetation near water • built by female • 3–12 olive-green, olive-buff, or cream eggs; elliptical to subelliptical or long oval, 5.6 cm long.

Plumage Sexes differ	Habitat 〰 ___ 〰〰	Migration Migratory	Weight 1.0 kg

DATE _____ TIME_____ LOCATION _____

| Family ANATIDAE | Species *Anas querquedula* | Length 38 cm | Wingspan 61–79 cm |

GARGANEY

A Eurasian dabbling duck, most Garganeys in eastern North America may be escaped birds. In flight males show prominent pale bluish-gray coverts and a shiny green speculum with white front and rear borders; the female's is less visible. Male and

MALE

broad white eyebrow

dark crown

dark bill

red-brown head

large bluish shoulder patches

pale eyebrow

grayish wing coverts

distinct dark line from bill through eyes to nape

white lore spot bordered by second dark line

FEMALE

female look similar in eclipse plumage, but the male retains his wing pattern.

• **SONG** Male makes distant rattling wooden note, *geg-geg-geg.* Female quacks.
• **BEHAVIOR** Feeds with bill scooping in shallow water. Eats mollusks and crustaceans.
• **BREEDING** Monogamous.

Similar Birds

BLUE-WINGED TEAL ♀ CINNAMON TEAL ♀
Rounder head; pale blue patch on forewing; no white border on both edges of speculum.

GREEN-WINGED TEAL ♀
Darker and smaller overall; no white border on both edges of speculum; no pale gray patch on forewing.

• **NESTING** Incubation 21–23 days by female. Precocial young leave nest first day of hatching. First flight at about 44 days. Tended by female.
• **POPULATION** Casual to accidental status.

Flight Pattern
Swift agile direct flight with rapid wing beats.

Nest Identification	
Shape ⌒⌒ ⬭ Location ✹✹✹ 🦆	In long grasses or under cover of bushes on ground in a dry place usually near water • built by female • 7–12 yellowish cream to light olive eggs, 4.7 x 3.3 cm long.

| Plumage Sexes differ | Habitat 🐦 ⌇ ⥵ | Migration Migratory | Weight 326 g |

DATE _____ TIME_____ LOCATION _____

Family ANATIDAE	Species *Anas formosa*	Length 41 cm	Wingspan 51–64 cm

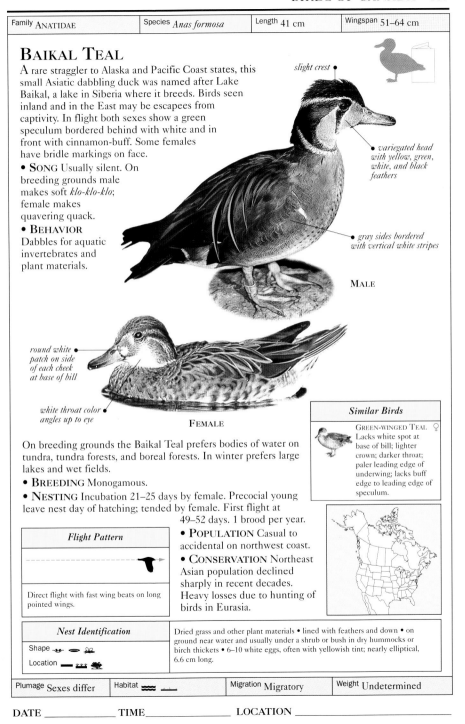

BAIKAL TEAL

A rare straggler to Alaska and Pacific Coast states, this small Asiatic dabbling duck was named after Lake Baikal, a lake in Siberia where it breeds. Birds seen inland and in the East may be escapees from captivity. In flight both sexes show a green speculum bordered behind with white and in front with cinnamon-buff. Some females have bridle markings on face.

• SONG Usually silent. On breeding grounds male makes soft *klo-klo-klo*; female makes quavering quack.

• BEHAVIOR Dabbles for aquatic invertebrates and plant materials.

slight crest

variegated head with yellow, green, white, and black feathers

gray sides bordered with vertical white stripes

MALE

round white patch on side of each cheek at base of bill

white throat color angles up to eye

FEMALE

On breeding grounds the Baikal Teal prefers bodies of water on tundra, tundra forests, and boreal forests. In winter prefers large lakes and wet fields.

• BREEDING Monogamous.

• NESTING Incubation 21–25 days by female. Precocial young leave nest day of hatching; tended by female. First flight at 49–52 days. 1 brood per year.

• POPULATION Casual to accidental on northwest coast.

• CONSERVATION Northeast Asian population declined sharply in recent decades. Heavy losses due to hunting of birds in Eurasia.

Similar Birds

GREEN-WINGED TEAL ♀
Lacks white spot at base of bill; lighter crown; darker throat; paler leading edge of underwing; lacks buff edge to leading edge of speculum.

Flight Pattern

Direct flight with fast wing beats on long pointed wings.

Nest Identification	
Shape	Dried grass and other plant materials • lined with feathers and down • on ground near water and usually under a shrub or bush in dry hummocks or birch thickets • 6–10 white eggs, often with yellowish tint; nearly elliptical, 6.6 cm long.
Location	

Plumage Sexes differ	Habitat	Migration Migratory	Weight Undetermined

DATE _____ TIME_____ LOCATION _____

Family ANATIDAE	Species *Anas crecca*	Length 30–41 cm	Wingspan 51–64 cm

GREEN-WINGED TEAL

The smallest dabbling duck in North America, the Green-winged Teal is also one of the most agile and fastest on the wing. Small compact flocks of Green-winged Teals often wheel and bank like Rock Doves in flight. Flying birds show no pale wing patches but rather a metallic green speculum bordered in front with chestnut and behind with white.

• **SONG** In courtship a *KRICK-et* note, from which species name is derived; it has been likened to the voice of the Spring Peeper. Female makes a faint *quack*.

• **BEHAVIOR** Forages in shallows by tipping up. Walks easily on land. Feeds in fields, wood lots, and agricultural areas. Primarily feeds on vegetable materials.

• **BREEDING** Monogamous with forced extra pair copulation. Solitary nester.

• **NESTING** Incubation 20–24 days by female. First flight at about 34 days. Precocial young are tended by female but find their own food.

dark glossy green patch from eye to nape with narrow white border below

MALE

rich chestnut head

black bill

vermiculated gray sides and back

buff-white breast with dark spotting

yellowish undertail coverts

vertical white bar separates breast from side

gray legs and feet

dusky brown body with buff mottling

EURASIAN RACE MALE

whitish belly

white undertail coverts with brown mottling

FEMALE

Similar Birds

BLUE-WINGED TEAL ♂
In flight shows white belly and pale blue forewing patches
• female has longer bill.

CINNAMON TEAL ♀
Female is darker brown with longer bill.

Flight Pattern	• **POPULATION** Common. Increasing. • **CONSERVATION** Vulnerable to ingesting spent lead shot from bottom mud while feeding.	
Swift, sometimes erratic, direct flight.		

Nest Identification	Grass, twigs, feathers, and leaves • lined with down • usually among grasses and weeds of meadows, sometimes in open woodlands or brush within 61 m of water • built by female • 6–18 cream, light olive, buff, or dull white eggs; elliptical to subelliptical, 4.6 cm long.
Shape 〜 Location 🌾 〰	

Plumage Sexes differ	Habitat 〰 〜	Migration Migratory	Weight 363 g

DATE _____ TIME_____ LOCATION _____

Family ANATIDAE	Species *Aythya valisineria*	Length 48–61 cm	Wingspan 71–91 cm

CANVASBACK

A sloping profile from the front of its crown to the tip of its long dark bill distinguishes this bird. It is one of the largest and heaviest ducks in North America. At a distance the male appears white with a black rear and breast. The long neck and head are rich rust-red. The female is grayer with a rusty tint to the neck and head.

- **SONG** Male makes grunt or croak; female makes quack.
- **BEHAVIOR** A wary species that often rafts well away from the shoreline. Flies high, frequently in formations.

sloping profile

MALE

long dark bill

rust-red neck and head

black breast

black tail and undertail coverts

whitish sides and back

rusty head and neck

FEMALE

grayish back and sides

Dives deeply to feed on aquatic vegetation and mollusks.

- **BREEDING** Monogamous. Solitary nester.
- **NESTING** Incubation 23–29 days by female. First flight at about 56–60 days. Tended by female. 1 brood per year.
- **POPULATION** Common to uncommon but local. Declining for some time, but has dropped drastically in recent years because of drought and drainage of marshes where they breed. Currently stable.
- **CONSERVATION** Nesting habitat loss primarily blamed for decline. Releases from hunting pressures and development of nesting habitats may have stabilized populations.

Similar Birds

REDHEAD
Lacks sloping profile • male has grayer sides • female is darker brown overall.

Flight Pattern

Strong direct flight with rapid wing beats. Flies in straight line or V formation.

Nest Identification

Shape ⬭ 🥄 🥄   Location 🌾 🌾

Dead vegetation lined with down • in marsh in stands of vegetation above shallow water; sometimes on dry ground • built by female • 7–12 grayish or greenish olive eggs. 6.1 cm in diameter.

Plumage Sexes differ	Habitat 〰️	Migration Migratory	Weight 1.3 kg

DATE _____ TIME_____ LOCATION _____

Family ANATIDAE	Species *Aythya americana*	Length 46–56 cm	Wingspan 74–89 cm

REDHEAD

A diving duck of freshwater marshes in summer, this bird congregates in large numbers on marine bays, estuaries, and big lakes in winter. The male's golden yellow eye is the most striking of North American waterfowl. In flight both sexes show a broad gray trailing edge to the wing.

• **SONG** Silent most of year. During courtship male utters mewing sounds, *whee-ough* or *keyair*. Also makes low trilling *rrrrrr*. Female has grating *squak*.

• **BEHAVIOR** Diving duck. Crepuscular activities, including flight and feeding. Some feeding at night.

round rufous-brown head

smoky gray upperparts and sides

black upper and lower tail coverts

black breast

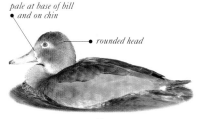

MALE

blue-gray bill with black tip and white subterminal ring

pale at base of bill and on chin

rounded head

Primary diet of aquatic vegetation. Female appears to take initiative in courtship, often chasing males.

• **BREEDING** Monogamous. Brood parasite.

FEMALE

Similar Birds

 CANVASBACK
Male is whiter on sides and back; longer all-dark bill; sloping profile.

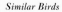 GREATER SCAUP
LESSER SCAUP
Pale color on wings of female does not extend to primaries.

RING-NECKED DUCK
Female has peaked head.

• **NESTING** Incubation 23–29 days by female. Young leave nest about 1 day after hatching. First flight at 56–73 days. Young tended by female but find own food. 1 brood per year.

• **POPULATION** Locally common. Declining in East. Far fewer than historical levels. Decrease due to loss of nesting habitat to agriculture, draining of wetlands, and drought.

• **CONSERVATION** Strictly regulated with hunting bag limits; some regions have no harvesting.

Flight Pattern
Rapid direct flight with strong wing beats. Flies in V formation.

Nest Identification	
Shape 🪹 Location	Dead vegetation and down anchored to standing growth • on bed of reeds and cattails connected to vegetation or set in thick marsh grasses above water • built by female • 9–14 pale olive, buff, or dull white eggs, 6.1 cm long • number of eggs hard to determine because females lay eggs in nests of other Redheads.

Plumage Sexes differ	Habitat 〰〰	Migration Migratory	Weight 1.2 kg

DATE _____ TIME_____ LOCATION _____

Family ANATIDAE	Species *Aythya collaris*	Length 36–46 cm	Wingspan 61–76 cm

RING-NECKED DUCK

This puffy-headed diving duck with a peaked crown prefers small freshwater ponds, wooded lakes, and swamps. On water the male appears dark with whitish gray sides separated from the black breast by a white crescent that is clearly discernible at a distance. Both sexes have a white ring on the bill, white bellies, bluish gray legs and feet, and show a gray wing stripe in flight. The cinnamon ring at the base of the neck, which gives the duck its name, is a poor field mark, seen only at close range in good light.

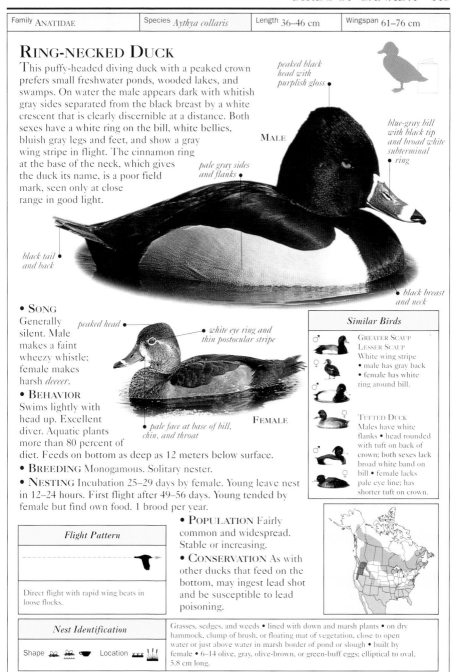

peaked black head with purplish gloss

MALE

blue-gray bill with black tip and broad white subterminal ring

pale gray sides and flanks

black tail and back

black breast and neck

peaked head

white eye ring and thin postocular stripe

pale face at base of bill, chin, and throat

FEMALE

• **SONG** Generally silent. Male makes a faint wheezy whistle; female makes harsh *deeeer*.

• **BEHAVIOR** Swims lightly with head up. Excellent diver. Aquatic plants more than 80 percent of diet. Feeds on bottom as deep as 12 meters below surface.

• **BREEDING** Monogamous. Solitary nester.

• **NESTING** Incubation 25–29 days by female. Young leave nest in 12–24 hours. First flight after 49–56 days. Young tended by female but find own food. 1 brood per year.

• **POPULATION** Fairly common and widespread. Stable or increasing.

• **CONSERVATION** As with other ducks that feed on the bottom, may ingest lead shot and be susceptible to lead poisoning.

Similar Birds

GREATER SCAUP
LESSER SCAUP
White wing stripe
• male has gray back
• female has white ring around bill.

TUFTED DUCK
Males have white flanks • head rounded with tuft on back of crown; both sexes lack broad white band on bill • female lacks pale eye line; has shorter tuft on crown.

Flight Pattern
Direct flight with rapid wing beats in loose flocks.

Nest Identification	Grasses, sedges, and weeds • lined with down and marsh plants • on dry hammock, clump of brush, or floating mat of vegetation, close to open water or just above water in marsh border of pond or slough • built by female • 6–14 olive, gray, olive-brown, or green-buff eggs; elliptical to oval, 5.8 cm long.
Shape ⬮⬮ ⬮⬮ ⬬ Location ▪▪▪ ⑊⑊	

Plumage Sexes differ	Habitat 〰〰	Migration Migratory	Weight 726 g

DATE _____ TIME_____ LOCATION _____

| Family ANATIDAE | Species *Aythya fuligula* | Length 46–56 cm | Wingspan 76–89 cm |

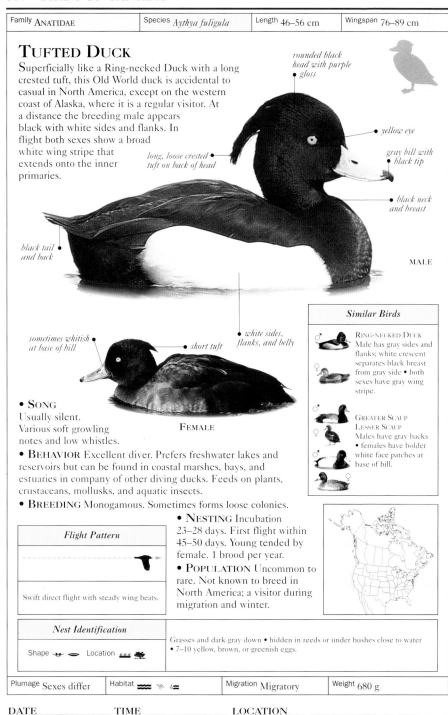

TUFTED DUCK

Superficially like a Ring-necked Duck with a long crested tuft, this Old World duck is accidental to casual in North America, except on the western coast of Alaska, where it is a regular visitor. At a distance the breeding male appears black with white sides and flanks. In flight both sexes show a broad white wing stripe that extends onto the inner primaries.

rounded black head with purple gloss

yellow eye

gray bill with black tip

black neck and breast

long, loose crested tuft on back of head

black tail and back

MALE

sometimes whitish at base of bill

short tuft

white sides, flanks, and belly

FEMALE

Similar Birds

RING-NECKED DUCK
Male has gray sides and flanks; white crescent separates black breast from gray side • both sexes have gray wing stripe.

GREATER SCAUP
LESSER SCAUP
Males have gray backs • females have bolder white face patches at base of bill.

• **SONG**
Usually silent.
Various soft growling notes and low whistles.
• **BEHAVIOR** Excellent diver. Prefers freshwater lakes and reservoirs but can be found in coastal marshes, bays, and estuaries in company of other diving ducks. Feeds on plants, crustaceans, mollusks, and aquatic insects.
• **BREEDING** Monogamous. Sometimes forms loose colonies.
• **NESTING** Incubation 23–28 days. First flight within 45–50 days. Young tended by female. 1 brood per year.
• **POPULATION** Uncommon to rare. Not known to breed in North America; a visitor during migration and winter.

Flight Pattern
Swift direct flight with steady wing beats.

Nest Identification
Shape   Location

Grasses and dark gray down • hidden in reeds or under bushes close to water
• 7–10 yellow, brown, or greenish eggs.

| Plumage Sexes differ | Habitat | Migration Migratory | Weight 680 g |

DATE _____ TIME_____ LOCATION _____

Family ANATIDAE	Species *Aythya marila*	Length 38–51 cm	Wingspan 76–86 cm

GREATER SCAUP

Breeding farther north than related species, this large diving duck prefers ponds and lakes in summer. It winters primarily along the coast, often in floating flocks or "rafts" of tens of thousands. The color of the gloss on the male's head usually greenish. From a distance on the water males appear black in front, white in the middle, and black behind. In flight the white wing stripe extends onto the primaries.

• SONG Usually quiet. Common note is loud *scaup*. Courting males make soft whistled *week-week-whew*; female makes low *harrrr*.

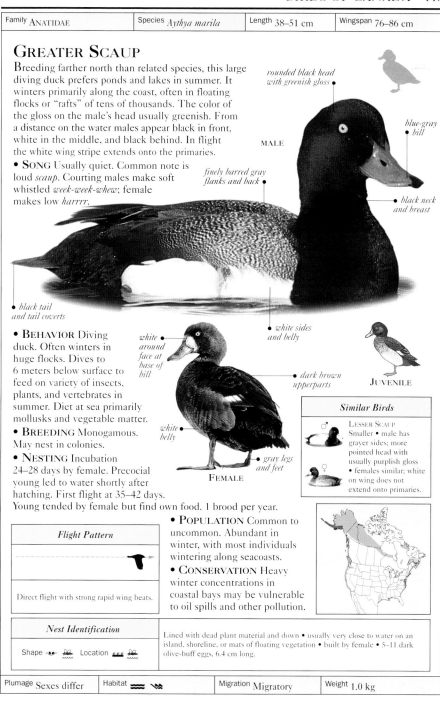

rounded black head with greenish gloss

blue-gray bill

MALE

finely barred gray flanks and back

black neck and breast

black tail and tail coverts

white around face at base of bill

white sides and belly

dark brown upperparts

JUVENILE

white belly

gray legs and feet

FEMALE

• BEHAVIOR Diving duck. Often winters in huge flocks. Dives to 6 meters below surface to feed on variety of insects, plants, and vertebrates in summer. Diet at sea primarily mollusks and vegetable matter.

• BREEDING Monogamous. May nest in colonies.

• NESTING Incubation 24–28 days by female. Precocial young led to water shortly after hatching. First flight at 35–42 days. Young tended by female but find own food. 1 brood per year.

Similar Birds

♂ LESSER SCAUP Smaller • male has grayer sides; more pointed head with usually purplish gloss • females similar; white on wing does not extend onto primaries.

♀

• POPULATION Common to uncommon. Abundant in winter, with most individuals wintering along seacoasts.

• CONSERVATION Heavy winter concentrations in coastal bays may be vulnerable to oil spills and other pollution.

Flight Pattern
Direct flight with strong rapid wing beats.

Nest Identification	
Shape 〜 Location 〜	Lined with dead plant material and down • usually very close to water on an island, shoreline, or mats of floating vegetation • built by female • 5–11 dark olive-buff eggs, 6.4 cm long.

Plumage Sexes differ	Habitat 〜 〜	Migration Migratory	Weight 1.0 kg

Family ANATIDAE	Species *Aythya affinis*	Length 38–46 cm	Wingspan 61–84 cm

LESSER SCAUP

Like the very similar Greater Scaup, at a distance the male appears dark in front, white in the middle, and dark behind. The Lesser Scaup has a more pointed head. The gloss on the male's head is usually purplish. In flight the white wing stripe confined to the secondaries. The Lesser Scaup is more commonly seen inland in winter than the Greater Scaup and is perhaps the most abundant diving duck in North America.

• **SONG** Courting males utter low, whistled *whew*. Females make odd rattling purr, *kwuh-h-h-h*.

• **BEHAVIOR** Diving duck. Behavior similar to closely related Greater Scaup. Diet varies with habitat but fairly evenly distributed between plant and animal materials.

• **BREEDING** Monogamous. Solitary nester.

• **NESTING** Incubation 21–28 days by female. Precocial young leave nest shortly after hatching. First flight after 45–50 days. Young tended by female but find own food.

• **POPULATION** Common. Slight decrease in 20th century.

• **CONSERVATION** Deaths due to fishing nets and lines may be significant. Like many other waterfowl, ingests lead shot on bottom while feeding, often resulting in death. Increased use of steel shot intended to eliminate this.

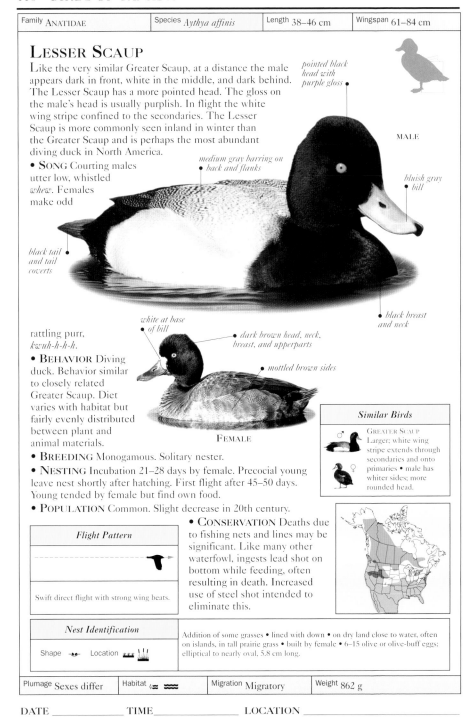

pointed black head with purple gloss

MALE

medium gray barring on back and flanks

bluish gray bill

black tail and tail coverts

black breast and neck

white at base of bill

dark brown head, neck, breast, and upperparts

mottled brown sides

FEMALE

Similar Birds

GREATER SCAUP Larger; white wing stripe extends through secondaries and onto primaries • male has whiter sides; more rounded head.

Flight Pattern
Swift direct flight with strong wing beats.

Nest Identification	
Shape	Location

Addition of some grasses • lined with down • on dry land close to water, often on islands, in tall prairie grass • built by female • 6–15 olive or olive-buff eggs; elliptical to nearly oval, 5.8 cm long.

Plumage Sexes differ	Habitat	Migration Migratory	Weight 862 g

DATE _____ TIME_____ LOCATION _____

Family ANATIDAE	Species *Somateria spectabilis*	Length 46–64 cm	Wingspan 89–102 cm

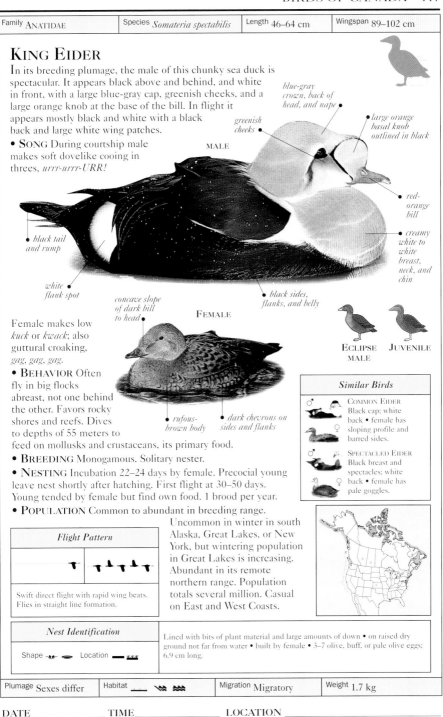

KING EIDER

In its breeding plumage, the male of this chunky sea duck is spectacular. It appears black above and behind, and white in front, with a large blue-gray cap, greenish cheeks, and a large orange knob at the base of the bill. In flight it appears mostly black and white with a black back and large white wing patches.

• **SONG** During courtship male makes soft dovelike cooing in threes, *urrr-urrr-URR!*

blue-gray crown, back of head, and nape

greenish cheeks

large orange basal knob outlined in black

MALE

red-orange bill

creamy white to white breast, neck, and chin

black tail and rump

white flank spot

concave slope of dark bill to head

FEMALE

black sides, flanks, and belly

ECLIPSE MALE   JUVENILE

Female makes low *kuck* or *kwack*; also guttural croaking, *gag, gag, gag.*

• **BEHAVIOR** Often fly in big flocks abreast, not one behind the other. Favors rocky shores and reefs. Dives to depths of 55 meters to feed on mollusks and crustaceans, its primary food.

rufous-brown body

dark chevrons on sides and flanks

• **BREEDING** Monogamous. Solitary nester.

• **NESTING** Incubation 22–24 days by female. Precocial young leave nest shortly after hatching. First flight at 30–50 days. Young tended by female but find own food. 1 brood per year.

• **POPULATION** Common to abundant in breeding range. Uncommon in winter in south Alaska, Great Lakes, or New York, but wintering population in Great Lakes is increasing. Abundant in its remote northern range. Population totals several million. Casual on East and West Coasts.

Similar Birds

♂ **COMMON EIDER** Black cap; white back • female has ♀ sloping profile and barred sides.

♂ **SPECTACLED EIDER** Black breast and spectacles; white ♀ back • female has pale goggles.

Flight Pattern
Swift direct flight with rapid wing beats. Flies in straight line formation.

Nest Identification	
Shape / Location	Lined with bits of plant material and large amounts of down • on raised dry ground not far from water • built by female • 3–7 olive, buff, or pale olive eggs; 6.9 cm long.

Plumage Sexes differ	Habitat	Migration Migratory	Weight 1.7 kg

DATE _____ TIME_____ LOCATION _____

Family ANATIDAE	Species *Somateria mollissima*	Length 58–69 cm	Wingspan 89–107 cm

COMMON EIDER

The largest sea duck is best known for the female's soft down, used for its softness and insulation in pillows, comforters, sleeping bags and jackets. Eiders use the down to line their nests. Rather than killing the eider, humans have learned to take the down a few days after the young leave the nest. To make a pound requires down from 35–40 nests. Juveniles are similar to females. Western females are duller brown; western males have a yellow-orange bill, and most

white head with black cap
feathers extend along side of bill
gray to green bill turns yellow-orange in summer
white back

EASTERN MALE

black tail

2 pale green patches on back of head

have a narrow black V on the throat.

black sides

sloping profile
feathers extend along side of bill
light brown with heavy dark brown barring

ECLIPSE MALE

• **SONG** Male makes pigeonlike *cooo* or hoarse *kor-er-korkorr-kor*; also moans. Female makes hoarse quacking sound. Silent in winter.

EASTERN FEMALE

Similar Birds

♂ KING EIDER
Male has black back; blue-gray crown; lacks sloping profile • female has chevron pattern and lacks sloping profile.

♂ SPECTACLED EIDER
Male has large white "goggles" with black border • female has pale brown "goggles."

• **BEHAVIOR** Feeds at low tide by day. Dives only 10–18 meters deep. Uses wings to swim underwater and can fly straight out of water. Breaks shellfish shells with gizzard.

• **BREEDING** Monogamous. Nests in colonies.

• **NESTING** Incubation 25–30 days by female. Young led to water by female after hatching. Female feeds young with help of another female. First flight at about 56 days. 1 brood per year.

• **POPULATION** Abundant to common; somewhat local.

• **CONSERVATION** Local populations vulnerable to oil spills and other forms of pollution. Females still pursued for valuable down. Heavily hunted in the Arctic.

Flight Pattern
Rapid direct flight, often low over water.

Nest Identification	
Shape 🦆 🥚 Location 🌿🌿 🏚	On bed of twigs, mosses, grass, and seaweed with large amounts of female down used for lining and wrapped around and under nest • sheltered by rocks or plants on ground • built by female • 3–5 light olive, brownish olive, or gray-olive eggs, 7.6 cm long.

Plumage Sexes differ	Habitat 〰️ ___	Migration Some migrate	Weight 2.2 kg

DATE _____ TIME_____ LOCATION _____

Family ANATIDAE	Species *Histrionicus histrionicus*	Length 38–53 cm	Wingspan 61–71 cm

HARLEQUIN DUCK

The male of this small diving duck appears entirely dark from a distance, but at close range the plumage consists of a wild pattern of bold white and black crescents, lines, and spots. Females are dark grayish brown with stubby bills and three white spots on each side of the face. Juveniles are similar to females.

• **SONG** Usually silent. In courtship male gives mouselike squeak. Both sexes have low croaking calls.

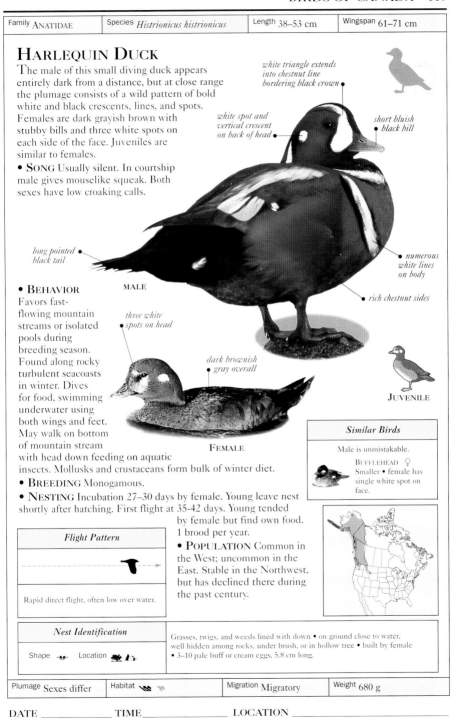

white triangle extends into chestnut line bordering black crown

white spot and vertical crescent on back of head

short bluish black bill

long pointed black tail

MALE

numerous white lines on body

rich chestnut sides

three white spots on head

dark brownish gray overall

JUVENILE

FEMALE

• **BEHAVIOR** Favors fast-flowing mountain streams or isolated pools during breeding season. Found along rocky turbulent seacoasts in winter. Dives for food, swimming underwater using both wings and feet. May walk on bottom of mountain stream with head down feeding on aquatic insects. Mollusks and crustaceans form bulk of winter diet.

• **BREEDING** Monogamous.

• **NESTING** Incubation 27–30 days by female. Young leave nest shortly after hatching. First flight at 35-42 days. Young tended by female but find own food. 1 brood per year.

• **POPULATION** Common in the West; uncommon in the East. Stable in the Northwest, but has declined there during the past century.

Similar Birds

Male is unmistakable.

BUFFLEHEAD ♀
Smaller • female has single white spot on face.

Flight Pattern

Rapid direct flight, often low over water.

Nest Identification

Shape   Location

Grasses, twigs, and weeds lined with down • on ground close to water, well hidden among rocks, under brush, or in hollow tree • built by female • 3–10 pale buff or cream eggs, 5.8 cm long.

Plumage Sexes differ	Habitat	Migration Migratory	Weight 680 g

DATE _____ TIME_____ LOCATION _____

Family ANATIDAE	Species *Melanitta perspicillata*	Length 43–54 cm	Wingspan 76–91 cm

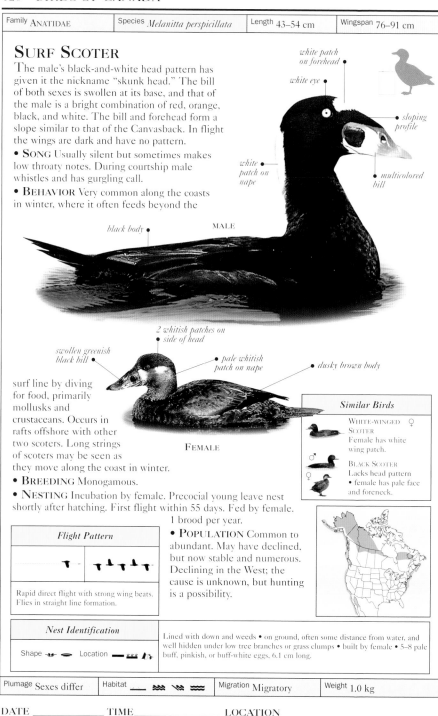

SURF SCOTER

The male's black-and-white head pattern has given it the nickname "skunk head." The bill of both sexes is swollen at its base, and that of the male is a bright combination of red, orange, black, and white. The bill and forehead form a slope similar to that of the Canvasback. In flight the wings are dark and have no pattern.

• **SONG** Usually silent but sometimes makes low throaty notes. During courtship male whistles and has gurgling call.

• **BEHAVIOR** Very common along the coasts in winter, where it often feeds beyond the

white patch on forehead
white eye
sloping profile
white patch on nape
multicolored bill

black body

MALE

2 whitish patches on side of head

swollen greenish black bill
pale whitish patch on nape
dusky brown body

surf line by diving for food, primarily mollusks and crustaceans. Occurs in rafts offshore with other two scoters. Long strings of scoters may be seen as they move along the coast in winter.

FEMALE

• **BREEDING** Monogamous.

• **NESTING** Incubation by female. Precocial young leave nest shortly after hatching. First flight within 55 days. Fed by female. 1 brood per year.

• **POPULATION** Common to abundant. May have declined, but now stable and numerous. Declining in the West; the cause is unknown, but hunting is a possibility.

Similar Birds

WHITE-WINGED ♀ SCOTER
Female has white wing patch.

♂
BLACK SCOTER ♀
Lacks head pattern • female has pale face and foreneck.

Flight Pattern

Rapid direct flight with strong wing beats. Flies in straight line formation.

Nest Identification

Shape ⌣ ⬭ Location ▬ ⚎ 🌿

Lined with down and weeds • on ground, often some distance from water, and well hidden under low tree branches or grass clumps • built by female • 5–8 pale buff, pinkish, or buff-white eggs, 6.1 cm long.

Plumage Sexes differ	Habitat ___ 〰 〰 〰	Migration Migratory	Weight 1.0 kg

Family ANATIDAE	Species *Melanitta fusca*	Length 48–61 cm	Wingspan 84–104 cm

WHITE-WINGED SCOTER

The largest of the scoters is the only one with a white speculum, which is seen easily in flight but may show as a white patch in the folded wing or be concealed. Scoters may fly in bunched flocks, long lines, or V formations. Winter duck hunters along the Atlantic Coast discovered that when these ducks were flying too high overhead or too distant to shoot, they often would come closer when shouted at loudly.

white "swish" mark passes through eye

brownish wash on sides

black body MALE

white speculum may show as patch in folded wing

red, white, black, and orange bill with black knob at base

brownish gray bill with small knob at base

2 indistinct white spots on face

sooty brown body

FEMALE

- **SONG** Both sexes utter whistle note in courtship; hoarse croak. In flight produces 6–8 bell-like notes.
- **BEHAVIOR** Dives to depths of 12 meters. Feeds primarily on shellfish, which it swallows whole and breaks up with grinding action of powerful gizzard.
- **BREEDING** Monogamous. Solitary nester.
- **NESTING** Incubation 25–31 days by female. First flight at 63–75 days. Tended by female. 1 brood per year.
- **POPULATION** Common to abundant. Perhaps the most common scoter.
- **CONSERVATION** Sea ducks are vulnerable to pollution of wintering habitats and oil spills close to coasts.

Similar Birds

SURF SCOTER
Lacks white wing patches • male has white forehead and patch on back of neck • female has 2 white patches on sides of face.

BLACK SCOTER
Lacks white wing patches • male has solid black head • female has whitish-brown cheeks, chin, throat, and sides of neck.

Flight Pattern

Direct flight with steady wing beats that sometimes seem heavy and labored. Flies in straight line or V formation.

Nest Identification

Shape 〰️ Location 👣 ▬

Lined with leaves, sticks, and down • on ground • built by female • 5–17 light ocher, pinkish, or creamy buff eggs; nearly elliptical, 6.6 cm long.

Plumage Sexes differ	Habitat 〰️ 〰️	Migration Migratory	Weight 1.8 kg

DATE _____ TIME_____ LOCATION _____

Family ANATIDAE	Species *Melanitta nigra*	Length 43–53 cm	Wingspan 76–89 cm

BLACK SCOTER

One of the large sea ducks, most birds of this species are seen on wintering grounds along both coasts. The male is the only all-black duck in North America. In flight both sexes show a silvery gray sheen on the flight feathers that contrasts with the black linings of the underwings. Wings make a whistling sound in flight. Males often winter further north than females, keeping in tight-knit flocks on the water. Adult males have brownish black feet and legs.

all-black plumage

yellow-orange knob on black bill

MALE

sooty brown cap

dark bill

center line to hindneck and body

pale brownish gray cheeks, sides of head, and foreneck

• **SONG** Usually silent. Male's melancholy mellow *cour-loo* thought by some to be the most musical duck call. In courtship male whistles; female has abrasive *cour-loo*.

• **BEHAVIOR** Diving duck. Usually feeds in shallower more protected waters about 8 meters deep. Primary diet is mollusks.

• **BREEDING** Monogamous.

brownish black legs and feet

FEMALE

Similar Birds
WHITE-WINGED SCOTER SURF SCOTER Both sexes show white patches on head in all plumages.

• **NESTING** Incubation 27–28 days by female. Precocial young; first flight at about 46 days. Female tends young but leaves after 7-21 days. 1 brood per year.

• **POPULATION** Common to fairly common; casual to uncommon in the winter in interior. Declining.

• **CONSERVATION** Vulnerable to coastal oil spills.

Flight Pattern
Strong direct flight with rapid wing beats. Flies in straight line and V formation.

Nest Identification	
Shape ⌄ ⌣ Location ⚘⚘ ⚘	Coarse grass • lined with feathers • on ground hidden in standing grass or under shrub • built by female • 5–8 buff to pink-buff eggs; elliptical to oval, 6.4 x 4.3 cm.

Plumage Sexes differ	Habitat ___ ≈≈ ≈≈	Migration Migratory	Weight 1.1 kg

DATE _____ TIME_____ LOCATION _____

Family ANATIDAE	Species *Clangula hyemalis*	Length 38–56 cm	Wingspan 66–79 cm

LONG-TAILED DUCK

Both the genus name and the former common name of Oldsquaw refer to the almost continuous chatter of this long-tailed sea duck. It is the only duck that undergoes two complete brilliant molts annually, plus an eclipse plumage. Winter males have a mostly white body with brownish black patches on the face, breast, and back, and a long black tail. Winter females appear similar but have a paler head. In flight both sexes show uniform dark wings without markings.

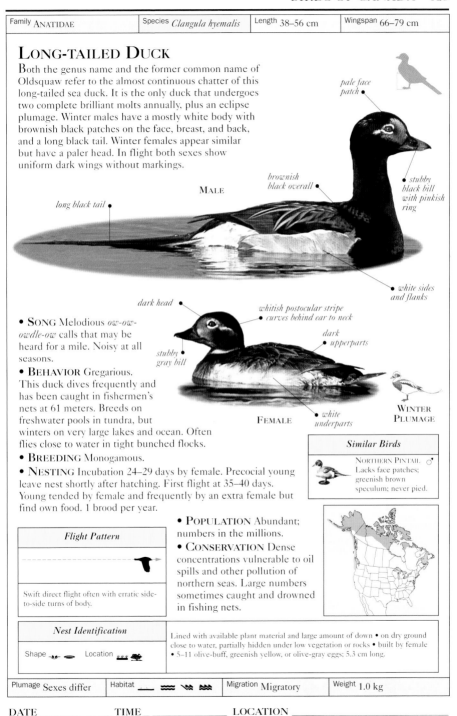

pale face patch

MALE

brownish black overall

stubby black bill with pinkish ring

long black tail

white sides and flanks

dark head

whitish postocular stripe curves behind ear to neck

dark upperparts

stubby gray bill

WINTER PLUMAGE

FEMALE

white underparts

• **SONG** Melodious *ow-ow-owdle-ow* calls that may be heard for a mile. Noisy at all seasons.

• **BEHAVIOR** Gregarious. This duck dives frequently and has been caught in fishermen's nets at 61 meters. Breeds on freshwater pools in tundra, but winters on very large lakes and ocean. Often flies close to water in tight bunched flocks.

• **BREEDING** Monogamous.

• **NESTING** Incubation 24–29 days by female. Precocial young leave nest shortly after hatching. First flight at 35–40 days. Young tended by female and frequently by an extra female but find own food. 1 brood per year.

Similar Birds

NORTHERN PINTAIL ♂ Lacks face patches; greenish brown speculum; never pied.

• **POPULATION** Abundant; numbers in the millions.

• **CONSERVATION** Dense concentrations vulnerable to oil spills and other pollution of northern seas. Large numbers sometimes caught and drowned in fishing nets.

Flight Pattern

Swift direct flight often with erratic side-to-side turns of body.

Nest Identification

Shape ⚬ ⬯   Location 🌾🌿

Lined with available plant material and large amount of down • on dry ground close to water, partially hidden under low vegetation or rocks • built by female • 5–11 olive-buff, greenish yellow, or olive-gray eggs; 5.3 cm long.

Plumage Sexes differ	Habitat ▬ ≈≈ ➤ ➤➤	Migration Migratory	Weight 1.0 kg

DATE _____ TIME_____ LOCATION _____

Family ANATIDAE	Species *Bucephala albeola*	Length 33–41 cm	Wingspan 51–61 cm

BUFFLEHEAD

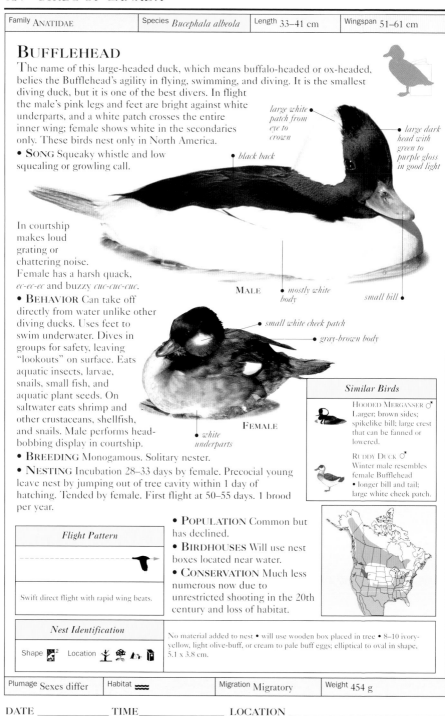

The name of this large-headed duck, which means buffalo-headed or ox-headed, belies the Bufflehead's agility in flying, swimming, and diving. It is the smallest diving duck, but it is one of the best divers. In flight the male's pink legs and feet are bright against white underparts, and a white patch crosses the entire inner wing; female shows white in the secondaries only. These birds nest only in North America.

• **SONG** Squeaky whistle and low squealing or growling call.

large white patch from eye to crown

large dark head with green to purple gloss in good light

black back

In courtship makes loud grating or chattering noise. Female has a harsh quack, *ec-ec-ec* and buzzy *cuc-cuc-cuc.*

MALE *mostly white body* *small bill*

• **BEHAVIOR** Can take off directly from water unlike other diving ducks. Uses feet to swim underwater. Dives in groups for safety, leaving "lookouts" on surface. Eats aquatic insects, larvae, snails, small fish, and aquatic plant seeds. On saltwater eats shrimp and other crustaceans, shellfish, and snails. Male performs head-bobbing display in courtship.

small white cheek patch

gray-brown body

FEMALE

white underparts

• **BREEDING** Monogamous. Solitary nester.

• **NESTING** Incubation 28–33 days by female. Precocial young leave nest by jumping out of tree cavity within 1 day of hatching. Tended by female. First flight at 50–55 days. 1 brood per year.

Similar Birds

HOODED MERGANSER ♂ Larger; brown sides; spikelike bill; large crest that can be fanned or lowered.

RUDDY DUCK ♂ Winter male resembles female Bufflehead • longer bill and tail; large white cheek patch.

• **POPULATION** Common but has declined.

• **BIRDHOUSES** Will use nest boxes located near water.

• **CONSERVATION** Much less numerous now due to unrestricted shooting in the 20th century and loss of habitat.

Flight Pattern
Swift direct flight with rapid wing beats.

Nest Identification
Shape Location	No material added to nest • will use wooden box placed in tree • 8–10 ivory-yellow, light olive-buff, or cream to pale buff eggs; elliptical to oval in shape, 5.1 x 3.8 cm.

Plumage Sexes differ	Habitat 〰	Migration Migratory	Weight 454 g

DATE _____ TIME_____ LOCATION _____

| Family ANATIDAE | Species *Bucephala clangula* | Length 41–51 cm | Wingspan 64–81 cm |

COMMON GOLDENEYE

In flight, on its whistling wings, the male shows more white plumage than any other North American duck except for the Common Merganser. Both sexes exhibit large white wing patches in flight. The small tight flocks often fly high.

• **SONG** During courtship male has grating *zee–zeee* or *zee-zee-at*, resembling call of Common Nighthawk. Female has abrasive low quack.

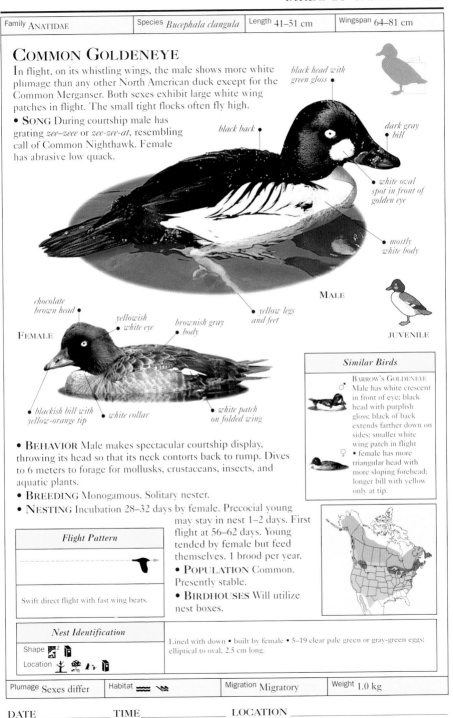

black head with green gloss

black back

black head with green gloss

dark gray bill

white oval spot in front of golden eye

mostly white body

MALE

JUVENILE

chocolate brown head

yellowish white eye

brownish gray body

yellow legs and feet

FEMALE

blackish bill with yellow-orange tip

white collar

white patch on folded wing

Similar Birds

BARROW'S GOLDENEYE
♂ Male has white crescent in front of eye; black head with purplish gloss; black of back extends farther down on sides; smaller white wing patch in flight

♀ • female has more triangular head with more sloping forehead; longer bill with yellow only at tip.

• **BEHAVIOR** Male makes spectacular courtship display, throwing its head so that its neck contorts back to rump. Dives to 6 meters to forage for mollusks, crustaceans, insects, and aquatic plants.
• **BREEDING** Monogamous. Solitary nester.
• **NESTING** Incubation 28–32 days by female. Precocial young may stay in nest 1–2 days. First flight at 56–62 days. Young tended by female but feed themselves. 1 brood per year.
• **POPULATION** Common. Presently stable.
• **BIRDHOUSES** Will utilize nest boxes.

Flight Pattern
Swift direct flight with fast wing beats.

Nest Identification	
Shape	Lined with down • built by female • 5–19 clear pale green or gray-green eggs; elliptical to oval, 2.5 cm long.
Location	

| Plumage Sexes differ | Habitat 〜〜 〜 | Migration Migratory | Weight 1.0 kg |

DATE _____ TIME_____ LOCATION _____

Family ANATIDAE	Species *Bucephala islandica*	Length 41–51 cm	Wingspan 76 cm

BARROW'S GOLDENEYE

In summer this puffy-headed duck plays in mountain streams and rides currents in large rivers. In winter it generally is found on saltwater along the coasts. The forehead rises abruptly from a short triangular bill to a crown that appears flattened, and the nape is puffy. Female bill color varies with season and may be mostly dark with a yellow tip in the winter; the amount of yellow gradually increases to the point the bill may be entirely yellow or have dark mottling at the base when breeding.

puffy black head with purplish sheen

golden eye

white crescent on face

white spots on scapulars

black tail

MALE

brown head

golden eye

FEMALE

darker gray-brown back

black of back extends as bar on sides in front of wing

JUVENILE

grayish brown mottling on breast

grayish brown mottling on sides and flanks

• **SONG**
Makes low grating croaks. During courtship male utters kittenlike squeals and muted grunts.

Similar Birds

COMMON GOLDENEYE
Male has large white spot on face, not crescent; more pointed head with greenish gloss; mostly white scapulars, not spotted • female has longer, more slender bill with yellow restricted to tip; more gently sloped forehead.

• **BEHAVIOR** Flies close to surface of water for some time after the running takeoff typical of diving ducks. Not as gregarious as many other waterfowl. Relatively tame. In western mountains may nest as high as 3,050 meters above sea level.

• **BREEDING** Monogamous.

• **NESTING** Incubation 28–34 days by female. Precocial young stay in nest 1–2 days. First flight at 56 days. Young tended by female but find own food. 1 brood per year.

• **POPULATION** Uncommon to fairly common.

Flight Pattern
Swift direct flight; wings make whistling noise.

Nest Identification	
Shape 🦆 Location 🌳	Up to 15.2 m off ground in large tree cavity, rock crevice, or abandoned building; also in burrow or on ground under bushes • built by female • 5–15 pale olive or blue-green eggs, 6.1 cm long.

Plumage Sexes differ	Habitat ≈ ≈	Migration Migratory	Weight 1.1 kg

DATE _____ TIME_____ LOCATION _____

| Family ANATIDAE | Species *Mergellus albellus* | Length 36–41 cm | Wingspan 61–66 cm |

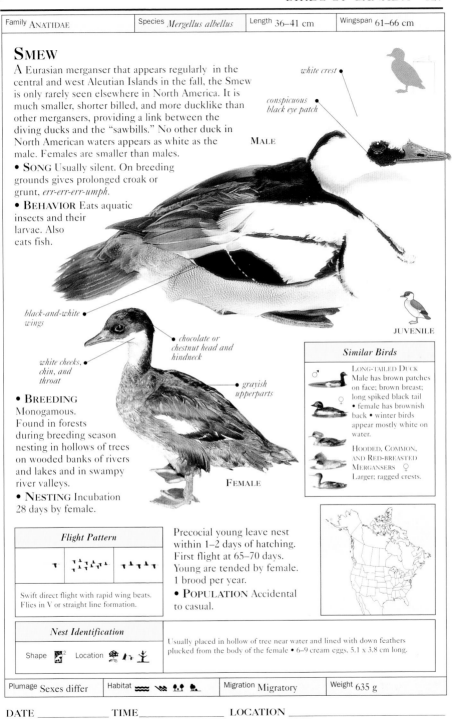

SMEW

A Eurasian merganser that appears regularly in the central and west Aleutian Islands in the fall, the Smew is only rarely seen elsewhere in North America. It is much smaller, shorter billed, and more ducklike than other mergansers, providing a link between the diving ducks and the "sawbills." No other duck in North American waters appears as white as the male. Females are smaller than males.

white crest

conspicuous black eye patch

MALE

• **SONG** Usually silent. On breeding grounds gives prolonged croak or grunt, *err-err-err-umph.*

• **BEHAVIOR** Eats aquatic insects and their larvae. Also eats fish.

black-and-white wings

chocolate or chestnut head and hindneck

white cheeks, chin, and throat

grayish upperparts

JUVENILE

• **BREEDING** Monogamous. Found in forests during breeding season nesting in hollows of trees on wooded banks of rivers and lakes and in swampy river valleys.

• **NESTING** Incubation 28 days by female.

FEMALE

Similar Birds

♂ **LONG-TAILED DUCK** Male has brown patches on face; brown breast; long spiked black tail • female has brownish back • winter birds appear mostly white on water.

HOODED, COMMON, AND RED-BREASTED MERGANSERS ♀ Larger; ragged crests.

Precocial young leave nest within 1–2 days of hatching. First flight at 65–70 days. Young are tended by female. 1 brood per year.

• **POPULATION** Accidental to casual.

Flight Pattern
Swift direct flight with rapid wing beats. Flies in V or straight line formation.

Nest Identification	
Shape	Location	Usually placed in hollow of tree near water and lined with down feathers plucked from the body of the female • 6–9 cream eggs, 5.1 x 3.8 cm long.

| Plumage Sexes differ | Habitat | Migration Migratory | Weight 635 g |

DATE _____ TIME_____ LOCATION _____

Family ANATIDAE	Species *Lophodytes cucullatus*	Length 41–48 cm	Wingspan 61–66 cm

HOODED MERGANSER

The smallest native North American merganser has the largest crest. The male's crest is a vertical white fan bordered with black that can be raised and lowered during display. When the crest is folded, the head appears puffy. Flying birds of both sexes show a white wing patch on the secondaries. On water the male's white breast broken by two black lines in front of the chestnut sides serves as a good field mark.

• **SONG** Hoarse grunts and chatters. Displaying male gives rolling froglike *crrrroooo*; sometimes utters hollow pop.

• **BEHAVIOR** Male raises and lowers crest frequently in display. Excellent diver.

white fan crest

black head

blackish bill

black neck

MALE

black tail and back

Uses both wings and feet to swim swiftly underwater. Thin, serrated bill is adapted for taking fish, but also feeds on crustaceans, aquatic insects, other animals, and plants. Flies quickly into the air off water.

dull brownish gray head

loose rusty crest

dull brownish gray body with blackish back

chestnut sides

white breast with 2 black bars

dark bill with yellowish lower mandible

FEMALE

Similar Birds

RED-BREASTED MERGANSER ♂
COMMON MERGANSER ♂
Red bill; paler and grayer; larger.

BUFFLEHEAD ♂
Lacks chestnut sides.

• **BREEDING** Monogamous. Solitary nester.

• **NESTING** Incubation 26–41 days by female. Young leave nest within 24 hours of hatching. First flight at about 71 days. Young tended by female but find own food. 1 brood per year.

• **POPULATION** After past decline, now increasing because of nest boxes, including those intended for Wood Ducks.

• **BIRDHOUSES** Will nest in artificial boxes.

Flight Pattern

Rapid direct flight with fast wing beats. Flies silently and swiftly.

Nest Identification

Shape 🥚 🕳 Location 🪺 🌿 🍃

Wood chips with debris in bottom • 4.5–6 m off ground • built by female • 6–18 white eggs, almost spherical; 5.3 cm long.

Plumage Sexes differ	Habitat 〰 〰	Migration Migratory	Weight 680 g

DATE _____ TIME_____ LOCATION _____

Family ANATIDAE	Species *Mergus merganser*	Length 56–69 cm	Wingspan 79–94 cm

COMMON MERGANSER

The Common Merganser is the largest merganser in North America. The male's mostly white body, dark head, and red bill easily distinguish it from the other mergansers at a distances or in flight. This is the only merganser in North America in which the female is crested and the male is not.

• **SONG** Male makes harsh croaks; female makes loud harsh *karr karr.*

• **BEHAVIOR** Expert diver pursues small fish under water. Also feeds on mollusks, crustaceans, aquatic insects, and some plants. In winter often stays as far north as open water will allow. Patters across water or land to build up speed for takeoff. Often flies low following stream courses.

• **BREEDING** Monogamous. Solitary nester.

• **NESTING** Incubation 28–35 days by female. Young remain in nest 1 day or more. First flight at 65–70 days. Young tended by female but find own food. 1 brood per year.

• **POPULATION** Fairly common. Stable in US; may be increasing in Europe.

• **BIRDHOUSES** Will use man-made nest boxes.

• **CONSERVATION** Some fishermen feel it competes for their catches and try to kill indiscriminately.

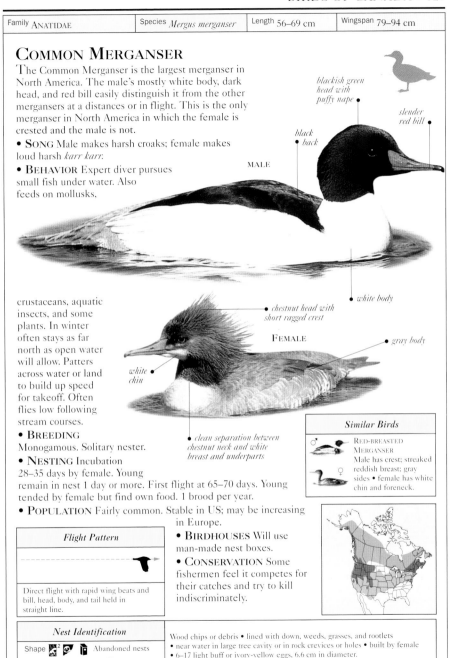

blackish green head with puffy nape

slender red bill

black back

MALE

white body

chestnut head with short ragged crest

FEMALE

gray body

white chin

clean separation between chestnut neck and white breast and underparts

Similar Birds

RED-BREASTED MERGANSER
Male has crest; streaked reddish breast; gray sides • female has white chin and foreneck.

Flight Pattern

Direct flight with rapid wing beats and bill, head, body, and tail held in straight line.

Nest Identification

Shape — Abandoned nests

Location —

Wood chips or debris • lined with down, weeds, grasses, and rootlets • near water in large tree cavity or in rock crevices or holes • built by female • 6–17 light buff or ivory-yellow eggs, 6.6 cm in diameter.

Plumage Sexes differ	Habitat	Migration Migratory	Weight 1.7 kg

DATE _____ TIME_____ LOCATION _____

Family ANATIDAE	Species *Mergus serrator*	Length 41–66 cm	Wingspan 79–89 cm

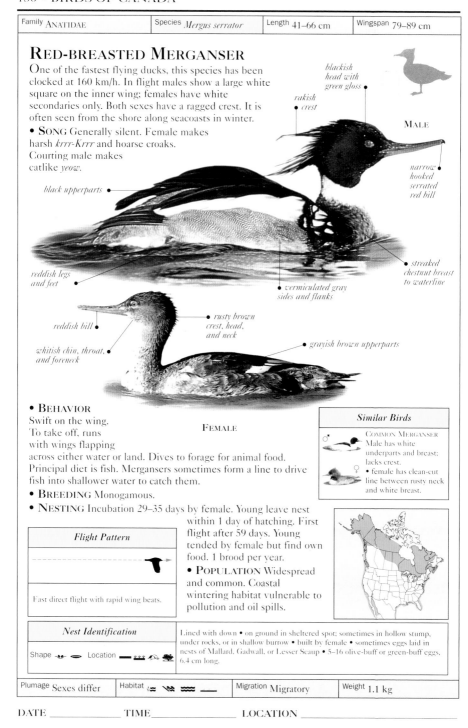

RED-BREASTED MERGANSER

One of the fastest flying ducks, this species has been clocked at 160 km/h. In flight males show a large white square on the inner wing; females have white secondaries only. Both sexes have a ragged crest. It is often seen from the shore along seacoasts in winter.

• **SONG** Generally silent. Female makes harsh *krrr-Krrr* and hoarse croaks. Courting male makes catlike *yeow*.

blackish head with green gloss

rakish crest

MALE

narrow hooked serrated red bill

black upperparts

reddish legs and feet

streaked chestnut breast to waterline

vermiculated gray sides and flanks

reddish bill

rusty brown crest, head, and neck

whitish chin, throat, and foreneck

grayish brown upperparts

FEMALE

• **BEHAVIOR** Swift on the wing. To take off, runs with wings flapping across either water or land. Dives to forage for animal food. Principal diet is fish. Mergansers sometimes form a line to drive fish into shallower water to catch them.

• **BREEDING** Monogamous.

• **NESTING** Incubation 29–35 days by female. Young leave nest within 1 day of hatching. First flight after 59 days. Young tended by female but find own food. 1 brood per year.

• **POPULATION** Widespread and common. Coastal wintering habitat vulnerable to pollution and oil spills.

Similar Birds

COMMON MERGANSER Male has white underparts and breast; lacks crest. • female has clean-cut line between rusty neck and white breast.

Flight Pattern

Fast direct flight with rapid wing beats.

Nest Identification

Shape ⚬ ⚬   Location ▬ ▬ ▰ ▰

Lined with down • on ground in sheltered spot; sometimes in hollow stump, under rocks, or in shallow burrow • built by female • sometimes eggs laid in nests of Mallard, Gadwall, or Lesser Scaup • 5–16 olive-buff or green-buff eggs, 6.4 cm long.

Plumage Sexes differ	Habitat ⚬ ▰ ≈ ▬	Migration Migratory	Weight 1.1 kg

DATE _____ TIME_____ LOCATION _____

Family ANATIDAE	Species *Oxyura jamaicensis*	Length 36–41 cm	Wingspan 53–61 cm

RUDDY DUCK

This big-headed chunky duck has a long stiff tail that is often cocked and fanned forward. Wings are uniform in color. In winter males become gray-brown with a gray bill. In breeding season found in pairs or small loose groups on freshwater lakes and ponds. After nesting, may occur in large flocks; in winter it can be found on salt bays.

• **SONG** Usually silent. In courtship male utters continual *chuck-chuck-chuck-chuck-churr*.

• **BEHAVIOR** Diving duck that can sink slowly beneath the surface like a grebe. When disturbed often swims away underwater instead of flying away. Gray legs and feet are placed so far beneath the body that it cannot walk upright. Primary diet of vegetable materials. A relatively tame bird.

• **BREEDING** Monogamous.

• **NESTING** Incubation 23–26 days by female. Young leave nest within a day of hatching. First flight at 42–48 days. Young tended by female but feed themselves. 1 brood per year, sometimes 2 in the South.

• **POPULATION** Fairly common to common. Current levels are lower than in the past.

• **CONSERVATION** Reasons for decline unknown, but this bird is very tame and easily killed by hunters. Shallow-water nesting areas are subject to draining for agriculture and droughts.

blackish cap reaches below eye

long stiff black tail

blue bill

white cheeks

MALE

rust-red body

whitish belly with light brown barring

blackish gray bill

white cheek with dark brown horizontal streak

brown-gray upperparts

WINTER PLUMAGE

FEMALE

pale underparts with fine brown barring

Similar Birds

MASKED DUCK
Male lacks white cheek
• female has 2 dark lines across face
• population very local.

CINNAMON TEAL
Lacks stiff tail and large pale blue forewing patch in flight
• female lacks line through face.

Flight Pattern
Jerky direct flight with rapid wing beats.

Nest Identification	
Shape	Location
Grasses and cattails • lined with down • in dense marsh vegetation over shallow water • sometimes uses abandoned nests • built by female • 5–17 creamy white or nest-stained eggs, 6.4 cm long • eggs huge compared to body size and similar in size to those laid by much larger ducks.	

Plumage Sexes differ	Habitat	Migration Migratory	Weight 590 g

DATE _____ TIME_____ LOCATION _____

Family ACCIPITRIDAE	Species *Pandion haliaetus*	Length 53–61 cm	Wingspan 137–183 cm

OSPREY

A kindred of other diurnal birds of prey, the Osprey is so distinctive it is sometimes placed in it own family. Its large size and uniquely curved claws allow the Osprey to carry a large fish a considerable distance to feed to its young in the nest. Occasionally an eagle dives upon an Osprey carrying a fish, forces a release, and catches the fish for itself before the fish hits the water.

dark brown upperparts with purplish gloss

• *mostly white head*

• *broad black mark through cheeks and sides of neck*

• **SONG** Series of loud whistled *kyews* or melodious whistle of *chewk-chewk-chewk* or *cheap-cheap-cheap*.

• *clear white belly*

• *long tail with narrow black bars*

• *toes equal in length on claws curved into one-third of a circle*

• **BEHAVIOR** Eats mainly fish. Dives into water to catch prey from 9–30.5 meters above surface. Holds fish with both feet, stops to shake water out of feathers, points fish head forward to decrease wind resistance, and carries to perch or to feed young. Often flies with distinctive crook or kink in wing bent at wrist, which has a black patch.

• **BREEDING** Monogamous. Colonial or solitary nester.

• **NESTING** Incubation 32–43 days by both sexes; however, female does more, while male brings food. Semialtricial young stay in nest 48–59 days. Fed by both parents. 1 brood per year.

JUVENILE

• **POPULATION** Uncommon inland; species is fairly common in its coastal range.

• **BIRDHOUSES** Osprey will build nest on man-made cartwheel on pole or on platforms built in marshes.

Similar Birds

BALD EAGLE
Entirely white head and tail; crown held flat; dark underparts and underwings • juvenile has entirely dark head and patchy tannish white underwings.

• **CONSERVATION** Endangered in 1950s because of chemical pollution (especially DDT), but has since made a comeback, at least partly by transplanting young into areas where entire populations had been extirpated.

Flight Pattern
Deep, slow wing beats alternate with glides; sometimes soars on thermals.

Nest Identification	
Shape ⌒⌒ Location 🌲 ⚡ 🏠 🏭	Sticks, sod, cow dung, seaweed, rubbish, and similar material • up to 61 m above ground in dead or live trees near or over water, or atop telephone poles or bridges • built by both sexes • usually 3 white or pinkish eggs marked with brown and olive; 6.1 x 2.5 cm long.

Plumage Sexes similar	Habitat 〰 〰	Migration Migratory	Weight 1.4 kg

DATE _____ TIME_____ LOCATION _____

Family ACCIPITRIDAE	Species *Haliaeetus leucocephalus*	Length 86–109 cm	Wingspan 183–244 cm

BALD EAGLE

The national bird of the United States has an awe-inspiring wingspan and striking white head and tail that make adults easy to identify. Big concentrations of these huge birds can be seen perched in trees and resting on sandbars when salmon run in rivers of the Northwest. Juveniles can be recognized by their large size; dark brown head, tail, and body; mottled white patches on underwings and underparts; grayish eyes; and light yellow feet.

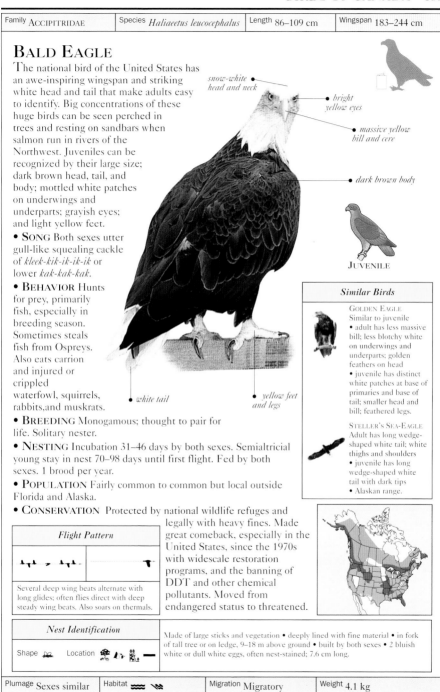

snow-white head and neck

bright yellow eyes

massive yellow bill and cere

dark brown body

JUVENILE

white tail

yellow feet and legs

- **SONG** Both sexes utter gull-like squealing cackle of *kleek-kik-ik-ik-ik* or lower *kak-kak-kak*.
- **BEHAVIOR** Hunts for prey, primarily fish, especially in breeding season. Sometimes steals fish from Ospreys. Also eats carrion and injured or crippled waterfowl, squirrels, rabbits, and muskrats.
- **BREEDING** Monogamous; thought to pair for life. Solitary nester.
- **NESTING** Incubation 31–46 days by both sexes. Semialtricial young stay in nest 70–98 days until first flight. Fed by both sexes. 1 brood per year.
- **POPULATION** Fairly common to common but local outside Florida and Alaska.
- **CONSERVATION** Protected by national wildlife refuges and legally with heavy fines. Made great comeback, especially in the United States, since the 1970s with widescale restoration programs, and the banning of DDT and other chemical pollutants. Moved from endangered status to threatened.

Similar Birds

GOLDEN EAGLE
Similar to juvenile
- adult has less massive bill; less blotchy white on underwings and underparts; golden feathers on head
- juvenile has distinct white patches at base of primaries and base of tail; smaller head and bill; feathered legs.

STELLER'S SEA-EAGLE
Adult has long wedge-shaped white tail; white thighs and shoulders
- juvenile has long wedge-shaped white tail with dark tips
- Alaskan range.

Flight Pattern
Several deep wing beats alternate with long glides; often flies direct with deep steady wing beats. Also soars on thermals.

Nest Identification	
Shape Location	Made of large sticks and vegetation • deeply lined with fine material • in fork of tall tree or on ledge, 9–18 m above ground • built by both sexes • 2 bluish white or dull white eggs, often nest-stained; 7.6 cm long.

Plumage Sexes similar	Habitat	Migration Migratory	Weight 4.1 kg

DATE _____ TIME_____ LOCATION _____

Family ACCIPITRIDAE	Species *Circus cyaneus*	Length 41–61 cm	Wingspan 97–122 cm

NORTHERN HARRIER

Its owl-like facial disk and white rump patch, which is prominent in flight, set the Northern Harrier apart from all other North American falconiformes. Males take several years to acquire their gray-plumaged upperparts. Their wings are long with black-tipped trailing edges, and the outermost four or five primaries are black.

• **SONG** Shrill calls *kek, kek, kek* or *keee, keee, keee*, especially around the nest.

• **BEHAVIOR** Hunts using low slow flight that consists of alternately flapping and gliding with the wings held in a shallow V above the back. Often quarters back and forth over low vegetation and can turn and drop rapidly on prey that it may detect initially by sound. Feeds on small mammals, especially rodents up to the size of a small rabbit, frogs, snakes, small birds, carrion, and large insects. Sometimes hunts the edges of grass fires to capture prey driven out by the flames. Courtship flight of males is thrillingly acrobatic.

• **BREEDING** Some pairs monogamous; some males are polygamous with up to 3 mates. Solitary nester. Both sexes very vocal with high-pitched screams when defending nest.

• **NESTING** Incubation 31–32 days by female. Semi-altricial young stay in nest 30–35 days, fed by both sexes. 1 brood per year.

• **POPULATION** Common but declining.

• **CONSERVATION** Populations have declined everywhere on its breeding range because of the loss of marshland habitat as well as pesticides. Formerly, many were lost to shooting.

gray upperparts

chestnut spotting on breast and throat

MALE

black wing tips and secondary tips

whitish underparts

very long tail

JUVENILE

disk of feathers around face

brown upperparts

FEMALE

Similar Birds
ROUGH-LEGGED HAWK ♀ Base of tail (not rump) white; broad blackish subterminal band on tail • does not course low over fields but hunts from perch or by hovering.

Flight Pattern
Several deep wing beats alternate with glides.

Nest Identification	
Shape 🪺 ➤ Location 🌿🌿	Sticks and grass lined with fine material • usually placed on the ground • may be 1.5 m above water or marshy terrain • built by both sexes, but female does most construction • 3–9 bluish white eggs, sometimes spotted with brown, 4.6 cm long.

Plumage Sexes differ	Habitat ___	Migration Some migrate	Weight 357 g

DATE _____ TIME_____ LOCATION _____

Family ACCIPITRIDAE	Species *Accipiter striatus*	Length 25–36 cm	Wingspan 51–71 cm

SHARP-SHINNED HAWK

A territorial bird, the Sharp-shinned Hawk occasionally strikes humans in defense of its nest. Its name describes its flattened, thin tarsus or shank. This is the smallest of the North American accipiters; the female is larger than the male. The head and neck seem small for its long, slender body. Its long tail has three to four narrow black crossbars, and is squared or notched on the tip. Juveniles have brown upperparts and white underparts with heavy brown streaking.

- **SONG** When disturbed utters *kek-kek-kek* or *kik-kik-kik*. Call is melancholy cry.
- **BEHAVIOR** Eats mostly small birds, including songbirds, taken off ground or twigs, or in air. Also eats small mammals (including bats), reptiles, grasshoppers, and other larger insects.
- **BREEDING** Monogamous. Solitary nester.
- **NESTING** Incubation 32–35 days by female. Semialtricial young stay in nest 23–27 days. Fed by both sexes. 1 brood per year.
- **POPULATION** Common to fairly common.
- **FEEDERS** Often attracted to concentrations of small birds at bird feeders, especially in winter.
- **CONSERVATION** Decline during 1950s through 1970s due to pesticides and heavy metal pollutants in environment. Some comeback in 1980s but is perhaps declining again.

finely streaked red-brown throat

red-brown bars across chest and belly

blue-gray upperparts

white undertail coverts

long bright yellow legs with "sharp shins"

square or slightly forked tail

narrow white tip on tail

JUVENILE

Similar Birds

COOPER'S HAWK
Rounded tail; larger (but female Sharp-shinned approach male Cooper's in size); larger head; more contrast between black crown and face; wide white band on tip of tail (can be tricky because of feather wear); sometimes lightly streaked undertail coverts.

Flight Pattern

More buoyant flight than other accipiters with several rapid wing beats between glides.

Nest Identification

Shape ⌒ ⌒   Location 🌲 🌳🌲

Made of sticks and twigs • lined with strips of bark, grass, and coniferous needles • sometimes in deciduous trees but usually conifers, 3–18 m above ground, next to trunk • 4–5 white or bluish eggs marked with browns, 3.8 cm long.

Plumage Sexes similar	Habitat 🌾 🌿🌿 🌱	Migration Some migrate	Weight 102 g

DATE _____ TIME_____ LOCATION _____

Family ACCIPITRIDAE	Species *Accipiter cooperii*	Length 36–53 cm	Wingspan 69–91 cm

COOPER'S HAWK

Sometimes called the Blue Darter or Chicken Hawk by farmers; however, studies show poultry are only a small portion of the Cooper's Hawk's diet. It is named after William Cooper, who was the first person to collect one of these birds and have it identified. Like most hawks, the juvenile has heavily streaked underparts and brown upperparts, whereas adults show blue-gray upperparts. Females are larger than males, and both show a blue-gray back. In flight the long tail appears rounded.

- **SONG** Alarm call is *kac-kac-kac* or *kuck, kuck kuck, kuck.*
- **BEHAVIOR** Territorial; will

not allow similar Sharp-shinned Hawk in same woodland. Attacks poultry, other birds, small mammals, and takes songbirds out of nest. Occasionally eats fish. Sometimes carries prey to water and kills it by drowning. Hunts by waiting in ambush or by dashing in swift low flight through wooded lot; surprises prey and catches it with talons.

- **BREEDING** Monogamous. Solitary nester.
- **NESTING** Incubation 32–36 days by both sexes, but more by female. Semialtricial young stay in nest 27–34 days, fed by both sexes. 1 brood per year.
- **POPULATION** Uncommon to rare. Steadily increasing after bottoming out in 1970s.
- **CONSERVATION** Decline in mid-20th century principally due to pesticides. Stable or increasing in most areas.

JUVENILE

dark gray or black on top of head

deep red to yellow eyes

yellow cere

white undertail coverts

rounded tail with dark bars and a white band on tip

reddish bars across breast and belly

yellow legs and feet

Similar Birds

SHARP-SHINNED HAWK Shorter tail with notched or squared end; smaller head; less contrast between back and crown; narrower white band at tip of tail
• male much smaller, but female approaches size of male Cooper's.

Flight Pattern

Rapid wing beats followed by short glide; often circles in flight on thermals.

Nest Identification	Sticks and twigs • lined with chips, outer bark strips, and occasionally green conifer needles • in crotch of conifer near trunk or in deciduous tree, 3–18 m above ground • built by both sexes, but male does more • 4–5 bluish white or greenish white eggs, spotted with browns and usually nest-stained; elliptical to subelliptical, 3.8 cm long.
Shape 🪺 Location 🌲🌳	

Plumage Sexes similar	Habitat 🌳🌳 🌿	Migration Some migrate	Weight 349 g

DATE _____ TIME_____ LOCATION _____

Family ACCIPITRIDAE	Species *Accipiter gentilis*	Length 48–69 cm	Wingspan 102–119 cm

NORTHERN GOSHAWK

An agile and proficient flier, the Northern Goshawk is not afraid to catch prey near humans when it is hungry. This bold hawk has been known to attack duck decoys. It appears pale gray at a distance, and in flight the shorter tail and longer, broad wings (for an accipiter) give the superficial appearance of a Red-tailed Hawk. The female is the larger and dominant partner in a pair.

- **SONG** Alarm call is harsher and deeper than Cooper's Hawk, *kac-kac-kac* or *kuk, kuk, kuk.* Female utters high-pitched melancholy whine, *kee-a-ah,* reminiscent of the Red-shouldered Hawk.
- **BEHAVIOR** Eats snowshoe hare, lemmings, and grouse; migrates south in irruptive numbers when their prey populations crash. Also eats small to medium mammals, large and small birds (including ducks and crows), and some large insects. Dives and kills prey on ground or in air with deadly grip of talons. Female very defensive of nest site to the point of attacking intruders, including humans.
- **BREEDING** Monogamous. Solitary nester.
- **NESTING** Incubation 36–42 days by both sexes, but female does more. Semialtricial young stay in nest 41–43 days. Fed by both sexes. First flight at 45 days. 1 brood per year.
- **POPULATION** Uncommon to rare.
- **CONSERVATION** Expanding range. Possible increase in the Northeast during recent decades. Southwestern mountain populations may be threatened by loss of habitat.

distinct white eyebrow over each eye widens posteriorly

black crown

wedge-shaped black postocular stripe

orange-red eyes

blue-gray back

white underparts with gray mottling

relatively long rounded wings

JUVENILE

long rounded to wedge-shaped tail

fluffy white undertail coverts

Similar Birds

COOPER'S HAWK Shorter wings; longer tail; darker blue-gray upperparts; barred rusty underparts.

Flight Pattern

Several strong rapid wing beats interspersed with glides; soars on thermals.

Nest Identification	
Shape · Location	Sticks and twigs • lined with bark strips, evergreen sprigs, grass, and feathers • in fork of branch or trunk of tree, 6–23 m above ground • built by both sexes, but male does more • 3–4 bluish or off-white eggs, occasionally nest-stained or spotted with brown; slightly elongate elliptical or oval, 5.8 cm long.

Plumage Sexes similar	Habitat	Migration Migratory	Weight 907 g

DATE _____ TIME_____ LOCATION _____

Family ACCIPITRIDAE	Species *Buteo lineatus*	Length 43–61 cm	Wingspan 81–127 cm

RED-SHOULDERED HAWK

This bird uses the same territory for years, and even succeeding generations may return to the same territory. The longest recorded continuous use of the same territory is forty-five years. Five races (*lineatus, alleni, extimus, elagans,* and *texanus*) show variations in color and size but all have barred rusty underparts, reddish wing linings, and shoulders with banded tails. In flight the long black tail displays numerous narrow white bands on adults and juveniles. Flight feathers are spotted and barred black and white and show a pale "window" at the base of the outer primaries. Male is larger than female.

• **SONG** Evenly spaced series of clear high loud and often rapidly repeated *kee-ah* or *clee-u clee-u clee-u* notes. Blue Jays can mimic the call perfectly.

• **BEHAVIOR** Stalks prey from perch. Catches and eats small to medium-sized mammals, small reptiles, amphibians, large insects, spiders, earthworms, snails, and an occasional bird. Prefers wet woodlands, often near water and swamps. Often perches low to hunt on posts, utility poles, and low to mid level in trees.

• **BREEDING** Monogamous. Solitary nester.

• **NESTING** Incubation 28 days by both sexes. Semialtricial young stay in nest 35–45 days. Fed by both sexes. 1 brood per year.

yellow cere
reddish shoulders
extensive pale spotting on upperparts

rust-red barring on underparts

JUVENILE

yellow feet and legs

FLORIDA RACE

long black tail with numerous narrow white bands

Similar Birds

BROAD-WINGED HAWK Smaller; shorter tail; lacks barring in flight feathers; fewer, wider white tail bands; lacks reddish shoulders; lacks wing windows; peweelike call.

• **POPULATION** Fairly common in range.

• **CONSERVATION** Some decline due to habitat loss and human encroachment particularly in West. Pesticides in Midwest interfered with reproduction during the 1970s.

Flight Pattern
Flies with fairly rapid stiff wing beats; soars on flat wings and glides on slightly drooped wings. Soars on thermals.

Nest Identification	
Shape ▱ Location 🪹 🌲	Made of sticks, twigs, inner bark strips, dry leaves, moss, lichen, and coniferous needles • usually by a tree trunk 3–61 m above ground • built by both sexes • 2–6 white or bluish white eggs, often nest-stained and marked with brown; short elliptical, 5.3 cm long.

Plumage Sexes similar	Habitat 🌳 〰 🌿 🏞	Migration Some migrate	Weight 499 g

DATE _____ TIME_____ LOCATION _____

Family ACCIPITRIDAE	Species *Buteo platypterus*	Length 33–48 cm	Wingspan 81–99 cm

BROAD-WINGED HAWK

The smallest of the North American buteos is similar in size to a stocky crow. These birds, which migrate in flocks of thousands, make up the bulk of hawk flights in September in the East. This peaceful bird is one of the tamest hawks. In flight the tips of the flight feathers appear dark, producing a black border along the trailing edge of the wing, and the underwing linings vary from white to rusty-buff. The black-and-white bands in the tail are approximately equal in width. Juveniles are similar to adults but appear more washed out and have fainter tail bands; underparts are pale with heavy dark streaking.

dark brown upperparts

red barring on underparts

- **SONG** Thin shrill whistle, *peeteee* or *peweeeeeeeeee*, often given in flight and similar to the high plaintive whistled note of an Eastern Wood-Pewee.
- **BEHAVIOR** Perches to watch for prey from utility poles and wires or near water along edge of woods. Hunts along wooded roads under the tree canopy. Swoops down to grab prey with talons. Eats amphibians, reptiles, small rodents, shrews, rabbits, some small birds, large insects, and insect larvae.
- **BREEDING** Monogamous. Solitary nester.
- **NESTING** Incubation 28–32 days by both sexes, but mostly by female. Semialtricial young stay in nest 29–35 days, fed by both sexes. 1 brood per year.
- **POPULATION** Common in eastern US and southern Canada west to a portion of eastern British Columbia. Rare in winter in California and Florida.

large black-and-white bands on tail

JUVENILE

Similar Birds

RED-SHOULDERED HAWK Larger in size; narrower, more rounded wings with barred and spotted black-and-white flight feathers; buff to rusty-red wing linings; longer, narrower tail with white bands much narrower than dark ones.

- **CONSERVATION** Large numbers once shot during migration, particularly along mountainous ridges in the East. Now protected by law. Neotropical migrant.

Flight Pattern
Several rapid shallow wing beats followed by a glide. Soars on thermals and updrafts.

Nest Identification	Sticks, twigs, and dead leaves • lined with inner bark strips with lichen, outer bark chips, evergreen sprigs, and green leaves • in crotch of deciduous tree, 9–15 m above ground • built by both sexes in slow process that takes 3–5 weeks • 2–4 white or bluish white eggs sometimes marked with brown; short elliptical, 4.8 cm long.
Shape Location	

Plumage Sexes similar	Habitat	Migration Migratory	Weight 420 g

DATE _____ TIME_____ LOCATION _____

Family ACCIPITRIDAE	Species *Buteo swainsoni*	Length 48–56 cm	Wingspan 117–147 cm

SWAINSON'S HAWK

Sometimes traveling in huge flocks, these birds migrate from North America to Argentina, about 17,700–27,350 km each year. This large buteo lives in open rangeland, hill country, plains, and grasslands where trees are sparse. Swainson's Hawk is about the same size as the Red-tailed Hawk and has three different color morphs: light, rufous (intermediate), and dark. This variety provides for a confusing array of plumages: dark morphs are dark brown overall; the rufous morph is similar but with variegated medium brown underparts. In flight the narrow, slightly pointed wings are held in a slight dihedral, and the bird tilts from side to side like a Turkey Vulture.

uniformly dark brown upperparts

white wing linings

black bill with yellow cere

white throat

wide chestnut band on chest

JUVENILE

pale buff to white belly

RUFOUS MORPH

DARK MORPH

LIGHT MORPH

narrowly banded gray tail with wide dark subterminal band

• **SONG** Plaintive whistle, *kr-e-e-eeeeer*, similar to that of the Broad-winged Hawk.

• **BEHAVIOR** Hunts, sometimes in flocks, for grasshoppers and crickets. Stalks ground squirrels at their burrows. Catches prey in talons. Also eats mice, rabbits, lizards, frogs, toads, and an occasional game bird. Frequents grasslands, agricultural grain fields, and open landscapes.

• **BREEDING** Monogamous. Solitary nester.

• **NESTING** Incubation 28–35 days by both sexes; female does more. Semialtricial young stay in nest 30–35 days. Fed by both sexes. First flight at 38–46 days. 1 brood per year.

• **POPULATION** Very common to common but numbers are recorded as declining.

• **CONSERVATION** Recent heavy losses in South American wintering grounds due to birds eating insects that have been poisoned by insecticides.

Similar Birds

SHORT-TAILED HAWK Shorter, broader wings and tail; wings with pale barring only in flight feathers • light morph has completely white underparts and white forehead • Florida range; casual to southeast Texas.

RED-TAILED HAWK Lacks breast band; pale flight feathers; reddish tail.

Flight Pattern

Alternates series of powerful deep wing beats with long glides. Soars on thermals, updrafts, wings bent upward in dihedral.

Nest Identification	
Shape	Location

Large sticks, twigs, brambles, grass, and similar materials • lined with inner bark, fresh leaves, flower clusters, down, and feathers • in tree 2–21.5 m above ground • 2–4 bluish greenish white eggs marked with pale brown; subelliptical to elliptical, 5.6 cm long.

Plumage Sexes similar	Habitat	Migration Migratory	Weight 907 g

DATE _____ TIME_____ LOCATION _____

Family ACCIPITRIDAE	Species *Buteo jamaicensis*	Length 48–64 cm	Wingspan 117–147 cm

RED-TAILED HAWK

This hawk is found in more habitats than any other North American buteo and, consequently, is the most common hawk on the continent. This species has five races: a pale pink-tailed Great Plains race known as "Krider's Red-tailed," *krideri;* the eastern *borealis,* the southwestern *fuertesi;* the western, *calurus;* and the rare "Harlan's Hawk" or *harlani,* once considered a separate species, which is very dark with a white-based tail. All adults show a dark brownish mantle in flight and dark brown bar on leading edge of underwing. All juveniles have a dark brown tail with a black band. Because it perches low on woodland edges and along roadsides this is one of the most conspicuous and easily observed hawks.

reddish tail ranges from pale buff-pink to deep rufous-red

whitish flight feathers with pale barring

pale wing linings

large bill with yellow cere

white belly with broad band of dark streaking

EASTERN ADULT
BOREALIS

- **SONG** Harsh descending slurred *keeeeer-r-r.* Also rasping hissing screamy, *p-s-s-s, kree-kree ree-e-e.*
- **BEHAVIOR** Across its vast range takes a wide variety of prey. Eats small to medium mammals, reptiles, amphibians, grasshoppers, spiders, earthworms, crustaceans, some fish, and an occasional small bird or bat. Carries small prey to perch; partially eats large prey on ground.
- **BREEDING** Monogamous; may mate for life. Solitary nester.
- **NESTING** Incubation 28–35 days by both sexes; more by female. Semialtricial young stay in nest 42–46 days. Fed by both sexes. 1 brood per year.

HARLAN'S HAWK

KRIDER'S RED-TAILED

Similar Birds

ROUGH-LEGGED HAWK Smaller bill and feet; feathered legs; white rump; white tail with multiple dark bands; black belly (light morph).

SWAINSON'S HAWK Multiple tail bands; dark flight feathers; pale wing linings; brown chest (light morph).

- **POPULATION** Very common. Some decline due to habitat loss.
- **CONSERVATION** Some eggshell thinning. Many still killed illegally, and some are accidentally killed by cars.

Flight Pattern	

Several rapid strong wing beats followed by a glide. Soars well on thermals and sometimes hangs on updrafts.

Nest Identification	
Shape Location	Sticks and twigs • lined with inner bark strips, evergreen sprigs, and green leaves • in crotch of large tree, on cliff ledge, or on artificial structure, as high as 36.5 m above ground • built by both sexes • 2–3 white or bluish white eggs sometimes spotted brown, 6.1 cm long.

Plumage Sexes similar	Habitat	Migration Migratory	Weight 1.0 kg

DATE _____ TIME_____ LOCATION _____

Family ACCIPITRIDAE	Species *Buteo regalis*	Length 56–71 cm	Wingspan 142 cm

FERRUGINOUS HAWK

One of the largest and most powerful buteos, this hawk is true to its Latin species name, meaning kingly or royal. This bird has light, dark, and reddish morphs; the light morph is the most common. Dark morphs are dark rufous to dark brown overall. In flight all three hold the long pointed wings in a dihedral, and show a white patch at base of primaries from above. The light morph appears almost completely white from below except for the reddish legs, which form a rusty red V beneath the body.

rufous-streaked head

yellow cere

reddish brown upperparts

white underparts with light reddish brown spotting

JUVENILE

- **SONG** Alarm call of *kree-a* or *kaah kaah.*
- **BEHAVIOR** Eats mainly ground squirrels; spots them from perch, flies high in air, and swoops down to catch them. Also hunts prairie dogs, rabbits, small rodents,

reddish leggings

yellow feet

DARK MORPH

pale tail with buff-gray tip

LIGHT MORPH

snakes, lizards, small to medium birds, and large insects. One of the few large hawks that hovers. Prefers open country, where it often hunts from low perches on fence posts, utility poles, or small trees.

- **BREEDING** Monogamous. Solitary nester.
- **NESTING** Incubation 31–33 days by both sexes, but female does more. Semialtricial young stay in nest 40–50 days; for first 21 days female stays on nest while male hunts, then both sexes hunt. First flight at 38–50 days. 1 brood per year.
- **POPULATION** Uncommon to fairly common. Rare to casual in migration or winter to states bordered by the Mississippi River and occasionally Florida.
- **CONSERVATION** Threatened and declining due to illegal shooting and loss of habitat. Some are accidentally killed by cars.

Similar Birds

ROUGH-LEGGED HAWK
Dark morph has banded tail with broad dark subterminal band; no rusty leggings.

"KRIDER'S RED-TAILED" HAWK
Juvenile is shorter; more rounded wings; dark subterminal tail band to tip; unfeathered tarsus.

Flight Pattern

Quarters back and forth close to ground; alternates several deep flaps with glides similar to Northern Harrier. Soars on thermals and hovers.

Nest Identification

Shape Location

Sticks and debris • lined with finer materials, including cow dung • usually on top of tree, 2–15 m above ground; in treeless areas may build on cliffs or ground • built by both sexes • 2–6 pale bluish white eggs blotched with pale to dark browns and buffs; between spherical and elliptical, 6.4 cm long.

Plumage Sexes similar	Habitat	Migration Migratory	Weight 1.0 kg

DATE _____ TIME_____ LOCATION _____

Family ACCIPITRIDAE	Species *Buteo lagopus*	Length 46–71 cm	Wingspan 122–142 cm

ROUGH-LEGGED HAWK

Named for the feathered shanks of its legs, this big high-soaring hawk of the open country often is seen perched on fence posts or dead trees. It flies low on long, thin pointed wings and is one of the few large hawks that regularly hovers. In flight the light morph's long grayish white tail with a broad dark subterminal band and white tail coverts contrast sharply with its black belly and dark back.

• **SONG** Usually silent in winter. Circling pairs in breeding season give melancholy whistle.

• **BEHAVIOR** Eats mostly small rodents and large insects. Usually catches prey on ground. Often hunts from low perch or by standing on ground on a mound or other elevation. When hunting in flight, flies low over open vegetation, quartering slowly back and forth, alternately flapping and gliding or hovering before plunging feet-first on prey. Irruptive flights when prey populations crash bring many south in winter.

• **BREEDING** Monogamous. Pairs have been recorded to remain together for many years.

• **NESTING** Incubation 28–31 days by female. Young leave nest at about 41 days and spend 21–42 days in Arctic after fledging and before migrating south for winter.

• **POPULATION** Common in breeding range; uncommon to fairly common with erratic numbers on wintering grounds.

• **CONSERVATION** Enormous numbers once were shot in western US because of tameness. In the West many killed while feeding on animal carcasses on highways.

whitish head

LIGHT MORPH FEMALE

small bill with yellow cere

whitish underparts with dark brown streaking (heaviest on upper chest and belly)

thin feathered legs

small, dainty yellow feet

1–3 narrow dark marks on tail

LIGHT MORPH JUVENILE

long grayish white tail with broad dark subterminal band

blackish brown overall

rarely, white mottling on head and chest

barred dark gray tail with broad dark subterminal band

DARK MORPH FEMALE

Similar Birds

RED-TAILED HAWK Dark morph is dark brown overall; rufous tail; shorter wings and tails; smaller bill.

FERRUGINOUS HAWK Dark morph has whitish carpal crescent on underwing; dark brown overall; brighter rufous on lesser upperwing coverts and tail coverts.

Flight Pattern

Alternates powerful flaps with glides. Hangs in wind and hovers over one spot; somewhat floppy wing beats at times.

Nest Identification

Shape — Location —

Small twigs and plant material; 61–76 cm in diameter • in river valleys, precipices, slopes in raised places • uses nest for several years; each pair can have several nests and use them alternately • 2–3 eggs when food is scarce; 5–7 eggs when food is abundant; blotched, white, or streaked with brown.

Plumage Sexes similar	Habitat	Migration Migratory	Weight 862 g

DATE _____ TIME_____ LOCATION _____

Family ACCIPITRIDAE	Species *Aquila chrysaetos*	Length 84–97 cm	Wingspan 183–244 cm

GOLDEN EAGLE

Like most other birds of prey, the female Golden Eagle is considerably larger than the male. This large dark eagle is fairly common in the West and rare to uncommon in the East. It has been clocked in a steep glide at 193 km/h and is estimated to swoop on prey in dives at more than 240 km/h. Juveniles in flight display "ringtail" plumage (a broad white tail band with a terminal band of black) and a broad white patch at the base of the primaries. Large birds of prey require large territories, and home ranges for a pair of this species have been recorded as large as 155 square km.

yellow cere

tawny-golden feathers on crown

tawny-golden feathers on nape and sides of neck

black bill

dark brown overall

feathered tarsus

yellow feet

- **SONG** Generally silent. Around nest makes yelping bark, *keya*, and whistled notes. During soaring courtship flight yelps or mews.
- **BEHAVIOR** Favors rabbit, ground squirrel, marmot, grouse, and ptarmigan. Also eats large insects, other small mammals, carrion, and reptiles, including turtles. Has been known to attack full-grown deer, antelopes, and birds as large as Great Horned Owls and cranes. Returns to the same nest yearly or every other year.

JUVENILE

Similar Birds

BALD EAGLE
Juvenile has larger head; shorter tail; mottled white patches on underparts make tail more blotchy; underwing pattern; bare tarsus.

- **BREEDING** Monogamous; may pair for life. Solitary nester.
- **NESTING** Incubation 43–45 days by both sexes; female does more. Young stay in nest 66–70 days, dependent on parents for first 30 days. First flight at 65–70 days. Usually has 1 brood every 2 years.
- **POPULATION** Uncommon to rare in the East but fairly common in the West. A total of only 4,000–5,000 pairs were estimated in 1964. Circumpolar.
- **CONSERVATION** Protected by law. Thousands once killed by ranchers in efforts to protect livestock from potential predation. Also killed in collisions with aircraft. Protected areas established.

Flight Pattern
Alternates deep slow powerful wing beats with glides or rides easily on thermals.

Nest Identification	
Shape 🪺 Location 🌲 🏔 🌴	Sticks woven with brush and leaves • lined with fine material • located 3–30.5 m high in trees • 2.4–3 m across and 91–122 cm deep • built by both sexes • 2 white or creamy buff eggs marked with brown or reddish brown, 7.4 cm long.

Plumage Sexes similar	Habitat ▲ ___	Migration Some migrate	Weight 1.6 kg

DATE _____ TIME_____ LOCATION _____

Family FALCONIDAE	Species *Falco tinnunculus*	Length 30–41 cm	Wingspan 69–76 cm

EURASIAN KESTREL

The Eurasian Kestrel can be differentiated from the American Kestrel by its larger size and its single, rather than double, black facial mark and wedge-shaped tail. Years ago in France, this species was trained in falconry to fly at bats. Accidental in winter on the northeast coast, Eurasian Kestrels have been known to travel across the Atlantic Ocean, either by flying or riding on a ship.

• **SONG** Creaking cackling shrill *kee-kee-kee* call.

• **BEHAVIOR** Feeds primarily on large insects, small rodents, and small birds. Prefers open country where it perches on fence posts, utility poles, and wires while it watches for prey. Often hunts by hovering in one spot over grasses or thickets.

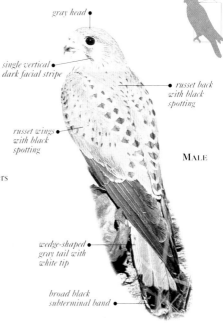

gray head •

single vertical • dark facial stripe

• russet back with black spotting

russet wings • with black spotting

MALE

wedge-shaped • gray tail with white tip

broad black • subterminal band

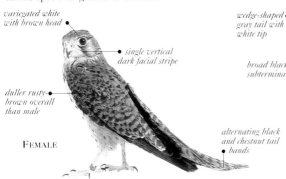

variegated white with brown head •

• single vertical dark facial stripe

duller rusty- brown overall than male

FEMALE

alternating black and chestnut tail bands •

Similar Birds

AMERICAN KESTREL Male has chestnut cap; chestnut nape with black splotch; chestnut tail • female has less-variegated darker cap • both have 2 facial stripes; square to rounded tail; smaller.

• **BREEDING** Monogamous. Solitary nester.

• **NESTING** Incubation 28–32 days primarily by female. Young stay in nest 30–35 days, fed by both sexes. 1 brood per year.

• **POPULATION** Accidental to casual, primarily in winter on the East Coast from the Maritimes to New Jersey and on the West Coast from islands in the Bering Sea to British Columbia.

• **CONSERVATION** Single greatest cause of death is being shot by humans.

Flight Pattern	

Flies with rapid wing beats followed by a glide. Soars on thermals and updrafts.

Nest Identification	Little, if any, nest material • uses abandoned nest of crow or magpie, split or cavity in tree, and ledges on cliffs or buildings • 4.5–23 m above ground • 3–6 cream to white eggs blotched heavily with browns and nest-stained, 3.8 cm long.
Shape	
Location	

Plumage Sexes differ	Habitat	Migration Migratory	Weight 187 g

DATE _____ TIME_____ LOCATION _____

Family FALCONIDAE	Species *Falco sparverius*	Length 23–30 cm	Wingspan 51–64 cm

AMERICAN KESTREL

The smallest most common North American falcon is found all over the continent and north to the tree line in summer. It is sometimes called the Sparrow Hawk, a misnomer as the bird is neither a hawk nor does its diet include a significant amount of sparrows or other small birds. In flight it shows the typical long tail and long pointed wings of a falcon. A bird of the open country, it often is seen perched on wires along roadsides.

• **SONG** Alarm call a loud quick *klee-klee-klee* or *killy, killy, killy.*

• **BEHAVIOR** When perched bobs tail. Hunts rodents and insects from perch or hovers. Also eats bats, small birds, small reptiles, and frogs. Not dependent on drinking water in desert because it extracts water from its diet.

• **BREEDING** Monogamous. Solitary nester. During courtship male brings food and feeds female in the air.

• **NESTING** Incubation 29–31 days by both sexes, mostly by female. Semialtricial young stay in nest 30–31 days, fed by female. Male calls female from nest to feed. 1 brood per year, sometimes 2 in the South.

• **POPULATION** Common.

• **BIRDHOUSES** Readily nests in bird boxes built especially for kestrels. Occasionally attracted to bird feeders to prey on birds.

black-and-white pattern on head

rufous back with dark barring

2 vertical dark facial lines

spotted tawny-buff breast

MALE

blue-gray wings and wing coverts

long slender pointed wings

rufous-red tail without barring

2 vertical dark facial lines

streaked pale underparts

rufous tail with brown barring, black band, and narrow white tip

FEMALE

Similar Birds

SHARP-SHINNED HAWK
Blue-gray upperparts; red-brown streaked and barred underparts; square or notched barred tail; short rounded wings.

MERLIN ♂
Larger; variegated head; lacks facial bars, blue-black tail and back; heavily streaked underparts • male has blue-black wings.

• **CONSERVATION** Migratory counts suggest recent decline in the Northeast; other populations seem stable. Expanded establishment of nest boxes in some areas, especially along highways, seems to have encouraged recovery.

Flight Pattern	

Several rapid wing beats followed by a glide; often hovers on rapidly beating wings. Also soars on thermals.

Nest Identification	
Shape	Location

Little, if any, nest material • in old flicker tree holes, niches in walls, and holes under gables, 4–24 m above ground • 3–7 white to cream or pale pink eggs, heavily blotched with browns, sometimes unmarked; 3.6 cm long.

Plumage Sexes differ	Habitat	Migration Migratory	Weight 111 g

DATE _____ TIME _____ LOCATION _____

| Family FALCONIDAE | Species *Falco columbarius* | Length 28–33 cm | Wingspan 58–66 cm |

MERLIN

This medium-sized falcon of northern coniferous forests hunts the openings in parklike grasslands, bogs, and shrubby barrens. In flight it shows the distinctive falcon "jizz" of long pointed wings and a long tail with a big-headed, powerful look, and it displays impressive bursts of speed when in pursuit of prey. Geographic variation in color exists, from pale prairie birds to dark Pacific Northwest forms.

- **SONG** *Ki-ki-kee*, *kek-kek-kek* rapidly repeated.
- **BEHAVIOR** A relatively tame bird, allowing close approach. Defensive of nest; often attacks intruders, including humans. The Merlin flies close to the ground and catches prey with bursts of speed while in pursuit, rather than by diving or hovering. It is a bird that often hunts from an open perch. Primary diet of small birds, mammals, and large insects. May frequent cities in winter.
- **BREEDING** Monogamous. Solitary nester.
- **NESTING** Incubation 28–32 days mostly by female. Semialtricial young stay in nest 25–35 days. Fed by both sexes. 1 brood per year.
- **POPULATION** Uncommon.

blue-gray crown

yellow enlarged area at base of bill

white chin and throat with streaking

whitish buff head and nape

narrow black mustache

blue-gray back and wings

whitish buff underparts heavily streaked brown to black

yellow legs and feet

MALE

blue-black tail with gray barring and white tip

brown upperparts

more heavily streaked underparts

FEMALE

Similar Birds

AMERICAN KESTREL ♂ Smaller; bobs tail and hovers; barred rufous back and tail.

PEREGRINE FALCON Larger; indistinct barring on tail; dark hood on head extends beneath eye like broad sideburn.

- **CONSERVATION** Some declines attributed to pesticides and heavy metals in food chain.

Flight Pattern
Swift direct flight with rapid powerful wing beats.

Nest Identification	
Shape / Location	Uses old tree nests of crows, magpies, and hawks, relined with bark and feathers • 4.5–11 m above ground • built by female • 2–7 white eggs, some marked with reddish brown; short elliptical, 4.1 cm long.

| Plumage Sexes differ | Habitat | Migration Most migrate | Weight 162 g |

DATE _____ TIME_____ LOCATION _____

Family FALCONIDAE	Species *Falco rusticolus*	Length 51–64 cm	Wingspan 122–163 cm

GYRFALCON

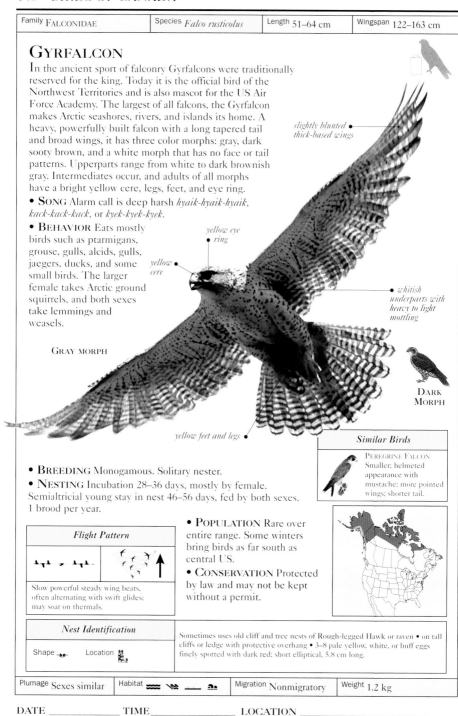

In the ancient sport of falconry Gyrfalcons were traditionally reserved for the king. Today it is the official bird of the Northwest Territories and is also mascot for the US Air Force Academy. The largest of all falcons, the Gyrfalcon makes Arctic seashores, rivers, and islands its home. A heavy, powerfully built falcon with a long tapered tail and broad wings, it has three color morphs: gray, dark sooty brown, and a white morph that has no face or tail patterns. Upperparts range from white to dark brownish gray. Intermediates occur, and adults of all morphs have a bright yellow cere, legs, feet, and eye ring.

- **SONG** Alarm call is deep harsh *hyaik-hyaik-hyaik, kack-kack-kack*, or *kyek-kyek-kyek*.
- **BEHAVIOR** Eats mostly birds such as ptarmigans, grouse, gulls, alcids, gulls, jaegers, ducks, and some small birds. The larger female takes Arctic ground squirrels, and both sexes take lemmings and weasels.

slightly blunted thick-based wings

yellow eye ring

yellow cere

whitish underparts with heavy to light mottling

GRAY MORPH

DARK MORPH

yellow feet and legs

- **BREEDING** Monogamous. Solitary nester.
- **NESTING** Incubation 28–36 days, mostly by female. Semialtricial young stay in nest 46–56 days, fed by both sexes. 1 brood per year.

Similar Birds

PEREGRINE FALCON
Smaller; helmeted appearance with mustache; more pointed wings; shorter tail.

- **POPULATION** Rare over entire range. Some winters bring birds as far south as central US.
- **CONSERVATION** Protected by law and may not be kept without a permit.

Flight Pattern

Slow powerful steady wing beats, often alternating with swift glides; may soar on thermals.

Nest Identification

Shape   Location

Sometimes uses old cliff and tree nests of Rough-legged Hawk or raven • on tall cliffs or ledge with protective overhang • 3–8 pale yellow, white, or buff eggs finely spotted with dark red; short elliptical, 5.8 cm long.

Plumage Sexes similar	Habitat	Migration Nonmigratory	Weight 1.2 kg

DATE _____ TIME_____ LOCATION _____

Family FALCONIDAE	Species *Falco peregrinus*	Length 41–51 cm	Wingspan 109–117 cm

PEREGRINE FALCON

A peregrine in a stoop is one of the fastest birds in the world, reaching speeds of 282 km/h or more.

• **SONG** Usually silent. On breeding grounds makes loud *witchew*, *witchew*, *witchew*. When disturbed gives loud repeated *cack, cack, cack, cack*.

• **BEHAVIOR** Prefers open areas with good vantage points on which to perch, often near water. Feeds almost exclusively on birds it takes in the air after a steep swift dive from above them. Wanders widely after nesting season, following prey south as far as southern South America. Faithful to nesting sites and aeries, some of which have been used by generations of peregrines for centuries. Lives on buildings in large cities.

• **BREEDING** Monogamous. Solitary nester.

• **NESTING** Incubation 28–32 days mostly by female. Semialtricial young stay in nest 35–42 days. Fed by both sexes. 1 brood per year.

• **POPULATION** Common to fairly common on tundra; fairly common in migration; uncommon to rare as breeding bird in US. Increasing since continental lows suffered in 1960s and 1970s.

• **CONSERVATION** Listed as threatened. Regulation of DDT along with captive breeding and release program have sparked comeback.

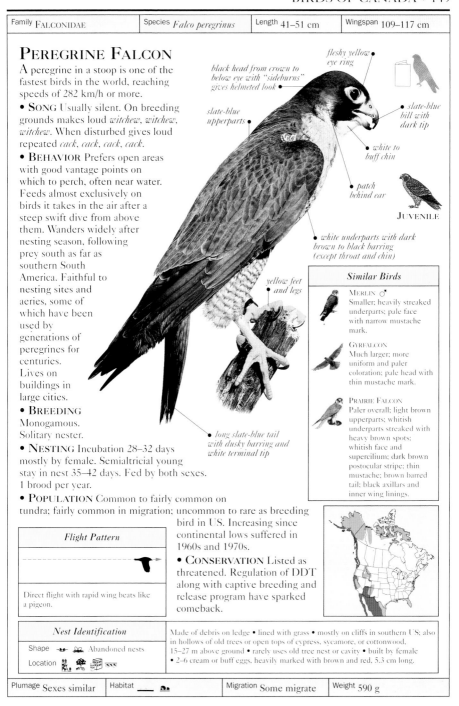

fleshy yellow eye ring

black head from crown to below eye with "sideburns" gives helmeted look

slate-blue upperparts

slate-blue bill with dark tip

white to buff chin

patch behind ear

JUVENILE

white underparts with dark brown to black barring (except throat and chin)

yellow feet and legs

long slate-blue tail with dusky barring and white terminal tip

Similar Birds

MERLIN ♂
Smaller; heavily streaked underparts; pale face with narrow mustache mark.

GYRFALCON
Much larger; more uniform and paler coloration; pale head with thin mustache mark.

PRAIRIE FALCON
Paler overall; light brown upperparts; whitish underparts streaked with heavy brown spots; whitish face and supercilium; dark brown postocular stripe; thin mustache; brown barred tail; black axillars and inner wing linings.

Flight Pattern
Direct flight with rapid wing beats like a pigeon.

Nest Identification	
Shape	Abandoned nests
Location	

Made of debris on ledge • lined with grass • mostly on cliffs in southern US; also in hollows of old trees or open tops of cypress, sycamore, or cottonwood, 15–27 m above ground • rarely uses old tree nest or cavity • built by female • 2–6 cream or buff eggs, heavily marked with brown and red, 5.3 cm long.

Plumage Sexes similar	Habitat	Migration Some migrate	Weight 590 g

DATE _____ TIME_____ LOCATION _____

| Family FALCONIDAE | Species *Falco mexicanus* | Length 38–48 cm | Wingspan 102–107 cm |

PRAIRIE FALCON

Found on open prairies and grasslands with suitable cliffs, bluffs, and outcroppings for nesting sites, this bird's dusty sandy browns blend with the landscape. It is paler overall than the similar-sized Peregrine Falcon, whose range it overlaps in the West. In flight the "armpits" are blackish on axillaries and inner wing linings. Juveniles are darker above than adults and more heavily streaked below.

• SONG Mostly silent. Common alarm or territorial cackling call is shrill yelping *kik-kik-kik* or *kek-kek-kek*.

• BEHAVIOR Ledge display and spectacular aerial displays in courtship. Often perches on rocks, ledges, posts, or utility poles while scanning for prey. Overtakes birds in flight with rapid bursts of speed or in a dive from above. Eats primarily small birds, small mammals, and large insects. Nests in mountains as high as 3,048 m and descends in winter to foothills and prairies.

• BREEDING Monogamous. Solitary nester.

• NESTING Incubation 29–33 days, mostly by female. Semialtricial young stay in nest 31–42 days. Fed by both sexes. 1 brood per year.

• POPULATION Uncommon to fairly common. Declining in Utah, western Canada, and agricultural California.

• CONSERVATION The Prairie Falcon has experienced some population declines which are for the most part attributed to disturbances from increasing human encroachment.

white eyebrow

dark postocular stripe

thin dark mustache

light brown upperparts edged with buff

yellow cere at base of bill

yellow bill with blue-gray tip

white throat, chin, and face

whitish underparts with heavy brown spots

yellow legs and feet

long dark brown tail with sandy bars

JUVENILE

Similar Birds

PEREGRINE FALCON
Adults slate-blue upperparts; darker head, helmeted appearance; in flight lacks black wing pits.

MERLIN ♂
Smaller • male has blue-gray back; more heavily streaked underparts; more contrasting barring in tail; lacks black in wing pits.

| *Flight Pattern* |
| Swift flight with rapid wing beats. Sometimes alternates several rapid wing beats with glide. |

| *Nest Identification* | On cliff ledge, occasionally in rock crevice • abandoned nests • always facing open habitat • 4–5 white eggs, heavily marked with brown and purple; short elliptical and subelliptical, 5.3 cm long. |
| Shape ～ ～ Location | |

| Plumage Sexes similar | Habitat ___ ☎ | Migration Nonmigratory | Weight 544 g |

DATE _____ TIME_____ LOCATION _____

Family PHASIANIDAE	Species *Alectoris chukar*	Length 36 cm	Wingspan 51–59 cm

CHUKAR

This bird was first introduced from Eurasia into the western United States and southwestern Canada as a game bird in the 1930s. Males are slightly larger than females and carry a small spur on each leg, but are otherwise similar. Adults show bold blackish brown flank and side bars. Juveniles lack flank barring and are scaly on the sides with mottling and spots on the upperparts.

- **SONG** Series of loud rapid *chuck chuck chuck chuck* notes that inspired its name; also a shrill *whitoo* alarm note.
- **BEHAVIOR** Spends most of breeding season on the ground in pairs; in flocks or coveys of 6–40 birds

sandy gray-brown upperparts

reddish bill

buffy throat and face

bold black line around face and throat

buffy underparts

chestnut outer tail feathers

reddish feet and legs

JUVENILE

the rest of the year. Roosts on the ground, sometimes sleeping in a "wagon-wheel" configuration similar to the bobwhite. Usually escapes danger by running.

- **BREEDING** Monogamous. A few males reported to be polygamous.
- **NESTING** Incubation 22–24 days by female. Precocial young; first flight at about 14 days. 1 brood per year.
- **POPULATION** Common, but can vary dramatically from year to year. Winters with heavy prolonged snow covering food can cause major drops in local populations.
- **FEEDERS** May feed on small grain seeds on ground; more commonly attracted to permanent sources of water such as farm ponds and cattle tanks.
- **CONSERVATION** Managed as a game species where population is established.

Similar Birds

GRAY PARTRIDGE
Rusty face and throat; chestnut bars on flanks; U-shaped chestnut splotch on belly; rusty tail; yellow-brown feet and legs; pale bill.

Flight Pattern

Direct flight with rapid deep wing beats.

Nest Identification

Shape   Location

Shallow scrape • lined with dried grasses or feathers • on ground sheltered by shrub, grassy tussock, or small boulder • built by female • 10–20 yellow-white eggs spotted or speckled with brown, 4.3 cm long.

Plumage Sexes similar	Habitat	Migration Altitudinal movements	Weight 635 g

DATE _____ TIME_____ LOCATION _____

Family PHASIANIDAE	Species *Perdix perdix*	Length 30 cm	Wingspan 46–56 cm

GRAY PARTRIDGE

Originally a native of Eurasia, this rotund gray-and-brown partridge was introduced into North America in the early 1900s and is now a widely established game bird. When this ground dweller takes off, its wings make a whirring sound, and the mottled brown back and rufous-chestnut outer tail feathers are visible. The white bill in the rusty face is framed by vermiculated gray underparts. Females may lack a chestnut patch on the belly; when present it is smaller than in the male.

rusty face and throat

grayish brown overall

reddish brown–barred flanks

dark chestnut patch on belly

MALE

• **SONG** Low grating *kee-ah* or *keep-keep* or *keee-UCK*. When alarmed or excited, *kuta-kut-kut-kut*.

• **BEHAVIOR** Eats seeds of grains, weeds, and grasses, as well as insects, including grasshoppers and beetles. Water source is dew. Requires grit to assist gizzard in grinding food; often finds this grit in gravel roads, where birds may be seen outside the dense cover they prefer.

grayish brown overall

rusty face and throat

rusty outer tail feathers

FEMALE

Pairs and family groups in summer; coveys of 15–20 birds in winter. Prefers to walk rather than fly.

• **BREEDING** Monogamous.

• **NESTING** Incubation 21–26 days mostly by female. Precocial young led from nest by both sexes after hatching; tended 13–15 days until first flight. 1 brood per year.

• **POPULATION** Introduced and established. Common but declining in part of range.

• **CONSERVATION** Managed for legal harvesting during hunting seasons. Many killed by mowing of fields and in collisions with utility wires, fences, and automobiles.

Similar Birds

CHUKAR
Larger; reddish bill and legs; sandy or gray-brown upperparts; white-buff cheeks; prominent black line extends across forehead through eyes; dark bars on sides and flanks • western range.

Flight Pattern
Flies with rapid stiff wing beats followed by a glide.

Nest Identification	Lined with weed stems, dead grasses, and a fine inner layer of soft leaves, grasses, and feathers • in wild grass, hayfield, or grain field, within 7.5–15 m of field edge or along fencerows or roadsides • built by female while male stands ground • 5–20 olive or white eggs; subelliptical to short oval or short pyriform, 3.6 cm long.
Shape Location	

Plumage Sexes differ	Habitat	Migration Nonmigratory	Weight 397 g

Family PHASIANIDAE	Species *Phasianus colchicus*	Length 53–91 cm	Wingspan 81 cm

RING-NECKED PHEASANT

First introduced as a game bird in California in 1857 and then in larger numbers elsewhere, the Asian Ring-necked Pheasant is one of the most widely distributed and most popular birds among hunters; thousands are harvested annually. The male has distinctive mottled brown plumage; a long, pointed tail; fleshy red eye patches; and a head that ranges in color from a glossy dark green to a purple hue.

- **SONG** When alarmed utters hoarse croaking notes. Male makes loud piercing double squawk *kok-cack*.
- **BEHAVIOR** Gregarious, forming flocks (sometimes large) in autumn and maintaining them into spring. Runs swiftly with tail cocked. Strong flight, rising off ground at steep angle with loud whirring takeoff.

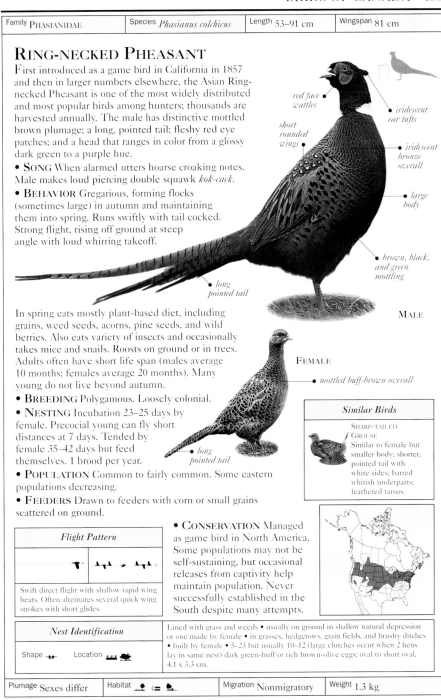

red face wattles

short rounded wings

iridescent ear tufts

iridescent bronze overall

large body

brown, black, and green mottling

long pointed tail

MALE

In spring eats mostly plant-based diet, including grains, weed seeds, acorns, pine seeds, and wild berries. Also eats variety of insects and occasionally takes mice and snails. Roosts on ground or in trees. Adults often have short life span (males average 10 months; females average 20 months). Many young do not live beyond autumn.

- **BREEDING** Polygamous. Loosely colonial.
- **NESTING** Incubation 23–25 days by female. Precocial young can fly short distances at 7 days. Tended by female 35–42 days but feed themselves. 1 brood per year.
- **POPULATION** Common to fairly common. Some eastern populations decreasing.
- **FEEDERS** Drawn to feeders with corn or small grains scattered on ground.

FEMALE

mottled buff-brown overall

long pointed tail

Similar Birds

SHARP-TAILED GROUSE Similar to female but smaller body; shorter, pointed tail with white sides; barred whitish underparts; feathered tarsus.

- **CONSERVATION** Managed as game bird in North America. Some populations may not be self-sustaining, but occasional releases from captivity help maintain population. Never successfully established in the South despite many attempts.

Flight Pattern

Swift direct flight with shallow rapid wing beats. Often alternates several quick wing strokes with short glides.

Nest Identification

Shape — Location —

Lined with grass and weeds • usually on ground in shallow natural depression or one made by female • in grasses, hedgerows, grain fields, and brushy ditches • built by female • 5–23 but usually 10–12 (large clutches occur when 2 hens lay in same nest) dark green-buff or rich brown-olive eggs; oval to short oval, 4.1 x 3.3 cm.

Plumage Sexes differ	Habitat	Migration Nonmigratory	Weight 1.3 kg

DATE _____ TIME_____ LOCATION _____

| Family PHASIANIDAE | Species *Bonasa umbellus* | Length 43 cm | Wingspan 56–64 cm |

RUFFED GROUSE

Both the male and female Ruffed Grouse are dramatic, not only in appearance but in action. In spring the drumming of the male can be heard from almost a kilometer away. The sound is so low-pitched that one might feel as if it is coming from within, and it can take a moment to realize that its source is a distant bird. The female is known for its crippled-bird act that distracts intruders from the nest. This grouse has two morphs: The gray morph is more widespread, while the red morph is plentiful only in the Appalachians and Pacific Northwest.

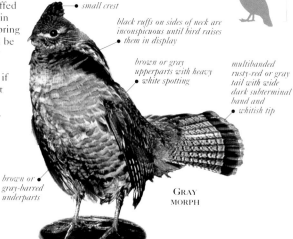

• small crest

black ruffs on sides of neck are inconspicuous until bird raises • them in display

brown or gray upperparts with heavy • white spotting

multibanded rusty-red or gray tail with wide dark subterminal band and • whitish tip

brown or • gray-barred underparts

GRAY MORPH

• **SONG** Short *quit-quit* noises when alarmed.

• **BEHAVIOR** Eats insects, berries, fruits, nuts, seeds of weeds and trees, tree leaf buds, and small reptiles and amphibians. Makes short flights.

• **BREEDING** Promiscuous. Solitary nester. Male exhibits display called drumming; he raises his crest, ruffs, and fan-shaped tail and makes whirring sounds by compressing air between his body and rapidly beating wings. This is done to claim territory and attract females. Normally shy and retiring but can be aggressive and has been known to run at humans in its territory.

RED MORPH

• **NESTING** Incubation 21–28 days by female. Precocial young leave nest within hours of hatching and in 10–12 days roost in trees with tending female. Young independent about 84 days after fledging. 1 brood per year.

• **POPULATION** Common. Local populations fluctuate, with irruptive dispersals into areas that are not normally occupied by grouse.

• **CONSERVATION** Managed as a game bird over much of its range; more killed annually than any other grouse species (3.5–3.7 million).

Similar Birds

SPRUCE GROUSE
Narrow chestnut band on tail tip • male has red eye comb; sharply defined black breast with white spots or bars on sides • female is dark rusty or grayish brown with white spotting and black barring on underparts.

BLUE GROUSE
Dark tail with gray terminal band; mottled gray underparts • male has yellow-orange eye combs.

| **Flight Pattern** |
| Strong rapid flight with rapid wing beats. |

| **Nest Identification** | |
| Shape 🐛   Location 🪹 🌳 ▬ | Lined with small sticks, pine needles, leaves, and feathers • usually near tree trunk or sheltered by shrub, log, boulder, or tree stump • built by female • 8–14 buff eggs, sometimes lightly spotted with browns, 3.8 cm long. |

| Plumage Sexes similar | Habitat 🌳 | Migration Nonmigratory | Weight 635 g |

Family PHASIANIDAE	Species *Centrocercus urophasianus*	Length 53–76 cm	Wingspan 71–97 cm

GREATER SAGE-GROUSE

This plump chickenlike bird is the largest of the North American grouse. It also has one of the most spectacular mating displays of all grouse. The male struts; rapidly inflates and deflates the air sacs of its breast, producing loud, far-carrying, bubbling, popping sounds; and spreads its pointed tail feathers. The much smaller female appears similar to the male but lacks eye combs, white ruff feathers on the breast, and the black bib on the throat.

long stiff spikelike tail feathers

yellow eye comb

black throat and bib

MALE

mottled gray-brown overall

white breast ruff

black belly

• **SONG** Flushing note, *kuk kuk kuk*. In courtship display male makes bubbling, popping sound with air sacs.

• **BEHAVIOR** Eats soft evergreen leaves, shoots of plain sagebrush, blossoms, leaves, pods, buds, and insects. Prefers to walk but when flushed rises rapidly in flight; usually doesn't fly far.

white throat

FEMALE

black belly

• **BREEDING** Promiscuous. Social. Males display together at traditional communal dancing areas called leks. Females attracted to the leks mate with only 1 or 2 males.

Similar Birds

SHARP-TAILED GROUSE Smaller; narrow pointed tail; white belly and undertail coverts; scaled spotted pale underparts.

GUNNISON SAGE-GROUSE Paler tail with more white barring • male has more prominent crown plumes.

• **NESTING** Incubation 25–27 days by female. Precocial young stay with female. First flight at 7–14 days.

• **POPULATION** Seems to have disappeared over much of range due to land clearing and over-grazing. Endangered in Canada.

• **CONSERVATION** Managed as a game bird in US.

Flight Pattern

Rises with rapid wing beats (female slips from side to side), then alternates series of rapid flaps with glides.

Nest Identification	
Shape	Location	Lined with grass and sage leaves • concealed under sagebrush • built by female • 6–9 pale green eggs evenly marked with brown spots and dots; short elliptical to oval, 5.6 cm long.

Plumage Sexes differ	Habitat	Migration Nonmigratory	Weight 3.2 kg

DATE _____ TIME_____ LOCATION _____

Family PHASIANIDAE	Species *Falcipennis canadensis*	Length 41 cm	Wingspan 58 cm

SPRUCE GROUSE

Also known as the Black Grouse, this bird is mainly a tree dweller. Sometimes called a "fool hen" because it seems fearless of man, it is an easy target for hunters. Franklin's Grouse, a subspecies in the northern Rockies and Cascades, lacks the chestnut band on the tail tip, and the uppertail coverts have white tips. In all other forms the tail has a dark tip and chestnut band. When flying over his territory, the male Franklin's Grouse makes a "wind cracking" sound with his wings to mark his claim.

• **SONG** Usually silent. Males make low hooting sounds. Makes clucking noise around intruders.

• **BEHAVIOR** Arboreal. Tame. Eats buds and needles of conifers, seeds of weeds and grasses, berries, mushrooms, fern fronds, some insects. Forages along wooded roadsides.

• **BREEDING** Promiscuous. Solitary nester.

• **NESTING** Incubation 17–24 days by female. Precocial young abandon nest upon hatching and can take short weak flights at 7–10 days. Young tended by female. 1 brood per year.

• **POPULATION** Common. Local populations fluctuate. Southern edge of range may have seen slight decline, but still common in far north.

• **CONSERVATION** Managed as a game bird.

crimson comb of bare skin above eyes

black chin, throat, and foreneck

white spots along sides of breast and neck

blackish tail with chestnut terminal band

black breast

mottled gray upperparts

MALE

lacks red comb and white spots

mottled brownish or grayish

dark barring and white spotting on underparts

FEMALE

Similar Birds

♂ RUFFED GROUSE Slightly larger; slight crest; dark subterminal tail band; dark patch on side of neck • male lacks red eye comb; slight crest; pale chin; barred pale breast; finely barred gray or reddish brown tail with dark subterminal band.

♂ BLUE GROUSE Dusky or sooty in color; broad pale band at tip of blackish tail; mottled gray underparts • male has yellow or orange ♀ comb above eyes • western range.

Flight Pattern	
	⊤ ᶜ⅂ᶜ ⌐ ᶜ⅂ᶜ ⌐

Strong rapid flight with series of rapid stiff wing beats alternating with short glides on downward-pointed wings.

Nest Identification	
Shape ·❥· Location ▬	Lined with dry grasses, leaves, twigs, and a few feathers • under low branch of spruce or bushes • built by female • 5–10 beautiful cinnamon to pink-buff or cream-buff eggs, usually marked with large rich brown spots and blotches, some thickly and evenly covered with small spots or dots; oval to short oval, 4.3 cm long.

Plumage Sexes differ	Habitat 🐾	Migration Migratory	Weight 499 g

DATE _____ TIME_____ LOCATION _____

| Family PHASIANIDAE | Species *Lagopus lagopus* | Length 38–43 cm | Wingspan 51–57 cm |

WILLOW PTARMIGAN

The ptarmigans are small Arctic birds that change their brown summer plumage to white in winter. Molting birds are often a patchwork of white and brown feathers, and white feathers grow to cover toes for winter. Unlike other ptarmigans, the male Willow stays with the female and staunchly defends its territory; this bird has been known to attack a grizzly bear that came too close to the nest. The male also will attack a human trying to catch one of its chicks. Among the most migratory of grouse, some casually winter as far south as the US–Canada border.

• **SONG** Low throaty rumbling sounds and noisy cackling. In display, male makes harsh barking *go-back-go-back-go-backa-go-backa-go-backa.*

• **BEHAVIOR** In summer eats flower buds and leaves of deciduous trees and shrubs, also fruits and insects. In winter eats catkins, twigs, and deciduous tree and shrub buds. Chicks eat spiders, insects, and caterpillars.

• **BREEDING** Mostly monogamous. In breeding season male chooses open area on ground. As his red combs swell he struts and barks, then flies up and flutters down.

• **NESTING** Incubation 21–22 days by female. Precocial young leave nest upon hatching. First flight at 7–12 days. Tended by both sexes. 1 brood per year.

• **POPULATION** Cycles from abundant to scarce. Generally common over northern range.

• **CONSERVATION** Harvested as game bird.

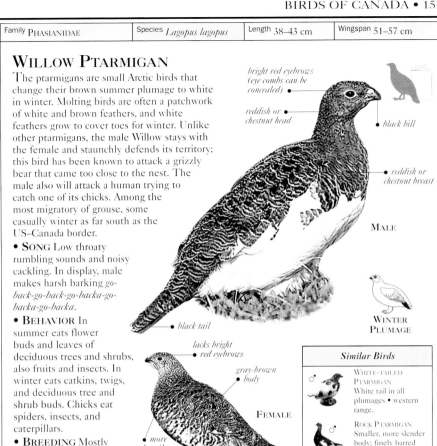

bright red eyebrows
(eye combs can be concealed)

reddish or chestnut head

black bill

reddish or chestnut breast

MALE

WINTER PLUMAGE

lacks bright red eyebrows

gray-brown body

FEMALE

more heavily barred on breast and flanks

black tail

black tail

Similar Birds

WHITE-TAILED PTARMIGAN
White tail in all plumages • western range.

ROCK PTARMIGAN
Smaller, more slender body; finely barred brownish gray plumage; less rufous than Willow; smaller bill • in winter male has black lore and narrow black postocular line.

Flight Pattern

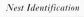

Strong and swift but relatively short flights. Alternates rapid, stiff wing beats with short glides.

Nest Identification

Shape ~ Location

Lined with grasses and feathers • at base of log, in bunch of grass, bush, or hammock on tundra, beach, or near marsh • built by female • 5–17 yellowish eggs splotched with brown; oval, 4.3 cm long.

| Plumage Sexes differ | Habitat | Migration Most do not migrate | Weight 590 g |

DATE _____ TIME_____ LOCATION _____

Family PHASIANIDAE	Species *Lagopus mutus*	Length 33–38 cm	Wingspan 43–51 cm

ROCK PTARMIGAN

This bird is perhaps the hardiest of the ptarmigans. It lives year-round in the cold northern mountain regions of Greenland and arctic North America and has been declared the official bird of Nunavut Territory. These birds have been seen flying directly into snowbanks to sleep. The Rock Ptarmigan develops two different plumages to match the predominant colors of the season: white in winter, brown in summer. Winter males retain their small red combs and show a black line running from the bill through the eye. Birds experience great and varying amounts of white patches in individual plumages during the sequence of the molt.

small red combs over eyes

MALE

mottled, barred brownish gray plumage

black tail

feathers on entire leg to toe

• **SONG** Low growls and croaks and noisy cackles.

• **BEHAVIOR** In summer eats spiders, insects, leaves, buds, fruits, seeds, and mosses. In winter finds food on top of snow such as twigs, buds, and seeds. Unusually resilient for a grouse in flight, it can travel up to 1.5 km before alighting.

mottled, barred blackish-brown on brownish-buff plumage

short black bill

WINTER PLUMAGE

• **BREEDING** Monogamous. Colonial. Male defends small territory on breeding ground; displays with swollen red combs to attract females and drive away rival males.

feathers on entire leg to toe

white wing feathers

FEMALE

Similar Birds

♂ WILLOW PTARMIGAN
Darker; less gray-brown summer plumage
• male has rufous-brown plumage; larger bill.

WHITE-TAILED PTARMIGAN
White tail; smaller
• western range.

• **NESTING** Incubation 21–24 days by female. Precocial young remain in nest 10–16 days, fed by female. 1 brood per year.

• **POPULATION** Common on tundra. Casual in winter south into taiga. Accidental elsewhere.

• **CONSERVATION** Harvested as a game bird.

Flight Pattern

Strong swift takeoff; in flight alternates several quick wing beats with glides on down-bowed wings.

Nest Identification

Shape ___ Location ___

Lined with grass, moss, and a few feathers • built by female • 6–13 buff or cinnamon eggs marked with dark browns and blacks; subelliptical, 4.1 cm long.

Plumage Sexes differ	Habitat ___	Migration Nonmigratory	Weight 422 g

Family PHASIANIDAE	Species *Lagopus leucurus*	Length 30–33 cm	Wingspan 41–43 cm

WHITE-TAILED PTARMIGAN

Making its home in high mountain peaks, this bird is the only ptarmigan to nest south of Canada. It is the smallest of the ptarmigans, distinguishable from others by its white tail. This bird of high-elevation alpine and subalpine tundra lives most of its life above the timberline. Small numbers have been successfully introduced into suitable habitat in Utah and the Sierras of eastern California and western Nevada. The plumage is molted three times annually and those who have seen this bird in its high mountain home know how well it matches the background in a habitat that seemingly offers little concealment. In winter the bird is entirely white except for its black eyes and bill and the small red comb arcing above the eye, while in other seasons it is a patchwork of white and mottled browns.

red comb over eye

back, neck, head, and breast are mottled brown, white, and black

MALE

white wings

white underparts and legs

white tail and rump

WINTER PLUMAGE

- **SONG** Soft clucking and mellow hooting.
- **BEHAVIOR** In winter eats buds and twigs of alpine shrubs and dwarf trees, alder catkins, and conifer needles and buds. In spring and summer eats leaves, flowers of herbaceous alpine plants, berries, buds of willows, some grit, seeds, and insects. Social in nonbreeding season, with dozens roosting together. Can fly up to 1.5 km before alighting.
- **BREEDING** Monogamous.
- **NESTING** Incubation 22–24 days by female. Precocial young leave nest upon hatching. First flight at 7–21 days. Tended by female. 1 brood per year.
- **POPULATION** Common above tree line but local.
- **CONSERVATION** Harvested as a game bird.

Similar Birds

WILLOW PTARMIGAN
ROCK PTARMIGAN
Larger in size; black on tail in all plumages.

Flight Pattern
Strong, swift, and rapid, but relatively short, flight; rises with explosive roar of wings; alternates wing beats with short glides.

Nest Identification	Lined with grasses, lichen, small leaves, and feathers • in fine grasses of steep slopes or between rocks above timberline, 3,050–4,270 m above ground • built by female • 3–9 pink or buff eggs with brown blotches or fine dots, 4.3 cm long.
Shape ⬤ Location ▬ ▨ ⚏	

Plumage Sexes similar	Habitat ▬ ▲	Migration Nonmigratory	Weight 360 g

DATE _____ TIME_____ LOCATION _____

Family PHASIANIDAE	Species *Dendragapus obscurus*	Length 46–53 cm	Wingspan 61–71 cm

BLUE GROUSE

During courtship this fowl-like bird will perch, inflate its colorful air sac, and make owl-like calls or moans that can be heard 180 meters away. The Blue Grouse of coastal areas has a yellow neck sac and a gray band at the end of its tail. Although nonmigratory, populations move up and down mountain slopes annually, spending summer in mixed deciduous forests at lower elevations and winter in conifers higher up the slope.

• **SONG** Series of hoots.

• **BEHAVIOR** Feeds along edges of coniferous forests. Eats berries, tree buds, tender twigs, leaves, conifer needles, seeds, and insects. Relatively tame; allows close approach. Solitary and arboreal. In courtship display male retracts white-based feathers to reveal neck sac.

• **BREEDING** Promiscuous. Solitary nester.

• **NESTING** Incubation 25–26 days by female. Precocial young leave nest soon after hatching. First flight at 7–10 days. Tended by female. After breeding male often moves to alpine meadows while female keeps incubating at nest on lower slopes; female and young follow 30-60 days later. 1 brood per year.

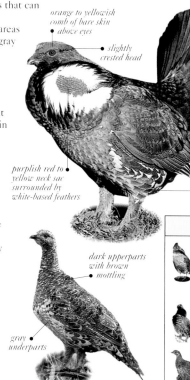

orange to yellowish comb of bare skin above eyes

slightly crested head

purplish red to yellow neck sac surrounded by white-based feathers

dark tail

MALE

gray or sooty overall plumage

dark upperparts with brown mottling

gray underparts

FEMALE

Similar Birds

RUFFED GROUSE Finely barred gray to rusty brown tail with dark subterminal band (broken in female); lacks eye combs.

♂ **SPRUCE GROUSE** Male has sharply defined black breast with white spots or bars on side • female has dark barring and white spotting on underparts • both sexes have chestnut band on tail tip (except birds in northern Rockies and Cascades). ♀

• **POPULATION** A fairly common species.

• **CONSERVATION** Affected by forest management; may increase after clear-cuts but declines as forest grows up. Seems to fare best in original old-growth forests.

Flight Pattern
Strong rapid direct flight; alternates series of rapid stiff wing beats with glides.

Nest Identification	
Shape ⚬ Location ▬	Conifer needles, grasses, and leaves • sheltered by log or rock, or near base of tree • built by female • 7–16 pink-buff eggs finely dotted with brown or sometimes unmarked; short subelliptical, 5.1 cm long.

Plumage Sexes differ	Habitat	Migration Nonmigratory	Weight 1.2 kg

DATE _____ TIME_____ LOCATION _____

Family PHASIANIDAE	Species *Tympanuchus phasianellus*	Length 41–48 cm	Wingspan 53–64 cm

SHARP-TAILED GROUSE

This gregarious bird performs fascinating mating rituals in spring at communal leks where the male "dances," with tail spread, purple neck sac exposed, and quills rattling; and fights with other males. Often seen on prairies in summer, Saskatchewan's provincial bird gets its name from its narrow pointed tail. There is a small stiff crest on the top of the head. In flight adults can be distinguished from female Ring-necked Pheasants by the white feathers on the side of the tail.

yellow-orange eye combs

brownish overall

narrow pointed tail

brown eyes

scaled, spotted underparts

• **SONG** Chattering noises and a soft *coo-oo*. Utters bold booming notes during breeding season.

• **BEHAVIOR** Eats grasshoppers, other large insects, rose hips, berries, corn, wheat, other grains, buds, leaves, and flowers; vegetable materials make up more than 90 percent of diet. Inhabits open grasslands in summer, where the lek is located; retreats to brushy shrub-scrub country after breeding season. Strong flier, occasionally traveling 3–5 km in a single flight.

• **BREEDING** Promiscuous.

• **NESTING** Incubation 21–24 days by female. Precocial young leave nest shortly after hatching. Tended by female. First flight at 7–14 days. 1 brood per year.

• **POPULATION** Uncommon to fairly common over most of range. Has increased in some areas because of timbering practices, but declining in others. Has disappeared from Nevada, New Mexico, and Oregon.

• **CONSERVATION** Managed as a game bird species with regulated hunting seasons and some habitat improvement.

Similar Birds

RING-NECKED PHEASANT ♀ Much longer pointed tail with white barring; no white tail feathers; lacks barring or scaling on underparts.

GREATER PRAIRIE-CHICKEN Barred underparts; shorter, squared tail.

Flight Pattern
Rises on rapidly beating wings when flushed; then alternates between series of rapid stiff wing beats and glides on slightly drooping wings.

Nest Identification	Lined with grasses, leaves, and feathers • on ground concealed in grass or under shrub, about a kilometer from dancing ground • built by female • 5–17 light brown eggs dotted with reddish brown and lavender, occasionally unmarked; ovate, 4.3 cm long.
Shape Location	

Plumage Sexes similar	Habitat	Migration Nonmigratory	Weight 953 g

DATE _____ TIME_____ LOCATION _____

Family PHASIANIDAE	Species *Meleagris gallopavo*	Length 94–117 cm	Wingspan 122–152 cm

WILD TURKEY

The largest game bird in North America, the Wild Turkey once was so widespread it was considered for the US national emblem. Male turkeys gobble year round, but in spring they are easily startled and will gobble at any abrupt noise. Today this unmistakable symbol of a US national holiday is becoming common again due to conservation efforts and its own adjustments to changes in its original woodland habitat.

• **SONG** Gobbling may be heard up to 1.5 km away and is easily imitated, with bird often responding to it. Several different clucking calls given by both sexes: *cluk, cluck, cut, putt,* and others.

• **BEHAVIOR** Powerful muscular gizzard can grind hardest foods. Eats nuts, seeds, large insects, frogs, lizards, wild fruits, and grapes. Flies to tree roosts for the night. Male displays by strutting with tail spread, wings drooped to ground, bare skin of head intensified in color, and frequent gobbling.

• **BREEDING** Polygamous.

• **NESTING** Incubation 27–28 days by female. First flight in about 14 days. Tended by female. 1 brood per year.

• **POPULATION** Rare to fairly common. Wild birds unlikely in areas of human habitation, though widely domesticated. Increasing.

bare blue and pink head

large iridescent dark body glistens with greens and bronzes

red wattles

MALE

white-barred flight feathers

blackish breast tuft or "beard"

proportionally smaller head

lacks breast tuft (small "beard" present in some older females)

spurred pinkish legs

duller in color and less iridescent than male

smaller than male

FEMALE

medium-length broad tail

• **CONSERVATION** Trap and transfer programs have helped reestablish some populations. Increased comeback of blocks of forest interspersed with agricultural areas, as well as wildlife management programs, have helped increase populations.

Flight Pattern
Swift powerful flight for short distances with rapid wing beats and deep strokes; often glides after several series of wing beats.

Nest Identification	
Shape 〰 Location ▬	Lined with a few dead leaves and grass • on ground concealed under shrub or in grass • built by female • 8–20 white to cream or buff eggs, sometimes blotched or spotted with brown or red, 6.4 cm long.

Plumage Sexes differ	Habitat 🌳 🏵 ⛰ ✸	Migration Nonmigratory	Weight 7.4 kg

DATE _____ TIME_____ LOCATION _____

Family ODONTOPHORIDAE	Species *Callipepla californica*	Length 25 cm	Wingspan 36–41 cm

CALIFORNIA QUAIL

Its curled topknot distinguishes the California Quail from others in its range, except Gambel's Quail, but scaly underparts distinguish it from Gambel's. Considered a dooryard bird in southern California, the California Quail often enters suburban areas and may be seen feeding on lawns or attending feeders with grain spilled on the ground, birdbaths, garden pools, and lawn sprinklers.

MALE

• **SONG** Low chattering and grunting. Bold distinct *chi-ca-go*.

pale forehead

• **BEHAVIOR**
Solitary or paired in breeding season. In fall, gathers in well-organized coveys of up to 100. Sentinel stands guard from perch while birds feed, at same place regularly, 1–2 hours before and after sunrise and sunset. Mostly vegetarian; eats some insects and spiders. Generally inactive midday.

black throat with white necklace border

chestnut patch on belly

JUVENILE

• **BREEDING** Polygamous. Female more gregarious.

short black teardrop-shaped plume or double plume

Similar Birds

GAMBEL'S QUAIL
Lacks scaled underparts, brown sides, and brown crown.

MOUNTAIN QUAIL
Gray-brown upperparts; 2 long thin straight head plumes that appear as a single plume; gray breast; chestnut sides with white barring • juvenile has grayer underparts and longer head plumes.

• **NESTING** Incubation 18–23 days, usually by female. Young leave nest soon after hatching and stay with parents on ground about 28 days. First flight at 10–14 days. 1 brood per year.

whitish stripe over eyes and across forehead

FEMALE

• **POPULATION** Common.

• **FEEDERS** Feeding stations with small seed on ground and man-made water sources.

scaly underparts

brown sides

Flight Pattern

Flies with explosive burst of speed over short distances. Alternates series of rapid stiff wing beats with short glides.

• **CONSERVATION** Adapts well to civilization but declining in some regions because of habitat loss from overbuilding. Hunted as a game bird.

Nest Identification

Shape

Location

Lined with grasses or leaves • on ground or in fork of tree branch about 3 m above ground • built by female • 12–16 cream-buff to very yellow eggs covered with large blotches or dots of brown-gray, 3.0 cm long.

Plumage Sexes differ	Habitat	Migration Nonmigratory	Weight 232 g

DATE _____ TIME _____ LOCATION _____

Family ODONTOPHORIDAE	Species *Colinus virginianus*	Length 23–25 cm	Wingspan 36–41 cm

NORTHERN BOBWHITE

This familiar eastern quail, named for the male's loud call, inhabits farmlands, fields, lightly grazed pastures, and grasslands. The "Masked Bobwhite," a southwestern race with a black face and cinnamon-rufous underparts, formerly of Mexico and southeast Arizona, has been reintroduced into Arizona grasslands.

conspicuous white stripe over eyes

rufous-red overall

short brown to black bill

white throat

whitish underparts with coarse black scalloping

dark gray tail

MALE

• **SONG** Rising clear whistle, *bob-WHITE!* or *bob-bob-WHITE!*, given most often by males in spring and summer. Also whistles *hoy*.

• **BEHAVIOR** Solitary or in pairs in spring; family groups in summer; coveys of 8–15 in fall and winter. Roosts on ground in groups of up to 30, tails pushed together and heads facing out of a tight wagon wheel–shaped circle. Eats seeds, insects, worms, and spiders.

• **BREEDING** Monogamous; some evidence of polygamy.

• **NESTING** Incubation 23–24 days by both sexes. Young leave nest soon after hatching; tended by both sexes. First flight at 12–14 days. 1 brood per year.

cinnamon-rufous flanks with broad white stripes

short dark bill

buff stripe over eyes

buff throat

whitish underparts with coarse black scalloping

cinnamon-rufous flanks with broad white stripes

FEMALE

Similar Birds

SCALED QUAIL
Pale gray-brown head; scaly body; prominent white tufted crest; prefers more arid habitat.

GAMBEL'S QUAIL ♂
Prominent crest plume; uniformly pale gray overall; sandy-buff underparts; rufous flanks with white streaks • inhabits desert scrublands of the Southwest.

• **POPULATION** Uncommon to common in brushlands and open woodland. Introduced into northwestern US. Significantly declining over much of range.

• **FEEDERS** Scattered grains on ground or man-made permanent sources of water.

• **CONSERVATION** Endangered in Canada. Hunted as a game bird in US; highly managed in some states. Decline may be due to habitat loss and changes in farming. Sensitive to cold winters; hard freezes may wipe out entire populations.

Flight Pattern
Rises swiftly with whirring rapid wing beats then sails away, wings curved downward. Alternates series of stiff wing beats with short glides on drooping wing tips.

Nest Identification
Shape ⌣ Location ⸬ ▬

Lined with grasses • leaves small openings in sides • on ground • built by both sexes • 14–16 white or cream-white eggs; subpyriform and sometimes quite pointed, 3.0 cm long.

Plumage Sexes differ	Habitat ▬ ♟♟ ♟	Migration Nonmigratory	Weight 179 g

DATE _____ TIME_____ LOCATION _____

Family RALLIDAE	Species *Coturnicops noveboracensis*	Length 15–18 cm	Wingspan 25–33 cm

YELLOW RAIL

The sparrow-sized Yellow Rail is one of the least-known rails. It is so reluctant to fly that trained dogs can catch it. If flushed it flies weakly with its feet dangling, showing a white patch on the trailing edge of the inner wing before dropping back into cover. Its narrow body, strong toes, and flexible wings help it survive in dense marsh grasses. Adults have olive-gray legs, a buff chest, dark brown flanks with white bars, white-spotted wing coverts, and cinnamon undertail coverts. Juveniles are darker gray-black above with slight buffy striping; more white spotting on head, neck, breast, and sides; and more black barring on the flanks.

dark brown upperparts with broad buff stripes and narrow white crossbars

dark brown crown

broad dark smudge through eye

short yellowish to greenish gray bill

- **SONG** Like pebbles tapping, *tick-tick*, *tick-tick-tick*. Usually at night.
- **BEHAVIOR** Secretive; difficult to see in the open; sticks to thick grasses and marsh vegetation. Prefers to walk or run if disturbed. Flutters in air when flushed, then quickly drops and runs on the ground to escape. Averse to flying yet able to migrate great distances. Eats insects, small snails, seeds, tender leaves of clover, and grasses.
- **BREEDING** Monogamous. Solitary nester.
- **NESTING** Incubation 16–18 days by female. Precocial young leave nest shortly after hatching. Probably tended by female. May be independent of parents at 35 days. 1 brood per year.
- **POPULATION** Uncommon to rare and poorly known. Declining due to loss of habitat.
- **CONSERVATION** Draining and development of wetlands negatively impacting populations. Considered a game bird in some states.

Similar Birds

SORA
Juveniles are twice as large; bright yellow bill; lack buff stripes on upperparts; lacks white wing patch in flight.

Flight Pattern	

Flutters weakly on floppy wings for short low flights. Direct flight when traveling longer distances.

Nest Identification	Canopy of vegetation pulled to cover mat of fine dead grass • above damp soil on bare ground or flattened vegetation • a little above water of marsh or meadow and screened by small blades of grass • built by both sexes • 7–10 creamy buff eggs occasionally spotted with reddish brown and capped; ovate but often markedly elongated, 2.8 cm long.
Shape ⚊ ⬛ Location ⟋⟋⟋	

Plumage Sexes similar	Habitat ⟋≈ ⎯⎯ ≋ ⋇	Migration Migratory	Weight 51 g

DATE _____ TIME_____ LOCATION _____

Family RALLIDAE	Species *Crex crex*	Length 27 cm	Wingspan 43–46 cm

CORN CRAKE

The *crek-crek* sound made by rubbing fingernails across the teeth of a comb often entices this timid bird to leave its hiding place. A native of Eurasia, rare vagrants have found their way to the farmlands of Canada and New England. Unlike most other rails, the Corn Crake does not live in marshes but rather in meadows and other grasslands. When flushed, the chestnut wings with darker flight feathers are distinctive. Juveniles are similar to adults but have lighter barring on sides, flanks, and on undertail coverts.

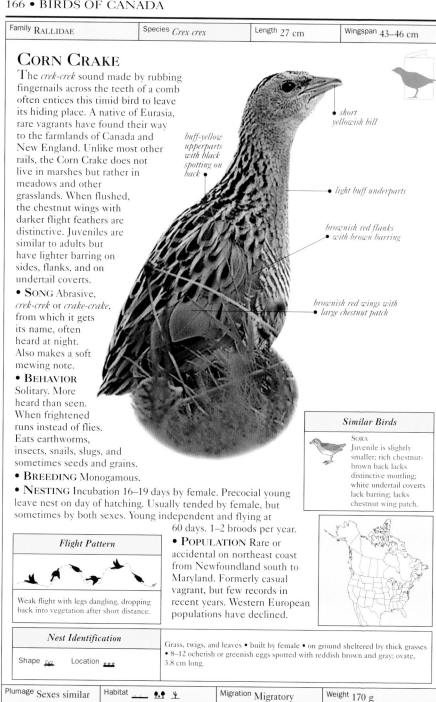

short yellowish bill

buff-yellow upperparts with black spotting on back

light buff underparts

brownish red flanks with brown barring

brownish red wings with large chestnut patch

• **SONG** Abrasive, *crek-crek* or *crake-crake*, from which it gets its name, often heard at night. Also makes a soft mewing note.

• **BEHAVIOR** Solitary. More heard than seen. When frightened runs instead of flies. Eats earthworms, insects, snails, slugs, and sometimes seeds and grains.

• **BREEDING** Monogamous.

• **NESTING** Incubation 16–19 days by female. Precocial young leave nest on day of hatching. Usually tended by female, but sometimes by both sexes. Young independent and flying at 60 days. 1–2 broods per year.

• **POPULATION** Rare or accidental on northeast coast from Newfoundland south to Maryland. Formerly casual vagrant, but few records in recent years. Western European populations have declined.

Similar Birds

SORA
Juvenile is slightly smaller; rich chestnut-brown back lacks distinctive mottling; white undertail coverts lack barring; lacks chestnut wing patch.

Flight Pattern

Weak flight with legs dangling, dropping back into vegetation after short distance.

Nest Identification

Shape 　　 Location 　　

Grass, twigs, and leaves • built by female • on ground sheltered by thick grasses • 8–12 ocherish or greenish eggs spotted with reddish brown and gray; ovate, 3.8 cm long.

Plumage Sexes similar	Habitat	Migration Migratory	Weight 170 g

DATE _____ TIME_____ LOCATION _____

Family RALLIDAE	Species *Rallus longirostris*	Length 36–41 cm	Wingspan 48–53 cm

CLAPPER RAIL

As with most rails the Clapper Rail is more often heard than seen. It is named for its noisy rattling call which is said to sound like old-time clappers. Abrupt noises cause these birds to cry in unison; noisiest at night. This large rail is locally known as "marsh hen" and often leaves the cover of the salt marshes it inhabits to work the muddy flats at low tide. As it walks it bobs its head and flips its short tail exposing white undertail coverts.

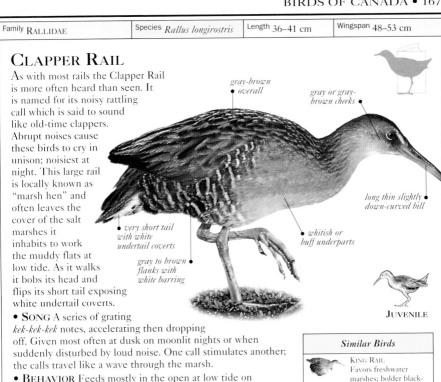

gray-brown overall

gray or gray-brown cheeks

long thin slightly down-curved bill

very short tail with white undertail coverts

whitish or buff underparts

gray to brown flanks with white barring

JUVENILE

• **SONG** A series of grating *kek-kek-kek* notes, accelerating then dropping off. Given most often at dusk on moonlit nights or when suddenly disturbed by loud noise. One call stimulates another; the calls travel like a wave through the marsh.

• **BEHAVIOR** Feeds mostly in the open at low tide on mudflats. At other times forages concealed in salt marsh vegetation. Eats crabs and other crustaceans, worms, amphibians, reptiles, mollusks, small fish, and aquatic insects.

• **BREEDING** Monogamous. Solitary nester.

• **NESTING** Incubation 20–23 days by both sexes. Precocial young abandon nest soon after hatching. Tended by both sexes. Independent after 35–42 days. First flight at 63–70 days. Possibly 2 broods per year.

• **POPULATION** Common in coastal salt marshes but declining on West Coast and in some places in the East. Casual on Atlantic Coast to the Maritimes.

Similar Birds

KING RAIL
Favors freshwater marshes; bolder black-and-white bars on flanks; bright rufous-brown neck and chest; tawny-buff cheeks; buff-edged back feathers; brown wing coverts; voice differs.

VIRGINIA RAIL
One-third the size; darker overall; blue-gray auriculars; bright rufous upperwing coverts.

• **CONSERVATION** The inland freshwater race on the lower Colorado River is considered endangered. Also endangered on the West Coast due to habitat loss and perhaps introduced predators.

Flight Pattern

Low fluttering flight over short distances with legs dangling.

Nest Identification	
Shape ⬭ Location 🏔️ 🌿 🌾	Basket of aquatic vegetation and tide-deposited materials • elevated on firm bank or under small bush • built by both sexes, but male does more • 5–12 buff or olive-buff eggs marked with brown; subelliptical to long subelliptical to ovate, 4.3 cm long.

Plumage Sexes similar	Habitat	Migration Migratory	Weight 323 g

DATE _____ TIME_____ LOCATION _____

Family RALLIDAE	Species *Rallus elegans*	Length 38–48 cm	Wingspan 53–64 cm

KING RAIL

This large freshwater rail migrates through the Mississippi Valley and along the Atlantic Coast. Oddly, this bird's population seems tied to that of the muskrat, which creates open spaces in the marsh providing feeding and drinking areas for the rail. Widely

olive-brown upperparts with buff-edged back feathers

olive-brown head and hindneck

long slender, slightly down-curved bill

cinnamon-rufous foreneck and chest

blackish upper bill, orange to red lower bill, and dusky tip

distributed in the East in summer, it is found in both freshwater and brackish marshes. Some consider it an inland freshwater race of the smaller Clapper Rail, but the King Rail is more rufous and has buff edging on the back feathers and brown to rufous wing coverts.

dark blackish brown and white barring on flanks

JUVENILE

• **SONG** Series of less than 10 notes of *kek-kek-kek* or *jupe-jupe-jupe* deeper than those of Clapper Rail and not descending. Various other clucking and grunting notes.

• **BEHAVIOR** Sometimes feeds in open, mostly in shallow water or mudflats exposed at low tide. Variable diet of aquatic and semiaquatic foods includes plant parts, invertebrates, and vertebrates. Terrestrial, yet migrates long distances.

• **BREEDING** Monogamous. Solitary nester.

• **NESTING** Incubation 21–24 days by both sexes. Precocial young abandon nest soon after hatching; stay with parents about 63 days. Possibly 2 broods per year.

• **POPULATION** Fairly common to common in freshwater and brackish habitat near the Gulf Coast. Declined or disappeared in some areas due to loss of and/or contamination of habitat.

• **CONSERVATION** Listed as endangered in Canada. Considered a game bird in some US states. Wetland management crucial.

Similar Birds

VIRGINIA RAIL
Much smaller; darker overall; blue-gray auriculars; bright rufous upperwing coverts.

CLAPPER RAIL
Slightly smaller; duller coloring; less barring on flanks; variable plumage, but grayish edge on brown-centered back feathers and olive-brown wing coverts; frequents salt marshes.

Flight Pattern
Slow floppy flight, often low above vegetation with feet dangling.

Nest Identification	
Shape 🐚 Location ✦✦✦ ⚊⚊	Dry aquatic vegetation • 15–20 cm above water amid aquatic vegetation • built by both sexes, but male does more • 6–15 buff eggs spotted with brown; ovate, 4.1 cm long.

Plumage Sexes similar	Habitat 〰 ▬▬	Migration Migratory	Weight 414 g

DATE _____ TIME_____ LOCATION _____

Family RALLIDAE	Species *Rallus limicola*	Length 23–25 cm	Wingspan 33–37 cm

VIRGINIA RAIL

Like all rails, the Virginia Rail generally does not fly when it is being pursued but will run swiftly through the marsh grasses. Note its gray cheeks and the reddish bill and legs. Flanks, lower belly, and undertail coverts are barred with black and white. In flight the wings show chestnut in the leading edge. Although this bird prefers freshwater and brackish marshes, it often inhabits salt marshes in winter. Juveniles have dark blackish brown upperparts and black, gray, and white mottling and barring on underparts.

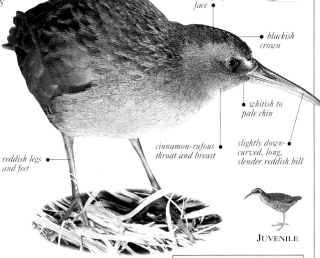

blue-gray face

blackish crown

whitish to pale chin

cinnamon-rufous throat and breast

slightly down-curved, long, slender reddish bill

reddish legs and feet

JUVENILE

- **SONG** Resembles the clicking of keys on an old typewriter, *kid-ick, kid-ick, kid-ick* or *tic-tic-tic*. Also makes *kik, kik, kik, ki-queea* "kicker" call and descending series of piglike grunts and other odd calls.
- **BEHAVIOR** Somewhat secretive and terrestrial. Feeds primarily on insects but also takes aquatic animals, including worms, spiders, crustaceans, and small fish. Diet is varied, especially in winter, with duckweed and seeds of marsh grasses, rushes, and sedges.
- **BREEDING** Monogamous.
- **NESTING** Incubation 18–20 days by both sexes. Precocial young leave nest soon after hatching. Tended by both parents. First flight at about 25 days. Possibly 2 broods per year.

Similar Birds

KING RAIL
About twice the size • olive-brown head; brown to gray cheeks; cinnamon-rufous underparts; black-and-white barring on flanks.

CLAPPER RAIL
Larger; grayish body; cinnamon to gray underparts; black-and-white barring on flanks; prefers salt marshes.

- **POPULATION** Fairly common to uncommon. Declining but still widespread despite loss of wetland habitat.
- **CONSERVATION** Still hunted as a game bird in some states. Wetland protection and management is crucial.

Flight Pattern

Weak brief fluttering flight with long legs dangling.

Nest Identification

Shape ⬤   Location ⸪⸪ ⋀⋀⋀

Pile of matted reeds and layers of coarse aquatic vegetation and grass • in tussock or clumped vegetation • built by both sexes • 5–13 off-white or buff eggs spotted with brown and often wreathed; oval to short oval, 3.3 cm long.

Plumage Sexes similar	Habitat 〰️	Migration Migratory	Weight 88 g

DATE _____ TIME_____ LOCATION _____

Family RALLIDAE	Species *Porzana carolina*	Length 20–25 cm	Wingspan 30–37 cm

SORA

In late summer large numbers of these birds gather in marshes to feed and build up fat reserves before migrating; they seem especially fond of smartweed seeds and wild rice. Like all rails, the Sora migrates at night, and for a group that hardly distinguishes itself in the air, this species may cover almost 4,850 km between wintering and breeding grounds. It is identifiable by its short yellow bill framed with black feathers around its base, black throat, and black center in the upper breast. Small and plump, it is one of the most common North American rails. Juveniles lack the black on the face and underparts and, with their buff coloration, sometimes are confused with the much smaller Yellow Rail.

black-and-buff spots on wings and back

black patch on face and throat

irregular barring of thin white lines on gray underparts

short chickenlike yellow bill

yellow-green legs

very long toes

JUVENILE

WINTER PLUMAGE

- **SONG** Descending melodious whinny and abrasive high-pitched *keek*. Makes froglike whistle of *ker-wheer* on breeding ground.
- **BEHAVIOR** Small bill prevents it from probing into marsh mud for animals like the long-billed rails. Eats mainly plant life such as seeds, wild rice, and algae. Also feeds on insects, spiders, small crustaceans, and snails. Often found in the open where it walks slowly with head down and short tail cocked and flicked above white undertail coverts. Can show up in almost any moist habitat, especially in migration.
- **BREEDING** Monogamous.
- **NESTING** Incubation 19–20 days. Precocial young abandon nest soon after hatching. 2 broods per year.

Similar Birds

VIRGINIA RAIL
Long, slender, slightly down-curved reddish bill; gray face; rusty-red throat and breast.

YELLOW RAIL
Much smaller; checkered pattern of buff stripes and white bars on a blackish back on upperparts; lacks black on chin and throat; shows white wing patch in flight.

- **POPULATION** Common and widespread despite loss of wetland habitat.
- **CONSERVATION** Recent loss of habitat due to draining and development of marshes; also due to loss of wintering coastal habitat.

Flight Pattern

Weak labored floppy flight for short distances and low over vegetation with legs dangling.

Nest Identification

Shape ⬚ Location 🌾 〽️

A bowl of cattails, dry leaves, grasses, and reeds • about 15 cm in diameter • connected to stems of marsh vegetation a few inches above water • in reeds, cattails, or grasses over deeper water • 10–12 rich buff eggs irregularly spotted with browns and grays; ovate, 3.0 cm long.

Plumage Sexes similar	Habitat 〰️ ~~~ ___	Migration Migratory	Weight 74 g

DATE _____ TIME_____ LOCATION _____

Family RALLIDAE	Species *Gallinula chloropus*	Length 36 cm	Wingspan 51–58 cm

COMMON MOORHEN

This is a fairly tame chickenlike bird of freshwater marshes, ponds, and lakes with heavy stands of cattails, rushes, sedges, and other aquatic vegetation.

- **SONG** No musical sounds are produced. Vocalizations range from explosive, froglike *hups* to loud, chickenlike grunts, clucks, and squeaks along with drawn-out whines and rapid *thicket-thicket-thicket* calls.

- **BEHAVIOR** This noisy bird of the wetlands, unlike most of the rail family, is often seen in the open walking over or climbing through aquatic vegetation. It swims with a pumping back-and-forth motion of its head and neck. When walking it often flicks its tail up and down, flashing the white undertail coverts with their dark center. Usually found in medium to large groups in which individuals can be aggressive toward other members in disputes over food, mates, or nesting areas. Feeds on aquatic vegetation, snails, grasshoppers, and other invertebrates.

- **BREEDING** Monogamous. Solitary to semicolonial, some cooperative breeding.

- **NESTING** Incubation 18–22 days by both sexes. Precocial young stay in nest 40–50 days, fed by both parents and extra birds. 1–3 broods per year.

- **POPULATION** Common, but loss of wetlands has resulted in decline, especially in northern range. Still widespread; may be common in good marsh habitat.

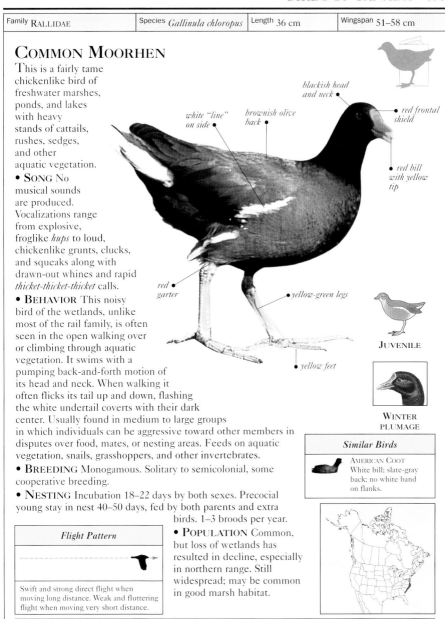

blackish head and neck

brownish olive back

white "line" on side

red frontal shield

red bill with yellow tip

red garter

yellow-green legs

yellow feet

JUVENILE

WINTER PLUMAGE

Similar Birds
AMERICAN COOT White bill; slate-gray back; no white band on flanks.

Flight Pattern
Swift and strong direct flight when moving long distance. Weak and fluttering flight when moving very short distance.

Nest Identification	Often with ramp of vegetation • made of bleached aquatic vegetation lined with grass • on ground near water or low shrub over water • built by both sexes • 2–13 cinnamon or buff eggs spotted with reddish brown or olive and overlaid with scattered fine dots, 4.3 cm long.
Shape Location	

Plumage Sexes similar	Habitat	Migration Some migrate	Weight 340 g

DATE _____ TIME_____ LOCATION _____

Family RALLIDAE	Species *Fulica americana*	Length 38 cm	Wingspan 58–71 cm

AMERICAN COOT

This close relative of the gallinules and moorhens lives on open water and is often mistaken for a duck. It pumps its small head back and forth like a chicken when walking or swimming and usually travels and feeds in flocks. A common and widely distributed species over much of North America, the American Coot is easily distinguished by its overall slate-gray plumage, which is

gray-black head and neck

reddish brown frontal shield

slate-gray body

short white bill

JUVENILE

blacker on the head and neck, its white bill, and small reddish brown frontal shield. Juveniles are similar to adults but paler, particularly on the underparts, with a darker bill.

• **SONG** Grunts, grating quacks, and hoarse chatters of *ke-yik* and *k-rrk!* or *krek!* Drawling *k-yew-r* and laughing *wah wahk* or *kuk-kuk-kuk-kuk-kuk.*

• **BEHAVIOR** Feeds by immersing head and neck in shallows with body and tail tipped up. May also pick food off surface. Dives 3–7.5 meters deep for fronds, leaves, seeds, and roots of aquatic plants, which make up most of diet. Also eats insects, amphibians, mollusks, and small fish. Runs with wings flapping rapidly to gain flight from water. Often aggressive toward other waterbirds, chasing them nosily from its vicinity.

• **BREEDING** Monogamous. Pairs display in front of each other on water in courtship. The male also chases the female across surface of water.

• **NESTING** Incubation 21–25 days by both sexes. Precocial young abandon nest shortly after hatching and drying off. Tended by both sexes. First flight at 49–56 days. 1–2 broods per year.

• **POPULATION** Common to abundant. Has decreased in the East in recent years.

Similar Birds

COMMON MOORHEN Red shield; yellow-tipped red bill; brown back; white-tipped flank feathers form line between flank and back • juvenile paler with white flank stripe.

PURPLE GALLINULE Dark bluish purple head, neck, and underparts; greenish brown back; yellow-tipped red bill; pale blue shield • juvenile has olive-brown upperparts; pale brown underparts; dull yellowish bill.

Flight Pattern
Fairly swift direct flight with rapid wing beats and feet protruding beyond tail.

Nest Identification	
Shape · Location ·	Made of dead stems • lined with finer material • floating and anchored to vegetation • built by both sexes • 2–12 pinkish buff eggs marked with blackish brown, 4.8 cm long.

Plumage Sexes similar	Habitat	Migration Migratory	Weight 726 g

DATE _____ TIME _____ LOCATION _____

| Family GRUIDAE | Species *Grus canadensis* | Length 86–122 cm | Wingspan 185–229 cm |

SANDHILL CRANE

The five North American subspecies of this crane (plus one in Cuba) differ in size and intensity of coloration. The small southern sedentary populations are the most threatened. On the ground cranes look stately with long necks, heavy straight bills, long legs, "bustle" of tertials drooping over the tail, and upright stance. In flight they are distinguished from herons because the neck and head are extended and the slow downward wing beat is jerked quickly upward. This bird may probe for food in mud that contains iron, which deposits on the bill and stains the feathers rusty-brown when the bird preens.

• **SONG** Noisy trumpetlike *garoo-oo-a-a-a-a*; can carry more than a mile.

• **BEHAVIOR** Roosts communally at night in winter, standing on damp low land or in shallow water. Courtship dances in late winter and spring involve bounding 2–2.5 meters into air with wings half spread and calling loudly. Eats variety of plants and animals. In summer feeds in breeding marshes or nearby meadows. Walks great distances for food. May soar on thermals and migrate so high it is invisible from the ground.

• **BREEDING** Monogamous. Thought to mate for life.

• **NESTING** Incubation 28–32 days by both sexes. Precocial young leave nest soon after hatching. First flight at 65 days. 1 brood per year.

• **POPULATION** Common to fairly common and local. Stable or increasing, though vulnerable to habitat loss.

• **CONSERVATION** Killing and habitat loss to agriculture depleted southern numbers in the last two centuries. Degradation of habitat at major migration stopping points seriously impacting species. Mississippi Sandhill Crane National Wildlife Refuge houses most remaining Mississippi Sandhill Cranes, and there is an active propagation program.

dull red skin on crown and lores

straight blackish gray bill

whitish cheeks, chin, and upper throat

long neck

gray body

black primaries

long blackish gray legs and feet

JUVENILE

Similar Birds

WHOOPING CRANE Rare; larger; white; reddish black mustache; black primaries visible in flight.

GREAT BLUE HERON Lacks "bustle"; gray upperparts; yellow bill; dull yellow-brown legs; white head; elongated black supercilium; flies with neck pulled back in S-curve on body.

Flight Pattern

Heavy, labored, steady wing beats with slow downstroke and rapid jerky upstroke. Flies in V or straight line formation.

Nest Identification

Shape ⬭ Location ⚬⚬⚬ ▬ ⑊⑊⑊

Dead sticks, moss, reeds, and grass • built by both sexes • 2 buff eggs marked with olive or 2 olive eggs marked with brown; subelliptical to long oval, 9.4–9.7 x 5.8 cm.

| Plumage Sexes similar | Habitat ⑊≋ ▬▬ | Migration Some migrate | Weight 3.4 kg |

DATE _____ TIME_____ LOCATION _____

Family GRUIDAE	Species *Grus grus*	Length 112–130 cm	Wingspan 201–231 cm

COMMON CRANE

This Eurasian bird has occurred in North America as an accidental vagrant to central Alaska, western Canada, the Great Plains, and the Midwest. These appearances almost always have been in the company of Sandhill Cranes. It is believed that Sandhills breeding in eastern Russia may be accompanied in migration by Common Cranes breeding in the same area. In flight note the black flight feathers and short tail. Juveniles have brown mottled gray plumage with a brown head and neck.

patch of red bare skin on crown

broad white postocular stripe extends from eye to back of long neck

long straight dull yellow bill

black face, chin, throat, and neck

gray overall

• **SONG** Bold piercing trumpeting, or at times a low mellow warble.

• **BEHAVIOR** Very wary. If threatened usually will leave nest quietly and not take flight until a distance away. Flies with head and legs outstretched. May allow close approach. Feeds in dry places, preferring seeds, berries, grain, and young shoots. Frequently eats insects and mollusks, occasionally small mammals, fish, and frogs.

long black legs and feet

• **BREEDING** Monogamous. Precocial. During breeding season several birds gather and take turns performing characteristic displays such as squatting, hopping, and calling, with half-opened wings.

• **NESTING** Nest sometimes used several years consecutively. Incubation 30 days by both sexes in turn; female incubates at night. Precocial young leave nest soon after hatching; tended by both parents. First flight at 65–70 days. 1 brood per year.

• **POPULATION** Accidental vagrant to Midwest, Great Plains, western Canada, and central Alaska. Uncommon to fairly common, local in Eurasia.

• **CONSERVATION** Not threatened; some concern due to loss of wetland habitat.

Similar Birds

SANDHILL CRANE
Gray body; red bare skin also on forehead and lores; lacks black-and-white pattern on head and neck; only primary feathers on wing are black • juveniles very similar but Common Crane has black in entire trailing edge of wing.

Flight Pattern

Straight flight with deep even wing beats, slow downstroke, and quick upstroke. Flies in V formation during migration.

Nest Identification

Shape ⬬   Location 🪺 🌾 🌿

Matted grasses • in shallow water or set on reeds or in a thicket • 2 brownish or olive eggs with red-brown spots; elongated ovoid, 9.7 x 5.8 cm.

Plumage Sexes similar	Habitat ▲ 〰 🌱	Migration Migratory	Weight 5.5 kg

DATE _____ TIME_____ LOCATION _____

Family GRUIDAE	Species *Grus americana*	Length 132 cm	Wingspan 221 cm

WHOOPING CRANE

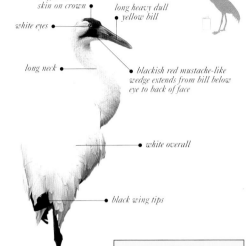

bright red bare skin on crown

long heavy dull yellow bill

white eyes

long neck

blackish red mustache-like wedge extends from bill below eye to back of face

white overall

black wing tips

long black legs and feet

The stately Whooping Crane is the tallest bird in North America and one of the most endangered. By 1941 only fifteen individuals wintering on the Texas coast were left in the wild. The breeding grounds of these birds were unknown until 1954 when they were discovered in Wood Buffalo National Park in Alberta in central Canada. Intensive conservation and management programs have slowly increased this flock to more than one hundred fifty individuals. Juveniles are white with a rusty red head and neck and have rusty red feathers scattered over the rest of the body.

• **SONG** Piercing trumpetlike *ker-loo ker-lee-loo* that can be heard for more than 3 km. This volume is achieved by the 1.5-meter-long trachea coiled within the keel of the breast bone.

• **BEHAVIOR** Eats fish, frogs, small mammals, mollusks, crustaceans, corn, other grains, and roots of water plants.

• **BREEDING** Monogamous; mates for life. In courtship dance, one of pair begins by lowering head and flapping wings. Bird leaps 1 meter in air with head back, bill pointed skyward, neck arched over back, legs stiff, and wings flapping. Mate runs forward a few steps, pumping head up and down and flapping wings. Then both leap into air and bounce up and down. The silent dance ends as suddenly as it begins. On wintering grounds do not form flocks but maintain family groups of 3–4 birds and hold winter territory.

• **NESTING** Incubation 29–35 days by both sexes. Precocial young abandon nest soon after hatching; tended by both parents. First flight at approximately 80–90 days. 1 brood per year.

• **POPULATION** Increasing. Populations introduced in Idaho and Florida.

• **CONSERVATION** Endangered, but public education as well as intensive management and protection programs, slowly succeeding.

Similar Birds

SANDHILL CRANE Smaller; lacks mustache; bare red skin also on forehead and lores; pale gray overall; black bill and legs; shows black primaries in flight.

AMERICAN WHITE PELICAN Larger; white with black outer secondaries, primaries, and upper primary coverts; short legs; flies with neck folded and long yellow-orange bill resting on breast.

Flight Pattern	

Typical crane flight of slow downward wing beat with powerful flick or jerk on upbeat. Flies in V formation in migration.

Nest Identification

Shape ⬟   Location ▬ ▪▪▪ ⑂

Soft or coarse grass, reeds, or sod • built on a mound by both sexes • 1–3 cream-olive buff eggs marked with brown; ovate or elliptical ovate, 9.9 x 6.4 cm.

Plumage Sexes similar	Habitat 〰	Migration Migratory	Weight 5.8 kg

DATE _____ TIME_____ LOCATION _____

Family CHARADRIIDAE	Species *Vanellus vanellus*	Length 30–33 cm	Wingspan 53–61 cm

NORTHERN LAPWING

Easily identified by its crest, the Northern Lapwing fits a niche in Eurasia similar to that of the Killdeer in North America. It is the only crested plover to occur in North America, usually in winter when the sides of its head and crest are buff-colored. On rare occasions winter storms have blown numbers of this bird across the Atlantic. The Northern Lapwing often feeds at night, especially during a full moon. Its broad rounded wings have black tips on all but the outer 3–4 primary feathers, which have white tips. When bird is in flight it shows white underwing linings and a white tail with a broad black subterminal band.

wispy but prominent black crest

irregular black patch beneath eye extends onto lores and auriculars

dark green-glossed upperparts

black breast

broad rounded wings

white underparts

tawny undertail coverts

• **SONG** A whistled *wee-ip* or *pee-wit*. A territorial song of *coo-wee-ip* and *wee-willuch-coo-wee-ip*. In flight, often calls *pee-wit* repeatedly.

• **BEHAVIOR** On breeding grounds in Greenland, Europe, and Asia, stays in large flocks when not breeding. Noisy and obvious in flight. Often chases larger birds, including raptors, from territory. Feeds chiefly on wide variety of invertebrates, taking some plant materials and their seeds.

• **BREEDING** Monogamous. Rather noisy when breeding. Male has bowing display, revealing its tawny undertail coverts and accompanied by wheezing sounds.

• **NESTING** Incubation 24–28 days by both sexes. Young precocial. First flight at 35–40 days. 1 brood per year.

• **POPULATION** Casual in fall and winter in northeastern states and provinces; accidental elsewhere in the the eastern US as far south as Florida. Common in Eurasia.

Flight Pattern
Strong direct flight on rapidly beating wings.

Nest Identification	
Shape 〜 Location 👣 ▬	Lined with grasses • usually on slightly raised ground • built by male • 4–5 pale brown eggs, blotched with black, 4.7 cm long.

Plumage Sexes similar	Habitat ⚲	Migration Migratory	Weight 210 g

DATE _____ TIME_____ LOCATION _____

Family CHARADRIIDAE	Species *Pluvialis squatarola*	Length 29–33 cm	Wingspan 56–64 cm

BLACK-BELLIED PLOVER

The largest of the North American plovers, this stocky bird has a cautious nature and tends to travel in flocks, which helped it survive during a period when many plovers were destroyed by market hunters. This is the grayest of all the New World plovers in both breeding and winter plumages. In flight it shows a bold white wing stripe, white uppertail coverts, and black axillars. Seen on

white stripe over eyes extends down sides of neck

gray-white forehead and crown

short stout black bill

gray-spotted black upperparts

black face, chin, and throat

black breast and belly

WINTER PLUMAGE

snow-white tail coverts

mudflats in winter, this bird is distinguished by its larger size, stout black bill, and gray plumage.

- **SONG** Long melancholy triple-note whistle, *tlee-oo-eee* or *pee-oo-ee*, with second note lower-pitched.
- **BEHAVIOR** Feeds along seacoasts on broad tidal sand, mudflats, or in salt marshes. Eats marine worms, insects, small mollusks, and crustaceans.
- **BREEDING** Monogamous.
- **NESTING** Incubation 26–27 days by both sexes. Young precocial; leave nest soon after hatching. Tended by both sexes for 14 days, then by male only. First flight at 23–35 days. 1 brood per year.
- **POPULATION** Uncommon to common migrant on both coasts and in Great Lakes; uncommon to rare elsewhere in interior. On tundra breeding grounds cycles between uncommon, common, and rare. Difficult to detect population trends.
- **CONSERVATION** Stopover staging areas for foraging migrants important to population stability.

Similar Birds

AMERICAN GOLDEN-PLOVER Winter adults and juveniles are smaller; long primary projection beyond tertials and tail; dusky underwings and axillars; in flight show uniform upperparts with indistinct, narrow whitish wing stripe.

PACIFIC GOLDEN-PLOVER Winter adults and juveniles are smaller; smaller black bill; buff cast to plumage; buff spots and bars on underparts.

Flight Pattern

Strong direct flight with rapid wing beats.

Nest Identification

Shape _____   Location _____

Tundra moss • lined with dried grasses, moss, and lichens • on dry ground with good visibility • male begins scrape; lined by female • 3–5 gray, green, whitish, or brown eggs spotted and scrawled with dark brown and black, 5.1 cm long.

Plumage Sexes similar	Habitat	Migration Migratory	Weight 221 g

DATE _____ TIME_____ LOCATION _____

Family CHARADRIIDAE	Species *Pluvialis dominica*	Length 25–28 cm	Wingspan 46–57 cm

AMERICAN GOLDEN-PLOVER

This expert long-distance migrant flies at a rate of 96.5 km/h and covers thousands of kilometers per year between Arctic tundra nesting grounds and winter quarters as far away as Argentina. Once an abundant bird, the American Golden-Plover was almost eradicted by market hunters during the late 1800s. Winter adults and juveniles are

short thin black bill

dark brown upperparts dappled profusely with golden spots

broad white stripe over eyes and forehead extends down sides of neck

black face and foreneck

black breast

WINTER PLUMAGE

brown overall with darker upperparts than underparts and lack the distinctive black-and-white markings. In flight in all plumages the uppertail coverts and back are the same color, the underwings are gray throughout, and there is an indistinct pale wing stripe. Primaries of standing birds extend well past the tail.

black underparts, including undertail coverts

- **SONG** Shrieking *ku-wheep* or *quee-dle*.
- **BEHAVIOR** Often flies in small swiftly moving flocks. Holds wings above back after alighting; often bobs head. Feeds on insects (mostly grasshoppers, crickets, and larvae), small mollusks, and crustaceans. On tundra often gorges on crowberry in preparation for autumn migration.
- **BREEDING** Monogamous.
- **NESTING** Incubation 26–27 days by both sexes in turn; male by day, female at night. Precocial young abandon nest soon after hatching. Tended by both sexes. First flight at 21–24 days. 1 brood per year.

Similar Birds

PACIFIC GOLDEN-PLOVER ♂ Longer tertials; shorter primary projection • juveniles and winter birds appear golden yellow overall with spangling and spotting on upperparts; less contrasting crown.

MOUNTAIN PLOVER Plainer overall without markings on lower breast or belly; pale legs.

BLACK-BELLIED PLOVER In winter plumage has black axillaries; white rump.

- **POPULATION** Uncommon. May be limited because of habitat loss on South American winter range; perhaps never fully recovered from 19th-century market hunting.

Flight Pattern
Swift strong direct flight on steady rapid wing beats. Flies in tight flocks that constantly change shape.

Nest Identification	
Shape	Location	Lined with lichens, moss, grass, and leaves • on ground in tundra • built by male • 3–4 cinnamon to light buff or cream eggs marked with black and brown spots and blotches, 4.8 cm long.

Plumage Sexes similar	Habitat	Migration Migratory	Weight 145 g

DATE _____ TIME_____ LOCATION _____

Family CHARADRIIDAE	Species *Pluvialis fulva*	Length 25 cm	Wingspan 46 cm

PACIFIC GOLDEN-PLOVER

The smallest of the Golden-Plovers is most likely to be seen in the Pacific Coast states of North America in winter. It breeds on the coast and river valleys of northwestern Alaska and winters in southern Asia and on many Pacific islands, including the Hawaiian Islands – a feat requiring pinpoint navigational skills. If grassland or coastal roosting sites are unavailable, these plovers may roost on flat roofs of buildings. In winter plumage bird has mottled tawny-buff and brown upperparts, and whitish buff underparts with spots and bars.

white line extends from forehead over eye and behind face; along side of neck, sides, and flanks; and onto undertail coverts

thick black bill

black throat and face

bright golden spangling and spotting on upperparts

MALE

black underparts to undertail coverts

long grayish black legs

white on flanks and undertail coverts

WINTER PLUMAGE

• **SONG** Repeated, plaintive *teee-chewee*; also loud *chu-wheet*.

• **BEHAVIOR** Eats variety of invertebrates, seeds, and berries. Feeds in small flocks, often associating with other shorebirds. Makes short runs and stops and quickly stabs at ground during feeding.

dusky-black postocular stripe and rear edge of ear coverts

face, chin, throat, and upper neck white with tiny black flecking

FEMALE

more extensive white feathering on sides, flanks, and undertail coverts

Similar Birds

AMERICAN GOLDEN-PLOVER
In winter dark streaking and tipping on breast feathers is broader and forms mottled or barred pattern; duller in color; primaries extend well beyond tail when standing; shorter bill and legs • in breeding plumage white stripe stops on side of neck; black undertail coverts.

• **BREEDING** Monogamous.

• **NESTING** Incubation 25 days by both sexes. Precocial young abandon nest shortly after hatching. Tended by both sexes but find own food. First flight at 26–28 days.

• **POPULATION** Uncommon to casual along Pacific Coast in winter. Common to fairly common on breeding grounds in western Alaska and Siberia.

Flight Pattern
Swift direct flight with rapid steady wing beats.

Nest Identification	
Shape	Location	Lined with lichens, moss, grass, and dead leaves • built by male • 4 whitish to buff, cinnamon-buff, creamy buff, greenish buff, or ivory-yellow eggs heavily marked with dark black or brown; ovate pyriform, 4.8 cm long.

Plumage Sexes differ	Habitat	Migration Migratory	Weight 153 g

DATE _____ TIME_____ LOCATION _____

Family CHARADRIIDAE	Species *Charadrius mongolus*	Length 18–20 cm	Wingspan 38–41 cm

MONGOLIAN PLOVER

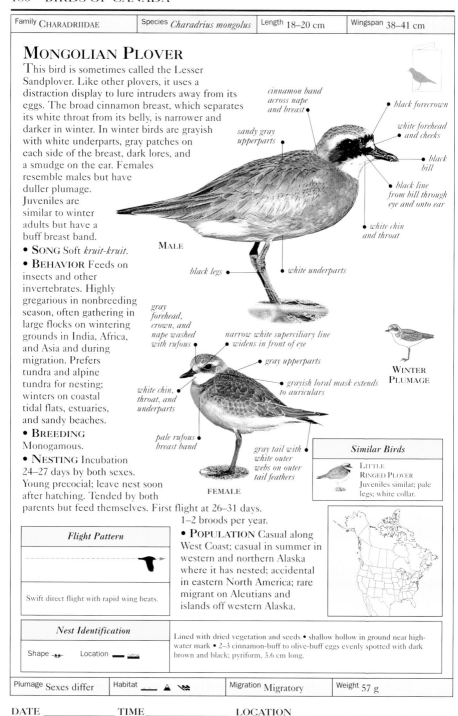

This bird is sometimes called the Lesser Sandplover. Like other plovers, it uses a distraction display to lure intruders away from its eggs. The broad cinnamon breast, which separates its white throat from its belly, is narrower and darker in winter. In winter birds are grayish with white underparts, gray patches on each side of the breast, dark lores, and a smudge on the ear. Females resemble males but have duller plumage. Juveniles are similar to winter adults but have a buff breast band.

- **SONG** Soft *kruit-kruit*.
- **BEHAVIOR** Feeds on insects and other invertebrates. Highly gregarious in nonbreeding season, often gathering in large flocks on wintering grounds in India, Africa, and Asia and during migration. Prefers tundra and alpine tundra for nesting; winters on coastal tidal flats, estuaries, and sandy beaches.
- **BREEDING** Monogamous.
- **NESTING** Incubation 24–27 days by both sexes. Young precocial; leave nest soon after hatching. Tended by both parents but feed themselves. First flight at 26–31 days. 1–2 broods per year.
- **POPULATION** Casual along West Coast; casual in summer in western and northern Alaska where it has nested; accidental in eastern North America; rare migrant on Aleutians and islands off western Alaska.

cinnamon band across nape and breast

black forecrown

sandy gray upperparts

white forehead and cheeks

black bill

black line from bill through eye and onto ear

white chin and throat

MALE

black legs

white underparts

gray forehead, crown, and nape washed with rufous

narrow white superciliary line widens in front of eye

gray upperparts

grayish loral mask extends to auriculars

white chin, throat, and underparts

WINTER PLUMAGE

pale rufous breast band

gray tail with white outer webs on outer tail feathers

FEMALE

Similar Birds

LITTLE RINGED PLOVER Juveniles similar; pale legs; white collar.

Flight Pattern

Swift direct flight with rapid wing beats.

Nest Identification

Shape ⚬ Location ▬ ▬

Lined with dried vegetation and seeds • shallow hollow in ground near high-water mark • 2–3 cinnamon-buff to olive-buff eggs evenly spotted with dark brown and black; pyriform, 3.6 cm long.

Plumage Sexes differ	Habitat ▬ ▲ 🐾	Migration Migratory	Weight 57 g

DATE _____ TIME_____ LOCATION _____

Family CHARADRIIDAE	Species *Charadrius alexandrinus*	Length 15–18 cm	Wingspan 34 cm

SNOWY PLOVER

The smallest and whitest of the North American plovers inhabits barren sandy beaches. Unlike all other "ringed" plovers in North America, breast band is never complete. Females and juveniles resemble males except for

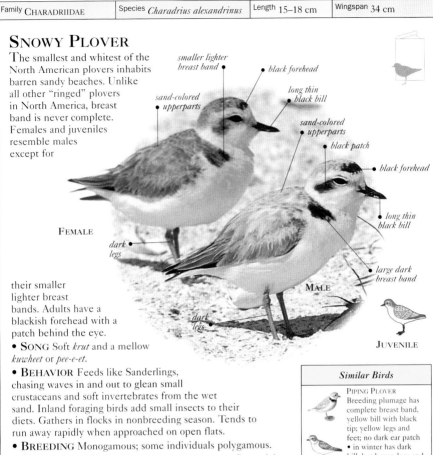

smaller lighter breast band

black forehead

long thin black bill

sand-colored upperparts

sand-colored upperparts

black patch

black forehead

long thin black bill

FEMALE

dark legs

large dark breast band

dark legs

MALE

JUVENILE

their smaller lighter breast bands. Adults have a blackish forehead with a patch behind the eye.

- **SONG** Soft *krut* and a mellow *kuwheet* or *pee-e-et*.
- **BEHAVIOR** Feeds like Sanderlings, chasing waves in and out to glean small crustaceans and soft invertebrates from the wet sand. Inland foraging birds add small insects to their diets. Gathers in flocks in nonbreeding season. Tends to run away rapidly when approached on open flats.
- **BREEDING** Monogamous; some individuals polygamous.
- **NESTING** Incubation 24–32 days by both sexes. Precocial young fed by both sexes. 1–2 broods per year.
- **POPULATION** Rare. Declining in some areas, especially Gulf Coast and parts of Pacific Coast.

Similar Birds

PIPING PLOVER
Breeding plumage has complete breast band, yellow bill with black tip; yellow legs and feet; no dark ear patch • in winter has dark bill, but larger; legs and feet dark but not black; lacks dark ear patch.

- **CONSERVATION** Human disturbance on beaches often causes failed nesting attempts. Considered threatened in parts of range. Declining populations have prompted management by state and federal agencies.

Flight Pattern
Direct flight with rapid wing beats.

Nest Identification	
Shape Location	Lined with bits of shell, grass, and pebbles by female • marked with twigs and debris • built by male • very often on edge of Least Tern colonies, whose eggs look remarkably similar • 2–3 pale, buff eggs dotted, spotted, and scrawled with black or gray; conical to elliptical, 3.0 cm long.

Plumage Sexes differ	Habitat	Migration Some migrate	Weight 40 g

Family CHARADRIIDAE	Species *Charadrius hiaticula*	Length 19 cm	Wingspan 38 cm

COMMON RINGED PLOVER

Small, bulky, and sporting a single band across its breast, the Common Ringed Plover is almost indistinguishable from the Semipalmated Plover. Morphologically, there is no easy way to distinguish the two species unless you have them in hand (this species has little or no webbing between the toes), but they have very different

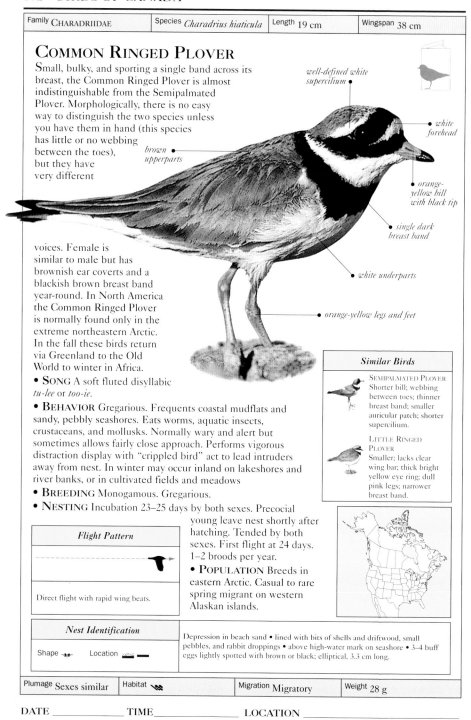

well-defined white supercilium

white forehead

brown upperparts

orange-yellow bill with black tip

single dark breast band

white underparts

orange-yellow legs and feet

voices. Female is similar to male but has brownish ear coverts and a blackish brown breast band year-round. In North America the Common Ringed Plover is normally found only in the extreme northeastern Arctic. In the fall these birds return via Greenland to the Old World to winter in Africa.

• **SONG** A soft fluted disyllabic *tu-lee* or *too-ie*.

• **BEHAVIOR** Gregarious. Frequents coastal mudflats and sandy, pebbly seashores. Eats worms, aquatic insects, crustaceans, and mollusks. Normally wary and alert but sometimes allows fairly close approach. Performs vigorous distraction display with "crippled bird" act to lead intruders away from nest. In winter may occur inland on lakeshores and river banks, or in cultivated fields and meadows

• **BREEDING** Monogamous. Gregarious.

• **NESTING** Incubation 23–25 days by both sexes. Precocial young leave nest shortly after hatching. Tended by both sexes. First flight at 24 days. 1–2 broods per year.

• **POPULATION** Breeds in eastern Arctic. Casual to rare spring migrant on western Alaskan islands.

Similar Birds

SEMIPALMATED PLOVER
Shorter bill; webbing between toes; thinner breast band; smaller auricular patch; shorter supercilium.

LITTLE RINGED PLOVER
Smaller; lacks clear wing bar; thick bright yellow eye ring; dull pink legs; narrower breast band.

Flight Pattern

Direct flight with rapid wing beats.

Nest Identification

Shape ⸺ Location ⸺

Depression in beach sand • lined with bits of shells and driftwood, small pebbles, and rabbit droppings • above high-water mark on seashore • 3–4 buff eggs lightly spotted with brown or black; elliptical, 3.3 cm long.

Plumage Sexes similar	Habitat 〰	Migration Migratory	Weight 28 g

DATE _____ TIME_____ LOCATION _____

Family CHARADRIIDAE	Species *Charadrius semipalmatus*	Length 18 cm	Wingspan 36–39 cm

SEMIPALMATED PLOVER

Migrating throughout the continent, flocks of these plovers often assemble near the water at sundown to roost with their heads tucked into their feathers. This small shorebird migrates by day or night, and some are killed during night migration when they strike lighthouses. Note the short black-tipped orange bill, single breast band, yellow-orange legs, and upperparts the color of wet sand. In winter the bill is entirely black, and the breast band turns gray-brown. In flight this plover shows a white wing stripe and white

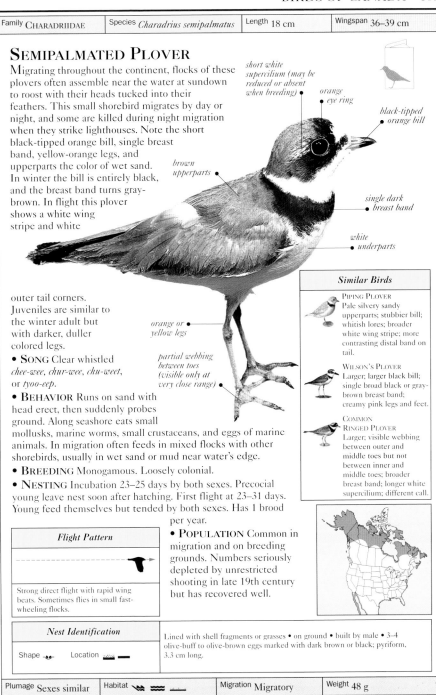

short white supercilium (may be reduced or absent when breeding)

orange eye ring

black-tipped orange bill

brown upperparts

single dark breast band

white underparts

outer tail corners. Juveniles are similar to the winter adult but with darker, duller colored legs.

orange or yellow legs

partial webbing between toes (visible only at very close range)

- **SONG** Clear whistled *chee-wee, chur-wee, chu-weet,* or *tyoo-eep.*
- **BEHAVIOR** Runs on sand with head erect, then suddenly probes ground. Along seashore eats small mollusks, marine worms, small crustaceans, and eggs of marine animals. In migration often feeds in mixed flocks with other shorebirds, usually in wet sand or mud near water's edge.
- **BREEDING** Monogamous. Loosely colonial.
- **NESTING** Incubation 23–25 days by both sexes. Precocial young leave nest soon after hatching. First flight at 23–31 days. Young feed themselves but tended by both sexes. Has 1 brood per year.
- **POPULATION** Common in migration and on breeding grounds. Numbers seriously depleted by unrestricted shooting in late 19th century but has recovered well.

Similar Birds

PIPING PLOVER
Pale silvery sandy upperparts; stubbier bill; whitish lores; broader white wing stripe; more contrasting distal band on tail.

WILSON'S PLOVER
Larger; larger black bill; single broad black or gray-brown breast band; creamy pink legs and feet.

COMMON RINGED PLOVER
Larger; visible webbing between outer and middle toes but not between inner and middle toes; broader breast band; longer white supercilium; different call.

Flight Pattern

Strong direct flight with rapid wing beats. Sometimes flies in small fast-wheeling flocks.

Nest Identification

Shape ⸺ Location ⸺

Lined with shell fragments or grasses • on ground • built by male • 3–4 olive-buff to olive-brown eggs marked with dark brown or black; pyriform, 3.3 cm long.

Plumage Sexes similar	Habitat	Migration Migratory	Weight 48 g

DATE _____ TIME_____ LOCATION _____

Family CHARADRIIDAE	Species *Charadrius melodus*	Length 18 cm	Wingspan 36–39 cm

PIPING PLOVER

This plover is difficult to spot until it moves, as its plumage blends in with the dry summer sand along the Atlantic Coast and south shores of the Great Lakes region. Endemic to central and eastern North America, and once common on beaches, this bird is now endangered because of human activity and disturbance during nesting season. Note the dry sand color of the upperparts, the yellow legs, and in flight the white wing stripe and white rump with contrasting black tail tip. Winter plumaged birds have a blackish orange bill, darker duller orange legs, and the sandy breast band may be broken. Juveniles are similar to winter adults.

white forehead and lores

sandy buff overall

orange bill with black tip

narrow blackish breast band (may be incomplete in females and East Coast birds)

white underparts

yellow-orange legs and feet

WINTER PLUMAGE

- **SONG** Clear *peep-lo.*
- **BEHAVIOR** Gregarious in post-breeding seasons, but territorial when nesting. Sprints, then stops to inspect sand with head cocked to one side; picks food off ground. Eats fly larvae, beetles, crustaceans, and marine worms. Often feeds higher on the beach (where upperparts more closely match sand) than other small plovers. In migration feeds in mixed flocks with other shorebirds.
- **BREEDING** Monogamous. Loosely colonial. Territorial during breeding season.
- **NESTING** Incubation 26–28 days by both sexes. Precocial young stay in nest 20–35 days. Fed by both sexes. Has 1 brood per year.
- **POPULATION** Uncommon to rare and declining in many parts of range, especially in Midwest and Great Lakes. Uncommon migrant inland.
- **CONSERVATION** Endangered; almost eliminated as a breeder in Great Lakes region due to human activity on beaches. Irregular pattern of water release from dams affects nesting on interior rivers.

Similar Birds

SEMIPALMATED PLOVER Dark brown upperparts the color of wet sand; dark rump in flight.

SNOWY PLOVER Smaller; long dark legs; slim dark bill; lateral dark breast patches; lacks white rump patch in flight.

Flight Pattern
Wild direct flight with twists and turns and rapid steady wing beats; often in small flocks.

Nest Identification	
Shape ••• Location ••• ▬	Lined with broken shells, small stones, or driftwood • on sandy shore of lake or ocean well above high-water mark • built by both sexes • 3–4 pale buff eggs blotched with black and dark brown; short oval to short pyriform, 3.0 cm long.

Plumage Sexes similar	Habitat ⌇ ▬	Migration Migratory	Weight 54 g

DATE _____ TIME_____ LOCATION _____

Family CHARADRIIDAE	Species *Charadrius vociferus*	Length 23–27 cm	Wingspan 48–53 cm

KILLDEER

Named for its distinctive call, this bird is the largest of the ringed plovers and the only double-banded plover within its range. Perhaps the most familiar shorebird in North America, in summer it is found across almost the entire continent south of the tundra. In flight note the long pointed wings with long white stripe and the rufous-gold rump and long tail with subterminal black tail band. Juveniles are similar in appearance but have only one black band across the chest.

red eye ring

slim black bill

gray-brown upperparts

long rounded tail with black subterminal band and white tip

bright rufous-orange rump and uppertail coverts

white underparts with 2 black bands across chest

creamy pink legs and feet

• **SONG** Loud cry, *kill-dee* or *kill-deear* or *kill-deeah-dee-dee*. And ascending *dee-ee*. Also long trilled *trrrrrrr* during display or when young are threatened.

• **BEHAVIOR** Alternately runs, then stands still as though to look or listen, then dabs suddenly with bill at ground. More than 98 percent of food consists of insects from riverbanks, golf courses, fields, and even lawns. Runs well. Leads intruders away from nest and young with "broken wing" act, rapid calls, one or both wings dragging, tail spread, and often limping or listing to one side. Once lured far enough from the nest/young, the "crippled" bird suddenly "heals" and flies away, calling all the while.

• **BREEDING** Monogamous. Solitary nester. Often returns to same mate and breeding site.

• **NESTING** Incubation 24–28 days by both sexes. Precocial young leave nest soon after hatching and feed themselves, but are tended by parents. First flight at 25 days. 2 broods per year.

• **POPULATION** Abundant to common in the northernmost regions of the range.

Similar Birds

SEMIPALMATED PLOVER Smaller; single breast band; rump and tail same color as back; yellow-orange legs.

WILSON'S PLOVER Smaller; single breast band; brown back, rump, and tail; large black bill.

Flight Pattern

Flies in wavering erratic manner on territory. Capable of swift direct flight.

Nest Identification	
Shape Location	Unlined or lined with pebbles, grass, and twigs • on ground with good visibility • built by male • 3–5 buff eggs with black and brown blotches; oval to pyriform, typically quite pointed; 3.6 cm long.

Plumage Sexes similar	Habitat	Migration Migratory	Weight 91 g

DATE _____ TIME_____ LOCATION _____

Family CHARADRIIDAE	Species *Charadrius montanus*	Length 23 cm	Wingspan 44–50 cm

MOUNTAIN PLOVER

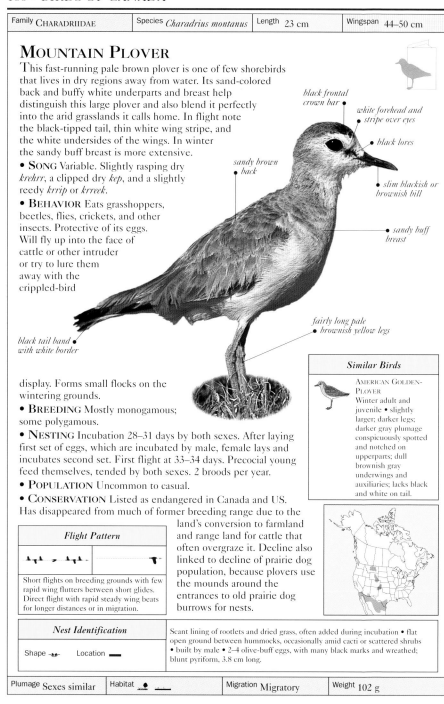

This fast-running pale brown plover is one of few shorebirds that lives in dry regions away from water. Its sand-colored back and buffy white underparts and breast help distinguish this large plover and also blend it perfectly into the arid grasslands it calls home. In flight note the black-tipped tail, thin white wing stripe, and the white undersides of the wings. In winter the sandy buff breast is more extensive.

black frontal crown bar

white forehead and stripe over eyes

black lores

slim blackish or brownish bill

sandy brown back

sandy buff breast

- **SONG** Variable. Slightly rasping dry *krehrr*, a clipped dry *kep*, and a slightly reedy *krrip* or *krreek*.
- **BEHAVIOR** Eats grasshoppers, beetles, flies, crickets, and other insects. Protective of its eggs. Will fly up into the face of cattle or other intruder or try to lure them away with the crippled-bird

fairly long pale brownish yellow legs

black tail band with white border

display. Forms small flocks on the wintering grounds.
- **BREEDING** Mostly monogamous; some polygamous.
- **NESTING** Incubation 28–31 days by both sexes. After laying first set of eggs, which are incubated by male, female lays and incubates second set. First flight at 33–34 days. Precocial young feed themselves, tended by both sexes. 2 broods per year.
- **POPULATION** Uncommon to casual.
- **CONSERVATION** Listed as endangered in Canada and US. Has disappeared from much of former breeding range due to the land's conversion to farmland and range land for cattle that often overgraze it. Decline also linked to decline of prairie dog population, because plovers use the mounds around the entrances to old prairie dog burrows for nests.

Similar Birds

AMERICAN GOLDEN-PLOVER Winter adult and juvenile • slightly larger; darker legs; darker gray plumage conspicuously spotted and notched on upperparts; dull brownish gray underwings and auxiliaries; lacks black and white on tail.

Flight Pattern

Short flights on breeding grounds with few rapid wing flutters between short glides. Direct flight with rapid steady wing beats for longer distances or in migration.

Nest Identification

Shape ~ Location ▬

Scant lining of rootlets and dried grass, often added during incubation • flat open ground between hummocks, occasionally amid cacti or scattered shrubs • built by male • 2–4 olive-buff eggs, with many black marks and wreathed; blunt pyriform, 3.8 cm long.

Plumage Sexes similar	Habitat ▴● ▬	Migration Migratory	Weight 102 g

DATE _____ TIME_____ LOCATION _____

Family HAEMATOPODIDAE	Species *Haematopus ostralegus*	Length 41–43 cm	Wingspan 76–86 cm

EURASIAN OYSTERCATCHER

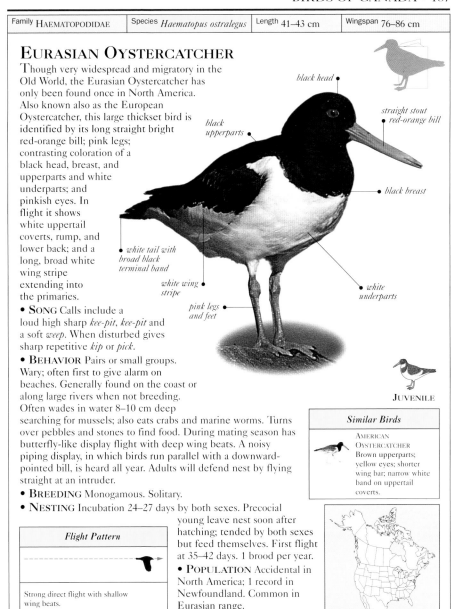

Though very widespread and migratory in the Old World, the Eurasian Oystercatcher has only been found once in North America. Also known also as the European Oystercatcher, this large thickset bird is identified by its long straight bright red-orange bill; pink legs; contrasting coloration of a black head, breast, and upperparts and white underparts; and pinkish eyes. In flight it shows white uppertail coverts, rump, and lower back; and a long, broad white wing stripe extending into the primaries.

black head

straight stout red-orange bill

black upperparts

black breast

white underparts

white tail with broad black terminal band

white wing stripe

pink legs and feet

• **SONG** Calls include a loud high sharp *kee-pit, kee-pit* and a soft *weep*. When disturbed gives sharp repetitive *kip* or *pick*.

• **BEHAVIOR** Pairs or small groups. Wary; often first to give alarm on beaches. Generally found on the coast or along large rivers when not breeding. Often wades in water 8–10 cm deep searching for mussels; also eats crabs and marine worms. Turns over pebbles and stones to find food. During mating season has butterfly-like display flight with deep wing beats. A noisy piping display, in which birds run parallel with a downward-pointed bill, is heard all year. Adults will defend nest by flying straight at an intruder.

• **BREEDING** Monogamous. Solitary.

• **NESTING** Incubation 24–27 days by both sexes. Precocial young leave nest soon after hatching; tended by both sexes but feed themselves. First flight at 35–42 days. 1 brood per year.

• **POPULATION** Accidental in North America; 1 record in Newfoundland. Common in Eurasian range.

JUVENILE

Similar Birds

AMERICAN OYSTERCATCHER
Brown upperparts; yellow eyes; shorter wing bar; narrow white band on uppertail coverts.

Flight Pattern

Strong direct flight with shallow wing beats.

Nest Identification

Shape   Location

Open depression lined with pebbles, shells, or vegetation • built by both sexes • on rocky or sandy spits, beaches, and islands • 2–4 yellowish or grayish buff eggs with dark spots and streaks; oval to long oval, 5.6 x 3.8 cm.

Plumage Sexes similar	Habitat	Migration Migratory	Weight 544 g

DATE _____ TIME_____ LOCATION _____

Family HAEMOTOPODIDAE	Species *Haematopus bachmani*	Length 44 cm	Wingspan 76–89 cm

BLACK OYSTERCATCHER

John James Audubon gave this oystercatcher its species name to honor his friend, Reverend John Bachman of Charleston, South Carolina. This stocky bird's mostly blackish brown coloring can make it difficult to spot against the dark rocks along the Pacific Coast. Juveniles are browner and have an orange-based dusky bill. In flight this large shorebird appears entirely dark without any white in the wings or tail.

yellow eyes

orange eye ring

long straight bright red-orange bill

black or blackish brown overall

pink legs and feet

• **SONG** Loud *keee, kee-ah* and a rapid series of *tees, whee-whee-tee-tee-tee.*
• **BEHAVIOR** Relatively tame. Usually found singly or in small groups. Eats mussels and marine worms, but feeds primarily on limpets and other shellfish that it pries open with its flattened bill. Often feeds on surf-hammered rocks, rocky reefs at low tide, or mudflats.
• **BREEDING** Monogamous. Performs piping display, where birds run side by side with heads down and bills pointing forward.
• **NESTING** Incubation 24–36 days by both sexes. Young leave nest soon after hatching. Tended by both sexes. First flight at 30–35 days or more. 1 brood per year.
• **POPULATION** Still widespread along the Pacific Coast from Baja California to the Aleutian Islands and numerous in some areas of range.
• **CONSERVATION** Vulnerable to disturbance at nesting sites. All oystercatchers are protected by federal law.

Similar Birds

AMERICAN OYSTERCATCHER
White underparts, wing bars, and tail base.

Flight Pattern

Rapid direct flight with slight shallow wing beats

Nest Identification

Shape ▄▄   Location ▄▄▄

Sparsely lined with pebbles and shells • on beach in small pebbles above high-water mark • built by both sexes • 1–4 pale buff to olive eggs spotted and scrawled with brown and black; ovate to pyriform, 5.6 cm long.

Plumage Sexes similar	Habitat 🌊	Migration Nonmigratory	Weight 590 g

DATE _____ TIME_____ LOCATION _____

Family RECURVIROSTRIDAE	Species *Himantopus mexicanus*	Length 36–39 cm	Wingspan 64–69 cm

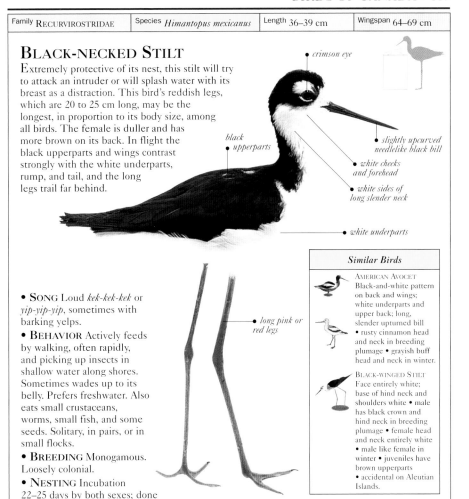

BLACK-NECKED STILT

Extremely protective of its nest, this stilt will try to attack an intruder or will splash water with its breast as a distraction. This bird's reddish legs, which are 20 to 25 cm long, may be the longest, in proportion to its body size, among all birds. The female is duller and has more brown on its back. In flight the black upperparts and wings contrast strongly with the white underparts, rump, and tail, and the long legs trail far behind.

crimson eye

black upperparts

slightly upcurved needlelike black bill

white cheeks and forehead

white sides of long slender neck

white underparts

long pink or red legs

• **SONG** Loud *kek-kek-kek* or *yip-yip-yip*, sometimes with barking yelps.
• **BEHAVIOR** Actively feeds by walking, often rapidly, and picking up insects in shallow water along shores. Sometimes wades up to its belly. Prefers freshwater. Also eats small crustaceans, worms, small fish, and some seeds. Solitary, in pairs, or in small flocks.
• **BREEDING** Monogamous. Loosely colonial.
• **NESTING** Incubation 22–25 days by both sexes; done by female at night, by male during day. Precocial young leave nest after hatching and feed themselves, but are tended by both sexes. First flight at 4–5 weeks. 1 brood per year.
• **POPULATION** Fairly common to uncommon. Casual north of breeding range. May be increasing as range expands.

Similar Birds

AMERICAN AVOCET
Black-and-white pattern on back and wings; white underparts and upper back; long, slender upturned bill • rusty cinnamon head and neck in breeding plumage • grayish buff head and neck in winter.

BLACK-WINGED STILT
Face entirely white; base of hind neck and shoulders white • male has black crown and hind neck in breeding plumage • female head and neck entirely white • male like female in winter • juveniles have brown upperparts • accidental on Aleutian Islands.

Flight Pattern

Strong swift direct flight with somewhat shallow wing beats.

Nest Identification

Shape ⚬ Location ▬

Lined with stems, weeds, sticks, grasses, fragments of shells, small rocks, fish bones, and rubbish • on ground • sometimes hidden by grasses • built by both sexes • 3–5 yellow or buff eggs heavily blotched with black or brown; pyriform, 4.3 cm long.

Plumage Sexes similar	Habitat	Migration Most migrate	Weight 167 g

DATE _____ TIME_____ LOCATION _____

Family RECURVIROSTRIDAE	Species *Recurvirostra americana*	Length 46–51 cm	Wingspan 69–97 cm

AMERICAN AVOCET

The tallest in its family, this graceful long-legged bird is the world's only avocet with distinct basic and alternate plumages. Winter (basic) plumage shows a gray head and neck, while breeding adults show rusty cinnamon on the head and neck. Females are similar to males but have a shorter and more upward-curved bill. In flight both sexes show a bold black-and-white pattern on the upperparts and black wing tips, primary coverts, and scapular bars.

rusty cinnamon head and neck

black-and-white upperparts

whitish scapulars

long slender upcurved black bill

white underparts

long blue-gray legs

- **SONG** Loud *wheet* or *pleeet*.
- **BEHAVIOR** Eats primarily insects, shrimp, and other crustaceans but also takes other aquatic invertebrates. Prefers to feed in flocks, sometimes with more than 100 birds walking shoulder to shoulder. Sometimes feeds in water up to its belly with bill in water. In shallow water brings food to surface by sweeping its open bill back and forth in the water. In deep water may feed like a dabbling duck by tipping over.
- **BREEDING** Monogamous. Loosely colonial. Pairs perform elaborate courtship display and group rituals.
- **NESTING** Incubation 22–29 days by both sexes. Precocial young leave nest soon after hatching. Tended by both sexes but feed themselves. First flight at 28–35 days. 1 brood per year.
- **POPULATION** The American Avocet is fairly common; stable and possibly increasing west of the Great Plains; uncommon and local in the East, where it is an uncommon transient in summer and a coastal species in winter.
- **CONSERVATION** Protected by law and currently making a comeback after overhunting depleted numbers in the 19th and early 20th centuries.

WINTER PLUMAGE

Similar Birds

BLACK-NECKED STILT Slightly upcurved black bill; black upperparts; white underparts; long reddish legs and feet.

Flight Pattern

Strong direct flight with neck extended slightly forward and long legs trailing behind tail.

Nest Identification

Shape ⌣ Location ▬ ⠿

Lined with dry grasses and mud chips • on flat ground or marsh near water • built by both sexes • 3–4 olive-buff eggs blotched with brown and black; pyriform to long pyriform, 5.1 cm long.

Plumage Sexes similar	Habitat ≈≈ ⌂ ⌇ ⌇	Migration Migratory	Weight 315 g

DATE _____ TIME_____ LOCATION _____

Family SCOLOPACIDAE	Species *Tringa melanoleuca*	Length 36 cm	Wingspan 58–66 cm

GREATER YELLOWLEGS

The largest of the North American *Tringa*, this common sandpiper is almost a third larger than the very similar Lesser Yellowlegs. It is closely related to the Old World "shanks," but differs from them by having a squarish white rump patch and a dark back. Its large size and long bright yellow legs distinguish this gray shorebird from most others. Paler winter plumage shows fainter streaking, spotting, and barring on the

long slender neck

dark gray-brown back with white speckles

long slightly upturned bill

white underparts speckled and barred brown

white tail

long bright yellow legs

neck, breast, sides, and flanks. In flight the dark wings and mantle contrast with the white rump and tail.

- **SONG** Loud repeated descending *teu-teu-teu* in series of 3 or more. Also territorial song of *too-whee*.
- **BEHAVIOR** Occurs either alone or in small flocks. Wary; known for its loud whistled alarm call that warns other shorebirds of approaching danger. Feeds by pecking or skimming water with its bill, not by probing. Sometimes dashes in pursuit of small fish. Also eats insects and their larvae, crabs, and snails.
- **BREEDING** Monogamous. Solitary.
- **NESTING** Incubation 23 days by both sexes. Precocial young leave nest soon after hatching and find own food but tended by both sexes. First flight at 18–20 days. 1 brood per year.
- **POPULATION** Fairly common even in migration. May be increasing.

Similar Birds

LESSER YELLOWLEGS
Smaller; shorter, thinner straight black bill; calls *tew* or *tew-tew*.

WILLET
Larger and stockier; straight dark bill; lacks white spotting on upperparts; grayish legs; striking black-and-white wing pattern in flight.

COMMON GREENSHANK
Slightly smaller; more distinctly upturned bill; less heavily streaked, barred, and spotted; greenish legs and feet; in flight rump and lower back show as large white wedge.

Flight Pattern

Swift direct flight, sometimes at great heights, with long legs extended beyond tail.

Nest Identification

Shape — Location

In moss on small hummock usually near water • lined with grass and leaves • 3–4 buff eggs blotched with gray and dark brown; ovate pyriform, 4.8 cm long.

Plumage Sexes similar	Habitat	Migration Migratory	Weight 170 g

DATE _____ TIME_____ LOCATION _____

Family SCOLOPACIDAE	Species *Tringa flavipes*	Length 27 cm	Wingspan 48–56 cm

LESSER YELLOWLEGS

Often seen walking gracefully on mudflats or shores, this sandpiper is tame and approachable. It is best distinguished from the Greater Yellowlegs by its smaller size and its bill, which is completely straight and only one-third the length of its cousin's bill, as well as by its different voice. Winter plumage is grayer and paler overall with little or no streaking. In flight the dark wings and back contrast sharply with the white tail and rump.

heavy brown streaks on head and neck

blackish grayish scapulars and mantle with white spots

long straight thin bill

blackish grayish tertials with white spots

heavy brown streaks on breast

sparse brown streaks on flanks

- **SONG** Harsh short *tew-tew* or *tew*. Alarm call is sharp *kip*. Also makes musical *pill-e-wee*.
- **BEHAVIOR** Gregarious; occurs in flocks, sometimes large, in winter and migration. Slowly picks food from surface of water. Feeds with a delicate high-stepping gait. Eats insects, small crustaceans, bloodworms, and small fish.
- **BREEDING** Monogamous. Loosely colonial. Noisy on nesting grounds.
- **NESTING** Incubation 22–23 days by both sexes. Precocial young leave nest soon after hatching and feed themselves, but are tended by both sexes for 18–20 days. 1 brood per year.

long orange-yellow legs

Similar Birds

GREATER YELLOWLEGS Larger; longer, often slightly upturned bill; more heavily barred breast and flanks; makes descending whistled series of 3 or more, *teu-teu-teu*.

SOLITARY SANDPIPER Slightly smaller; darker brown upperparts; heavier brownish streaking on neck and breast; white eye ring; dull greenish yellow legs; dark rump; in flight shows barred dark tail edged with white.

- **POPULATION** Common on breeding grounds. In migration, common in the East and the Midwest; uncommon in the far West. Fairly common in winter in Baja and on the Gulf Coast. Stable or slightly increasing.

Flight Pattern
Swift direct flight with rapid wing beats.

Nest Identification	In grass marshes and bogs surrounded by black spruce trees • on raised pile of leaves or vegetation near water • lined with small amount of grass and leaves • built by female • 3–4 buff to yellow or gray eggs with brown blotches; ovate pyriform, 4.3 x 3.0 cm.
Shape ⚬ Location ⚬⚬⚬	

Plumage Sexes similar	Habitat	Migration Migratory	Weight 82 g

DATE _____ TIME _____ LOCATION _____

Family SCOLOPACIDAE	Species *Tringa totanus*	Length 28 cm	Wingspan 56 cm

COMMON REDSHANK

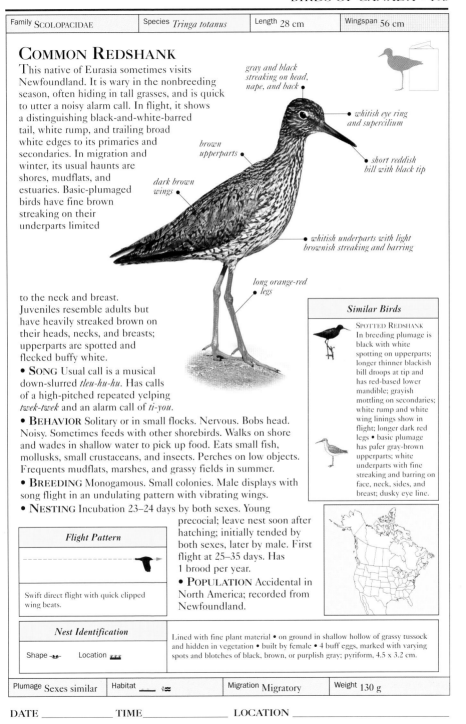

This native of Eurasia sometimes visits Newfoundland. It is wary in the nonbreeding season, often hiding in tall grasses, and is quick to utter a noisy alarm call. In flight, it shows a distinguishing black-and-white-barred tail, white rump, and trailing broad white edges to its primaries and secondaries. In migration and winter, its usual haunts are shores, mudflats, and estuaries. Basic-plumaged birds have fine brown streaking on their underparts limited

gray and black streaking on head, nape, and back

whitish eye ring and supercilium

brown upperparts

short reddish bill with black tip

dark brown wings

whitish underparts with light brownish streaking and barring

long orange-red legs

to the neck and breast. Juveniles resemble adults but have heavily streaked brown on their heads, necks, and breasts; upperparts are spotted and flecked buffy white.

• **SONG** Usual call is a musical down-slurred *tleu-hu-hu*. Has calls of a high-pitched repeated yelping *twek-twek* and an alarm call of *ti-you*.

• **BEHAVIOR** Solitary or in small flocks. Nervous. Bobs head. Noisy. Sometimes feeds with other shorebirds. Walks on shore and wades in shallow water to pick up food. Eats small fish, mollusks, small crustaceans, and insects. Perches on low objects. Frequents mudflats, marshes, and grassy fields in summer.

• **BREEDING** Monogamous. Small colonies. Male displays with song flight in an undulating pattern with vibrating wings.

• **NESTING** Incubation 23–24 days by both sexes. Young precocial; leave nest soon after hatching; initially tended by both sexes, later by male. First flight at 25–35 days. Has 1 brood per year.

• **POPULATION** Accidental in North America; recorded from Newfoundland.

Similar Birds

SPOTTED REDSHANK
In breeding plumage is black with white spotting on upperparts; longer thinner blackish bill droops at tip and has red-based lower mandible; grayish mottling on secondaries; white rump and white wing linings show in flight; longer dark red legs • basic plumage has paler gray-brown upperparts; white underparts with fine streaking and barring on face, neck, sides, and breast; dusky eye line.

Flight Pattern
Swift direct flight with quick clipped wing beats.

Nest Identification	
Shape	Location	Lined with fine plant material • on ground in shallow hollow of grassy tussock and hidden in vegetation • built by female • 4 buff eggs, marked with varying spots and blotches of black, brown, or purplish gray; pyriform, 4.5 x 3.2 cm.

Plumage Sexes similar	Habitat	Migration Migratory	Weight 130 g

DATE _____ TIME_____ LOCATION _____

Family SCOLOPADAE	Species *Tringa erythropus*	Length 32 cm	Wingspan 58–64 cm

SPOTTED REDSHANK

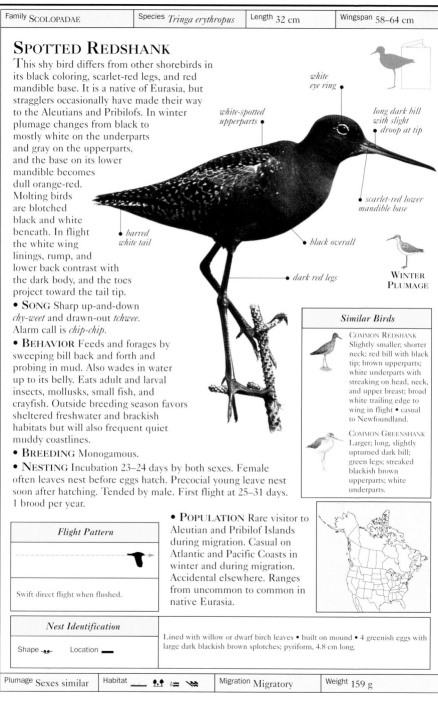

This shy bird differs from other shorebirds in its black coloring, scarlet-red legs, and red mandible base. It is a native of Eurasia, but stragglers occasionally have made their way to the Aleutians and Pribilofs. In winter plumage changes from black to mostly white on the underparts and gray on the upperparts, and the base on its lower mandible becomes dull orange-red. Molting birds are blotched black and white beneath. In flight the white wing linings, rump, and lower back contrast with the dark body, and the toes project toward the tail tip.

white eye ring

white-spotted upperparts

long dark bill with slight droop at tip

scarlet-red lower mandible base

barred white tail

black overall

dark red legs

WINTER PLUMAGE

• **SONG** Sharp up-and-down *chy-weet* and drawn-out *tchwee*. Alarm call is *chip-chip*.

• **BEHAVIOR** Feeds and forages by sweeping bill back and forth and probing in mud. Also wades in water up to its belly. Eats adult and larval insects, mollusks, small fish, and crayfish. Outside breeding season favors sheltered freshwater and brackish habitats but will also frequent quiet muddy coastlines.

• **BREEDING** Monogamous.

• **NESTING** Incubation 23–24 days by both sexes. Female often leaves nest before eggs hatch. Precocial young leave nest soon after hatching. Tended by male. First flight at 25–31 days. 1 brood per year.

Similar Birds

COMMON REDSHANK Slightly smaller; shorter neck; red bill with black tip; brown upperparts; white underparts with streaking on head, neck, and upper breast; broad white trailing edge to wing in flight • casual to Newfoundland.

COMMON GREENSHANK Larger; long, slightly upturned dark bill; green legs; streaked blackish brown upperparts; white underparts.

• **POPULATION** Rare visitor to Aleutian and Pribilof Islands during migration. Casual on Atlantic and Pacific Coasts in winter and during migration. Accidental elsewhere. Ranges from uncommon to common in native Eurasia.

Flight Pattern
Swift direct flight when flushed.

Nest Identification	
Shape **⌣** Location **▬**	Lined with willow or dwarf birch leaves • built on mound • 4 greenish eggs with large dark blackish brown splotches; pyriform, 4.8 cm long.

Plumage Sexes similar	Habitat	Migration Migratory	Weight 159 g

DATE _____ TIME_____ LOCATION _____

Family SCOLOPACIDAE	Species *Tringa solitaria*	Length 20–23 cm	Wingspan 38–43 cm

SOLITARY SANDPIPER

As its name suggests, this sandpiper is often seen alone or in small loose groups in its habitat of freshwater lakes, ponds, marshes, and rivers. This shorebird is not wary around humans and often exhibits an up-and-down bobbing or jerking motion with its head and body similar to a Spotted Sandpiper's bobbing. In flight the dark

dark brown upperparts with dense whitish buff spotting

slender body

dark wings

whitish eye ring

black central tail feathers

blackish brown streaks on lower throat and breast

blackish brown streaks on sides

white underparts

greenish yellow legs

rump patch and central tail feathers contrast with the white outer tail feathers, which have black bars. Also note the dark wings without a wing stripe, dark underwings.

- **SONG** High shrill *pit-peet-wheet* or *peet.*
- **BEHAVIOR** Searches for food by stirring up water, especially in stagnant pools, with bill and feet. Picks food from surface or probes with bill. Eats insects and insect larvae, small fish, small crustaceans, and other invertebrates. Somewhat aggressive toward other birds when feeding. Migrates singly or in small groups. Upon landing holds wings above back before folding.
- **BREEDING** Monogamous.
- **NESTING** Incubation 23–24 days by female. Precocial young leave nest soon after hatching and are tended by female. First flight at 17–20 days. 1 brood per year.
- **POPULATION** Fairly common on breeding grounds; fairly common and widespread in migration. Seems stable.

Similar Birds

SPOTTED SANDPIPER Smaller; less upright stance; teeters body; yellowish or creamy pink legs; pink bill with dark tip; white supercilium; white wing stripe; shallow stiff wing beats • spotted underparts in summer.

Flight Pattern	
Often zigzags on takeoff; light buoyant swallowlike direct flight.	

Nest Identification	
Shape 〰 Location 🐦	Female strengthens abandoned nest with other material • most often in conifers, 1–12 m above ground • 4–5 olive eggs marked with brown, usually in wreath shape; pyriform to oval, 3.8 x 2.8 cm.

Plumage Sexes similar	Habitat	Migration Migratory	Weight 48 g

DATE _____ TIME_____ LOCATION _____

| Family SCOLOPACIDAE | Species *Catoptrophorus semipalmatus* | Length 33–41 cm | Wingspan 61–79 cm |

WILLET

This large gray sandpiper is named for its song of *pill-will-willet* given loudly and frequently on the breeding grounds. A rather nondescript shorebird, the Willet may initially thwart your efforts at identification as it sleeps standing on one leg with its head tucked in on its back or probes in mud with its long gray-black bill. But the moment it takes flight it is readily identified by the mostly white tail, white rump, bold black-and-white wing pattern, and loud call of its name. In winter the light upperparts lack the variegated/barred pattern.

white spectacles

variegated light brownish gray to light gray overall

light underparts

bold black-and-white wing pattern

blue-gray legs

WINTER PLUMAGE

- **SONG** Alarm or scolding call of *kip* or *wiek*. In flight makes *wee-wee-wee*. Well-known call of *pill-will-will, pill-o-will-o-willet,* or *pill-will-willet.*

- **BEHAVIOR** Generalist. Wades, probing for food with bill. In water eats aquatic insects, marine worms, crabs, mollusks, and small fish. On land eats seeds, fresh shoots, and rice. On breeding grounds often perches high on rocks, posts, shrubs, or other tall objects, from which it may scold intruders in its territory. Becomes noisy when alarmed. Mobs will attack interlopers, especially at nesting time.

- **BREEDING** Monogamous. Semicolonial. Nests are 61 or more meters apart.

- **NESTING** Incubation 22–29 days by both sexes (male at night; female at other times). Precocial young leave nest soon after hatching but tended by both sexes. Parents sometimes abandon unhatched eggs after first young leaves nest even though they have well-developed embryos. First flight at about 28 days. 1 brood per year.

Similar Birds

GREATER YELLOWLEGS Slimmer; grayer; thinner, more needlelike, often slightly upturned bill; yellow legs; in flight has white rump and tail with distal tail bands; no wing pattern.

- **POPULATION** Common. Has recovered from hunting in late 19th century and expanded into new or parts of ranges where it had been extirpated.

- **CONSERVATION** Habitat disturbance is beginning to negatively affect population.

Flight Pattern

Short low flight; series of rapid wing beats alternates with glides. Over long distances direct flight with steady rapid wing beats.

Nest Identification

Shape ⌣ Location ⚬⚬⚬

Lined with dry grass • on sand away from shrubbery, tucked in cups of vegetation or tall grasses • 4–5 grayish to olive-buff eggs blotched with brown; 5.3 cm long.

| Plumage Sexes similar | Habitat 🪶 🌿 | Migration Migratory | Weight 215 g |

Family SCOLOPACIDAE	Species *Heteroscelus incanus*	Length 28 cm	Wingspan 56 cm

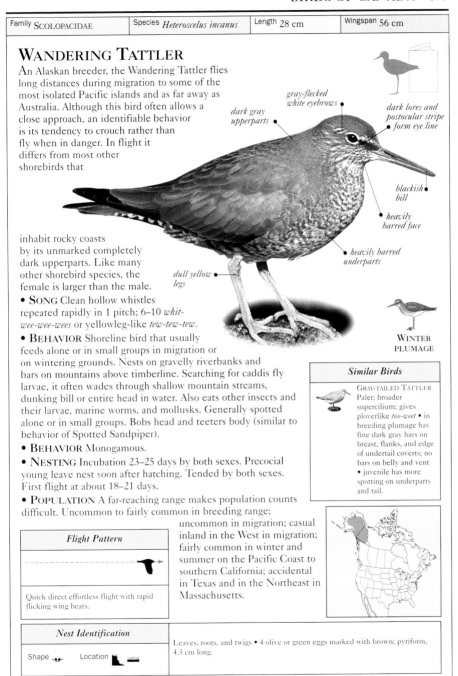

WANDERING TATTLER

An Alaskan breeder, the Wandering Tattler flies long distances during migration to some of the most isolated Pacific islands and as far away as Australia. Although this bird often allows a close approach, an identifiable behavior is its tendency to crouch rather than fly when in danger. In flight it differs from most other shorebirds that

gray-flecked white eyebrows

dark gray upperparts

dark lores and postocular stripe form eye line

blackish bill

heavily barred face

heavily barred underparts

dull yellow legs

inhabit rocky coasts by its unmarked completely dark upperparts. Like many other shorebird species, the female is larger than the male.

- **SONG** Clean hollow whistles repeated rapidly in 1 pitch; 6–10 *whit-wee-wee-wees* or yellowleg-like *tew-tew-tew*.
- **BEHAVIOR** Shoreline bird that usually feeds alone or in small groups in migration or on wintering grounds. Nests on gravelly riverbanks and bars on mountains above timberline. Searching for caddis fly larvae, it often wades through shallow mountain streams, dunking bill or entire head in water. Also eats other insects and their larvae, marine worms, and mollusks. Generally spotted alone or in small groups. Bobs head and teeters body (similar to behavior of Spotted Sandpiper).
- **BEHAVIOR** Monogamous.
- **NESTING** Incubation 23–25 days by both sexes. Precocial young leave nest soon after hatching. Tended by both sexes. First flight at about 18–21 days.
- **POPULATION** A far-reaching range makes population counts difficult. Uncommon to fairly common in breeding range; uncommon in migration; casual inland in the West in migration; fairly common in winter and summer on the Pacific Coast to southern California; accidental in Texas and in the Northeast in Massachusetts.

WINTER PLUMAGE

Similar Birds

GRAY-TAILED TATTLER Paler; broader supercilium; gives ploverlike *too-weet* • in breeding plumage has fine dark gray bars on breast, flanks, and edge of undertail coverts; no bars on belly and vent • juvenile has more spotting on underparts and tail.

Flight Pattern

Quick direct effortless flight with rapid flicking wing beats.

Nest Identification

Shape ___ Location ___

Leaves, roots, and twigs • 4 olive or green eggs marked with brown; pyriform, 4.3 cm long.

Plumage Sexes similar	Habitat	Migration Migratory	Weight 116 g

DATE _____ TIME_____ LOCATION _____

Family SCOLOPACIDAE	Species *Actitis macularia*	Length 19 cm	Wingspan 33–36 cm

SPOTTED SANDPIPER

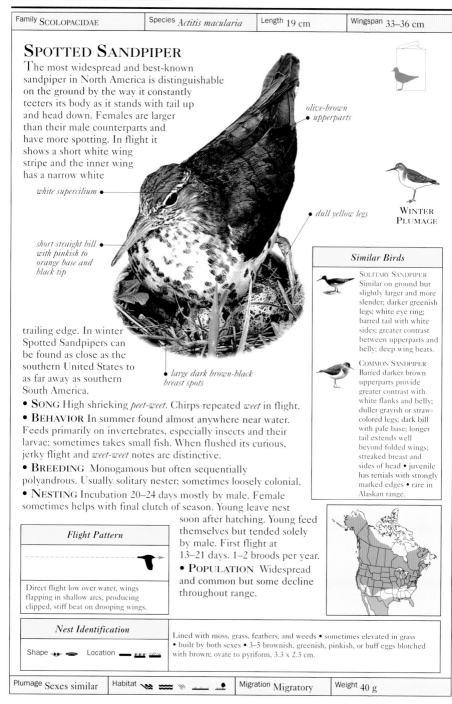

The most widespread and best-known sandpiper in North America is distinguishable on the ground by the way it constantly teeters its body as it stands with tail up and head down. Females are larger than their male counterparts and have more spotting. In flight it shows a short white wing stripe and the inner wing has a narrow white

olive-brown upperparts

white supercilium

dull yellow legs

WINTER PLUMAGE

short straight bill with pinkish to orange base and black tip

trailing edge. In winter Spotted Sandpipers can be found as close as the southern United States to as far away as southern South America.

large dark brown-black breast spots

Similar Birds

SOLITARY SANDPIPER Similar on ground but slightly larger and more slender; darker greenish legs; white eye ring; barred tail with white sides; greater contrast between upperparts and belly; deep wing beats.

COMMON SANDPIPER Barred darker brown upperparts provide greater contrast with white flanks and belly; duller grayish or straw-colored legs; dark bill with pale base; longer tail extends well beyond folded wings; streaked breast and sides of head • juvenile has tertials with strongly marked edges • rare in Alaskan range.

• **SONG** High shrieking *peet-weet*. Chirps repeated *weet* in flight.
• **BEHAVIOR** In summer found almost anywhere near water. Feeds primarily on invertebrates, especially insects and their larvae; sometimes takes small fish. When flushed its curious, jerky flight and *weet-weet* notes are distinctive.
• **BREEDING** Monogamous but often sequentially polyandrous. Usually solitary nester; sometimes loosely colonial.
• **NESTING** Incubation 20–24 days mostly by male. Female sometimes helps with final clutch of season. Young leave nest soon after hatching. Young feed themselves but tended solely by male. First flight at 13–21 days. 1–2 broods per year.
• **POPULATION** Widespread and common but some decline throughout range.

Flight Pattern

Direct flight low over water, wings flapping in shallow arcs, producing clipped, stiff beat on drooping wings.

Nest Identification

Shape — Location

Lined with moss, grass, feathers, and weeds • sometimes elevated in grass • built by both sexes • 3–5 brownish, greenish, pinkish, or buff eggs blotched with brown; ovate to pyriform, 3.3 x 2.3 cm.

Plumage Sexes similar	Habitat	Migration Migratory	Weight 40 g

DATE _____ TIME_____ LOCATION _____

Family SCOLOPACIDAE	Species *Xenus cinereus*	Length 23 cm	Wingspan 41 cm

TEREK SANDPIPER

A very busy feeder, the Terek Sandpiper can be seen foraging in water, chasing its prey along the beach, and returning to the water to wash its catch before running back up the beach to feed again. This thrush-sized Eurasian bird is the only sandpiper with short legs and an upcurved bill. Winter plumage is mostly dull gray without mottling. In flight

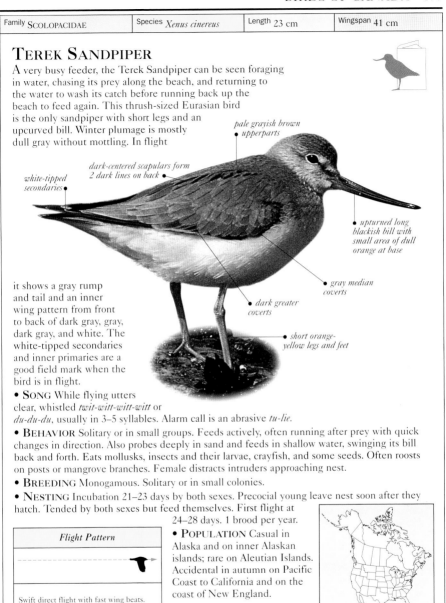

pale grayish brown upperparts

dark-centered scapulars form 2 dark lines on back

white-tipped secondaries

upturned long blackish bill with small area of dull orange at base

gray median coverts

dark greater coverts

short orange-yellow legs and feet

it shows a gray rump and tail and an inner wing pattern from front to back of dark gray, gray, dark gray, and white. The white-tipped secondaries and inner primaries are a good field mark when the bird is in flight.

• **SONG** While flying utters clear, whistled *twit-witt-witt-witt* or *du-du-du*, usually in 3–5 syllables. Alarm call is an abrasive *tu-lie*.

• **BEHAVIOR** Solitary or in small groups. Feeds actively, often running after prey with quick changes in direction. Also probes deeply in sand and feeds in shallow water, swinging its bill back and forth. Eats mollusks, insects and their larvae, crayfish, and some seeds. Often roosts on posts or mangrove branches. Female distracts intruders approaching nest.

• **BREEDING** Monogamous. Solitary or in small colonies.

• **NESTING** Incubation 21–23 days by both sexes. Precocial young leave nest soon after they hatch. Tended by both sexes but feed themselves. First flight at 24–28 days. 1 brood per year.

• **POPULATION** Casual in Alaska and on inner Alaskan islands; rare on Aleutian Islands. Accidental in autumn on Pacific Coast to California and on the coast of New England.

Flight Pattern
Swift direct flight with fast wing beats.

Nest Identification	
Shape Location	Lined with grasses, bits of tree material, and pine needles • on ground near water • often sheltered by shrub • built by female • 4 pearl-gray eggs with blackish to brownish speckles; pyriform, 3.8 cm long.

Plumage Sexes similar	Habitat	Migration Migratory	Weight 71 g

DATE _____ TIME_____ LOCATION _____

Family SCOLOPACIDAE	Species *Bartramia longicauda*	Length 30 cm	Wingspan 43–51 cm

UPLAND SANDPIPER

The distinctive silhouette of the Upland Sandpiper is often seen perched on fences, utility poles, rocks, and stumps watching for intruders and predators in the grasslands and prairies it inhabits in summer. This large pale sandpiper has a long slender neck, small dovelike head, large dark eyes, and long tail. In winter the Upland Sandpiper migrates long distances to eastern South America.

small dovelike head

large dark brown eye

long slender neck

brown-streaked buff-edged upperparts

short thin yellow-brown bill slightly decurved toward tip

buff neck and breast with streaks, bars, and chevrons

whitish belly and undertail coverts

yellow-green legs and feet

dark rump

wedge-shaped tail with white border and thin black bars

• **SONG** Trilling *pulip pulip*. In low circling stiff-winged flight on breeding grounds, emits wolflike whistle *wheelooooooooo*. Usual flight call is piping *quip-ip-ip-ip*.

• **BEHAVIOR** Has ploverlike feeding patterns: runs, stops, then runs again. Not a bird of shores and wetlands like most sandpipers, it frequents hay fields, pastures, and prairies and often perches on poles. Feeds on insects, other invertebrates, and seeds of weeds, grasses, and grains. Upon landing often holds wings above body for 1–2 seconds before folding them.

• **BREEDING** Monogamous. Loose colonies. During courtship flight spreads wings and circles high in sky, singing a melodious song that can be heard up to a mile away.

• **NESTING** Incubation 21–27 days. Precocial young leave nest soon after hatching. First flight at about 30–31 days. Young feed themselves but are tended and protected by both sexes. 1 brood per year.

• **POPULATION** Mostly recovered since large decline in late 1800s. Common in parts of the Great Plains; some decline has been recorded in local populations throughout much of the East and the Northeast.

• **CONSERVATION** Eastern decline due to habitat loss and increased human disturbance.

Similar Birds

BUFF-BREASTED SANDPIPER
Smaller; black bill; short yellow legs; buff face and underparts; wings project beyond tail.

Flight Pattern

Swift direct flight when traveling some distance. In breeding display flies slowly with flickering wing beats.

Nest Identification

Shape ⟋⟍ Location ▬ ▬▬▬

Lined with dry grass • built by both sexes • 4 creamy pale buff to pinkish buff eggs speckled red-brown; pyriform, 4.6 cm long.

Plumage Sexes similar	Habitat 🌾 🌿 🌱 🌲	Migration Migratory	Weight 136 g

DATE _____ TIME_____ LOCATION _____

Family SCOLOPACIDAE	Species *Numenius phaeopus*	Length 43–46 cm	Wingspan 79–84 cm

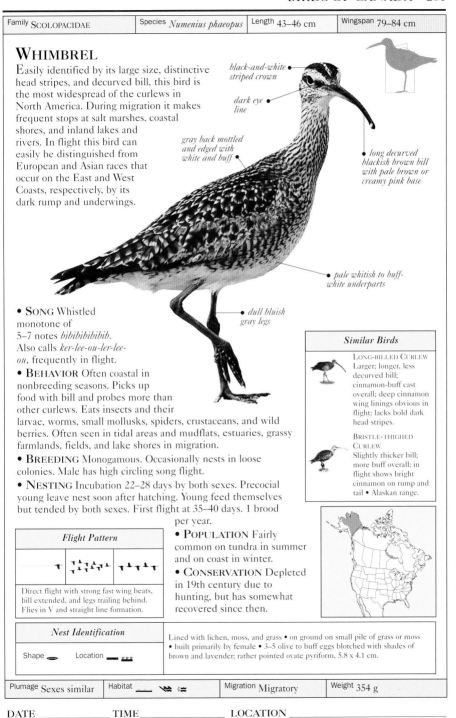

WHIMBREL

Easily identified by its large size, distinctive head stripes, and decurved bill, this bird is the most widespread of the curlews in North America. During migration it makes frequent stops at salt marshes, coastal shores, and inland lakes and rivers. In flight this bird can easily be distinguished from European and Asian races that occur on the East and West Coasts, respectively, by its dark rump and underwings.

black-and-white striped crown

dark eye line

gray back mottled and edged with white and buff

long decurved blackish brown bill with pale brown or creamy pink base

pale whitish to buff-white underparts

dull bluish gray legs

- **SONG** Whistled monotone of 5–7 notes *bibibibibibib*. Also calls *ker-lee-ou-ler-lee-ou*, frequently in flight.
- **BEHAVIOR** Often coastal in nonbreeding seasons. Picks up food with bill and probes more than other curlews. Eats insects and their larvae, worms, small mollusks, spiders, crustaceans, and wild berries. Often seen in tidal areas and mudflats, estuaries, grassy farmlands, fields, and lake shores in migration.
- **BREEDING** Monogamous. Occasionally nests in loose colonies. Male has high circling song flight.
- **NESTING** Incubation 22–28 days by both sexes. Precocial young leave nest soon after hatching. Young feed themselves but tended by both sexes. First flight at 35–40 days. 1 brood per year.
- **POPULATION** Fairly common on tundra in summer and on coast in winter.
- **CONSERVATION** Depleted in 19th century due to hunting, but has somewhat recovered since then.

Similar Birds

LONG-BILLED CURLEW Larger; longer, less decurved bill; cinnamon-buff cast overall; deep cinnamon wing linings obvious in flight; lacks bold dark head stripes.

BRISTLE-THIGHED CURLEW Slightly thicker bill; more buff overall; in flight shows bright cinnamon on rump and tail • Alaskan range.

Flight Pattern
Direct flight with strong fast wing beats, bill extended, and legs trailing behind. Flies in V and straight line formation.

Nest Identification	
Shape	Location	Lined with lichen, moss, and grass • on ground on small pile of grass or moss • built primarily by female • 3–5 olive to buff eggs blotched with shades of brown and lavender; rather pointed ovate pyriform, 5.8 x 4.1 cm.

Plumage Sexes similar	Habitat	Migration Migratory	Weight 354 g

DATE _____ TIME_____ LOCATION _____

Family SCOLOPACIDAE	Species *Numenius tahitiensis*	Length 43–46 cm	Wingspan 81–88 cm

BRISTLE-THIGHED CURLEW

Little is known about the biology of this rare curlew that nests only in western Alaska. In 1948 its nesting location was one of the last to be revealed among the North American species. Its migratory flight is more than 4,000 km nonstop from Alaska to Hawaii or other islands in the Pacific Ocean. This bird is most often seen alone or in groups of five or six. Similar in size and shape to the Whimbrel, the Bristle-thighed Curlew is more buff-colored overall, and in flight it shows cinnamon-buff wing linings, an unbarred bright tawny-buff rump, and barred tail in flight. The long, stiff, shiny bristles on the thighs and flanks for which the bird is named are not a good field character, for the bird must be practically in the hand to view them.

dark lateral crown stripes border a pale central crown stripe

pale supercilium

dark eye line

upperparts heavily marked with cinnamon-chestnut

long decurved dark bill with creamy pink base

streaked pinkish neck and breast

whitish buff underparts

barred bright rusty tail

short thick bluish gray legs

- **SONG** Long whistle of *chu-a-whit* similar to voice of Black-bellied Plover.
- **BEHAVIOR** On wintering grounds has unusual habit of eating the eggs of other nesting birds, including frigatebirds, albatrosses, boobies, and terns. Sometimes steals eggs from beneath incubating birds. On breeding grounds eats insects, berries, crustaceans, and mollusks. In winter, roosts in trees or sometimes on the roofs of houses or buildings; normally roosts on the ground in rocky tundra breeding areas.
- **BREEDING** Monogamous. Solitary.
- **NESTING** Incubation 25 days by both sexes. Precocial young leave nest soon after hatching; feed themselves but tended by both sexes. Female usually leaves, but male continues to tend young. 1 brood per year.

Similar Birds

WHIMBREL
Lacks bright cinnamon-chestnut rump and uppertail; paler, whiter underparts without buff washes; more slender bill; different voice.

MARBLED GODWIT
Brighter cinnamon on wings and underwing linings; barred rump; upcurved bill.

- **POPULATION** Rare vagrant to Pacific Coast in migration.
- **CONSERVATION** Population well under 10,000. Most vulnerable during flightless stage in winter and long migration over water.

Flight Pattern
Strong swift direct flight with head and neck extended and long legs trailing behind tail.

Nest Identification	
Shape 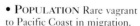 Location ▬ ✱✱	Lined with bits of lichen, moss, and leaves • on ground hidden in vegetation • built by both sexes • 4 olive-buff eggs blotched with brown; pyriform, 6.6 cm long.

Plumage Sexes similar	Habitat ▬▬ ✹	Migration Migratory	Weight 377 g

DATE _____ TIME_____ LOCATION _____

Family SCOLOPACIDAE	Species *Numenius madagascariensis*	Length 56–66 cm	Wingspan 81–89 cm

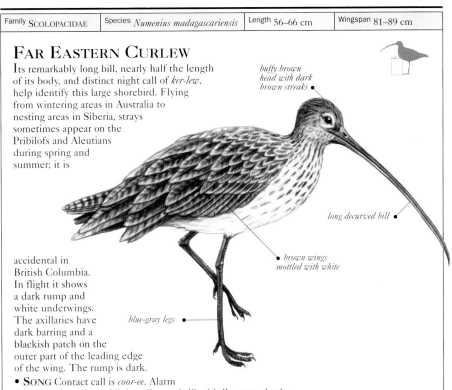

FAR EASTERN CURLEW

Its remarkably long bill, nearly half the length of its body, and distinct night call of *ker-lew*, help identify this large shorebird. Flying from wintering areas in Australia to nesting areas in Siberia, strays sometimes appear on the Pribilofs and Aleutians during spring and summer; it is

buffy brown head with dark brown streaks

long decurved bill

brown wings mottled with white

blue-gray legs

accidental in British Columbia. In flight it shows a dark rump and white underwings. The axillaries have dark barring and a blackish patch on the outer part of the leading edge of the wing. The rump is dark.

• **SONG** Contact call is *coor-ee*. Alarm call of *ker ker-ee-ker-ee*. Night call sounds like bird's name, *ker-lew*.

• **BEHAVIOR** Wary; solitary to large and somewhat dispersed flocks. Active and vocal at night. Sometimes roosts in tall trees or shrubs. Uses beak to probe for burrowing prey. Also picks prey from the surface. Eats crustaceans, marine worms, insects and insect larvae, and other invertebrates.

• **BREEDING** Monogamous. Colonial.

• **NESTING** Incubation 27–29 days by both sexes. Precocial young tended by both parents; leave nest soon after hatching. First flight at 32–38 days. 1 brood per year.

• **POPULATION** Casual on Aleutians and Pribilofs in spring and summer. Accidental in coastal British Columbia. Fairly common to common in breeding range of southeastern Eurasia. Perhaps declining on winter grounds in Australia.

Similar Birds

LONG-BILLED CURLEW Cinnamon overall, including underwings.

Flight Pattern
Steady strong direct flight on rapidly beating wings. Flies in straight line or V formation when in flocks or migrating.

Nest Identification	
Shape 〰 Location ▬	Lined with leaves and grasses • on knoll or dry hill • 4 olive-green eggs marked with brown to greenish brown blotches; oval to short elliptical, 7.1 cm long.

Plumage Sexes similar	Habitat 〰 〰 〰 ▬	Migration Migratory	Weight 771 g

DATE _____ TIME_____ LOCATION _____

| Family SCOLOPACIDAE | Species *Numenius tenuirostris* | Length 38–41 cm | Wingspan 69–79 cm |

SLENDER-BILLED CURLEW

Very little is known about this nearly extinct bird, which breeds in the taiga zone of Siberia. It was recorded just once in Ontario in the 1920s; there are no other recorded sightings of this shorebird in North America. This is the palest of the curlews. The tail is barred brown. The uppertail and rump are mostly white with the white extending up the back in a white wedge.

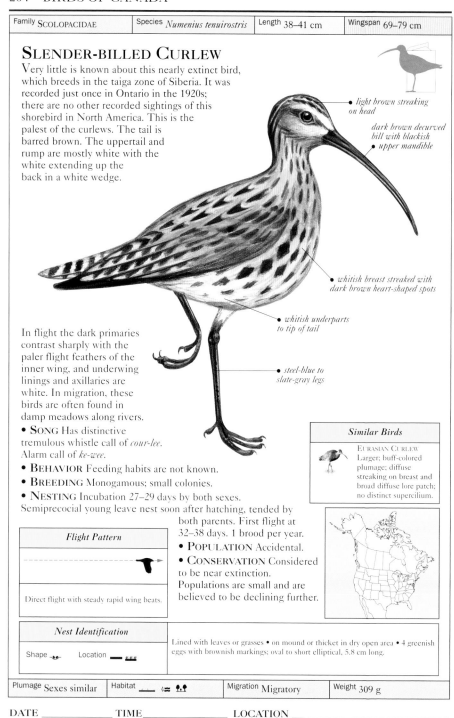

light brown streaking on head

dark brown decurved bill with blackish upper mandible

whitish breast streaked with dark brown heart-shaped spots

whitish underparts to tip of tail

steel-blue to slate-gray legs

In flight the dark primaries contrast sharply with the paler flight feathers of the inner wing, and underwing linings and axillaries are white. In migration, these birds are often found in damp meadows along rivers.

• **SONG** Has distinctive tremulous whistle call of *cour-lee*. Alarm call of *ke-wee*.

• **BEHAVIOR** Feeding habits are not known.

• **BREEDING** Monogamous; small colonies.

• **NESTING** Incubation 27–29 days by both sexes. Semiprecocial young leave nest soon after hatching, tended by both parents. First flight at 32–38 days. 1 brood per year.

• **POPULATION** Accidental.

• **CONSERVATION** Considered to be near extinction. Populations are small and are believed to be declining further.

Similar Birds

EURASIAN CURLEW Larger; buff-colored plumage; diffuse streaking on breast and broad diffuse lore patch; no distinct supercilium.

Flight Pattern

Direct flight with steady rapid wing beats.

Nest Identification

Shape •_• Location ▬ ▰▰▰

Lined with leaves or grasses • on mound or thicket in dry open area • 4 greenish eggs with brownish markings; oval to short elliptical, 5.8 cm long.

| Plumage Sexes similar | Habitat ▬ ⸙≈ ♠♦ | Migration Migratory | Weight 309 g |

DATE _____ TIME_____ LOCATION _____

| Family SCOLOPACIDAE | Species *Numenius americanus* | Length 58 cm | Wingspan 91–102 cm |

LONG-BILLED CURLEW

The largest North American member of the sandpiper family has a very long, slender decurved bill. The male claims and defends large territories with a flapping gliding flight. After courtship and mating, these birds usually nest in dry uplands often near rivers but sometimes rangelands or farmlands. As with other curlews the female is larger than the male. It is distinguished in flight by the long decurved bill and cinnamon underwing linings.

cinnamon-brown upperparts

indistinct eye line

long decurved bill

pinkish or grayish brown base on lower mandible

buff-brown underparts

dull blue-gray legs

- **SONG** Solid melodic ascending *cur-lee*. On breeding grounds gives bubbling warbled *curleeeeeeeeeuuu*.
- **BEHAVIOR** Feeds by probing mud with bill or dunking head under water. Eats adult insects, fly larvae, aquatic insects, mollusks, crustaceans, and small amphibians. Often flies in wedge-shaped flocks, especially in migration.
- **BREEDING** Monogamous. Colonial or semicolonial.
- **NESTING** Incubation 27–30 days by both sexes. Incubating bird sits motionless on nest even if approached. Precocial young leave nest soon after hatching. Tended by both sexes. First flight at 32–45 days. 1 brood per year.
- **POPULATION** Common and widespread in nesting area. Casual to rare on southeastern Atlantic Coast in winter.
- **CONSERVATION** Overgrazing in nesting areas has caused some decline.

Similar Birds

WHIMBREL Smaller; grayer overall; gray-brown head with distinctive stripes; pale whitish gray underparts.

MARBLED GODWIT Smaller; straight or slightly upturned bill; cinnamon secondaries; brighter inner primaries with fewer brown markings.

Flight Pattern

Steady strong wing beats in direct flight. Gliding flight in display on breeding grounds.

Nest Identification

Shape ⌒ ⌒ Location ▬

Lined with a few bits of grass, weeds, and chips • on ground in open prairie • 3–5 pale to olive-buff eggs with brown and olive spotting, 6.6 cm long.

| Plumage Sexes similar | Habitat | Migration Migratory | Weight 544 g |

DATE _____ TIME_____ LOCATION _____

| Family SCOLOPACIDAE | Species *Limosa limosa* | Length 41 cm | Wingspan 76 cm |

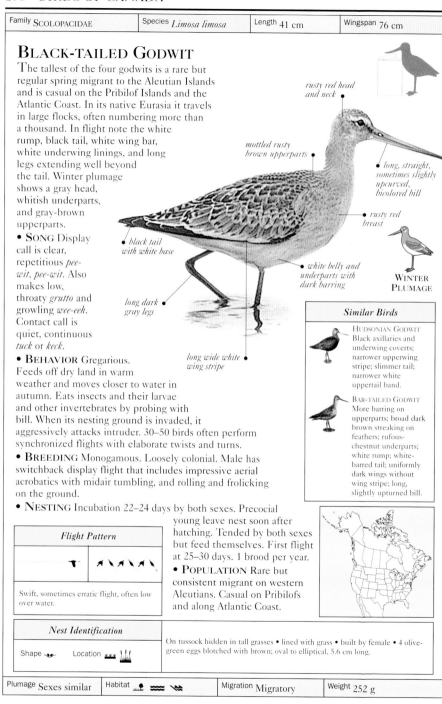

BLACK-TAILED GODWIT

The tallest of the four godwits is a rare but regular spring migrant to the Aleutian Islands and is casual on the Pribilof Islands and the Atlantic Coast. In its native Eurasia it travels in large flocks, often numbering more than a thousand. In flight note the white rump, black tail, white wing bar, white underwing linings, and long legs extending well beyond the tail. Winter plumage shows a gray head, whitish underparts, and gray-brown upperparts.

rusty red head and neck

mottled rusty brown upperparts

long, straight, sometimes slightly upcurved, bicolored bill

rusty red breast

• **SONG** Display call is clear, repetitious *pee-wit, pee-wit*. Also makes low, throaty *grutto* and growling *wee-eeh*. Contact call is quiet, continuous *tuck* or *keck*.

black tail with white base

white belly and underparts with dark barring

WINTER PLUMAGE

long dark gray legs

• **BEHAVIOR** Gregarious. Feeds off dry land in warm weather and moves closer to water in autumn. Eats insects and their larvae and other invertebrates by probing with bill. When its nesting ground is invaded, it aggressively attacks intruder. 30–50 birds often perform synchronized flights with elaborate twists and turns.

long wide white wing stripe

• **BREEDING** Monogamous. Loosely colonial. Male has switchback display flight that includes impressive aerial acrobatics with midair tumbling, and rolling and frolicking on the ground.

• **NESTING** Incubation 22–24 days by both sexes. Precocial young leave nest soon after hatching. Tended by both sexes but feed themselves. First flight at 25–30 days. 1 brood per year.

Similar Birds

HUDSONIAN GODWIT
Black axillaries and underwing coverts; narrower upperwing stripe; slimmer tail; narrower white uppertail band.

BAR-TAILED GODWIT
More barring on upperparts; broad dark brown streaking on feathers; rufous-chestnut underparts; white rump; white-barred tail; uniformly dark wings without wing stripe; long, slightly upturned bill.

• **POPULATION** Rare but consistent migrant on western Aleutians. Casual on Pribilofs and along Atlantic Coast.

Flight Pattern	

Swift, sometimes erratic flight, often low over water.

Nest Identification	
Shape ⌣ Location	On tussock hidden in tall grasses • lined with grass • built by female • 4 olive-green eggs blotched with brown; oval to elliptical, 5.6 cm long.

| Plumage Sexes similar | Habitat | Migration Migratory | Weight 252 g |

DATE _____ TIME_____ LOCATION _____

Family SCOLOPACIDAE	Species *Limosa haemastica*	Length 38 cm	Wingspan 69 cm

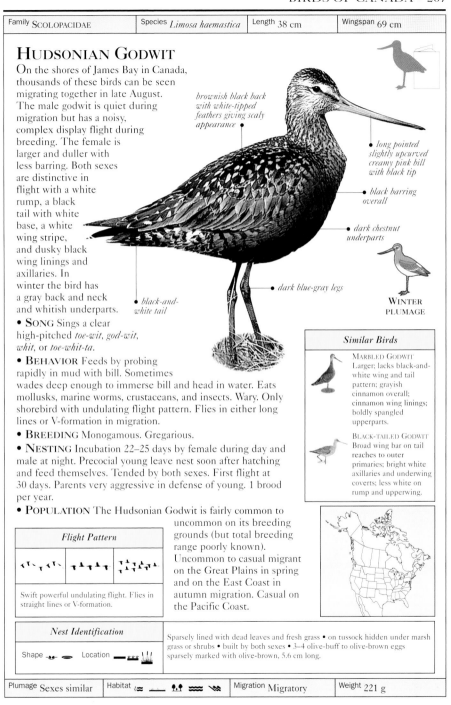

HUDSONIAN GODWIT

On the shores of James Bay in Canada, thousands of these birds can be seen migrating together in late August. The male godwit is quiet during migration but has a noisy, complex display flight during breeding. The female is larger and duller with less barring. Both sexes are distinctive in flight with a white rump, a black tail with white base, a white wing stripe, and dusky black wing linings and axillaries. In winter the bird has a gray back and neck and whitish underparts.

brownish black back with white-tipped feathers giving scaly appearance

long pointed slightly upcurved creamy pink bill with black tip

black barring overall

dark chestnut underparts

dark blue-gray legs

black-and-white tail

WINTER PLUMAGE

- **SONG** Sings a clear high-pitched *toe-wit, god-wit, whit*, or *toe-whit-ta*.
- **BEHAVIOR** Feeds by probing rapidly in mud with bill. Sometimes wades deep enough to immerse bill and head in water. Eats mollusks, marine worms, crustaceans, and insects. Wary. Only shorebird with undulating flight pattern. Flies in either long lines or V-formation in migration.
- **BREEDING** Monogamous. Gregarious.
- **NESTING** Incubation 22–25 days by female during day and male at night. Precocial young leave nest soon after hatching and feed themselves. Tended by both sexes. First flight at 30 days. Parents very aggressive in defense of young. 1 brood per year.
- **POPULATION** The Hudsonian Godwit is fairly common to uncommon on its breeding grounds (but total breeding range poorly known). Uncommon to casual migrant on the Great Plains in spring and on the East Coast in autumn migration. Casual on the Pacific Coast.

Similar Birds

MARBLED GODWIT
Larger; lacks black-and-white wing and tail pattern; grayish cinnamon overall; cinnamon wing linings; boldly spangled upperparts.

BLACK-TAILED GODWIT
Broad wing bar on tail reaches to outer primaries; bright white axillaries and underwing coverts; less white on rump and upperwing.

Flight Pattern

Swift powerful undulating flight. Flies in straight lines or V-formation.

Nest Identification

Shape ⌣ ⬭   Location ▬ ▬ ▥

Sparsely lined with dead leaves and fresh grass • on tussock hidden under marsh grass or shrubs • built by both sexes • 3–4 olive-buff to olive-brown eggs sparsely marked with olive-brown, 5.6 cm long.

Plumage Sexes similar	Habitat	Migration Migratory	Weight 221 g

DATE _____ TIME _____ LOCATION _____

Family SCOLOPACIDAE	Species *Limosa lapponica*	Length 41 cm	Wingspan 71 cm

BAR-TAILED GODWIT

This bird was considered a delicacy in the fifteenth century. It can be distinguished from the similar curlews by its upturned bill. These large shorebirds fly in big flocks and perform elaborate aerial movements. The female is larger and paler overall with streaked light chestnut or pinkish underparts. In winter both sexes are gray. In flight toes extend beyond the tip of the tail, and the rump is either whitish or

long slightly upturned two-toned bill

solid red-chestnut underparts

gray-brown or black barring on tail

dark gray legs

WINTER PLUMAGE

barred, as are the wing linings. The wings are dark and lack stripes, and the white tail has dark brown to black bars.

• **SONG** Usually silent. On breeding grounds gives trilling song; slightly nasal dry *kek*; barking *kak-kak;* or *keewick.*

• **BEHAVIOR** Feeds by wading into water and picking from mud's surface and by probing with side-to-side motion. Eats insects, crustaceans, marine worms, and mollusks. Nests on tundra and in swampy areas near lakes. Flocks in winter.

• **BREEDING** Monogamous. Colonial.

• **NESTING** Incubation 20–21 days by both sexes. Soon after hatching precocial young are led to nearby marshes where they stay until they are able to fly. Young feed themselves but are tended by both sexes. 1 brood per year.

• **POPULATION** Uncommon breeder in western Alaska. Casual along Pacific Coast. Very rare migrant along Atlantic Coast.

Similar Birds

MARBLED GODWIT
Bright cinnamon wings, rump, and tail.

BLACK-TAILED GODWIT
Longer legs and neck; flatter forehead; slightly more blunt, less up-curved bill; white rump and belly; heavy, irregular barring on lower breast and belly; wide black terminal tail band; bold white stripe in wing.

Flight Pattern

Direct flight with strong steady wing beats.

Nest Identification

Shape ⌒ ⬬ Location ⟱ 🌱

Usually on moist or mossy tundra hidden in grass on tussock • lined with moss, lichen, birch leaves, and grasses • built by both sexes • 2–4 olive or pale brown eggs sparsely spotted with brown, 5.6 cm long.

Plumage Sexes similar	Habitat	Migration Migratory	Weight 306 g

Family SCOLOPACIDAE	Species *Limosa fedoa*	Length 46–51 cm	Wingspan 81 cm

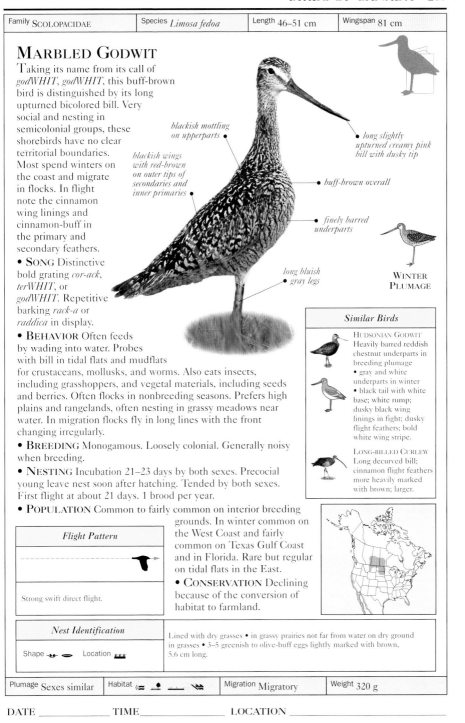

MARBLED GODWIT

Taking its name from its call of *god*WHIT, *god*WHIT, this buff-brown bird is distinguished by its long upturned bicolored bill. Very social and nesting in semicolonial groups, these shorebirds have no clear territorial boundaries. Most spend winters on the coast and migrate in flocks. In flight note the cinnamon wing linings and cinnamon-buff in the primary and secondary feathers.

blackish mottling on upperparts

blackish wings with red-brown on outer tips of secondaries and inner primaries

long slightly upturned creamy pink bill with dusky tip

buff-brown overall

finely barred underparts

long bluish gray legs

WINTER PLUMAGE

• **SONG** Distinctive bold grating *cor-ack*, *ter*WHIT, or *god*WHIT. Repetitive barking *rack-a* or *raddica* in display.

• **BEHAVIOR** Often feeds by wading into water. Probes with bill in tidal flats and mudflats for crustaceans, mollusks, and worms. Also eats insects, including grasshoppers, and vegetal materials, including seeds and berries. Often flocks in nonbreeding seasons. Prefers high plains and rangelands, often nesting in grassy meadows near water. In migration flocks fly in long lines with the front changing irregularly.

• **BREEDING** Monogamous. Loosely colonial. Generally noisy when breeding.

• **NESTING** Incubation 21–23 days by both sexes. Precocial young leave nest soon after hatching. Tended by both sexes. First flight at about 21 days. 1 brood per year.

• **POPULATION** Common to fairly common on interior breeding grounds. In winter common on the West Coast and fairly common on Texas Gulf Coast and in Florida. Rare but regular on tidal flats in the East.

• **CONSERVATION** Declining because of the conversion of habitat to farmland.

Similar Birds

HUDSONIAN GODWIT Heavily barred reddish chestnut underparts in breeding plumage • gray and white underparts in winter • black tail with white base; white rump; dusky black wing linings in fight; dusky flight feathers; bold white wing stripe.

LONG-BILLED CURLEW Long decurved bill; cinnamon flight feathers more heavily marked with brown; larger.

Flight Pattern
Strong swift direct flight.

Nest Identification	
Shape	Location	Lined with dry grasses • in grassy prairies not far from water on dry ground in grasses • 3–5 greenish to olive-buff eggs lightly marked with brown, 5.6 cm long.

Plumage Sexes similar	Habitat	Migration Migratory	Weight 320 g

| Family SCOLOPACIDAE | Species *Arenaria interpres* | Length 23–25 cm | Wingspan 43–46 cm |

RUDDY TURNSTONE

The alarm cry of this stout little ploverlike shorebird alerts other birds to possible danger. It often is seen probing the drift line on beaches, even cleaning up leftovers from beach picnics. Some will take bread from a human hand. In flight the vividly patterned body and wings are unmistakable in bold rusty reds, blacks, and white. Winter plumage shows a brown-and-white face, dull brown wings and back, and a brown bib but retains the striking white stripes on the wings, back, and tail.

black-and-white face

short pointed dark bill tilts up at tip

black, white, and rusty red harlequin-patterned back and wings

white chin

black bib on breast

• **SONG** Low guttural rattle. Alarm call is *chick-ik* or *kewk*. Flight call is *ket-ah-kek* or *kit-it-it*. While feeding gives contact call of *tut*.

white underparts

short orange-red legs (duller in winter)

• **BEHAVIOR** Roots through seaweed and tips over stones, shells, and other things washed up onto shore. Feeds on insects, mollusks, crustaceans and their eggs, worms, and bird eggs. Sometimes eats discards of birds such as oystercatchers, including carrion. May eat coconut meat as well. Forages alone or in small flocks often mixed with other shorebirds. Other shorebirds may nest near Turnstones to gain protection from predators.

WINTER PLUMAGE

• **BREEDING** Monogamous.

• **NESTING** Incubation 21–24 days by both sexes, but female does more. Precocial young leave nest soon after hatching but feed themselves. Tended by both sexes, but female leaves before first flight at 19–21 days. 1 brood per year.

Similar Birds

BLACK TURNSTONE
Dark chin; lacks chestnut or rust coloring; dark reddish brown legs
• Alaskan and West Coast range.

• **POPULATION** Common and widespread on tundra breeding grounds and on coasts in winter. Casual to rare inland in migration, except around the Great Lakes where the species is more common.

Flight Pattern
Swift direct flight with rapid wing beats.

Nest Identification	
Shape ⌣ Location ⁙ ▬	Lined with bits of dry plants, withered leaves, moss, grass, or seaweed • in open tundra • built by female • 2–4 olive-green to olive-buff eggs marked with browns and blacks, 4.1 cm long.

| Plumage Sexes similar | Habitat ⌣ 〰 | Migration Migratory | Weight 111 g |

DATE _____ TIME_____ LOCATION _____

Family SCOLOPACIDAE	Species *Arenaria melanocephala*	Length 23 cm	Wingspan 43–46 cm

BLACK TURNSTONE

Stockier, with broader wings than the Ruddy Turnstone, this bird blends so well with its rocky habitat that it can barely be seen when still. The male displays by zigzagging around the female, flying high, then diving downward so

dusky gray-black uppparts, head, and neck

white spot in front of eye

black bill slightly upturned on end

dusky gray-black breast sprinkled and edged white

WINTER PLUMAGE

fast that its feathers make an audible vibration. It breeds in coastal Alaska and winters along the Pacific Coast from south-central Alaska to Mexico. In flight it shows a white back, white wing stripe, and a white base to the tail. In winter plumage the Black Turnstone lacks the spot in front of the eye and the white spotting on the breast, and it displays duller yellow legs.

dusky orange legs

white belly

Similar Birds

RUDDY TURNSTONE White chin; harlequin black-and-white face pattern; black bib; rusty chestnut upperparts; orange legs; white underparts.

SURFBIRD Winter • larger; darker gray head, breast, and upperparts; white chin and underparts; dark gray chevrons and streaks on lower breast, sides, flanks, and undertail coverts; dull yellow legs and feet; stouter bill has dull yellow base to lower mandible • in flight shows white wing stripe and white tail with black terminal band.

• **SONG** Guttural rattle, *skirrr*, higher than that of Ruddy Turnstone. A thin *peet-weet-weet* on breeding grounds.

• **BEHAVIOR** Using its wedgelike bill, turns seashells and rocks to forage for insects, as its name suggests. Also eats barnacles, crustaceans, and mollusks. Uses beak to pry food off rocks or inserts beak into shell to open. Solitary feeder or forages in small flocks; often with other species of shorebirds.

• **BREEDING** Monogamous. Colonial.

• **NESTING** Incubation 21–24 days by both sexes. Precocial young leave nest soon after hatching; feed themselves. First flight at 23 days. 1 brood per year.

• **POPULATION** Common, but has declined in past 20 years; reason undetermined.

Flight Pattern

Swift direct flight on rapidly beating wings. On breeding grounds male has zigzag display in flight.

Nest Identification
Shape 〜 Location ▬ 〜 〜

Lined with grass • built by both sexes • 3–4 yellow-green to olive eggs with dark brown blotches; oval to pyriform, 4.1 cm long.

Plumage Sexes similar	Habitat 〜	Migration Migratory	Weight 113 g

DATE _____ TIME_____ LOCATION _____

Family SCOLOPACIDAE	Species *Aphriza virgata*	Length 25 cm	Wingspan 51 cm

SURFBIRD

The Surfbird is distinguished from similar species by its short thick blunt black-tipped, yellow-based bill and distinctive plumage showcased in flight. Aloft the bird is easily spotted with its white wing bar and broad white tail with broad black triangle at the tip. The Surfbird's wintering range

head and upperparts heavily streaked with dusky black spots

white- and chestnut-edged upperparts

mostly golden rufous scapulars

short stout black bill with yellow base

heavily streaked and spotted dusky throat, breast, sides, and flanks

yellowish green legs

WINTER PLUMAGE

extends on the coasts from southeastern Alaska to southern Chile, where it forages in the spray of the surf line. During this time the bird's head, upperparts, and breast plumage are a solid dark gray.

- **SONG** A short *wickee-doo* or *week-doo* or *pee-weet*. Sometimes a series of calls, *tee tee teet*, *krrree krree*, and *tew tew* or *tew-it-tewit*.
- **BEHAVIOR** During nesting season often seen scampering across mountain rocks and feeding on beetles, flies, wasps, caterpillars, and other insects. Near stony or rocky shores eats small mollusks, crustaceans, and soft parts of barnacles. Highly defensive of nests, the Surfbird will guard eggs from grazing sheep, caribou, and other threatening animals, including humans, by delaying flight until the final moments of a predator's approach. Then it explodes into flight in the predator's face, forcing it to step back from the nest site.
- **BREEDING** Monogamous. Gregarious.
- **NESTING** Incubation performed by both sexes, but time unknown. Precocial young leave nest soon after hatching, feeding themselves, but tended by both parents. First flight estimated at 19–21 days. 1 brood per year.
- **POPULATION** Stable, but uncommon.

Similar Birds

ROCK SANDPIPER
In breeding season has black lower breast patch; chestnut-edged black crown and back; white wing stripe and dark tail show in flight; long slender dark bill.

BLACK TURNSTONE
Winter plumage • short bill, slightly upturned at tip; blackish gray upperparts and breast; bold black-and-white wing pattern; white back; black rump; white base to black tail.

Flight Pattern

Swift flight on rapidly beating wings. Darts away over water in closely knit flock of 30–50 that turns and twists in unison.

Nest Identification

Shape ⚬   Location ▬

Moss-lined with lichen and dead leaves • shallow depression of bare dry rock on ledge or natural depression above timberline • built by male and female • 4 buff eggs with reddish brown spots; piriform, 4.3 x 3.0 cm.

Plumage Sexes similar	Habitat ▲ 🦃	Migration Migratory	Weight 184 g

DATE _____ TIME_____ LOCATION _____

Family SCOLOPACIDAE	Species *Calidris canutus*	Length 25–28 cm	Wingspan 51 cm

RED KNOT

At one time the Red Knot was one of the most abundant shorebirds in North America, but 19th-century market hunters diminished its population by slaughtering it in both spring and autumn migrations. It can be distinguished by its chunky body, short bill, and short greenish legs. Known as classic high-arctic breeders and long-distance migrants, Red Knots winter mostly in the lower half of South America and may travel 30,575 km per year. Dappled brown-black upperparts and chestnut underparts turn to pale gray upperparts and white underparts in winter.

buff-chestnut face

dappled brown-black upperparts

WINTER PLUMAGE

short, slightly curved black bill

buff-chestnut breast

finely barred pale grayish white tail and rump

short greenish legs

- **SONG** Generally silent. Feeding birds and flocks in flight emit harsh monosyllabic *knut.* Males on breeding grounds whistle a melodious *poor-me.*
- **BEHAVIOR** Generally feeds on beaches, tidal flats, and lagoons. Eats mollusks, crabs, and insects and their larvae. When feeding in mud probes for food with bill. Often migrates and winters in large flocks that wheel, bank, and roll together in tight, dashing formations. Breeding display flight involves high, circling flight on still or quivering wings, ending with a rapid, tumbling fall, and landing with wings upraised.
- **BREEDING** Monogamous. Gregarious.
- **NESTING** Incubation 21–23 days by both sexes. Precocial young leave nest soon after hatching. Tended by both sexes. First flight at 18–20 days. Female leaves before first flight. 1 brood per year.
- **POPULATION** Uncommon to fairly common on breeding grounds and in migration on Atlantic Coast. Uncommon transient on Pacific Coast. A rare transient inland.
- **CONSERVATION** Federal protection has helped increase populations of this bird.

Similar Birds

CURLEW SANDPIPER
Slim and small; longer curved bill; pale rump • red underparts in breeding plumage.

GREAT KNOT
Longer bill; large body; lacks robin-red face, neck, and underparts; heavily spotted white underparts; heavy black spotting on breast; black streaking on neck and head; more heavily barred pale rump and tail • spring migrant in western Alaska.

Flight Pattern
Swift direct flight with rapid wing beats. Flies in V or straight line formation.

Nest Identification	Lined with leaves, lichen, and moss • hollow in clumps of lichens among rocks and scant plant life near water • built by both sexes, but male does most • 3–4 olive-buff eggs marked with brown-black spot; pyriform, 4.1 cm long.
Shape 〜 Location ▬ ▦ ▦	

Plumage Sexes similar	Habitat ▬ 〜	Migration Migratory	Weight 125 g

DATE _____ TIME_____ LOCATION _____

Family SCOLOPACIDAE	Species *Calidris alba*	Length 20 cm	Wingspan 38 cm

SANDERLING

This sandpiper runs back and forth on the beach with the ebb and flow of the water, chasing receding waves to snatch up exposed invertebrates. It also stands on one leg for long periods. The palest of the sandpipers, this bird differs from others in its family by its lack of a hind toe. Its light-colored winter plumage blends in with dry sand. The Sanderling nests in the arctic of both hemispheres and winters to the southern end of both, traveling as far as 12,875 km between its summer and winter homes. In flight the wings show a broad white stripe, black leading and trailing edges, and white underwings. Its white tail has black central tail feathers.

rusty wash over head and back

JUVENILE

black bill

black shoulders

white underparts

rusty wash over breast

black legs and feet

WINTER PLUMAGE

- **SONG** Harsh *kree*. Also gives a *twick* or *kip* while in flight.
- **BEHAVIOR** Hunts for sand crabs and mollusks in the sand at the water's edge. Also eats other crustaceans, marine worms, amphipods, isopods, and insects. On arctic breeding grounds eats insects and insect larvae, some plants, leaves, and algae. In flight flocks often wheel and turn, changing direction with flashing wings and a change of color, first showing dark backs then light underparts.
- **BREEDING** Monogamous or polyandrous. Colonial.
- **NESTING** Incubation 24–31 days usually by male, while female often lays second clutch, incubating 1 while male incubates other. Some females take 2 mates, lay a clutch in each nest, then leave the males to tend the eggs and young in their respective nests. Precocial young leave nest soon after hatching; feed themselves but tended by at least 1 parent; female leaves if male is present. First flight at 17 days. 1–2 broods per year.
- **POPULATION** Common.
- **CONSERVATION** Decline due to destruction of habitat.

Similar Birds

RED KNOT
Larger; in breeding plumage rusty red underparts extend onto lower breast and upper belly; barred flanks and undertail coverts; barred rump; in nonbreeding lacks black in shoulders.

DUNLIN
Slightly larger; stout bill droops at the tip
• in winter has gray-brown upperparts, lores, and cheeks; grayish throat and upper breast with fine dusky streaking; lacks black in bend of wing.

Flight Pattern

Swift direct flight with rapid wing beats.

Nest Identification

Shape ••• 🥚 Location ▬ ▬

Lined with small leaves, grass, lichen, mosses, or willow leaves • on high, well-drained, rocky tundra • built by both sexes, but male does more • 3–4 dull olive-green or brown eggs sparsely spotted with brown and black, 3.6 cm long.

Plumage Sexes similar	Habitat 〰 〰 ▬	Migration Migratory	Weight 119 g

DATE _____ TIME_____ LOCATION _____

Family SCOLOPACIDAE	Species *Calidris pusilla*	Length 17 cm	Wingspan 28–33 cm

SEMIPALMATED SANDPIPER

This coastal inhabitant gets its name from the partial webbing it has between its front toes. This bird often mingles with other shorebirds such as sanderlings and Semipalmated Plovers around the time of high tide. Like most shorebirds, Semipalmated Sandpipers will frequently sleep standing on one or both legs, with their bill tucked into their back feathers. Sometimes they will travel along the beach hopping on one leg. Grayer in all plumages than most peeps and have less streaking on the breast and no spotting on the flanks.

trace wash of rufous on crown, auriculars, and scapulars

dusky smudge across eye

gray-brown upperparts, crown, and nape

white face and throat

black semi-straight blunt-tipped bill, deep at base

dusky dark-brown-streaked chest side patches

thick short body

black legs and feet

white underparts

- **SONG** Short *churk* or *churp*. On breeding ground, song given in flight is a monotonous *kee-kee-kee-kee*.

- **BEHAVIOR** The bird is often seen running along the beach, pecking and occasionally probing the sand, searching for insects, worms, small mollusks, and small crustaceans. Generally feeds farther from the water's edge than other peeps. Often gathers in large flocks in migration.

- **BREEDING** Monogamous. Gregarious. Aggressive during breeding season.

- **NESTING** Incubation 18–22 days by both sexes. Precocial young leave nest on day of hatching and feed themselves, tended by both parents. Female abandons after few days. First flight at 14–19 days. 1 brood per year.

- **POPULATION** Fairly common to common on breeding grounds. Common migrant from Atlantic Coast to central Great Plains; rare migrant in the West, south of Canada. Casual to rare in Florida in winter.

- **CONSERVATION** Species still abundant but is being threatened due to diminishing stopover points.

WINTER PLUMAGE

Similar Birds

WESTERN SANDPIPER Bright rufous on scapulars, back, ear patch, and crown; gray plumage, less uniformly brown; larger and lankier; longer legs; longer, slightly decurved bill (especially female).

Flight Pattern

Swift flight on rapidly beating wings. Flushed birds rise in zigzag pattern. Flocks twist and turn as precise unit.

Nest Identification

Shape ~ Location ***

Grass-lined with leaves and moss • nests generally built on grassy slope or mound surrounded by short vegetation • built by both sexes • 2–4 whitish to olive-buff eggs, blotched with brown, chestnut, or gray; ovate pyriform to subpyriform, 2.0 x 3.0 cm.

Plumage Sexes similar	Habitat	Migration Migratory	Weight 31 g

| Family SCOLOPACIDAE | Species *Calidris mauri* | Length 15–18 cm | Wingspan 30–36 cm |

WESTERN SANDPIPER

A long-distance migrant, the Western Sandpiper flies southeast and remains on North and South American coasts during the winter months. It is the western relative of the Semipalmated Sandpiper, which it closely resembles

bright rufous crown

rufous base of scapulars

long tapered black bill slightly drooped at the tip

bright rufous ear patches

arrow-shaped spots on sides

partially webbed toes

black legs and feet

WINTER PLUMAGE

except for a longer bill that usually appears slightly drooped at the tip. In breeding plumage it has arrow-shaped spots on the sides and breast and rufous on the crown, ear patches, and scapulars. In winter plumage it is one of the palest "peeps," with almost no contrast in the faintly mottled upperparts.

• **SONG** High raspy *jeet* or *cheet*.
• **BEHAVIOR** Often can be identified by a distinctive feeding pattern: while snatching invertebrates it occasionally eats with its head immersed in the water. Feeds primarily on insects but also takes small crustaceans, mollusks, and worms. In migration and on wintering grounds, often occurs in large flocks. Coastal outside breeding season, but fairly common inland in migration.
• **BREEDING** Monogamous. Colonial. Highly gregarious.
• **NESTING** Incubation 18–21 days by both sexes. Precocial young leave nest a few hours after hatching. Female departs, but male tends young. Young feed themselves. First flight at 17–21 days. 1 brood per year.
• **POPULATION** Common to abundant on breeding grounds; common in migration and on US coastal wintering grounds.
• **CONSERVATION** Abundant but still vulnerable to habitat loss at stopover points.

Similar Birds

SEMIPALMATED SANDPIPER
Shorter bill without drooped tip; duller in color; less rufous; faint or nonexistent mantle and scapular lines; dark brown upperparts edged with buff; makes harsh *churk*.

LEAST SANDPIPER
Smaller; brown wash on head, head, neck, and breast with dark brown streaking; yellow-green legs and feet.

Flight Pattern

Swift direct flight with rapid wing beats. Large tight flocks twist and turn in coordinated movements.

Nest Identification

Shape ⚬ Location ▬ ❧

Lined with leaves, grass, and lichens • slightly elevated on moist or dry tundra near water • male hollows out several sites; female chooses one and lines nest • 3–5 whitish brown eggs marked with red-brown spots; pyriform, 2.2 x 3.0 cm inches.

| Plumage Sexes similar | Habitat ▬ ▲ 🦆 | Migration Migratory | Weight 23 g |

DATE _____ TIME_____ LOCATION _____

Family SCOLOPACIDAE	Species *Calidris ruficollis*	Length 16 cm	Wingspan 28–30 cm

RED-NECKED STINT

Previously called the Rufous-necked Sandpiper, this native of Asia is a rare breeder in the summer in western and northern Alaska. It is one of the easier "peeps" to identify in breeding plumage, with rufous on the head, neck, and mantle. Adults migrate before juveniles and sometimes

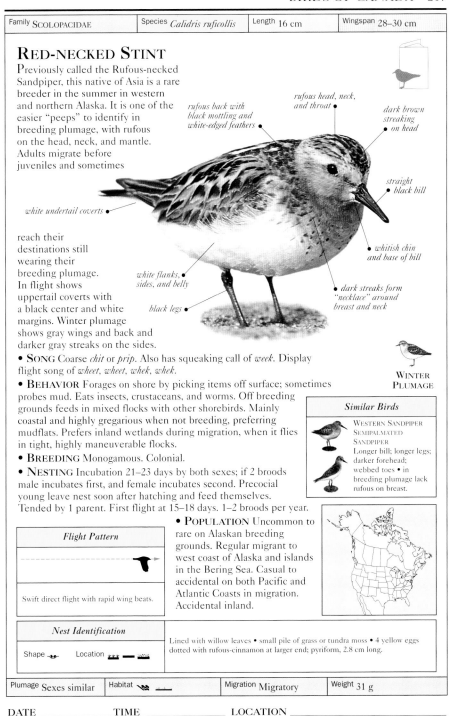

rufous back with black mottling and white-edged feathers

rufous head, neck, and throat

dark brown streaking on head

straight black bill

white undertail coverts

whitish chin and base of bill

reach their destinations still wearing their breeding plumage. In flight shows uppertail coverts with a black center and white margins. Winter plumage shows gray wings and back and darker gray streaks on the sides.

white flanks, sides, and belly

black legs

dark streaks form "necklace" around breast and neck

WINTER PLUMAGE

- **SONG** Coarse *chit* or *prip*. Also has squeaking call of *week*. Display flight song of *wheet, wheet, whek, whek*.
- **BEHAVIOR** Forages on shore by picking items off surface; sometimes probes mud. Eats insects, crustaceans, and worms. Off breeding grounds feeds in mixed flocks with other shorebirds. Mainly coastal and highly gregarious when not breeding, preferring mudflats. Prefers inland wetlands during migration, when it flies in tight, highly maneuverable flocks.
- **BREEDING** Monogamous. Colonial.
- **NESTING** Incubation 21–23 days by both sexes; if 2 broods male incubates first, and female incubates second. Precocial young leave nest soon after hatching and feed themselves. Tended by 1 parent. First flight at 15–18 days. 1–2 broods per year.

Similar Birds

WESTERN SANDPIPER
SEMIPALMATED SANDPIPER
Longer bill; longer legs; darker forehead; webbed toes • in breeding plumage lack rufous on breast.

- **POPULATION** Uncommon to rare on Alaskan breeding grounds. Regular migrant to west coast of Alaska and islands in the Bering Sea. Casual to accidental on both Pacific and Atlantic Coasts in migration. Accidental inland.

Flight Pattern

Swift direct flight with rapid wing beats.

Nest Identification

Shape — Location

Lined with willow leaves • small pile of grass or tundra moss • 4 yellow eggs dotted with rufous-cinnamon at larger end; pyriform, 2.8 cm long.

Plumage Sexes similar	Habitat	Migration Migratory	Weight 31 g

DATE _____ TIME_____ LOCATION _____

Family SCOLOPACIDAE	Species *Calidris minuta*	Length 15 cm	Wingspan 28–30 cm

LITTLE STINT

This sparrow-sized native of the Arctic regions was first recognized in North America in 1975. Since that time it has been found as a casual migrant on both coasts and as a rare visitor, usually in spring migration, to islands off western Alaska. In breeding plumage its small size; short straight black bill; black legs; and rusty red head, upperparts, and breast are good clues to its identity. Its winter plumage shows dull grayish brown upperparts, individual black feathers with rusty and white edgings, and a gray wash with dark grayish brown streaks over its breast. In all plumages the long primary projection separates this species from other similar "peeps."

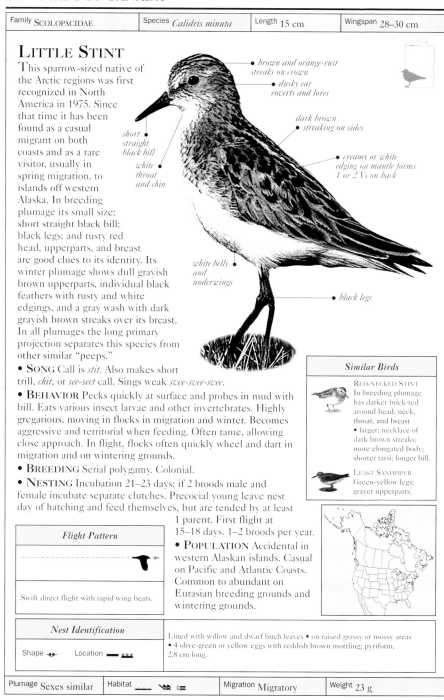

brown and orange-rust streaks on crown

dusky ear coverts and lores

dark brown streaking on sides

creamy or white edging on mantle forms 1 or 2 Vs on back

short straight black bill

white throat and chin

white belly and underwings

black legs

- **SONG** Call is *stit*. Also makes short trill, *chit*, or *see-seet* call. Sings weak *svee-svee-svee*.
- **BEHAVIOR** Pecks quickly at surface and probes in mud with bill. Eats various insect larvae and other invertebrates. Highly gregarious, moving in flocks in migration and winter. Becomes aggressive and territorial when feeding. Often tame, allowing close approach. In flight, flocks often quickly wheel and dart in migration and on wintering grounds.
- **BREEDING** Serial polygamy. Colonial.
- **NESTING** Incubation 21–23 days; if 2 broods male and female incubate separate clutches. Precocial young leave nest day of hatching and feed themselves, but are tended by at least 1 parent. First flight at 15–18 days. 1–2 broods per year.
- **POPULATION** Accidental in western Alaskan islands. Casual on Pacific and Atlantic Coasts. Common to abundant on Eurasian breeding grounds and wintering grounds.

Similar Birds

RED-NECKED STINT
In breeding plumage has darker brick-red around head, neck, throat, and breast.
- larger; necklace of dark brown streaks; more elongated body; shorter tarsi; longer bill.

LEAST SANDPIPER
Green-yellow legs; grayer upperparts.

Flight Pattern
Swift direct flight with rapid wing beats.

Nest Identification	
Shape 🐦 Location ▬ ▬▬	Lined with willow and dwarf birch leaves • on raised grassy or mossy areas • 4 olive-green or yellow eggs with reddish brown mottling; pyriform, 2.8 cm long.

Plumage Sexes similar	Habitat ▬ 🦆 ≈	Migration Migratory	Weight 23 g

DATE _____ TIME_____ LOCATION _____

Family SCOLOPACIDAE	Species *Calidris subminuta*	Length 13–15 cm	Wingspan 28–30 cm

LONG-TOED STINT

Longer toes, particularly middle and hind digits, easily distinguish this East Asian shorebird from other stints and "peeps." However, this is a very difficult characteristic to see in the field. More useful field marks are the long neck, rufous cap, white superciliary stripe, and dark forehead extending to the base of the bill, sometimes joining the dusky lores. The legs and feet are yellow-green. Juveniles are similar to breeding adults, which have a buffy wash on the breast and a dark eye stripe expanding into a dark auricular patch. A long-distance migrant, this bird winters on the coasts of India, Asia, and Australia. In flight it shows a narrow white wing stripe and a gray tail with dark central tail feathers.

dark rufous-brown-streaked crown

gray-brown and rufous-buff-edged upperparts

thin blackish bill

green base to lower mandible

gray-brown-streaked breast and neck

white underparts

JUVENILE

• **SONG** Slow repeated *roer*. Most common call is soft bubbling brief *prrt, chrrup,* or *chulip*. Other calls include grating *tik-tik-tik*.

• **BEHAVIOR** Frequents grassy swampy regions and alpine tundra. Feeds in small flocks or alone, either slowly and mouselike or actively with quick little runs. Eats a variety of invertebrates in vegetation at water's edge. Lures intruders from nest with intensive distraction display. When alarmed, freezes crouched flat or stands upright with neck extended.

• **BREEDING** Monogamous. Colonial. Displaying male circles high while singing.

• **NESTING** Incubation 18–22 days by both sexes. Precocial young leave nest few hours after hatching and feed themselves. Female often deserts, leaving male to care for young. First flight at 17–21 days. 1 brood per year.

• **POPULATION** Uncommon to rare in native Eurasia. Casual in migration to islands in Bering Sea; fairly common in spring migration on outer Aleutians. Rare to accidental on West Coast and elsewhere.

• **CONSERVATION** Common to fairly common, though vulnerable to habitat loss at stopover grounds.

Similar Birds

LITTLE STINT
Smaller and darker black legs; shorter toes; similar coloring; short straight bill; rufous upperparts and sides of breast, with dark spotting pattern; white underparts.

LEAST SANDPIPER
Closely resembles; mouselike bird; medium-length slightly decurved bill; gray-brown head, chest, and upperparts; white underparts; indistinct whitish supercilium; yellow legs and feet.

Flight Pattern
Swift direct flight with rapid wing beats. If flushed rises quickly with fast jerking flight, wing beats weak and fluttery.

Nest Identification	Grass- and leaf-lined with sedges and lichen • on slightly elevated moist to dry tundra by water, usually under shrub • male builds several scrapes, female chooses one and lines • 3–5 whitish brown eggs, marked with red-brown spots; pyriform to subpyriform, 3.0 x 2.3 cm.
Shape 〰 Location ▬	

Plumage Sexes similar	Habitat ___ 〰 ≈	Migration Migratory	Weight 31 g

DATE _____ TIME_____ LOCATION _____

Family SCOLOPACIDAE	Species *Calidris minutilla*	Length 15 cm	Wingspan 28–30 cm

LEAST SANDPIPER

During migration a small sandpiper on the edge of an inland pool or wet area is likely to be this species. The Least Sandpiper is the smallest of the native North American sandpipers and among the smallest waders

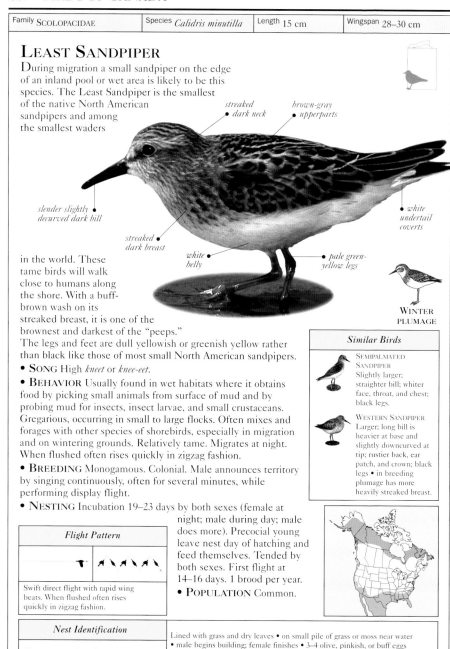

streaked dark neck

brown-gray upperparts

slender slightly decurved dark bill

streaked dark breast

white belly

white undertail coverts

pale green-yellow legs

WINTER PLUMAGE

in the world. These tame birds will walk close to humans along the shore. With a buff-brown wash on its streaked breast, it is one of the brownest and darkest of the "peeps." The legs and feet are dull yellowish or greenish yellow rather than black like those of most small North American sandpipers.

• **SONG** High *kneet* or *knee-eet*.

• **BEHAVIOR** Usually found in wet habitats where it obtains food by picking small animals from surface of mud and by probing mud for insects, insect larvae, and small crustaceans. Gregarious, occurring in small to large flocks. Often mixes and forages with other species of shorebirds, especially in migration and on wintering grounds. Relatively tame. Migrates at night. When flushed often rises quickly in zigzag fashion.

• **BREEDING** Monogamous. Colonial. Male announces territory by singing continuously, often for several minutes, while performing display flight.

• **NESTING** Incubation 19–23 days by both sexes (female at night; male during day; male does more). Precocial young leave nest day of hatching and feed themselves. Tended by both sexes. First flight at 14–16 days. 1 brood per year.

• **POPULATION** Common.

Similar Birds

SEMIPALMATED SANDPIPER Slightly larger; straighter bill; whiter face, throat, and chest; black legs.

WESTERN SANDPIPER Larger; long bill is heavier at base and slightly downcurved at tip; rustier back, ear patch, and crown; black legs • in breeding plumage has more heavily streaked breast.

Flight Pattern

Swift direct flight with rapid wing beats. When flushed often rises quickly in zigzag fashion.

Nest Identification

Shape ⚬⚬   Location ⚬⚬⚬ ▬

Lined with grass and dry leaves • on small pile of grass or moss near water • male begins building; female finishes • 3–4 olive, pinkish, or buff eggs with dark brown spots; ovate pyriform, 3.0 x 2.2 cm.

Plumage Sexes similar	Habitat	Migration Migratory	Weight 23 g

DATE _____ TIME_____ LOCATION _____

Family SCOLOPACIDAE	Species *Calidris fuscicollis*	Length 18–20 cm	Wingspan 36–42 cm

WHITE-RUMPED SANDPIPER

The white rump, best seen in flight, can sometimes be glimpsed on a standing bird when it spreads its wings slightly. At rest the wing tips extend well beyond the tail. In flight the rump is a distinctive field mark shared by only one other small sandpiper, the Curlew Sandpiper (a casual to rare Eurasian species). A long-distance champion flier, this bird migrates from the Canadian Arctic to southern South America, a distance of more than 12,875 km. It appears larger in flight than it does on the ground. Crown and back are rusty.

whitish face and throat

gray to gray-brown head

straight slightly tapered bill

small streaks on head and neck

gray to gray-brown upperparts

wingtips extend beyond tail

yellow or greenish brown spot often at base of lower mandible

small streaks on breast, sides, and flanks

blackish legs

whitish underparts

• **SONG** High-pitched *jeet* described as insectlike, mouselike, or batlike.

WINTER PLUMAGE

• **BEHAVIOR** Gregarious. Often wades when foraging and may immerse entire head in water. Also probes with bill in mud for food. Feeds on marine worms, insects, weed seeds, snails, and crustaceans. Often forms single-species flocks or mixes with other shorebirds.

• **BREEDING** Polygamous. Male leaves breeding ground once eggs are laid.

• **NESTING** Incubation 21–22 days by female. Precocial young leave nest soon after hatching and feed themselves. Tended by female. First flight at 16–17 days. 1 brood per year.

• **POPULATION** Fairly common. Casual in the West.

• **CONSERVATION** Vulnerable to habitat destruction in staging areas.

Similar Birds

BAIRD'S SANDPIPER More brown overall; less-contrasting supercilium; buff edging on upperparts; buff wash on face and across streaked breast; lacks white uppertail patch.

WESTERN SANDPIPER Smaller; shorter wings do not extend past tail; dark-centered uppertail.

Flight Pattern

Strong direct flight with rapid wing beats.

Nest Identification

Shape ⚬ Location ••• ▬

Lichens, moss, and leaves, especially dry willow • on pile of grass or moss near water • built by female • 3–4 olive-buff to light green eggs marked with brown; pyriform to ovate, 2.3 x 3.6 cm.

Plumage Sexes similar	Habitat	Migration Migratory	Weight 34 g

DATE _____ TIME_____ LOCATION _____

Family SCOLOPACIDAE	Species *Calidris bairdii*	Length 19 cm	Wingspan 38–42 cm

BAIRD'S SANDPIPER

In early autumn large flocks of these thrush-sized birds gather on the Great Plains and fly to South America. Although they often join other small sandpipers during migration, these birds will separate from

buff head with fine streaks

indistinct pale eye stripe

streaked back with scaly appearance

wingtips extend beyond tail

straight dark bill slightly drooped at tip

buff breast with fine streaks

white underparts

blackish legs and feet

JUVENILE

WINTER PLUMAGE

those flocks and feed by themselves. This buff sandpiper has long wings that protrude well beyond the tip of the tail when standing, and its rump and uppertail are broadly dark-centered with very narrow whitish sides. Juveniles are similar to adults but have buffy tips to feathers on back and wings that give the young bird a more distinct scaly appearance. Winter plumage shows more gray and less streaking, but the combination of short bill, short legs, and long wings distinguish it.

• SONG Low raspy *kreep* or *preeet*.
• BEHAVIOR Fairly tame. Essentially an inland species in migration. On migration prefers to feed in higher and dryer areas than other small sandpipers. Runs across mud and through shallow water, picking up bits of food. Does not probe with bill. Eats algae, amphipods, insects, and insect larvae. Sometimes flies in mixed flocks with other shorebirds.
• BREEDING Monogamous. Less gregarious than most other birds in genus.
• NESTING Incubation 19–22 days by both sexes. Precocial young leave nest soon after hatching. Tended by both sexes. First flight at 16–20 days. 1 brood per year.
• POPULATION Fairly common inland; uncommon on both coasts in migration.
• CONSERVATION Vulnerable to habitat changes on staging areas.

Similar Birds

WHITE-RUMPED SANDPIPER
Brighter breeding and juvenile plumage with rusty wash on crown and back • grayer nonbreeding plumage • streaking on underparts to flanks; lacks buff wash on head and breast; white tail base.

LEAST SANDPIPER
Smaller; shorter, thinner bill; dull yellow legs.

Flight Pattern

Swift direct flight with rapid wing beats.

Nest Identification

Shape — Location —

No nest material • under low plants or moss-covered rocks or on small pile of grass • 4 pink to olive-buff eggs marked with dark browns; pyriform, 2.3 x 3.6 cm.

Plumage Sexes similar	Habitat	Migration Migratory	Weight 40 g

Family SCOLOPACIDAE	Species *Calidris melanotos*	Length 20–23 cm	Wingspan 38–41 cm

PECTORAL SANDPIPER

This bird is named for the two saclike structures under the neck and breast of the male. During courtship the male inflates these sacs, thus enhancing the appearance of the heavy streaking on its breast. The streaking ends abruptly in a sharp line, separating it from the snow-white belly. During flight the sacs pump up and down in rhythm with the bird's hooting calls. In flight this bird shows a blackish brown rump and tail. Males and females are similar but the male has darker brown streaking on the throat and breast with white mottling. Winter plumage is pale brown overall.

dark brown crown with black, chestnut, and pale olive-brown stripes

white stripe over each eye

thin white stripes on back and scapulars

slender black bill with greenish yellow base to lower mandible

streaked brown breast

scapular, tertial, and mantle feathers have blackish brown centers with chestnut to buff fringes

whitish underparts

greenish yellow legs

- **SONG** Low reedy *churk* or *churrrt*. Male has hooting courtship call; murmuring foghornlike *khoor, khoor*, or loud coarse *gr, gr, gr* repeated several times per second.
- **BEHAVIOR** Forages in vegetation. Feeds by pecking and shallow probing. Eats insects and larvae, small crustaceans, spiders, seeds, and amphipods. In migration prefers meadows, marshes, pond edges, tidal flats, and mudflats. Usually in small flocks of 20–40 birds. Relatively tame. May fly short distance, then pitch back into grass.
- **BREEDING** Promiscuous. Males mate several times. Females visit territories of other males. Males leave territories prior to hatching of eggs.
- **NESTING** Incubation 19–23 days by female. Precocial young leave nest soon after hatching and feed themselves, tended by female. First flight at 18–21 days. 1 brood per year.
- **POPULATION** Fairly common to common on breeding grounds and in migration on East Coast and in Midwest; uncommon from Great Plains to West Coast.

Similar Birds

SHARP-TAILED SANDPIPER
Lacks sharply defined streaked breast; buff wash across breast • in breeding plumage has streaking on crissum, sides, and flanks
• juvenile has buff-orange breast and rusty crown.

RUFF ♀
Larger; longer neck; gray-brown breast with heavy spotting and blotches; in flight shows large white ovals on uppertail and stronger wing bars.

Flight Pattern

Swift direct flight with rapid wing beats. When flushed climbs with zigzag flight.

Nest Identification	
Shape	Location	Grass and leaves • on dry ground near water • built by female • whitish to olive-buff eggs splotched with dark browns; pyriform to oval, 3.8 x 2.5 cm.

Plumage Sexes similar	Habitat	Migration Migratory	Weight 99 g

DATE _____ TIME_____ LOCATION _____

Family SCOLOPACIDAE	Species *Calidris acuminata*	Length 22 cm	Wingspan 43 cm

SHARP-TAILED SANDPIPER

This native of Eurasian tundra regions is a casual to uncommon spring migrant and common autumn migrant in western Alaska, and is a rare autumn migrant along the Pacific Coast to California. These sandpipers usually travel in the company of other shorebirds. In flight it shows mostly white underwing coverts and axillaries, white lateral uppertail coverts with dark shaft streaks, and

bright rufous cap

white eyebrows broaden behind eyes

white eye ring

brownish plumage

short, slightly decurved blackish brown bill with hint of pale gray or yellowish brown at base

a wedge-shaped tail. Juveniles have a white supercilium, reddish cap, and rufous lores and auriculars. All plumages show streaked undertail coverts.

buff breast with light spots and streaks

dull greenish gray legs and feet

• **SONG** Soft clear *pleep-pleep-trrt*, sometimes in a twittering sequence reminiscent of a Barn Swallow's vocalizations.

• **BEHAVIOR** Solitary or in pairs on breeding grounds. Male performs song flight with short, low-level upward flights followed by downward glides on upraised wings. Gregarious in migration and on wintering grounds, often mixing with other shorebirds. Eats many small insects and other invertebrates, including mollusks and crustaceans. On breeding grounds feeds primarily on mosquito larvae. Often feeds in grasslands and drier margins of wetlands similar to the Pectoral Sandpiper.

• **BREEDING** Polygynous; male mates with one or more females, each of which nests and incubates a set of eggs; solitary.

• **NESTING** Incubation estimated at 19–23 days by female. Precocial young leave nest soon after hatching and feed themselves. Tended by female. First flight estimated at 18–21 days. 1 brood per year.

• **POPULATION** Casual to common migrant in Alaska. Casual to rare across the rest of North America.

Similar Birds

PECTORAL SANDPIPER Longer neck; longer bill; dark cap; sharp contrast between brownish-streaked breast and white belly; yellow-green legs; white undertail coverts.

Flight Pattern

Swift direct flight with rapid wing beats.

Nest Identification

Shape ⚬ Location ▬ ▪▪▪

Lined with willow leaves • on moist ground sheltered by tall grasses or a bush • 4 brownish olive or greenish eggs speckled with browns, often more concentrated at one end; pyriform to oval, 3.8 x 2.5 cm.

Plumage Sexes similar	Habitat ▬ ≈≈ ⟆	Migration Migratory	Weight 71 g

DATE _____ TIME_____ LOCATION _____

Family SCOLOPACIDAE	Species *Calidris maritima*	Length 23 cm	Wingspan 36–39 cm

PURPLE SANDPIPER

This bird is named for a faint purplish gloss on the back and scapular feathers, visible in bright light in the hand but rarely in the field. It winters along rocky coasts, jetties, and reefs. Flocks of these stocky birds can be seen following the coast during migration. Nonbreeding plumage shows a dark slate-gray head, breast, flanks,

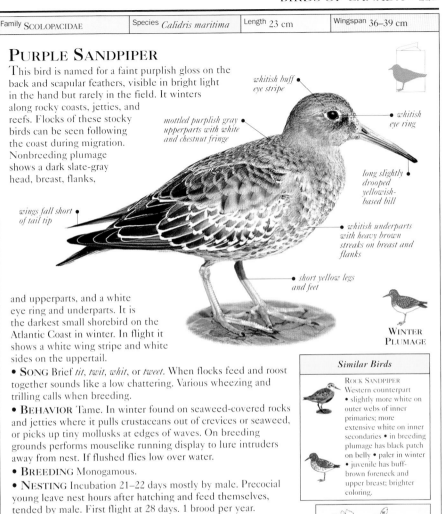

whitish buff eye stripe

mottled purplish gray upperparts with white and chestnut fringe

whitish eye ring

long slightly drooped yellowish-based bill

wings fall short of tail tip

whitish underparts with heavy brown streaks on breast and flanks

short yellow legs and feet

WINTER PLUMAGE

and upperparts, and a white eye ring and underparts. It is the darkest small shorebird on the Atlantic Coast in winter. In flight it shows a white wing stripe and white sides on the uppertail.

- **SONG** Brief *tit, twit, whit,* or *tweet.* When flocks feed and roost together sounds like a low chattering. Various wheezing and trilling calls when breeding.
- **BEHAVIOR** Tame. In winter found on seaweed-covered rocks and jetties where it pulls crustaceans out of crevices or seaweed, or picks up tiny mollusks at edges of waves. On breeding grounds performs mouselike running display to lure intruders away from nest. If flushed flies low over water.
- **BREEDING** Monogamous.
- **NESTING** Incubation 21–22 days mostly by male. Precocial young leave nest hours after hatching and feed themselves, tended by male. First flight at 28 days. 1 brood per year.
- **POPULATION** Fairly common on breeding grounds and on the East Coast in winter; rare to casual inland and as far south as the Gulf Coast. Seem to be increasing, perhaps due to numerous jetties constructed along Atlantic Coast.

Similar Birds

ROCK SANDPIPER
Western counterpart
• slightly more white on outer webs of inner primaries; more extensive white on inner secondaries • in breeding plumage has black patch on belly • paler in winter • juvenile has buff-brown foreneck and upper breast; brighter coloring.

Flight Pattern

Swift direct flight on shallow clipped wing beats (somewhat like that of a Spotted Sandpiper).

Nest Identification

Shape — Location ——

Lined with grass • on dry or damp tundra • male makes several scrapes; female chooses one • 3–4 olive-buff eggs blotched with brown or black; pyriform, 3.8 cm long.

Plumage Sexes similar	Habitat	Migration Migratory	Weight 77 g

DATE _____ TIME_____ LOCATION _____

Family SCOLOPACIDAE	Species *Calidris ptilocnemis*	Length 23 cm	Wingspan 36–39 cm

ROCK SANDPIPER

A close relative of the Purple Sandpiper, the Rock Sandpiper occurs in the Pacific. The two species are similarly plumaged in winter with a slate-gray head, breast, flanks, and upperparts. The nonbreeding Rock Sandpiper's bill has a greenish yellow base, and its legs appear greenish yellow. It is often seen with two similar shorebirds in winter, the Surfbird and the

black chestnut-edged crown and back

white eye stripe

long slender decurved blackish bill

Black Turnstone. In flight both are distinguishable from the Rock Sandpiper by a white band across the base of the tail.

white belly

black patch on lower breast

• **SONG** Call is a flickerlike whistle, *tu-tu-tu-tu-tu* repeated. On breeding grounds, a loud rippling *chirrup* or *prierrr* or complex series of chatters, trills, and whines.

short blackish legs

• **BEHAVIOR** Gleans food from seaweed-covered rocks at water's edge. Eats small mollusks, crustaceans, insects, seeds, and worms. Relatively tame, allowing close approach. Breeding males perform a song flight around claimed territory and display with slow wing beats and glides.

WINTER PLUMAGE

• **BREEDING** Monogamous. Colonial.

• **NESTING** Incubation 20 days by both sexes, occasionally only the male. Precocial young leave nest soon after hatching and feed themselves, tended by male. First flight estimated at 21 days. 1 brood per year.

• **POPULATION** Fairly common. Breeds in Alaska and winters south on coast to northern California; casual to central California. Has declined since 1970s.

Similar Birds

PURPLE SANDPIPER
Eastern counterpart
• slightly more white on inner primaries and secondaries • in nonbreeding plumage, more sharply defined spotting on lower breast and flanks, and lacks blackish breast spot • in juvenile plumage, brighter buff-brown foreneck and upper breast and more sharply defined spotting on lower breast and flanks • difficult to separate in winter.

BLACK TURNSTONE
Winter plumage
• shorter, slightly upturned bill; darker upperparts; white band across upper tail.

SURFBIRD
Winter plumage
• shorter bill with yellow base; white band across upper tail.

Flight Pattern

Swift flight with shallow clipped wing beats. Often flies low over water. When flushed, often zigzags while climbing.

Nest Identification

Shape ~ Location ▬ ~

Lined with lichens, leaves, and grass • on ground in pile of lichen or moss, above beaches on tundra, to hills or mountain tops, or ground on open dry tundra, often slightly elevated • male begins scrape, female finishes and lines • 4 olive to buff eggs, marked with brown; pyriform, 3.8 cm long.

Plumage Sexes similar	Habitat ▬ ▲ ⚏	Migration Migratory	Weight 77 g

DATE _____ TIME_____ LOCATION _____

Family SCOLOPACIDAE	Species *Calidris alpina*	Length 19–22 cm	Wingspan 37–40 cm

DUNLIN

Impressive fliers, these small brown sandpipers are able to migrate at speeds of more than 160 km per hour and travel in flocks that can be so large they look like a swarm of insects. Once known as the Red-backed Sandpiper, the breeding bird is unmistakable with its long sturdy droop-tipped bill, rusty red upperparts, and black belly patch. Females are similar to males but have brown napes. When feeding it often gives the appearance of being hunchbacked.

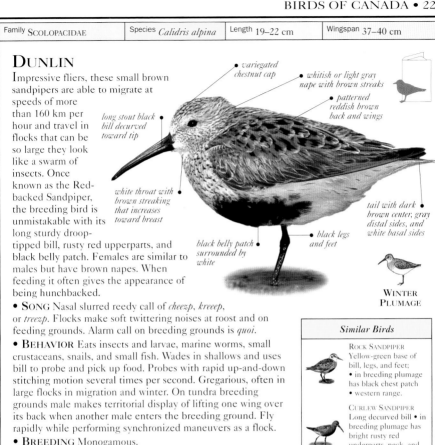

- variegated chestnut cap
- whitish or light gray nape with brown streaks
- patterned reddish brown back and wings
- long stout black bill decurved toward tip
- white throat with brown streaking that increases toward breast
- tail with dark brown center, gray distal sides, and white basal sides
- black belly patch surrounded by white
- black legs and feet

WINTER PLUMAGE

- **SONG** Nasal slurred reedy call of *cheezp, kreeep,* or *treezp.* Flocks make soft twittering noises at roost and on feeding grounds. Alarm call on breeding grounds is *quoi.*
- **BEHAVIOR** Eats insects and larvae, marine worms, small crustaceans, snails, and small fish. Wades in shallows and uses bill to probe and pick up food. Probes with rapid up-and-down stitching motion several times per second. Gregarious, often in large flocks in migration and winter. On tundra breeding grounds male makes territorial display of lifting one wing over its back when another male enters the breeding ground. Fly rapidly while performing synchronized maneuvers as a flock.
- **BREEDING** Monogamous.
- **NESTING** Incubation 20–23 days by both sexes. Precocial young leave nest day of hatching. Tended by both sexes, but primarily by male, for several days. First flight at 19–23 days. 1 brood per year.
- **POPULATION** Common on breeding grounds, both coasts, and inland to the Great Plains in migration. Rare on the Great Plains. Common on coastal wintering grounds. Has been declining since the 1970s for undetermined reasons.
- **CONSERVATION** Vulnerable to habitat loss in staging and wintering areas.

Similar Birds

ROCK SANDPIPER
Yellow-green base of bill, legs, and feet;
- in breeding plumage has black chest patch
- western range.

CURLEW SANDPIPER
Long decurved bill • in breeding plumage has bright rusty red underparts, neck, and head; white belly, undertail coverts, and rump patch • in winter plumage has white rump without black center line.

Flight Pattern

Swift direct flight with rapid wing beats.

Nest Identification

Shape ➤   Location ***

Leaves and grasses • hummock or raised dry area on wet, grass, or sedge tundra • both sexes make scrapes, but female chooses one and completes nest • 4 olive, bluish green, or buff eggs blotched with browns or gray; pyriform, 3.6 cm long.

Plumage Sexes similar	Habitat 〰〰	Migration Migratory	Weight 54 g

DATE _____ TIME_____ LOCATION _____

Family SCOLOPACIDAE	Species *Calidris himantopus*	Length 19–22 cm	Wingspan 39–43 cm

STILT SANDPIPER

This long-legged sandpiper can be seen during migration feeding in dense flocks in shallow waters along the Atlantic coast. It is unwary and approachable, attributes that were exploited by early nineteenth-century market hunters to the point that it became rare and irregular in New England, where it was once common. Today this slender, long-necked, long-legged shorebird seems to be increasing in numbers and is once again common. In flight it shows a white rump. In winter, the Stilt Sandpiper displays gray upperparts and white underparts.

rufous patch on cheeks

long, slender, slightly decurved black bill

- **SONG** Low hoarse whistled *whu* or rattling trill *querrp*. Also brays, whines, and utters guttural trills on breeding ground.
- **BEHAVIOR** Eats mostly insects and their larvae, but also takes small crustaceans and mollusks and some plant materials, including seeds. May wade belly-deep in water and feed by thrusting head underwater while probing mud with beak in a stitching motion. Usually tame around humans; however, this bird has been known to attack when an intruder approaches the nest.

dark-patterned wings show narrow white bar in flight

horizontal barlike marking on chest and belly

long greenish yellow legs

WINTER PLUMAGE

- **BREEDING** Monogamous. Male chases female in flight until he flies ahead, then male dives downward singing and raising wings over back.
- **NESTING** Incubation 19–21 days by both parents; male by day, female at night. Precocial young leave nest shortly after hatching, tended by parents for about 14 days. First flight at 17–18 days. 1 brood per year.
- **POPULATION** Common on breeding grounds and in the interior east of the Rockies during migration. Rare on West Coast, primarily in fall. Uncommon on East Coast in spring; common in fall. Rare in winter in coastal southern US.
- **CONSERVATION** Populations seem to be slowly on the increase.

Similar Birds

CURLEW SANDPIPER
Winter plumage • black legs; beak more curved.

LESSER YELLOWLEGS
Winter plumage • larger; darker gray upperparts with extensive white speckling; dusky lores; white supralorals; white eye ring; bright yellow legs and feet; long straight black bill.

Flight Pattern
Strong powerful direct flight on long, rapidly beating wings.

Nest Identification	
Shape Location	On small piles of sedge or low well-drained rocky ledges • pair may return to former nest site from year to year • male scrapes, but female decides which nest to use • 4 pale green to olive-green or cream eggs with brown spots; pyriform, 3.6 cm long.

Plumage Sexes similar	Habitat	Migration Migratory	Weight 60 g

DATE _____ TIME_____ LOCATION _____

Family SCOLOPACIDAE	Species *Eurynorhynchus pygmeus*	Length 15 cm	Wingspan 28–30 cm

SPOONBILL SANDPIPER

The Spoonbill Sandpiper is easy to identify, with its spoon-shaped bill; however, the bill is not easily seen in profile and requires a close view. This very uncommon sparrow-size sandpiper nests in Siberia and spends winters in parts of Asia. On rare occasions, North American birders have spotted this unusual bird in Alaska and coastal British Columbia. Juveniles and adults are similar, but adults have brown-streaked rusty plumage that extends from the head onto the face and breast, plus a more defined eye line. In flight, the center of the tail and rump is dark and there is a small white bar across the wing. Feet and legs are black. Winter adults show gray to gray-brown upperparts and white forehead, supercilium, chin, and underparts.

chestnut- and black-mottled back, edged buff and white

brown-streaked rusty head

brown wings

JUVENILE

black bill with spoonlike tip

white belly

BREEDING ADULT

- **SONG** Has contact call of *wheet* or *preep*. Courtship call of *preer-prr-prr*, a buzzing trill descending in pitch and resembling cicada.
- **BEHAVIOR** Wades in shallow water, using bill to forage. Eats mostly insects but takes small crustaceans and other invertebrates. Searches for food using side-to-side sweeping motion like an avocet instead of sewing-machine motion of most sandpipers. Often in the company of other species of sandpipers in migration and on wintering grounds.
- **BREEDING** Monogamous. During courtship the male performs a courtship display in which he circles, plummets, and hovers while singing.
- **NESTING** Incubation 21–22 days, mostly by male. Young precocial; leave nest day of hatching, tended by male. First flight at 15–18 days. 1 brood per year.
- **POPULATION** Casual to accidental in Alaska and islands in Bering Sea; accidental elsewhere on the northern Pacific Coast.
- **CONSERVATION** This sandpiper is a rare species with world population estimated at only 2,000–2,800 pairs. Numbers are of some concern.

Similar Birds

RED-NECKED STINT
Gray scapulars; straight bill with pointed tip; fainter streaking on breast and nape.

Flight Pattern

Swift direct flight with rapid wing beats.

Nest Identification

Shape   Location

Lined with willow leaves • on ground in grassy area near freshwater puddles or in dry meadow • 3–4 pale brownish eggs with small brown spots; pyriform, 2.8 cm long.

Plumage Sexes similar	Habitat	Migration Migratory	Weight 28 g

DATE _____ TIME_____ LOCATION _____

Family SCOLOPACIDAE	Species *Tryngites subruficollis*	Length 19–21 cm	Wingspan 41–43 cm

BUFF-BREASTED SANDPIPER

Birders can spot this shorebird during migration when it stops to forage in the wet fields, turf farms, and rice fields of inland North America; it also favors golf courses and airports. This species generally is approachable, but when frightened it usually runs from danger rather than flying. It has a short pigeonlike bill, and an upright stance like a plover. In flight the silvery white axillars and underwing linings contrast with the buff underparts and darker back. Juveniles have more scaly upperparts.

buff head and face with streaked and spotted brown crown

prominent dark eye with light eye ring

streaked and spotted brown hindneck

short straight dark brown bill

long buff neck

buff-edged brown upperparts appear scaly

buff breast with streaked and spotted brown sides

white belly and undertail coverts

buff-edged brown tail

yellowish orange legs and feet

• **SONG** During migration a soft hoarse call of *pr-r-r-reet*. During display makes quick clucking sounds. Otherwise mostly silent.

• **BEHAVIOR** Gregarious. Eats insects, fly larvae and pupae, some spiders, and seeds. Prefers short dry grasslands in migration. Travels in small flocks, often mixing with other species. Rarely forages beside water.

• **BREEDING** Promiscuous. Males display together at a communal area called a lek. During the display the male flash the silvery white undersides of its wings. Successful males may mate with several females. Males leave shortly after breeding.

• **NESTING** Female incubates 19–21 days; precocial young leave nest soon after hatching. First flight at about 21 days. 1 brood per year.

• **POPULATION** Uncommon to fairly common on breeding grounds and in interior during migration. Rare to casual or uncommon in autumn migration on both coasts.

• **CONSERVATION** Once abundant, but tameness and flock density have made it vulnerable to slaughter by market hunters. Protective laws have helped population recover from near extinction.

Similar Birds

UPLAND SANDPIPER
Larger; streaked brown plumage with no conspicuous marks on upperparts; streaking on breast, sides, and flanks; long, thin neck; small dovelike head; short yellow bill with black tip.

RUFF
Juvenile larger; smaller head; shorter, droopy bill; long neck; deep-bellied, hump-backed body; U-shaped white rump band • rare to casual.

Flight Pattern

Swift direct flight with rapid wing beats. When flushed twists and turns like a snipe as it climbs away.

Nest Identification

Shape — Location —

Lined with grasses or moss • on ground in pile of vegetation or in tree stump • built by female • 4 white, buff, or olive eggs with brown blotches; pyriform, 3.3 cm long.

Plumage Sexes similar	Habitat ___	Migration Migratory	Weight 71 g

DATE _____ TIME_____ LOCATION _____

Family SCOLOPACIDAE	Species *Philomachus pugnax*	Length 23–32 cm	Wingspan 41–64 cm

RUFF

The male Ruff in breeding plumage is unique, dressed in his frilly tufts and plumes that can range from black to rufous to white to speckled or barred. The much smaller female lacks the tufts and plumes, and the breast is heavily blotched with dark browns and blacks. In flight, females show a U-shaped white band on a dark brown rump; males show a white oval patch on each side of the dark tail and white underwings.

- **SONG** Usually silent, except during migration when birds in flocks give cries of *who-eeee*. Otherwise has a range of low grunting notes, *koock* or *kuh-uck*.
- **BEHAVIOR** Prefers marshlands or wet meadows where it probes in mud for food or wades in water. Eats a variety of terrestrial and aquatic insects, crustaceans, and worms; some plant materials.
- **BREEDING** Polygamous. Colonial. Male performs display at lek, in which it raises ear tufts and ruffs, then bows and begins kicking and pecking other males. Females visit the lek and are chosen by one or several males. Male leaves female shortly after courtship.
- **NESTING** Incubation 20–23 days by female. Precocial young leave nest day of hatching and feed themselves but tended by female. First flight at 25–28 days. 1 brood per year by female; several by male.
- **POPULATION** Old World species. Casual to rare on both West and East Coasts, around Great Lakes, and inland.

variously colored ruff, ear tufts, and neck plumes

small head

red, greenish, yellowish, or orange facial warts and wattles

plump body with humpback and potbelly

MALE

short slightly decurved bill

chestnut to black scapulars, mantle, and tertials

white underparts with multicolored barring

orange, yellow, or red legs

JUVENILE

WINTER PLUMAGE

grayish brown upperparts mottled black with buffy white edging

black-mottled and blotched plumage on breast and flanks

FEMALE

Similar Birds

PECTORAL SANDPIPER
Smaller; shorter necked; shorter yellow legs; wide dark center to rump with white sides.

UPLAND SANDPIPER
Long thin neck; small head; dark barred tail and rump.

Flight Pattern
Has low but swift direct flight with rapid wing beats.

Nest Identification
Shape 〜 ⬯ Location ▬ ⋀⋀⋀ ⋔

Lined with grasses and leaves • on ground or in marsh on small pile of grass or reeds, hidden in dense vegetation • built by female • 4 gray-green or buff eggs, with brown spots; pyriform, 4.3 cm long.

Plumage Sexes differ	Habitat ⋀⋀ 〰	Migration Migratory	Weight 170 g

DATE _____ TIME_____ LOCATION _____

| Family SCOLOPACIDAE | Species *Limnodromus griseus* | Length 27–30 cm | Wingspan 46–56 cm |

SHORT-BILLED DOWITCHER

This snipelike sandpiper is commonly seen in open marshes and mudflats during migration. Dowitchers are known by the long bill, a white wedge from the barred tail to the back that is only visible in flight, and a light belly. Although its call differs from that of the Long-billed Dowitcher, they are difficult to distinguish in the field because of the variety of breeding plumages in its three races and the overlap in bill length between the two species. Juveniles are the easiest to separate by plumage from August to October. Winter plumage is gray overall. The female is similar to the male but larger.

white supercilium

dark brownish upperparts with rufous-buff-edged feathers

whitish chin

long blackish brown bill

chunky body

white to cinnamon-red breast with heavy brownish spotting or barring

barred tail

short greenish legs

WINTER PLUMAGE

- **SONG** Generally silent. Utters clear mellow or abrasive *chi-too-too* or *kee-you*. Also sings *tiddle-whee*, especially in spring.
- **BEHAVIOR** Gregarious; feeds and roosts in large flocks and associates with other species. Eats mostly insects, also eggs of king or horseshoe crabs. Probes with fast up-and-down motion of bill. Often submerges head in water. May freeze in standing position when approached. Often flies at considerable heights.
- **BREEDING** Monogamous. Colonial. Male displays with a hovering flight song over breeding territory.

Similar Birds

LONG-BILLED DOWITCHER
Slightly larger; longer legs; darker overall; darker tail with white bars narrower than dark bars; different voice • females may have longer bill than males • in breeding plumage lacks white underparts.

- **NESTING** Incubation 21 days by female, sometimes by both sexes. Precocial young leave nest soon after hatching. Tended by male but feed themselves. 1 brood per year.
- **POPULATION** Common.

Flight Pattern
Strong swift direct flight with rapid wing beats.

Nest Identification	
Shape ⚬ Location ⚬⚬ ▬	Sticks, leaves, and grasses • on ground in small pile of grass or moss • built by both sexes • 4 buff-green or brownish eggs speckled and blotched with brown; pyriform, 4.1 x 2.8 cm.

| Plumage Sexes similar | Habitat 🏝️ 🌾 〰️ 〰️ 〰️ | Migration Migratory | Weight 108 g |

DATE _____ TIME_____ LOCATION _____

Family SCOLOPACIDAE	Species *Limnodromus scolopaceus*	Length 28–32 cm	Wingspan 46–51 cm

LONG-BILLED DOWITCHER

Despite its name, only the female has a slightly longer bill than its cousin, the Short-billed Dowitcher. The Long-billed prefers freshwater habitats and migrates south later in the season than the Short-billed. Winter plumage shows gray overall. In breeding plumage birds show no white on the underparts, and the tail is darker than that of the Short-billed,

dense dark barring on throat and upper breast

bright white scapular tips

pale chestnut to buff supercilium

pale chestnut to buff chin

long straight bill

dark barring on lower breast and belly

reddish underparts

greenish yellow legs and feet

WINTER PLUMAGE

with smaller light bars than dark ones. Juveniles have darker upperparts and duller underparts than the juvenile Short-billed. The scapulars have narrow dark rust edges, while the tertials have narrow, very even pale edges. On the Short-billed these feathers are broadly edged with reddish buff, and many have internal markings.

• **SONG** Fast high-pitched thin nasal *keek* or *keek-keek-keek* usually uttered as a single or triple note. Also sings *peter-wee-too.*

• **BEHAVIOR** Gregarious. When feeding rapidly probes up and down with long bill. Often puts entire head in water to probe for insects. Eats mostly insects and insect larvae but also takes crustaceans, mollusks, and plant seeds. Favors freshwater mudflats in migration and winter. Often flies high in migration.

• **BREEDING** Monogamous. Small colonies. Male sings while performing hovering display flight.

• **NESTING** Incubation 20 days by both sexes in first week, then just by male. Precocial young leave nest day of hatching, then tended by male but feed themselves. 1 brood per year.

• **POPULATION** Varies from common to uncommon.

Similar Birds

SHORT-BILLED DOWITCHER
Slightly smaller; shorter legs; paler upperparts; some white in underparts; paler tail with white bars as wide or wider than dark bars; different call.

COMMON SNIPE
Long bill; boldly striped head; buff stripes on back; barred flanks; rusty red tail.

Flight Pattern
Swift direct flight with rapid wing beats.

Nest Identification	
Shape ✏ Location ✏	Lined with leaves and grass • atop small pile of grasses or moss • built by female • 4 brown to olive eggs with brown and gray blotches; pyriform, 4.1 x 2.8 cm.

Plumage Sexes similar	Habitat	Migration Migratory	Weight 99 g

DATE _____ TIME_____ LOCATION _____

Family SCOLOPACIDAE	Species *Gallinago gallinago*	Length 25–28 cm	Wingspan 43–51 cm

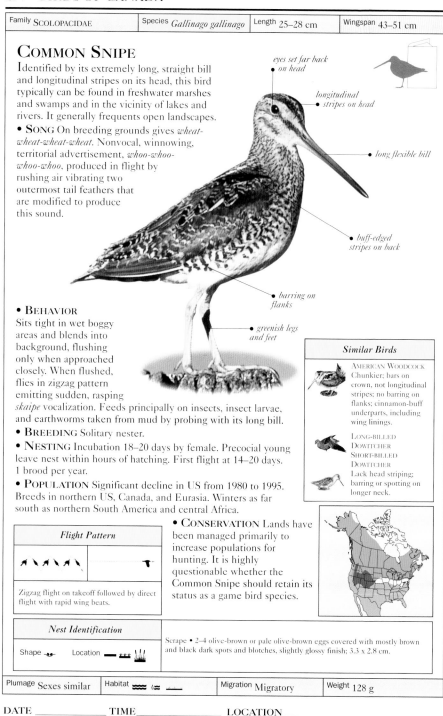

COMMON SNIPE

Identified by its extremely long, straight bill and longitudinal stripes on its head, this bird typically can be found in freshwater marshes and swamps and in the vicinity of lakes and rivers. It generally frequents open landscapes.

• **SONG** On breeding grounds gives *wheat-wheat-wheat-wheat*. Nonvocal, winnowing, territorial advertisement, *whoo-whoo-whoo-whoo*, produced in flight by rushing air vibrating two outermost tail feathers that are modified to produce this sound.

eyes set far back on head

longitudinal stripes on head

long flexible bill

buff-edged stripes on back

barring on flanks

greenish legs and feet

• **BEHAVIOR** Sits tight in wet boggy areas and blends into background, flushing only when approached closely. When flushed, flies in zigzag pattern emitting sudden, rasping *skaipe* vocalization. Feeds principally on insects, insect larvae, and earthworms taken from mud by probing with its long bill.

• **BREEDING** Solitary nester.

• **NESTING** Incubation 18–20 days by female. Precocial young leave nest within hours of hatching. First flight at 14–20 days. 1 brood per year.

• **POPULATION** Significant decline in US from 1980 to 1995. Breeds in northern US, Canada, and Eurasia. Winters as far south as northern South America and central Africa.

• **CONSERVATION** Lands have been managed primarily to increase populations for hunting. It is highly questionable whether the Common Snipe should retain its status as a game bird species.

Similar Birds

AMERICAN WOODCOCK Chunkier; bars on crown, not longitudinal stripes; no barring on flanks; cinnamon-buff underparts, including wing linings.

LONG-BILLED DOWITCHER SHORT-BILLED DOWITCHER Lack head striping; barring or spotting on longer neck.

Flight Pattern	
Zigzag flight on takeoff followed by direct flight with rapid wing beats.	

Nest Identification	
Shape ⬐ Location ▬ ▪▪▪ ⅢⅢ	Scrape • 2–4 olive-brown or pale olive-brown eggs covered with mostly brown and black dark spots and blotches, slightly glossy finish; 3.3 x 2.8 cm.

Plumage Sexes similar	Habitat ≋ ⫽≋ ⏤⏤	Migration Migratory	Weight 128 g

DATE _____ TIME_____ LOCATION _____

Family SCOLOPACIDAE	Species *Scolopax rusticola*	Length 34 cm	Wingspan 56 cm

EURASIAN WOODCOCK

The plumage of this rare visitor to North America serves as camouflage in the European and Asian forests where it lives. Its long flexible bill with a sensitive tip helps it probe for food in the cold ground. Females have been reported to move chicks away from intruders by carrying them in flight. The pale chestnut-brown rump shows in flight.

thick blackish bars on back of crown and nape

upperparts mottled with chestnut, brown, gray, and buff

pale buff forehead and forecrown, with brown streaks

narrow dark eye stripe from bill to behind eye

long straight bill

buff-brown sides of cheeks with a dark bar

blackish tail with silvery white terminal band

pale chestnut-buff underparts, dark brown barred

broad pointed wings

yellow-buff and chestnut-brown barred tertials and coverts

short gray-brown legs and feet

- **SONG** Generally silent, except on breeding territory. During breeding, male gives accelerating series of low, barely audible grunts, *kwoor-kwoor-kwo-ro* or *ook-ook-tsseee*, followed by sharp loud *pee-tzz*, as he performs courtship flights at dawn and dusk low over the treetops. When flushed has grating repetitive call of *shraaap*.

- **BEHAVIOR** Solitary. Nocturnal. Probes for worms by inserting bill deep in soil. Eats mostly earthworms but also slugs and insects; some plant materials. When feeding, walks deliberately with constant rocking motion of body.

- **BREEDING** Polygamous; loose colonies. Male performs courtship display at dusk and in early morning. Males circle above treetops for 20 minutes at a time, calling to attract females into territory for mating.

- **NESTING** Incubation 22 days by female. Precocial young leave nest within 1–2 days of hatching to feed themselves, tended by female. First flight at 15–20 days. 1 brood per year.

- **POPULATION** Rare to accidental. Recorded in northeast Canada, northeast United States, Virginia, and Alabama, mostly in 19th century. No recent records.

- **CONSERVATION** Still hunted throughout most of native range in Eurasia.

Similar Birds

AMERICAN WOODCOCK Smaller in size; more distinctive stripes down back; more narrow outer primaries; shorter and more rounded wings; lacks barring on underparts and underwings.

Flight Pattern

Swift direct flight with rapid wing beats. When flushed, zigzags away.

Nest Identification

Shape ___ Location ___

Lined with leaves and grasses • a grassy tussock, sheltered by bush, tree trunk, or stump • built by female • 4 ocherous eggs, spotted with brownish red; oval, 4.3 cm long.

Plumage Sexes similar	Habitat	Migration Migratory	Weight 306 g

DATE _____ TIME _____ LOCATION _____

| Family SCOLOPACIDAE | Species *Scolopax minor* | Length 27–28 cm | Wingspan 46 cm |

AMERICAN WOODCOCK

The long bill of this upland shorebird is sensitive and flexible, allowing it to feel for worms in deep soil. Woodcocks are rarely seen during the day unless flushed and escaping straightaway in flight on twittering rounded wings. Chunky, short-necked, and short-legged, its plumage matches the dead leaves of the forest floor and old fields where it roosts by day.

• **SONG** Generally silent. In spring, male on display ground has nasal call of *peeant*, similar to that of the Common Nighthawk. During display flights male produces a musical twittering with wings and a liquid, bubbling song from high overhead.

• **BEHAVIOR** Crepuscular and nocturnal.

short black tail with silvery white terminal band

gray-striped upperparts

black and brown barring on crown

big eyes set high on head

long, thin creamy pinkish brown bill

overall black and brown barring and markings

rusty underparts and underwing linings

Solitary. Eats mostly earthworms, but also takes slugs, insects, and some seeds and berries. Before probing into soil with bill, often stamps foot on ground, causing earthworms to move. During feeding, walks slowly with a back and forth rocking motion.

• **BREEDING** Polygamous; loose colonies. Male has complex courtship flight: he flies from ground, circling as high as 91 meters, hovers, chirps, and glides earthward in a series of zigzags.

• **NESTING** Incubation 20–21 days by female. Precocial young leave nest 1–2 days after hatching to feed themselves, tended by female. First flight at 14 days; independent at 42–56 days. 1 brood per year.

• **POPULATION** Fairly common. Casual to eastern Colorado and eastern New Mexico; accidental to southeastern California.

• **CONSERVATION** Hunted and managed as a game bird.

Similar Birds

COMMON SNIPE
More slender overall; longer bill; striped head pattern; pointed wings; barred sides, flanks, and undertail coverts; streaked neck and upper breast; buffy white stripes on back; reddish tail with white terminal band; longer greenish legs and feet.

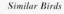

EURASIAN WOODCOCK
Accidental — no recent records • much larger; brown- and pale buff-barred underparts; pointier, longer wings.

Flight Pattern
Most often has swift direct flight; when flushed, flies low for short distance before dropping back into cover.

Nest Identification	
Shape 〜 Location 〜	Lined with twigs and dried leaves • on ground, hidden in tall grasses, weeds, or near stump of tree • built by female • 4 buff or cinnamon eggs, with gray, purple, and brown spots; oval, 3.8 x 2.8 cm.

| Plumage Sexes similar | Habitat 🌾 🌳 🌿 | Migration Migratory | Weight 176 g |

DATE _____ TIME_____ LOCATION _____

Family SCOLOPACIDAE	Species *Phalaropus tricolor*	Length 20–24 cm	Wingspan 37–41 cm

WILSON'S PHALAROPE

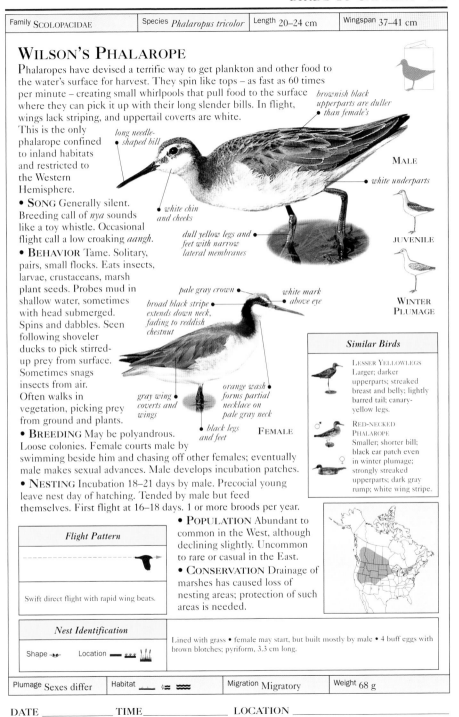

Phalaropes have devised a terrific way to get plankton and other food to the water's surface for harvest. They spin like tops – as fast as 60 times per minute – creating small whirlpools that pull food to the surface where they can pick it up with their long slender bills. In flight, wings lack striping, and uppertail coverts are white.

This is the only phalarope confined to inland habitats and restricted to the Western Hemisphere.

brownish black upperparts are duller than female's

long needle-shaped bill

MALE

white underparts

white chin and cheeks

dull yellow legs and feet with narrow lateral membranes

JUVENILE

- **SONG** Generally silent. Breeding call of *nya* sounds like a toy whistle. Occasional flight call a low croaking *aangh*.
- **BEHAVIOR** Tame. Solitary, pairs, small flocks. Eats insects, larvae, crustaceans, marsh plant seeds. Probes mud in shallow water, sometimes with head submerged. Spins and dabbles. Seen following shoveler ducks to pick stirred-up prey from surface. Sometimes snags insects from air. Often walks in vegetation, picking prey from ground and plants.

pale gray crown
broad black stripe extends down neck, fading to reddish chestnut

white mark above eye

WINTER PLUMAGE

gray wing coverts and wings
orange wash forms partial necklace on pale gray neck

black legs and feet
FEMALE

Similar Birds

LESSER YELLOWLEGS Larger; darker upperparts; streaked breast and belly; lightly barred tail; canary-yellow legs.

RED-NECKED PHALAROPE Smaller; shorter bill; black ear patch even in winter plumage; strongly streaked upperparts; dark gray rump; white wing stripe.

- **BREEDING** May be polyandrous. Loose colonies. Female courts male by swimming beside him and chasing off other females; eventually male makes sexual advances. Male develops incubation patches.
- **NESTING** Incubation 18–21 days by male. Precocial young leave nest day of hatching. Tended by male but feed themselves. First flight at 16–18 days. 1 or more broods per year.
- **POPULATION** Abundant to common in the West, although declining slightly. Uncommon to rare or casual in the East.
- **CONSERVATION** Drainage of marshes has caused loss of nesting areas; protection of such areas is needed.

Flight Pattern
Swift direct flight with rapid wing beats.

Nest Identification	
Shape ~ Location ▬ ▬ ⋔⋔	Lined with grass • female may start, but built mostly by male • 4 buff eggs with brown blotches; pyriform, 3.3 cm long.

Plumage Sexes differ	Habitat ▬ ▬ ≈≈	Migration Migratory	Weight 68 g

DATE _____ TIME_____ LOCATION _____

| Family SCOLOPACIDAE | Species *Phalaropus lobatus* | Length 20 cm | Wingspan 36–38 cm |

RED-NECKED PHALAROPE

Formerly called the Northern Phalarope, this bird is the smallest of the phalaropes, as well as the most abundant and widely distributed. Like all birds in its genus, the male is the only gender with brood patches with which to incubate the clutch. Male and female have similar plumage, but male looks more washed-out. White wing bars show in flight. In winter plumage both sexes have heavily streaked gray upperparts, whitish underparts, a black line through the eyes, and dark legs and feet.

streaked gray forehead and crown

straight, needlelike black bill

dark gray back with buff striping and feather edging

white throat

MALE

• **SONG** Flight call is soft *clipp* or *twit*, *tirric* or *twik*. Utters various insectlike alarm calls on breeding grounds.

• **BEHAVIOR** Very tame. Gregarious in migration and winter; also pelagic in winter. Turns in circles while feeding in shallow water and picks up zooplankton stirred up to surface. Turns over rocks, picks larvae off water. Eats brine shrimp, aquatic vegetation, insect larvae, mollusks, and plankton. Female initiates courtship, selects scrape, and deserts male as soon as incubation begins; sometimes mates with a second male.

white underparts

short blue-gray legs and feet

small white spot in front of eye

black face and crown

rufous-red on neck

JUVENILE

gray sides of breast

gray streaking on sides and flanks

FEMALE

WINTER PLUMAGE

• **BREEDING** Monogamous, or female serially polyandrous (at least 10 percent). Solitary or in pairs.

• **NESTING** Incubation 17–21 days by male. Precocial young leave nest soon after hatching and are able to swim immediately. Tended by male but feed themselves. First flight at 20–21 days. 1 brood by male and 1–2 broods by female per year.

• **POPULATION** Abundant. Common off West Coast and inland in the West during migration; rare inland in the Midwest and the East; uncommon off Atlantic Coast; fairly common offshore in Maritimes and New England.

• **CONSERVATION** Vulnerable to marine pollution and oil spills.

Similar Birds

RED PHALAROPE
Larger; longer wings • thicker yellowish bill in breeding season • in winter has thicker blackish bill; more uniform pale gray upperparts without whitish streaking.

Flight Pattern
Swift swallowlike flight with rapid wing beats and quick movements and turns.

Nest Identification	
Shape ⌣ Location ▬ ⁂	Lined with grasses, dried leaves, and stalks • in tussock of grasses or sunken in mosses, often sheltered by vegetation • built by male, often in company of female • 3–4 buff-olive eggs spotted with brown; oval to pyriform, 3.0 x 2.0 cm.

| Plumage Sexes differ | Habitat ⥥ ≈≈ ▬ ⧼⧽ | Migration Migratory | Weight 34 g |

DATE _____ TIME_____ LOCATION _____

Family SCOLOPACIDAE	Species *Phalaropus fulicaria*	Length 20–23 cm	Wingspan 36–41 cm

RED PHALAROPE

Of all phalaropes, the Red is most pelagic, nests farthest north, and migrates farthest south. It breeds well north of the Arctic Circle and winters at sea off both Atlantic and Pacific Coasts. Its bill is shorter and thicker than that of other phalaropes. In flight it shows a white wing stripe, a uniformly gray back (in winter), and brownish legs and feet.

black wing tips

MALE

• **SONG** Bell-like *clink-clink*. Also a shrieking shrill *wit-wit* and *tink* or *tsik*.

white face

• **BEHAVIOR** Tame. Solitary or in small flocks; at sea occasionally in very large flocks. Pelagic in winter. Swims readily. Wades into water to feed; finds food on surface and in shallow water. Swims and spins often, picking up planktonic food particles with its bill from the surface. Eats small insects, fish, and aquatic invertebrates.

black crown and forehead

black at base of bill

dark gray upperparts have feathers fringed with rufous-buff

yellowish bill with black tip

• **BREEDING** Female polyandrous; male promiscuous. Semicolonial. Female selects territory, leaves area shortly after laying eggs; and sometimes mates again.

JUVENILE

• **NESTING** Incubation 18–20 days by male. Precocial young leave nest soon after hatching. Tended by male but feed themselves. First flight at 16–20 days. 1 brood per year by male and 2 broods by female.

chestnut-red underparts

WINTER PLUMAGE

more brightly colored

FEMALE

chestnut-red underparts

Similar Birds

♂ RED-NECKED PHALAROPE Thinner, needlelike bill; smaller • in winter plumage is darker with heavily striped back; blacker crown; more contrasting wing stripe.

• **POPULATION** Abundant on breeding grounds. In winter and migration fairly common off the West Coast; uncommon off the East Coast. Rare inland.

• **CONSERVATION** Accidents occur during migration, such as collisions with lighthouses. Storms at sea can blow birds inland. Vulnerable to oil spills.

Flight Pattern
Swift direct flight with rapid wing beats.

Nest Identification	
Shape Location	Domed with grass • lined with grasses and other fine materials • on ground near water • built by male • 3–4 olive-green eggs blotched with black or brown; oval to pyriform, 3.0 x 2.3 cm.

Plumage Sexes differ	Habitat	Migration Migratory	Weight 51 g

DATE _____ TIME _____ LOCATION _____

Family LARIDAE	Species *Stercorarius skua*	Length 51–56 cm	Wingspan 137–150 cm

GREAT SKUA

Sometimes called a sea hawk because its habits resemble those of
inland raptors, this skua is known to steal food from other
seabirds. A native of Iceland and northern Europe, it can be
seen off the north Atlantic Coast year-round. About the size
of a stocky Herring Gull, this bird will attack gannets. It
likes to tend large fishing boats where it may take
scraps, throwbacks, and garbage. A dark chunky
heavy-looking bird with wide wings that show
patches of white at the base of the primaries, it
looks somewhat hunchbacked in flight. It
displays pale and dark color phases.

broad white markings on upper primaries

dark brown underwing

brownish overall, streaked with gold and reddish brown

heavy blackish gray bill with dark tip

cinnamon- and buff-marked chestnut-brown underparts

DARK MORPH

short blackish brown wedge-shaped tail

PALE MORPH

• **SONG**
Calls *skooo-aa,
skoooo-aa*. When
defending nest,
cries *tuk-tuk-tuk*.

• **BEHAVIOR**
Spends much time at sea.
Eats fishes, small seabirds, ducks,
small mammals, carrion, and refuse. Steals fish from other
birds by attacking them from the air and causing them to release
or disgorge prey. Usually initiates pursuit-chases with low-level
attack, harassing birds as large as gannets by chasing them and
grabbing their tail or wing until they disgorge their catch, which
the skua often catches before it hits the water.

• **BREEDING** Usually monogamous, but have been known to
be polygamous; small colonies. Raises wings in display flight.

• **NESTING** Incubation 26–29 days by both sexes, but mostly
by female. Semiprecocial young stay in nest 42–49 days, fed by
both parents. First flight at about 60 days, but young stay near nest
for 21–28 more days, tended by
both parents. 1 brood per year.

• **POPULATION** Uncommon
off the north and middle
Atlantic Coast south to North
Carolina from November
through March.

Similar Birds

POMARINE, PARASITIC,
AND LONG-TAILED
JAEGERS
Dark morphs • smaller;
not barrel chested; may
have tail points (unless
molted); narrower
wings; less striking wing
patch.

SOUTH POLAR SKUA
Lacks reddish tones and
streaking on upperparts
• "blond phase" much
paler with less streaking
and much paler head.

Flight Pattern

Strong purposeful direct flight with
shallow constant wing beats; hugs wave
contours or flies up to 45.5 m high.

Nest Identification

Shape ～ Location ▟ ▬

Lined with leaves, moss, and grass • on rocky ground at base of bank or slope
• built by both sexes • 1–3 yellow to green or brown eggs, marked with purple
and brown splotches; short elliptical, 6.6 cm long.

Plumage Sexes similar	Habitat 〰 ___	Migration Migratory	Weight 414 g

DATE _____ TIME_____ LOCATION _____

Family LARIDAE	Species *Stercorarius maccormicki*	Length 53 cm	Wingspan 132 cm

SOUTH POLAR SKUA

Rarely seen from shore, this skua spends much of its time at sea, scavenging around fishing boats and chasing gulls and shearwaters. It nests along the coast of Antarctica but winters (our summer) in northern oceans; vagrants have been spotted in the Aleutians and once in North Dakota. They may be seen well off the Atlantic and Pacific coasts from May to November. In flight, the South Polar Skua looks stout-bodied and chunky, with a "hunched shoulder" appearance. The smallest of the skuas, this bird has a smaller head than the Great Skua; both a light and dark morph with gradations in between may range from almost white-bodied to blackish. The intermediate morph has a medium-brown nape and underparts.

white base to primaries forms bar on middle of forewing

brown unstreaked mantle

short broad tail

- **SONG** Usually silent away from breeding areas. Gull-like *scoo-ah*.
- **BEHAVIOR** Solitary outside breeding season. Aggressive hunter. Eats fish, penguin eggs, lemmings, and carrion. Shakes birds with its bill

broad rounded wings

PALE MORPH

to make them let go of their prey then seizes it. Dives into water from air to catch fish. Tends fishing trawlers. Defensive at nest; often flies straight at the head of a human intruder.
- **BREEDING** Monogamous; small colonies. Male feeds female during courtship.
- **NESTING** Incubation 24–34 days by both parents; female does more. Young semiprecocial; one nestling may be forced by its sibling to leave nest shortly after hatching; usually dies. The remaining one is fed by both parents by regurgitation.

First flight at 49–59 days. 1 brood per year.
- **POPULATION** Casual May to November well offshore on both Pacific and Atlantic Coasts, as postbreeding birds disperse northward from Antarctica.

Similar Birds

GREAT SKUA
Larger; reddish streaking on upperparts; lacks pale nape
• eastern range.

Flight Pattern

Strong swift direct flight with constant shallow wing beats.

Nest Identification

Shape   Location

Moss or bare soil • on rocky slopes, bottom of hill • male begins nest, female completes • 1–3 yellow to green or brown eggs marked with purples and browns; short elliptical, 6.1 cm long.

Plumage Sexes similar	Habitat	Migration Migratory	Weight 1.1 kg

DATE _____ TIME_____ LOCATION _____

Family LARIDAE	Species *Stercorarius pomarinus*	Length 51–58 cm	Wingspan 122 cm

POMARINE JAEGER

The largest and strongest jaeger is about the size of a Ring-billed or Heermann's Gull, with a bulky body, thick neck, and wide-based wings. Like many of the skuas, its nesting is related to lemming populations on the Arctic tundra. When the brown lemming is numerous these seabirds nest, and when the rodent is not abundant they may not breed at all.

It has a light color morph and a more rare dark morph. Adults

yellowish wash over nape and cheeks

chocolate-brown back, upperwing coverts, secondary flight feathers, and tail feathers

2 long central tail feathers twisted 90 degrees

dark helmeted appearance

heavy hooked bill

LIGHT MORPH

have 2 blunt central tail feathers with vanes twisted vertically. In flight this bird appears bulkier, with a slower wing beat, than other jaegers, and displays a larger white patch at the base of the primaries, often with a second smaller and fainter patch nearby.

dark band mottled across chest

chocolate-brown underwing coverts

white to pale base of primary flight feathers, darker toward tips

- **SONG** Often silent, except on breeding grounds. Sharp *which-yew* or *yeew*; high-pitched *week-week* or *yeew-eee*.

- **BEHAVIOR** Solitary or in pairs. Predatory. Eats small mammals, fish, birds, carrion, and refuse. Often steals from other seabirds. Picks up prey with bill, never talons. Found at sea outside breeding season.

DARK MORPH

- **BREEDING** Monogamous; small colonies. During courtship, male and female face one another and vibrate wings while singing.

JUVENILE

- **NESTING** Incubation 25–27 days by both sexes. Semiprecocial young leave nest after a few days, but tended 42 days or more. First flight at 21–27 days after fledging nest. Average less than 1 brood per year.

- **POPULATION** Uncommon to fairly common on tundra breeding grounds. Common to uncommon far offshore on both coasts outside breeding season.

Similar Birds

PARASITIC JAEGER Smaller; more slender; two central tail feathers extended and pointed but not twisted; smaller bill; less white at base of primaries.

SOUTH POLAR SKUA Bulky, heavy body; golden streaking on nape; hunchback appearance; short wedge-shaped tail with central tail feathers not extended.

Flight Pattern
Strong steady flight with slow deep wing beats like a large gull; may alternate several wing beats with long glide.

Nest Identification	
Shape Location	Lined with plant material • on ground • built by both parents • 2 olive to brown eggs, with dark brown blotches; short elliptical, 6.6 cm long.

Plumage Sexes similar	Habitat	Migration Migratory	Weight 635 g

DATE _____ TIME_____ LOCATION _____

Family LARIDAE	Species *Stercorarius parasiticus*	Length 38–53 cm	Wingspan 91 cm

PARASITIC JAEGER

This skua can sometimes be seen from shore, intruding upon migrating flocks of terns and stealing food from other seabirds. It has two distinct color morphs, light and dark, and many intermediates. Falconlike in pursuit, it is about the size of a Laughing or Mew Gull and normally flies with quick wing beats broken by short glides. It is not known to breed until three to five years of age.

• **SONG** Usually silent when not on breeding grounds. Yelping notes and rising *skooo-a* or *ka-aaow*.

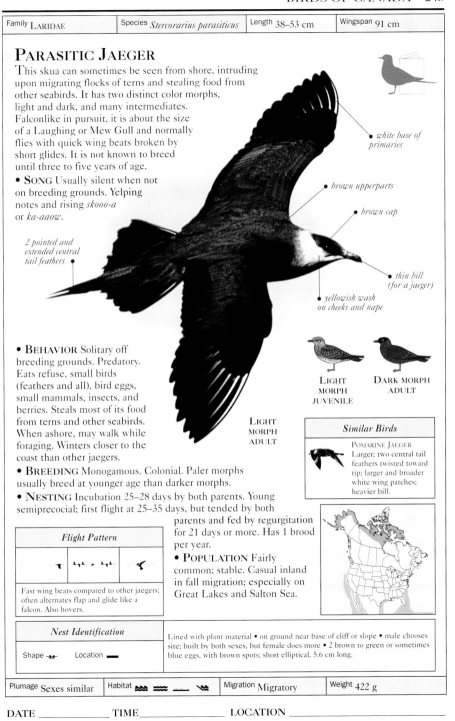

white base of primaries

brown upperparts

brown cap

thin bill (for a jaeger)

yellowish wash on cheeks and nape

2 pointed and extended central tail feathers

LIGHT MORPH JUVENILE

DARK MORPH ADULT

LIGHT MORPH ADULT

• **BEHAVIOR** Solitary off breeding grounds. Predatory. Eats refuse, small birds (feathers and all), bird eggs, small mammals, insects, and berries. Steals most of its food from terns and other seabirds. When ashore, may walk while foraging. Winters closer to the coast than other jaegers.

• **BREEDING** Monogamous. Colonial. Paler morphs usually breed at younger age than darker morphs.

• **NESTING** Incubation 25–28 days by both parents. Young semiprecocial; first flight at 25–35 days, but tended by both parents and fed by regurgitation for 21 days or more. Has 1 brood per year.

• **POPULATION** Fairly common; stable. Casual inland in fall migration; especially on Great Lakes and Salton Sea.

Similar Birds

POMARINE JAEGER Larger; two central tail feathers twisted toward tip; larger and broader white wing patches; heavier bill.

Flight Pattern

Fast wing beats compared to other jaegers; often alternates flap and glide like a falcon. Also hovers.

Nest Identification

Shape ～ Location ▬

Lined with plant material • on ground near base of cliff or slope • male chooses site; built by both sexes, but female does more • 2 brown to green or sometimes blue eggs, with brown spots; short elliptical, 5.6 cm long.

Plumage Sexes similar	Habitat ～～ ～～ ～ ～	Migration Migratory	Weight 422 g

DATE _____ TIME_____ LOCATION _____

Family LARIDAE	Species *Stercorarius longicaudus*	Length 51–58 cm	Wingspan 76–84 cm

LONG-TAILED JAEGER

Distinguished by its 20- to 25-cm central tail feathers, this jaeger is rarely seen from land outside breeding season in the Arctic. These birds migrate in family groups to the central Pacific and south Atlantic in winter, but their route is unknown. The smallest of the jaegers, it is the least likely to steal food from other seabirds and is highly dependent on the tundra's small rodent populations in summer. In flight adults do not show a breast band, as do other jaegers. They have light grayish brown upperparts and long slender wings without a white patch at the base of the primaries (shafts of three outer primaries are white) and a slender body. Juveniles have a short tail and a white patch at the base of the primaries under the wing.

white collar

black cap

yellow cheeks

dark brown flight feathers contrast with gray coverts

blue-gray legs and feet

long pointed inner tail feathers

- **SONG** While flying, *pheu-pheu-pheu*. When irritated utters *kr-r-r-r; kr-r-r-r, kir-kri-kri*.

- **BEHAVIOR** In summer eats mostly lemmings and other small rodents, but also takes birds, eggs, insects, carrion, and berries. In winter eats fish, squid, carrion, and refuse. Uses beak to pick up food. Catches insects and other prey in flight. Often flies low over land or water. Most pelagic jaeger in postbreeding season.

- **BREEDING** Monogamous. Colonial. Does not breed until 3–4 years old. Courtship display features zigzag chasing flight. During courtship, male feeds female from the ground.

- **NESTING** Incubation 23–25 days by both sexes. Young semiprecocial; first flight at 22–27 days, but both sexes tend and feed by regurgitation for 7–21 days. 1 brood per year unless lemmings are scarce, then birds will not breed at all.

DARK MORPH JUVENILE

LIGHT MORPH JUVENILE

Similar Birds

PARASITIC JAEGER Larger; black legs; larger white patch on outer wings; grayish breast band; short, pointed central tail feathers.

- **POPULATION** Common on tundra breeding grounds. Trends stable. Disperses widely at sea outside breeding season. Fairly common to uncommon off West Coast; casual in Gulf of Mexico and on East Coast. Rare to accidental inland.

Flight Pattern

Light floating buoyant ternlike flight is graceful compared with other jaegers. Hovers before dipping to pick up prey.

Nest Identification

Shape — Location — ▪▪▪

Lined with grasses, moss, and leaves • on ground near edge of slope • built mostly by female • 2 brown to olive eggs with dark brown and gray blotches; short elliptical, 5.6 cm long.

Plumage Sexes similar	Habitat	Migration Migratory	Weight 281 g

DATE _____ TIME_____ LOCATION _____

Family LARIDAE	Species *Larus atricilla*	Length 38–43 cm	Wingspan 102–107 cm

LAUGHING GULL

Named for its laughterlike call, this gull was threatened by the feather trade in the early 20th century. Now this coastal inhabitant forms colonies with thousands of nests. A distinguishing habit is its tendency to steal food from the Brown Pelican by snatching it out of the pelican's pouch after it surfaces with a catch. This three-year gull passes through two different winter plumages prior to attaining adult plumage. Adults have a white tail year round. In winter adults the black head is replaced by a gray smudge on the nape, and the bill, legs, and feet are dull blackish.

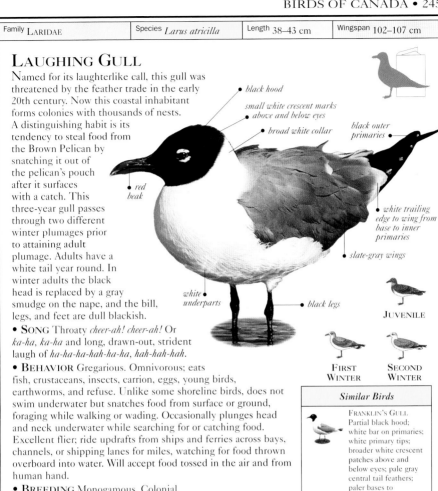

black hood

small white crescent marks above and below eyes

broad white collar

black outer primaries

red beak

white trailing edge to wing from base to inner primaries

slate-gray wings

white underparts

black legs

JUVENILE

FIRST WINTER

SECOND WINTER

• **SONG** Throaty *cheer-ah! cheer-ah!* Or *ka-ha, ka-ha* and long, drawn-out, strident laugh of *ha-ha-ha-hah-ha-ha, hah-hah-hah.*

• **BEHAVIOR** Gregarious. Omnivorous; eats fish, crustaceans, insects, carrion, eggs, young birds, earthworms, and refuse. Unlike some shoreline birds, does not swim underwater but snatches food from surface or ground, foraging while walking or wading. Occasionally plunges head and neck underwater while searching for or catching food. Excellent flier; ride updrafts from ships and ferries across bays, channels, or shipping lanes for miles, watching for food thrown overboard into water. Will accept food tossed in the air and from human hand.

• **BREEDING** Monogamous. Colonial.

• **NESTING** Incubation about 20 days by both sexes. Young leave nest to hide in nearby vegetation after a few days. Both sexes feed first by regurgitation, solid food later. First flight at 35 days. 1 brood per year.

• **POPULATION** Common. Probably stable over much of range, but numbers have been increasing in the northeastern US in recent years.

Similar Birds

FRANKLIN'S GULL
Partial black hood; white bar on primaries; white primary tips; broader white crescent patches above and below eyes; pale gray central tail feathers; paler bases to underwing primaries.

Flight Pattern

Slow flight with deep wing beats. May soar on updrafts and deflected wind over dunes, beaches, parking lots, and ships.

Nest Identification

Shape ⌣ ⌣   Location ⋯ ⋯

Little lining in scrape; cup lined with grass, sticks, and debris • built by both sexes • 3 olive to buff eggs with brownish marks; ovate to elliptical ovate or pyriform, 4.8–5.8 x 4.8–5.8 cm.

Plumage Sexes similar	Habitat 〰 ▭	Migration Migratory	Weight 326 g

DATE _____ TIME _____ LOCATION _____

Family LARIDAE	Species *Larus pipixcan*	Length 33–38 cm	Wingspan 91 cm

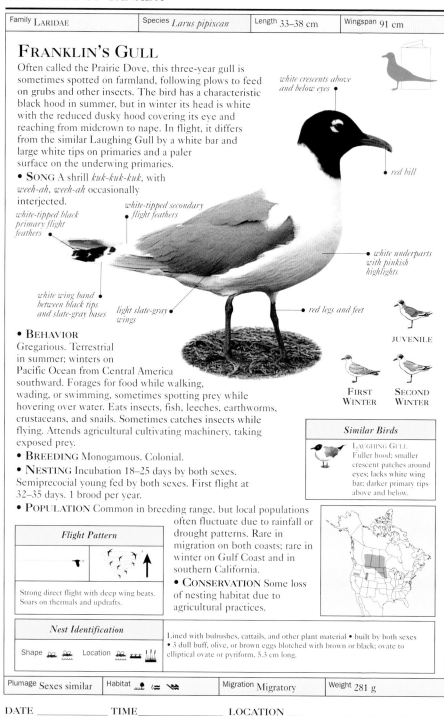

FRANKLIN'S GULL

Often called the Prairie Dove, this three-year gull is sometimes spotted on farmland, following plows to feed on grubs and other insects. The bird has a characteristic black hood in summer, but in winter its head is white with the reduced dusky hood covering its eye and reaching from midcrown to nape. In flight, it differs from the similar Laughing Gull by a white bar and large white tips on primaries and a paler surface on the underwing primaries.

white crescents above and below eyes

red bill

• **SONG** A shrill *kuk-kuk-kuk*, with *weeh-ah, weeh-ah* occasionally interjected.

white-tipped secondary flight feathers

white-tipped black primary flight feathers

white underparts with pinkish highlights

white wing band between black tips and slate-gray bases

light slate-gray wings

red legs and feet

JUVENILE

• **BEHAVIOR** Gregarious. Terrestrial in summer; winters on Pacific Ocean from Central America southward. Forages for food while walking, wading, or swimming, sometimes spotting prey while hovering over water. Eats insects, fish, leeches, earthworms, crustaceans, and snails. Sometimes catches insects while flying. Attends agricultural cultivating machinery, taking exposed prey.

FIRST WINTER

SECOND WINTER

• **BREEDING** Monogamous. Colonial.

• **NESTING** Incubation 18–25 days by both sexes. Semiprecocial young fed by both sexes. First flight at 32–35 days. 1 brood per year.

Similar Birds

LAUGHING GULL
Fuller hood; smaller crescent patches around eyes; lacks white wing bar; darker primary tips above and below.

• **POPULATION** Common in breeding range, but local populations often fluctuate due to rainfall or drought patterns. Rare in migration on both coasts; rare in winter on Gulf Coast and in southern California.

• **CONSERVATION** Some loss of nesting habitat due to agricultural practices.

Flight Pattern
Strong direct flight with deep wing beats. Soars on thermals and updrafts.

Nest Identification	
Shape	Location

Lined with bulrushes, cattails, and other plant material • built by both sexes • 3 dull buff, olive, or brown eggs blotched with brown or black; ovate to elliptical ovate or pyriform, 5.3 cm long.

Plumage Sexes similar	Habitat	Migration Migratory	Weight 281 g

Family LARIDAE	Species *Larus minutus*	Length 25–30 cm	Wingspan 61–66 cm

LITTLE GULL

This European native is rarely encountered in great numbers in North America. The first Little Gull nest in North America was discovered in 1962. The smallest of all gulls, this shoreline inhabitant sometimes is seen alongside Bonaparte's Gulls and terns. In winter months, the Little Gull sports a gray cap, a gray spot behind both eyes, and a black bill. Breeding adults have a black cap. In flight, note the rounded wing with dark gray to black underwings, contrasting with the pale upperwing and body and square tail. Juveniles show a black bar on the upperwings in flight. This is a two- to three-year gull.

white-tipped flight feathers

WINTER PLUMAGE

rounded pale gray wings

dark red bill with black tip

white underparts

JUVENILE

red legs

BREEDING PLUMAGE

• **SONG** Calls include a *kek-kek-kek* with a repeated *kay-e*.

• **BEHAVIOR** Forages for food by flying low over land or the water's surface, sometimes dipping down while in flight to catch prey. Also forages while swimming and wading in shallow water. Feeds primarily on insects in summer; otherwise crustaceans, mollusks, spiders, small fish, and marine worms. Feeding flight is hesitant, wavering, and ternlike as it dips down, legs trailing, to pick up food from water.

• **BREEDING** Monogamous. Colonial.

• **NESTING** Incubation 23–25 days by both sexes. Semiprecocial young remain in nest 21–24 days, fed by both sexes. 1 brood per year.

• **POPULATION** Rare to uncommon. North American populations scattered and irregular. Common in Eurasian countries.

• **CONSERVATION** North American numbers probably not large enough to be self-sustaining, but birds migrating from Europe maintain a small but steady population.

Similar Birds

BONAPARTE'S GULL
Larger; black bill; white wedge on outer wing (primaries); black-tipped primaries; pale underwing surface.

BLACK-HEADED GULL
Significantly larger; dark brown-black head; red bill; white wedge on outer wing; black-tipped primaries.

Flight Pattern
Strong direct flight with deep wing beats, particularly on downstroke.

Nest Identification	
Shape ⟋⟍ Location ▬	Grass- and leaf-lined with weeds and reeds • on wet ground, sometimes built higher • built by both sexes • 1–5 yellowish, olive-brown, greenish gray eggs, marked with reddish brown and gray; ovate, 4.1 x 4.6 cm.

Plumage Sexes similar	Habitat 〜〜 ⩘	Migration Migratory	Weight 119 g

Family LARIDAE	Species *Larus ridibundus*	Length 36–41 cm	Wingspan 102 cm

BLACK-HEADED GULL

Despite its name, the Black-headed Gull has a chocolate-brown head during the breeding season. In its native Eurasian habitat it is usually found in freshwater; however, while wintering in North America it lives in coastal waters. In flight this two-year gull shows blackish primaries on the underwing, a white wedge on the

pale gray wings and back

white nape, neck, and underparts

chocolate-brown hood

maroon bill

white tail and rump

wing fore-edge, and black-tipped primaries. Winter adults lose the dark hood and have a black ear spot. Juveniles are similar to winter adults but have a paler bill, legs, and feet; a black tail tip; and a brown carpal bar.

maroon legs and feet

JUVENILE

WINTER PLUMAGE

• **SONG** Resembles laughter; harsh nasal varied *kraah*. Remains very vocal outside breeding season.

• **BEHAVIOR** Eats insects, crustaceans, earthworms, marine worms, mollusks, small fish, carrion, seeds, and berries. Swoops down while flying and picks up prey from water. Also steals food from other birds. Follows plows to pick up exposed prey.

• **BREEDING** Monogamous. Colonial.

• **NESTING** Incubation 23–26 days by both sexes. Semiprecocial young remain in nest for 10 days, fed by both sexes. First flight at 35 days. 1 brood per year.

• **POPULATION** Fairly common in winter in Newfoundland where there are small breeding colonies. Rare in winter off the coast of the Maritimes and New England; accidental to western Alaska. Casual to accidental elsewhere.

Similar Birds

BONAPARTE'S GULL
Smaller; pale underwing, including primaries; black hood; black bill.

Flight Pattern

Light buoyant direct flight on long pointed angled wings. Soars on thermals and updrafts.

Nest Identification

Shape 〜 Location ▬ ▬ ⩫ 〰

Lined with leaves, moss, and grasses • on ground hidden by vegetation • built by both sexes • 2–4 gray-green to tan or yellowish eggs marked with brown or olive; oval to elliptical, 5.1 cm long.

Plumage Sexes similar	Habitat 〜 〜 〜 〜	Migration Migratory	Weight 284 g

DATE _____ TIME_____ LOCATION _____

| Family LARIDAE | Species *Larus philadelphia* | Length 30–36 cm | Wingspan 84–91 cm |

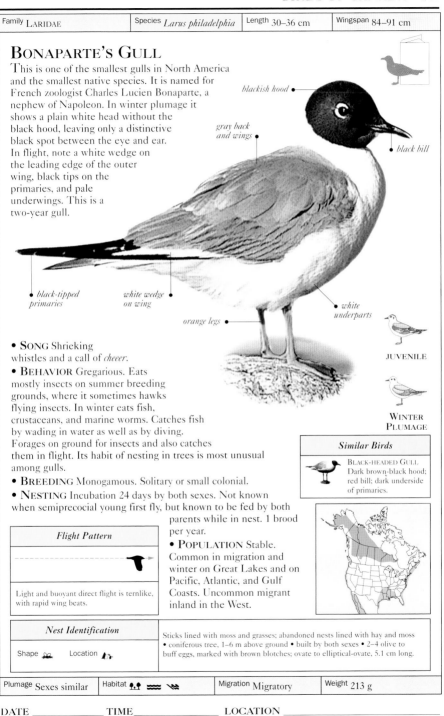

BONAPARTE'S GULL

This is one of the smallest gulls in North America and the smallest native species. It is named for French zoologist Charles Lucien Bonaparte, a nephew of Napoleon. In winter plumage it shows a plain white head without the black hood, leaving only a distinctive black spot between the eye and ear. In flight, note a white wedge on the leading edge of the outer wing, black tips on the primaries, and pale underwings. This is a two-year gull.

blackish hood

gray back and wings

black bill

black-tipped primaries

white wedge on wing

orange legs

white underparts

JUVENILE

WINTER PLUMAGE

- **SONG** Shrieking whistles and a call of *cheeer*.
- **BEHAVIOR** Gregarious. Eats mostly insects on summer breeding grounds, where it sometimes hawks flying insects. In winter eats fish, crustaceans, and marine worms. Catches fish by wading in water as well as by diving. Forages on ground for insects and also catches them in flight. Its habit of nesting in trees is most unusual among gulls.
- **BREEDING** Monogamous. Solitary or small colonial.
- **NESTING** Incubation 24 days by both sexes. Not known when semiprecocial young first fly, but known to be fed by both parents while in nest. 1 brood per year.
- **POPULATION** Stable. Common in migration and winter on Great Lakes and on Pacific, Atlantic, and Gulf Coasts. Uncommon migrant inland in the West.

Similar Birds

BLACK-HEADED GULL
Dark brown-black hood; red bill; dark underside of primaries.

Flight Pattern

Light and buoyant direct flight is ternlike, with rapid wing beats.

Nest Identification

Shape Location

Sticks lined with moss and grasses; abandoned nests lined with hay and moss • coniferous tree, 1–6 m above ground • built by both sexes • 2–4 olive to buff eggs, marked with brown blotches; ovate to elliptical-ovate, 5.1 cm long.

| Plumage Sexes similar | Habitat | Migration Migratory | Weight 213 g |

DATE _____ TIME_____ LOCATION _____

Family LARIDAE	Species *Larus heermanni*	Length 46–53 cm	Wingspan 122–130 cm

HEERMANN'S GULL

The overall dark coloring distinguishes this gull from others and makes it one of the easiest gulls in the West to identify. No other Pacific Coast gull combines the characteristics of white head, dark gray body, black tail with white tip, and red bill. When perched, the wing tips protrude well beyond the tip of the tail, covering the bird's pale gray rump and uppertail coverts. This somewhat aggressive bird is common along the Pacific Coast and spends most of its time at sea. First and second winter birds are very dark. This is a four-year gull.

• SONG A whiny *whee-ee*. While flying, repeatedly utters *cow-auk*, *cow-eek*.

white head and neck

red bill

gray breast and underparts

blue-gray legs and feet

white tips of flight feathers on inner wing

black tail with white band on terminal tip

JUVENILE

SECOND WINTER

THIRD WINTER

• BEHAVIOR Habits almost exclusively marine. Spends less time on beaches than any other western gull on the Pacific Coast south of Alaska. Eats fish, crustaceans, mollusks, insects, carrion, and sometimes eggs of other birds. Dives into ocean to catch fish. Tends flocks of feeding pelicans and cormorants, following them and sometimes stealing food from them or retrieving dropped or discarded prey. Also tends sea otters and seals.

• BREEDING Monogamous. Colonial.

• NESTING Incubation 28 days by both sexes. Semiprecocial young fed by both sexes. Age at first flight undetermined. 1 brood per year.

• POPULATION Common postbreeding-season visitor to West Coast; rare to casual inland in the Southwest.

Similar Birds

WESTERN GULL
Dark gray mantle and wings; white head, tail, and underparts; yellow bill; pink legs and feet.

• CONSERVATION Vulnerable to pollution of marine environments and disturbance on nesting grounds in Gulf of California and coastal islands off Baja California and western Mexico.

Flight Pattern

Buoyant direct flight on rather long wings, with a rhythmic, flicking wing beat.

Nest Identification

Shape ⚬ ⚬   Location ▬

Unlined if scrape; cup made of sticks, grass, and weeds, then lined with feathers • on ground between rocks or hidden in vegetation • built by both sexes • 2–3 pale gray to blue-gray eggs, with lavender, brown, and blue blotches, sometimes wreathed; ovate to elliptical ovate, 6.7 cm long.

Plumage Sexes similar	Habitat 〰 ⚏ 〰	Migration Migratory	Weight 499 g

DATE _____ TIME_____ LOCATION _____

Family LARIDAE	Species *Larus canus*	Length 41–46 cm	Wingspan 109 cm

MEW GULL

Heard from the tops of conifers with its catlike *mee-you*, the Mew Gull is common along the Pacific coast. It breeds along the coast and on lakes in the interior of extreme northwestern North America. Separated from similar gulls by the short unmarked yellow bill and the white spots (mirrors) in the black-tipped primaries. Winter adults have a white head washed with brown and a

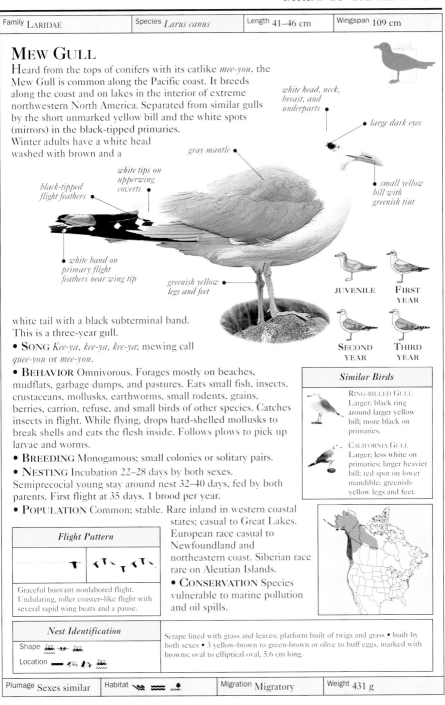

white head, neck, breast, and underparts

large dark eyes

gray mantle

small yellow bill with greenish tint

white tips on upperwing coverts

black-tipped flight feathers

white band on primary flight feathers near wing tip

greenish yellow legs and feet

JUVENILE

FIRST YEAR

SECOND YEAR

THIRD YEAR

white tail with a black subterminal band. This is a three-year gull.

- **SONG** *Kee-ya, kee-ya, kee-ya*; mewing call *quee-you* or *mee-you*.

- **BEHAVIOR** Omnivorous. Forages mostly on beaches, mudflats, garbage dumps, and pastures. Eats small fish, insects, crustaceans, mollusks, earthworms, small rodents, grains, berries, carrion, refuse, and small birds of other species. Catches insects in flight. While flying, drops hard-shelled mollusks to break shells and eats the flesh inside. Follows plows to pick up larvae and worms.

- **BREEDING** Monogamous; small colonies or solitary pairs.

- **NESTING** Incubation 22–28 days by both sexes. Semiprecocial young stay around nest 32–40 days, fed by both parents. First flight at 35 days. 1 brood per year.

- **POPULATION** Common; stable. Rare inland in western coastal states; casual to Great Lakes. European race casual to Newfoundland and northeastern coast. Siberian race rare on Aleutian Islands.

- **CONSERVATION** Species vulnerable to marine pollution and oil spills.

Similar Birds

RING-BILLED GULL Larger; black ring around larger yellow bill; more black on primaries.

CALIFORNIA GULL Larger; less white on primaries; larger heavier bill; red spot on lower mandible; greenish-yellow legs and feet.

Flight Pattern

Graceful buoyant nonlabored flight. Undulating, roller coaster–like flight with several rapid wing beats and a pause.

Nest Identification

Shape

Location

Scrape lined with grass and leaves; platform built of twigs and grass • built by both sexes • 3 yellow-brown to green-brown or olive to buff eggs, marked with browns; oval to elliptical oval, 5.6 cm long.

Plumage Sexes similar	Habitat	Migration Migratory	Weight 431 g

DATE _____ TIME_____ LOCATION _____

| Family LARIDAE | Species *Larus delawarensis* | Length 46–48 cm | Wingspan 122 cm |

RING-BILLED GULL

One of the most widespread and familiar gulls in North America, the Ring-billed Gull can be distinguished by the black subterminal band on its yellow bill.

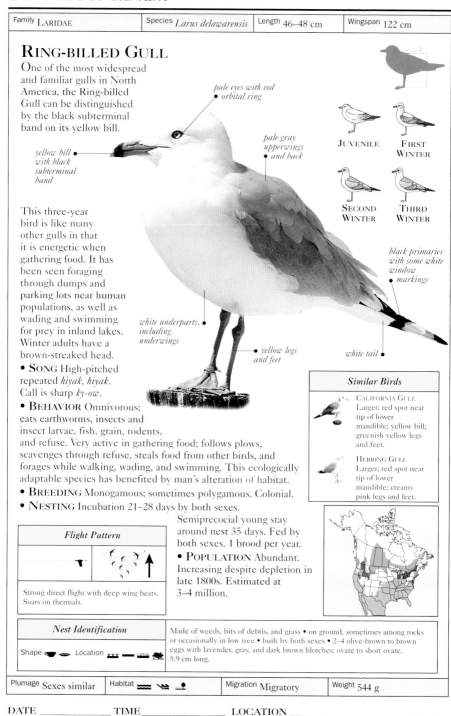

pale eyes with red orbital ring

yellow bill with black subterminal band

pale gray upperwings and back

JUVENILE   FIRST WINTER

SECOND WINTER   THIRD WINTER

black primaries with some white window markings

This three-year bird is like many other gulls in that it is energetic when gathering food. It has been seen foraging through dumps and parking lots near human populations, as well as wading and swimming for prey in inland lakes. Winter adults have a brown-streaked head.

white underparts, including underwings

yellow legs and feet

white tail

• **SONG** High-pitched repeated *hiyak, hiyak.* Call is sharp *ky-ow.*

• **BEHAVIOR** Omnivorous; eats earthworms, insects and insect larvae, fish, grain, rodents, and refuse. Very active in gathering food; follows plows, scavenges through refuse, steals food from other birds, and forages while walking, wading, and swimming. This ecologically adaptable species has benefited by man's alteration of habitat.

• **BREEDING** Monogamous; sometimes polygamous. Colonial.

• **NESTING** Incubation 21–28 days by both sexes.

Semiprecocial young stay around nest 35 days. Fed by both sexes. 1 brood per year.

• **POPULATION** Abundant. Increasing despite depletion in late 1800s. Estimated at 3–4 million.

Similar Birds

CALIFORNIA GULL
Larger; red spot near tip of lower mandible; yellow bill; greenish yellow legs and feet.

HERRING GULL
Larger; red spot near tip of lower mandible; creamy pink legs and feet.

Flight Pattern
Strong direct flight with deep wing beats. Soars on thermals.

Nest Identification	
Shape ⬤ ◢ Location ▦ ▬ ▦ ⬥	Made of weeds, bits of debris, and grass • on ground, sometimes among rocks or occasionally in low tree • built by both sexes • 2–4 olive-brown to brown eggs with lavender, gray, and dark brown blotches; ovate to short ovate, 5.9 cm long.

| Plumage Sexes similar | Habitat ≈ ⬥ ⬥ | Migration Migratory | Weight 544 g |

DATE _____ TIME_____ LOCATION _____

| Family LARIDAE | Species *Larus californicus* | Length 53–56 cm | Wingspan 122–137 cm |

CALIFORNIA GULL

The monument to the gull in Salt Lake City was inspired by the California Gull, because it saved the crops of the Mormon settlers from the grasshopper plague of 1848. Today, this four-year gull is the state bird of Utah. It builds its nests close to freshwater marshes and lakes, but at other times, it is frequently seen on inland fields and nearby farms, foraging through trash and eating insects. In flight, note that adults have

white head, neck, and breast

gray back and upperwings

yellow bill with red and black spot on lower mandible

DARK JUVENILE

FIRST WINTER

black-tipped wings with white windows

white underparts and tail

greenish yellow to gray-green legs and feet

SECOND WINTER

a dusky gray stripe on the trailing edge of the underwing. Winter adults have brownish streaking on the head and hindneck.

- **SONG** Has soft call of *kow-kow-kow*, *kee-ou*, or *klee-ah*. Has alarm call of *yowww*; also a quiet repeated *waaaaaaaah*.
- **BEHAVIOR** Primarily an inland species during summer months. Feeds on a host of agricultural pests, from grasshoppers and many other insects to rodents. Also takes fish, eggs and young from other birds, worms, spiders, refuse, and carrion. Like most gulls it is an active forager.
- **BREEDING** Monogamous. Colonial.
- **NESTING** Incubation 23–27 days by both sexes. Semiprecocial young tended by both sexes; it is not known how long they stay in nest. First flight at about 45 days. 1 brood per year.
- **POPULATION** Increasing. Abundant. Casual on Gulf Coast and East Coast in winter.
- **CONSERVATION** Vulnerable to human disturbance at nesting colonies on large western lakes and pollution of lakes and habitat loss. Mono Lake has 50,000 seriously threatened pairs.

Similar Birds

RING-BILLED GULL
Smaller; black ring around beak; lighter eyes; lacks dusky trailing edge to underwing.

HERRING GULL
Larger; red spot only on lower mandible; yellow eye; creamy pink legs and feet; lacks dusky trailing edge to underwing; lighter gray back and upperwings.

Flight Pattern	
Strong direct flight with deep wing beats. Soars on thermals and updrafts.	

Nest Identification	
Shape ⬤ ⬤ Location ▬	Twigs, dried feathers, bits of debris, grass, and weeds; 36–46 cm • on ground • built by both sexes • 2–3 olive-buff eggs, often blotched with deep grays and browns; oval to short oval; if third egg is laid, shape is short, subelliptical; 7.1 cm long.

| Plumage Sexes similar | Habitat ≋ ⬤ ≋ | Migration Migratory | Weight 635 g |

DATE _____ TIME_____ LOCATION _____

Family LARIDAE	Species *Larus argentatus*	Length 56–66 cm	Wingspan 137–147 cm

HERRING GULL

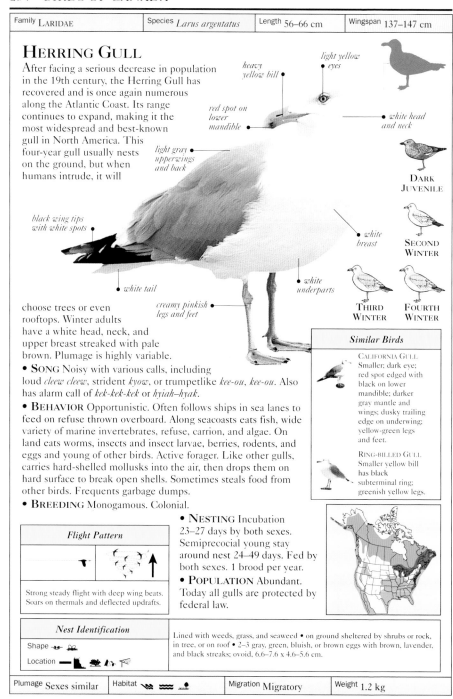

After facing a serious decrease in population in the 19th century, the Herring Gull has recovered and is once again numerous along the Atlantic Coast. Its range continues to expand, making it the most widespread and best-known gull in North America. This four-year gull usually nests on the ground, but when humans intrude, it will

heavy yellow bill

light yellow eyes

red spot on lower mandible

light gray upperwings and back

white head and neck

DARK JUVENILE

black wing tips with white spots

white breast

SECOND WINTER

white tail

creamy pinkish legs and feet

white underparts

THIRD WINTER

FOURTH WINTER

choose trees or even rooftops. Winter adults have a white head, neck, and upper breast streaked with pale brown. Plumage is highly variable.

• **SONG** Noisy with various calls, including loud *cleew cleew*, strident *kyow*, or trumpetlike *kee-ou, kee-ou*. Also has alarm call of *kek-kek-kek* or *hyiah–hyak*.

• **BEHAVIOR** Opportunistic. Often follows ships in sea lanes to feed on refuse thrown overboard. Along seacoasts eats fish, wide variety of marine invertebrates, refuse, carrion, and algae. On land eats worms, insects and insect larvae, berries, rodents, and eggs and young of other birds. Active forager. Like other gulls, carries hard-shelled mollusks into the air, then drops them on hard surface to break open shells. Sometimes steals food from other birds. Frequents garbage dumps.

• **BREEDING** Monogamous. Colonial.

Similar Birds

CALIFORNIA GULL
Smaller; dark eye; red spot edged with black on lower mandible; darker gray mantle and wings; dusky trailing edge on underwing; yellow-green legs and feet.

RING-BILLED GULL
Smaller yellow bill has black subterminal ring; greenish yellow legs.

• **NESTING** Incubation 23–27 days by both sexes. Semiprecocial young stay around nest 24–49 days. Fed by both sexes. 1 brood per year.

• **POPULATION** Abundant. Today all gulls are protected by federal law.

Flight Pattern	

Strong steady flight with deep wing beats. Soars on thermals and deflected updrafts.

Nest Identification	
Shape	Lined with weeds, grass, and seaweed • on ground sheltered by shrubs or rock, in tree, or on roof • 2–3 gray, green, bluish, or brown eggs with brown, lavender, and black streaks; ovoid, 6.6–7.6 x 4.6–5.6 cm.
Location	

Plumage Sexes similar	Habitat	Migration Migratory	Weight 1.2 kg

DATE _____ TIME_____ LOCATION _____

Family LARIDAE	Species *Larus cachinnans*	Length 61 cm	Wingspan 137–145 cm

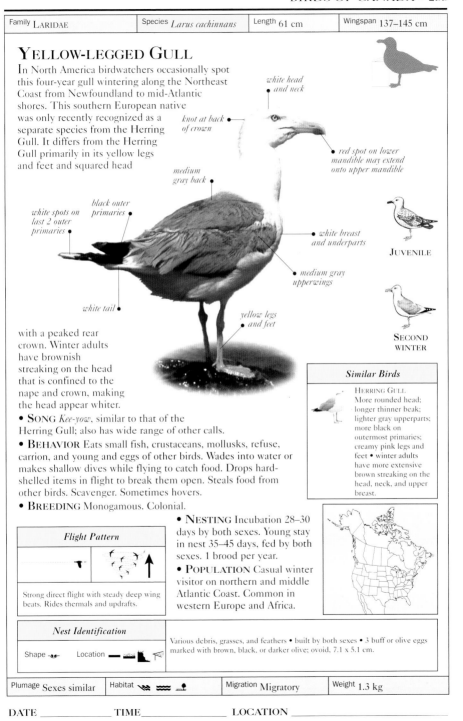

YELLOW-LEGGED GULL

In North America birdwatchers occasionally spot this four-year gull wintering along the Northeast Coast from Newfoundland to mid-Atlantic shores. This southern European native was only recently recognized as a separate species from the Herring Gull. It differs from the Herring Gull primarily in its yellow legs and feet and squared head

white head and neck

knot at back of crown

red spot on lower mandible may extend onto upper mandible

medium gray back

black outer primaries

white spots on last 2 outer primaries

white breast and underparts

medium gray upperwings

white tail

yellow legs and feet

JUVENILE

SECOND WINTER

with a peaked rear crown. Winter adults have brownish streaking on the head that is confined to the nape and crown, making the head appear whiter.

• **SONG** *Kee-yow*, similar to that of the Herring Gull; also has wide range of other calls.

• **BEHAVIOR** Eats small fish, crustaceans, mollusks, refuse, carrion, and young and eggs of other birds. Wades into water or makes shallow dives while flying to catch food. Drops hard-shelled items in flight to break them open. Steals food from other birds. Scavenger. Sometimes hovers.

• **BREEDING** Monogamous. Colonial.

Similar Birds

HERRING GULL
More rounded head; longer thinner beak; lighter gray upperparts; more black on outermost primaries; creamy pink legs and feet • winter adults have more extensive brown streaking on the head, neck, and upper breast.

• **NESTING** Incubation 28–30 days by both sexes. Young stay in nest 35–45 days, fed by both sexes. 1 brood per year.

• **POPULATION** Casual winter visitor on northern and middle Atlantic Coast. Common in western Europe and Africa.

Flight Pattern
Strong direct flight with steady deep wing beats. Rides thermals and updrafts.

Nest Identification	
Shape	Location

Various debris, grasses, and feathers • built by both sexes • 3 buff or olive eggs marked with brown, black, or darker olive; ovoid, 7.1 x 5.1 cm.

Plumage Sexes similar	Habitat	Migration Migratory	Weight 1.3 kg

DATE _____ TIME_____ LOCATION _____

Family LARIDAE	Species *Larus thayeri*	Length 58–64 cm	Wingspan 140 cm

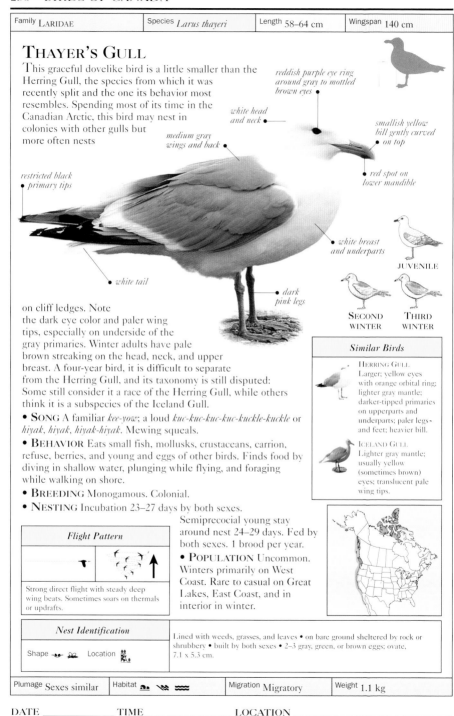

THAYER'S GULL

This graceful dovelike bird is a little smaller than the Herring Gull, the species from which it was recently split and the one its behavior most resembles. Spending most of its time in the Canadian Arctic, this bird may nest in colonies with other gulls but more often nests

reddish purple eye ring around gray to mottled brown eyes

white head and neck

smallish yellow bill gently curved on top

medium gray wings and back

red spot on lower mandible

restricted black primary tips

white breast and underparts

JUVENILE

white tail

dark pink legs

SECOND WINTER

THIRD WINTER

on cliff ledges. Note the dark eye color and paler wing tips, especially on underside of the gray primaries. Winter adults have pale brown streaking on the head, neck, and upper breast. A four-year bird, it is difficult to separate from the Herring Gull, and its taxonomy is still disputed: Some still consider it a race of the Herring Gull, while others think it is a subspecies of the Iceland Gull.

• **SONG** A familiar *kee-yow*; a loud *kuc-kuc-kuc-kuc-kuckle-kuckle* or *hiyak, hiyak, hiyak-hiyak*. Mewing squeals.

• **BEHAVIOR** Eats small fish, mollusks, crustaceans, carrion, refuse, berries, and young and eggs of other birds. Finds food by diving in shallow water, plunging while flying, and foraging while walking on shore.

• **BREEDING** Monogamous. Colonial.

• **NESTING** Incubation 23–27 days by both sexes. Semiprecocial young stay around nest 24–29 days. Fed by both sexes. 1 brood per year.

• **POPULATION** Uncommon. Winters primarily on West Coast. Rare to casual on Great Lakes, East Coast, and in interior in winter.

Similar Birds

HERRING GULL
Larger; yellow eyes with orange orbital ring; lighter gray mantle; darker-tipped primaries on upperparts and underparts; paler legs and feet; heavier bill.

ICELAND GULL
Lighter gray mantle; usually yellow (sometimes brown) eyes; translucent pale wing tips.

Flight Pattern

Strong direct flight with steady deep wing beats. Sometimes soars on thermals or updrafts.

Nest Identification

Shape Location

Lined with weeds, grasses, and leaves • on bare ground sheltered by rock or shrubbery • built by both sexes • 2–3 gray, green, or brown eggs; ovate, 7.1 x 5.3 cm.

Plumage Sexes similar	Habitat	Migration Migratory	Weight 1.1 kg

DATE _____ TIME_____ LOCATION _____

Family LARIDAE	Species *Larus glaucoides*	Length 58–64 cm	Wingspan 137 cm

ICELAND GULL

Restricted to the North Atlantic Ocean where it is in the company of larger, more robust gulls, this highly variable four-year gull spends its summers on the coasts of northeastern Canada and Greenland. It has two morphs: the typical form, which nests in Greenland and has white wing tips, and the Kumlien's, which nests in Canada and has gray wing tips. The pale primaries look translucent in

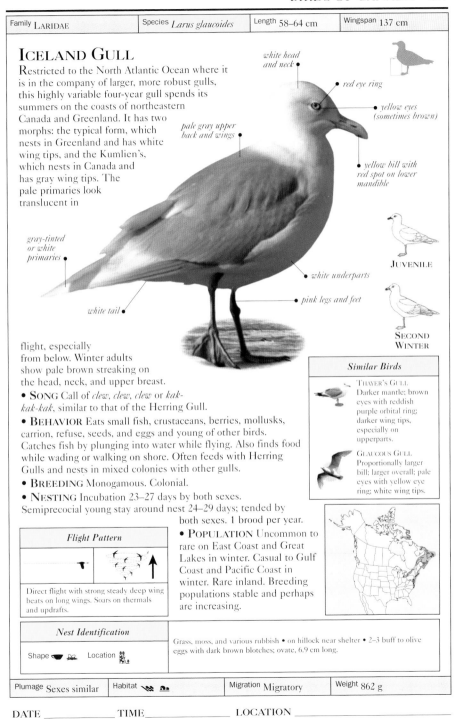

white head and neck

red eye ring

yellow eyes (sometimes brown)

pale gray upper back and wings

yellow bill with red spot on lower mandible

gray-tinted or white primaries

white underparts

pink legs and feet

white tail

JUVENILE

SECOND WINTER

flight, especially from below. Winter adults show pale brown streaking on the head, neck, and upper breast.

• **SONG** Call of *clew, clew, clew* or *kak-kak-kak*, similar to that of the Herring Gull.

• **BEHAVIOR** Eats small fish, crustaceans, berries, mollusks, carrion, refuse, seeds, and eggs and young of other birds. Catches fish by plunging into water while flying. Also finds food while wading or walking on shore. Often feeds with Herring Gulls and nests in mixed colonies with other gulls.

• **BREEDING** Monogamous. Colonial.

• **NESTING** Incubation 23–27 days by both sexes. Semiprecocial young stay around nest 24–29 days; tended by both sexes. 1 brood per year.

• **POPULATION** Uncommon to rare on East Coast and Great Lakes in winter. Casual to Gulf Coast and Pacific Coast in winter. Rare inland. Breeding populations stable and perhaps are increasing.

Similar Birds

THAYER'S GULL
Darker mantle; brown eyes with reddish purple orbital ring; darker wing tips, especially on upperparts.

GLAUCOUS GULL
Proportionally larger bill; larger overall; pale eyes with yellow eye ring; white wing tips.

Flight Pattern

Direct flight with strong steady deep wing beats on long wings. Soars on thermals and updrafts.

Nest Identification

Shape — Location

Grass, moss, and various rubbish • on hillock near shelter • 2–3 buff to olive eggs with dark brown blotches; ovate, 6.9 cm long.

Plumage Sexes similar	Habitat	Migration Migratory	Weight 862 g

DATE _____ TIME_____ LOCATION _____

Family LARIDAE	Species *Larus fuscus*	Length 53–56 cm	Wingspan 137 cm

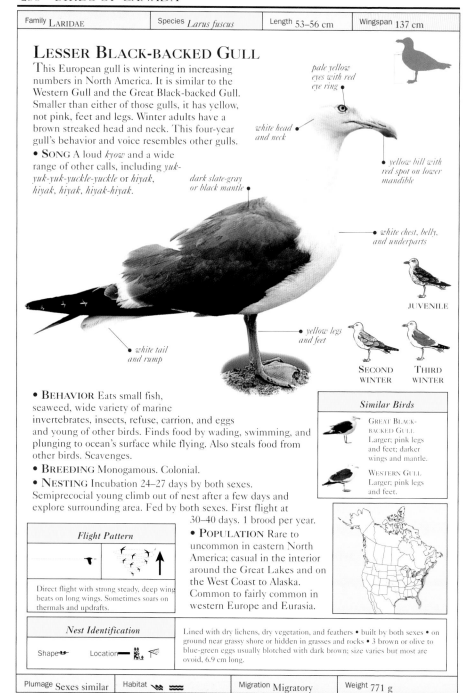

LESSER BLACK-BACKED GULL

This European gull is wintering in increasing numbers in North America. It is similar to the Western Gull and the Great Black-backed Gull. Smaller than either of those gulls, it has yellow, not pink, feet and legs. Winter adults have a brown streaked head and neck. This four-year gull's behavior and voice resembles other gulls.

- **SONG** A loud *kyow* and a wide range of other calls, including *yuk-yuk-yuk-yuckle-yuckle* or *hiyak, hiyak, hiyak, hiyak-hiyak.*

pale yellow eyes with red eye ring

white head and neck

yellow bill with red spot on lower mandible

dark slate-gray or black mantle

white chest, belly, and underparts

JUVENILE

white tail and rump

yellow legs and feet

SECOND WINTER

THIRD WINTER

- **BEHAVIOR** Eats small fish, seaweed, wide variety of marine invertebrates, insects, refuse, carrion, and eggs and young of other birds. Finds food by wading, swimming, and plunging to ocean's surface while flying. Also steals food from other birds. Scavenges.
- **BREEDING** Monogamous. Colonial.
- **NESTING** Incubation 24–27 days by both sexes. Semiprecocial young climb out of nest after a few days and explore surrounding area. Fed by both sexes. First flight at 30–40 days. 1 brood per year.
- **POPULATION** Rare to uncommon in eastern North America; casual in the interior around the Great Lakes and on the West Coast to Alaska. Common to fairly common in western Europe and Eurasia.

Similar Birds

GREAT BLACK-BACKED GULL
Larger; pink legs and feet; darker wings and mantle.

WESTERN GULL
Larger; pink legs and feet.

Flight Pattern

Direct flight with strong steady, deep wing beats on long wings. Sometimes soars on thermals and updrafts.

Nest Identification

Shape ⌣ Location 🐦 ⚐

Lined with dry lichens, dry vegetation, and feathers • built by both sexes • on ground near grassy shore or hidden in grasses and rocks • 3 brown or olive to blue-green eggs usually blotched with dark brown; size varies but most are ovoid, 6.9 cm long.

Plumage Sexes similar	Habitat 〰〰 〰	Migration Migratory	Weight 771 g

DATE _____ TIME_____ LOCATION _____

Family LARIDAE	Species *Larus schistisagus*	Length 64–69 cm	Wingspan 147 cm

SLATY-BACKED GULL

This four-year Asian gull spends most of its time near the Bering Sea, but occasionally wanders to the islands near Alaska. It is similar to but smaller than the Atlantic Coast's Great Black-backed Gull. In flight note the dark slate-gray mantle and wings, the broad

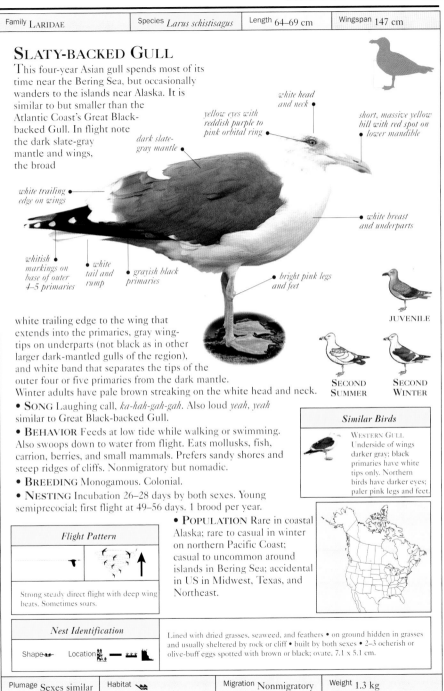

white head and neck

yellow eyes with reddish purple to pink orbital ring

short, massive yellow bill with red spot on lower mandible

dark slate-gray mantle

white trailing edge on wings

white breast and underparts

whitish markings on base of outer 4–5 primaries

white tail and rump

grayish black primaries

bright pink legs and feet

JUVENILE

SECOND SUMMER

SECOND WINTER

white trailing edge to the wing that extends into the primaries, gray wing-tips on underparts (not black as in other larger dark-mantled gulls of the region), and white band that separates the tips of the outer four or five primaries from the dark mantle. Winter adults have pale brown streaking on the white head and neck.

• **SONG** Laughing call, *ka-hah-gah-gah*. Also loud *yeah, yeah* similar to Great Black-backed Gull.

• **BEHAVIOR** Feeds at low tide while walking or swimming. Also swoops down to water from flight. Eats mollusks, fish, carrion, berries, and small mammals. Prefers sandy shores and steep ridges of cliffs. Nonmigratory but nomadic.

• **BREEDING** Monogamous. Colonial.

• **NESTING** Incubation 26–28 days by both sexes. Young semiprecocial; first flight at 49–56 days. 1 brood per year.

• **POPULATION** Rare in coastal Alaska; rare to casual in winter on northern Pacific Coast; casual to uncommon around islands in Bering Sea; accidental in US in Midwest, Texas, and Northeast.

Similar Birds

WESTERN GULL Underside of wings darker gray; black primaries have white tips only. Northern birds have darker eyes; paler pink legs and feet.

Flight Pattern

Strong steady direct flight with deep wing beats. Sometimes soars.

Nest Identification

Shape   Location

Lined with dried grasses, seaweed, and feathers • on ground hidden in grasses and usually sheltered by rock or cliff • built by both sexes • 2–3 ocherish or olive-buff eggs spotted with brown or black; ovate, 7.1 x 5.1 cm.

Plumage Sexes similar	Habitat	Migration Nonmigratory	Weight 1.3 kg

DATE _____ TIME_____ LOCATION _____

Family LARIDAE	Species *Larus occidentalis*	Length 61–69 cm	Wingspan 137–147 cm

WESTERN GULL

Rarely seen far inland from shore and residing almost exclusively on the Pacific Coast, this four-year gull often lives near nesting colonies of other birds and sea lions because it includes in its diet various types of eggs, small birds, and carrion. Two races exist: the northern *occidentalis* and southern *wymani*; *occidentalis* has a paler mantle and slightly darker eyes. In flight shows a white trailing edge on its wings, a dark slate-gray mantle, and a white tail, tail coverts, and rump. Winter adults of the

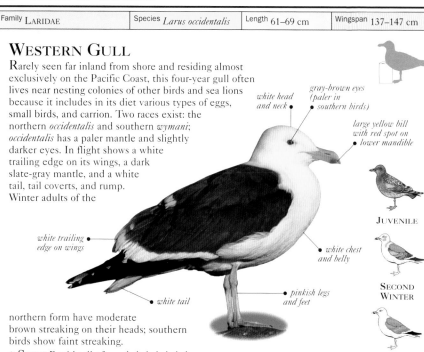

white head and neck •

gray-brown eyes (*paler in southern birds*)

large yellow bill with red spot on lower mandible

JUVENILE

white trailing edge on wings •

• white chest and belly

SECOND WINTER

• white tail

• pinkish legs and feet

THIRD WINTER

northern form have moderate brown streaking on their heads; southern birds show faint streaking.

• **SONG** Rapid call of *quock, kuk, kuk, kuk*.

• **BEHAVIOR** Inhabits coastal areas. Eats fish, a great variety of marine invertebrates, carrion, refuse, small mammals, and eggs and young of other birds. Catches fish by diving from the air to the water's surface, or by wading in water. Harasses cormorants and pelicans to force them to disgorge their catch. Drops hard shellfish in flight to ground to break shell. Follows fishing boats. Commonly found around seacoast towns and on wharves, jetties, docks, pillions, buildings, and moored ships.

• **BREEDING** Monogamous. Colonial. On offshore islands.

• **NESTING** Incubation 25–32 days by both sexes, mostly female. Semiprecocial young stay around nest 29–32 days. Fed by both sexes. 1 brood per year.

Similar Birds

YELLOW-FOOTED GULL Slightly larger; yellow legs and feet; lighter mantle.

GLAUCOUS-WINGED GULL Lighter mantle; gray primaries; dark eyes with red orbital ring.

• **POPULATION** Common. Stable along Pacific Coast from Baja to southern British Columbia. Casual north to southern Alaska. Rare inland.

• **CONSERVATION** Vulnerable to pollution of coastal marine environment.

Flight Pattern

Direct flight with strong steady wing beats. Often soars to great heights on updrafts along coastal sea cliffs.

Nest Identification	
Shape 〰 Location 🏘 ▬ ⚬⚬⚬ 🏚	Moss, weeds, and grass • on ground near ridge of rock or sand • built by both sexes • 1–6 buff to olive-gray eggs with dark brown blotches; ellipsoid to ovoid, 6.6–7.6 cm x 4.8–5.1 cm.

Plumage Sexes similar	Habitat 〰 〰	Migration Nonmigratory	Weight 1.0 kg

Family LARIDAE	Species *Larus glaucescens*	Length 61–69 cm	Wingspan 137–147 cm

GLAUCOUS-WINGED GULL

Its name is derived from the Greek word *glaukos*, which means blue-gray or bluish. This bird is the most abundant and widespread gull in the northeastern Pacific Ocean. It often nests with other gulls and sometimes produces hybrids. Falling somewhere between the Herring Gull and the Glaucous Gull in appearance, this four-year gull is rather chunky and robust. Its increasing population and predatory habits make it a major predator on other seabird colonies in its range.

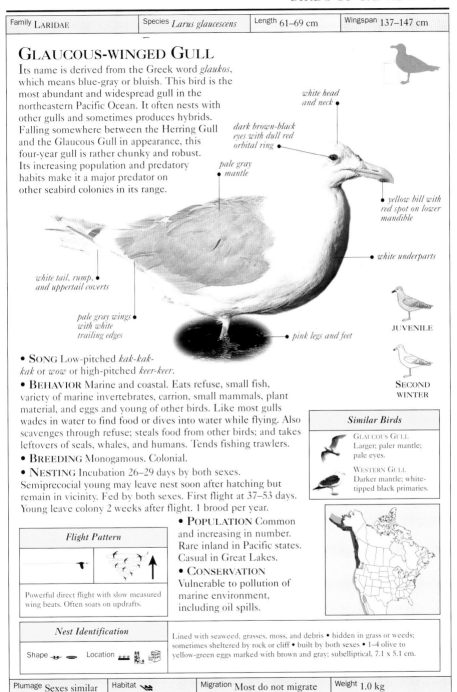

white head and neck

dark brown-black eyes with dull red orbital ring

pale gray mantle

yellow bill with red spot on lower mandible

white underparts

white tail, rump, and uppertail coverts

pale gray wings with white trailing edges

pink legs and feet

JUVENILE

SECOND WINTER

- **SONG** Low-pitched *kak-kak-kak* or *wow* or high-pitched *keer-keer*.
- **BEHAVIOR** Marine and coastal. Eats refuse, small fish, variety of marine invertebrates, carrion, small mammals, plant material, and eggs and young of other birds. Like most gulls wades in water to find food or dives into water while flying. Also scavenges through refuse; steals food from other birds; and takes leftovers of seals, whales, and humans. Tends fishing trawlers.
- **BREEDING** Monogamous. Colonial.
- **NESTING** Incubation 26–29 days by both sexes. Semiprecocial young may leave nest soon after hatching but remain in vicinity. Fed by both sexes. First flight at 37–53 days. Young leave colony 2 weeks after flight. 1 brood per year.
- **POPULATION** Common and increasing in number. Rare inland in Pacific states. Casual in Great Lakes.
- **CONSERVATION** Vulnerable to pollution of marine environment, including oil spills.

Similar Birds

GLAUCOUS GULL
Larger; paler mantle; pale eyes.

WESTERN GULL
Darker mantle; white-tipped black primaries.

Flight Pattern

Powerful direct flight with slow measured wing beats. Often soars on updrafts.

Nest Identification

Shape — Location —

Lined with seaweed, grasses, moss, and debris • hidden in grass or weeds; sometimes sheltered by rock or cliff • built by both sexes • 1–4 olive to yellow-green eggs marked with brown and gray; subelliptical, 7.1 x 5.1 cm.

Plumage Sexes similar	Habitat	Migration Most do not migrate	Weight 1.0 kg

DATE _____ TIME_____ LOCATION _____

Family LARIDAE	Species *Larus hyperboreus*	Length 66–76 cm	Wingspan 142–152 cm

GLAUCOUS GULL

The palest of the large gulls, this bird is also the most northerly breeder of the *Larus* gulls. It can be found nesting on the Arctic coasts of North America and Greenland. A heavy-bodied, stocky, barrel-chested gull, its short wings barely extend beyond the tail when standing. Winter adults show head and neck lightly streaked pale brown. This is a four-year gull.

• **SONG** Usually silent. While flying, makes a prattling-like quack. Also has various shrieking cries, similar to those of Herring Gull.

• **BEHAVIOR** Marine habits. Predatory and aggressive, especially in summer when it feeds primarily on eggs and young of other birds, especially ducks, alcids, shorebirds, and gulls. Also eats fish, marine invertebrates, refuse, insects, and berries. Major predator on lemmings and other small mammals during their peak population cycles. Steals food from other seabirds. Also finds food by wading in water and diving to surface while flying. Catches smaller birds and insects in air.

• **BREEDING** Monogamous. Colonial.

• **NESTING** Incubation 27–28 days by both sexes. Semiprecocial young leave nest within days of hatching, but remain in vicinity. Fed by both sexes. Independent soon after first flight at 45–50 days. Usually 1 brood per year.

• **POPULATION** Common on breeding grounds. Closely tied to lemming population near its nesting grounds. Uncommon to fairly common in winter on the north Atlantic and north Pacific Coasts. Rare south and inland.

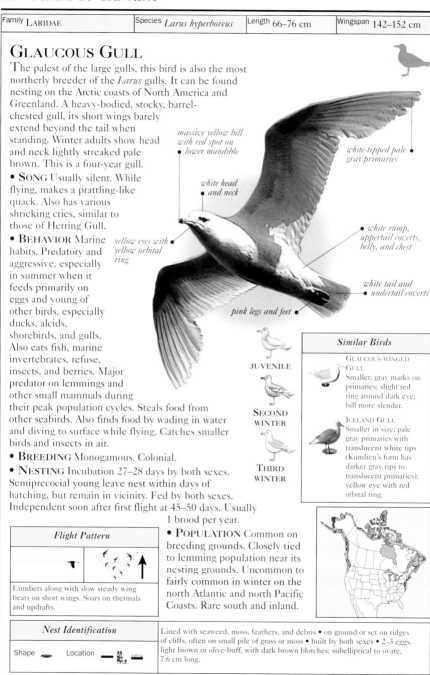

massive yellow bill with red spot on lower mandible

white-tipped pale gray primaries

white head and neck

yellow eyes with yellow orbital ring

white rump, uppertail coverts, belly, and chest

white tail and undertail coverts

pink legs and feet

JUVENILE

SECOND WINTER

THIRD WINTER

Similar Birds

GLAUCOUS-WINGED GULL
Smaller; gray marks on primaries; slight red ring around dark eye; bill more slender.

ICELAND GULL
Smaller in size; pale gray primaries with translucent white tips (Kumlien's form has darker gray tips to translucent primaries); yellow eye with red orbital ring.

Flight Pattern
Lumbers along with slow steady wing beats on short wings. Soars on thermals and updrafts.

Nest Identification	
Shape ⬤ Location ▬ 🪹 ▬	Lined with seaweed, moss, feathers, and debris • on ground or set on ridges of cliffs, often on small pile of grass or moss • built by both sexes • 2–3 eggs, light brown or olive-buff, with dark brown blotches; subelliptical to ovate, 7.6 cm long.

Plumage Sexes similar	Habitat 〰 〰 🦪	Migration Migratory	Weight 1.5 kg

DATE _____ TIME_____ LOCATION _____

| Family LARIDAE | Species *Larus marinus* | Length 71–79 cm | Wingspan 152–167 cm |

GREAT BLACK-BACKED GULL

This predatory and domineering bird is the largest gull in North America. It is highly aggressive toward other birds but will nest harmoniously in colonies with other gulls. A four-year gull, it frequents the northern Atlantic Coast of North America. The adult is snow-white below with a white tail and black mantle and upperwings. Winter adults have very little streaking on the white head and nape. In all plumages it has pink legs and feet. The prevalence of garbage dumps in coastal areas has led to an increase in population of this species.

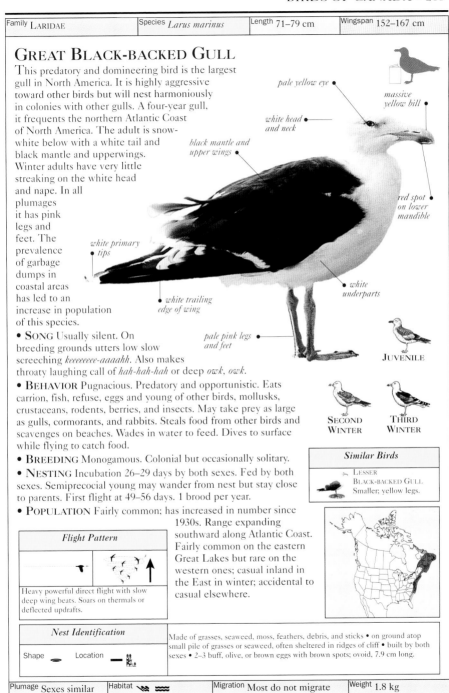

pale yellow eye

massive yellow bill

white head and neck

black mantle and upper wings

red spot on lower mandible

white primary tips

white underparts

white trailing edge of wing

pale pink legs and feet

JUVENILE

SECOND WINTER

THIRD WINTER

- **SONG** Usually silent. On breeding grounds utters low slow screeching *keeeeeeee-aaaahh*. Also makes throaty laughing call of *hah-hah-hah* or deep *owk, owk*.
- **BEHAVIOR** Pugnacious. Predatory and opportunistic. Eats carrion, fish, refuse, eggs and young of other birds, mollusks, crustaceans, rodents, berries, and insects. May take prey as large as gulls, cormorants, and rabbits. Steals food from other birds and scavenges on beaches. Wades in water to feed. Dives to surface while flying to catch food.
- **BREEDING** Monogamous. Colonial but occasionally solitary.
- **NESTING** Incubation 26–29 days by both sexes. Fed by both sexes. Semiprecocial young may wander from nest but stay close to parents. First flight at 49–56 days. 1 brood per year.
- **POPULATION** Fairly common; has increased in number since 1930s. Range expanding southward along Atlantic Coast. Fairly common on the eastern Great Lakes but rare on the western ones; casual inland in the East in winter; accidental to casual elsewhere.

Similar Birds
LESSER BLACK-BACKED GULL Smaller; yellow legs.

Flight Pattern
Heavy powerful direct flight with slow deep wing beats. Soars on thermals or deflected updrafts.

Nest Identification	
Shape	Location	Made of grasses, seaweed, moss, feathers, debris, and sticks • on ground atop small pile of grasses or seaweed, often sheltered in ridges of cliff • built by both sexes • 2–3 buff, olive, or brown eggs with brown spots; ovoid, 7.9 cm long.

| Plumage Sexes similar | Habitat | Migration Most do not migrate | Weight 1.8 kg |

DATE _____ TIME_____ LOCATION _____

Family LARIDAE	Species *Xema sabini*	Length 33–36 cm	Wingspan 84–91 cm

SABINE'S GULL

This two-year gull summers near the arctic coasts of North America, but after nesting season it is rarely spotted from shore because it spends most of its time at sea. Nesting in the tundra, parents are very protective of the nest and will attack intruders or use silent distraction methods to lure them away. In flight birds have a striking black, white, and gray wing pattern; black primaries; and a gray mantle separated by a wide white triangle on the back of the wing. It is the only North American

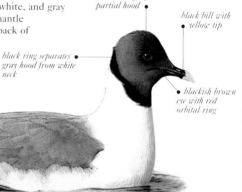

dark slate-gray partial hood

black bill with yellow tip

black ring separates gray hood from white neck

blackish brown eye with red orbital ring

black primaries with white tips

forked white tail

gull with a distinctly forked tail. Winter adults have a white head with dusky gray on the back of the crown and nape.

• **SONG** Short, harsh ternlike cry of *creeeee*.

• **BEHAVIOR** Largely pelagic. Eats insects, fish, crustaceans, mollusks, and marine worms in breeding season; otherwise, eats mostly fish. Runs along mudflats like a plover searching for food. Also feeds by dipping to water's surface from flight and foraging while swimming.

• **BREEDING** Monogamous. Small colonies. Often in company of Arctic Terns.

• **NESTING** Incubation 23–26 days by both sexes. Semiprecocial young. Shortly after hatching, nestlings led to water by parents. Young feed themselves. First flight at about 35 days. 1 brood per year.

• **POPULATION** Common on breeding grounds. Winters at sea mainly in Southern Hemisphere. Common migrant well off West Coast; casual on and off East Coast. Rare to casual in migration in interior of the West and on Great Lakes.

JUVENILE   WINTER ADULT

Similar Birds

BONAPARTE'S GULL
Black bill; black hood; orange legs and feet; white outer primaries form triangle at wing tip; square tail.

Flight Pattern

Ternlike airy direct flight with continuous wing beats, a few glides, and numerous dives. Also hovers.

Nest Identification

Shape ⬯   Location ▬ ⚬⚬⚬

Seaweed, grasses, moss, and feathers • on ground atop pile of vegetation near water • may be built by both sexes • 1–3 olive-buff eggs spotted with darker olive-brown and occasionally wreathed; ovate to subelliptical, 4.6 cm long.

Plumage Sexes similar	Habitat ▬▬ ≈≈≈	Migration Migratory	Weight 204 g

DATE _____ TIME_____ LOCATION _____

| Family LARIDAE | Species *Rissa tridactyla* | Length 41–43 cm | Wingspan 86 cm |

BLACK-LEGGED KITTIWAKE

Named for its call of *kittiwake*, this pelagic three-year gull nests on high narrow cliffs on arctic and sub-arctic coasts. Unlike most gulls it does not scavenge at garbage dumps but spends most of its time at sea and drinks only saltwater. Adults have a white body, gray mantle and wings, pale whitish underwings, a square to slightly notched tail, and black legs and feet. The black tips of the outer primaries lack white spotting and produce a clean, straight-edged dark tip. Winter adults show a dark smudge across the nape. Juveniles have a black collar across the back of the neck, a black-tipped tail, and a black W stretching from wing tip to wing tip across the back.

black-tipped outer primaries

light gray wings with paler gray flight feathers

light gray back

white tail coverts and tail

dark eyes

unmarked thin pale yellow bill

white head and neck

JUVENILE WINTER ADULT

- **SONG** Series of piercing *kittiwake*'s. Also makes quieter *ock-ock-ock*.
- **BEHAVIOR** Pelagic outside breeding season. Eats primarily small fish but also takes crustaceans, mollusks, squid, insects, and refuse from ships. Forages for food while swimming and dips while flying to snatch items from surface. Often hovers briefly above water before dropping on prey at surface.
- **BREEDING** Monogamous. Colonial.
- **NESTING** Incubation 25–32 days by both sexes. First flight at 34–58 days. Young return to nest at night after first flight and are fed by both sexes. 1 brood per year.
- **POPULATION** Abundant on breeding grounds. In migration and winter common to uncommon on open ocean; usually not seen from shore in the East, seen uncommonly in the West. Casual to accidental inland in winter.
- **CONSERVATION** Large nesting colonies vulnerable to human disturbance.

Similar Birds

SABINE'S GULL
Winter plumage
- notched white tail; wings black from "wrist" to tip, forming black triangle; inner primaries and secondaries white; black half-collar over nape; yellow-tipped black bill
- Pacific Coast range.

RED-LEGGED KITTIWAKE
Bright reddish coral legs; shorter broader bill; darker upperparts
- Pacific Coast range.

Flight Pattern

Buoyant graceful swift flight with rapid wing beats and shallow strokes alternating with several rapid wing beats and a glide.

Nest Identification

Shape   Location

Mud, seaweed, moss, and sod • on cliff ledge, side of building, or in cave • built by both sexes with materials brought by male • 1–3 buff to olive or pale blue eggs with brown or gray speckles; subelliptical, 5.6 x 4.1 cm.

| Plumage Sexes similar | Habitat | Migration Migratory | Weight 422 g |

DATE _____ TIME_____ LOCATION _____

Family LARIDAE	Species *Rissa brevirostris*	Length 36–41 cm	Wingspan 84 cm

RED-LEGGED KITTIWAKE

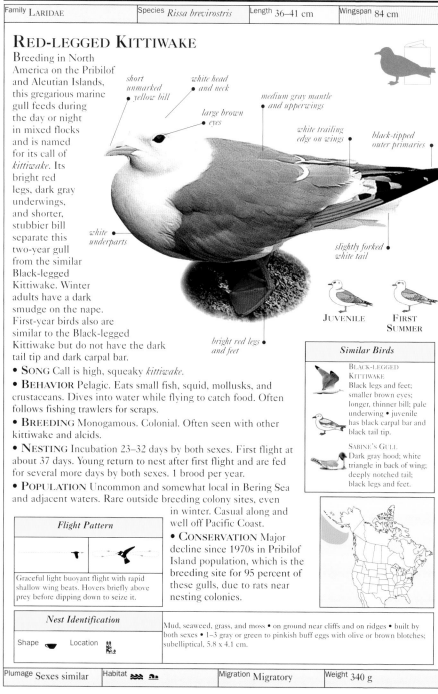

Breeding in North America on the Pribilof and Aleutian Islands, this gregarious marine gull feeds during the day or night in mixed flocks and is named for its call of *kittiwake*. Its bright red legs, dark gray underwings, and shorter, stubbier bill separate this two-year gull from the similar Black-legged Kittiwake. Winter adults have a dark smudge on the nape. First-year birds also are similar to the Black-legged Kittiwake but do not have the dark tail tip and dark carpal bar.

short unmarked yellow bill

white head and neck

large brown eyes

medium gray mantle and upperwings

white trailing edge on wings

black-tipped outer primaries

white underparts

slightly forked white tail

bright red legs and feet

JUVENILE

FIRST SUMMER

• **SONG** Call is high, squeaky *kittiwake*.

• **BEHAVIOR** Pelagic. Eats small fish, squid, mollusks, and crustaceans. Dives into water while flying to catch food. Often follows fishing trawlers for scraps.

• **BREEDING** Monogamous. Colonial. Often seen with other kittiwake and alcids.

• **NESTING** Incubation 23–32 days by both sexes. First flight at about 37 days. Young return to nest after first flight and are fed for several more days by both sexes. 1 brood per year.

• **POPULATION** Uncommon and somewhat local in Bering Sea and adjacent waters. Rare outside breeding colony sites, even in winter. Casual along and well off Pacific Coast.

• **CONSERVATION** Major decline since 1970s in Pribilof Island population, which is the breeding site for 95 percent of these gulls, due to rats near nesting colonies.

Similar Birds

BLACK-LEGGED KITTIWAKE
Black legs and feet; smaller brown eyes; longer, thinner bill; pale underwing • juvenile has black carpal bar and black tail tip.

SABINE'S GULL
Dark gray hood; white triangle in back of wing; deeply notched tail; black legs and feet.

Flight Pattern

Graceful light buoyant flight with rapid shallow wing beats. Hovers briefly above prey before dipping down to seize it.

Nest Identification

Shape   Location

Mud, seaweed, grass, and moss • on ground near cliffs and on ridges • built by both sexes • 1–3 gray or green to pinkish buff eggs with olive or brown blotches; subelliptical, 5.8 x 4.1 cm.

Plumage Sexes similar	Habitat	Migration Migratory	Weight 340 g

DATE _____ TIME_____ LOCATION _____

| Family LARIDAE | Species *Rhodostethia rosea* | Length 33–36 cm | Wingspan 84 cm |

ROSS'S GULL

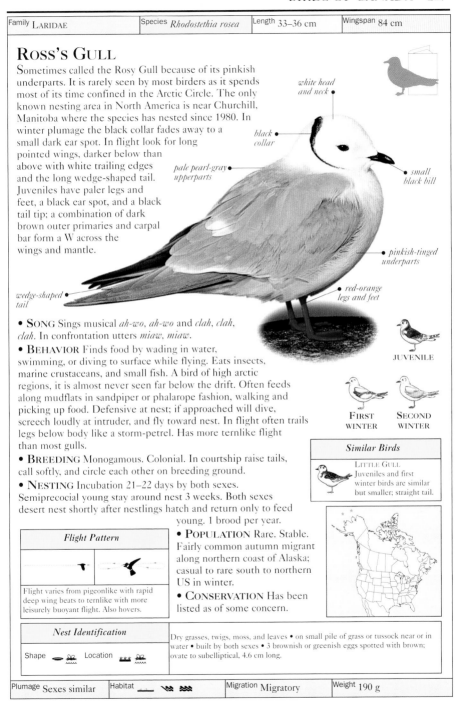

Sometimes called the Rosy Gull because of its pinkish underparts. It is rarely seen by most birders as it spends most of its time confined in the Arctic Circle. The only known nesting area in North America is near Churchill, Manitoba where the species has nested since 1980. In winter plumage the black collar fades away to a small dark ear spot. In flight look for long pointed wings, darker below than above with white trailing edges and the long wedge-shaped tail. Juveniles have paler legs and feet, a black ear spot, and a black tail tip; a combination of dark brown outer primaries and carpal bar form a W across the wings and mantle.

white head and neck

black collar

pale pearl-gray upperparts

small black bill

pinkish-tinged underparts

red-orange legs and feet

wedge-shaped tail

JUVENILE

FIRST WINTER

SECOND WINTER

- **SONG** Sings musical *ah-wo, ah-wo* and *clah, clah, clah*. In confrontation utters *miaw, miaw*.
- **BEHAVIOR** Finds food by wading in water, swimming, or diving to surface while flying. Eats insects, marine crustaceans, and small fish. A bird of high arctic regions, it is almost never seen far below the drift. Often feeds along mudflats in sandpiper or phalarope fashion, walking and picking up food. Defensive at nest; if approached will dive, screech loudly at intruder, and fly toward nest. In flight often trails legs below body like a storm-petrel. Has more ternlike flight than most gulls.
- **BREEDING** Monogamous. Colonial. In courtship raise tails, call softly, and circle each other on breeding ground.
- **NESTING** Incubation 21–22 days by both sexes. Semiprecocial young stay around nest 3 weeks. Both sexes desert nest shortly after nestlings hatch and return only to feed young. 1 brood per year.
- **POPULATION** Rare. Stable. Fairly common autumn migrant along northern coast of Alaska; casual to rare south to northern US in winter.
- **CONSERVATION** Has been listed as of some concern.

Similar Birds

LITTLE GULL
Juveniles and first winter birds are similar but smaller; straight tail.

Flight Pattern
Flight varies from pigeonlike with rapid deep wing beats to ternlike with more leisurely buoyant flight. Also hovers.

Nest Identification	
Shape Location	Dry grasses, twigs, moss, and leaves • on small pile of grass or tussock near or in water • built by both sexes • 3 brownish or greenish eggs spotted with brown; ovate to subelliptical, 4.6 cm long.

| Plumage Sexes similar | Habitat | Migration Migratory | Weight 190 g |

DATE _____ TIME_____ LOCATION _____

Family LARIDAE	Species *Pagophila eburnea*	Length 38–43 cm	Wingspan 94 cm

IVORY GULL

This pigeon-sized pure white two-year gull blends with the ice and snow surrounding its breeding grounds near the arctic seas. One of the hardiest gulls in the world, it is almost never found far from snow and ice and rarely winters farther south than drifting ice and pack ice. Juveniles are white with dark smudges on the face, brownish to black speckles on the back and wings, black tips on the primaries and a dark tail band. The all-white adult plumage is not acquired until its second year.

black eyes

bold white overall

yellow-tipped dark bill

black legs and feet

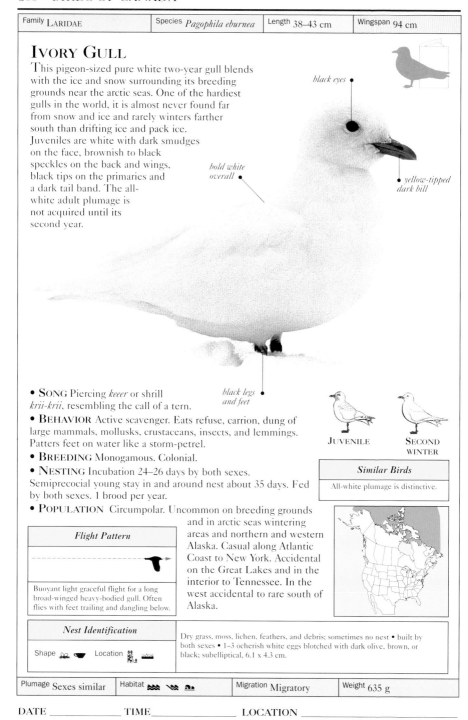

JUVENILE

SECOND WINTER

- **SONG** Piercing *keeer* or shrill *krii-krii*, resembling the call of a tern.
- **BEHAVIOR** Active scavenger. Eats refuse, carrion, dung of large mammals, mollusks, crustaceans, insects, and lemmings. Patters feet on water like a storm-petrel.
- **BREEDING** Monogamous. Colonial.
- **NESTING** Incubation 24–26 days by both sexes. Semiprecocial young stay in and around nest about 35 days. Fed by both sexes. 1 brood per year.
- **POPULATION** Circumpolar. Uncommon on breeding grounds and in arctic seas wintering areas and northern and western Alaska. Casual along Atlantic Coast to New York. Accidental on the Great Lakes and in the interior to Tennessee. In the west accidental to rare south of Alaska.

Similar Birds

All-white plumage is distinctive.

Flight Pattern

Buoyant light graceful flight for a long broad-winged heavy-bodied gull. Often flies with feet trailing and dangling below.

Nest Identification

Shape ___ ___   Location ___ ___

Dry grass, moss, lichen, feathers, and debris; sometimes no nest • built by both sexes • 1–3 ocherish white eggs blotched with dark olive, brown, or black; subelliptical, 6.1 x 4.3 cm.

Plumage Sexes similar	Habitat ___ ___ ___	Migration Migratory	Weight 635 g

DATE _____ TIME_____ LOCATION _____

Family LARIDAE	Species *Sterna caspia*	Length 48–58 cm	Wingspan 127–140 cm

CASPIAN TERN

The largest and least sociable tern is easily distinguished by its large size, stout red-orange bill, and tail forked to a quarter of its length. In flight the underside of the outer primaries are dark. Caspian Terns are known for their predatory feeding habits, sometimes stealing catches from other seabirds and eating eggs and young of other terns and gulls. Many Caspian Terns migrate to coastal regions during winter months, moving as far south as the West Indies and the northern regions of South America. Some remain in coastal locales year-round. Juveniles and winter adults have a streaked dusky-and-white cap that extends below the eye.

black cap covers head from bill to nape and extends below eye

pale gray upperparts

large thick red-orange bill often with black tip (sometimes tip is yellow or orange)

white underparts

forked tail

black legs and feet

dusky to dark gray undersides of primaries

WINTER PLUMAGE

- **SONG** Call is harsh deep *kaark* and *ka-arr*. Young whistle a distinctive *whee-you*.
- **BEHAVIOR** This common coastal inhabitant also visits inland wetlands in summer. Gull-like, it often feeds on water surfaces but sometimes dives into water for small fish, its principal food. When patrolling flies with bill pointed down. Often hovers before plunge diving into water for prey.
- **BREEDING** Monogamous. Colonial. Rarely solitary.
- **NESTING** Incubation 20–28 days by both sexes. Semiprecocial young may leave nest for nearby shore a few days after hatching. First flight at 28–35 days. Young may remain with parents up to 8 months. 1 brood per year.
- **POPULATION** Stable range; some populations increasing. Small colonies scattered over breeding range.
- **CONSERVATION** Vulnerable to disturbance of coastal nesting colonies and habitat loss on beaches and inland wetlands.

Similar Birds

ROYAL TERN
Smaller; longer more deeply forked tail; lacks blackish wedge on underwing tips; mostly white forehead and anterior crown except early in breeding season, when entire crown is black; black crest on nape; less stout orange bill without black tip.

ELEGANT TERN
Smaller; long thin red-orange bill without black tip; black crest; white underparts with pinkish tinge • western range.

Flight Pattern
Strong swift graceful flight. Bulk makes it appear gull-like. Sometimes hovers briefly over prey before dipping down to seize it.

Nest Identification	
Shape	Location	Lined with seaweed, moss, grass, and occasional debris • sometimes concealed among shells, driftwood, and rubbish • built by both sexes • 1–3, sometimes 4–5, pinkish buff eggs with brown markings; ovate, elliptical ovate, or subelliptical. 6.4 x 4.6 cm.

Plumage Sexes similar	Habitat	Migration Migratory	Weight 635 g

DATE _____ TIME _____ LOCATION _____

Family LARIDAE	Species *Sterna elegans*	Length 41–43 cm	Wingspan 86 cm

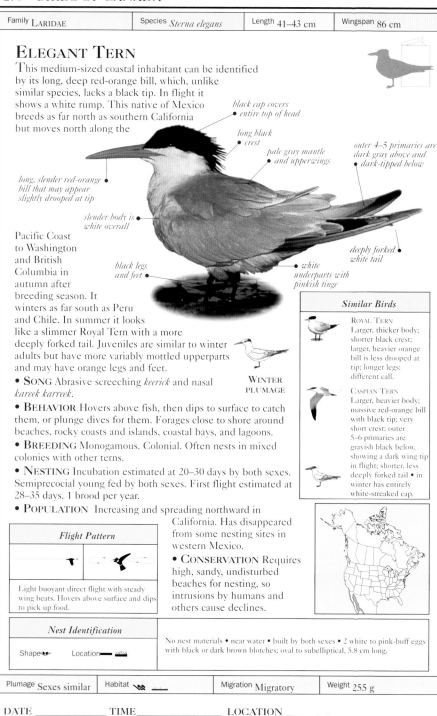

ELEGANT TERN

This medium-sized coastal inhabitant can be identified by its long, deep red-orange bill, which, unlike similar species, lacks a black tip. In flight it shows a white rump. This native of Mexico breeds as far north as southern California but moves north along the Pacific Coast to Washington and British Columbia in autumn after breeding season. It winters as far south as Peru and Chile. In summer it looks like a slimmer Royal Tern with a more deeply forked tail. Juveniles are similar to winter adults but have more variably mottled upperparts and may have orange legs and feet.

black cap covers entire top of head

long black crest

pale gray mantle and upperwings

outer 4–5 primaries are dark gray above and dark-tipped below

long, slender red-orange bill that may appear slightly drooped at tip

slender body is white overall

black legs and feet

white underparts with pinkish tinge

deeply forked white tail

WINTER PLUMAGE

- **SONG** Abrasive screeching *keerick* and nasal *kareek karreek*.
- **BEHAVIOR** Hovers above fish, then dips to surface to catch them, or plunge dives for them. Forages close to shore around beaches, rocky coasts and islands, coastal bays, and lagoons.
- **BREEDING** Monogamous. Colonial. Often nests in mixed colonies with other terns.
- **NESTING** Incubation estimated at 20–30 days by both sexes. Semiprecocial young fed by both sexes. First flight estimated at 28–35 days. 1 brood per year.
- **POPULATION** Increasing and spreading northward in California. Has disappeared from some nesting sites in western Mexico.
- **CONSERVATION** Requires high, sandy, undisturbed beaches for nesting, so intrusions by humans and others cause declines.

Similar Birds

ROYAL TERN
Larger, thicker body; shorter black crest; larger, heavier orange bill is less drooped at tip; longer legs; different call.

CASPIAN TERN
Larger, heavier body; massive red-orange bill with black tip; very short crest; outer 5–6 primaries are grayish black below, showing a dark wing tip in flight; shorter, less deeply forked tail • in winter has entirely white-streaked cap.

Flight Pattern

Light buoyant direct flight with steady wing beats. Hovers above surface and dips to pick up food.

Nest Identification

Shape ⌣   Location ▬ ▬

No nest materials • near water • built by both sexes • 2 white to pink-buff eggs with black or dark brown blotches; oval to subelliptical, 5.8 cm long.

Plumage Sexes similar	Habitat ⌇ ▬	Migration Migratory	Weight 255 g

DATE _____ TIME _____ LOCATION _____

Family LARIDAE	Species *Sterna hirundo*	Length 33–41 cm	Wingspan 76–79 cm

COMMON TERN

Often called the Mackerel Gull, the Common Tern is seen tending areas where large fish, such as mackerel and tuna, drive schools of smaller fish to the surface. By following the Common Tern, fishermen often find the best place to cast their nets. Although common throughout their range, today's northeastern populations of this tern are lower than previously recorded. Inland populations are suspected to be on the decline as well. The upperwings and mantle are a

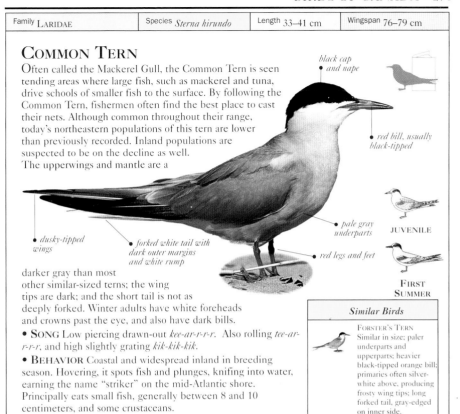

- black cap and nape
- red bill, usually black-tipped
- pale gray underparts
- dusky-tipped wings
- forked white tail with dark outer margins and white rump
- red legs and feet

JUVENILE

FIRST SUMMER

darker gray than most other similar-sized terns; the wing tips are dark; and the short tail is not as deeply forked. Winter adults have white foreheads and crowns past the eye, and also have dark bills.

- **SONG** Low piercing drawn-out *kee-ar-r-r-r*. Also rolling *tee-ar-r-r-r*, and high slightly grating *kik-kik-kik*.
- **BEHAVIOR** Coastal and widespread inland in breeding season. Hovering, it spots fish and plunges, knifing into water, earning the name "striker" on the mid-Atlantic shore. Principally eats small fish, generally between 8 and 10 centimeters, and some crustaceans.
- **BREEDING** Monogamous. Colonial. Often nests in mixed colonies with other terns.
- **NESTING** Incubation 21–27 days by both sexes. Young leave nest after a few days, but remain nearby. First flight at 22–28 days, but may remain with parents at least another 2 months. Fed by both sexes. 1–2 broods per year.
- **POPULATION** Common on breeding grounds and in migration on both coasts; rare in winter on southern California coast and Gulf Coast.
- **CONSERVATION** Almost completely extirpated in early 1900s by plume hunters for fashion markets. Has largely recovered since full protection established in 1913.

Similar Birds

FORSTER'S TERN
Similar in size; paler underparts and upperparts; heavier black-tipped orange bill; primaries often silver-white above, producing frosty wing tips; long forked tail, gray-edged on inner side.

ARCTIC TERN
Similar in size; shorter neck; darker gray underparts and upperparts; white cheeks; red bill without black tip; paler wing tips.

Flight Pattern	
Direct flight is light and buoyant. Hovers when feeding prior to plunge-diving into water for prey.	

Nest Identification	
Shape **⌣** Location **▬ ▬ ✕✕**	Lined with vegetation and debris, including grass, shells, and seaweed • built by both sexes • 1–3 buff to cinnamon-brown eggs, generally heavily spotted and overlaid with shades of dark brown and black; generally wreathed; oval to subelliptical, 4.1 cm long.

Plumage Sexes similar	Habitat ~~ ♙♙ ~~ ➤	Migration Migratory	Weight 119 g

DATE _____ TIME_____ LOCATION _____

| Family LARIDAE | Species *Sterna paradisaea* | Length 36–43 cm | Wingspan 74–84 cm |

ARCTIC TERN

Distinguishable from similar terns by its short red bill, neck and legs, the Arctic Tern sometimes appears to huddle on the ground. It is perhaps the champion long-distance migrant of the world, nesting in the Arctic and wintering in Antarctica during their summer, traveling an annual distance of more than 40,000 km. In flight, note the translucent flight feathers with a narrow trailing black border on the primaries; gray underparts; and deeply forked tail. Winter adults have white foreheads and crowns to the back of the eye, and dark bills and feet. Juveniles have white foreheads, and silvery white secondaries and outer coverts.

medium gray wings and mantle

JUVENILE

black cap and nape

white cheeks

white rump and deeply forked tail with gray outer margins

FIRST SUMMER

somewhat short, deep red bill

pale gray underparts

short red legs and small feet

• **SONG** Calls include a throaty *tr-tee-ar* and a shrieking *kee-kee*, similar to Common Tern, but higher and harsher, with emphasis on second or third note. Alarm call sounds like a brief *kee-kahr*.

• **BEHAVIOR** Often observed hovering 9–12 meters above water while searching for prey. Plunge dives to catch fish. Eats small fish and marine invertebrates, including small crustaceans. Very defensive at nest, often flying out and striking intruder while continuously vocalizing. Often follows fishing vessels.

• **BREEDING** Monogamous. Pairs or colonial.

• **NESTING** Incubation 20–24 days by both sexes. Semiprecocial young leave nest 1–3 days after hatching to hide nearby. First flight at 21–28 days. Young remain with parents additional 30 to 60 days, fed by both sexes. 1 brood per year.

• **POPULATION** Common to fairly common on breeding grounds. Casual to uncommon well offshore during migration. Steadily declining on southern end of breeding range along Atlantic Coast.

Similar Birds

FORSTER'S TERN
Similar in size; longer, orange, black-tipped bill and orange legs and feet; white underparts; frosty wing-tips; forked white tail with dusky inner margins; rarely seen well offshore.

COMMON TERN
Slightly stockier; flatter crown; longer neck and long red, black-tipped bill; shorter notched tail; dusky gray wing-tips above and below.

Flight Pattern
Buoyant graceful flight with nearly constant wing beats. Hovers above prey before plunge diving or dipping to surface.

Nest Identification	
Shape ⌣ Location ▬ ▬ ▬	Vegetation lined with debris, occasionally grass and shells • built by both sexes • 1–3 buff to pale olive eggs, blotched with black and brown markings; oval to subelliptical, 4.1 cm long.

| Plumage Sexes similar | Habitat ▬ ▬ ≈≈≈ ≈≈≈ | Migration Migratory | Weight 108 g |

DATE _____ TIME_____ LOCATION _____

Family LARIDAE	Species *Sterna forsteri*	Length 36–38 cm	Wingspan 76–79 cm

FORSTER'S TERN

Frequenting inland marshes as well as the coast, this widespread tern feeds and flocks with other terns. It can be distingushed by its long tail and orange-red bill. In flight note the pale frosty wing tips, white rump, and deeply forked

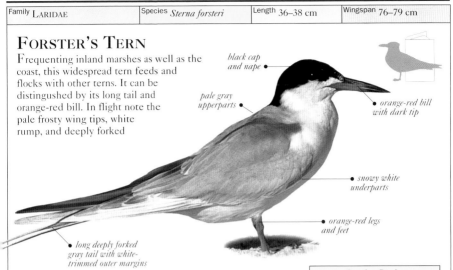

black cap and nape

pale gray upperparts

orange-red bill with dark tip

snowy white underparts

orange-red legs and feet

long deeply forked gray tail with white-trimmed outer margins

gray tail with white outer margins. Winter plumage shows dull yellow feet, a dark bill, and a white head with a black patch through the eye and ear. Juveniles are like winter adults but have a shorter tail, a ginger crown, and darker upperwings.

• **SONG** Throaty nasal *ki-arr, za-a-ap,* or *zrurrr,* with nighthawklike quality. Also gives piercing *kit, kit, kit* cry.

• **BEHAVIOR** Catches insects in flight. Eats dragonflies and other insects. Hovers above water, then plunge dives for small fish. Dips to water's surface to catch floating insects, keeping its feathers dry.

• **BREEDING** Monogamous. Loose colonies.

• **NESTING** Incubation 23–25 days by both sexes. Semiprecocial young leave nest after a few days but tended by both sexes until able to fly. 1 brood per year.

JUVENILE

WINTER PLUMAGE

Similar Birds

COMMON TERN
Shorter legs and bill; dark wing tips; white tail with dark outer margins • winter adults and juveniles have white forehead and forecrown; dark shoulder; dark eye patch joins at nape; higher-pitched call.

ARCTIC TERN
Shorter red bill without dark tip; shorter legs; gray underparts; gray throat and chin contrast with white face; white tail with dark outer margins; pale underwing with black trailing margins.

• **POPULATION** Common. Declining in some areas because of loss of marshlands.

• **CONSERVATION** Vulnerable to habitat loss to agriculture and development in draining of wetlands.

Flight Pattern
Shallow slow graceful strong flight with body moving up and down. Hovers over water prior to diving for prey.

Nest Identification		Atop floating dried reeds and lined with grass and reeds; in mud or sand and lined with bits of shells and grass; sometimes uses old grebe nests or muskrat houses • built by both sexes • 1–4 olive or buff eggs with brown or olive splotches and sometimes marked with dark brown lines; oval to short elliptical, 4.3 cm long.
Shape 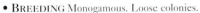		
Location		

Plumage Sexes similar	Habitat	Migration Migratory	Weight 159 g

DATE _____ TIME_____ LOCATION _____

Family LARIDAE	Species *Sterna aleutica*	Length 33–38 cm	Wingspan 74–81 cm

ALEUTIAN TERN

First discovered in 1868 on Kodiak Island, this tern was not spotted on the Aleutian Islands until 1962, despite its name. The Aleutian Tern often flocks with Arctic Terns and sometimes can be seen off the coast of British Columbia in spring. Its mantle and upperwings are darker lead-gray than other terns of the region and contrast with the white underparts, short tail, and rump. It has a black crown, nape, and lores and a white forehead; the trailing edges of the secondaries produce a dark gray bar bordered with white. Juveniles have brown upperparts with buff feather edging and a reddish bill, legs, and feet. Winter adults show white streaking on the crown.

• **SONG** Whistles drawn-out *twee-ee-ee*. Also calls *chif-chif-chu-ak* and gives hoarse un-ternlike *tee-ar-r-r* that sounds more like a shorebird's call.

• **BEHAVIOR** Eats crustaceans, small fish, and insects. Usually hovers while flying and dips to water to pick up food. Often nests in colonies with Arctic Tern. Very defensive in colonies, often aggressively attacking intruders. Follows fishing trawlers. Little known about behavior on wintering grounds.

• **BREEDING** Monogamous. Colonial.

• **NESTING** Incubation 22–23 days by both sexes. Young semiprecocial; first flight at about 25–31 days. Fed by both sexes. 1 brood per year.

white trim on inner edge of outer primaries produces window effect

black cap and eyeline

white forehead

secondary flight feathers have dark subterminal and thin white terminal bars

black bill

gray underparts

forked white tail

white throat and chin

blackish legs and feet

pale underwing

JUVENILE

Similar Birds

ARCTIC TERN
Black forehead and crown extend onto nape; red bill, legs, and feet; pale underwing; lacks dark bar on secondary tips; pale gray upperparts.

• **POPULATION** Uncommon to locally common on breeding grounds in summer. Casual in spring migration off British Columbia coast.

• **CONSERVATION** Nests sometimes disturbed by predators and humans.

Flight Pattern
Strong direct flight with graceful deep wing beats often high above water. Often hovers before dipping to water for food.

Nest Identification	
Shape	Location

Lined with plant matter, including moss and matted grasses • on ground near water • built by both sexes • 1–3 olive to buff eggs with heavy dark brown markings; ovate to elongate ovate, 4.3 x 3.0 cm.

Plumage Sexes similar	Habitat	Migration Migratory	Weight 119 g

DATE _____ TIME_____ LOCATION _____

| Family LARIDAE | Species *Sterna fuscata* | Length 41–43 cm | Wingspan 81–86 cm |

SOOTY TERN

For years, tuna fishermen have followed feeding flocks of Sooty Terns to locate schools of tuna. Sailors sometimes call this bird "wide-awake," because of its loud night call from the nesting colony, which sounds like *wide-a-wake*. These birds do not breed until they are at least four to eight years of age. Adults have clean-cut black upperparts and white underparts, wing linings, forehead, and short eye stripe.

Juvenile is sooty brown overall with white speckling on mantle and upperwings, white lower belly and undertail coverts, white underwing lining, and forked tail.

blackish brown cap

white forehead patch

blackish brown upperparts

black bill

white underparts

dark forked tail with white edges

black legs and feet

• **SONG** A high nasal *ker-wacky-wack* or *wide-a-wake*.

• **BEHAVIOR** Highly gregarious. Eats small fish and small squid. It is believed these birds sleep "on the wing," because they do not land on water and return to shore only when nesting. Banding in Dry Tortugas indicates adults are not highly migratory but that juveniles migrate as far as west Africa and may be gone 2–6 years before returning to the Florida Keys.

• **BREEDING** Monogamous. Colonial. Often nests in mixed colonies with Bridled Terns.

• **NESTING** Incubation 27–30 days by both sexes. Semiprecocial young wander around nest shortly after hatching, but remain close to parents. First flight at 56–63 days. May not leave colony for another 14–21 days, fed by both sexes. 1 brood per year.

• **POPULATION** Abundant. Widespread throughout tropical oceans. Large nesting colony on the Dry Tortugas; also nests on islands off Texas and Louisiana and on barrier islands of North Carolina. Regular in summer in Gulf Stream to North Carolina; casual to southern coastal California. Storm-blown birds to Maritimes and Great Lakes.

• **CONSERVATION** Strict protection laws on the Tortugas and some Hawaiian colonies. Vulnerable to human disturbance and introduced predators on breeding islands.

JUVENILE

Similar Birds

BRIDLED TERN White patch on forehead extends beyond eye; more pointed wings; paler lead-gray upperparts; white collar separates crown from back; forked tail paler with more white edging on tip.

Flight Pattern

Buoyant direct flight with strong, steady, shallow wing beats. Hovers above water before dipping to surface to pick up food.

Nest Identification

Shape ⚬ Location ▬ ▬

Lined with leaves • built by both sexes • 1 white to buff egg, with brown, gray, lavender, or black markings; oval, 5.1 x 3.6 cm.

| Plumage Sexes similar | Habitat ≋ ≋ | Migration Migratory | Weight 179 g |

DATE _____ TIME _____ LOCATION _____

Family LARIDAE	Species *Chlidonias niger*	Length 23–25 cm	Wingspan 51–61 cm

BLACK TERN

A black-bodied tern that prefers to breed and nest in the inland marshes of the North American prairie country but winters at sea. It is distinguishable by its overall black breeding plumage, gray upperparts, and dark red legs and feet. Its head and underparts turn white in winter and produce a strange-looking pied bird in late summer as winter molt begins. Winter adults have a black crown with an attached ear patch, a white collar, and a dusky black side bar. Juveniles are similar to winter adults with brownish mottling on the back and a dark carpal bar.

black head and neck

broad wings

short notched dark gray tail

black bill

uniformly pale gray underwings

dark gray upperwings

- **SONG**
Drawn-out squeaky *ka-sheek* and abrasive *kik-kik-kik*.

- **BEHAVIOR**
In summer prefers inland lakes and freshwater marshes. Hovers to spot insects. Catches insects in air or swoops down to water or ground to pick up with bill. Plunge dives on occasion. Eats mostly large flying insects but also takes spiders, small fish, crayfish, and small mollusks. Follows people tilling soil and feeds on disturbed insects.

black underparts

JUVENILE

WINTER PLUMAGE

- **BREEDING** Monogamous. Colonial.
- **NESTING** Incubation 17–22 days by both sexes. Semiprecocial young leave nest after 2–3 days but remain in nearby grasses. First flight at 19–25 days, but may be fed by both sexes for up to 2 additional weeks. 1 brood per year in most regions; 2 broods per year in the South.

Similar Birds
WHITE-WINGED TERN Dark red bill; black body and underwing linings; white upperwings and underwing flight feathers; white rump; slightly notched white tail.

- **POPULATION** Common to fairly common in the East; common in middle and western parts of range; uncommon to rare on the West Coast.
- **CONSERVATION** Has declined inland and on the East Coast from wetlands drainage.

Flight Pattern
Buoyant direct flight with deep rapid wing beats. Hovers for insects. Uneven foraging flight with much stopping and starting.

Nest Identification	
Shape Location	Dried reeds, stalks, and grasses • on floating dried vegetation • built by both sexes • 2–4 light buff to olive eggs with black, brown, and greenish buff blotches, usually wreathed; oval to long oval, 4.3 x 3.0 cm.

Plumage Sexes similar	Habitat	Migration Migratory	Weight 65 g

Family ALCIDAE	Species *Alle alle*	Length 22 cm	Wingspan 33 cm

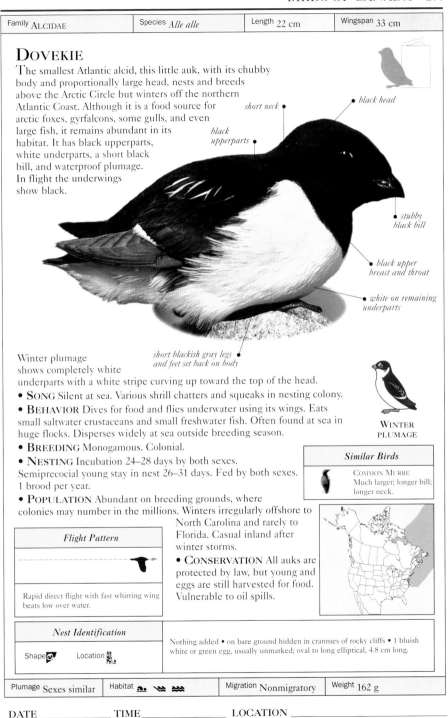

DOVEKIE

The smallest Atlantic alcid, this little auk, with its chubby body and proportionally large head, nests and breeds above the Arctic Circle but winters off the northern Atlantic Coast. Although it is a food source for arctic foxes, gyrfalcons, some gulls, and even large fish, it remains abundant in its habitat. It has black upperparts, white underparts, a short black bill, and waterproof plumage. In flight the underwings show black.

short neck

black head

black upperparts

stubby black bill

black upper breast and throat

white on remaining underparts

short blackish gray legs and feet set back on body

Winter plumage shows completely white underparts with a white stripe curving up toward the top of the head.

WINTER PLUMAGE

- **SONG** Silent at sea. Various shrill chatters and squeaks in nesting colony.
- **BEHAVIOR** Dives for food and flies underwater using its wings. Eats small saltwater crustaceans and small freshwater fish. Often found at sea in huge flocks. Disperses widely at sea outside breeding season.
- **BREEDING** Monogamous. Colonial.
- **NESTING** Incubation 24–28 days by both sexes. Semiprecocial young stay in nest 26–31 days. Fed by both sexes. 1 brood per year.
- **POPULATION** Abundant on breeding grounds, where colonies may number in the millions. Winters irregularly offshore to North Carolina and rarely to Florida. Casual inland after winter storms.
- **CONSERVATION** All auks are protected by law, but young and eggs are still harvested for food. Vulnerable to oil spills.

Similar Birds	
	COMMON MURRE Much larger; longer bill; longer neck.

Flight Pattern

Rapid direct flight with fast whirring wing beats low over water.

Nest Identification

Shape ◖ Location 🪹

Nothing added • on bare ground hidden in crannies of rocky cliffs • 1 bluish white or green egg, usually unmarked; oval to long elliptical, 4.8 cm long.

Plumage Sexes similar	Habitat 🐚 🌊 🌊	Migration Nonmigratory	Weight 162 g

DATE _____ TIME _____ LOCATION _____

Family ALCIDAE	Species *Uria aalge*	Length 44 cm	Wingspan 71–76 cm

COMMON MURRE

This large-bodied, crow-sized seabird is one of the most adept divers in the alcid family and is capable of diving to depths of more than 73 meters. Like all murres its pear-shaped egg is adapted to turn in a circle rather than roll off the precipitous cliffs where these birds nest. It has dark sooty brown upperparts, including the neck and head; a long thin black bill; and white underparts. Some Atlantic birds have a narrow white eye ring and stripe extending behind eye, but most East Coast birds and all Pacific Coast birds lack the eye adornment. Winter and juvenile birds show a white throat and cheeks and a black postocular stripe.

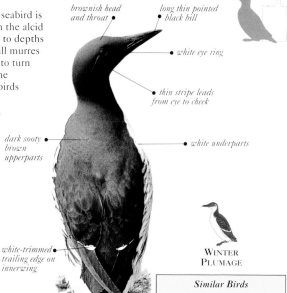

brownish head and throat

long thin pointed black bill

white eye ring

thin stripe leads from eye to cheek

dark sooty brown upperparts

white underparts

white-trimmed trailing edge on innerwing

WINTER PLUMAGE

- **SONG** Silent at sea. In flight makes soft *murrrr* sound. On nesting ground makes various low growling sounds, *arrrrrrrrrrhh*.
- **BEHAVIOR** Gregarious. Forms large rafts on water. Feeds in flocks, diving and swimming for food. Can stay underwater for 60 seconds. Carries fish lengthwise in mouth and sticks out tail while flying. Eats mostly various fish but also takes marine invertebrates, including shrimp and squid. Droppings from huge colonies provide important fertilizer to food chain of surrounding waters.
- **BREEDING** Monogamous. Colonial.
- **NESTING** Incubation 28–33 days by both sexes. Semiprecocial young stay in nest 19–21 days, then leave colony and accompany adults in water while completing development. Fed by both sexes. Typically 1 brood per year.
- **POPULATION** Abundant off West and East Coasts.
- **CONSERVATION** All alcids protected by law, but still vulnerable to marine oil spills.

Similar Birds

THICK-BILLED MURRE Shorter, thicker bill arched at tip with narrow white line along gape; white of underparts rises to sharp peak at throat • winter birds have darker face and neck; lack thin postocular stripe.

RAZORBILL Larger head; deeper bill; more pointed tail; blacker upperparts • Atlantic range.

Flight Pattern
Strong flight on rapidly whirring wings. Low over water near colonies. High for long distances, often twisting and turning.

Nest Identification	
Shape 🐾 Location 🪨	No nest materials • on bare ridge of cliff; sometimes placed against pebbles held together by droppings to guard egg from rolling off ledge • 1 white, green, blue, or brown egg with dark brown spots and blotches; spindle-shaped or elongated pyriform, 8.1 cm long.

Plumage Sexes similar	Habitat 🌊 🪶 🌊	Migration Nonmigratory	Weight 1.0 kg

DATE _____ TIME_____ LOCATION _____

| Family ALCIDAE | Species *Uria lomvia* | Length 46 cm | Wingspan 71–81 cm |

THICK-BILLED MURRE

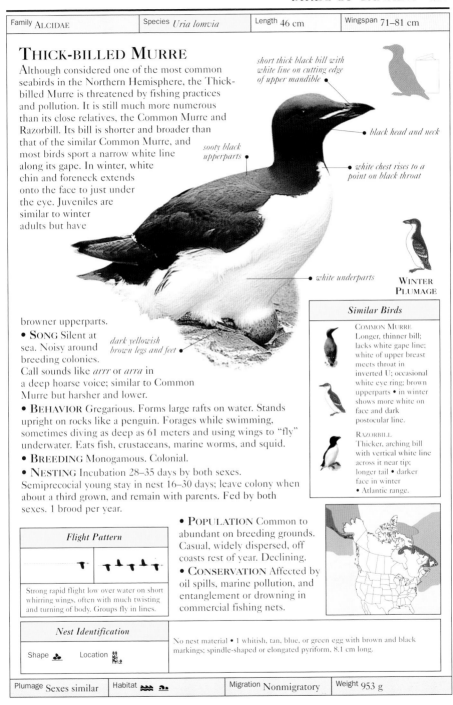

Although considered one of the most common seabirds in the Northern Hemisphere, the Thick-billed Murre is threatened by fishing practices and pollution. It is still much more numerous than its close relatives, the Common Murre and Razorbill. Its bill is shorter and broader than that of the similar Common Murre, and most birds sport a narrow white line along its gape. In winter, white chin and foreneck extends onto the face to just under the eye. Juveniles are similar to winter adults but have browner upperparts.

short thick black bill with white line on cutting edge of upper mandible

black head and neck

sooty black upperparts

white chest rises to a point on black throat

white underparts

WINTER PLUMAGE

- **SONG** Silent at sea. Noisy around breeding colonies. Call sounds like *arrr* or *arra* in a deep hoarse voice; similar to Common Murre but harsher and lower.

dark yellowish brown legs and feet

- **BEHAVIOR** Gregarious. Forms large rafts on water. Stands upright on rocks like a penguin. Forages while swimming, sometimes diving as deep as 61 meters and using wings to "fly" underwater. Eats fish, crustaceans, marine worms, and squid.
- **BREEDING** Monogamous. Colonial.
- **NESTING** Incubation 28–35 days by both sexes. Semiprecocial young stay in nest 16–30 days; leave colony when about a third grown, and remain with parents. Fed by both sexes. 1 brood per year.

Similar Birds

COMMON MURRE
Longer, thinner bill; lacks white gape line; white of upper breast meets throat in inverted U; occasional white eye ring; brown upperparts • in winter shows more white on face and dark postocular line.

RAZORBILL
Thicker, arching bill with vertical white line across it near tip; longer tail • darker face in winter • Atlantic range.

- **POPULATION** Common to abundant on breeding grounds. Casual, widely dispersed, off coasts rest of year. Declining.
- **CONSERVATION** Affected by oil spills, marine pollution, and entanglement or drowning in commercial fishing nets.

Flight Pattern

Strong rapid flight low over water on short whirring wings, often with much twisting and turning of body. Groups fly in lines.

Nest Identification

Shape 🐦   Location 🪺

No nest material • 1 whitish, tan, blue, or green egg with brown and black markings; spindle-shaped or elongated pyriform, 8.1 cm long.

| Plumage Sexes similar | Habitat 〰️ ⌇ | Migration Nonmigratory | Weight 953 g |

DATE _____ TIME_____ LOCATION _____

Family ALCIDAE	Species *Alca torda*	Length 41–46 cm	Wingspan 64–69 cm

RAZORBILL

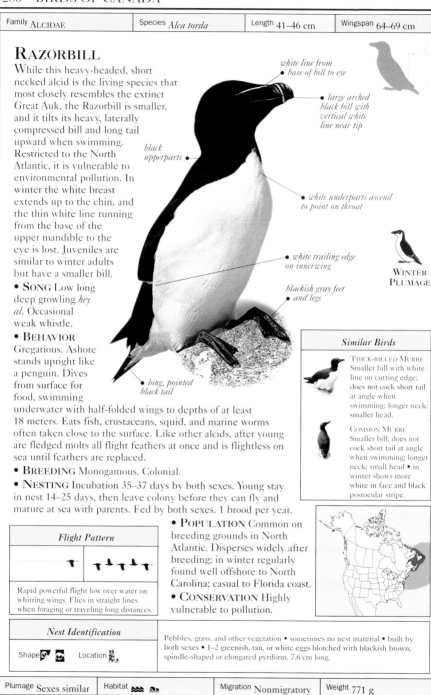

While this heavy-headed, short necked alcid is the living species that most closely resembles the extinct Great Auk, the Razorbill is smaller, and it tilts its heavy, laterally compressed bill and long tail upward when swimming. Restricted to the North Atlantic, it is vulnerable to environmental pollution. In winter the white breast extends up to the chin, and the thin white line running from the base of the upper mandible to the eye is lost. Juveniles are similar to winter adults but have a smaller bill.

white line from base of bill to eye

large arched black bill with vertical white line near tip

black upperparts

white underparts ascend to point on throat

white trailing edge on innerwing

blackish gray feet and legs

WINTER PLUMAGE

• **SONG** Low long deep growling *hey al.* Occasional weak whistle.

• **BEHAVIOR** Gregarious. Ashore stands upright like a penguin. Dives from surface for food, swimming underwater with half-folded wings to depths of at least 18 meters. Eats fish, crustaceans, squid, and marine worms often taken close to the surface. Like other alcids, after young are fledged molts all flight feathers at once and is flightless on sea until feathers are replaced.

long, pointed black tail

Similar Birds

THICK-BILLED MURRE Smaller bill with white line on cutting edge; does not cock short tail at angle when swimming; longer neck; smaller head.

COMMON MURRE Smaller bill; does not cock short tail at angle when swimming; longer neck; small head • in winter shows more white in face and black postocular stripe.

• **BREEDING** Monogamous. Colonial.

• **NESTING** Incubation 35–37 days by both sexes. Young stay in nest 14–25 days, then leave colony before they can fly and mature at sea with parents. Fed by both sexes. 1 brood per year.

• **POPULATION** Common on breeding grounds in North Atlantic. Disperses widely after breeding; in winter regularly found well offshore to North Carolina; casual to Florida coast.

• **CONSERVATION** Highly vulnerable to pollution.

Flight Pattern
Rapid powerful flight low over water on whirring wings. Flies in straight lines when foraging or traveling long distances.

Nest Identification	
Shape ⬤ ⬛ Location 🪺	Pebbles, grass, and other vegetation • sometimes no nest material • built by both sexes • 1–2 greenish, tan, or white eggs blotched with blackish brown; spindle-shaped or elongated pyriform, 7.6 cm long.

Plumage Sexes similar	Habitat 〰️ 🦆	Migration Nonmigratory	Weight 771 g

DATE _____ TIME_____ LOCATION _____

| Family ALCIDAE | Species *Cepphus grylle* | Length 30–36 cm | Wingspan 58 cm |

BLACK GUILLEMOT

A shoreline inhabitant, the Black Guillemot is usually observed closer to shore than most other alcids, especially in the North Atlantic. While its population is widely dispersed, it is not as gregarious as other birds in its family. Black Guillemots sometimes can be spotted coaxing their young to fly off cliffs, dangling prey just beyond reach for encouragement. In flight note the large white wing patch, white axillaries, and white underwing linings. The inside of this bird's mouth is bright coral orange. Winter adults and juveniles are white with mottled black upperparts.

black bill

black plumage

• **SONG** Weak, high-pitched whistle of *peeee*.

large white shoulder patch

• **BEHAVIOR** Not gregarious but may occur in small flocks; usually in pairs or alone. Eats rock eels, small fish, mollusks, crustaceans, insects, marine worms, and some vegetation. Often surface dives 9–30.5 meters underwater to forage for food under loose stones while swimming with wings. In flight flashes white patches and dangles red feet behind tail.

WINTER PLUMAGE

• **BREEDING** Monogamous. Semicolonial to colonial (colonies of only a few pairs).

• **NESTING** Incubation 23–39 days by both sexes. Semiprecocial young stay in nest 35 days. Fed by both sexes. 1 brood per year.

• **POPULATION** Fairly common on breeding grounds; disperses after breeding.

Similar Birds

PIGEON GUILLEMOT
Dusky wing linings and axillaries; black bar on white shoulder patch.
• Pacific Coast range.

• **CONSERVATION** Introduction of predators to nesting areas poses danger, but birds still numerous, Geographically dispersed nesting areas help offset the threat. Vulnerable to oil spills.

Flight Pattern
Direct flight with rapid wing beats low over water.

Nest Identification	
Shape ◐ ⬠ Location 🐦 ▬	Made of debris and small stones • often near driftwood • built by both sexes • 1–2 white eggs, sometimes tinted with bluish green, with black, brown, and gray markings; long elliptical to pyriform, 5.8 cm long.

| Plumage Sexes similar | Habitat ≈≈ ⚓ | Migration Most do not migrate | Weight 405 g |

DATE _____ TIME_____ LOCATION _____

Family ALCIDAE	Species *Cepphus columba*	Length 33–36 cm	Wingspan 58 cm

PIGEON GUILLEMOT

This western species, like other alcids, "flies" underwater as it searches for food, swimming with its wings. During breeding season flocks of these birds participate in a complicated water dance, gathering in lines above the water, then diving under the surface and playing tag with one another. This coastal species often can be spotted from shore. Look for the large white wing patch bisected by a black bar or wedge. In flight the axillars and underwings are dusky gray. Winter adults are white with black mottling on the upperparts, hindneck, and crown. Juveniles are similar to winter adults but duskier.

black bill

black plumage

large white wing patch bisected by black bar

WINTER PLUMAGE

- **SONG** Usually silent at sea. Nesting birds give weak hissing whistle, *peeeeee*.
- **BEHAVIOR** Semigregarious. Occurs alone or in pairs or small groups. Dives underwater to feed on small fish at bottom. Also eats mollusks, crustaceans, and marine worms.

reddish legs and feet

- **BREEDING** Monogamous. Small colonies or individual.
- **NESTING** Incubation 29–32 days by both sexes. Semiprecocial young stay in nest 29–39 days. Fed by both sexes. 1 brood per year.
- **POPULATION** Fairly common along northern Pacific Coast from Alaska to southern California. Winter distribution is not very well known.
- **CONSERVATION** Declining because of pollution, oil spills, and warming climatic trends.

Similar Birds

BLACK GUILLEMOT White underwing lining; solid white wing patch.

Flight Pattern

Strong swift direct flight low over water, often in wide circle, wings beating rapidly.

Nest Identification

Shape   Location

Rock chips, pebbles, and debris • on bare rock, in deserted holes of puffins and rabbits, under railroad ties, or on buildings and wharves • built by both sexes • 1–2 off-white, pale bluish, or very pale yellow eggs with gray and dark brown blotches; conical to pyriform, rounder toward end, 6.1 cm long.

Plumage Sexes similar	Habitat	Migration Nonmigratory	Weight 499 g

DATE _____ TIME_____ LOCATION _____

Family ALCIDAE	Species *Brachyramphus marmoratus*	Length 25 cm	Wingspan 41 cm

MARBLED MURRELET

Its marbled camouflage protects this bird from predators during the breeding season. Generally these birds nest in the open on the tundra, but farther south they nest in trees. When threatened this murrelet will fly rather than dive to escape, skittering rapidly just above the water. Note the heavy barring and mottling.

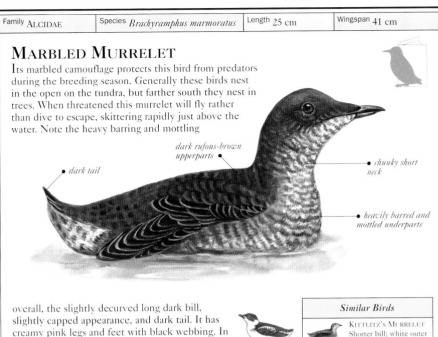

dark rufous-brown upperparts

dark tail

chunky short neck

heavily barred and mottled underparts

overall, the slightly decurved long dark bill, slightly capped appearance, and dark tail. It has creamy pink legs and feet with black webbing. In winter it has dark gray upperparts, white underparts from the eyes down, and a white line on the scapulars. Juveniles are similar to winter adults but have mottled underparts.

WINTER PLUMAGE

• **SONG** Often vocal. Gives series of loud high notes, *kree* or *meer-meer-meer-meer*.

• **BEHAVIOR** Gregarious in nonbreeding season. Feeds by diving from water's surface. Beats wings 2–3 times per second while underwater to swim as deep below the surface as 30.5 meters. Feeds on fish and crustaceans.

• **BREEDING** Monogamous. Usually a solitary nester.

• **NESTING** Incubation 27–30 days by both sexes. Semiprecocial young stay in nest 27 days. Fed by both sexes. 1 brood per year. Nests inland in trees south of tundra.

Similar Birds

KITTLITZ'S MURRELET Shorter bill; white outer tail feathers; white above eyes • in breeding season has white belly • in winter has dusky breast band.

LONG-BILLED MURRELET Paler throat; small pale oval patches on sides of nape; in flight shows white median underwing primary coverts • in breeding plumage has less rufous upperparts • in winter lacks white collar.

• **POPULATION** Common in its breeding range; rare on the Pacific Coast from southern California south.

• **CONSERVATION** Threatened by old-growth timber harvesting and oil spills.

Flight Pattern
Swift direct flight with whirring rapid wing beats. Rises quickly from water and flies low over surface.

Nest Identification	
Shape ⌒ Location ▬ ♨ ♨ ♨ ⚘ 🐦	No material added • on bare rocks on ground, on limbs, or in cavities of evergreen trees • built by both sexes • 1 light greenish yellow egg with blackish brown spots; subelliptical, 6.1 x 3.8 cm.

Plumage Sexes similar	Habitat ▬ ▲ 🦢 🐾	Migration Migratory	Weight 221 g

DATE _____ TIME _____ LOCATION _____

Family ALCIDAE	Species *Synthliboramphus antiquus*	Length 25 cm	Wingspan 41 cm

ANCIENT MURRELET

This little auk is named for the gray coloring on its back, thought to resemble a shawl worn across the shoulders of an elderly person, and for the white streaking on the sides of the crown in breeding plumage, which adds to the "ancient look." In flight it crooks its head upward and shows a black side bar contrasting with the white wing linings and white underparts; legs and feet are grayish. Juveniles are similar to winter adults but have a whitish throat and chin and lack any white streaking on the sides of the crown.

black on head extends to throat

straw to whitish yellow bill with blackish tip and culmen

• **SONG** Soft whistles and chirps during nesting. Shrill *chirrup* while at sea.

black-and-white-streaked half collar

pale slate-gray upperparts

WINTER PLUMAGE

white underparts

heavy blackish mottling on flanks

• **BEHAVIOR** Nomadic. Nocturnal on breeding grounds. Dives and swims underwater using wings. Eats crustaceans and small fish brought to surface by tides. Young raised at sea and recognize parents through auditory means.

BREEDING PLUMAGE

• **BREEDING** Monogamous. Colonial.

• **NESTING** Incubation 32–36 days by both sexes. Young remain in nest for 3 days, then are led to sea by parents. Not fed in nest. Young are tended by both sexes at sea for 28 days. 1 brood per year.

Similar Birds

MARBLED MURRELET Smaller; black bill • in winter has black back with white line bordering scapulars.

• **POPULATION** Uncommon to common on Aleutians and other islands in Bering Sea. Winters offshore to central California and rarely to southern California. Casual to accidental inland throughout continent.

Flight Pattern
Swift direct flight on rapidly whirring wings close to water; often stops midflight and drops into water.

• **CONSERVATION** Declining because of accidental introduction of rats on nesting islands and introduction of foxes and raccoons for fur production. Is vulnerable to offshore oil spills.

Nest Identification	
Shape	Lined with dry grass, twigs, and leaves • built by both sexes • 1–2 light brown or olive-brown eggs, sometimes tinged with blue and brown evenly distributed speckles; elongated, 5.8 x 3.8 cm.
Location	

Plumage Sexes similar	Habitat	Migration Nonmigratory	Weight 207 g

DATE _____ TIME _____ LOCATION _____

Family ALCIDAE	Species *Ptychoramphus aleuticus*	Length 23 cm	Wingspan 34 cm

CASSIN'S AUKLET

After hiding by day on its breeding islands, this bird is busy at night, constructing burrows for its nest or renovating a used one. The male and female take turns digging, stopping to bow to one another. It may take sixty days to dig a new burrow. One of the most widespread and abundant of the northeast Pacific alcids, it is a chunky little seabird with brownish gray upperparts and paler gray-brown underparts. At close range the short thick bill shows a light spot at the base. In flight the underwings are gray-brown, and the belly is whitish. Juveniles are lighter in color with dark eyes, whiter throats, and browner wings and tails.

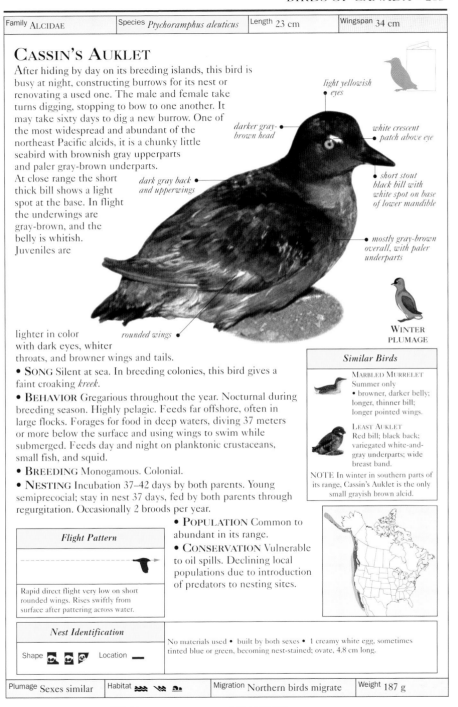

light yellowish eyes

darker gray-brown head

white crescent patch above eye

dark gray back and upperwings

short stout black bill with white spot on base of lower mandible

mostly gray-brown overall, with paler underparts

rounded wings

WINTER PLUMAGE

• **SONG** Silent at sea. In breeding colonies, this bird gives a faint croaking *kreek*.

• **BEHAVIOR** Gregarious throughout the year. Nocturnal during breeding season. Highly pelagic. Feeds far offshore, often in large flocks. Forages for food in deep waters, diving 37 meters or more below the surface and using wings to swim while submerged. Feeds day and night on planktonic crustaceans, small fish, and squid.

• **BREEDING** Monogamous. Colonial.

• **NESTING** Incubation 37–42 days by both parents. Young semiprecocial; stay in nest 37 days, fed by both parents through regurgitation. Occasionally 2 broods per year.

• **POPULATION** Common to abundant in its range.

• **CONSERVATION** Vulnerable to oil spills. Declining local populations due to introduction of predators to nesting sites.

Similar Birds

MARBLED MURRELET
Summer only
• browner, darker belly; longer, thinner bill; longer pointed wings.

LEAST AUKLET
Red bill; black back; variegated white-and-gray underparts; wide breast band.

NOTE In winter in southern parts of its range, Cassin's Auklet is the only small grayish brown alcid.

Flight Pattern

Rapid direct flight very low on short rounded wings. Rises swiftly from surface after pattering across water.

Nest Identification

Shape — Location —

No materials used • built by both sexes • 1 creamy white egg, sometimes tinted blue or green, becoming nest-stained; ovate, 4.8 cm long.

Plumage Sexes similar	Habitat	Migration Northern birds migrate	Weight 187 g

DATE _____ TIME_____ LOCATION _____

Family ALCIDAE	Species *Aethia psittacula*	Length 25 cm	Wingspan 39 cm

PARAKEET AUKLET

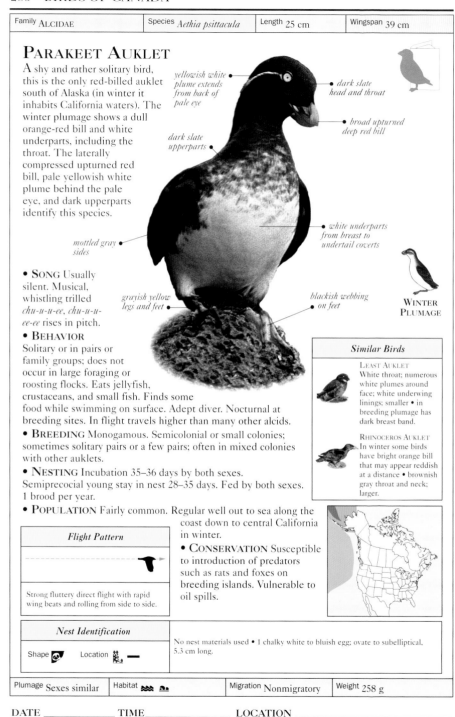

A shy and rather solitary bird, this is the only red-billed auklet south of Alaska (in winter it inhabits California waters). The winter plumage shows a dull orange-red bill and white underparts, including the throat. The laterally compressed upturned red bill, pale yellowish white plume behind the pale eye, and dark upperparts identify this species.

yellowish white plume extends from back of pale eye

dark slate head and throat

broad upturned deep red bill

dark slate upperparts

white underparts from breast to undertail coverts

mottled gray sides

blackish webbing on feet

WINTER PLUMAGE

grayish yellow legs and feet

- **SONG** Usually silent. Musical, whistling trilled *chu-u-u-ee, chu-u-u-ee-ee* rises in pitch.
- **BEHAVIOR** Solitary or in pairs or family groups; does not occur in large foraging or roosting flocks. Eats jellyfish, crustaceans, and small fish. Finds some food while swimming on surface. Adept diver. Nocturnal at breeding sites. In flight travels higher than many other alcids.
- **BREEDING** Monogamous. Semicolonial or small colonies; sometimes solitary pairs or a few pairs; often in mixed colonies with other auklets.
- **NESTING** Incubation 35–36 days by both sexes. Semiprecocial young stay in nest 28–35 days. Fed by both sexes. 1 brood per year.
- **POPULATION** Fairly common. Regular well out to sea along the coast down to central California in winter.
- **CONSERVATION** Susceptible to introduction of predators such as rats and foxes on breeding islands. Vulnerable to oil spills.

Similar Birds

LEAST AUKLET
White throat; numerous white plumes around face; white underwing linings; smaller • in breeding plumage has dark breast band.

RHINOCEROS AUKLET
In winter some birds have bright orange bill that may appear reddish at a distance • brownish gray throat and neck; larger.

Flight Pattern

Strong fluttery direct flight with rapid wing beats and rolling from side to side.

Nest Identification

Shape ◕ Location 🐾 ▬

No nest materials used • 1 chalky white to bluish egg; ovate to subelliptical, 5.3 cm long.

Plumage Sexes similar	Habitat 〰️ ⚓	Migration Nonmigratory	Weight 258 g

DATE _____ TIME _____ LOCATION _____

Family ALCIDAE	Species *Aethia pusilla*	Length 15 cm	Wingspan 24 cm

LEAST AUKLET

Common in the Bering Sea and Aleutian Islands, this sparrow-sized bird is arguably the most abundant seabird of the North Pacific. It is the smallest and one of the most gregarious members of the alcid family. Pairs often mate for more than one season. The combination of its small size, white throat, and dark breast band in summer are diagnostic. In flight it shows white underwing

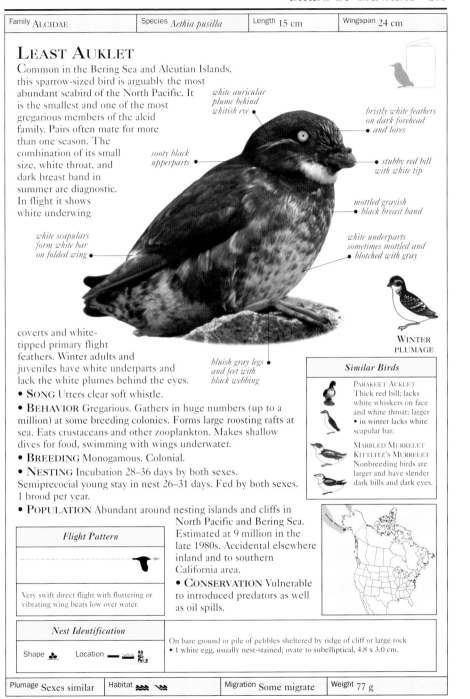

white auricular plume behind whitish eye

bristly white feathers on dark forehead and lores

sooty black upperparts

stubby red bill with white tip

mottled grayish black breast band

white scapulars form white bar on folded wing

white underparts sometimes mottled and blotched with gray

coverts and white-tipped primary flight feathers. Winter adults and juveniles have white underparts and lack the white plumes behind the eyes.

bluish gray legs and feet with black webbing

WINTER PLUMAGE

- **SONG** Utters clear soft whistle.
- **BEHAVIOR** Gregarious. Gathers in huge numbers (up to a million) at some breeding colonies. Forms large roosting rafts at sea. Eats crustaceans and other zooplankton. Makes shallow dives for food, swimming with wings underwater.
- **BREEDING** Monogamous. Colonial.
- **NESTING** Incubation 28–36 days by both sexes. Semiprecocial young stay in nest 26–31 days. Fed by both sexes. 1 brood per year.
- **POPULATION** Abundant around nesting islands and cliffs in North Pacific and Bering Sea. Estimated at 9 million in the late 1980s. Accidental elsewhere inland and to southern California area.
- **CONSERVATION** Vulnerable to introduced predators as well as oil spills.

Similar Birds

PARAKEET AUKLET
Thick red bill; lacks white whiskers on face and white throat; larger
- in winter lacks white scapular bar.

MARBLED MURRELET
KITTLITZ'S MURRELET
Nonbreeding birds are larger and have slender dark bills and dark eyes.

Flight Pattern
Very swift direct flight with fluttering or vibrating wing beats low over water.

Nest Identification	
Shape	Location	On bare ground or pile of pebbles sheltered by ridge of cliff or large rock • 1 white egg, usually nest-stained; ovate to subelliptical, 4.8 x 3.0 cm.

Plumage Sexes similar	Habitat	Migration Some migrate	Weight 77 g

DATE _____ TIME_____ LOCATION _____

Family ALCIDAE	Species *Aethia cristatella*	Length 23 cm	Wingspan 36 cm

CRESTED AUKLET

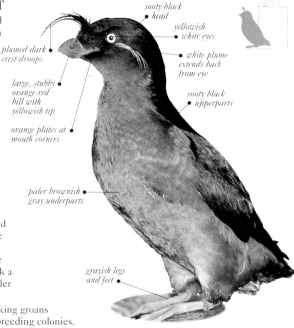

sooty black head

yellowish white eyes

plumed dark crest droops

white plume extends back from eye

large, stubby orange-red bill with yellowish tip

sooty black upperparts

orange plates at mouth corners

paler brownish gray underparts

grayish legs and feet

The bill of this gregarious bird emits a citruslike aroma, which may play a role in attracting a mate. Its stubby shape, quail-like size, and long forward-curling plume have engendered the local name of "sea quail." In breeding plumage slightly upturned, fleshy bright orange plates appear on the bill gape and present a curious grinning appearance, and the curled head crest and white postocular plume are enlarged. Dusky brown underwing linings show when the bird is in flight. In winter the crest and plume become shorter, and the bill turns brown and loses its decorative plates. Juveniles are similar to winter adults but lack a crest or plumes and have a duller yellow-brown bill.

• **SONG** Garrulous. Loud honking groans and chirps, especially around breeding colonies.

• **BEHAVIOR** Gregarious. Often forms flocks that may include other auklet species. Eats zooplankton, including crustaceans, as well as small fish and squid. Swims with wings underwater to search for food. Dives up to 61 meters below surface. In breeding areas forms huge concentrations, with countless birds wheeling and swirling through the air like smoke or swarms of bees.

• **BREEDING** Monogamous. Colonial.

• **NESTING** Incubation 29–41 days (average 34 days) by both sexes. Semiprecocial young stay in nest 27–36 days. Fed by both sexes, more by female. 1 brood per year.

Similar Birds

WHISKERED AUKLET
3 white plumes on sides of face; white-tipped bill lacks orange plates; thinner, more erect plume from forehead.

CASSIN'S AUKLET
Similar to juvenile but has darker bill and white belly.

• **POPULATION** Common to locally abundant. Accidental offshore in winter to the Baja California area.

• **CONSERVATION** Affected by oil spills, pollution, and introduction of predators to nesting islands.

Flight Pattern
Swift buzzing direct flight with rapid whirring wing beats close to water.

Nest Identification	
Shape 🐦 🐛 Location 🪨 ▬ 🌊	No nest materials • 1 white egg, usually nest-stained; oval to short oval, 5.3 cm long.

Plumage Sexes similar	Habitat 〰️ 🦆 〰️	Migration Nonmigratory	Weight 264 g

DATE _____ TIME_____ LOCATION _____

| Family ALCIDAE | Species *Cerorhinca monocerata* | Length 38 cm | Wingspan 56 cm |

RHINOCEROS AUKLET

Named for the unusual hornlike protrusion on its bill during breeding season, this bird digs and nests in burrows to which it returns each year along with its same mate. In flight it appears puffinlike but has more pointed wings, a whitish belly that blends into a darker breast and upperparts, and dark brownish gray underwings. In winter this bird lacks the horn on its upper mandible, and the color of its bill and plumes fade.

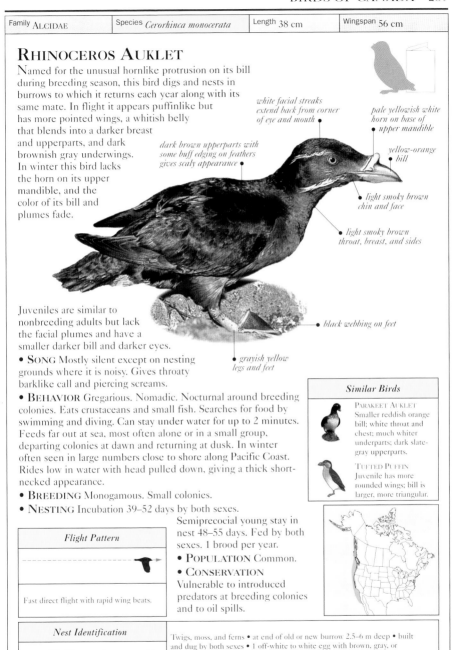

white facial streaks extend back from corner of eye and mouth

pale yellowish white horn on base of upper mandible

dark brown upperparts with some buff edging on feathers gives scaly appearance

yellow-orange bill

light smoky brown chin and face

light smoky brown throat, breast, and sides

black webbing on feet

grayish yellow legs and feet

Juveniles are similar to nonbreeding adults but lack the facial plumes and have a smaller darker bill and darker eyes.

• **SONG** Mostly silent except on nesting grounds where it is noisy. Gives throaty barklike call and piercing screams.

• **BEHAVIOR** Gregarious. Nomadic. Nocturnal around breeding colonies. Eats crustaceans and small fish. Searches for food by swimming and diving. Can stay under water for up to 2 minutes. Feeds far out at sea, most often alone or in a small group, departing colonies at dawn and returning at dusk. In winter often seen in large numbers close to shore along Pacific Coast. Rides low in water with head pulled down, giving a thick short-necked appearance.

• **BREEDING** Monogamous. Small colonies.

• **NESTING** Incubation 39–52 days by both sexes. Semiprecocial young stay in nest 48–55 days. Fed by both sexes. 1 brood per year.

• **POPULATION** Common.

• **CONSERVATION** Vulnerable to introduced predators at breeding colonies and to oil spills.

Similar Birds

PARAKEET AUKLET Smaller reddish orange bill; white throat and chest; much whiter underparts; dark slate-gray upperparts.

TUFTED PUFFIN Juvenile has more rounded wings; bill is larger, more triangular.

Flight Pattern
Fast direct flight with rapid wing beats.

Nest Identification	
Shape	Location

Twigs, moss, and ferns • at end of old or new burrow 2.5–6 m deep • built and dug by both sexes • 1 off-white to white egg with brown, gray, or lavender blotches; elliptical or subelliptical, 6.9 x 4.6 cm.

| Plumage Sexes similar | Habitat | Migration Nonmigratory | Weight 499 g |

DATE _____ TIME _____ LOCATION _____

Family ALCIDAE	Species *Fratercula arctica*	Length 30 cm	Wingspan 53–61 cm

ATLANTIC PUFFIN

Formerly called the Common Puffin, this, the provincial bird of Newfoundland, is the only puffin nesting on the Atlantic Coast. Because the eggs are laid in burrows, incubating birds are able to take long breaks, often walking around the nesting grounds socializing with other puffins. In flight it shows rounded grayish underwings and white underparts separated by a black collar. Winter birds have smaller yellow-edged bills and darker faces. Juveniles have even smaller bills.

- **SONG** Usually silent at sea. In flight makes soft purring sounds. At breeding sites this bird gives a low growl-like *arrr*.

- **BEHAVIOR** Tame and trusting at colonies. Upright posture. Eats crustaceans and small fish. Searches for food 15–61 meters underwater. Can carry 10 or more fish at once; arranges fish crosswise in bill as they are caught and transports them back to nest with heads and tails dangling out on either side. Winters at sea far from land, where prenuptial molt renders birds briefly flightless just prior to breeding season. Often patters across water to become airborne.

- **BREEDING** Monogamous. Colonial. Males fight each other on water during courtship.

- **NESTING** Incubation 39–45 days by both sexes. Semiprecocial young stay in nest 38–44 days. Fed by both sexes, then abandoned by parents who swim out to sea. Nestling fasts in burrow for about a week until able to swim out to sea, usually departing colony at dark. First flight at about 49 days. 1 brood per year.

- **POPULATION** Common but local in breeding season. In winter casual at sea to North Carolina.

- **CONSERVATION** Has been declining since the 19th Century due to hunting and introduction of predators such as rats, cats, dogs, and foxes to nesting grounds. Vulnerable to oil spills.

triangular black line from eye to below crown

narrow black line extends backward from eye

large triangular bill has red-orange tip and blue-gray base surrounded by yellow

pale gray to white face and cheeks

black upperparts

black of forehead, crown, and nape extends around throat to form black collar

white underparts

red-orange legs and feet

JUVENILE

WINTER PLUMAGE

Similar Birds

RAZORBILL
Black bill; black hood; lacks black collar; black legs and feet; white trailing edge on wing; white underwing linings.

Flight Pattern

Swift direct flight with rapid wing beats often close to water.

Nest Identification

Shape ⬡ ⬡ ⬡ Location — 🪨 ⚏

Burrow in loose soil with entrance hidden by rocks • lining, if present, composed of grass, feathers, seaweed, and leaves • male does most of excavating with some help from female • 1 white egg, sometimes with brown or lavender blotches; round, 6.4 cm long.

Plumage Sexes similar	Habitat 〰 🦆 〰	Migration Nonmigratory	Weight 377 g

DATE _____ TIME_____ LOCATION _____

Family ALCIDAE	Species *Fratercula corniculata*	Length 38 cm	Wingspan 56–58 cm

HORNED PUFFIN

Named for the fleshy erectile hornlike protrusions above each eye, this bird resembles the Atlantic Puffin, its East Coast counterpart, but their ranges do not overlap. In flight note the black upperparts and white face surrounded by black-and-white underparts that contrast with the black collar and dark grayish underwings. In winter the horns disappear, the

black upperparts

white face and cheeks

black forehead and crown

fleshy hornlike black protrusion extends from eye to crown

large triangular yellow bill with orange-red tip and orange wattle at gape

black collar

white chest and belly

orange-red legs and feet

JUVENILE · WINTER PLUMAGE

cheeks turn gray, and the bill becomes darker and smaller. Juveniles are similar to winter adults but have smaller bills without any red-orange.

- **SONG** Usually silent at sea. Around breeding colonies utters various throaty growls.
- **BEHAVIOR** Gregarious. Pelagic; winters at sea. Eats crustaceans, mollusks, fish, squid, and marine worms. Swims buoyantly, springing clear of water before diving under. Uses wings to propel itself underwater to catch food. Like other puffins carries multiple fish crosswise in bill back to colony.
- **BREEDING** Monogamous. Colonial. Often in mixed colonies with other seabirds.
- **NESTING** Incubation 40–42 days by both sexes. Semiprecocial young stay in nest 34–40 days. Fed by both sexes. 1 brood per year.

Similar Birds

TUFTED PUFFIN
Dark underparts • in breeding plumage has pale yellow head plumes.

COMMON MURRE
THICK-BILLED MURRE
Entirely dark head; small dark bill; white trailing margin on inner wing.

- **POPULATION** Abundant to very common but local. Rare to casual offshore in late spring to southern California.
- **CONSERVATION** Some decline due to introduced predators at nesting area, oil spills, and pollution.

Flight Pattern
Strong purposeful direct flight with rapid wing beats, often high above water.

Nest Identification	
Shape 🪹🪺 Location ▬ 🏠	Lined with grasses, if lined • in burrow 30–90 cm long or in rock crevices • built by both sexes • 1 chalky white egg with brown and lavender blotches; round to short elliptical, 7.1 cm long.

Plumage Sexes similar	Habitat ≈≈≈ ♒ ⌇	Migration Nonmigratory	Weight 635 g

DATE _____ TIME_____ LOCATION _____

Family ALCIDAE	Species *Fratercula cirrhata*	Length 39 cm	Wingspan 58–61 cm

TUFTED PUFFIN

The largest of the puffins is
distinguished by its odd-looking
head plumes in breeding season.
The combination of a massive
red, orange, and yellow bill;
long ivory-yellow head tufts;
white face; and stout black
body is unmistakable.
Though it always nests
in colonies, it travels
and feeds alone at sea.
In flight birds show
grayish wing linings.
In winter the plumes
disappear, the bill
becomes smaller and duller,
and the overall plumage,
including the face, becomes
blackish gray-brown. Juveniles are
smaller and darker and have small
dull yellow bills.

black crown
white face and cheeks
yellow eyes with red orbital ring
long buff-yellow plumes hang from behind eyes and run down neck
orange-red bill has yellowish or greenish gray basal third of upper mandible and yellow ridge
black overall
orange-red legs and feet

JUVENILE

• **SONG** Usually silent at sea. Around
nesting colony makes low, throaty growls.

• **BEHAVIOR** Nomadic. Eats crustaceans,
mollusks, fish, squid, and algae. Uses wings
to propel itself underwater, often chasing
schools of fish. Also dives for prey. Forages
widely from colony, often traveling far out to sea
and leaving nesting sites early in the morning for
the day. Must run across water prior to takeoff.
Walks and stands upright.

WINTER
PLUMAGE

• **BREEDING** Monogamous. Colonial. Requires headlands or
islands with soil or peat deep enough for nesting burrows.

• **NESTING** Incubation 41 days by both sexes. Semiprecocial
young stay in nest 45 days. Fed by both sexes. Usually 1 brood
per year, but 2 per year in the South.

• **POPULATION** Common to abundant in breeding areas of
northern part of range;
uncommon to rare off southern
California coast. Accidental in
the East.

• **CONSERVATION** Vulnerable
to predators in nesting areas and
oil spills.

Similar Birds

HORNED PUFFIN
Lacks ear tufts; white
underparts. • Pacific
Coast range.

RHINOCEROS AUKLET
Winter adults and
juveniles similar to
juvenile but have
whitish bellies; grayish
yellow legs and feet;
pale eye • Pacific Coast
range.

NOTE: No similar species in
the East.

Flight Pattern

Strong, purposeful direct flight with rapid
beats on rounded wings, often from 18 to
30.5 meters above water.

Nest Identification

Shape ⬠ ⬠ ⬠   Location ▬ 🏠

Lined with grass and feathers • burrow in soft sand or soil; sometimes in crevice
• built by both sexes • 1 chalky white or blue-tinged egg with brown, gray, and
lavender blotches; round to short elliptical, 7.1 cm long.

Plumage Sexes similar	Habitat ≈≈≈ ⌒ ≈≈	Migration Nonmigratory	Weight 771 g

DATE _____ TIME_____ LOCATION _____

Family COLUMBIDAE	Species *Columba livia*	Length 33–36 cm	Wingspan 61–64 cm

ROCK DOVE

Introduced into North America by Europeans in the early 1600s, the Rock Dove is often called homing pigeon or carrier pigeon. Early Romans are said to have used the Rock Dove to carry the report of Caesar's conquest of Gaul back to Rome, and legend says the Rock Dove brought news of Napoleon's defeat at Waterloo to England days before messages sent via horses and ships. Although native to wild rocky habitats, today these birds are most common in urban and rural settings, and they are still raised in coops or pigeon lofts.

blue-gray overall

• *iridescent feathers on head and neck reflect green, bronze, and purple*

• *2 thick broad bars across each wing*

WILDTYPE

They can vary in color from wildtype to browns, grays, white-gray, mosaics, or pure white, but they always show a white rump pattern.

COLOR VARIATIONS

• **SONG** Sings a repetitive cooing *coo-a-roo, coo-roo-cooo* or *cock-a-war* or *coo-cuk-cuk*.

• **BEHAVIOR** In wild eats grass, weed seeds, grains, clover, and berries. In cities eats bread crumbs and garbage. Will take food from the hand, but when frightened claps wings over the back while flying up. Able to fly faster than 135 km/h.

• **BREEDING** Male displays by turning in circles while cooing. Monogamous.

• **NESTING** Incubation 16–19 days by both sexes. Altricial young remain in nest about 27–35 days. Fed by both parents. Young thrust bills into parents' mouths to eat regurgitated food. 5 or more broods per year.

• **POPULATION** Common, especially in urban settings.

Similar Birds

BAND-TAILED PIGEON West • white bar on nape; broad gray tail band; lacks white rump.

MOURNING DOVE Much smaller; long pointed tail; lacks white rump patch.

Flight Pattern
Swift direct flight with rapid wing beats.

Nest Identification	
Shape ___ Location ___	Unlined platform of sticks, twigs, leaves, grasses • building ledges, barn rafters, gutters, sheltered cliff edges, or rocks • built by female with materials gathered by male • 2 white eggs, about 4.1 cm long.

Plumage Sexes similar	Habitat ___	Migration Nonmigratory	Weight 369 g

DATE _____ TIME_____ LOCATION _____

Family COLUMBIDAE	Species *Columba fasciata*	Length 36–38 cm	Wingspan 64 cm

BAND-TAILED PIGEON

Reduced in numbers by overhunting, the Band-tailed Pigeon has recovered as a result of bans on hunting in several states. It is generally is found in woods and wooded canyons in mountains, where it perches for long periods of time in the tops of leafless trees. Large flocks often gather at water holes and salt licks.

purplish head

narrow white band on nape of neck

yellow bill with dark tip

- **SONG** An owl-like repetitive *oo-whoo* or *whoo-oo-whoo*. During nesting season male utters deep smooth tremulous *whoo-whoo-hoo* or two-syllable *whoo-uh*.

- **BEHAVIOR** Not as gregarious as some other species of doves and pigeons, these birds often perch in small groups high in trees on open branches. Small flocks may fly together to water holes or to forage. In winter these flocks may number several hundred birds, rarely thousands. Flutters among branches to pick berries.

purplish wings and breast

yellow legs and feet

conspicuous wide dark gray terminal band across tail

Also eats wild peas, grains, seeds, nuts, and insects.

- **BREEDING** Male calls to female from open perch in tree. Monogamous. Scattered pairs or occasionally small colonies.

- **NESTING** Incubation 18–20 days by both sexes. Young stay in nest 25–30 days. Tended by both parents. Young fed by regurgitation of seeds, fruits, berries, and pigeons' milk. 2–3 broods per year.

- **POPULATION** Uncommon to fairly common; local.

- **CONSERVATION** Nearly extirpated from overhunting, but has recovered with restraints on hunting.

Similar Birds

ROCK DOVE
White rump; no contrasting gray band at end of tail.

Flight Pattern

Swift strong direct flight.

Nest Identification

Shape ⌒ Location 🐦 🪹

Flimsy platform of twigs • usually in tree branches or forks 2.5–12 m above ground • built by female with materials gathered by male • 1–2 unmarked white eggs, 4.1 x 2.5 cm.

Plumage Sexes similar	Habitat 🌳 ⛰ 🌿	Migration Migratory	Weight 354 g

DATE _____ TIME _____ LOCATION _____

Family COLUMBIDAE	Species *Streptopelia orientalis*	Length 34 cm	Wingspan 62 cm

ORIENTAL TURTLE-DOVE

On rare occasions birdwatchers on Vancouver Island have spotted an Oriental Turtle-Dove that perhaps lost its way migrating to the Bering Strait or occasionally on to the Aleutian Islands. Native to Russia and parts of Asia, where it is sometimes called the Rufous Turtle-Dove because of the rusty brown edging to the feathers on its back and scapulars, this large, stocky bird travels in small flocks during nonbreeding season. It can be found in open forests with deciduous and coniferous trees.

streaked black-and-white patch on neck

grayish rump

black feathers with buff, gray, or reddish fringes create scaly pattern

red legs

- **SONG** Low, grating *hoo-boo, hoo-boo, hoo-boo.*
- **BEHAVIOR** Solitary during breeding season; somewhat gregarious after nesting, foraging, roosting, and going to water in small groups. Feeds on various seeds. Somewhat tame, often allowing close approach. Builds a large, bulky nest for a dove. Frequents woodlands, especially riparian stands, with saplings and thick undergrowth.
- **BREEDING** Monogamous.
- **NESTING** Incubation 17–21 days mostly by female. Young fed regurgitated seeds and "pigeons' milk." Young leave nest 34–37 days after hatching. 2 or more broods per year.

white band on tip of long gray tail

Similar Birds
MOURNING DOVE Long pointed tail; dark eye; lacks black-and-white neck patch.

- **POPULATION** Accidental on Vancouver Island; casual to western Aleutians and Bering Sea; common in Russia.

Flight Pattern
Strong swift direct flight.

Nest Identification	
Shape Location	Larger than most dove nests • made of twigs and small branches • on low tree branches • 2 white or yellowish eggs in May.

Plumage Sexes similar	Habitat	Migration Migratory	Weight 201 g

DATE _____ TIME_____ LOCATION _____

Family COLUMBIDAE	Species *Zenaida macroura*	Length 30 cm	Wingspan 43–48 cm

MOURNING DOVE

A familiar sight across the continental United States and much of southern Canada, this dove can be distinguished from similar species by its long pointed tail bordered by large white tips on all feathers but the four innermost. Young have a more scaly appearance to the upperparts and more spots on the wings.

• **SONG** A melancholy *ooah-woo-woo-woo* by male throughout breeding season.

• **BEHAVIOR** Males aggressively defend territories. After breeding season, doves gather to roost in sheltered groves. Like other pigeons and doves, they drink by sucking up water instead of lifting their heads to swallow.

• **BREEDING** Monogamous. According to some research, may pair for life.

• **NESTING** Incubation about 14 days by both sexes. Altricial young stay in nest 12–14 days, fed by both sexes. "Pigeon's milk" is produced in the parent's crop and regurgitated with seeds held in the same organ to feed young. 5–6 broods per year in the South; 2–3 elsewhere.

• **POPULATION** Common and increasing. Have adapted well to habitat changes by humans.

• **FEEDERS** Sunflower seeds, millet, milo, and cracked corn on the ground or in platform feeders.

• **CONSERVATION** Managed as a game species in 31 states in the US and protected in the US and Canada. More than 30 million birds are legally harvested as game every year.

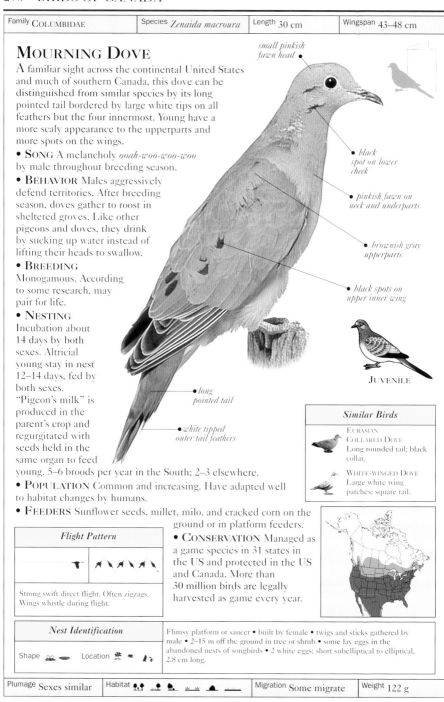

small pinkish fawn head

black spot on lower cheek

pinkish fawn on neck and underparts

brownish gray upperparts

black spots on upper inner wing

long pointed tail

white tipped outer tail feathers

JUVENILE

Similar Birds

EURASIAN COLLARED DOVE
Long rounded tail; black collar.

WHITE-WINGED DOVE
Large white wing patches; square tail.

Flight Pattern

Strong swift direct flight. Often zigzags. Wings whistle during flight.

Nest Identification

Shape   Location

Flimsy platform or saucer • built by female • twigs and sticks gathered by male • 2–15 m off the ground in tree or shrub • some lay eggs in the abandoned nests of songbirds • 2 white eggs; short subelliptical to elliptical, 2.8 cm long.

Plumage Sexes similar	Habitat	Migration Some migrate	Weight 122 g

DATE _____ TIME_____ LOCATION _____

| Family CUCULIDAE | Species *Coccyzus erythropthalmus* | Length 28–30 cm | Wingspan 38–43 cm |

BLACK-BILLED CUCKOO

This shy bird spends most of its time skulking in deep wooded forests. In rare instances, instead of incubating its own eggs it will lay its eggs in the nests of Yellow-billed Cuckoos, Gray Catbirds, Wood Thrushes, Yellow Warblers, or Chipping Sparrows. In flight note the long tail, which has small crescent-shaped white spots on the tips of all but the two central tail feathers, and the uniformly grayish brown wings and back. Juveniles are similar to adults but have a buff eye ring, paler undertail, and buff wash on the underparts, especially the undertail coverts.

narrow red eye ring

decurved black bill

grayish brown upperparts

white underparts

gray legs and feet

long graduated brown tail

- **SONG** Generally silent. Repeated monotone *cu-cu-cu* or *cu-cu-cu-cu* in series of 3–4 notes. Also gives series of rapid *kowk-kowk-kowk* notes all on a single pitch. Sometimes sings at night.
- **BEHAVIOR** Skulks through thick vegetation in shrubs and trees. Often sits quietly on branch scanning in all directions before changing perches. Eats primarily caterpillars, especially hairy tent caterpillars, and other insects; occasionally eats small mollusks, fish, and some wild fruits. Often found in damp thickets and wet places. Engages in courtship feeding.
- **BREEDING** Monogamous.
- **NESTING** Incubation 10–14 days by both sexes. Altricial young stay in nest 7–9 days; fed by both sexes. Young leave nest before they can fly and climb around on nest tree or shrub for about 14 days. 1 brood per year.
- **POPULATION** Uncommon to fairly common. Somewhat dependant on caterpillar populations; larger clutches laid when food is plentiful.

Similar Birds

YELLOW-BILLED CUCKOO
Yellow bill with dark tip; rufous primaries contrast with wing coverts and upperparts; larger white spots on undertail.

Flight Pattern

Often flies low and makes short flights from one tree to the next.

Nest Identification

Shape ⬯ ⬯   Location 🌳 🌲

Dried twigs • lined with fresh grass, leaves, pine needles, catkins, and vegetation • in tree or shrub 60 cm–6 m above ground • 2–5 blue-green eggs with dark blotches, 2.8 x 2.0 cm.

| Plumage Sexes similar | Habitat 🌳 ⛰ 🌾 | Migration Migratory | Weight 102 g |

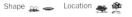

DATE _____ TIME_____ LOCATION _____

Family CUCULIDAE	Species *Coccyzus americanus*	Length 28–33 cm	Wingspan 38–43 cm

YELLOW-BILLED CUCKOO

Like most of the cuckoos, this bird prefers to perch unobtrusively in thick forests or shrubs. Many rural people know this bird as the "Rain Crow." Sometimes it lays its eggs in nests of the Black-billed Cuckoo but rarely in nests of other birds. It is often a casualty at "tower kills" while migrating at night. In flight, note the long tail and the contrast of rufous primaries against gray-brown wing coverts and upperparts. The juvenile shows a paler undertail pattern, and the lower mandible may not be yellow.

decurved bill with dark upper mandible and tip

grayish brown upperparts

rufous primaries

yellow lower mandible

white underparts

gray feet and legs

• **SONG** Often silent; song heard more often in summer. A monotonous throaty *ka-ka-ka-ka-kow-kow-kow-kow-kowlp—kowlp——kowl*, pruning down and slowing at the end.

• **BEHAVIOR** Slips quietly and somewhat stealthily through tangles; flies easily from tree to tree. Often sits motionless on an interior branch and slowly surveys the surrounding vegetation. Eats mostly hairy caterpillars; also insects, larvae, and small fruits and berries. Sometimes eats small frogs and lizards and the eggs of other birds. Engages in courtship feeding in which the male lands by perched female, climbs on her shoulder, and places food in her bill.

large white spots on black undertail

Similar Birds

BLACK-BILLED CUCKOO Entirely black bill; red eye ring; no rufous in wing; gray underside of tail with smaller crescent-shaped white spots; voice differs.

MANGROVE CUCKOO Gray-brown wings and coverts; black mask extends past eye; tawny-buff lower breast, sides, belly, flanks, and undertail coverts; decurved black bill, yellow at base of lower mandible • limited range in Florida; accidental on Gulf Coast.

• **BREEDING** Monogamous. Solitary nester.

• **NESTING** Incubation 9–11 days by both sexes. Altricial young stay in nest 7–9 days, fed by both sexes. Young leave nest before able to fly but remain in vicinity, climbing in branches; fed by parent for about 14 more days. 1 brood per year.

• **POPULATION** Uncommon to common. Somewhat dependent on caterpillar population; species produces greater number of eggs when plentiful.

• **CONSERVATION** Neotropical migrant that has declined significantly over much of its range.

Flight Pattern

Direct flight with slow light steady wing beats; often flies low from tree to tree with flash of rufous in wings.

Nest Identification	Small sticks, with lining of leaves, grasses, mosses, bits of fabric, and catkins from oaks and willow trees • so flimsy eggs can sometimes be seen from beneath • in tree or shrub, 60 cm–4 m above ground • built by both sexes • 1–5 pale bluish green eggs that fade to light greenish yellow, unmarked; elliptical to cylindrical, 3.0 x 2.3 cm.
Shape Location	

Plumage Sexes similar	Habitat	Migration Migratory	Weight 102 g

DATE _____ TIME_____ LOCATION _____

Family TYTONIDAE	Species *Tyto alba*	Length 36–51 cm	Wingspan 109–119 cm

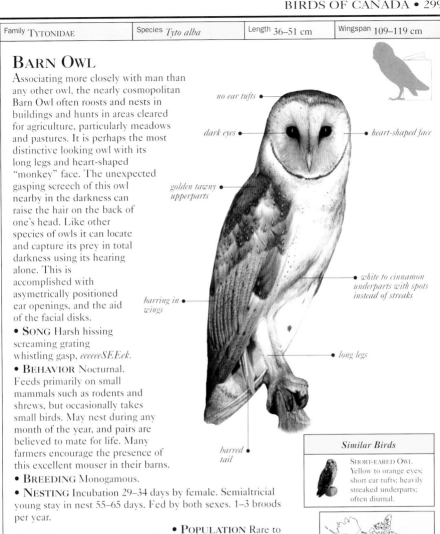

BARN OWL

Associating more closely with man than any other owl, the nearly cosmopolitan Barn Owl often roosts and nests in buildings and hunts in areas cleared for agriculture, particularly meadows and pastures. It is perhaps the most distinctive looking owl with its long legs and heart-shaped "monkey" face. The unexpected gasping screech of this owl nearby in the darkness can raise the hair on the back of one's head. Like other species of owls it can locate and capture its prey in total darkness using its hearing alone. This is accomplished with asymetrically positioned ear openings, and the aid of the facial disks.

- **SONG** Harsh hissing screaming grating whistling gasp, *eeeeeeSEEek*.
- **BEHAVIOR** Nocturnal. Feeds primarily on small mammals such as rodents and shrews, but occasionally takes small birds. May nest during any month of the year, and pairs are believed to mate for life. Many farmers encourage the presence of this excellent mouser in their barns.
- **BREEDING** Monogamous.
- **NESTING** Incubation 29–34 days by female. Semialtricial young stay in nest 55–65 days. Fed by both sexes. 1–3 broods per year.

no ear tufts
dark eyes
heart-shaped face
golden tawny upperparts
white to cinnamon underparts with spots instead of streaks
barring in wings
long legs
barred tail

Similar Birds

SHORT-EARED OWL Yellow to orange eyes; short ear tufts; heavily streaked underparts; often diurnal.

- **POPULATION** Rare to uncommon. Stable in most areas, but declines noted in the East.
- **BIRDHOUSES** Nest boxes.
- **CONSERVATION** Listed as threatened in some states. The eastern population is listed as endangered in Canada.

Flight Pattern
Slow light silent mothlike flight.

Nest Identification	
Shape	Debris arranged into crude depression • in tree cavity, barn loft, building, nest box, crevice, mine shaft, or cave • 2–12 whitish eggs, sometimes nest-stained; short subelliptical, 4.3 cm long.
Location	

Plumage Sexes similar	Habitat	Migration Some migrate	Weight 499 g

DATE _____ TIME_____ LOCATION _____

Family STRIGIDAE	Species *Otus flammeolus*	Length 15–18 cm	Wingspan 33 cm

FLAMMULATED OWL

One of the smallest owls in North America, the Flammulated Owl is also the only small owl with dark, not yellow, eyes. This owl's ear tufts are minute and hardly noticeable. The Flammulated Owl has two color phases, reddish and gray, with the former being more common in the southeastern part of the bird's range. The natural history of this diminutive North American owl is poorly known.

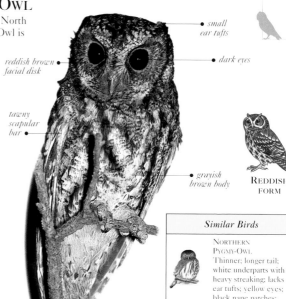

small ear tufts

reddish brown facial disk

dark eyes

tawny scapular bar

grayish brown body

REDDISH FORM

• **SONG** *Boo-BOOT* with emphasis on the second note of the song. A series of single paired low hoarse hollow hoots is given repeatedly at intervals of 2–3 seconds.

• **BEHAVIOR** Little is known. The bird is nocturnal. It feeds primarily on insects, including moths taken in flight and arachnids such as spiders and scorpions gleaned from the ground or the foliage of trees in its habitat. Sometimes will take as its prey various small mammals or other birds. It frequents primarily open pine and oak forests and spruce-fir forests in mountains as high as 2,450 meters.

• **BREEDING** Monogamous. Sometimes has been observed living in loose colonies.

• **NESTING** Incubation 21–26 days by female. Semialtricial young remain in nest about 25 days. Young are fed by both sexes. 1 brood per year.

Similar Birds

NORTHERN PYGMY-OWL
Thinner; longer tail; white underparts with heavy streaking; lacks ear tufts; yellow eyes; black nape patches; chiefly diurnal.

WESTERN SCREECH-OWL
Yellow eyes; lacks brown bar in scapulars; has different voice.

WHISKERED SCREECH-OWL
Longer ear tufts; yellow eyes; different voice.

NOTE: These are all permanent residents of the woodlands in the West. There are no similar birds ranging in the East.

• **POPULATION** Widespread and common in range, though slight declines are possible. Highly migratory; strays have made it to Florida and the Gulf Coast.

Flight Pattern
Slow light steady wing beats.

Nest Identification	
Shape	Location	Old woodpecker hole • no lining • 4.5–12 m above ground • 2–4 white or creamy white eggs; about oval, 2.8 cm long.

Plumage Sexes similar	Habitat	Migration Migratory	Weight 54 g

DATE _____ TIME_____ LOCATION _____

Family STRIGIDAE	Species *Otus kennicottii*	Length 20–25 cm	Wingspan 46–61 cm

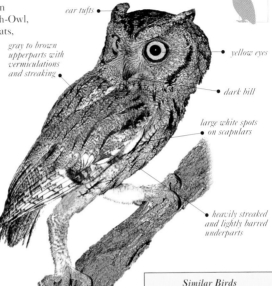

WESTERN SCREECH-OWL

This small tufted owl, the western counterpart of the Eastern Screech-Owl, is found in a wide variety of habitats, from wooded canyons, riparian thickets, and deserts to orchards and the suburbs. It is more often heard than seen. Over most of its range its plumage is generally gray, but Pacific Coast birds are more brownish in color.

ear tufts

gray to brown upperparts with vermiculations and streaking

yellow eyes

dark bill

large white spots on scapulars

heavily streaked and lightly barred underparts

• **SONG** Repeated brief whistles accelerating in tempo in the pattern of a dropped ball bouncing to a stop; a short trill followed by a drawn-out trill.

• **BEHAVIOR** Nocturnal; becomes active at dusk. Feeds on variety of small mammals, birds, reptiles, large insects, and arachnids, but the primary food is large insects. Small mammals carried to the nest to feed the young often are decapitated by the adults. Surplus food is cached in winter roosting cavities. Roosts by day in cavities or thick vegetation. Sedentary, often staying in the same home range throughout the year; males may defend a territory for as long as 10 months. Courtship begins as early as February when the male begins calling each night shortly after sunset to attract a mate. The calls cease when a pair is formed.

• **BREEDING** Monogamous.

• **NESTING** Incubation 21–30 days by female. Semialtricial young stay in nest about 28 days, fed by both sexes. 1 brood per year.

• **POPULATION** Common; widely distributed over range.

• **BIRDHOUSES** Will use man-made nest boxes.

Similar Birds

EASTERN SCREECH-OWL
May have rufous-red plumage; pale bill; different voice.

WHISKERED SCREECH-OWL
Pale bill; different voice; bolder streaking on underparts.

FLAMMULATED OWL
Dark eyes; brown bar in scapulars; different voice.

Flight Pattern

Buoyant silent flight with rapid wing beats.

Nest Identification

Shape

Location

Natural hole in tree or woodpecker hole • may use old magpie nests • no lining added • 1.5–10.5 m off ground • 2–6 white eggs, 3.6 cm long.

Plumage Sexes similar	Habitat	Migration Nonmigratory	Weight 153 g

DATE _____ TIME_____ LOCATION _____

Family STRIGIDAE	Species *Otus asio*	Length 20–25 cm	Wingspan 46–61 cm

EASTERN SCREECH-OWL

Perhaps the best-known owl in eastern North America, this small tufted bird is found in a great variety of habitats, from wooded lots to urban gardens. It is able to flatten its ear tufts, which gives the head a rounded appearance. There are two distinct color phases, reddish brown and gray, plus there are brown intermediates. Its voice is not a screech but rather a mournful whinny familiar to many.

• **SONG** Series of melancholy tremulous whistles descending in pitch; drawn-out trilling note. Simple to imitate.

• **BEHAVIOR** Nocturnal; becomes active at dusk. Feeds on wide variety of small vertebrates and invertebrates, including insects, arachnids, crayfish, mammals, amphibians, reptiles, birds, and fish. When using a cavity for a day roost, often will sit in the entrance. When approached on its roost, will flatten its body, erect its ear tufts, and close its eyes in an attempt to hide by blending into the background.

• **BREEDING** Monogamous.

• **NESTING** Incubation about 26 days mostly by female. Semialtricial young stay in nest about 28 days. Fed by both sexes. 1 brood per year.

• **POPULATION** Widespread and fairly common, but with gradual decline.

• **BIRDHOUSES** Will roost and nest in nesting boxes sized for wood ducks or flickers.

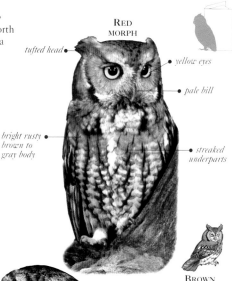

RED MORPH

tufted head

yellow eyes

pale bill

bright rusty brown to gray body

streaked underparts

BROWN INTERMEDIATE

GRAY MORPH

white spots on scapulars

Similar Birds

NORTHERN SAW-WHET OWL
Smaller; lacks ear tufts; blackish bill; large white spots on upperparts; small white streaking on forehead, crown, and nape.

WESTERN SCREECH-OWL
Gray to brown; dark bill; different voice
• western range.

Flight Pattern
Buoyant flight with silent wing beats.

Nest Identification	
Shape Location	Lined with feathers and debris from food • 3–9 m above ground in tree • 2–8 white eggs; round oval, 3.6 cm long.

Plumage Sexes similar	Habitat	Migration Nonmigratory	Weight 167 g

Family STRIGIDAE	Species *Bubo virginianus*	Length 46–64 cm	Wingspan 91–152 cm

GREAT HORNED OWL

The most widespread owl in North America and perhaps the most powerful, this owl often attacks animals much larger and heavier than itself, including domestic cats, skunks, and porcupines. Its color varies regionally from pale arctic birds to dark northwestern ones. It has been the official bird of Alberta since 1977.

large "horns" on head

yellow eyes

rusty facial disks

white chin and throat

mottled barred brownish gray upperparts

• **SONG** Series of 3–8 bold deep hoots, with the second and third hoots often running together, *Whoo! Whoo-whoo-whoo! Whoo! Whoo!* Often described as "You awake? Me too!" Female's hooting is higher in pitch.

• **BEHAVIOR** Chiefly nocturnal; becomes active at dusk. Sometimes hunts during the day. Takes wide variety of vertebrates; primarily feeds on mammals, but also eats birds, reptiles, and amphibians. Often aggressively defends nest and young to the point of striking humans who venture too close.

• **BREEDING** Monogamous. One of the earliest nesting species, with eggs laid in winter.

• **NESTING** Incubation 28–35 days mostly by female. Young stay in nest 35–45 days. Fed by both sexes. 1 brood per year.

• **POPULATION** Fairly common to common. Widespread.

• **BIRDHOUSES** Accepts artificial nesting platforms.

• **CONSERVATION** Many are killed by hunters and farmers.

Similar Birds

LONG-EARED OWL
Smaller and thinner; ear tufts closer together; vertical streaking, not horizontal barring, on underparts.

GREAT GRAY OWL
Larger; lacks ear tufts; large grayish white facial disks ringed with dark brown concentric circles; brown upperparts barred with dark browns and white; whitish underparts barred and streaked with browns; yellowish bill; long brownish tail barred with dark browns and white.

Flight Pattern

Direct flap-and-glide flight with strong, silent wing beats.

Nest Identification

Shape

Location

Abandoned nest of larger bird • large cavities, broken-off snags, buildings, ledges • 6–18 m above ground • 1–5 dull whitish eggs; elliptical, 6.9 cm long.

Plumage Sexes similar	Habitat	Migration Nonmigratory	Weight 1.4 kg

DATE _____ TIME _____ LOCATION _____

Family STRIGIDAE	Species *Nyctea scandiaca*	Length 51–69 cm	Wingspan 137–168 cm

SNOWY OWL

This heavy-bodied owl breeds on Arctic tundra and winters on grasslands, marshes, coastal beaches, and dunes. Regional crashes of Arctic lemming populations force these owls far south in some winters. This is our only all-white owl. Females and juveniles are similar, and show more dusky barring than males. Adopted as Quebec's official bird in 1987.

- yellow eyes
- large head without ear tufts
- all-white plumage

MALE

- **SONG** Piercing whistle and bold, growling bark, *krow-ow*, which can carry for more than a mile. Usually silent outside breeding season.
- **BEHAVIOR** Active in daylight and darkness. Often perches on ground or close to it on posts, rocks, dunes, ice, hay bales, or buildings. Eats primarily small mammals (voles and lemmings on breeding grounds) but some birds and fish. Male defends nest and young fearlessly; will do "crippled bird" act to lure predators away from nest.
- **BREEDING** Monogamous.
- **NESTING** Incubation 31–34 days by both sexes or female only. Young stay in nest 14–21 days, fed by both sexes. First flight at 43–57 days. 1 brood per year. Number of eggs depends on food supply; in poor lemming years, pairs may not breed.

more dusky barring

dusky spots and bars on feather tips

FEMALE

Similar Birds

BARN OWL
White to cinnamon-buff underparts; golden-buff upperparts; heart-shaped face; dark eyes.

- **POPULATION** Fairly common on breeding grounds; rare to casual south of breeding range. Stable because of remoteness from human disturbance.
- **CONSERVATION** No issues reported, but many birds are killed when wintering south of normal range.

Flight Pattern

Direct flap-and-glide flight with strong, deep wing beats.

Nest Identification

Shape ⚬⚬   Location ▬▬ ▦ ▨▨ ▲

Simple depression • unlined or minimally lined with moss, lichen, and plucked grass • on raised site with good visibility • built by female • 3–11 whitish eggs that become nest-stained, short elliptical or subelliptical, 5.6 cm long.

Plumage Sexes differ	Habitat ▬▬ ⩰ ⩳	Migration Irregular	Weight 1.8 kg

DATE _____ TIME_____ LOCATION _____

Family STRIGIDAE	Species *Surnia ulula*	Length 36–43 cm	Wingspan 84 cm

NORTHERN HAWK-OWL

This crow-sized hawklike owl of boreal forests and northern muskegs often perches conspicuously at the top of a conifer and slowly raises and lowers its long rounded tail in the manner of a kestrel. It has no ear tufts or "horns."

- **SONG** Rolling trilling, 2-syllable whistle, *killy-killy-killy-killy*.
- **BEHAVIOR** Chiefly diurnal but sometimes hunts at night. Very tame, often allowing close approach. Flies close to ground with rapid flapping and gliding when hunting; sometimes hovers. Eats small mammals up to the size of young snowshoe hares and birds as large as ptarmigans.

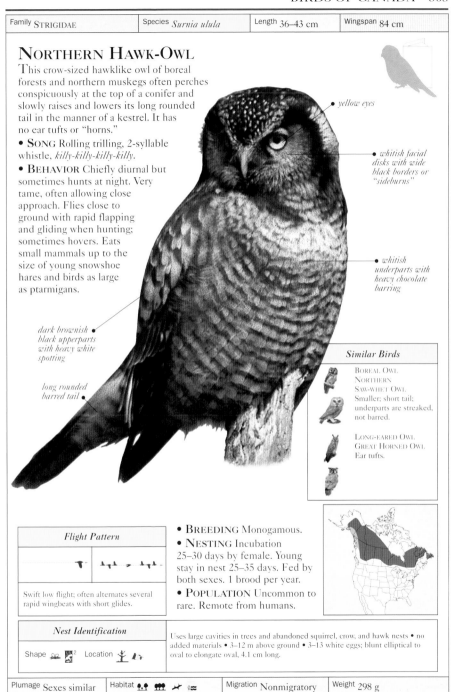

yellow eyes

whitish facial disks with wide black borders or "sideburns"

whitish underparts with heavy chocolate barring

dark brownish black upperparts with heavy white spotting

long rounded barred tail

Similar Birds

BOREAL OWL
NORTHERN
SAW-WHET OWL.
Smaller; short tail; underparts are streaked, not barred.

LONG-EARED OWL.
GREAT HORNED OWL.
Ear tufts.

Flight Pattern
Swift low flight; often alternates several rapid wingbeats with short glides.

- **BREEDING** Monogamous.
- **NESTING** Incubation 25–30 days by female. Young stay in nest 25–35 days. Fed by both sexes. 1 brood per year.
- **POPULATION** Uncommon to rare. Remote from humans.

Nest Identification	
Shape · Location	Uses large cavities in trees and abandoned squirrel, crow, and hawk nests • no added materials • 3–12 m above ground • 3–13 white eggs; blunt elliptical to oval to elongate oval, 4.1 cm long.

Plumage Sexes similar	Habitat	Migration Nonmigratory	Weight 298 g

DATE _____ TIME_____ LOCATION _____

| Family STRIGIDAE | Species *Glaucidium gnoma* | Length 15–18 cm | Wingspan 38 cm |

NORTHERN PYGMY-OWL

This little owl of the West is about the size of a bluebird, but it fearlessly attacks prey larger than itself. In turn, it becomes the victim of harassment by songbirds and even hummingbirds when they locate it during the day. The noisy mobbing activities of these birds may reveal the owl's presence to birders. When perched, it often cocks its long tail upward at an angle. Two black spots on the nape of its neck look almost like a pair of eyes. Regional variations in color produce birds with brown to gray plumage.

rounded head without ear tufts

brown to gray upperparts with white spots

yellow eyes

yellowish bill

heavily streaked whitish underparts

• **SONG** Smooth whistled *hoo* or *hoo hoo*. Also rapid repeated *hoo* or *took* notes followed by a single *took*. Imitation of the call often attracts the owl or songbirds looking to mob it.

long brown tail with white barring

ROCKY MOUNTAIN

• **BEHAVIOR** Chiefly nocturnal but often active in daylight, especially at dawn or dusk. Eats insects, small mammals, small birds, and an occasional small reptile. Relatively tame, allowing a close approach. Inhabits densely wooded canyons in foothills and mountains.

PACIFIC COAST

Similar Birds

FERRUGINOUS PYGMY-OWL Rufous tail with dark barring; brown streaking on underparts.

ELF OWL Smaller; short tail; lacks eyespots on nape; faint streaking on underparts.

• **BREEDING** Monogamous.

• **NESTING** Incubation about 28 days by female. Semialtrical young stay in nest about 27–28 days. Fed by both sexes. Probably 1 brood per year.

• **POPULATION** Fairly common to uncommon. Widespread. No evidence of decline in range.

Flight Pattern
Direct flight close to ground with rapid wing beats.

Nest Identification	
Shape	Location	In natural tree cavity or woodpecker hole • no lining • 2.5–7.5 m above ground • 2–7 white eggs, 2.8 cm long.

| Plumage Sexes similar | Habitat | Migration Nonmigratory | Weight 62 g |

DATE _____ TIME_____ LOCATION _____

Family STRIGIDAE	Species *Athene cunicularia*	Length 23–28 cm	Wingspan 51–61 cm

BURROWING OWL

This long-legged, short-tailed little owl inhabits grassland and prairies, but in its range it also can be found in similar habitats near humans such as golf courses and airports. In the West the Burrowing Owl often is associated with prairie dog towns, and the historical poisoning of the prairie dogs also brought declines in the owl's populations. The owls use an abandoned burrow for their nest and daytime roost, usually after some additional digging to enlarge and reshape it.

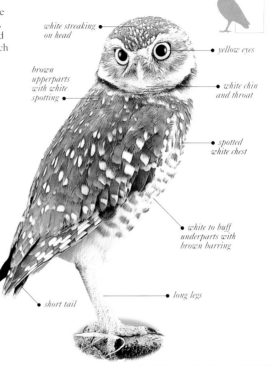

white streaking on head

yellow eyes

brown upperparts with white spotting

white chin and throat

spotted white chest

white to buff underparts with brown barring

short tail

long legs

• **SONG** High melancholy cry, *coo-coo-roo* or *co-hoo;* twittering series of *chack* notes. If disturbed in nest, young give alarm that mimics the buzzing of a rattlesnake.

• **BEHAVIOR** Terrestrial. Primarily nocturnal and crepuscular. Perches on ground, fence posts, utility wires, rocks, or mounds near burrow during day. Inhabits open country where it feeds primarily on large insects, some of which it catches in flight, and small mammals.

• **BREEDING** Monogamous. Often colonial.

• **NESTING** Incubation 21–30 days by female. Semialtricial young remain in nest 28 days, fed by both sexes. Typically 1–2 broods per year.

• **POPULATION** Fairly common to common but local.

• **BIRDHOUSES** Will nest in artificial man-made burrows.

• **CONSERVATION** Endangered or threatened over much of its range. Declining because of prairie dog and ground squirrel poison-control programs and habitat loss. Many killed by automobiles. Some attempts at management being made due to declining local populations.

Similar Birds

SHORT-EARED OWL Larger; long tail; short legs; buff-brown; heavily streaked upperparts and underparts.

Flight Pattern

Buoyant, sometimes erratic flight, with show silent wing beats; may hover briefly above prey.

Nest Identification

Shape Location ▬

Lined with cow manure, horse dung, food debris, dry grass, weeds, pellets, and feathers • built by both sexes, but male does more • 7–10 white nest-stained eggs (4–6 in Florida); round to ovate, 3.0 cm long.

Plumage Sexes similar	Habitat 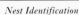	Migration Some migrate	Weight 150 g

DATE _____ TIME_____ LOCATION _____

Family STRIGIDAE	Species *Strix occidentalis*	Length 41–48 cm	Wingspan 114–122 cm

SPOTTED OWL

Although it is the western counterpart of the Barred Owl in shape, size, and habitat preference, this owl lacks the barring and streaking of that species. Its dark brown plumage is heavily spotted with white on the underparts and upperparts. This secretive bird inhabits dense, moist old-growth forests and deeply wooded canyons.

large, puffy head without ear tufts

dark eyes

rich dark brown and liberally spotted white overall

• **SONG** 3–4 barking notes, *Whoo-whoo-hoo-hoo*. Also gives low, hollow, ascending whistle, sounding like *coooo-wee*.

• **BEHAVIOR** Nocturnal and seldom seen. Perches inconspicuously in dense cover during the day. Feeds primarily on small mammals, some birds, and large insects. Hybridizes with Barred Owl, which is becoming more common in its northwestern range.

• **BREEDING** Monogamous.

• **NESTING** Incubation 28–32 days by female. Young stay in nest 34–36 days. Fed by both sexes. 1 brood per year.

• **POPULATION** Rare to uncommon. Listed as endangered in the Pacific Northwest and threatened in the Southwest. Does poorly in second-growth forests.

• **CONSERVATION** Federally protected. Affected by loss of old-growth forest habitat from logging and by hybridization with expanding populations of Barred Owl.

Similar Birds

BARRED OWL
Barred chest and upper breast; streaked underparts.

GREAT GRAY OWL
Larger; grayer; streaked underparts; yellow eyes.

Flight Pattern

Short flights with quick wing strokes; longer flights series of silent strong wing beats followed by short glides.

Nest Identification

Shape

Location

Simple scrape • hollow in tree, cave, or crevice • on cliff or in tree 9–49 m above ground • sometimes uses abandoned nests • built by female • 1–4 white eggs with faint tinge of buff; elliptical, 5.1 cm long.

Plumage Sexes similar	Habitat	Migration Nonmigratory	Weight 590 g

DATE _____ TIME_____ LOCATION _____

Family STRIGIDAE	Species *Strix varia*	Length 43–61 cm	Wingspan 127–152 cm

BARRED OWL

The "hoot owl" of southern swamps, this puffy-headed owl can also be found in woodlands. It lacks ear tufts, is stoutly built, and is heavily streaked, spotted, and variegated brown, buff, and white. This is one of only three large owls with dark eyes in North America.

large, round head

brown upperparts with heavy white spotting

dark eyes

horizontal barring on upper breast

heavily streaked paler underparts

long barred tail

• **SONG** Usually 8 or more drawn-out notes, *"Who cooks for you; who cooks for you-all?"* Call is drawn-out, descending *hoooAwllll.* Group of 2 or more owls make a loud, excited caterwauling. Often heard in daytime. Responds readily to imitations of its call by coming closer and often calling back.

• **BEHAVIOR** Mostly nocturnal and crepuscular but often active in daylight. Prefers deep woods; inhabits conifer, riparian, and swampy habitats. Feeds on wide variety of animals, including small mammals, birds, frogs, salamanders, lizards, snakes, fish, large insects, crabs, and crayfish.

• **BREEDING** Monogamous. Thought to pair for life.

• **NESTING.** Incubation 28–33 days by female. Young stay in nest 42 days. Fed by both sexes. 1 brood per year.

• **POPULATION** Very common to common and widespread. Swamp habitat population in the South has diminished. Range increasing now in the Northwest, where hybridizes with Spotted Owl.

Similar Birds

GREAT GRAY OWL Much larger and grayer; yellow eyes.

SPOTTED OWL White spotting on underparts, not barring or streaking • western range.

Flight Pattern

Short flights with steady, shallow wing beats, longer flights on silent rapid wing strokes followed by short glide.

Nest Identification

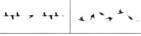

Shape   Location

In the East uses abandoned nests • 4.5–24 m above ground in tree • 2–3 white eggs, 5.1 cm long.

Plumage Sexes similar	Habitat	Migration Nonmigratory	Weight 635 g

DATE _____ TIME _____ LOCATION _____

Family STRIGIDAE	Species *Strix nebulosa*	Length 61–84 cm	Wingspan 137–152 cm

GREAT GRAY OWL

This is the largest North American owl, though the Great Horned Owl is heavier. Long-tailed and large-headed, the Great Gray Owl has huge facial disks crossed by a series of dark gray concentric circles that make the eyes seem small. It inhabits deep boreal forests and open muskeg bogs. Named Manitoba's official bird in 1987.

• SONG A bold, deep, booming *hoo-hoo-hooo*; also utters single-note hoots.

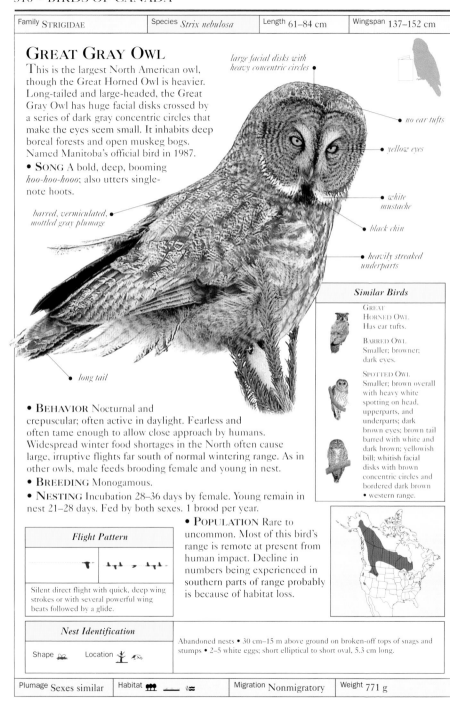

large facial disks with heavy concentric circles

no ear tufts

yellow eyes

white mustache

black chin

heavily streaked underparts

barred, vermiculated, mottled gray plumage

long tail

Similar Birds

GREAT HORNED OWL Has ear tufts.

BARRED OWL Smaller; browner; dark eyes.

SPOTTED OWL Smaller; brown overall with heavy white spotting on head, upperparts, and underparts; dark brown eyes; brown tail barred with white and dark brown; yellowish bill; whitish facial disks with brown concentric circles and bordered dark brown • western range.

• BEHAVIOR Nocturnal and crepuscular; often active in daylight. Fearless and often tame enough to allow close approach by humans. Widespread winter food shortages in the North often cause large, irruptive flights far south of normal wintering range. As in other owls, male feeds brooding female and young in nest.

• BREEDING Monogamous.

• NESTING Incubation 28–36 days by female. Young remain in nest 21–28 days. Fed by both sexes. 1 brood per year.

• POPULATION Rare to uncommon. Most of this bird's range is remote at present from human impact. Decline in numbers being experienced in southern parts of range probably is because of habitat loss.

Flight Pattern

Silent direct flight with quick, deep wing strokes or with several powerful wing beats followed by a glide.

Nest Identification

Shape | Location

Abandoned nests • 30 cm–15 m above ground on broken-off tops of snags and stumps • 2–5 white eggs; short elliptical to short oval, 5.3 cm long.

Plumage Sexes similar	Habitat	Migration Nonmigratory	Weight 771 g

DATE _____ TIME_____ LOCATION _____

Family STRIGIDAE	Species *Asio otus*	Length 33–41 cm	Wingspan 91–107 cm

LONG-EARED OWL

The most slender and most nocturnal of the large owls is perhaps the most overlooked. It is hard to detect because of its cryptic coloration, shy habits, and the ability to "freeze" against a perch with body flattened. This owl often uses the same winter perch day after day, resulting in a large accumulation of pellets and droppings beneath it; this telltale evidence can be used to locate the roosting owl above. Although the female is larger, both sexes appear similar. Frequents a wide range of habitats, from desert oases to riparian thickets to dense coniferous woodlands.

long close-set blackish ear tufts

yellow eyes

rusty facial disks

mottled brown

mottled buffy-white with heavy vertical streaking

• **SONG** Melodic low hoots, *quoo-quoo-quoo*, and long *hoos*. Sometimes sounds like a barking, whining puppy. Virtually mute outside breeding season.
• **BEHAVIOR** Nocturnal. Roosts perched close to tree trunk in thick cover during day. Hunts over open fields and marshes. Feeds primarily on mouse-size mammals; sometimes takes small birds. Often gregarious on roosts in winter. Accumulated pellet contents below roost can reveal local diet, as the undigested bones, teeth, and exoskeletons of its *long tail*

prey are compacted within them. Chooses abandoned nest of squirrel, crow, hawk, or heron as its own nesting site.
• **BREEDING** Monogamous.

Similar Birds

GREAT HORNED OWL Much larger, stouter build; ear tufts farther apart on head; horizontal barring beneath (not vertical streaking).

SHORT-EARED OWL Buffier below; shorter ear tufts; diurnal.

• **NESTING** Incubation 26–28 days by female. Semialtricial young stay in nest 23–26 days, fed by both sexes. 1 brood per year.
• **POPULATION** Uncommon to locally common; may be more common than suspected.

Flight Pattern
Buoyant silent wing beats. Ear tufts flattened back on head in flight.

Nest Identification	
Shape Location	Typically does not build nest • uses abandoned nests; sometimes tree cavity • suspected of sometimes evicting crow • 1–9 m above ground in a tree • 2–10 white eggs; elliptical, 4.1 cm long.

Plumage Sexes similar	Habitat	Migration Northern birds migrate	Weight 244 g

DATE _____ TIME_____ LOCATION _____

Family STRIGIDAE	Species *Asio flammeus*	Length 33–43 cm	Wingspan 97–112 cm

SHORT-EARED OWL

A big-headed, short-necked owl of grasslands and marshes, this bird is often seen quartering low over vegetation during the day. With tawny to buff-brown plumage, it shows large buff wing patches on the upperwing and a dark "wrist" mark on the underwing in flight. The ear tufts are very small and difficult to see unless the bird is perched. It has a streaked buff to whitish belly and white undertail coverts with faint streaking. Its diurnal activities make it frequently visible.

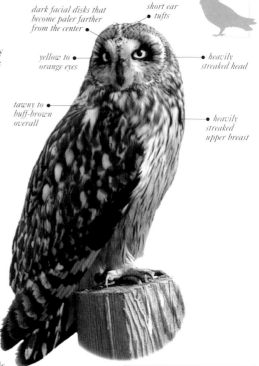

dark facial disks that become paler farther from the center

short ear tufts

yellow to orange eyes

heavily streaked head

tawny to buff-brown overall

heavily streaked upper breast

• **SONG** On breeding grounds this owl gives a loud *eeee-yerp*; a high-pitched grating *waowk, waowk, waowk*, like the barking of a dog; or a *toot-toot-toot-toot-toot*. When on its wintering grounds, the Short-eared Owl usually remains silent.

• **BEHAVIOR** Nocturnal and crepuscular; may hunt in late afternoons or on overcast days. Flies back and forth low over the ground, dropping feet first with wings held high onto prey. May perch on post or shrub to watch for prey. Feeds primarily on small rodents but also takes some small birds of open habitats and large insects. Uses crippled-bird display to lure intruders away from the nest or young on the ground.

• **BREEDING** Monogamous. Sometimes forms small colonies.

• **NESTING** Incubation 24–37 days by female. Semialtricial young stay in nest 21–36 days. Fed by both sexes. Typically 1 brood per year.

• **POPULATION** Fairly common. It has disappeared in parts of its southern range because of habitat loss.

• **CONSERVATION** The main conservation concern for this owl is a degree of habitat loss to agriculture and also loss due to killing by shooting.

Similar Birds

LONG-EARED OWL Smaller buff upperwing and black wrist patches; heavily barred underparts; large ear tufts; nocturnal.

Flight Pattern

Buoyant erratic flight with flopping wing beats.

Nest Identification

Shape ⌒ ⬬ ◖   Location ⚘ 𝀱

Shallow depression • lined with grass and feathers • on ground • built by female • 3–11 white eggs that become nest-stained; short elliptical, 3.8 cm long.

Plumage Sexes similar	Habitat ___ ⤳	Migration Some migrate	Weight 315 g

Family STRIGIDAE	Species *Aegolius funereus*	Length 20–30 cm	Wingspan 51–66 cm

BOREAL OWL

This small flat-headed owl is seldom seen because it is strictly nocturnal and sits concealed close to the trunk of a thick conifer when on its daytime perch. Its white facial disks are bordered with black. During irruptive flight in winter, when this owl comes far south of its normal winter range into the middle and eastern US, most individuals seem to be females and many are found seeking shelter in buildings. Juveniles are similar to adults on the upperparts, but they are a rich chocolate brown below with a dark brown facial disk, whitish upturned mustache, and a white wedge between the eyes that spreads above them on the forehead.

flat-topped head

whitish gray facial disks with black border

yellow eyes

pale bill

deep brown upperparts with heavy white spotting

whitish underparts with heavy chocolate streaking

JUVENILE

- **SONG** Resembles high-pitched ringing *ting, ting, ting, ting.* Brief series of tremulous *hoo* notes.
- **BEHAVIOR** Nocturnal. Solitary. Prefers thick old growth coniferous forests. Feeds primarily on small rodents and other small mammals, rarely on small birds. Males cease singing after they are mated.
- **BREEDING** Polygamous.
- **NESTING** Incubation 26–37 days by both sexes. Semialtricial young stay in nest 28–36 days. Fed by female with food brought by male. 1 brood per year.

Similar Birds

NORTHERN SAW-WHET OWL
Smaller; dark bill; white streaked head, not spotted • juvenile has tawny-cinnamon underparts without streaking.

- **POPULATION** Uncommon. Northern populations in no danger; status of western populations not well known, but the Boreal Owl is vulnerable to logging operations.
- **BIRDHOUSES** Will use man-made nest boxes.

Flight Pattern
Short flights on rapidly beating wings; longer ones more buoyant with shallow somewhat fluttering silent wing beats.

Nest Identification	
Shape Location	In tree cavity, usually a woodpecker hole • no lining added • 6–24.5 m above ground • 2–6 white eggs, 3.3 cm long.

Plumage Sexes similar	Habitat	Migration Irregular	Weight 102 g

DATE _____ TIME_____ LOCATION _____

Family STRIGIDAE	Species *Aegolius acadicus*	Length 18–20 cm	Wingspan 43–51 cm

NORTHERN SAW-WHET OWL

The incessant call of the male Northern Saw-whet Owl during breeding season sounds like a saw being sharpened or whetted. Some winters numbers of this little owl are found well south of the normal breeding range. This species is one of the smallest owls. Note the lack of ear tufts, dark bill, and white eyebrows. Females are larger than males. Juveniles have tawny-cinnamon underparts, chocolate-brown upperparts with white spotting, and a bold white Y from beak to eyebrows.

brown forehead and crown with liberal white streaking

pale buff to brownish facial disks

whitish eyebrows

white patch between eyes

blackish bill

chestnut-brown upperparts with heavy white and buff spotting

• **SONG** Repeated 1-note whistle of *too, too, too, too, too* or *sch-whet, sch-whet*, sometimes for hours at a time. Sings during breeding season only; singing decreases after mate is attracted. Voice may carry 0.5 km or more.

white underparts with reddish brown and dark brown blotches and streaks

• **BEHAVIOR** Solitary or in pairs. Eats small rodents, large insects, birds, and bats. Hunts primarily at night. Perches low, searching for prey, then flies down and snatches it with talons. Territorial birds often respond to imitations of their call by speeding up the rate of their calling; often attracted to playbacks of their call.

unmarked white undertail coverts

JUVENILE

• **BREEDING** Monogamous. Solitary.

• **NESTING** Incubation 26–29 days by female. Semialtricial young stay in nest 27–34 days. Fed by both sexes: Male brings food, then female feeds young for about first 18 days. 1 brood per year.

• **POPULATION** Fairly common. Declining.

Similar Birds

BOREAL OWL.
Larger; white face with blackish border; darker brown head with contrasting white spots; pale bill.

• **BIRDHOUSES** Uses nest boxes about the size of Wood Duck boxes.

• **CONSERVATION** Declining in parts of range due to habitat loss from logging, air pollution, and adelgid tree kills in high peaks of southern Appalachians.

Flight Pattern
Silent buoyant direct flight with fluttering wing beats.

Nest Identification
Shape Location

No nest materials • in tree cavity, abandoned woodpecker hole, or nesting box, 4–18 m above ground • 4–7 white eggs; oval to ovate, 3.0 cm long.

Plumage Sexes similar	Habitat	Migration Most do not migrate	Weight 74 g

DATE _____ TIME_____ LOCATION _____

Family CAPRIMULGIDAE	Species *Chordeiles minor*	Length 20–25 cm	Wingspan 53–61 cm

COMMON NIGHTHAWK

Like all members of the nightjar family, the adult bird flutters its gular pouch during intense heat to cool itself. The eggs and nestlings are sometimes carried to another location if temperatures become extreme. The female is similar to the male, but has a buffy, rather than white, throat and lacks the white tail band. Juveniles also lack this tail band. Note the long pointed wings with the white bar through the primaries, and the mothlike flight of the "bullbat," which is the colloquial name used for this nighthawk in the South. Although predominantly grayish brown overall, there is much color variation over the large North American range.

grayish brown overall

long dark pointed wings

white throat

notched tail with thick white band

distinctive white bar across primaries

- **SONG** Has raspy nasal somewhat froglike call of *peeant* or *beant*.
- **BEHAVIOR** Solitary or in small groups. Sometimes migrates in large flocks in fall. Crepuscular and nocturnal, but often feeds day or night, catching insects in flight. Eats a wide range of flying insects. Attracted to street lights and other outdoor lights at night to scoop up swarming insects. Bird species seen by many because of its habit of feeding over towns and cities. Skims over lakes and streams to drink water from surface.
- **BREEDING** Monogamous. Solitary. Male displays with a courtship power-dive, at the end of which the air rushes through his wings, making a loud *sw-r-r-r-oonk* sound like a rubber band or banjo string being plucked.
- **NESTING** Incubation 19–20 days, mostly by female. Young semiprecocial; first flight at 21 days, fed by both sexes. 1–2 broods per year.
- **POPULATION** Common but declining in parts of continent.
- **CONSERVATION** Neotropical migrant. Became common in towns and cities with the introduction of flat graveled roofs in mid-1800s as well as increased use of outside lighting, which attracts insects.

Similar Birds

LESSER NIGHTHAWK Shorter, more rounded wings; whitish bar across primaries slightly closer to tip; paler upperparts with more uniform mottling; generally flies closer to ground; does not power-dive; voice differs.

ANTILLEAN NIGHTHAWK Smaller; shorter wings; more fluttery flight; much more buffy overall; voice differs • rare in eastern range.

Flight Pattern
Darting flight on long pointed wings with erratic twists and turns and changes of direction. Wing beats slow and steady.

Nest Identification	
Shape	Lays eggs on rocks, small pebbles, abandoned fields, stumps, fence rails, and even on tarred or graveled roofs; 0–2.5 m above ground • female chooses site • 2 creamy white to pale olive-buff eggs, with brown and gray speckles; oval to elliptical oval, 3.0 x 2.3 cm.
Location	

Plumage Sexes similar	Habitat	Migration Migratory	Weight 62 g

DATE _____ TIME_____ LOCATION _____

Family CAPRIMULGIDAE	Species *Phalaenoptilus nuttallii*	Length 18–20 cm	Wingspan 28–33 cm

COMMON POORWILL

The smallest of the North American nightjars, this bird is the western counterpart of the eastern Whip-poor-will. It primarily feeds at night. Though all but its southernmost population migrates, the Common Poorwill is the only bird known to hibernate. It sometimes returns to the same rock crevice each winter. In flight, note its small size, short, rounded wings that

mixed mottled brownish gray to pale gray plumage

black throat and sides of face

broad white band over throat and dark breast

white-tipped black outer tail feathers

grayish underparts mottled dark gray and black

lack white patches, and the rounded tail with white tail corners. Male and female are similar, but the male has a larger bolder patch on its tail. This bird is more often heard than seen.

• **SONG** Has cry of *poor-will* or *poor-willy* or *poor-willow*, repeated 30–40 times per minute.
• **BEHAVIOR** Solitary. Nocturnal. During day, roosts hidden on ground in shrubs and grasses. Flies close to the ground at night searching for food or sits on ground watching for prey. Eats night-flying moths and other insects. Birds have been found in a state of hibernation during extremely cold weather.
• **BREEDING** Monogamous. Solitary.

Similar Birds

WHIP-POOR-WILL
Locally in Southwest
• larger longer tail with large white corners (male) or buffy tips (female); voice differs.

• **NESTING** Incubation 20–21 days by both sexes. Young semiprecocial; fed by both sexes; first flight at 20–23 days. 1–2 broods per year.
• **POPULATION** In US, fairly common; widespread, stable.

Flight Pattern

Flits on silent wings with quick shallow wing beats.

Nest Identification

Shape 🌿 🍂 Location ▬ ▬ 🌾

On bare soil, pebbles, or atop small pile of leaves, usually shaded by bush or grasses • 2 white to pinkish white eggs, sometimes spotted or mottled with violet; oval to elliptical oval, 2.5 x 2.0 cm.

Plumage Sexes similar	Habitat ✈ ⚘ ⚘ ▲	Migration Migratory	Weight 51 g

DATE _____ TIME_____ LOCATION _____

| Family CAPRIMULGIDAE | Species *Caprimulgus vociferus* | Length 23–25 cm | Wingspan 41–50 cm |

WHIP-POOR-WILL

The Whip-poor-will is best located and identified by its
distinctive calls. It is nearly impossible to see because it
tends to sit on the ground or lengthwise on a branch,
and its pattern closely matches the leaf litter of the
wood lots it frequents. "Whips" have rounded wings
that when folded do not reach to the tip of the tail.
Males are similar to females but the throat is
bordered with white and the tail has large
white patches.

• **SONG** A loud, clear *whip-poor-will*
often repeated at night in eastern
birds; call is more coarse among
southwestern birds.

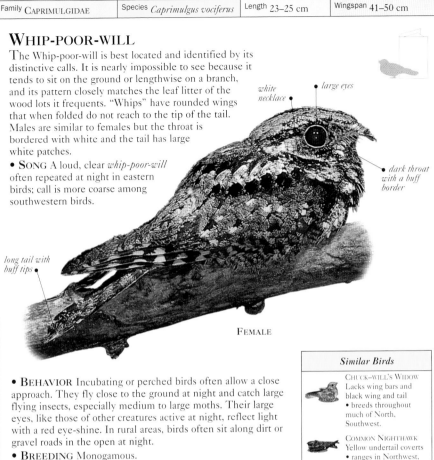

white necklace

large eyes

dark throat with a buff border

long tail with buff tips

FEMALE

• **BEHAVIOR** Incubating or perched birds often allow a close
approach. They fly close to the ground at night and catch large
flying insects, especially medium to large moths. Their large
eyes, like those of other creatures active at night, reflect light
with a red eye-shine. In rural areas, birds often sit along dirt or
gravel roads in the open at night.

• **BREEDING** Monogamous.

• **NESTING** Incubation 19–20 days by female.
Semiprecocial young stay in nest 20 days. Fed by both sexes.
1–2 broods per year.

• **POPULATION** Uncommon.
Has declined in the East in
recent decades because of
habitat loss caused by
forest fragmentation
and development.

• **CONSERVATION** Species
federally protected in the US.

Similar Birds

CHUCK–WILL'S WIDOW
Lacks wing bars and
black wing and tail
• breeds throughout
much of North,
Southwest.

COMMON NIGHTHAWK
Yellow undertail coverts
• ranges in Northwest,
Rockies, and much of
the Southwest.

Flight Pattern
Erratic mothlike flight. Male hovers during display, with slow smooth flight.

Nest Identification		
Shape 🐾	Location ▬	Eggs laid on flat ground on leaf litter • 2 whitish eggs marked with brown and gray overlaid with brown, olive, and lavender; 3.0 cm long.

| Plumage Sexes similar | Habitat 🌱 🌿 ▲ 🌳 | Migration Most migrate | Weight 57 g |

DATE _____ TIME_____ LOCATION _____

| Family APODIDAE | Species *Cypseloides niger* | Length 18–19 cm | Wingspan 38 cm |

BLACK SWIFT

The largest of the North American swifts, the Black Swift is rarely seen away from nesting sites because it spends most of its time hundreds of meters in the air, traveling over the lofty mountains and canyons of its habitat. Flocks of these strong fast high-flying birds will follow storm clouds for as far as 500 km to feed where insects gather in the warm air mass. In flight, juveniles of this species show faintly blacker underwing linings.

• **SONG** Heard infrequently. A harsh clear call of *ci-chi-chi-chit* or *plik-plik-plik-plik-plik*.

• **BEHAVIOR** Gregarious. Flies and travels in flocks, although the flocks often are small.

silvery forehead

blackish overall

long curved scimitar-shaped wings

MALE

Its habit is to feed while flying, eating various insects and spiders that are floating and flying in air columns. It also drinks water on the wing and dips its body on the surface of the water to bathe. Males and females copulate in midair. Often this bird soars with its tail spread. It prefers to make its nest on seaside cliffs, in the mouths of caves, or behind waterfalls in canyons. The Black Swift may become torpid during extended cold periods, and its young are able to survive without food for several days when cold stressed.

• **BREEDING** Monogamous. Colonial.

• **NESTING** Incubation 24–27 days by both sexes. Altricial young do not develop strong feet and grasping ability early as do other swifts, and as a result they stay in the nest for about 45–49 days, fed by both sexes. 1 brood per year.

• **POPULATION** Uncommon.

• **CONSERVATION** Neotropical migrant.

Similar Birds

VAUX'S SWIFT
Smaller; short, squared tail; paler underparts and rump.

Flight Pattern

Stiff shallow wing beats, slow and more leisurely than other swifts. Soars on thermals and updrafts.

Nest Identification

Shape ⬭ Location 🪺 🏞

Little mud; mostly ferns, algae, moss, and other plant material • lined with fine rootlets • on ridge of cliff near water, mouth of cave, or behind waterfall • 1 white egg, may be nest-stained; long oval to cylindrical, 3.0 cm long.

| Plumage Sexes similar | Habitat ▲ 🌊 | Migration Migratory | Weight 45 g |

Family APODIDAE	Species *Chaetura pelagica*	Length 14 cm	Wingspan 30–32 cm

CHIMNEY SWIFT

Often referred to as "a cigar with wings" because of its flight silhouette, this is the only swift normally found in eastern North America. Named for its habit of building nests inside chimneys or air shafts, it uses its gluelike saliva to attach its nest to the brick or concrete and to bind together the individual sticks. Adult birds feed their young until they are old enough to fly out of the chimney. In fall migration, hundreds may swirl above a large chimney at dusk before dropping into it to roost for the night. This bird has become so adapted to life in man-made structures that it now is a common summer species sweeping the skies over our towns, cities, and suburbs.

sooty gray overall

blackish gray bill

short cigar-shaped body

blackish gray legs and feet

long narrow curved wings

- **SONG** Bold chattering; rapid twittering calls cascade down from above.
- **BEHAVIOR** Gregarious. Eats flying insects and ballooning spiders in the air column. Catches food while flying. Roosted and nested in hollow trees before Europeans settled North America; now uses chimneys and air shafts. Almost always seen on the wing. Aerial courtship and mating with courtship V-ing display – pairs flying with wings held in extreme dihedral V above their backs.
- **BREEDING** Monogamous. Solitary or colonial. Sometimes with helpers at the nest.
- **NESTING** Incubation 19–21 days by both sexes, sometimes with the aid of helpers. Young altricial; stay in nest 30 days, fed by both sexes, but female feeds more. 1 brood per year.
- **POPULATION** Fairly common to common in range. Has increased dramatically with the abundance of artificial nesting sites created by European settlement of North America. Rare in southern California.
- **CONSERVATION** Neotropical migrant that winters in South America's Amazon Basin.

Similar Birds

VAUX'S SWIFT
Smaller; shorter wings; paler underparts and rump; voice differs; soars less frequently.

Flight Pattern

Rapid batlike flight on stiff swept-back wings alternates with long sweeping glides. Darts erratically. Soars on thermal drafts.

Nest Identification

Shape ⬛ Location

Half saucer of sticks and saliva • hollow interior of tree, chimney, air shaft, vertical pipe, silo, barn, open well or cistern, fruit cellar, or side of building • nest built by both sexes • 2–7 white eggs, may be nest stained; long oval to cylindrical, 2.0 x 1.3 cm.

Plumage Sexes similar	Habitat	Migration Migratory	Weight 23 g

DATE _____ TIME_____ LOCATION _____

Family APODIDAE	Species *Chaetura vauxi*	Length 10–11 cm	Wingspan 29 cm

VAUX'S SWIFT

This small swift of the forested regions of the Northwest is similar in appearance and actions to the Chimney Swift, but their ranges do not overlap. Furthermore, this little swift soars much less frequently. Its sooty brown plumage is paler below, especially on the throat and upper breast, as well as on the grayish to brownish gray rump and uppertail coverts. This species has only recently begun to adapt to nesting in chimneys.

• **SONG** Often gives high thin chippering and twittering calls. In courtship flights it utters faint rapid twitter, *chip-chip-chip-cheweet-cheweet.*

• **BEHAVIOR** Gregarious. Singles, pairs, or flocks of 20 or more birds. Aerial. Catches insects in flight. Practices courtship and copulation while flying. Breaks off twigs for nesting materials with feet in midair. In the beginning of the breeding season courting birds display by flying with wings upraised in a V position. Frequently feeds over water, flying close to the surface, and often flies rapidly and fairly low over foothills and highlands; may also fly at great heights. Frequents burned-over forest areas, where it nests in hollow snags. Like other swifts it cannot perch but clings to vertical walls to roost at night.

• **BREEDING** Monogamous. Loosely colonial.

• **NESTING** Incubation about 18–20 days by both sexes. Altricial young remain in nest 20–28 days, fed by both sexes. 1 brood per year.

• **POPULATION** Fairly common in woodlands near water. It is rare in winter in southern California. Casual along Gulf Coast.

blackish gray bill

pale gray throat and upper chest

sooty brown overall

short rounded tail with spiny tips

short cigar-shaped body

blackish gray legs and feet

Similar Birds

CHIMNEY SWIFT
Larger in size; longer wings; darker overall; broader darker rump; dark underparts extend up to throat. Louder chattering call; greater tendency to soar; different geographical range.

BLACK SWIFT
Larger; darker overall; slightly notched tail; silvery white forehead; soars frequently.

• **CONSERVATION** Neotropical migrant, wintering from central Mexico to northern South America. Vulnerable to old-growth timber harvesting as well as the removal of large snags from the forest.

Flight Pattern

Fast low flight with bursts of rapid fluttery wing beats, alternating with glides for short periods.

Nest Identification

Shape ⬤   Location 🌲 🏚

Twigs and conifer pine needles held together with saliva to inside wall of hollow tree, hollow snag, and occasionally a chimney • built by both sexes • 3–6 white eggs, may become nest stained; long oval to cylindrical, 1.8 x 1.0 cm.

Plumage Sexes similar	Habitat	Migration Migratory	Weight 17 g

DATE _____ TIME_____ LOCATION _____

Family APODIDAE	Species *Aeronautes saxatalis*	Length 15–18 cm	Wingspan 33–36 cm

WHITE-THROATED SWIFT

Possibly the most rapid flying North American bird, the White-throated Swift has been seen fleeing from Peregrine Falcons at estimated speeds of more than 320 km/h. This darting black-and-white swift is associated with steep cliff faces in mountain canyons and on the coast; recently it has started to nest under freeway overpasses and bridges. In flight from below it shows white underparts from the chin to midline at the end of the belly, a large white oval patch on each flank that is visible from above and below, and a long, forked tail that often looks pointed in flight when not spread.

• SONG 2–3 birds flying together utter piercing laughing *he he he he*. Distinctive high liquid to slightly screechy twittering and trilling calls.

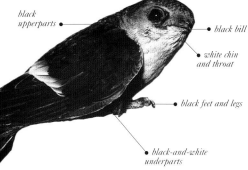

black upperparts

black bill

white chin and throat

long narrow wings

black feet and legs

black-and-white underparts

long forked tail

Similar Birds

VIOLET-GREEN SWALLOW Shorter broader wings; entirely white underparts; solid white flank patches extend onto sides of rump; metallic green upperparts with purple gloss; slightly notched tail; slower more buoyant flight.

• BEHAVIOR Gregarious. Aerial. Eats wide variety of flying insects and ballooning spiders. Catches food while in flight with the cavernous gaping mouth that is characteristic of all swifts.
• BREEDING Monogamous. Colonial. Courtship is performed entirely in flight; birds copulate in air, with male and female coming together from opposite directions, locking on, and pinwheeling downward through the air, sometimes for more than 150 meters.
• NESTING Incubation 19–21 days by both sexes. Young altricial; leave nest at approximately 30 days, fed by both sexes. 1 brood per year.
• POPULATION Common in mountainous country near canyons, cliffs, and sea cliffs.
• CONSERVATION Neotropical migrant that winters from Mexico south into Central America.

Flight Pattern

Swift flight, alternating rapid shallow wing beats with long glides. Soars and glides at high speeds. Darts, swoops, and abruptly changes direction.

Nest Identification

Shape ⬤ 🥢   Location 🪨 🏚 🏛

Sometimes flimsy or well-rounded cup of feathers and grasses cemented together with saliva and glued to wall of deep crack or crevice • built by both sexes • 3–6 white eggs; long-oval to cylindrical, 2.0 x 1.3 cm.

Plumage Sexes similar	Habitat ⛰ 🌊 ⚓	Migration Migratory	Weight 31 g

Family TROCHILIDAE	Species *Colibri thalassinus*	Length 10 cm	Wingspan 13–15 cm

GREEN VIOLET-EAR

This large dark hummingbird with shiny dark green upperparts and bluish green underparts is often noisy and first attracts attention when it is perched and giving its loud *chi-it, chi-I-it* notes. It vocalizes frequently and sometimes persistently. Generally associated with mountain forests, forest clearings, and the forest edge, it is common from Central Mexico southward into northern South America. However, vagrant individuals may show up almost anywhere, and there are numerous records from the eastern United States and as far north as Alberta and Ontario. The blue-violet ear patch and large spot on the chest are difficult to see in some light, and often the dark green of the body appears black in shadow or strong backlighting. The broad dark blue tail is often fanned when the bird is hovering, revealing a wide subterminal black band. Females and juveniles are similar to males but appear more faded in color.

slightly decurved black bill

blue-violet ear patch

blue-violet patch on breast

bluish green underparts

dark metallic green body

squared blue-green tail with dark subterminal band

• **SONG** Repeated, loud *tsip-tsip*. Jerky, dry rattle, *t'-iiiissk, t'-iiiissk, t'-iiiissk*.

• **BEHAVIOR** Solitary. Feeds high to low in vegetation on nectar and insects. Often aggressive toward other hummers at feeding areas. Perches inside shrub or tree on exposed bare twigs and often calls from perch.

• **BREEDING** Solitary.

• **NESTING** Incubation 14–18 days by female. Altricial young fledge at about 18–23 days. 1–2 broods per year.

• **POPULATION** Accidental to casual in Canada and the US; fairly common to common in native Mexico.

• **FEEDERS** Attracted to feeders with sugar water.

Similar Birds

BLUE-THROATED HUMMINGBIRD ♂ Larger; blue throat; white tips on tail feathers; 2 white lines on face.

Flight Pattern

Direct and hovering flight with very rapid wing beats.

Nest Identification

Shape   Location

Down, dry grass blades, and mosses; bound with cobwebs • decorated with bits of moss and lichen • on drooping twig or rootlet at forest edge, streamside, or on overhanging road bank • built by female • 2 white eggs; elliptical with one end more pointed, 1.3 x 0.8 cm.

Plumage Sexes similar	Habitat	Migration Nonmigratory	Weight 6.0 g

DATE _____ TIME_____ LOCATION _____

Family TROCHILIDAE	Species *Archilochus colubris*	Length 8–10 cm	Wingspan 11 cm

RUBY-THROATED HUMMINGBIRD

The only hummer known by most Easterners has a range that covers most of eastern North America. This is the hummingbird that frequents Eastern gardens and feeders. Both sexes have glittering green crown and upperparts, and the underparts are grayish to white. Males have black faces and a deep red to orange-red throat, or gorget. The humming of its wings is clearly discernible from some distance.

- **SONG** Series of rapid squeaky *chipping* notes.
- **BEHAVIOR** Feeds primarily on nectar but takes some insects and spiders, also sap from sapsucker drill wells. In courtship flight male makes huge a 180-degree arc back and forth, emitting a buzzing sound at its lowest point. Males often arrive on breeding grounds well ahead of females. These birds are strongly attracted to the color red, as are many other hummers.
- **BREEDING** Solitary.
- **NESTING** Incubation 11–16 days by female. Altricial young stay in nest 20–22 days. Fed by female. 1–3 broods per year.
- **POPULATION** Common to fairly common in breeding range. A few winter regularly in south Florida. Rare elsewhere.
- **FEEDERS** Red columbine in spring; saliva, trumpet or coral honeysuckle, and bee balm later in year. Also jewelweed, phlox, petunias, lilies, trumpet creeper, Siberian peatree, nasturtium, cone-shaped red flowers (wild and domesticated), and sugar water.
- **CONSERVATION** Red food dyes added to sugar water may harm birds. Sometimes attracted to red supporting insulators on electrical fences, then killed.

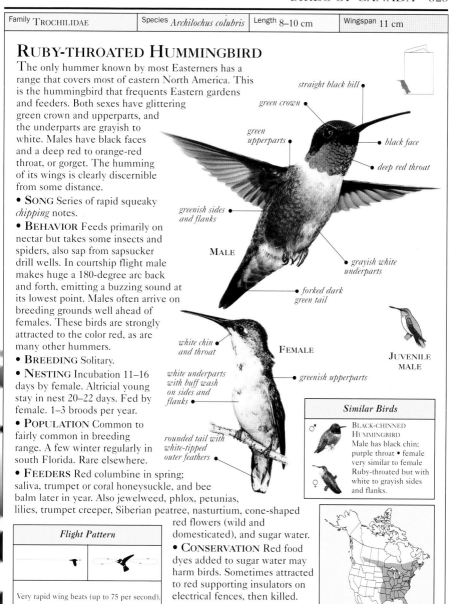

straight black bill
green crown
green upperparts
black face
deep red throat
greenish sides and flanks
MALE
grayish white underparts
forked dark green tail
white chin and throat
FEMALE
greenish upperparts
white underparts with buff wash on sides and flanks
rounded tail with white-tipped outer feathers
JUVENILE MALE

Similar Birds

BLACK-CHINNED HUMMINGBIRD Male has black chin; purple throat • female very similar to female Ruby-throated but with white to grayish sides and flanks.

Flight Pattern
Very rapid wing beats (up to 75 per second).

Nest Identification	
Shape ◖ Location 🌳 🌲	Soft plant down, fireweed, milkweed thistles, and leaves; bound with spider webs and cocoon material; trimmed with moss and lichens • looks like knot on a branch • 1.5–6 m above ground, often on downsloping branch over brook and sheltered by leaves • built by female • 2 white eggs; elliptical, 1.3 x 0.8 cm.

Plumage Sexes differ	Habitat 🏞 🌿 🌱	Migration Migratory	Weight 3.0 g

DATE _____ TIME_____ LOCATION _____

Family TROCHILIDAE	Species *Archilochus alexandri*	Length 9–10 cm	Wingspan 10–13 cm

BLACK-CHINNED HUMMINGBIRD

Like others in its genus, this western hummingbird has a complex courtship display. While flying in a pendulum pattern, the male vibrates its wings to make a buzzing noise when diving downward past the perched female. The black throat and distinctive white collar set this bird apart from its close cousin, the Ruby-throated Hummingbird. In good light the lower throat glistens in a violet band. Juveniles resemble adult females, and juvenile males begin to show some violet on the lower throat in late summer.

greenish head

greenish upperparts

straight black bill

black throat

partial white collar

whitish underparts

dusky green sides and flanks

MALE

• **SONG** Repetitive *teew* or *tchew*. When defending feeding territory or giving chase, combines *teew* note with high-pitched twitters and squeaks.

• **BEHAVIOR** Solitary. Eats nectar, pollen, and insects. Hovers by flowers to gather nectar or sallies from perch to catch tiny insects in midair. Often twitches tail while hovering. Prefers arid areas. Bathes in water or by hovering against wet foliage.

notched greenish tail with blackish outer tail feathers

FEMALE

greenish upperparts

whitish throat may show faint greenish streaking

dusky sides and flanks

whitish underparts

rounded green tail with white corners

• **BREEDING** Polygamous. Solitary nester.

• **NESTING** Incubation 13–16 days by female. Young stay in nest 13–21 days. Fed by female. 2–3 broods per year.

• **POPULATION** Neotropical migrant. Common in lowlands and mountain foothills. Casual in the Southeast in winter.

• **FEEDERS** Visits feeders with sugar water.

Similar Birds

RUBY-THROATED HUMMINGBIRD ♀
Female twitches tail less while feeding; shorter bill; greener crown; buff wash on sides; different voice.

COSTA'S HUMMINGBIRD ♀
Smaller; generally grayer upperparts and whiter underparts; squared tail with white tips and black central tail feathers; different voice
• does not stray to the Southeast.

Flight Pattern
Swift direct flight. Hovers with rapid wing beats (approximately 75 times per second) to feed. Can fly backward.

Nest Identification	
Shape 🥣 Location 🌿🌳	Plant down and spider's silk • decorated outside with small leaves and flowers • set in fork of small branch 1–2.5 m above ground (sometimes up to 9 m) • built by female • 1–3 white eggs; elliptical, with 1 end slightly more pointed, 1.3 x 0.8 cm.

Plumage Sexes differ	Habitat 🐾🦅🔵〰️	Migration Migratory	Weight 3.0 g

DATE _____ TIME_____ LOCATION _____

Family TROCHILIDAE	Species *Calypte anna*	Length 9–10 cm	Wingspan 12 cm

ANNA'S HUMMINGBIRD

Able to adapt to suburban habitat, this hummingbird is expanding geographically and becoming more numerous. Although predominantly nonmigratory, some have been reported to migrate. It eats more insects and spiders than any other hummingbird. The male, which often vocalizes while perched, is the only North American hummingbird with rose-red crown and throat. Juveniles are similar to females, but juvenile males have some red on the crown as well as the throat.

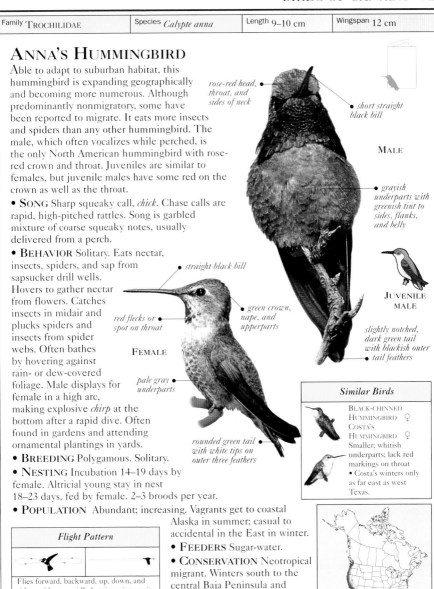

rose-red head, throat, and sides of neck

short straight black bill

MALE

grayish underparts with greenish tint to sides, flanks, and belly

JUVENILE MALE

straight black bill

green crown, nape, and upperparts

red flecks or spot on throat

slightly notched, dark green tail with blackish outer tail feathers

FEMALE

pale gray underparts

rounded green tail with white tips on outer three feathers

• **SONG** Sharp squeaky call, *chick*. Chase calls are rapid, high-pitched rattles. Song is garbled mixture of coarse squeaky notes, usually delivered from a perch.

• **BEHAVIOR** Solitary. Eats nectar, insects, spiders, and sap from sapsucker drill wells. Hovers to gather nectar from flowers. Catches insects in midair and plucks spiders and insects from spider webs. Often bathes by hovering against rain- or dew-covered foliage. Male displays for female in a high arc, making explosive *chirp* at the bottom after a rapid dive. Often found in gardens and attending ornamental plantings in yards.

• **BREEDING** Polygamous. Solitary.

• **NESTING** Incubation 14–19 days by female. Altricial young stay in nest 18–23 days, fed by female. 2–3 broods per year.

• **POPULATION** Abundant; increasing. Vagrants get to coastal Alaska in summer; casual to accidental in the East in winter.

• **FEEDERS** Sugar-water.

• **CONSERVATION** Neotropical migrant. Winters south to the central Baja Peninsula and northwestern Mexico.

Similar Birds

BLACK-CHINNED HUMMINGBIRD ♀
COSTA'S HUMMINGBIRD ♀
Smaller; whitish underparts; lack red markings on throat • Costa's winters only as far east as west Texas.

Flight Pattern	

Flies forward, backward, up, down, and side to side on rapidly beating wings as it feeds. Swift darting flight from place to place. Wing beats a blur.

Nest Identification	
Shape 〰 Location 🌿🌳	Plant down bound with spider silk and lined with plant down and feathers • on small tree branch, on ledge of cliff, or sometimes on utility wire • 45 cm–9 m above ground • built by female • 1–3 white eggs; elliptical oval or subelliptical, with similar curvatures at each end, 1.3 x 0.8 cm.

Plumage Sexes differ	Habitat 🌿🪶🌲🌾🌾🍃	Migration Nonmigratory	Weight 3.0 g

DATE _____ TIME_____ LOCATION _____

Family TROCHILIDAE	Species *Calypte costae*	Length 9 cm	Wingspan 11 cm

COSTA'S HUMMINGBIRD

Living primarily in the desert, these birds breed early before the season warms up, then migrate south to avoid the extreme heat of middle to late summer. It is the second smallest bird in North America, a distinctly grayish looking hummingbird from a distance. Females are similar to males but show white corners on the green tail and lack the violet crown and coloring down the sides of the neck. The striking gorget feathers can be elevated to stick out along the sides of the throat. Juveniles are similar to females, but juvenile males often have purple feathers forming a small chevron in the center of a dusky-streaked throat.

short straight black bill

violet crown

iridescent violet gorget down sides of neck

white underparts

grayish green upperparts

greenish wash on sides and flanks

short greenish tail with black outer tail feathers

MALE

gray-green cap to eyes, nape, and upperparts

straight black bill

JUVENILE MALE

greenish wash on sides

white underparts

FEMALE

• **SONG** Shrill hissing or piercing whistle in display flight. Calls include liquid twittering *chip*.

• **BEHAVIOR** Solitary. Feeds and perches at low to middle levels. Eats nectar, insects, spiders, and sap. Hovers to gather nectar from flowers and catches insects in air. Plucks trapped insects and spiders from webs. Often feeds with tail wagging. Frequents desert and arid scrub foothill habitats. Sometimes soars between clumps of flowers.

• **BREEDING** Polygamous. Solitary.

• **NESTING** Incubation 15–18 days by female. Altricial young stay in nest 20–23 days, fed by female. Males often leave late-nesting females still incubating eggs to avoid heat of summer. 1 brood per year.

• **POPULATION** Fairly common. Casual to western Texas and northward to southern Alaska.

• **FEEDERS** Sugar water.

• **CONSERVATION** Neotropical migrant. Development of desert habitats for housing and agriculture could be potentially harmful to overall population.

Similar Birds

BLACK-CHINNED HUMMINGBIRD ♀
Larger; greener upperparts; grayer underparts; voice differs.

ANNA'S HUMMINGBIRD ♀
Larger; green upperparts; gray underparts with greenish wash on sides; white tips on outer three tail feathers; straight black bill; red on throat.

Flight Pattern

Moves swiftly from place to place on a whir of wings. Hovers, moving in all directions while feeding.

Nest Identification

Shape ◗   Location 🌲 🌿 🌳

Plant down, forb leaves, bud scales, flowers, and bark strips, bound with spider silk • on fork of tree, shrub, yucca, or dead cactus • 1–3 m above ground • built by female • 2 white eggs; elliptical to oval, with occasional tendency toward elliptical ovate, 1.3 x 0.8 cm.

Plumage Sexes differ	Habitat 🌿 ⚘ ⚘ ✈	Migration Migratory	Weight 3.0 g

DATE _____ TIME_____ LOCATION _____

Family TROCHILIDAE	Species *Stellula calliope*	Length 7–8 cm	Wingspan 11 cm

CALLIOPE HUMMINGBIRD

This is the smallest bird north of Mexico. As the female incubates her eggs in the extreme cold of the high mountains, she does not become torpid but is able to maintain her body heat from the insulation in the nest and by remaining at rest. In addition to the small size, note the short black bill and the short tail. Its primaries extend beyond the tail when the bird is perched.

• **SONG** Relatively silent. High shrill sharp chips, *si tsi-tsi, tsi-tsi*, repeated.

• **BEHAVIOR** Solitary. Often dominated by other hummingbirds at flowers. Hovers over low flowers to feed and snatches insects in midair. Plucks insects and spiders from web and also drinks sap from holes drilled by sapsuckers. Hardy; inhabits open coniferous, montane forests and mountain meadows. Courting males fly in huge U-shaped pattern in front of the female, rising as high as 20 meters before darting back down to repeat the pattern. Gives high-pitched *bzzt* note at bottom of dive.

• **BREEDING** Polygamous. Solitary.

• **NESTING** Incubation 15–16 days by female. Young stay in nest 18–23 days, fed by female. 1 brood per year; may have 2 broods.

• **POPULATION** Common. Rare in the Southeast in the fall and winter.

• **FEEDERS** Sugar water.

• **CONSERVATION** Neotropical migrant. Species is vulnerable to loss of habitat.

reddish violet-streaked, V-shaped gorget on white background of throat

short straight black bill

greenish upperparts

white underparts with green speckling on sides

MALE

short tail

greenish upperparts

reddish violet-speckled throat

buff underparts with light rufous tint to sides

FEMALE

Similar Birds

RUFOUS HUMMINGBIRD ♀ Larger; more rufous sides; rufous at base of tail feathers; wings fall short of tail end when bird is perched.

BROAD-TAILED HUMMINGBIRD ♀ Larger; tail extends beyond primaries; rufous at base of tail feathers.

Flight Pattern

Hovers on whirring wings when feeding; moves up, down, back, and forward. Swift, zipping direct flight from place to place.

Nest Identification

Shape 〰 Location 🐦

Shredded bark, bits of cones, and plant down, covered with lichen • bound with cocoon material and spider's silk, with lining of plant down • on dead or live tree limbs or on conifer cone, protected by larger tree branches • sometimes built on previous year's nest • 60 cm–21.5 m above ground • built by female • 2 white eggs; elliptical to oval, 1.3 x 0.8 cm.

Plumage Sexes differ	Habitat 🌿 ▲ 🌲	Migration Migratory	Weight 3.0 g

DATE _____ TIME_____ LOCATION _____

Family TROCHILIDAE	Species *Selasphorus rufus*	Length 10 cm	Wingspan 12 cm

RUFOUS HUMMINGBIRD

This tenacious hummingbird aggressively defends its territory and will attack not only larger birds such as blackbirds and thrushes, but also chipmunks. At feeders it is intolerant of all other would-be visitors and spends much of its time driving them away from the nectar. Like most hummingbirds, highly attracted to the color red, it has been known to examine human clothing, magazine covers, and other items showing this color. This is the only hummingbird in North America with a rufous back, and the one most likely to be seen in the East in the fall and winter after the Ruby-throated Hummingbirds have migrated south. The male has green markings on his rufous back, a rufous tail, and his gorget sparkles copper-red in good light; the female also has small spots on her throat that appear red in certain light.

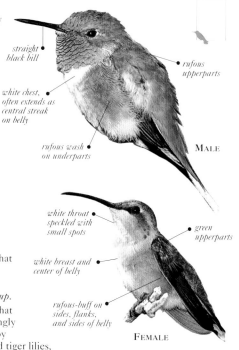

straight black bill

rufous upperparts

white chest, often extends as central streak on belly

rufous wash on underparts

MALE

white throat speckled with small spots

green upperparts

white breast and center of belly

rufous-buff on sides, flanks, and sides of belly

FEMALE

• **SONG** Call is sibilant *chewp chewp*; in defense chases, proclaims *zeee-chupppity-chup*.

• **BEHAVIOR** Solitary. A hardy hummer that nests as far north as southern Alaska. Strongly prefers red to any other color and hovers by red tubular flowers, such as columbine and tiger lilies, to gather nectar. Feeds and perches at low to middle levels. Catches insects in midair and eats sap from holes drilled by sapsuckers. Plucks spiders and insects from webs. Wings make buzzy whistle in flight. Male displays for female in U-shaped or oval pattern; ascends with back to female, then dives, turning toward her on whistling wings with orange-red gorget flashing.

• **BREEDING** Polygamous. Solitary in small loose semicolonies.

• **NESTING** Incubation 12–14 days by female. Altricial young stay in nest 20 days, fed by female. 1–2 broods per year.

Similar Birds

ALLEN'S HUMMINGBIRD
Male has green back
• females cannot be distinguished in the field
• in the hand, tail feathers more slender.

• **POPULATION** Abundant to common. Rare in the East in fall and winter.

• **FEEDERS** Sugar water.

• **CONSERVATION** Neotropical migrant. Possible decline in recent years; no noted cause.

Flight Pattern

Hovers while feeding; darts up and down, in and out, and backwards; swift and dashing flight on a blur of whirring wings.

Nest Identification

Shape 🐦   Location 🪹

Plant down, covered with lichen, moss, bud scales, leaves, shredded bark, and plant fibers; bound with spider silk and lined with plant down • most often on drooping limb; occasionally in fork of tree or shrub, 1.5–15 m above ground • built by female • 2 white eggs; elliptical oval or subelliptical, 1.8 x 0.8 cm.

Plumage Sexes differ	Habitat 🌿 🏞 ⛰	Migration Migratory	Weight 3.0 g

DATE _____ TIME_____ LOCATION _____

Family ALCEDINIDAE	Species *Ceryle alcyon*	Length 28–37 cm	Wingspan 56–66 cm

BELTED KINGFISHER

Widely distributed and common along freshwater
bodies of water as well as the coast, this is the
only kingfisher across most of its range, except
along the Mexican border. It is one of the few
North American birds in which the female is
more colorful than the male. The male has
blue-gray upperparts with a blue-gray
band across the breast and appears big-
headed with its large bill and ragged
crest. In flight it shows a white
patch on the upperwing at the
base of the primaries.

• **SONG** Bold raspy rattle sounds
like a heavy fishing reel.

• **BEHAVIOR** Generally solitary.
Plunges headfirst into water from
perch or a hover up to 6 meters
or more above water to catch
fish. Feeds primarily on
fish but also takes
amphibians, reptiles,
insects, crustaceans,
and mollusks.
Frequents favorite
perches along
waterways for
hunting. Pair digs
burrow in bank
1–2 m deep (can
be up to 4.5 m).

• **BREEDING**
Monogamous; solitary nester.

• **NESTING** Incubation
23–24 days by both sexes.
Altricial young stay in nest 27–29 days.
Fed by both sexes. 1–2 broods per year.

• **POPULATION** Slight decline in North America.

• **CONSERVATION** Often
viewed as problem at fish
hatcheries; before regulation
they were shot and killed at
hatcheries and along trout
streams. This may still occur at
some hatcheries.

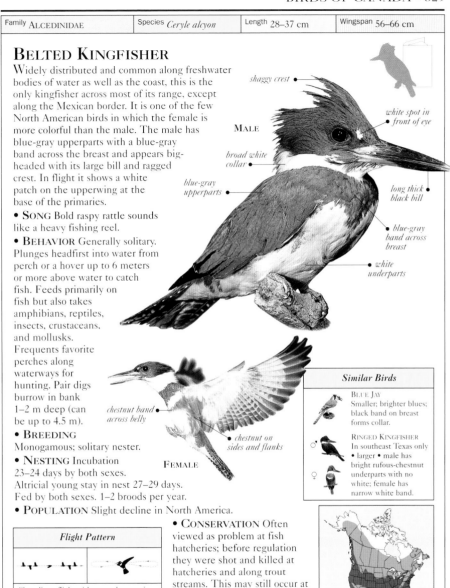

shaggy crest

white spot in front of eye

MALE

broad white collar

blue-gray upperparts

long thick black bill

blue-gray band across breast

white underparts

chestnut band across belly

chestnut on sides and flanks

FEMALE

Similar Birds

BLUE JAY
Smaller; brighter blues;
black band on breast
forms collar.

RINGED KINGFISHER
In southeast Texas only
• larger • male has
bright rufous-chestnut
underparts with no
white; female has
narrow white band.

Flight Pattern
Slow direct flight with somewhat erratic pattern. Hovers above water to search for prey.

Nest Identification	
Shape Location	Horizontal burrow, occasionally slanted upward, in bank beside fresh water • usually no lining but debris and undigested fish bones and scales • may be far from water • 1–2 m long • built by both sexes • 5–8 white eggs, about 3.3 x 2.5 cm.

Plumage Sexes differ	Habitat	Migration Some migrate	Weight 147 g

DATE _____ TIME_____ LOCATION _____

Family PICIDAE	Species *Melanerpes lewis*	Length 25–29 cm	Wingspan 51–53 cm

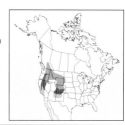

LEWIS'S WOODPECKER

Discovered by and named for Meriwether Lewis of the Lewis and Clark expedition of 1803–1806, this bird often is mistaken for a crow in flight because of its overall blackish appearance and its direct flight pattern, which is unlike most woodpeckers. It is the only North American woodpecker that is mostly black with iridescent green highlights and a pinkish belly. In flight it shows a blackish green crissum. The female is similar to the male but smaller. Juveniles have a brownish head and underparts and lack the gray collar, red face, and pink belly.

blackish green head

wide gray collar

dark red face patch

black back and upperparts with glossy green sheen

black bill

wide blackish green wings

black legs and feet

pinkish red belly

blackish green tail

• **SONG** Usually silent. Grating repetitive call of *churrr-churrr* or *chea-er*. Alarm call is *yick-yick*.

• **BEHAVIOR** Solitary or in pairs. May perch on wires to catch insects in flight, which is unusual for woodpeckers; also probes for insects in trees. Diet also includes nuts and fruits. Stores surplus food in crevice of tree in nonbreeding season, modifying acorns and nuts to fit the hole by removing the shell and shaping them. Defends cache from would-be robbers. Frequents logged areas, burns, riparian woodlands, and orchards.

• **BREEDING** Monogamous. Pairs may mate for life. Solitary nester.

• **NESTING** Incubation 13–14 days by both sexes (male at night, female during day). Altricial young stay in nest 28–34 days. Fed by both sexes. 1 brood per year.

JUVENILE

• **POPULATION** Uncommon to fairly common. Declined in recent years, especially on northwest coast. Some individuals are nomadic. Accidental in the East.

• **FEEDERS** Visits feeders with suet and other foods.

• **CONSERVATION** Listed as a species of special concern by the National Audubon Society, but populations have appeared stable in recent decades.

Flight Pattern

Crowlike flight with slow deliberate wing beats. Sallies from perch to take insects in flight, returning to same or nearby perch.

Nest Identification	
Shape Location	A few wood chips or pieces of bark • in trunks of dead or live trees or poles; often in snag of living tree • 5- to 8-cm entrance hole; 23- to 76-cm-deep cavity; 1.5–52 m high • built by both sexes, but male does most of excavating • 4–9 white eggs; oval to elliptical, 2.5 cm in diameter.

Plumage Sexes similar	Habitat	Migration Some migrate	Weight 116 g

DATE _____ TIME_____ LOCATION _____

Family PICIDAE	Species *Melanerpes erythrocephalus*	Length 22–23 cm	Wingspan 41–46 cm

RED-HEADED WOODPECKER

The ecological eastern counterpart of Lewis's Woodpecker, this is the only woodpecker in the East with an entirely red head. Unlike many other woodpeckers, the Red-headed Woodpecker catches most of its food in flight, from the ground, or by gleaning it from tree trunks and limbs; it rarely bores holes in trees to probe for insects. The male does, however, vigorously drill its nest cavity with the aid of its mate. In flight the white underparts, white rump, and large white secondary patches contrast sharply with the black tail, wings, and back. Juveniles have brownish black upperparts and brown heads.

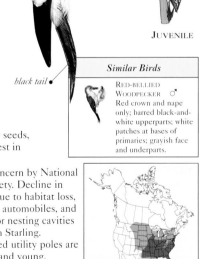

red head, neck, and throat

black bill

red upper breast

black back

black wing coverts and primaries

black legs and feet

white underparts

JUVENILE

• **SONG** Fairly noisy. In breeding season has bold grating *queark* or *queer, queer, queer*. Also sounds like a chicken clucking, *kerr-uck, kerr-uck*.

• **BEHAVIOR** Solitary or in pairs. Eats various insects, spiders, millipedes, and centipedes; sometimes takes eggs and young of other birds, mice, corn, grains, various nuts, and berries. Often hunts from low perches, flying to ground to pick up prey or nut. Caches acorns and nuts, removing shells and storing the meat for winter.

• **BREEDING** Monogamous. Solitary nester.

• **NESTING** Incubation 12–14 days by both sexes. Altricial young stay in nest 27–31 days. Fed by both sexes. 1–2 broods per year.

black tail

• **POPULATION** Uncommon and declining. Casual to accidental west of the Rocky Mountains.

• **FEEDERS AND BIRDHOUSES** Suet, sunflower seeds, cracked corn, raisins, nuts, and bread. Some will nest in birdhouse built for woodpeckers.

Similar Birds

RED-BELLIED WOODPECKER ♂
Red crown and nape only; barred black-and-white upperparts; white patches at bases of primaries; grayish face and underparts.

• **CONSERVATION** Listed as species of special concern by National Audubon Society. Decline in past century due to habitat loss, collisions with automobiles, and competition for nesting cavities with European Starling. Creosote-coated utility poles are lethal to eggs and young.

Flight Pattern
Strong flight with slow steady shallow wing beats. Sallies for flying insects, then returns to same or nearby perch.

Nest Identification	
Shape Location	In snag, limb of living tree, stump, or dead tree • 4.5-cm entrance; 20–61 cm deep; 2.5–24.5 m above ground • drilled mostly by male • 4–7 white eggs; oval to elliptical, 2.5 cm in diameter.

Plumage Sexes similar	Habitat	Migration Some migrate	Weight 71 g

Family PICIDAE	Species *Melanerpes carolinus*	Length 23–27 cm	Wingspan 38–46 cm

RED-BELLIED WOODPECKER

This noisy common woodpecker of eastern US forests and forest edges has adapted to different habitats, from southern pine forests to northern hardwoods, scattered trees, and urban parks. The bird's upperparts have black-and-white barring in a zebra pattern. The "red belly" that gives the bird its name is a reddish wash low on the belly and between the legs that is actually difficult to see in the field. In flight it shows a white rump, white patches at the base of the primaries, and white-barred central tail feathers. Juvenile birds are similar to adults but have a gray-brown head.

pale grayish tan face and chin

red crown and nape

black-and-white barring on upperparts

MALE

pale grayish tan underparts

gray crown

red nape

FEMALE

• **SONG** Quavering *churr-churr* or *querrr-querrr* and abrupt *chuck, chuck, chuck,* softer than Golden-fronted Woodpecker.

• **BEHAVIOR** Conspicuous, with noisy vocalizations and drumming in breeding season. Nests and roosts nightly in tree cavities. Eats wide variety of fare, including insects, fruits, vegetables, seeds, and sap from sapsucker drill wells.

• **BREEDING** Monogamous. Solitary nester.

• **NESTING** Incubation 11–14 days by both sexes; male at night, female during day. Young stay in nest 22–27 days. Fed by both sexes. 1 brood per year in the North; 2–3 broods per year in the South.

Similar Birds

GOLDEN-FRONTED WOODPECKER Black tail without white barring; golden-orange nape; yellow patch at base of upper mandible; indistinct yellowish wash on belly • male has red cap.

• **POPULATION** Common to fairly common. Expanding northward in recent decades to southern border of Canada. Seems stable overall; may be increasing slightly.

• **FEEDERS** Nuts, sunflower seeds, peanut butter, and suet.

Flight Pattern

Undulating flight with fairly rapid wing beats interspersed with periods of roller-coaster flight with wings folded.

Nest Identification

Shape   Location 🐦 🌳

In tree 1.5–22 m above ground • built by both sexes • sometimes uses abandoned holes of other woodpeckers • 3–8 white eggs, 2.5 cm in diameter.

Plumage Sexes differ	Habitat 🌲 🌳 🪵	Migration Nonmigratory	Weight 68 g

Family PICIDAE	Species *Sphyrapicus thyroideus*	Length 23 cm	Wingspan 43 cm

WILLIAMSON'S SAPSUCKER

The male and female plumages are so different that they once were thought to be of different species. This shy bird makes its home among the coniferous trees in the mountains of western North America. In strong sunlight the male's head, neck, back, breast, wings, and tail shine with a green iridescent sheen. Males in flight often appear entirely black with a white rump and white shoulder patches. Females in flight show brown upperparts with whitish barring and a white rump. Juveniles are similar to adults, but the juvenile male has a white throat, and the juvenile female lacks the black breast patch.

- **SONG** Often quiet. Loud shrieking *cheeeeer* is similar to Red-tailed Hawk's call. Also makes trilling *k-k-r-r-r-r-r* and soft nasal *whang* or *wheather*. Males make staccato tapping sounds.
- **BEHAVIOR** Solitary or in pairs. Shy and wary. Bores holes in trees to drink sap, and picks insects off tree bark. Eats various insects and their larvae, spiders, berries, and cambium. Courtship involves mutual head bobbing, crest raising, holding wings above back, and fluttering mothlike flights.
- **BREEDING** Monogamous. Small, very loose colonies.
- **NESTING** Incubation 12–14 days by both sexes (male at night, female during day). Altricial young stay in nest 21–35 days. Fed by both sexes. 1 brood per year.
- **POPULATION** Fairly common to uncommon in western mountains. Accidental in eastern North America.
- **FEEDERS** Visits feeders filled with sugar water and suet.

black head and neck

2 white facial stripes

narrow red throat patch

black breast

lemon-yellow belly

black back

white shoulder patch

barred black-and-white sides, flanks, and undertail coverts

MALE

brown head

black breast patch

brown-and-white barring on back

lemon-yellow belly

FEMALE

brown barring on sides, flanks, and undertail coverts

black tail

Similar Birds

YELLOW-BELLIED SAPSUCKER
Red forehead and forecrown; white shoulder patches; pale yellow belly.

RED-NAPED SAPSUCKER
Red forehead, forecrown, and nape; white shoulder patches; pale yellow belly
- only in the West.

Flight Pattern

Alternates between several rapid shallow wing beats and periods of short glides.

Nest Identification

Shape   Location

No lining except a few bark chips • in dead or live conifer or aspen 1–18.5 m above ground; excavation takes 3–4 weeks; excavates new nest annually but often uses same tree as previous year • built by male • 3–7 porcelain-white eggs; oval to elliptical, 2.3 x 1.8 cm.

Plumage Sexes differ	Habitat	Migration Migratory	Weight 48 g

Family PICIDAE	Species *Sphyrapicus varius*	Length 20–23 cm	Wingspan 41–46 cm

YELLOW-BELLIED SAPSUCKER

Eastern counterpart to the Red-naped Sapsucker, this is the most widespread of the four North American sapsuckers. In breeding season male and female perform continual loud drumming duets, including ritual tapping at the nest entrance. The female is similar to the male but has a white throat. In flight birds show a white rump and white shoulder patches. Juveniles have brown mottling on the chest, head, and upperparts, and a white shoulder patch but lack the bright head and throat colors.

red forehead and forecrown

red throat

black bib

bold black-and-white patterned face

white shoulder patch

black-and-white barring on back

pale yellow wash on underparts

barred and streaked undertail coverts, sides, and flanks

MALE

black tail with white bars on central feathers

JUVENILE

- **SONG** Often silent. Low, growling nasal *mew* sounds somewhat catlike. Alarm call of *cheee-er, cheeee-er*. During courtship display cries *hoih-hoih*. Males make staccato drumming sounds.

- **BEHAVIOR** Solitary or in pairs. Bores series of small holes, often in horizontal rows, in trees to drink the sap that collects. Eats insects attracted to drill wells, plus fruits, berries, and tree buds. Guards wells from other birds, including hummingbirds, and small mammals. Nests in soft deciduous trees, often near water.

- **BREEDING** Monogamous. Small, very loose colonies.

- **NESTING** Incubation 12–13 days by both sexes (male at night, female during day). Altricial young stay in nest 25–29 days; fed mixture of sap and insects by both sexes. Taught sapsucking by both sexes. 1 brood per year.

- **POPULATION** Common to fairly common in deciduous and mixed forests. Accidental to rare in West during migration and winter.

- **FEEDERS** In winter, mixture of suet and sugar. Will eat sweets, like jelly or doughnuts. Drinks sugar water from hummingbird feeders.

- **CONSERVATION** People dislike the drill wells created in their shade and fruit trees; fearing the tree will be injured or diseased, they often kill sapsuckers, although the birds are protected by law.

Similar Birds

RED-NAPED SAPSUCKER
Red on nape.
- only in the West.

Flight Pattern

Alternates several rapid shallow wing beats with short glides, producing undulating flight as the bird progresses.

Nest Identification

Shape ▨ ⅄   Location 🌳

Usually no materials except bark chips • in dead or live tree (prefers live tree); 2–18.5 m above ground • built by both sexes in 7–10 days • 3–4-cm entrance hole; 13 x 36-cm gourd-shaped cavity • 4–7 white eggs; oval to elliptical, 2.3 x 1.8 cm.

Plumage Sexes similar	Habitat 🌲🌳	Migration Migratory	Weight 51 g

DATE _____ TIME_____ LOCATION _____

Family PICIDAE	Species *Sphyrapicus nuchalis*	Length 20–23 cm	Wingspan 41–46 cm

RED-NAPED SAPSUCKER

South and west of the Rocky Mountains, this is the counterpart to the Yellow-bellied Sapsucker, which it very much resembles. Adept at drilling sap wells, these birds carry sap in their crops to feed their nestlings and teach them to "sapsuck" shortly after fledging. Its white rump patch is conspicuous in flight. Females are similar to males but usually have a whitish chin with variable amounts of red on the throat. Juveniles lack the red head and have brown-mottled upperparts and underparts, but do have the white shoulder patch.

- **SONG** Often silent. Low growling mewing *meeah*, similar to that of Yellow-bellied Sapsucker. Males make staccato drumming sounds.
- **BEHAVIOR** Solitary or in pairs. Bores small regularly spaced holes in trees to drink the sap that collects in them. Feeds mainly on sap, pine pitch, cambium, and some insects and berries. Males and females perform drumming duets during courtship and ritual tapping at nest hole. Important provider of preformed cavities for nests and dens of other species in its habitat, where it often is one of the only woodpecker species.
- **BREEDING** Monogamous. Small, very loose colonies.
- **NESTING** Incubation 12–13 days by both sexes; male incubates at night. Altricial young stay in nest 25–29 days, fed by both sexes. 1 brood per year.
- **POPULATION** Common in deciduous forest. Casual or accidental in southwest Canada, the Midwest, and in southeastern Louisiana.
- **FEEDERS** Mixture of sugar and suet.

red forehead, forecrown, and nape

2 white stripes on black face

2 converging, chainlike stripes on back

white shoulder patches

white underparts with yellow wash on breast and belly

black-and-white barring on back and wings

chevron-shaped spots and streaks on undertail coverts, sides, and flanks

black-and-white barring on central tail feather

Similar Birds

YELLOW-BELLIED SAPSUCKER
More obscure mottled pattern on back; lacks red nape; red on throat smaller and more confined by black borders at sides
- female lacks any red on throat.

RED-BREASTED SAPSUCKER
All-red head, neck, and breast; less mottling and barring on back.

Flight Pattern

Alternates several rapid shallow wing beats with periods of short glides, producing undulating flight pattern.

Nest Identification

Shape | Location

Usually no materials, except a few bark chips • in dead or live tree, more frequently live deciduous, 3–11 m above ground • built by both sexes • gourd-shaped, 13 x 36 cm; entrance hole 3–4 cm • 5–6 white eggs; oval to elliptical, 2.3 x 1.8 cm.

Plumage Sexes differ	Habitat	Migration Migratory	Weight 68 g

DATE _____ TIME_____ LOCATION _____

Family PICIDAE	Species *Sphyrapicus ruber*	Length 20–23 cm	Wingspan 41–46 cm

RED-BREASTED SAPSUCKER

Its bold red hood makes this bird easy to spot as it drills sap wells in trees along the Pacific Coast. It is one of few woodpecker species with identical male and female plumages. This bird often hybridizes with the Red-naped Sapsucker. The amount of white to yellow spotting and barring on the back varies; the southern subspecies has much more white. In flight look for the white rump and white shoulder patches. Juveniles are brownish with little or no red on the head, neck, and breast.

completely red breast

variable pale yellowish wash on belly, sides, and flanks

completely red head and neck

large white shoulder patch

black back with white bars

black tail with barred white central tail feathers

• **SONG** Often silent. Low growling *meww* similar to call of Yellow-bellied Sapsucker. Also utters bold *yew-ick*, *yew-ick* and *kew-yew*. Males make staccato tapping sounds.

• **BEHAVIOR** Solitary or in pairs. Drills holes in tree trunks to drink sap; also strips bark to produce sap flow. Eats mostly sap, insects, and some fruits. Northern populations nest at lower elevations. Birds at higher elevations retreat to lower forests in winter. Birds nesting in lower elevations choose living deciduous trees; those in higher elevation choose conifers, alders, or willows along streams or around lakes.

• **BREEDING** Monogamous. Small, loose colonies.

• **NESTING** Incubation 12–13 days; female role not fully established. Altricial young stay in nest 25–29 days. Fed by male; female's role undetermined. 1 brood per year.

Similar Birds

RED-NAPED SAPSUCKER
Red restricted to forehead, crown, and nape; more heavily mottled and barred back; black-and-white striped face pattern; black bib.

• **POPULATION** Common in mixed forests in coastal ranges.

• **FEEDERS** Sugar water, suet.

• **CONSERVATION** Logging activities reduce habitat.

Flight Pattern

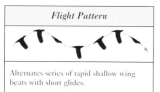

Alternates series of rapid shallow wing beats with short glides.

Nest Identification

Shape [icon]   Location [icons]

Usually no materials except a few bark chips • in dead or live tree 4.5–30.5 m above ground • 3.8-cm entrance hole; 13 x 38-cm gourd-shaped chamber • built by male; female role undetermined • 4–5 white eggs; oval to elliptical, 2.3 x 1.8 cm.

Plumage Sexes similar	Habitat [icons]	Migration Migratory	Weight 48 g

Family PICIDAE	Species *Picoides pubescens*	Length 17–18 cm	Wingspan 28–30 cm

DOWNY WOODPECKER

The smallest woodpecker in North America is found across most of the continent, ranging from coast to coast and from the northern tree line south to the Gulf and the deserts and dry grassland just north of the Mexican border. The combination of small size, white back, and small stubby bill distinguishes this common woodpecker. The female differs from the male only in that it lacks the red occipital patch. In the Pacific Northwest these birds show pale brownish gray underparts and back.

- **SONG** Downslurred soft high-pitched whinny. Call is flat *pik* or *pick* and not as high-pitched as that given by the Hairy Woodpecker.
- **BEHAVIOR** Both sexes drum on dead limbs or tree trunks with good resonating qualities or on utility poles, buildings, or other man-made objects to advertise their presence and proclaim territorial rights. Eats primarily insects and their larvae and eggs, but also takes seeds, nuts, berries (including those of poison ivy), spiders, and snails. The agility that comes with its small size allows it to feed on smaller branches and farther out on their tips than other woodpeckers. Roosts in cavities at night.
- **BREEDING** Monogamous.
- **NESTING** Incubation 12 days by both sexes (male at night). Young stay in nest 20–25 days. Fed by both sexes. 1 brood per year, possibly 2 in the South.
- **POPULATION** Widespread and common. Species can be found almost anywhere there are trees.
- **FEEDERS AND BIRDHOUSES** Will come to feeders for suet, peanut butter, sunflower seeds, and bread. Will nest in bird box designed for it.

white face

short stubby black bill shorter than depth of head

red occipital patch

black malar mark

wedge-shaped black postocular stripe

black nape and shoulders

white back

black wings with white spotting

white underparts

3 outermost tail feathers of black tail are white with dark spots or bars

Similar Birds

HAIRY WOODPECKER Larger; longer bill; white outer feathers of black tail lack spots or bars; call is *peek*.

Flight Pattern

Undulating flight with rapid wing beats alternating with pauses on folded wings, which produces bouncing flight.

Nest Identification

Shape Location

Excavated in dead tree trunk or branch; pair usually leaves chips in bottom • usually 3.5–9 m above ground, sometimes 1.5–18.5 m • built by both sexes • 3–7 white eggs, 2 cm in diameter.

Plumage Sexes similar	Habitat	Migration Nonmigratory	Weight 28 g

DATE _____ TIME_____ LOCATION _____

Family PICIDAE	Species *Picoides villosus*	Length 22–27 cm	Wingspan 38–44 cm

HAIRY WOODPECKER

The Hairy Woodpecker and the Northern Flicker are the two most widely distributed woodpeckers in North America. This woodpecker is found almost anywhere forests exist. Similar in appearance to the smaller Downy Woodpecker, it is noisier but less confiding in humans and does not often allow a close approach before it flies away. Learning its high-pitched *peek* call note will make this shy bird easier to locate. Look for a white back when bird is in flight. The only difference between male and female birds is that the female lacks the red occipital patch. Birds in the Pacific Northwest show pale brownish gray underparts.

long black bill is nearly as long as head is deep

red occipital patch

black nape

white face with black malar mark and wedge-shaped postocular stripe

black shoulders

white underparts

black wings with white spotting/barring

black tail with 3 entirely white outermost feathers on each side

• **SONG** Loud downslurred whinny reminiscent of Belted Kingfisher's rattle. Call is bold, grating, sharp *peek*.

• **BEHAVIOR** Roosts in cavities at night. Feeds primarily on wood-boring insects and their larvae, other insects, nuts, seeds, and from the drill wells of sapsuckers. Both sexes drum to advertise presence and maintain territory.

• **BREEDING** Monogamous. Some individuals known to remain with same mate for at least 4 years.

• **NESTING** Incubation 11–15 days by both sexes (male at night). Altricial young remain in nest 28–30 days. Fed by both sexes. 1 brood per year unless nest is robbed or disturbed.

• **POPULATION** Fairly common, but sometimes local, over most of range. Sometimes more common in northern hardwood and boreal forests; rare in the Deep South and in Florida.

• **FEEDERS** Sometimes comes for sunflower seeds, nuts, fruits, peanut butter, and suet.

Similar Birds

DOWNY WOODPECKER
Smaller; shorter, stubby bill (length much less than depth of head); white outer tailfeathers with dark spots/bars.

THREE-TOED WOODPECKER
Black-and-white barring on back; dark barred sides • male has yellow crown.

Flight Pattern

Undulating flight with rapid wing beats alternating with pauses on folded wings, which produces bouncing flight.

Nest Identification

Shape 　　Location

1–18.5 m above ground • built by both sexes • 3–6 white eggs, 2.5 cm in diameter.

Plumage Sexes differ	Habitat	Migration Most do not migrate	Weight 71 g

DATE _____ TIME_____ LOCATION _____

Family PICIDAE	Species *Picoides albolarvatus*	Length 23 cm	Wingspan 43 cm

WHITE-HEADED WOODPECKER

The only North American woodpecker with a white head, this bird makes its home in the coniferous forests of the mountains of the western United States. Sometimes it can be observed perching upside-down or sideways, nuthatchlike, on tree trunks or branches. The female is similar to the male, but lacks the red patch on the back of her head. In flight the white head and white patches in the primaries contrast with the black body.

white head, throat, and upper breast

narrow red patch on back of head

small black bill

black postocular stripe

black body

- **SONG** Calls include a sharp *pee-dink* or *pee-dee-dink*. Also utters abrasive *chick* or *ick*, and a rattle that descends at the end, similar to that of a Downy Woodpecker.
- **BEHAVIOR** Solitary or in pairs. Gleans insects off pinecones, branches, and trunks of trees. Wedges bark off trees to expose food or sometimes flycatches. Eats a variety of insects and their larvae, spiders, seeds, and berries. In the southern part of the range, more than half the diet may be made up of pinecone seeds. Males and females tend to forage separately in winter, partitioning the resources, with females feeding low on ponderosa pine and incense cedar, while males forage higher in the same trees and additionally on Coulter pines.
- **BREEDING** Monogamous.
- **NESTING** Incubation 14 days by both sexes. Young altricial; stay in nest 26 days before first flight, fed by both sexes. 1 brood per year.

large white wing patch at base of primaries

Similar Birds

The entirely white head is unique among North American woodpeckers.

- **POPULATION** Fairly common in mountainous conifer forests from 1,220–2,743 meters; rare and local in the northern parts of the range.
- **CONSERVATION** Vulnerable to logging operations. Listed as endangered in Canada.

Flight Pattern

Relatively slow flight, alternating several deep rapid wing beats and short glides with wings partially folded to sides.

Nest Identification

Shape | Location

A few bark chips • tree stump or tree, 1–7.5 m above ground; sometimes bores several cavities in one trunk • built by both sexes • 3–7 white eggs; oval to elliptical, 2.5 x 2.0 cm.

Plumage Sexes similar	Habitat	Migration Nonmigratory	Weight 62 g

DATE _____ TIME_____ LOCATION _____

Family PICIDAE	Species *Picoides tridactylus*	Length 20–23 cm	Wingspan 36–38 cm

THREE-TOED WOODPECKER

Formerly called Northern Three-toed Woodpecker. Black-and-white barring on sides and flanks, with black-and-white-barred back, set it apart from similar species. Barring on the back varies with geography, with Rocky Mountain birds having almost white backs and birds in the Northeast having mostly black backs with thin white bars. Not as active as many birds in its family; easily overlooked, spending long periods of time simply clinging to the trunk of a tree. The female is similar to the male but has a speckled crown, rather than a yellow cap. Juveniles are duller, with yellow spotting on the crown which later disappears in females.

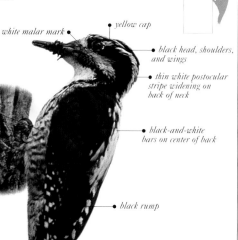

white malar mark

yellow cap

black head, shoulders, and wings

thin white postocular stripe widening on back of neck

black-and-white bars on center of back

whitish underparts with heavy blackish barring on sides and flanks

black rump

black tail with white outer tail feathers and some black spotting

• **SONG** Generally silent. Calls soft; has a timid squeaking sound reminiscent of the *mew* of a Yellow-bellied Sapsucker; also a soft *pik*.

• **BEHAVIOR** Tame. Slow and deliberate. Peels long strips of bark off trees to find wood-boring insects. Eats various insects and their larvae, spiders, some berries, and cambium. Frequents coniferous forests, often in mountains. Attracted to burned forests; often feeds on downed timber and rotting logs. Females tend to forage higher in trees than males.

• **BREEDING** Monogamous. Pair bond may last several years.

• **NESTING** Incubation 12–14 days by both sexes; male incubates at night. Young altricial; stay in nest 22–26 days, fed by both sexes. 1 brood per year.

• **POPULATION** Common to fairly common, especially in burned-over forest.

• **CONSERVATION** Vulnerable to habitat loss due to logging operations.

Similar Birds

BLACK-BACKED WOODPECKER Solid black back without white barring or patch; short white postocular stripe.

HAIRY WOODPECKER Unmarked white underparts; lacks barred sides and flanks; white back; black crown; unspotted white outer tail feathers • male has red occipital patch • rarely, juvenile may have orange to yellow crown but never has barred sides and flanks.

Flight Pattern

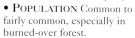

Alternates several rapid wing beats with short glide with wings partially folded to sides.

Nest Identification

Shape Location

Usually no materials except a few bark chips • in stump or tree, 1.5–13.5 m above ground • built by both sexes • 3–6 white eggs; subelliptical, 2.3 x 1.9 cm.

Plumage Sexes similar	Habitat	Migration Nonmigratory	Weight 71 g

DATE _____ TIME_____ LOCATION _____

Family PICIDAE	Species *Picoides arcticus*	Length 24 cm	Wingspan 43 cm

BLACK-BACKED WOODPECKER

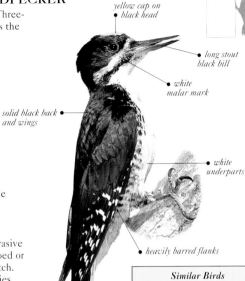

yellow cap on black head

long stout black bill

white malar mark

solid black back and wings

white underparts

heavily barred flanks

Formerly called the Black-backed Three-toed Woodpecker, this species shares the anatomical distinction of three toes with the Three-toed Woodpecker. It is closely related to the latter species but is distinguished by its black back, the lack of a long white postocular stripe and the male's more solidly yellow cap. Both species often leave behind rows of bark-stripped conifers in the boreal pine forests of North America they frequent. Both are attracted to burned-over forests, areas of windfall, and swampy areas with standing dead trees. The female has a solid black head, without the yellow cap of the male.

- **SONG** Often silent and easily overlooked. Call is a single-note, abrasive sharp *pick* or *chik*, similar to Three-toed or Hairy Woodpeckers, but lower in pitch. Sometimes repeated rapidly in a series.
- **BEHAVIOR** Solitary or in pairs. Tame; deliberate in its movements. Somewhat nomadic and may erupt in numbers where insect outbreaks provide abundant food source. Peels large pieces of bark off trunk of tree to find wood-boring insects. Eats a variety of insects, including ants; also takes spiders, cambium, wild fruits, and nuts.
- **BREEDING** Monogamous.
- **NESTING** Incubation 12–14 days by both sexes, but mostly by female. Young altricial; stay in nest 25 days, fed by both sexes. 1 brood per year.
- **POPULATION** Uncommon to fairly common; sometimes local. In the East, some may wander south of breeding range during the winter.
- **CONSERVATION** Vulnerable to habitat loss due to logging operations.

black tail with unmarked white outer tail feathers

Similar Birds

THREE-TOED WOODPECKER Black-and-white barring down center of back; much longer white postocular stripe.

HAIRY WOODPECKER White back; wider, longer white postocular stripe; unmarked white underparts, including sides and flanks; white spots and barring on wings and wing coverts; • male has red occipital patch.

Flight Pattern
Alternates between several rapid wing beats and short glides with wings partially folded to sides.

Nest Identification	Cavity lined with chips • excavated in dead stubs or trunks of dead trees, 60 cm–24.5 m above ground, usually within opening in forest; sloped entry used as doorstep • built by both sexes, mostly by male • 2–6 white eggs; subelliptical, 2.3 x 1.9 cm.
Shape Location	

Plumage Sexes similar	Habitat	Migration Nonmigratory	Weight 71 g

DATE _____ TIME_____ LOCATION _____

Family PICIDAE	Species *Colaptes auratus*	Length 32–36 cm	Wingspan 48–53 cm

NORTHERN FLICKER

This large woodpecker is often found in open spaces where it spends considerable time on the ground foraging for ants. Two distinct geographical groups, which were considered separate species until the early 1980s, occur: in the East and Northwest, Yellow-shafted Flicker has yellow underwings and undertail, and a black mustache; and, in the West, Red-shafted Flicker has bright salmon-red to red-orange underwings and undertail, and a red mustache. Although the two forms have similar bodies, the Red-shafted form shows a different pattern on its head with colors that are basically reversed from those of the Yellow-shafted form: a gray face and brown forehead, crown, and nape with no red crescent. Females are similar to males, lacking only the mustache. All birds have brown backs and wings with dark barring, a black crescent bib, buff to grayish underparts with heavy spotting, and a white rump patch.

red crescent on back of crown

gray crown and forehead

gray nape

brown back and upperwings with black barring

tan face

black mustache

YELLOW-SHAFTED MALE

buff-white underparts with heavy black spotting

RED-SHAFTED MALE

• **SONG** In breeding season, long bold repeated *wick-er, wick-er, wick-er* notes. Year-round, makes single loud *klee-yer* or *clearrrr*.

• **BEHAVIOR** Most terrestrial North American woodpecker. An analysis of the contents of a single flicker stomach revealed 3,000 ants. Spring courtship displays are noisy and animated, as pair bonds are established and rivals are driven away.

• **BREEDING** Monogamous. Solitary nester.

• **NESTING** Incubation 11–16 days by both sexes. Altricial young stay in nest 4 weeks, fed by both sexes. Usually 1 brood per year, sometimes 2 in the South.

• **POPULATION** Yellow-shafted form common. Red-shafted form is fairly common to common. Both thought to be declining.

• **BIRDHOUSES** Nests in houses and boxes.

• **CONSERVATION** Declining. Introduced European Starlings successfully compete for nest sites.

Similar Birds

GILDED FLICKER Limited range but overlaps with Red-shafted form; like a smaller, more washed out Red-shafted Flicker; yellow wash under wings and tail • only in the West.

Flight Pattern

Several rapid wing beats followed by a pause with wings folded at sides produces up-and-down flight pattern.

Nest Identification	In snag, poles, posts, buildings, nest boxes, and banks (sometimes driving out the kingfisher or Bank Swallow tenants) • 2–6 m above ground, sometimes higher • built by both sexes • sometimes uses same nest hole for second season • 3–12 white eggs; oval to short-oval; 2.8 x 2.0 cm.
Shape 🪶 Location 🌳 🏠 �’ 🔲	

Plumage Sexes differ	Habitat 🌲🌳 🌾 🏔	Migration Most do not migrate	Weight 136 g

DATE _____ TIME_____ LOCATION _____

Family PICIDAE	Species *Dryocopus pileatus*	Length 42–50 cm	Wingspan 69–76 cm

PILEATED WOODPECKER

These crow-sized woodpeckers drum on trees to claim territory and attract a mate; the loud heavy sound is as if the tree is being hit with a wooden mallet. Each member of a mated pair excavates several roosting cavities and may retire for the evening in one of them. The male roosts in the current nesting cavity before the eggs are laid and afterward incubates them there at night. In flight both sexes show a large white patch at the base of the primaries as well as white underwing linings.

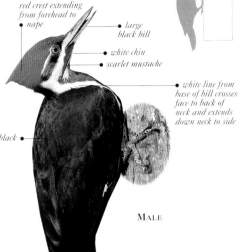

red crest extending from forehead to nape

large black bill

white chin

scarlet mustache

white line from base of bill crosses face to back of neck and extends down neck to side

solid black back

MALE

black forehead

black mustache

FEMALE

- **SONG** Location call to mate is a deliberate loud *cuck, cuck, cuck*. Both sexes have a call of *yucka, yucka, yucka*, similar to a flicker, that changes in pitch, loudness, and in its cadence.
- **BEHAVIOR** Solitary or in pairs. Loud and often conspicuous. Bores deep into trees and peels off large strips of bark for food. Also digs on ground and on fallen logs. Eats ants, beetles, and a variety of other insects, especially tree-boring ones, acorns, beechnuts, seeds of tree cones, nuts, and various fruits.
- **BREEDING** Monogamous.
- **NESTING** Incubation 15–18 days by both sexes, mostly male. Young altricial; brooded by female; stay in nest 26–28 days, fed by both sexes. 1 brood per year.
- **POPULATION** Common to fairly common in the Southeast; uncommon and local elsewhere.
- **FEEDERS** Mixture of melted suet, pecans, and walnut meats.

Similar Birds

♂ IVORY- BILLED WOODPECKER Probably extinct • larger; 2 white stripes on back extending from sides of neck; white secondaries make white patch on back when wings fold; black chin; ivory-white bill; in flight, shows white secondaries and tips of inner primaries; white lining one dge of underwing • female has black crest.

- **CONSERVATION** Vulnerable to habitat loss and forest fragmentation. Sharp decline in early 20th century, but has adapted to habitat changes. Competes for excavated nesting cavities with European Starlings.

Flight Pattern
Strong powerful wing beats when traveling distances; alternates rapid wing strokes with brief periods of wings folded to sides on short flights beneath the canopy.

Nest Identification	
Shape Location	Few wood chips • dead or live tree in shaded area, 4.5–26 m above ground • excavated by both sexes; female sometimes does more • 3–8 white eggs; oval to elliptical, 3.3 x 2.5 cm.

Plumage Sexes differ	Habitat	Migration Nonmigratory	Weight 309 g

DATE _____ TIME_____ LOCATION _____

Family TYRANNIDAE	Species *Contopus cooperi*	Length 19 cm	Wingspan 33 cm

OLIVE-SIDED FLYCATCHER

This is a stout large-headed flycatcher with dark olive sides and flanks and distinctive white rump side tufts, which are often concealed or obscured by the folded wings. The Olive-sided Flycatcher is often observed perched high on an exposed dead limb in a tree or on lookout in the tops of dead or living trees. Populations are on the decline in many regions, believed to be the result of disappearing winter habitats. Migration begins in late spring and early fall; these birds spend the winter as far away as Central and South America.

proportionally short neck

brownish olive upperparts

large mostly black bill with center and base of lower mandible a dull orange

dull white throat, center breast strip, belly, and undertail coverts

brownish olive sides of breast, streaked sides, and flanks

large stout body

black legs and feet

• **SONG** Call sounds like *quick three beers* with second note higher. Other calls include a trebled *pip*.

• **BEHAVIOR** Solitary. Reclusive. Often perched on high exposed branches. Hawks a wide variety of flying insects in midair, often taking larger insects the size of, and including, honeybees, beetles, and cicadas. Characteristic tendency is to vigorously defend nesting areas against predators and humans. Frequents open montane and boreal coniferous forests, burns, bogs, swamps, and areas around mountain lakes; uses dead trees for hunting perches.

• **BREEDING** Monogamous. Solitary.

• **NESTING** Incubation 14–17 days by female. Young altricial; fed by both sexes; first flight at 21–23 days. 1 brood per year.

proportionally short tail

Similar Birds

GREATER PEWEE
Longer tail; tufted crest; more uniform gray plumage overall; white chin and throat; dark upper mandible and bright orange lower mandible; lacks rump tufts; voice differs.
• casual in winter in Arizona and California.

EASTERN WOOD-PEWEE
Smaller, sparrow-sized body; pale whitish to olive-gray underparts; lacks rump tufts; 2 narrow white wing bars; voice differs.

• **POPULATION** Fairly common; casual in winter in coastal mountains of southern California. Declining; one factor may be deforestation and loss of habitat on wintering grounds.

• **CONSERVATION** Neotropical migrant.

Flight Pattern
Swift flight on rapidly beating wings. Sallies from perch to take flying insects with audible snap of bill; returns to perch.

Nest Identification	
Shape ◣ Location ⋔	Lined with lichen, grass, roots, twigs, weeds, and pine needles • in conifer, usually on horizontal branch, 1.5–21.5 m above ground • built by female • 3–4 white to pinkish buff eggs with brown and gray spots concentrated at larger end; oval to short oval, 2.3 x 1.5 cm.

Plumage Sexes similar	Habitat ▲ 🌲	Migration Migratory	Weight Undetermined

DATE _____ TIME_____ LOCATION _____

Family TYRANNIDAE	Species *Contopus sordidulus*	Length 16 cm	Wingspan 27 cm

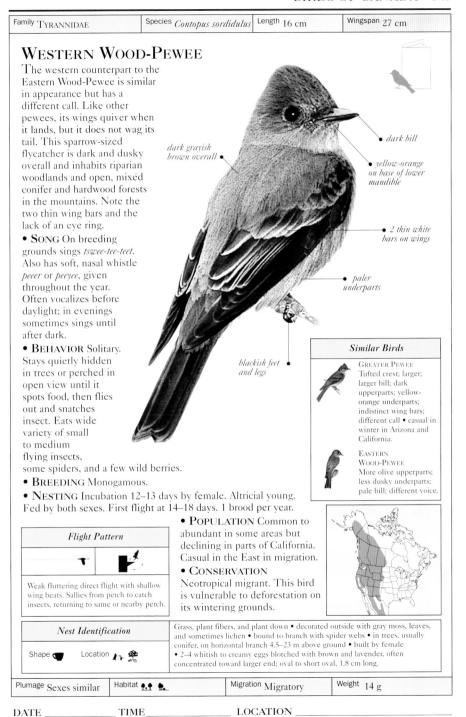

WESTERN WOOD-PEWEE

The western counterpart to the Eastern Wood-Pewee is similar in appearance but has a different call. Like other pewees, its wings quiver when it lands, but it does not wag its tail. This sparrow-sized flycatcher is dark and dusky overall and inhabits riparian woodlands and open, mixed conifer and hardwood forests in the mountains. Note the two thin wing bars and the lack of an eye ring.

- **SONG** On breeding grounds sings *tswee-tee-teet*. Also has soft, nasal whistle *peeer* or *peeyee*, given throughout the year. Often vocalizes before daylight; in evenings sometimes sings until after dark.
- **BEHAVIOR** Solitary. Stays quietly hidden in trees or perched in open view until it spots food, then flies out and snatches insect. Eats wide variety of small to medium flying insects, some spiders, and a few wild berries.
- **BREEDING** Monogamous.
- **NESTING** Incubation 12–13 days by female. Altricial young. Fed by both sexes. First flight at 14–18 days. 1 brood per year.
- **POPULATION** Common to abundant in some areas but declining in parts of California. Casual in the East in migration.
- **CONSERVATION** Neotropical migrant. This bird is vulnerable to deforestation on its wintering grounds.

dark grayish brown overall

dark bill

yellow-orange on base of lower mandible

2 thin white bars on wings

paler underparts

blackish feet and legs

Similar Birds

GREATER PEWEE
Tufted crest; larger; larger bill; dark upperparts; yellow-orange underparts; indistinct wing bars; different call • casual in winter in Arizona and California.

EASTERN WOOD-PEWEE
More olive upperparts; less dusky underparts; pale bill; different voice.

Flight Pattern

Weak fluttering direct flight with shallow wing beats. Sallies from perch to catch insects, returning to same or nearby perch.

Nest Identification

Shape   Location

Grass, plant fibers, and plant down • decorated outside with gray moss, leaves, and sometimes lichen • bound to branch with spider webs • in trees, usually conifer, on horizontal branch 4.5–23 m above ground • built by female • 2–4 whitish to creamy eggs blotched with brown and lavender, often concentrated toward larger end; oval to short oval, 1.8 cm long.

Plumage Sexes similar	Habitat	Migration Migratory	Weight 14 g

DATE _____ TIME_____ LOCATION _____

Family TYRANNIDAE	Species *Contopus virens*	Length 16 cm	Wingspan 27 cm

EASTERN WOOD-PEWEE

Although this bird is very difficult to distinguish visually from its western counterpart, the Western Wood-Pewee, their ranges barely overlap and their voices differ. Like most flycatchers, it tends to perch on an open lookout among thick trees or shrubs, sailing into the open only to feed. It is often first detected by its voice, because it often calls its distinctive *pee-a-wee* while perched, awaiting its next chance at a flying insect. Juveniles are similar to adults but both upper and lower mandibles showing dark coloration.

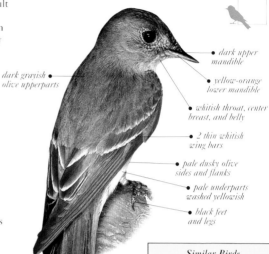

dark grayish olive upperparts

dark upper mandible

yellow-orange lower mandible

whitish throat, center breast, and belly

2 thin whitish wing bars

pale dusky olive sides and flanks

pale underparts washed yellowish

black feet and legs

- **SONG** During the day whistles distinctive, slow plaintive *pee-a-wee*, with second note lower; on second or third repeat, often followed by *pee-yeer*; second note lower. At dusk and early dawn, sings *ah-de-deee*.
- **BEHAVIOR** Solitary. Perches on open and/or dead branches in trees to spot prey; flies out to catch food. Eats a wide variety of flying insects, including beetles, flies, moths, wasps, and bees. Takes some spiders and a few berries. Like other flycatchers, it often defends its territory even from larger birds by flying at them and pecking at their backs.
- **BREEDING** Monogamous.
- **NESTING** Incubation 12–13 days by female. Young altricial; stay in nest 14–18 days, fed by both sexes. 1 brood per year.
- **POPULATION** Fairly common and widespread. Casual in the West in migration.
- **CONSERVATION** Neotropical migrant. Infrequent host to cowbird's eggs. Decline due to possible loss of South American wintering habitat.

Similar Birds

WESTERN WOOD-PEWEE
Ranges barely overlap; very similar in size and appearance; duskier and darker overall; darker lower mandible; voice is different.

EASTERN PHOEBE
Slightly larger; paler whitish to yellow underparts; lacks wing bars; both mandibles dark; pumps tail up and down while perched, especially upon landing; voice differs.

Flight Pattern	
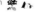	
Rather slow fluttering direct flight on shallowly beating wings. Sallies forth to catch insects in midair, returning to perch.	

Nest Identification	
Shape 🍵 Location 🌲 🐦	Grass, plant fibers, and spider web, covered with thick layer of lichens • fork of tree or saddled on horizontal branch, 4.5–15 m above ground • built by female • 2–4 whitish eggs, with brown blotches and purple, often wreathed at large end; oval to short ovate, 1.8 x 1.3 cm.

Plumage Sexes similar	Habitat 🌿🌿 🌳	Migration Migratory	Weight 14 g

DATE _____ TIME_____ LOCATION _____

| Family TYRANNIDAE | Species *Empidonax flaviventris* | Length 14 cm | Wingspan 22 cm |

YELLOW-BELLIED FLYCATCHER

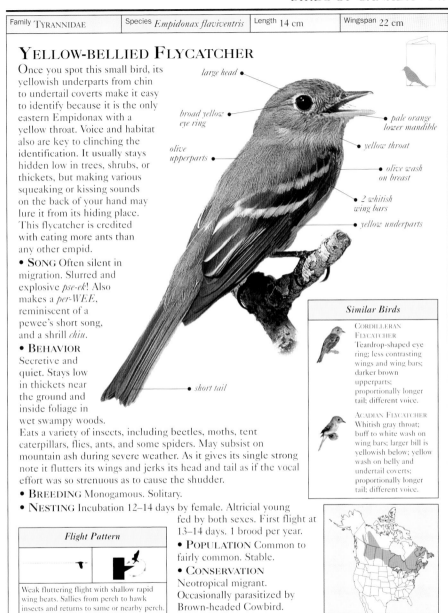

Once you spot this small bird, its yellowish underparts from chin to undertail coverts make it easy to identify because it is the only eastern Empidonax with a yellow throat. Voice and habitat also are key to clinching the identification. It usually stays hidden low in trees, shrubs, or thickets, but making various squeaking or kissing sounds on the back of your hand may lure it from its hiding place. This flycatcher is credited with eating more ants than any other empid.

- **SONG** Often silent in migration. Slurred and explosive *pse-ek*! Also makes a *per-WEE*, reminiscent of a pewee's short song, and a shrill *chiu*.
- **BEHAVIOR** Secretive and quiet. Stays low in thickets near the ground and inside foliage in wet swampy woods. Eats a variety of insects, including beetles, moths, tent caterpillars, flies, ants, and some spiders. May subsist on mountain ash during severe weather. As it gives its single strong note it flutters its wings and jerks its head and tail as if the vocal effort was so strenuous as to cause the shudder.
- **BREEDING** Monogamous. Solitary.
- **NESTING** Incubation 12–14 days by female. Altricial young fed by both sexes. First flight at 13–14 days. 1 brood per year.
- **POPULATION** Common to fairly common. Stable.
- **CONSERVATION** Neotropical migrant. Occasionally parasitized by Brown-headed Cowbird.

large head

broad yellow eye ring

olive upperparts

pale orange lower mandible

yellow throat

olive wash on breast

2 whitish wing bars

yellow underparts

short tail

Similar Birds

CORDILLERAN FLYCATCHER Teardrop-shaped eye ring; less contrasting wings and wing bars; darker brown upperparts; proportionally longer tail; different voice.

ACADIAN FLYCATCHER Whitish gray throat; buff to white wash on wing bars; larger bill is yellowish below; yellow wash on belly and undertail coverts; proportionally longer tail; different voice.

Flight Pattern

Weak fluttering flight with shallow rapid wing beats. Sallies from perch to hawk insects and returns to same or nearby perch.

Nest Identification

Shape

Location

Twigs, rootlets, weeds, and moss • lined with thin rootlets, grass, and fresh leaves • atop hillock of moss or on upturned stumps among roots of fallen trees, 0–60 cm above ground • built by female • 3–5 white eggs with light brown dots that become heavier near larger end; oval to short oval, 1.8 x 1.3 cm.

| Plumage Sexes similar | Habitat | Migration Migratory | Weight 11 g |

DATE _____ TIME _____ LOCATION _____

Family TYRANNIDAE	Species *Empidonax virescens*	Length 15 cm	Wingspan 22 cm

ACADIAN FLYCATCHER

Its scientific genus name, which means "mosquito king," widely misses the mark in describing this bird's feeding habits, but it is an apt description of the small size of a flycatcher that lords over a realm of small insects. It is the only Empidonax flycatcher to breed in the deep southern states of North America, where it rules in heavily wooded deciduous bottomlands, swamps, and riparian thickets, and in the wooded ravines of drier uplands. Like other empids it is best known by its voice.

pale yellow eye ring

olive upperparts

2 buffy or whitish wing bars

long broad-based bill with yellow lower mandible

pale grayish throat

white lower breast

• **SONG** Soft call of *peace* or *peeet.* Its explosive *PIZ-zza!!* sounds like a bird sneezing. On territory, males utter a mechanical *ti, ti, ti, ti* as they move from one perch to the next beneath the canopy.

• **BEHAVIOR** Solitary. Easily overlooked except for its occasional vocalizations. Perches in shade on lower to mid-level branches in thick trees to search for food, then dashes out to snatch insect. Eats wide variety of flying insects. Frequents wet areas in open woodlands where it aggressively drives away larger birds and other intruders from the breeding territory.

yellowish undertail coverts and belly

long primary projection

• **BREEDING** Monogamous.

• **NESTING** Incubation 13–15 days by female. Young altricial; fed by both sexes, but more by female. First flight at 13–15 days; male may feed fledglings while female starts second clutch. 2 broods per year.

• **POPULATION** Common; range expanding in Northeast.

• **CONSERVATION** Endangered in Canada. Neotropical migrant. Frequently nest parasitized by Brown-headed Cowbird.

Similar Birds

LEAST FLYCATCHER
Smaller bill; more brownish olive upperparts; grayish white underparts; bright white wingbars and eye ring; shorter primary projection • voice and breeding habitat differ.

**WILLOW FLYCATCHER
ALDER FLYCATCHER**
Less distinct eye ring, less contrasting wings with dull wingbars; and more brown upperparts • voice and breeding habitat differ.

Flight Pattern	
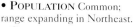	
Weak fluttering flight with shallow wing beats on rapidly beating wings. Sallies out from perch and takes insects in flight, then returns to same or nearby perch.	

Nest Identification	
Shape Location	Sticks, grass, dried stems, and bits of bark and cobweb; lined with grass, hair, and plant down • sloppy/messy-looking with long streamers of grasses hanging beneath cup • in fork of horizontal limb well out from trunk • 90 cm–7.5 m up • built by female • 2–4 creamy white eggs, with sparse brown spots; oval to short oval; 1.8 x 1.5 cm.

Plumage Sexes similar	Habitat	Migration Migratory	Weight 14 g

DATE _____ TIME_____ LOCATION _____

Family TYRANNIDAE	Species *Empidonax alnorum*	Length 15 cm	Wingspan 20–23 cm

ALDER FLYCATCHER

Perhaps the most green-brown of the eastern empids, this bird was formerly known as Traill's Flycatcher, from which both it and the Willow Flycatcher were split into separate species in the 1970s. This shy bird is easily overlooked; during nesting season it stays hidden within the thick trees and shrubs of its alder swamp and wet meadow-thicket habitat. Occasionally it can be spotted dashing out of hiding to catch passing insects or perching conspicuously on an exposed branch to sing.

brownish olive head

white eye ring

brownish olive upperparts

blackish bill with pinkish orange lower mandible

whitish throat

dusky wash on chest

pale yellow wash on sides and flanks

2 white bars on wings

whitish belly

darker wings

whitish undertail coverts

blackish legs and feet

darker tail

• **SONG** Raspy *fee-bee-o* or *way-bee-o* on breeding grounds. Also has call of bold *pep*.

• **BEHAVIOR** Male sings repeatedly for first 2 weeks after returning to territory in late spring, but after he bonds with female is largely silent. Stays low in thick vegetation, often hunting inside umbrella of thicket canopy. Perches in shrubs to spot prey, then catches it in flight. Eats wide variety of flying insects; gleans some from vegetation, including spiders and millipedes. Also feeds on some types of small berries.

• **BREEDING** Monogamous.

• **NESTING** Incubation 12–14 days by female. Altricial young. Fed by both sexes. First flight at 13–14 days. 1 brood per year.

• **POPULATION** Common and considered stable.

• **CONSERVATION** Neotropical migrant. Occasionally nest parasitized by Brown-headed Cowbird.

Similar Birds

WILLOW FLYCATCHER
Different call; more brown overall; less-prominent wing bars and eye ring; *whit* call note • different breeding habitat.

ACADIAN FLYCATCHER
Greener upperparts; longer tail; yellowish eye ring; yellow wash on belly and undertail coverts; different voice and habitat.

Flight Pattern
Weak fluttering direct flight with shallow wing beats. Sallies to hawk flying insects, often returning to same or nearby perch.

Nest Identification	
Shape Location	Grass, weeds, bark strips, small twigs, and rootlets • lined with plant down or other soft materials • in horizontal or upright fork of shrub or low tree 30–120 cm (sometimes as high as 9 m) above ground • built by female • 3–4 white eggs dotted with brown on larger end; oval, 1.8 x 1.4 cm.

Plumage Sexes similar	Habitat	Migration Migratory	Weight 14 g

DATE _____ TIME_____ LOCATION _____

Family TYRANNIDAE	Species *Empidonax traillii*	Length 15 cm	Wingspan 20–23 cm

WILLOW FLYCATCHER

This bird can be distinguished from other Empidonax flycatchers by its voice and breeding habitat preference, plus it is perhaps the most brown of the eastern Empidonax and lacks a prominent eye ring. Much variation occurs in overall color: northwestern races have dark heads, while southwestern races are very pale. The compact, intricate nests of these birds often have streamers hanging underneath. Formerly this species was lumped together with the Alder Flycatcher as the Traill's Flycatcher.

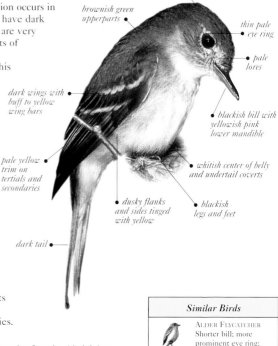

brownish to brownish green head

brownish green upperparts

thin pale eye ring

pale lores

dark wings with buff to yellow wing bars

blackish bill with yellowish pink lower mandible

pale yellow trim on tertials and secondaries

whitish center of belly and undertail coverts

dusky flanks and sides tinged with yellow

blackish legs and feet

dark tail

- **SONG** Often silent in migration. Utters harsh, burry *fitz-bew* or *fritz-be-yew*, resembling a sneeze with accent on first syllable. Call a loud, thick *whit!*
- **BEHAVIOR** Inhabits swamps and willow thickets along streams. Often perches low below crown of vegetation; when singing uses exposed perch. Males chase females in courtship flights similar to those of other empids. Perches to spot prey, then catches it in flight. Eats wide variety of flying insects and those gleaned from foliage; also takes spiders and some berries.
- **BREEDING** Monogamous.
- **NESTING** Incubation 12–15 days by female. Altricial young. Fed by both sexes. First flight at 12–14 days. 1 brood per year.
- **POPULATION** Fairly common and expanding southern range in the East; uncommon to rare in parts of the West; declining on West Coast. Decline due to loss of streamside habitat.
- **CONSERVATION** Neotropical migrant. Nests parasitized by Brown-headed Cowbird. Populations increase with reduced cattle grazing in breeding habitats and cessation of killing and removing streamside willow thickets.

Similar Birds

ALDER FLYCATCHER Shorter bill; more prominent eye ring; more olive-gray to olive-brown back; bolder buff wing bars • different voice and habitat.

Flight Pattern
Weak fluttering flight with shallow rapid wing beats. Sallies from perch to hawk flying insects, returning to perch.

Nest Identification	
Shape Location	Bark, grass, rootlets, and bits of plants • lined with plant down and other soft vegetation • in fork of deciduous tree or shrub 60 cm–4.5 m above ground • built by female • 2–4 pale buff to whitish eggs with brown spots that become thicker on the larger end; oval to short oval, 1.8 x 1.4 cm.

Plumage Sexes similar	Habitat	Migration Migratory	Weight 14 g

DATE _____ TIME_____ LOCATION _____

Family TYRANNIDAE	Species *Empidonax minimus*	Length 13 cm	Wingspan 19–22 cm

LEAST FLYCATCHER

A common summer breeding resident in Canada and the smallest of the eastern empids, the Least Flycatcher is perhaps the most often-encountered small flycatcher in the East. During breeding season the male makes a noisy territorial display, calling *chee-BECK* more than sixty times per minute while chasing other flycatchers in its territory. Note its small size, small bill, brown to olive wash on the upperparts, and conspicuous eye ring and wing bars.

large head
short triangular bill
white eye ring
whitish throat
pale lower mandible with dusky tip
gray wash on breast
olive-green to brown upperparts
paler underparts
white wing bars
short primary projection
pale yellow belly
pale yellow undertail coverts

- **SONG** Sings raspy repetitive *chee-BECK*. Call is piercing *whitt-whitt-whitt*.
- **BEHAVIOR** Active, often changing perches. Flicks tail and wings a lot; jerks tail strongly upward. Chases female in courtship; chases ecologically similar American Redstart out of nesting territory. Perches to spot prey, then catches it in the air while flying. Also gleans insects from branches and foliage. Eats wide variety of insects, some spiders, and a few berries and seeds.
- **BREEDING** Monogamous. Sometimes in loose colonies.
- **NESTING** Incubation 13–15 days by female. Altricial young stay in nest 12–17 days. Fed by both sexes. 1–2 broods per year.
- **POPULATION** Common and widespread but declining in parts of range.
- **CONSERVATION** Neotropical migrant. Uncommon host to cowbird. Declining population noted by National Audubon Society.

Similar Birds

WILLOW, ALDER, AND ACADIAN FLYCATCHERS Larger; larger bills; greener upperparts; longer primary extensions; different voices • Willow Flycatcher has less prominent eye ring but similar *whit* call note.

DUSKY FLYCATCHER Slightly longer, narrower bill; longer tail; grayer throat; less contrast in wings; more narrow eye ring; different song.

HAMMOND'S FLYCATCHER Small narrow bill; part of lower mandible is orangish; gray throat; darker olive-gray breast; more distinct teardrop-shaped eye ring; long primary projection; different voice.

Flight Pattern

Weak fluttering direct flight with shallow wing beats. Sallies to take insects in flight and returns to same or nearby perch.

Nest Identification

Shape | Location

Grass, bark strips, twigs, lichens, and plant fibers; bound by spider or caterpillar webs • in fork of tree or shrub 60 cm–18.5 m above ground • built by female • 3–6 creamy white eggs; ovate, 1.5 x 1.3 cm.

Plumage Sexes similar	Habitat	Migration Migratory	Weight 11 g

DATE _____ TIME_____ LOCATION _____

Family TYRANNIDAE	Species *Empidonax hammondii*	Length 14 cm	Wingspan 23 cm

HAMMOND'S FLYCATCHER

This small bird avoids competition for nest sites and food by living higher on mountains in open coniferous forests and nesting at higher elevations and farther north than most other Empidonax flycatchers. Spending much of its day perched high in the trees, this rather large-headed, short-tailed empid has a relatively horizontal stance, with the tail on the same plane as the body or slightly cocked. It often shows a small patch of orangish color at the base of the lower mandible.

large grayish head

teardrop-shaped white eye ring

grayish olive back

narrow short blackish bill

whitish to buff wing bars

gray or olive wash on breast and sides

darker wings and tail

pale yellow wash on belly

whitish to pale yellow tertials

short tail

• **SONG** Often silent for long periods of time. Low, rapid, hoarse, sharp two-syllable *sill-it* or *chi-pit* and low-pitched, rough *greeep* or *pweeet*. Call is raspy, sharp *peet*.

• **BEHAVIOR** Active, flicking tail frequently and often flicking wings at same time. Perches in tree to spot prey, then quickly catches it in flight. Eats wide variety of flying insects and others it gleans from foliage.

• **BREEDING** Monogamous.

• **NESTING** Incubation 12–16 days by female. Altricial young stay in nest 16–18 days. Fed by both sexes. 1 brood per year.

• **POPULATION** Common and widespread. Casual in East.

• **CONSERVATION** Neotropical migrant. Vulnerable to loss of habitat from logging of montane coniferous forests.

Similar Birds

DUSKY FLYCATCHER More open, scrubby habitat; longer bill; pale lower mandible with dusky tip; pale gray throat; shorter primary projection; longer tail; different voice.

LEAST FLYCATCHER Slightly smaller; actively flicks wings and tail; grayer above, whiter below; more prominent eye ring; lower mandible mostly yellowish; different voice.

Flight Pattern
Weak, fluttering direct flight with shallow wing beats. Sallies to take flying insects and returns to same or nearby perch.

Nest Identification	
Shape ⬤ Location 🌿 🪹	Made of weed stems, grass, bark strips, and lichens • lined with finer materials, hair, feathers, and grass • on horizontal branch or fork of tree 3–18.5 m above ground • built by female • 3–4 creamy white eggs, sometimes dotted with brown; ovate, 1.8 x 1.4 cm.

Plumage Sexes similar	Habitat 🌳 🦌	Migration Migratory	Weight 11 g

DATE _____ TIME _____ LOCATION _____

Family TYRANNIDAE	Species *Empidonax wrightii*	Length 15 cm	Wingspan 24 cm

GRAY FLYCATCHER

This shy bird is at home in the Great Basin spending most of its day in arid, open woodland, perched on piñon or juniper trees or in sagebrush. When frightened, it dives for cover and stays hidden in thick bushes until the intruder has passed. Its gray coloration and long tail, which it slowly bobs like a phoebe, make it the easiest empid to identify visually. By late fall, its whitish underparts show a pale yellow wash. Juveniles display two buffy rather than whitish wing bars.

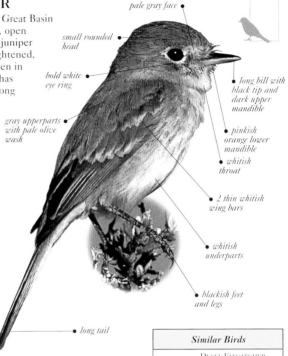

pale gray face

small rounded head

bold white eye ring

gray upperparts with pale olive wash

long bill with black tip and dark upper mandible

pinkish orange lower mandible

whitish throat

2 thin whitish wing bars

whitish underparts

blackish feet and legs

long tail

- **SONG** Sings an energetic irregular low-pitched *chee-whipp* or *chuwip*. Call note is a *whipp*.
- **BEHAVIOR** The tail-dipping trait is the most distinctive of any empid and differs from the upward tail jerks of several other species. The long tail is quickly twitched, then slowly lowered, and finally raised back to the original position. Tends to perch low and fly down, taking insects on or near the ground. Eats grasshoppers, beetles, wasps, bees, moths, and other small insects.
- **BREEDING** Monogamous.
- **NESTING** Incubation 14 days by female. Young altricial; stay in nest 16 days, fed by both sexes. First flight at 16 days. 1 brood per year.
- **POPULATION** Fairly common in semiarid habitat of the Great Basin. Casual to uncommon migrant in coastal California; accidental in the East.
- **CONSERVATION** Neotropical migrant. Vulnerable to habitat loss due to development and overgrazing.

Similar Birds

DUSKY FLYCATCHER Frequents arid to semiarid scrub habitat • shorter bill with dark orange base; pale throat; olive-gray upperparts; fairly conspicuous eye ring; voice differs, but call note is similar.

Flight Pattern

Weak fluttering flight on shallow wing beats. Sallies forth to hawk insects in flight, often returning to same perch.

Nest Identification	
Shape Location	Weeds, bark, grasses, and twigs, lined with plant down, fine bark fibers, animal fur, and feathers • fork of shrub or conifer, 60 cm–2.5 m above ground • female builds; male sometimes helps • 3–4 creamy white eggs; oval to short oval, 1.8 x 1.5 cm.

Plumage Sexes similar	Habitat	Migration Migratory	Weight 11 g

DATE _____ TIME_____ LOCATION _____

Family TYRANNIDAE	Species *Empidonax oberholseri*	Length 15 cm	Wingspan 20–23 cm

DUSKY FLYCATCHER

This bird prefers to breed and nest in the open woodlands and brushlands of high mountain chaparrals of western North America. It is similar to Hammond's Flycatcher but stays lower in elevation and less sheltered in trees, outside the dense spruce-fir forests preferred by Hammond's. It is intermediate between the Hammond's and Gray Flycatchers in body size, bill size, and tail length, and sometimes shows a yellowish wash on its underparts.

pale lores more conspicuous than other empids

white eye ring

grayish olive upperparts

bill has orange-based lower mandible fading into dark tip

whitish throat

pale olive wash on upper breast

- **SONG** Song is variable in pattern. On breeding grounds, sings a melancholy *dee-hick* or *sill-it*, given in late evening or early morning. Also has songs of a rough *grrreeep* and a clear high-pitched *pweet*. Call note is a dry *whit*.
- **BEHAVIOR** Solitary. Occasionally flicks tail upward while perched, but only flicks wings irregularly. Usually builds nests below 4 meters high, unlike Hammond's, which usually builds higher than 4 meters. Often perches in trees to sing. Feeds by gleaning insects from foliage and by hawking sallies; eats moths and other flying insects.
- **BREEDING** Monogamous.
- **NESTING** Incubation 12–16 days by female. Young altricial; stay in nest 15–20 days, fed by both sexes, but female does more. Parents tend young another 21 days after leaving nest. 1 brood per year.
- **POPULATION** Common and increasing. Accidental in the eastern US.
- **CONSERVATION** Neotropical migrant.

Similar Birds

GRAY FLYCATCHER Frequents more open desert scrub and piñon-juniper • longer bill; long tail; overall gray coloration; gray-white throat; dips tail down like a phoebe.

HAMMOND'S FLYCATCHER Frequents higher-elevation dense conifer forests • narrow, short bill with flesh-orange basal half to lower mandible; long primary extension; call differs.

Flight Pattern

Weak fluttering flight with shallow wing beats. Sallies forth and picks off flying insects, often returning to the same perch.

Nest Identification

Shape **◗**   Location **🌲 🌿**

Grasses, weeds, and bark, lined with plant down, soft grasses, feathers, and animal hair • fork of tree or shrub, 90 cm–2 m above ground • built by female • 3–4 chalky white eggs; ovate, 1.8 cm long.

Plumage Sexes similar	Habitat 🌿🌿 ▲ ▲	Migration Migratory	Weight 11 g

DATE _____ TIME_____ LOCATION _____

Family TYRANNIDAE	Species *Empidonax difficilis*	Length 14 cm	Wingspan 22 cm

PACIFIC-SLOPE FLYCATCHER

This bird was formerly lumped together with the Cordilleran Flycatcher as one species; collectively they were called the Western Flycatcher. It is impossible to distinguish the two species in the field except by voice and breeding range. This common forest inhabitant often is spotted perched in deep shade, singing repetitive notes and catching insects in midair. In winter it migrates to western and southern Mexico. This empid has a big head, teardrop-shaped eye ring, brownish green upperparts, and a yellow wash on its underparts.

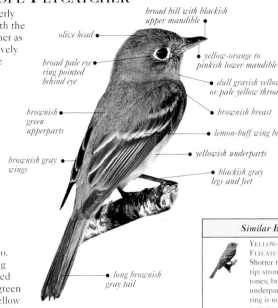

olive head

broad pale eye ring pointed behind eye

brownish green upperparts

brownish gray wings

broad bill with blackish upper mandible

yellow-orange to pinkish lower mandible

dull grayish yellow or pale yellow throat

brownish breast

lemon-buff wing bars

yellowish underparts

blackish gray legs and feet

long brownish gray tail

• **SONG** Variable. Male gives distinguishing slurred, high-pitched, thin *psee-yeet*, whistled on rising scale and usually repeated in 3 parts. Male's call is *pit-peet*. Female's common call is sharp, thin, high-pitched *seet*.

• **BEHAVIOR** Solitary but not shy or elusive. Often found in shaded spots, rarely in open habitats. Active; often flicks tail and wings when perched. Hawks flying insects or gleans them from foliage. Sometimes eats berries and seeds.

• **BREEDING** Monogamous.

• **NESTING** Incubation 14–15 days by female. Altricial young stay in nest 14–18 days. Fed by both sexes. 1–2 broods per year.

Similar Birds

YELLOW-BELLIED FLYCATCHER
Shorter tail; longer wing tip; stronger green tones; brighter yellow underparts; rounder eye ring is not pointed at rear; more rounded head; darker wings and back; greater contrasting wing bars and tertial edges; different voice • ranges barely overlap.

CORDILLERAN FLYCATCHER
Male has more disyllabic call of *wi-seet* or *wi-seen* • in breeding season has separate western range.

• **POPULATION** Widespread and common despite forest cutting. Common Southwest migrant; accidental in the East.

• **CONSERVATION** Neotropical migrant. Rarely parasitized by cowbirds. Vulnerable to habitat loss from logging operations.

Flight Pattern

Weak, fluttering direct flight with shallow wing beats. Sallies to catch flying insects, then returns to perch.

Nest Identification	
Shape	Location

Made of plant materials, including moss, grass, roots, bark, lichens, and leaves, along with hair and feathers • on stream bank, rootlets of upturned tree, cliff ledge, eave of building, or in tree • 0–9 m above ground • built by female • 3–5 whitish eggs with brown blotches near larger end; oval to short oval, 1.8 x 1.4 cm.

Plumage Sexes similar	Habitat	Migration Migratory	Weight 11 g

DATE _____ TIME_____ LOCATION _____

Family TYRANNIDAE	Species *Empidonax occidentalis*	Length 14 cm	Wingspan 22 cm

CORDILLERAN FLYCATCHER

At one time the Cordilleran Flycatcher and the Pacific-Slope Flycatcher were considered the same species, called the Western Flycatcher. Visually inseparable from the Pacific-Slope in the field, the Cordilleran is only reliably distinguished by the male's song, a double-note *pit peet*, and by its range during the breeding season. In September the Cordilleran Flycatcher migrates to Mexico, settling in foothills and mountains, where it is also a resident. The bird arrives in May on its breeding grounds.

teardrop-shaped pale lemon eye ring

broad bill with blackish upper mandible and creamy pinkish orange lower mandible

olive to brownish upperparts and olive head

lemon to pale lemon throat and underparts

dusky to brownish chest

dark brownish wings and tail

lemon-buff wing bars

blackish gray feet and legs

lemon-buff to pale lemon tertial edges, panel on secondaries

• **SONG** Male's song is a double-noted *pit peet*. Call is a thin high-pitched sharp *seet*.

• **BEHAVIOR** Solitary. Often perches in conspicuous place, but frequents shady spots rather than open places. Hawks flying insects and gleans insects from branches and foliage; insects include ants, bees, wasps, moths, caterpillars, and beetles. Sometimes eats berries and seeds.

• **BREEDING** Monogamous.

• **NESTING** Incubation 14–15 days by female. Altricial young remain in nest 14–18 days, fed by both sexes. 1 brood per year, perhaps 2.

• **POPULATION** Widespread and common in montane coniferous forests and wooded canyons. Casual on the Great Plains in migration.

• **CONSERVATION** Neotropical migrant. Sometimes parasitized by cowbirds. Vulnerable to habitat loss caused by logging operations.

Similar Birds

PACIFIC-SLOPE FLYCATCHER Smaller body; paler brownish green upperparts and head; bright yellowish and olive underparts; brownish breast; broad pale eye ring is pointed behind eye; breeding range differs; voice of male differs.

Flight Pattern

Weak fluttering flight with shallow wing beats. Hawks insects by flying forth to take them in air and returning to perch.

Nest Identification

Shape 🍵 Location 🌿🪹 🪺

Lined with lichen, leaves, bark, moss, grass, and roots • variety of locations such as stream banks, roots of upturned trees, cliff ledges, buildings, tree branches • 0–9 m above ground • built by female • 3–5 whitish eggs, with brown blotches concentrated near larger end; oval to short-oval, 1.8 x 1.4 cm.

Plumage Sexes similar	Habitat	Migration Migratory	Weight 11 g

DATE _____ TIME_____ LOCATION _____

Family TYRANNIDAE	Species *Sayornis phoebe*	Length 18 cm	Wingspan 29 cm

EASTERN PHOEBE

An early migration makes the Eastern Phoebe a common harbinger of spring north of the Mason-Dixon Line. It is easily identified by its wagging tail and distinctive, harsh *fee-be* calls. The subject of the first bird-banding experiment in North America, by John James Audubon in 1840, the Eastern Phoebe has provided researchers with much information about longevity, site fidelity, dispersal, and migratory movements. Phoebes are hardy birds that often winter near water as far north as the Ohio River. This is the only species of flycatcher to winter in the eastern United States. In the bird's nesting range it seems almost every concrete bridge and culvert over small to medium streams has a phoebe nest beneath it.

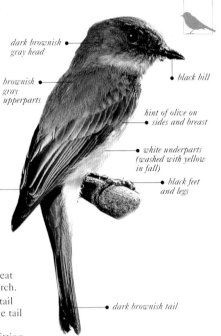

dark brownish gray head

black bill

brownish gray upperparts

hint of olive on sides and breast

white underparts (washed with yellow in fall)

black feet and legs

dark brownish wings

dark brownish tail

- **SONG** Sharp *chip* is one of most common calls. Also issues brusque pointed *FEE-be* accented on first syllable. Song often repeated, especially when male establishes territory and attempts to attract mate; may repeat many times per minute from high, exposed perch.
- **BEHAVIOR** Solitary or in pairs. Often bobs tail when perched, especially after landing with the tail swept downward, then raised upward, and sometimes pushed sideways in an arc. While sitting atop tree branches and other perches, watches for insects and sallies to catch them in midair. Also catches food in foliage and on ground. In addition to insects, also eats small fish, berries, and fruit.
- **BREEDING** Monogamous. Solitary nester.
- **NESTING** Incubation about 16 days by female. Altricial young stay in nest 15–16 days. Fed by both sexes. 2 broods per year, sometimes 3 in the South.
- **POPULATION** Common and increasing.
- **BIRDHOUSES** Accepts nesting ledges glued to vertical walls under concrete bridges.
- **CONSERVATION** Neotropical migrant. Parasitized by cowbirds. Buildings, dams, bridges, and culverts have provided more nesting areas.

Similar Birds

EASTERN WOOD-PEWEE Darker underparts; yellowish lower mandible; 2 whitish wing bars; does not pump tail; different voice.

Flight Pattern	

Weak buoyant fluttering flight with shallow wing beats. Hawks insects by flying from perch and taking insect in flight with audible pop of the mandibles.

Nest Identification		Mud pellets covered with moss • lined with grass, weeds, leaves, hair, and feathers • often built on top of remains of old nest • attached to a vertical wall or on a shelf or beam • built by female • 2–8 white eggs with occasional reddish brown spots; oval, 2.0 x 1.5 cm.
Shape	Location	

Plumage Sexes similar	Habitat	Migration Most migrate	Weight 20 g

DATE _____ TIME_____ LOCATION _____

Family TYRANNIDAE	Species *Sayornis saya*	Length 19 cm	Wingspan 32 cm

SAY'S PHOEBE

Unlike other phoebes, Say's Phoebe is not as commonly tied to habitats near water but inhabits semiarid regions such as savannas, farmlands, and open brushlands. This active bird is rarely sedentary and is often spotted darting for insects and wagging its tail. Its gray-brown upperparts and rusty underparts make it superficially resemble the American Robin, but its upright posture and aerial acrobatics quickly reveal its identity as a flycatcher.

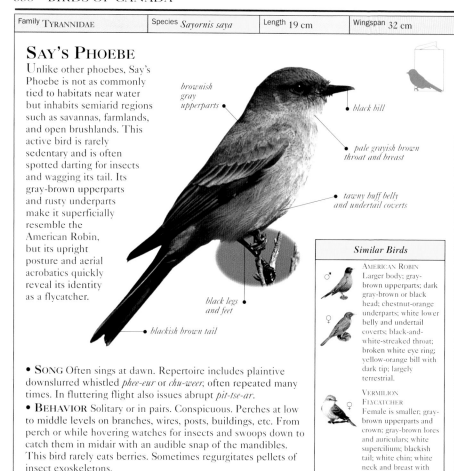

brownish gray upperparts

black bill

pale grayish brown throat and breast

tawny buff belly and undertail coverts

black legs and feet

blackish brown tail

Similar Birds

AMERICAN ROBIN Larger body; gray-brown upperparts; dark gray-brown or black head; chestnut-orange underparts; white lower belly and undertail coverts; black-and-white-streaked throat; broken white eye ring; yellow-orange bill with dark tip; largely terrestrial.

VERMILION FLYCATCHER Female is smaller; gray-brown upperparts and crown; gray-brown lores and auriculars; white supercilium; blackish tail; white chin; white neck and breast with dusky streaking; salmon-peach belly and undertail coverts.

• **SONG** Often sings at dawn. Repertoire includes plaintive downslurred whistled *phee-eur* or *chu-weer*, often repeated many times. In fluttering flight also issues abrupt *pit-tse-ar*.

• **BEHAVIOR** Solitary or in pairs. Conspicuous. Perches at low to middle levels on branches, wires, posts, buildings, etc. From perch or while hovering watches for insects and swoops down to catch them in midair with an audible snap of the mandibles. This bird rarely eats berries. Sometimes regurgitates pellets of insect exoskeletons.

• **BREEDING** Monogamous. Solitary nester.

• **NESTING** Incubation 12–14 days by female. Altricial young stay in nest 14–16 days. Fed by both sexes. 1–2 broods per year, sometimes 3 in the Southwest along the Mexican border.

• **POPULATION** Stable and fairly common. Casual in eastern US.

• **CONSERVATION** Neotropical migrant. Rare host to cowbird parasitism.

Flight Pattern

Weak fluttering buoyant flight with shallow wing beats. Hawks from perch to catch flying insects; also hovers.

Nest Identification

Shape 🦃 Location 🏕️ 🔺 〰️ 🏚️

Adherent • mud pellets, moss, and grass • lined with grass, weeds, moss, spider webs, and wool • attached to vertical walls • built by female • 3–7 white eggs with occasional brown or reddish spots; ovate to short ovate, 2.0 x 1.5 cm.

Plumage Sexes similar	Habitat 🛩️ ⚊ 🌱 ⚘ 🌿	Migration Migratory	Weight 20 g

DATE _____ TIME _____ LOCATION _____

Family TYRANNIDAE	Species *Myiarchus crinitus*	Length 22 cm	Wingspan 30–36 cm

GREAT CRESTED FLYCATCHER

This big eastern flycatcher with a rusty tail and shaggy crest stays hidden in tall trees, but its coarse song is heard throughout the forest. Although similar in size to the Eastern Kingbird, the Great Crested Flycatcher prefers thickly wooded areas. Males defend their large territories by battling in the air with other males, clawing one another and sometimes pulling out feathers. Like some other members of its genus, it often tops off the nest with a discarded snakeskin, but in today's throwaway society it more readily finds cellophane and plastic. Upperparts are olive-green, and the bird shows two white wing bars.

darker gray crown

heavy black bill

gray throat and upper breast

lemon-yellow belly and undertail coverts

- **SONG** Bold melodic whistle of *wheeep!* and rolling *prrrrrrrrrrreeeet*. *Wheeep* notes often given in rapid succession in series of 3 or more.

primaries show cinnamon-rufous edges

rufous inner webs on tail feathers

- **BEHAVIOR** Solitary or in pairs. Often ranges high in the canopy, sitting on exposed limbs in the crown of a tall tree or on top of a dead snag. Catches prey higher above ground than most flycatchers. Sallies from perch to snatch insects from foliage and catch them in midair, often returning to same or nearby perch. Eats variety of larger insects, including beetles, crickets, katydids, caterpillars, moths, and butterflies. Also eats some fruits and berries. Male chases female in courtship flight close to possible nesting cavity.
- **BREEDING** Monogamous. Solitary nester.
- **NESTING** Incubation 13–15 days by female. Altricial young remain in nest 12–21 days. Fed by both sexes. 1 brood per year.
- **POPULATION** Common in open wooded lots and on forest edge. Rare on California coast in autumn migration.
- **BIRDHOUSES** Sometimes uses nest boxes placed on trees or buildings 2–15 meters high.
- **CONSERVATION** Neotropical migrant. Vulnerable to habitat loss.

Similar Birds

ASH-THROATED FLYCATCHER
Smaller bill; paler underparts with whitish throat and pale gray breast; pale yellow belly and crissum; brown-tipped outer tail feathers; different voice.

BROWN-CRESTED FLYCATCHER
Bigger heavier bill; paler gray throat and breast; paler yellow belly; different voice.

Flight Pattern

Fairly swift buoyant direct flight. Hawks insects in flight, returning to perch. Hovers over foliage or ground then dips for food.

Nest Identification

Shape | Location

Filled and lined with grass, weeds, bark strips, rootlets, feathers, fur, snakeskin, onion skin, cellophane, and clear plastic • in cavity, abandoned holes of other birds, or bird boxes • built by both sexes • 4–8 creamy white to pale buff eggs marked with brown, olive, and lavender; ovate to short ovate, sometimes elliptical ovate or elongate ovate, 2.3 x 1.7 cm.

Plumage Sexes similar	Habitat	Migration Migratory	Weight 34 g

DATE _____ TIME_____ LOCATION _____

Family TYRANNIDAE	Species *Tyrannus crassirostris*	Length 24 cm	Wingspan 38–41 cm

THICK-BILLED KINGBIRD

In the 1950s this native of Mexico first arrived in the southwestern part of North America in Guadalupe Canyon on the southern border between Arizona and New Mexico. Its population has been slowly increasing in size ever since. Bold and gregarious, some refer to it as the noisiest bird in Arizona. It has a fondness for sycamore trees along streams, and it perches high in them to watch for passing insects. It is a large chunky kingbird with a large head and a very stout, broad black bill. Birds in fresh fall plumage and first year juveniles can show bright yellow underparts.

dark grayish brown head and nape

dark brownish black ear patch

grayish olive-brown upperparts

dusky brown wings, narrowly edged with pale cinnamon

large black bill

dirty white chin, throat, and underparts

pale yellowish wash on belly and undertail coverts

black feet and legs

FIRST FALL

dusky brown tail, lightly edged cinnamon

slightly notched or square-tipped tail

• **SONG** Noisy. A loud, whistled metallic nasal *pureet* or *di-diweek*. Often calls after returning to perch. Also has bold piercing calls of *cut-a-reap* and *kiterreer*.
• **BEHAVIOR** Solitary or in pairs. Conspicuous, often perching in high open areas near tops of trees or on dead branches or tree top. Spots prey from perches, sallies out to catch in midair, and returns to perch to eat. Feeds on large flying insects, including grasshoppers, beetles, and cicadas; also hovers and takes insects and berries from foliage or ground. Frequents riparian woodlands with large sycamores or grasslands with scattered trees.
• **BREEDING** Monogamous. Solitary.
• **NESTING** Breeding biology poorly known. Estimated incubation 18–20 days by female. Young altricial; fed by both sexes. Estimated to fledge nest at 15–20 days. 1 brood per year.
• **POPULATION** Common in Guadalupe Canyon; uncommon and local elsewhere in southeastern Arizona. Casual in fall and winter in western Arizona and southern California. Accidental along the West Coast north to British Columbia.
• **CONSERVATION** Neotropical migrant. Vulnerable to loss of riparian habitats.

Similar Birds

TROPICAL KINGBIRD Smaller bill; lighter gray head; dark grayish brown upperparts; much brighter yellow underparts with less extensive white; notched tail; voice differs.

WESTERN KINGBIRD CASSIN'S KINGBIRD Paler heads and upperparts; much smaller bills; squared tails with white edging or tips; brighter and more extensive yellow underparts; voices differ.

Flight Pattern

Buoyant fluttering flight with shallow wing beats. Hawks insects and returns to perch. Hovers, dipping to pick up prey.

Nest Identification

Shape ⌣   Location 🪺

Twigs, grasses, weeds, and leaves, lined with plant down • untidy and flimsy; unfinished in appearance; can sometimes see eggs or nestlings through bottom • on horizontal tree branch, 15–18.5 m above ground • built by both sexes • 3–4 whitish eggs, blotched with brown; oval to long oval or subelliptical, 2.5 x 1.8 cm.

Plumage Sexes similar	Habitat 🌳 ⛰️	Migration Migratory	Weight 57 g

Family TYRANNIDAE	Species *Tyrannus verticalis*	Length 22 cm	Wingspan 38–41 cm

WESTERN KINGBIRD

The most common and well-known kingbird in the West has easily adapted to the ongoing development of its habitat. It even takes advantage of it by using telephone poles and other artificial structures as nesting areas and fences and utility wires as hunting perches. Often found in urban areas, it is more gregarious than any other kingbird, with two or more pairs occasionally nesting in the same tree. Aggressive, it also is known for its tenacity for chasing hawks, crows, ravens, and other large birds away from its nesting territory. It can be distinguished from other large flycatchers and kingbirds by the black tail with white edging on each side. A red-orange crown patch usually is concealed.

pale ashy gray head, neck, and breast

dark thin gray eye patch

olive-green tinted back

small black bill

bright lemon-yellow underparts

black legs and feet

dark brownish black wings contrast with paler back

black squared tail with white edges

• **SONG** Call is a rather quiet clipped *bek*. Has an abrasive and bickering chatter of *ker-er-ip, ker-er-ip, pree pree pr-prrr*.

• **BEHAVIOR** Solitary or in pairs or small groups. Gregarious in winter. Conspicuous. Hunts from open perches at low, middle, and high levels. Sits on perch to spot prey, flies out to catch in midair, and returns to perch to eat. Often hovers above foliage or ground and dips down to pick up food. Feeds on various insects, fruits, and berries. Male performs hectic courtship flight, darting upward into air, fluttering, vibrating feathers, and delivering trilling song.

• **BREEDING** Monogamous. Solitary. Sometimes can be found in loose semicolonies.

• **NESTING** Incubation 18–19 days by female. Young stay in nest 16–17 days, fed by both sexes. 1–2 broods per year.

• **POPULATION** Common in semiarid open country. Range has expanded during the 20th century as expansion of agriculture has created more suitable nesting and foraging areas. Some winter in southern Florida. Accidental in fall migration to New England and the Atlantic Coast.

• **CONSERVATION** Neotropical migrant.

Similar Birds

CASSIN'S KINGBIRD
Darker gray head, breast, and neck; darker olive-brown back; pale buffy white tips on dusky brown tail feathers; whiter throat; voice differs.

TROPICAL AND COUCH'S KINGBIRDS
Larger, longer bills; darker ear patches; darker upperparts; yellow of underparts extends upward to throats; slightly notched tails; voices differ.

Flight Pattern

Buoyant fluttering flight on shallow wing beats. Sallies for insects in flight, returns to perch. Hovers over prey and dips down.

Nest Identification

Shape ⬤ Location 🪺 🌲 🏠 🏚

Grass, weeds, twigs, and plant fibers, lined with finer materials, including hair, plant down, and cotton • near trunk on horizontal limb or fork of tree, 2.5–12 m above ground • sometimes on brace or cross-arm of utility pole, church steeple, or other man-made structure • built by both sexes • 3–7 whitish eggs, heavily blotched with brown, lavender, and black; oval to short oval, 2.5 x 1.5 cm.

Plumage Sexes similar	Habitat	Migration Migratory	Weight 40 g

Family TYRANNIDAE	Species *Tyrannus tyrannus*	Length 22 cm	Wingspan 36–38 cm

EASTERN KINGBIRD

True to its name, this kingbird is the only one nesting in the East north of southern Florida. It has an extensive breeding range that covers most of North America: from the Atlantic Coast north almost to the treeline in the southern Yukon. Its Latin name means "king of the tyrants," and when defending its nest this aggressive bird sometimes will land on the backs of hawks, crows, and vultures, pecking and pulling their feathers. In winter flocks fly to South America and survive on a diet of mostly berries. This species is fashionably decked with blackish upperparts, white underparts, and a distinctive white terminal tail band. A red stripe on its crown, usually concealed, is seen only when the bird is displaying.

black cap, forehead, and sides of face

black bill

charcoal-gray back and rump

white throat

grayish wash on breast

charcoal-gray wings

white underparts

• **SONG** Utters grating buzzing high-pitched *dzeet* note combined with a rapid *tzi, tzeet, tzi, tzeet, tzi, tzeet.*

• **BEHAVIOR** Solitary or in pairs. Gregarious in migration and winter. Often sits on exposed, low- to mid-level perches and high on trees, shrubs, weed stalks, fences, utility wires, etc. Sits on perch to spot prey, hawks insects in air, and returns to perch to eat them. Also hovers to pick food off leaves or ground. Eats various insects, fruits, and berries. Male performs erratic courtship flights, hovering, circling, and tumbling with tail spread and crown patch revealed.

black feet and legs

black tail with white terminal band

• **BREEDING** Monogamous. Solitary nester.

• **NESTING** Incubation 16–18 days mostly by female. Altricial young stay in nest approximately 16–18 days. Fed by both sexes. 1 brood per year.

• **POPULATION** Common, widespread, and conspicuous. Has expanded its range and increased its numbers along with agricultural expansion.

• **CONSERVATION** Neotropical migrant. Common cowbird host, but often damages cowbird eggs.

Similar Birds

GRAY KINGBIRD
Pale gray upperparts; white underparts; black mask through eyes; forked tail lacks white terminal band • limited US range.

Flight Pattern

Fluttering stiff-winged direct flight with shallow wing beats. Sallies to snatch insects in flight, then returns to perch.

Nest Identification	
Shape 🥄 Location 🌳 🌿 🏠	Weed stalks, twigs, and grass • lined with fine grass, sometimes animal hair • far to midway out on horizontal tree branch or shrub; sometimes on post or stump; 2–18.5 m above ground, usually near water • built by female with help from male • 3–5 white to pinkish white eggs with heavy brown, lavender, and gray blotches; long and pointed to very round, but most ovate, 2.3 x 1.8 cm.

Plumage Sexes similar	Habitat 🌲 🌾 🌿	Migration Migratory	Weight 43 g

DATE _____ TIME_____ LOCATION _____

Family TYRANNIDAE	Species *Tyrannus savana*	Length 37 cm	Wingspan 38 cm

FORK-TAILED FLYCATCHER

Also known as the Swallow-tailed Flycatcher, this bird often is seen at ground level and in flocks of more than fifty birds in its normal tropical range from southern Mexico to southern South America. The Fork-tailed Flycatcher is easily identified by its deeply forked black tail and black cap. A yellow patch on its crown is usually concealed. Wandering vagrants are casual in Texas and along the Atlantic Coast and accidental elsewhere from the Gulf Coast to California to the Great Lakes states and southern Canada. Many observations have been of juveniles, which resemble adults but have shorter tails.

black head

pale gray upperparts

black bill

white underparts, throat, and, chin

dark brown wings with white edges

extremely long, deeply forked black tail with white-edged outer feathers

- **SONG** Call is abrasive repeated liquid *sik* or *plik*. Also utters lower, bleating *ek-ek-ek-ek-ek-ek*, etc. During courtship flights male makes rapid, clicking, sharp dry rattle with wings.
- **BEHAVIOR** Solitary or in pairs. At night roosts communally (except nesting females) with up to several hundred birds. Gregarious during nonbreeding season. Often perches low within a meter of ground in savannas and other open, grassy country. Sallies up and hawks insects in air or drops to pick them off ground. Plucks berries and fruits in flight and eats them. Males perform a slow butterfly-like courtship flight.
- **BREEDING** Monogamous. Solitary nester.
- **NESTING** Breeding biology poorly known. Incubation estimated 14–17 days by female. Altricial young estimated to fly at 14–17 days. Fed by both sexes. 1–2 broods per year.
- **POPULATION** Casual to accidental in North America.
- **CONSERVATION** Deforestation in tropics and expansion of agricultural lands, including grassy fields, has probably aided this species.

Similar Birds

SCISSOR-TAILED FLYCATCHER
Pale pearly gray upperparts and head; salmon-pink sides, flanks, and underwing linings; red axillars.

Flight Pattern

Swift flight with shallow wing beats and long rippling tail streamers. Sallies to snatch insects in flight, then returns to perch.

Nest Identification

Shape ⬗   Location 🌲 🌿 🌳

Grasses, plant fibers, leaves, and bark shreds • lined with seed down, plant down, and hair • on horizontal branch of tree or shrub 90 cm–11 m above ground • built by female • 2–3 glossy white eggs wreathed with chocolate and lilac spots; oval to long oval, 2.3 x 1.5 cm.

Plumage Sexes similar	Habitat ___ 🌿 〰	Migration Migratory	Weight 28 g

Family LANIIDAE	Species *Lanius cristatus*	Length 19 cm	Wingspan 32 cm

BROWN SHRIKE

Occasionally this Eurasian native strays to the western Aleutians, St. Lawrence Island, south-coastal Alaska, and, more rarely, California and Maritime Canada. It usually perches quietly in trees, searching for prey; when alarmed it calls and wags its tail from side to side. Juveniles resemble females but have more distinct barring on their sides and flanks, and the white borders of their masks are restricted to the areas around the eyes.

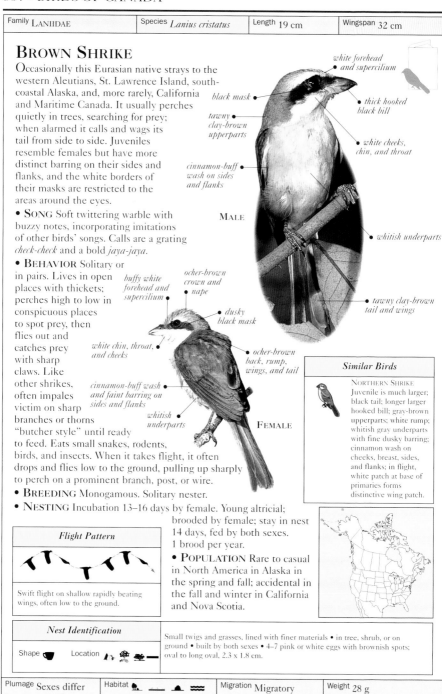

white forehead and supercilium

black mask

tawny clay-brown upperparts

thick hooked black bill

white cheeks, chin, and throat

cinnamon-buff wash on sides and flanks

MALE

whitish underparts

tawny clay-brown tail and wings

ocher-brown crown and nape

buffy white forehead and supercilium

dusky black mask

white chin, throat, and cheeks

ocher-brown back, rump, wings, and tail

cinnamon-buff wash and faint barring on sides and flanks

whitish underparts

FEMALE

- **SONG** Soft twittering warble with buzzy notes, incorporating imitations of other birds' songs. Calls are a grating *check-check* and a bold *jaya-jaya*.
- **BEHAVIOR** Solitary or in pairs. Lives in open places with thickets; perches high to low in conspicuous places to spot prey, then flies out and catches prey with sharp claws. Like other shrikes, often impales victim on sharp branches or thorns "butcher style" until ready to feed. Eats small snakes, rodents, birds, and insects. When it takes flight, it often drops and flies low to the ground, pulling up sharply to perch on a prominent branch, post, or wire.
- **BREEDING** Monogamous. Solitary nester.
- **NESTING** Incubation 13–16 days by female. Young altricial; brooded by female; stay in nest 14 days, fed by both sexes. 1 brood per year.
- **POPULATION** Rare to casual in North America in Alaska in the spring and fall; accidental in the fall and winter in California and Nova Scotia.

Similar Birds

NORTHERN SHRIKE Juvenile is much larger; black tail; longer larger hooked bill; gray-brown upperparts; white rump; whitish gray underparts with fine dusky barring; cinnamon wash on cheeks, breast, sides, and flanks; in flight, white patch at base of primaries forms distinctive wing patch.

Flight Pattern

Swift flight on shallow rapidly beating wings, often low to the ground.

Nest Identification

Shape ☕ Location 🌿 🌳 🌾

Small twigs and grasses, lined with finer materials • in tree, shrub, or on ground • built by both sexes • 4–7 pink or white eggs with brownish spots; oval to long oval, 2.3 x 1.8 cm.

Plumage Sexes differ	Habitat 🌿 ___ 🌲 〰️	Migration Migratory	Weight 28 g

DATE _____ TIME_____ LOCATION _____

Family LANIIDAE	Species *Lanius ludovicianus*	Length 23 cm	Wingspan 32–33 cm

LOGGERHEAD SHRIKE

This large-headed bird with whitish underparts is one of two shrike species that nest and breed in North America. Known as the "Butcher Bird" across its range, this adept hunter usually perches in the open to watch for prey. It has the unusual behavior of caching the bodies of its prey by suspending them impaled on a plant spine or the barbed wire of a fence. The caches may serve as larder for future use, to soften the food for easier rendering, or to passively advertise the presence of the territory and its owner. Juveniles have brownish upperparts and more distinct barring on their underparts.

• large head

• black hooked beak

• black mask meets in a slender line over beak

• bluish gray upperparts

• black wings with white patch

• grayish to whitish rump

JUVENILE

slender black tail with white outer feathers •

• **SONG** Variety of squeaking notes and low warbles, delivered in slow deliberate phrases, often repeated, *queedle, queedle*. Call is a grating *shak-shak*.
• **BEHAVIOR** Solitary. Pairs in breeding season. Often sits immobile, hawklike, watching for prey for long periods. Flies down to catch prey with bill or sharp claws; also catches insects in flight. Eats small rodents, birds, reptiles, amphibians, and insects. Pair defends territory in breeding season but defend separate territories in winter.
• **BREEDING** Monogamous. Solitary nester.
• **NESTING** Incubation 16–17 days by female. Young altricial; brooded by female; stay in nest 17–21 days, fed by both sexes. 2 broods per year (occasionally 3 in the South).
• **POPULATION** Fairly common in habitats with open fields and scattered trees. Now rare over much of central part of range.
• **CONSERVATION** Some are neotropical migrants. Declining seriously in coastal California, the Northeast, and the eastern Midwest due to habitat loss and insecticide/pesticide use.

Similar Birds

NORTHERN SHRIKE Larger; paler head and back; narrower mask does not meet above bill; larger, more deeply hooked bill, often pale at base of lower mandible; barred underparts; bobs tail • juvenile much browner in color.

NORTHERN MOCKINGBIRD Longer thinner straighter bill; lighter wings with larger white patches; paler tail with more extensive white in outer feathers; head proportionally smaller.

Flight Pattern
Rapid flight on rapidly beating wings with brief periods of wings pulled to sides. Often flies low across the ground.

Nest Identification	
Shape 🐦 Location 🌳 🌿 🌲	Twigs lined with grasses, string, feathers, and hair • in bush or tree, 2.5–4.5 m above ground (but as high as 15 m) • built by female or sometimes both sexes • 4–7 white to grayish buff eggs, marked with grays, browns, or blacks, often concentrated near large end; oval to long oval, 2.5 x 1.9 cm.

Plumage Sexes similar	Habitat	Migration Migratory	Weight 48 g

DATE _____ TIME_____ LOCATION _____

Family LANIIDAE	Species *Lanius excubitor*	Length 23–25 cm	Wingspan 34–42 cm

NORTHERN SHRIKE

Perched high in the treetops, this robin-sized bird acts as a sentry, often uttering loud warning calls to other birds as it scans the landscape for prey. The larger and more northerly distributed of the two shrikes that nest and breed in North America, it is aggressive and will attack Blue Jays or other birds larger than itself, especially in defending its caches. Irruptive movements south in the winter seem to be correlated with the availability of prey species, especially small mammals. In flight the white wing patches, white rump, and white outer tail feathers contrast against the black wings and tail. The female is similar to the male but duller and sometimes more brown. Young birds are browner than adults and have heavier barring on their underparts.

white feathering above bill
black eye patch
pale gray upperparts and head
large hooked bill, often with pale base to lower mandible
whitish underparts with faint barring

FIRST WINTER

JUVENILE

- **SONG** Sings a low disjointed jerky thrasherlike song of clear notes and phrases, some musical, interspersed with grating shrieks. Call is a *shak-shak*. Also imitates calls of other birds.
- **BEHAVIOR** Solitary. Pairs in breeding season. Hunts in daytime. Perches in prominent lookout to spot prey; catches prey with beak, stuns it, and often impales it on sharp thorns or branches until ready to eat. Caches food for later use in this manner. Feeds on small mammals, mostly rodents, small birds, and insects. Aggressive in pursuit of prey. White in tail and white wing patches flash in flight.
- **BREEDING** Monogamous. Solitary nester.
- **NESTING** Incubation 15–16 days by female. Young altricial; brooded by female; stay in nest 20 days, fed by both sexes. First flight at about 20 days, but fed by both sexes for 10 more days or longer. 1 brood per year.
- **POPULATION** Uncommon in taiga (boreal forest) in clearings, open areas, and edges.
- **FEEDERS** Raw hamburger, suet. Also hunts feeder visitors.

Similar Birds

LOGGERHEAD SHRIKE Smaller; darker head and back; gray to white rump; wider mask extending above eye and across bill; smaller and less strongly hooked black bill; gray underparts with very faint or no barring • juveniles are gray-brown and lightly barred.

Flight Pattern

Swift undulating flight on shallow rapid wing beats, often low to the ground.

Nest Identification

Shape ☕   Location 🌳 🌿

Sticks lined with feathers, hair, and fine materials • in tree or shrub, 3.5–6 m above ground • built by both sexes • 4–9 grayish or greenish white eggs, heavily blotched with olive, brown, and lavender; oval to long oval, 2.8 x 2.0 cm.

Plumage Sexes similar	Habitat 🌾 🏚 🌲 ⛰	Migration Migratory	Weight 65 g

DATE _____ TIME_____ LOCATION _____

| Family VIREONIDAE | Species *Vireo griseus* | Length 13 cm | Wingspan 20 cm |

WHITE-EYED VIREO

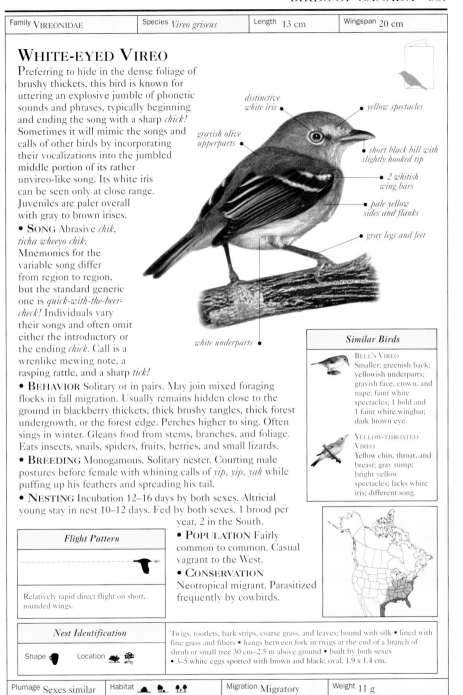

Preferring to hide in the dense foliage of brushy thickets, this bird is known for uttering an explosive jumble of phonetic sounds and phrases, typically beginning and ending the song with a sharp *chick!* Sometimes it will mimic the songs and calls of other birds by incorporating their vocalizations into the jumbled middle portion of its rather unvireo-like song. Its white iris can be seen only at close range. Juveniles are paler overall with gray to brown irises.

distinctive white iris

yellow spectacles

grayish olive upperparts

short black bill with slightly hooked tip

2 whitish wing bars

pale yellow sides and flanks

gray legs and feet

white underparts

• **SONG** Abrasive *chik, ticha wheeyo chik.* Mnemonics for the variable song differ from region to region, but the standard generic one is *quick-with-the-beer-check!* Individuals vary their songs and often omit either the introductory or the ending *chick.* Call is a wrenlike mewing note, a rasping rattle, and a sharp *tick!*

• **BEHAVIOR** Solitary or in pairs. May join mixed foraging flocks in fall migration. Usually remains hidden close to the ground in blackberry thickets, thick brushy tangles, thick forest undergrowth, or the forest edge. Perches higher to sing. Often sings in winter. Gleans food from stems, branches, and foliage. Eats insects, snails, spiders, fruits, berries, and small lizards.

• **BREEDING** Monogamous. Solitary nester. Courting male postures before female with whining calls of *yip, yip, yah* while puffing up his feathers and spreading his tail.

• **NESTING** Incubation 12–16 days by both sexes. Altricial young stay in nest 10–12 days. Fed by both sexes. 1 brood per year, 2 in the South.

• **POPULATION** Fairly common to common. Casual vagrant to the West.

• **CONSERVATION** Neotropical migrant. Parasitized frequently by cowbirds.

Similar Birds

BELL'S VIREO Smaller; greenish back; yellowish underparts; grayish face, crown, and nape; faint white spectacles; 1 bold and 1 faint white wingbar; dark brown eye.

YELLOW-THROATED VIREO Yellow chin, throat, and breast; gray rump; bright yellow spectacles; lacks white iris; different song.

Flight Pattern
Relatively rapid direct flight on short, rounded wings.

Nest Identification	
Shape	Location	Twigs, rootlets, bark strips, coarse grass, and leaves; bound with silk • lined with fine grass and fibers • hangs between fork in twigs at the end of a branch of shrub or small tree 30 cm–2.5 m above ground • built by both sexes • 3–5 white eggs spotted with brown and black; oval, 1.9 x 1.4 cm.

| Plumage Sexes similar | Habitat | Migration Migratory | Weight 11 g |

DATE _____ TIME_____ LOCATION _____

Family VIREONIDAE	Species *Vireo bellii*	Length 12 cm	Wingspan 18–20 cm

BELL'S VIREO

This small plain bird is the western counterpart of the White-eyed Vireo. It is a frequent victim of the Brown-headed Cowbird, which often lays eggs in its nest – the vireo often responds by building a new floor in the nest, covering the cowbird's eggs and its own. Although these birds actively forage during the day they are most often detected by their frequent singing. Overall plumage varies across its range, from the eastern and midwestern birds, which have greenish upperparts and yellowish underparts, to the West Coast race, which has gray upperparts and whitish underparts.

very faint white spectacles

greenish to grayish back

grayish crown, face, and nape

2 (sometimes only 1) faint white bars on each wing

blackish bill, slightly flattened with hooked tip

gray legs and feet

white to yellowish underparts

- **SONG** Male sings husky rapid jumble of question-and-answer-sounding phrases such as *cheadle cheadle chee? cheadle cheadle chew*! Often a phrase with rising inflection, followed by one that ends with a descending note. An active singer, may sing 8–17 songs a minute. Incubating males may sometimes sing from the nest. Call notes are harsh and scolding.
- **BEHAVIOR** Secretive and active. Often pumps tail. Sings often, revealing its presence in the thickets (particularly riparian), hedgerows, and scrub that it frequents. Eats variety of insects gleaned from the stems, branches, and foliage; also some fruits and berries. Courting male actively chases female, spreading tail, fluttering wings, and constantly singing.
- **BREEDING** Monogamous. Solitary.
- **NESTING** Incubation 14 days by both sexes. Young altricial; stay in nest 11–12 days, fed by both sexes. 2 broods per year.
- **POPULATION** Uncommon; declining in some regions. Some western riparian populations endangered.
- **CONSERVATION** Declining in Midwest and California from habitat loss, especially riparian habitat in arid and semiarid landscapes; frequent cowbird parasitism. Neotropical migrant.

Similar Birds

GRAY VIREO
Larger; gray overall; paler underparts; 1 or 2 faint wing bars; distinct eye ring; different song.

WHITE-EYED VIREO
Juvenile • dark eyes; grayish olive upperparts; whitish underparts with wash of yellow on sides and flanks; yellow spectacles; 2 white wing bars; voice differs.

Flight Pattern
Relatively rapid direct flight with shallow wing beats.

Nest Identification	
Shape ◖ Location 🌿 🐦	Dry leaves, shredded bark, plant fibers, and spider cocoons, lined with fine grass, down, and hair • hung from fork in tree or shrub or suspended by rim between two limbs • 30 cm–1.5 m above ground • built by both sexes • 3–5 white eggs, usually dotted with black or brown; oval, 1.8 x 1.3 cm.

Plumage Sexes similar	Habitat	Migration Migratory	Weight 9.0 g

DATE _____ TIME_____ LOCATION _____

Family VIREONIDAE	Species *Vireo flavifrons*	Length 14 cm	Wingspan 24 cm

YELLOW-THROATED VIREO

Considered the most brilliantly colored vireo, this bird
is most often observed in deciduous forests. Its
characteristic song is a series of short phrases similar in
pattern to several other vireos in its range but with
long pauses between phrases and a coarse quality.

• **SONG** Burry series of 2-note or sometimes
3-note phrases with hesitantly long pauses
between them sounding like *three-EIGHT,
three-EIGHT . . . three-EIGHT*, repeated
with the pattern and quality of a
Blue-headed Vireo with a
sore throat. Calls harsh,
nasal, accelerating,
rapid series of *cheh,
cheh, cheh* notes.

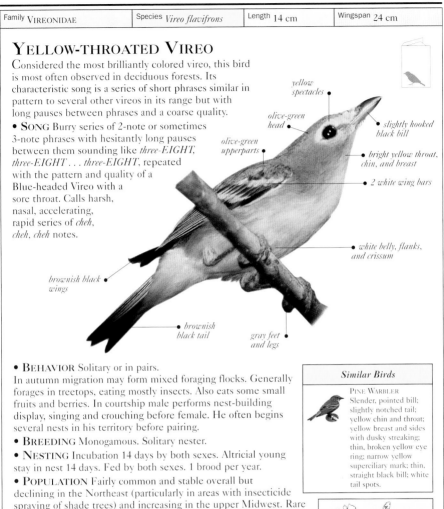

yellow
spectacles

olive-green
head

olive-green
upperparts

slightly hooked
black bill

bright yellow throat,
chin, and breast

2 white wing bars

white belly, flanks,
and crissum

brownish black
wings

brownish
black tail

gray feet
and legs

• **BEHAVIOR** Solitary or in pairs.
In autumn migration may form mixed foraging flocks. Generally
forages in treetops, eating mostly insects. Also eats some small
fruits and berries. In courtship male performs nest-building
display, singing and crouching before female. He often begins
several nests in his territory before pairing.

• **BREEDING** Monogamous. Solitary nester.

• **NESTING** Incubation 14 days by both sexes. Altricial young
stay in nest 14 days. Fed by both sexes. 1 brood per year.

• **POPULATION** Fairly common and stable overall but
declining in the Northeast (particularly in areas with insecticide
spraying of shade trees) and increasing in the upper Midwest. Rare
vagrant in the West; casual in
winter in south Florida.

• **CONSERVATION** Neotropical
migrant. Common brood
parasite host for Brown-headed
Cowbird; sometimes builds
second floor to cover its own
eggs as well as cowbird's.

Similar Birds

PINE WARBLER
Slender, pointed bill;
slightly notched tail;
yellow chin and throat;
yellow breast and sides
with dusky streaking;
thin, broken yellow eye
ring; narrow yellow
superciliary mark; thin,
straight black bill; white
tail spots.

Flight Pattern
Relatively weak fluttering direct flight with rapid wing beats.

Nest Identification	
Shape	Location

Grass covered with lichens • lined with grass, shredded bark, spider webs, and
cocoons • in deciduous trees 90 cm–18.5 m above ground • built by both sexes
• 3–5 white to pinkish white eggs with brown spots, especially near large end;
oval, 1.8 x 1.3 cm.

Plumage Sexes similar	Habitat	Migration Migratory	Weight 17 g

DATE _____ TIME_____ LOCATION _____

Family VIREONIDAE	Species *Vireo cassinii*	Length 13 cm	Wingspan 22 cm

CASSIN'S VIREO

Until the 1990s this bird and the Blue-headed and Plumbeous Vireos were classified as one species – the Solitary Vireo. Although similar to the Blue-headed Vireo, Cassin's differs in range and is duller in color with less white edging on flight feathers and tail. The male catches the female's attention by fluffing out

olive-washed grayish head

grayish olive to olive upperparts

blackish brown wings with grayish olive trim on secondaries

dusky lores break ring of white spectacles

blackish bill

grayish white throat and underparts

2 thick white to pale yellow wing bars and narrow tertial edgings

blackish brown tail with white-trimmed outer feathers and olive-trimmed central feathers

lemon feathers on flanks

olive wash on sides

blue-gray legs and feet

his bright yellow flank feathers and bowing up and down to her. Juvenile Cassin's females sometimes have greenish heads.

• **SONG** A mixed jumble of hesitant phrases, punctuated by short deliberate pauses, such as *chreu ... ch'ree ... choo'reet* or *ch-ree ... ch-ri'chi-roo*, often repeated.

• **BEHAVIOR** Solitary or in pairs. Forages high in trees by gleaning food from bark, branches, or foliage; sometimes hovers briefly to pick food off vegetation or catch insects in flight. Eats insects, larvae, and various fruits. Frequents open coniferous, coniferous-deciduous, pine-oak, or oak woodlands. Male performs nest-building display for female with no nesting material in mouth. Fairly tame on nest, allowing close approach.

• **BREEDING** Monogamous. Solitary.

• **NESTING** Incubation 11–12 days by both sexes, but female does more. Young altricial; stay in nest 12–14 days, fed by both sexes. 1–2 broods per year.

• **POPULATION** Fairly common. Casual in winter in northwest California. Accidental in southeast Alaska, Oklahoma, New York, and New Jersey.

• **CONSERVATION** Neotropical migrant. Vulnerable to habitat loss due to logging.

Similar Birds

PLUMBEOUS VIREO
Slightly larger; thicker bill; gray head and upperparts; more contrast between white throat and head and sides of breast; grayish sides and flanks with grayish streaking and without strong yellow wash.

HUTTON'S VIREO
Smaller; white eye ring breaks above eye; pale lores; grayish olive upperparts; different voice • only in the West.

Flight Pattern

Somewhat weak fluttering direct flight on rapidly beating wings. May hover briefly to pick insect or fruit off vegetation.

Nest Identification

Shape   Location

Twigs, fine grasses, and stems, lined with finer grasses and hair • in fork of twig of tree or bush or set in middle of conifer, 1–9 m above ground • built by both sexes • 3–5 white to creamy white eggs, with black and brown speckles; oval, 1.8 x 1.3 cm.

Plumage Sexes similar	Habitat	Migration Migratory	Weight Undetermined

DATE _____ TIME_____ LOCATION _____

Family VIREONIDAE	Species *Vireo solitarius*	Length 13 cm	Wingspan 22 cm

BLUE-HEADED VIREO

This bird makes its home in the thick coniferous and mixed coniferous-deciduous forests of Canada and the eastern United States, where it breeds southward through the southern Appalachians. The Appalachian race is larger, with a bluish gray back and the

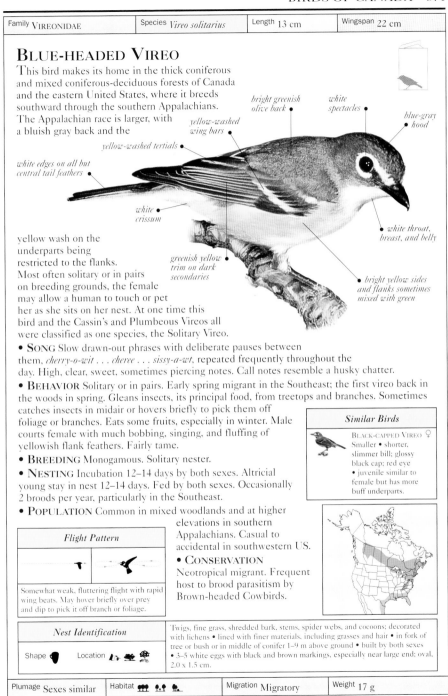

bright greenish olive back

white spectacles

blue-gray hood

yellow-washed wing bars

yellow-washed tertials

white edges on all but central tail feathers

white crissum

white throat, breast, and belly

greenish yellow trim on dark secondaries

bright yellow sides and flanks sometimes mixed with green

yellow wash on the underparts being restricted to the flanks. Most often solitary or in pairs on breeding grounds, the female may allow a human to touch or pet her as she sits on her nest. At one time this bird and the Cassin's and Plumbeous Vireos all were classified as one species, the Solitary Vireo.

• **SONG** Slow drawn-out phrases with deliberate pauses between them, *cherry-o-wit . . . cheree . . . sissy-a-wt*, repeated frequently throughout the day. High, clear, sweet, sometimes piercing notes. Call notes resemble a husky chatter.

• **BEHAVIOR** Solitary or in pairs. Early spring migrant in the Southeast; the first vireo back in the woods in spring. Gleans insects, its principal food, from treetops and branches. Sometimes catches insects in midair or hovers briefly to pick them off foliage or branches. Eats some fruits, especially in winter. Male courts female with much bobbing, singing, and fluffing of yellowish flank feathers. Fairly tame.

• **BREEDING** Monogamous. Solitary nester.

• **NESTING** Incubation 12–14 days by both sexes. Altricial young stay in nest 12–14 days. Fed by both sexes. Occasionally 2 broods per year, particularly in the Southeast.

• **POPULATION** Common in mixed woodlands and at higher elevations in southern Appalachians. Casual to accidental in southwestern US.

• **CONSERVATION** Neotropical migrant. Frequent host to brood parasitism by Brown-headed Cowbirds.

Similar Birds

BLACK-CAPPED VIREO ♀ Smaller • shorter, slimmer bill; glossy black cap; red eye • juvenile similar to female but has more buff underparts.

Flight Pattern

Somewhat weak, fluttering flight with rapid wing beats. May hover briefly over prey and dip to pick it off branch or foliage.

Nest Identification

Shape | Location

Twigs, fine grass, shredded bark, stems, spider webs, and cocoons; decorated with lichens • lined with finer materials, including grasses and hair • in fork of tree or bush or in middle of conifer 1–9 m above ground • built by both sexes • 3–5 white eggs with black and brown markings, especially near large end; oval, 2.0 x 1.5 cm.

Plumage Sexes similar	Habitat	Migration Migratory	Weight 17 g

DATE _____ TIME_____ LOCATION _____

Family VIREONIDAE	Species *Vireo huttoni*	Length 12–13 cm	Wingspan 18–20 cm

HUTTON'S VIREO

This small, kingletlike vireo actively forages high in the treetops, where it can be easily overlooked save for its very vocal nature. It may rapidly repeat the same song hundreds of times within a short period. Its olive-tinged plumage serves as a camouflage in the southwestern mountains and Pacific coastal woodlands where this bird makes its home. The West Coast race has greener upperparts than the interior southwestern race, which has grayer plumage.

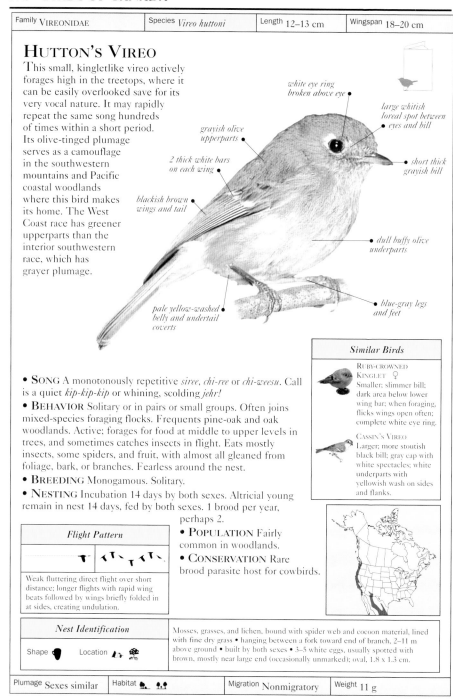

white eye ring broken above eye

large whitish loreal spot between eyes and bill

grayish olive upperparts

short thick grayish bill

2 thick white bars on each wing

blackish brown wings and tail

dull buffy olive underparts

pale yellow-washed belly and undertail coverts

blue-gray legs and feet

Similar Birds

RUBY-CROWNED KINGLET ♀
Smaller; slimmer bill; dark area below lower wing bar; when foraging, flicks wings open often; complete white eye ring.

CASSIN'S VIREO
Larger; more stoutish black bill; gray cap with white spectacles; white underparts with yellowish wash on sides and flanks.

• **SONG** A monotonously repetitive *siree, chi-ree* or *chi-weesu*. Call is a quiet *kip-kip-kip* or whining, scolding *jehr!*
• **BEHAVIOR** Solitary or in pairs or small groups. Often joins mixed-species foraging flocks. Frequents pine-oak and oak woodlands. Active; forages for food at middle to upper levels in trees, and sometimes catches insects in flight. Eats mostly insects, some spiders, and fruit, with almost all gleaned from foliage, bark, or branches. Fearless around the nest.
• **BREEDING** Monogamous. Solitary.
• **NESTING** Incubation 14 days by both sexes. Altricial young remain in nest 14 days, fed by both sexes. 1 brood per year, perhaps 2.
• **POPULATION** Fairly common in woodlands.
• **CONSERVATION** Rare brood parasite host for cowbirds.

Flight Pattern

Weak fluttering direct flight over short distance; longer flights with rapid wing beats followed by wings briefly folded in at sides, creating undulation.

Nest Identification

Shape ● Location ↟ ✿

Mosses, grasses, and lichen, bound with spider web and cocoon material, lined with fine dry grass • hanging between a fork toward end of branch, 2–11 m above ground • built by both sexes • 3–5 white eggs, usually spotted with brown, mostly near large end (occasionally unmarked); oval, 1.8 x 1.3 cm.

Plumage Sexes similar	Habitat 🌲 🌿	Migration Nonmigratory	Weight 11 g

DATE _____ TIME_____ LOCATION _____

Family VIREONIDAE	Species *Vireo gilvus*	Length 13–14 cm	Wingspan 22 cm

WARBLING VIREO

Wintering in Mexico and Central America, this bird has the largest breeding range of any vireo in the woodlands of North America. Although common over most of its range, it is not well known by many people other

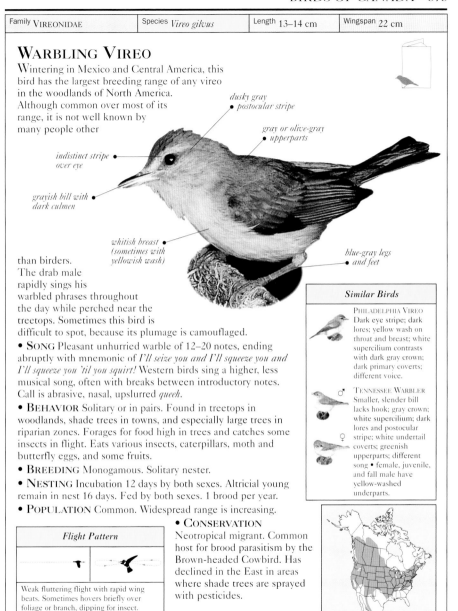

dusky gray postocular stripe

gray or olive-gray upperparts

indistinct stripe over eye

grayish bill with dark culmen

whitish breast (sometimes with yellowish wash)

blue-gray legs and feet

than birders. The drab male rapidly sings his warbled phrases throughout the day while perched near the treetops. Sometimes this bird is difficult to spot, because its plumage is camouflaged.

• **SONG** Pleasant unhurried warble of 12–20 notes, ending abruptly with mnemonic of *I'll seize you and I'll squeeze you and I'll squeeze you 'til you squirt!* Western birds sing a higher, less musical song, often with breaks between introductory notes. Call is abrasive, nasal, upslurred *queeh.*

• **BEHAVIOR** Solitary or in pairs. Found in treetops in woodlands, shade trees in towns, and especially large trees in riparian zones. Forages for food high in trees and catches some insects in flight. Eats various insects, caterpillars, moth and butterfly eggs, and some fruits.

• **BREEDING** Monogamous. Solitary nester.

• **NESTING** Incubation 12 days by both sexes. Altricial young remain in nest 16 days. Fed by both sexes. 1 brood per year.

• **POPULATION** Common. Widespread range is increasing.

• **CONSERVATION** Neotropical migrant. Common host for brood parasitism by the Brown-headed Cowbird. Has declined in the East in areas where shade trees are sprayed with pesticides.

Similar Birds

PHILADELPHIA VIREO
Dark eye stripe; dark lores; yellow wash on throat and breast; white supercilium contrasts with dark gray crown; dark primary coverts; different voice.

TENNESSEE WARBLER
Smaller, slender bill lacks hook; gray crown; white supercilium; dark lores and postocular stripe; white undertail coverts; greenish upperparts; different song • female, juvenile, and fall male have yellow-washed underparts.

Flight Pattern

Weak fluttering flight with rapid wing beats. Sometimes hovers briefly over foliage or branch, dipping for insect.

Nest Identification

Shape 🔻   Location 🌿🌳

Bark strips, leaves, vegetation fibers, and grass • hangs between fork toward end of branch, twig, or sometimes shrub, usually 1–4.5 m above ground • built by both sexes • 3–5 white eggs spotted with brown and black; oval, 2.0 x 1.3 cm.

Plumage Sexes similar	Habitat 🌾 🌳 〰 🌿	Migration Migratory	Weight 14 g

DATE _____ TIME_____ LOCATION _____

| Family VIREONIDAE | Species *Vireo philadelphicus* | Length 12–13 cm | Wingspan 20–23 cm |

PHILADELPHIA VIREO

First discovered near Philadelphia in the 1840s, this quiet bird is the least known of the East Coast vireos. A late spring migrant, it is easily overlooked in the company of warblers, with which it often travels. Furthermore, it seldom sings in migration, a characteristic that serves to draw even less attention to it. Superficially similar to the Red-eyed Vireo in appearance and voice,

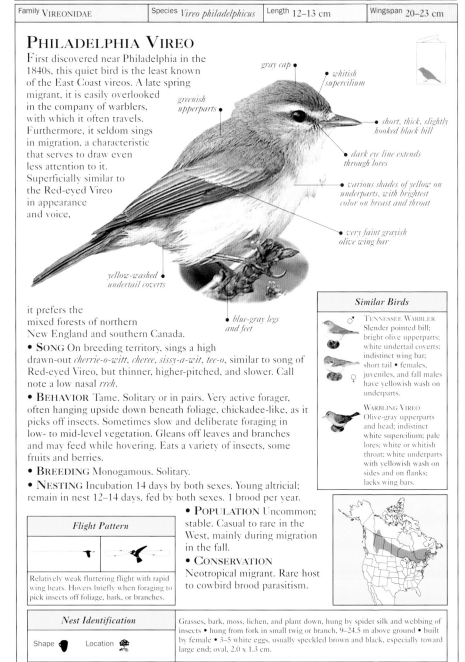

gray cap

whitish supercilium

greenish upperparts

short, thick, slightly hooked black bill

dark eye line extends through lores

various shades of yellow on underparts, with brightest color on breast and throat

very faint grayish olive wing bar

yellow-washed undertail coverts

blue-gray legs and feet

it prefers the mixed forests of northern New England and southern Canada.

• **SONG** On breeding territory, sings a high drawn-out *cherrie-o-witt, cheree, sissy-a-wit, tee-o*, similar to song of Red-eyed Vireo, but thinner, higher-pitched, and slower. Call note a low nasal *rreh*.

• **BEHAVIOR** Tame. Solitary or in pairs. Very active forager, often hanging upside down beneath foliage, chickadee-like, as it picks off insects. Sometimes slow and deliberate foraging in low- to mid-level vegetation. Gleans off leaves and branches and may feed while hovering. Eats a variety of insects, some fruits and berries.

• **BREEDING** Monogamous. Solitary.

• **NESTING** Incubation 14 days by both sexes. Young altricial; remain in nest 12–14 days, fed by both sexes. 1 brood per year.

• **POPULATION** Uncommon; stable. Casual to rare in the West, mainly during migration in the fall.

• **CONSERVATION** Neotropical migrant. Rare host to cowbird brood parasitism.

Similar Birds

TENNESSEE WARBLER ♂
Slender pointed bill; bright olive upperparts; white undertail coverts; indistinct white wing bar; short tail • females, juveniles, and fall males have yellowish wash on underparts. ♀

WARBLING VIREO
Olive-gray upperparts and head; indistinct white supercilium; pale lores; white or whitish throat; white underparts with yellowish wash on sides and on flanks; lacks wing bars.

Flight Pattern

Relatively weak fluttering flight with rapid wing beats. Hovers briefly when foraging to pick insects off foliage, bark, or branches.

Nest Identification

Shape 〇 Location 🪹

Grasses, bark, moss, lichen, and plant down, hung by spider silk and webbing of insects • hung from fork in small twig or branch, 9–24.5 m above ground • built by female • 3–5 white eggs, usually speckled brown and black, especially toward large end; oval, 2.0 x 1.3 cm.

| Plumage Sexes similar | Habitat 🌾🐛 🦆 🌲 | Migration Migratory | Weight 11 g |

DATE _____ TIME_____ LOCATION _____

Family VIREONIDAE	Species *Vireo olivaceus*	Length 15 cm	Wingspan 25 cm

RED-EYED VIREO

One of the most abundant in North American deciduous forests, this bird sings almost nonstop from dawn to dusk and often all night. It delivers its brief trilled phrases as it sits on the nest, forages for food, even as it swallows insects. A researcher once totaled the number of song repetitions uttered by an individual in one summer day as a remarkable 22,197 songs. These "sermons" have lent it the handle of "preacher bird." The black-bordered white eyebrow stripe distinguishes this bird from other vireos. The red iris is not visible at a distance; juveniles have a brown iris. Juveniles and autumn birds may have a yellowish wash on the flanks.

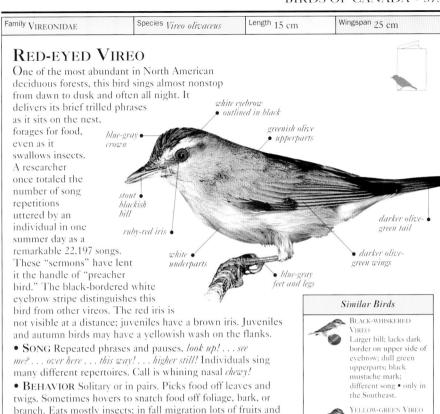

white eyebrow outlined in black
greenish olive upperparts
blue-gray crown
stout blackish bill
ruby-red iris
white underparts
darker olive-green tail
darker olive-green wings
blue-gray feet and legs

• **SONG** Repeated phrases and pauses, *look up! . . . see me? . . . over here . . . this way! . . . higher still!* Individuals sing many different repertoires. Call is whining nasal *chewy!*

• **BEHAVIOR** Solitary or in pairs. Picks food off leaves and twigs. Sometimes hovers to snatch food off foliage, bark, or branch. Eats mostly insects; in fall migration lots of fruits and berries. Defensive at nest. Responds readily to pishing and squeaking noises. In migration often joins mixed feeding flocks.

• **BREEDING** Monogamous. Solitary nester.

• **NESTING** Incubation 11–14 days by female. Altricial young stay in nest 10–12 days. Fed by both sexes. 1–2 broods per year.

• **POPULATION** Common in eastern woodlands. Some decline due to clearing of forests in the East. Rare vagrant in migration in the Southwest and on the Pacific Coast.

• **CONSERVATION** Neotropical migrant. Frequent cowbird brood parasitism. Vulnerable to poisoning by ingesting insects sprayed with pesticides and Gypsy Moth control programs.

Similar Birds

BLACK-WHISKERED VIREO
Larger bill; lacks dark border on upper side of eyebrow; dull green upperparts; black mustache mark; different song • only in the Southeast.

YELLOW-GREEN VIREO
Olive-green upperparts; whitish throat and underparts; bright yellow sides, flanks, and undertail coverts; pale gray or whitish supercilium; gray crown; pale olive auriculars; dusky lores; red eyes.

Flight Pattern

Alternates series of rapid wing beats with short glides within forest. Also hovers briefly to pick insects or berries off foliage.

Nest Identification

Shape | Location

Grapevine bark, fine grasses, rootlets, paper from wasp nests, lichens, spider webs, and cocoons • hanging on fork of tree branch or shrub 60 cm–18.5 m above ground • built by both sexes, but mostly by female • 3–5 white eggs, most often with fine brown and black dots, especially toward large end; oval, 2.0 x 1.4 cm.

Plumage Sexes similar	Habitat	Migration Migratory	Weight 17 g

DATE _____ TIME_____ LOCATION _____

Family CORVIDAE	Species *Perisoreus canadensis*	Length 29 cm	Wingspan 41–43 cm

GRAY JAY

Sometimes called the "camp robber," the Gray Jay is known for its bold behavior. Often observed at cabins and campsites, it will steal food and nonedible items. With its large salivary glands, it secretes mucous that allows it to store food by sticking it on twigs, pine needles, and tree branches. Several geographical races exist across its coast-to-coast range. These races vary most noticeably in the extent of the dark patch on the nape and crown, from almost none in the Rocky Mountain races to extensive patches in the races inhabiting the northwest coast. Juveniles are entirely sooty gray with a whitish mustache. Although nonmigratory, birds practice some altitudinal migration in winter.

black head patch

pale gray head

dark smoky gray upperparts

short black bill

white throat

gray breast

gray underparts range from pale to dark depending on race

dark smoky gray wings and tail

black legs and feet

• **SONG** Has a large repertoire of calls, including a fluted *wheeoo* and a low *chuck*. Calls also include a bold hawklike whistle, as well as a *cla-cla-cla-cla-cla*. Sometimes mimics hawk cries and songs sung by small birds.

JUVENILE

• **BEHAVIOR** Tame, bold, and curious. Caches food. Omnivorous. Eats mice, eggs, and young of other birds. Takes a variety of insects, carrion, camp food, seeds, nuts, and berries. Shows no fear of humans and comes close to snatch food and other objects. Males engage in courtship feeding of females.

• **BREEDING** Monogamous. Small colonies.

• **NESTING** Incubation 16–18 days by female. Young altricial; stay in nest 15–21 days, fed by both sexes. 1 brood per year.

• **POPULATION** Common to fairly common in conifer and mixed-conifer forests. Declining in some areas due to timber harvesting. Casual in winter in midwestern and northeastern states just south of breeding range.

Similar Birds

CLARK'S NUTCRACKER Chunky; medium gray upperparts and underparts; short white tail with black central feathers; black wings with white secondaries creating patch on inner wing in flight; entirely gray head; white eye ring; long black bill.

• **FEEDERS** Will attend feeders with corn, suet, and sunflower seeds.

• **CONSERVATION** Vulnerable to habitat loss from logging operations as well as forest fragmentation.

Flight Pattern
Light buoyant flight on steady wing beats; often glides between perches within or between trees and from perch to ground.

Nest Identification	Lined with moss, grass, sticks, bark, feathers, and fur, fastened together with spider webs and insect cocoons • on horizontal branch near trunk or in crotch of tree, 1–9 m above ground but can be up to 26 m • built by both sexes • 2–5 grayish white, pale green, pale gray, sometimes white eggs, with fine olive-buff, brown, or gray spots; oval, 3.0 x 2.0 cm.
Shape 🥄 Location 🌿 🌲	

Plumage Sexes similar	Habitat 🌳 🌲 🌿 〜〜	Migration Nonmigratory	Weight 74 g

Family CORVIDAE	Species *Cyanocitta stelleri*	Length 29 cm	Wingspan 43 cm

STELLER'S JAY

Recognized as the only crested jay in the West, Steller's Jay is named after Arctic explorer Georg Wilhelm Steller, who discovered this bird on the Alaska coast in 1741. In 1987, it was designated the provincial bird of British Columbia. The darkest jay in North America, it has a black head and crest and a sooty black back and breast. The extent of black on the body is variable among local populations, as is the amount of blue or white striping on the head or throat.

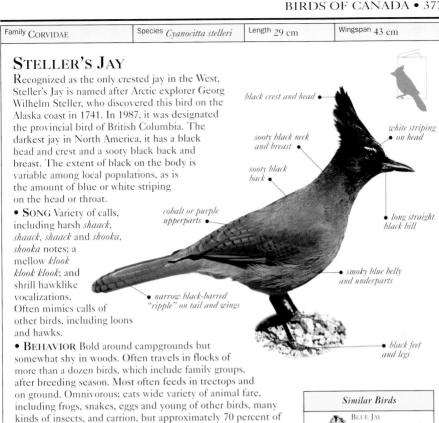

black crest and head

white striping on head

sooty black neck and breast

sooty black back

long straight black bill

cobalt or purple upperparts

smoky blue belly and underparts

narrow black-barred "ripple" on tail and wings

black feet and legs

• **SONG** Variety of calls, including harsh *shaack, shaack, shaack* and *shooka, shooka* notes; a mellow *klook klook klook*; and shrill hawklike vocalizations. Often mimics calls of other birds, including loons and hawks.

• **BEHAVIOR** Bold around campgrounds but somewhat shy in woods. Often travels in flocks of more than a dozen birds, which include family groups, after breeding season. Most often feeds in treetops and on ground. Omnivorous; eats wide variety of animal fare, including frogs, snakes, eggs and young of other birds, many kinds of insects, and carrion, but approximately 70 percent of annual diet (90–99 percent in winter) consists of pine seeds, acorns, and fruit. Caches seeds and acorns for winter larder.

• **BREEDING** This species is known to be monogamous and a solitary nester. Courtship feeding is done by the male Steller's Jay.

• **NESTING** Incubation 16–18 days mostly by female. Altricial young remain in nest 17–21 days. Fed by both sexes. 1 brood per year.

• **POPULATION** Steller's Jay is common in pine-oak and coniferous woodlands. Its population is both stable and increasing. Casual at lower elevations during the winter season. Accidental in the East.

• **FEEDERS** In winter family groups often frequent feeders.

Similar Birds

BLUE JAY
Purple-gray crest and back; grayish white underparts; black collar extends around body from breast to nape; white spots, bars, and patches in wings and tail; blue wings and tail with fine black barring.

Flight Pattern

Direct flight with steady buoyant wing beats. Often glides between perches in or among trees, or from tree to ground.

Nest Identification

Shape ⬤   Location 🐦 🌿

Cemented with mud • includes pine needles, twigs, dry leaves, roots, and grass • on horizontal limb near trunk or in crotch of conifer; occasionally in deciduous tree; 2.5–30.5 m above ground • built by both sexes • 2–6, but most often 4, pale greenish blue or bluish green eggs with brown markings; subelliptical to short subelliptical, 3.0 x 2.3 cm.

Plumage Sexes similar	Habitat 🐾 🌾 🍂 ⛰	Migration Nonmigratory	Weight 128 g

DATE _____ TIME_____ LOCATION _____

| Family CORVIDAE | Species *Cyanocitta cristata* | Length 28 cm | Wingspan 41 cm |

BLUE JAY

Once considered primarily a forest dweller, the Blue Jay has adapted to cities, parks, gardens, and forest fragmentation. Some populations remain in locales year-round, while more northern ones migrate south in flocks of 50–100. Common despite clear-cutting in eastern forests, its range is expanding northwest. It is easily recognized by its large size; blue-purple upperparts, wings, and tail; and jaunty bluish purple crest. It was voted the official bird of Prince Edward Island in 1976.

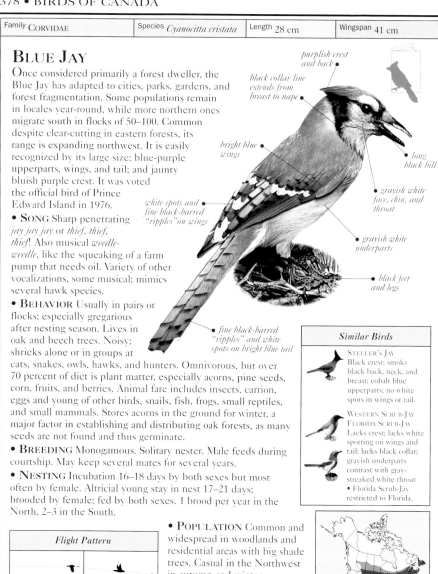

purplish crest and back

black collar line extends from breast to nape

bright blue wings

long black bill

grayish white face, chin, and throat

white spots and fine black-barred "ripples" on wings

grayish white underparts

black feet and legs

fine black-barred "ripples" and white spots on bright blue tail

• **SONG** Sharp penetrating *jay jay jay* or *thief, thief, thief*! Also musical *weedle-weedle*, like the squeaking of a farm pump that needs oil. Variety of other vocalizations, some musical; mimics several hawk species.

• **BEHAVIOR** Usually in pairs or flocks; especially gregarious after nesting season. Lives in oak and beech trees. Noisy; shrieks alone or in groups at cats, snakes, owls, hawks, and hunters. Omnivorous, but over 70 percent of diet is plant matter, especially acorns, pine seeds, corn, fruits, and berries. Animal fare includes insects, carrion, eggs and young of other birds, snails, fish, frogs, small reptiles, and small mammals. Stores acorns in the ground for winter, a major factor in establishing and distributing oak forests, as many seeds are not found and thus germinate.

• **BREEDING** Monogamous. Solitary nester. Male feeds during courtship. May keep several mates for several years.

• **NESTING** Incubation 16–18 days by both sexes but most often by female. Altricial young stay in nest 17–21 days; brooded by female; fed by both sexes. 1 brood per year in the North, 2–3 in the South.

Similar Birds

STELLER'S JAY
Black crest; smoky black back, neck, and breast; cobalt blue upperparts; no white spots in wings or tail.

WESTERN SCRUB-JAY
FLORIDA SCRUB-JAY
Lacks crest; lacks white spotting on wings and tail; lacks black collar; grayish underparts contrast with gray-streaked white throat • Florida Scrub-Jay restricted to Florida.

• **POPULATION** Common and widespread in woodlands and residential areas with big shade trees. Casual in the Northwest in autumn and winter.

• **FEEDERS** Suet, sunflower seeds, peanuts, cracked nuts; birdbaths.

Flight Pattern

Direct flight with steady, buoyant wing beats. Often glides between perches within or between trees, or to ground.

Nest Identification

Shape ◣ Location 🌳 🌿 🌳

Twigs, bark, moss, lichens, grass, and sometimes paper and string • built by both sexes • on horizontal branch near trunk or in crotch or vines 1.5–6 m above ground; sometimes up to 15 m • 3–7 pale greenish blue or bluish green eggs with dark brown markings; subelliptical, 2.8 x 2.2 cm.

| Plumage Sexes similar | Habitat 🌳 🌿 🍂 | Migration Migratory | Weight 85 g |

Family CORVIDAE	Species *Nucifraga columbiana*	Length 32 cm	Wingspan 46 cm

CLARK'S NUTCRACKER

Far from shy, this fearless bird can be seen chasing coyotes, barging into tents of campers, or flying toward the sound of an imitation owl call. It is named after Captain William Clark of the Lewis and Clark expedition. An avid forager, this bird gathers and stores its surplus pine nuts and seeds in caches in the ground by tens of thousands per year. They become its principal food from late winter to early summer, and those that germinate become important for the distribution of conifers. In flight the white tail with black central tail feathers and white secondary patch on the black wings contrast with the pale gray body. It resides in coniferous forests in the mountains between 915–3,960 meters near the timberline.

long black bill

stocky pale gray body

black wings with white secondaries forming patch on back of inner wing

white tail with black central tail feathers

black legs and feet

- **SONG** Noisy. Gives a very nasal rasping drawling dragged-out caw or *kra-a-a*.
- **BEHAVIOR** Gregarious; tame; curious. Eats insects and nuts, including the shell. Can carry 70–95 pine seeds at a time in sublingual pouch in mouth for winter cache. Sometimes invades human habitation, campgrounds, or picnic tables for scraps. Forages for food by walking or hopping on ground, or by pecking trees, woodpecker-style, for insects; may hawk flying insects like a flycatcher. Also takes bird eggs, nestlings, lizards, small mammals, and carrion. Can find thousands of buried seeds annually by memory.
- **BREEDING** Monogamous. Colonial.
- **NESTING** Incubation 16–18 days by both sexes. Altricial young stay in nest 18–21 days. Brooded by female. Fed by both sexes. 1 brood per year.
- **POPULATION** Common. Fluctuates from year to year but remains stable. Eruptions to desert and lowlands every 10–20 years. Accidental in East.
- **FEEDERS** Sunflower seeds.
- **CONSERVATION** Vulnerable to habitat loss due to logging operations in mountain coniferous forests.

Similar Birds

GRAY JAY
Slimmer; longer, uniformly gray tail; lacks white in wings; uniformly dark gray wings; black nape; short black bill.

Flight Pattern
Crowlike flight with slow steady deep deliberate wing beats. Sometimes alternates several rapid wing beats with long glides.

Nest Identification	Platform of small sticks and pieces of bark • lined with pine needles, leaves, and grass • on far end of horizontal branch of conifer 2.5–15 m above ground • built by both sexes • 2–6 pale green or gray-green eggs marked with brown, olive, or gray; long oval pointed at small end; vary from ovate to elliptical ovate, 3.3 cm long.
Shape ⬮ ⬮ Location 🌿	

Plumage Sexes similar	Habitat 🌲 🌿 ⛰	Migration Nonmigratory	Weight 142 g

DATE _____ TIME_____ LOCATION _____

| Family CORVIDAE | Species *Pica hudsonia* | Length 44–56 cm | Wingspan 61 cm |

BLACK-BILLED MAGPIE

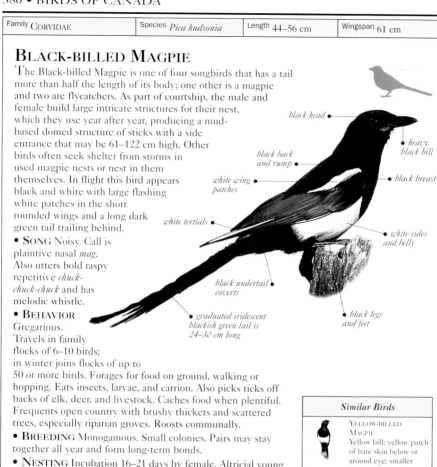

The Black-billed Magpie is one of four songbirds that has a tail more than half the length of its body; one other is a magpie and two are flycatchers. As part of courtship, the male and female build large intricate structures for their nest, which they use year after year, producing a mud-based domed structure of sticks with a side entrance that may be 61–122 cm high. Other birds often seek shelter from storms in used magpie nests or nest in them themselves. In flight this bird appears black and white with large flashing white patches in the short rounded wings and a long dark green tail trailing behind.

black head •

• heavy black bill

black back and rump •

white wing patches •

• black breast

white tertials •

• white sides and belly

black undertail coverts •

graduated iridescent blackish green tail is 24–30 cm long

• black legs and feet

• **SONG** Noisy. Call is plaintive nasal *mag*. Also utters bold raspy repetitive *chuck-chuck-chuck* and has melodic whistle.

• **BEHAVIOR** Gregarious. Travels in family flocks of 6–10 birds; in winter joins flocks of up to 50 or more birds. Forages for food on ground, walking or hopping. Eats insects, larvae, and carrion. Also picks ticks off backs of elk, deer, and livestock. Caches food when plentiful. Frequents open country with brushy thickets and scattered trees, especially riparian groves. Roosts communally.

• **BREEDING** Monogamous. Small colonies. Pairs may stay together all year and form long-term bonds.

• **NESTING** Incubation 16–21 days by female. Altricial young brooded by female but fed by both sexes. First flight at 25–32 days. 1 brood per year.

• **POPULATION** Common and widespread in rangeland and scrubland with open woodlands and thickets, especially near water. Casual in the East and the Southwest in winter. Some eastern birds may be escapees.

• **CONSERVATION** Thousands have been killed by accidentally ingesting poisoned bait intended for predators in rangeland.

Similar Birds

YELLOW-BILLED MAGPIE
Yellow bill; yellow patch of bare skin below or around eye; smaller
• western range, but Black-billed may casually wander into Yellow-billed's range.

Flight Pattern
Direct flight with slow, steady deliberate somewhat shallow wing beats. Often glides between perches or from perch to ground.

Nest Identification	
Shape ◎ Location 🌳 🌿 🌾	60–120-cm-high outside platform and roof made of sticks, mud, and thorny material • inside cup made of stems, rootlets, and horsehair • on limb of tree or shrub, typically no more than 7.5 m above ground but up to 15 m • built by female with materials brought by male • 7–13 greenish gray eggs marked with browns; usually subelliptical but sometimes long oval, 3.3 cm long.

| Plumage Sexes similar | Habitat 🌱 🐾 ✈ 🏞 | Migration Nonmigratory | Weight 187 g |

DATE _____ TIME_____ LOCATION _____

Family CORVIDAE	Species *Corvus monedula*	Length 33 cm	Wingspan 44 cm

EURASIAN JACKDAW

Since 1983 this active Eurasian bird has been making its way as a casual visitor to southeastern Canada and the northeastern United States. For a period of time, a pair even nested in Pennsylvania; however, the species has been unable to survive there and the small population is almost gone. It is believed that most, if not all, of the little corvids were ship-assisted in making the Atlantic crossing to North America. Its smaller size, gray ear patches and nape, and light gray eyes set it apart from other crows in the Northeast.

pale gray eyes

gray nape and ear patches

dark glossy blue-black metallic sheen on back and shoulders

black overall

- **SONG** Calls include a soft *chack* and a grating clipped metallic *kow* or *kyow*. Often repeats calls several times.
- **BEHAVIOR** Gregarious. Found in pairs or small groups. Joins other corvids in foraging and often uses communal roosts. Hops or walks on ground with quicker jerkier gait than most other crows. Hops on branches in trees. Forages in open and cultivated country. Omnivorous, eating seeds, fruits, berries, large insects, small reptiles, amphibians, small rodents, and eggs and nestlings of other birds. Unusual among corvids, it nests in holes in trees, rocks, buildings, pipes, cliffs, and even rabbit burrows. Nomadic.
- **BREEDING** Monogamous. Solitary or colonial.
- **NESTING** Incubation 18–19 days by female. Young altricial; brooded by female; stay in nest 30–35 days, fed by both sexes. 1 brood per year.

Similar Birds

No other black bird, and especially no other corvid in North America, has the combination of light eyes and gray nape and earpatches.

- **POPULATION** Accidental to casual in southeastern Canada from Ontario to Nova Scotia and to northeastern US from Pennsylvania to New England.
- **FEEDERS** Will come to feeders for sunflower seed, bread, and suet.

Flight Pattern

Flies with somewhat jerky buoyant wing beats. Glides between perches within trees, between trees, and from perch to ground.

Nest Identification	
Shape ⬤ Location 🐦 🌿 🏠 🏚️ 📦	Twigs and grasses, lined with finer grasses and wool • in tree holes, ridges of cliffs, burrows, under roofs, crevices, pipes, etc. • built by both sexes • 4–6 light bluish green or buff eggs, with fine dots of brown; oval to long oval, 3.6 x 2.5 cm.

Plumage Sexes similar	Habitat	Migration Northern birds migrate	Weight 244 g

DATE _____ TIME_____ LOCATION _____

Family CORVIDAE	Species *Corvus brachyrhynchos*	Length 44 cm	Wingspan 84–102 cm

AMERICAN CROW

One of the most widely distributed and recognized birds in North America, the American Crow is entirely black from beak to toe to tail with a glossy violet sheen. Studies of these intelligent birds have shown that they can count, solve puzzles, learn symbols, and retain information. They often are seen chasing and mobbing owls and hawks. Huge flocks from a few hundred to as many as 200,000 birds may assemble in winter to roost, travel, and feed together. Often persecuted, shot, poisoned, and even bombed on its roost in the past, this crow still lives among us by its intelligence and adaptability and is common throughout its range.

brown eyes

black bill

black overall with iridescent violet gloss on body

iridescent blue-violet and green-blue gloss on wings

black feet and legs

fan-shaped tail

• **SONG** Familiar loud call of *caw-caw* with many variations. Nasal begging call like *uh-uah* of the Fish Crow.

• **BEHAVIOR** Gregarious. Omnivorous; eats insects, many other small invertebrates from millipedes to snails, small amphibians, small reptiles, small mammals, eggs and young of other birds, waste corn and other grains, fruits, field crops, garbage, and carrion. Mobs avian predators, calling gangs of crows together to harass a large hawk or owl on a perch or drive it out of the area. Catches up to a soaring hawk and repeatedly dives on it from above, often forcing it down into the shelter of trees below. Breaks mollusk shells by dropping them on rocks from above.

• **BREEDING** Monogamous. Solitary nester. Sometimes known to be cooperative.

• **NESTING** Incubation 18 days by both sexes. Altricial young stay in nest 28–35 days. Brooded by female. Fed by both sexes and extra birds. 1 brood per year, 2 in the South.

• **POPULATION** Abundant. Adapting as habitat developed by humans.

• **CONSERVATION** Widely persecuted in the past by farmers and hunters. Still legally hunted for sport in many states.

Similar Birds

COMMON RAVEN
Larger; heavier stout bill; shaggy throat feathers; wedge-shaped tail; different voice.

FISH CROW
Smaller; more pointed wings; proportionally smaller more slender bill and longer tail; nasal, higher-pitched call • eastern range.

Flight Pattern
Slow steady deliberate direct flight with deep wing beats. Glides with slight dihedral from altitude to perch or ground, between perches, and from perch to ground.

Nest Identification	Made of twigs and branches • lined with tree material, grass, feathers, moss, leaves, and hair • in fork of tree or shrub or cross arms of utility pole 0–30.5 m above ground; sometimes on ground in prairie • built by both sexes and sometimes extra birds • 3–7 bluish green to olive-green eggs marked with brown and gray; oval, 4.1 x 2.8 cm.
Shape 〇〇 ⬤ Location 🌲 🌿🌳 ▬ 🏠	

Plumage Sexes similar	Habitat 🌾 🌳 🌿 ▬ 〰	Migration Some migrate	Weight 454 g

DATE _____ TIME_____ LOCATION _____

Family CORVIDAE	Species *Corvus caurinus*	Length 41 cm	Wingspan 76–91 cm

NORTHWESTERN CROW

A beachcomber often seen walking around like a tame chicken in coastal towns and villages in the Pacific Northwest, this crow occupies a niche similar to that of the Fish Crow in the East. Its range barely overlaps that of the American Crow; in fact, some believe it is a race or subspecies of that widespread species, although its voice is lower-pitched and huskier. Flocks of these birds can be seen harassing bald eagles, hawks, and owls.

iridescent violet gloss on head

iridescent violet gloss on back

black bill

black overall

iridescent violet gloss on breast

blue-violet and green-blue sheen on wings

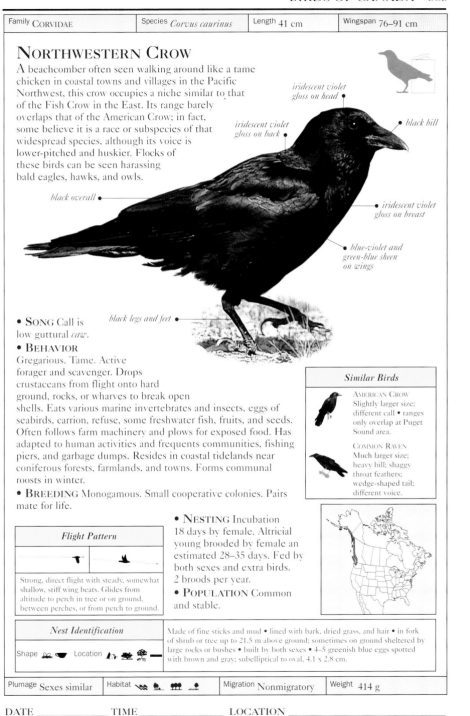

black legs and feet

- **SONG** Call is low guttural *caw*.
- **BEHAVIOR** Gregarious. Tame. Active forager and scavenger. Drops crustaceans from flight onto hard ground, rocks, or wharves to break open shells. Eats various marine invertebrates and insects, eggs of seabirds, carrion, refuse, some freshwater fish, fruits, and seeds. Often follows farm machinery and plows for exposed food. Has adapted to human activities and frequents communities, fishing piers, and garbage dumps. Resides in coastal tidelands near coniferous forests, farmlands, and towns. Forms communal roosts in winter.
- **BREEDING** Monogamous. Small cooperative colonies. Pairs mate for life.
- **NESTING** Incubation 18 days by female. Altricial young brooded by female an estimated 28–35 days. Fed by both sexes and extra birds. 2 broods per year.
- **POPULATION** Common and stable.

Similar Birds

AMERICAN CROW Slightly larger size; different call • ranges only overlap at Puget Sound area.

COMMON RAVEN Much larger size; heavy bill; shaggy throat feathers; wedge-shaped tail; different voice.

Flight Pattern

Strong, direct flight with steady, somewhat shallow, stiff wing beats. Glides from altitude to perch in tree or on ground, between perches, or from perch to ground.

Nest Identification

Shape | Location

Made of fine sticks and mud • lined with bark, dried grass, and hair • in fork of shrub or tree up to 21.5 m above ground; sometimes on ground sheltered by large rocks or bushes • built by both sexes • 4–5 greenish blue eggs spotted with brown and gray; subelliptical to oval, 4.1 x 2.8 cm.

Plumage Sexes similar	Habitat	Migration Nonmigratory	Weight 414 g

DATE _____ TIME _____ LOCATION _____

Family CORVIDAE	Species *Corvus corax*	Length 61–66 cm	Wingspan 117–142 cm

COMMON RAVEN

This magnificent flier is the aerial equal of hawks and falcons and North America's largest passerine. If any bird truly enjoys flying to the point of playing, it must be this raven. Intelligent resourceful hunters and scavengers, groups of these birds have been observed working together to capture prey too large for one bird to conquer. It is a revered totem and spirit to many Native Americans. The adults of this bird, which is Yukon Territory's avian emblem, are glossy black overall, with a huge "Roman nose," and shaggy throat feathers that can be elevated or sleeked down. The female is similar to the male but smaller.

nostrils hidden by stiff tufts of feathers extending about a third of the way out the bill

black overall with iridescent purple and violet sheen

long wedge-shaped tail with long central tail feathers

long heavy bill

black legs and feet

• **SONG** Variety of vocalizations, some quite musical, but most often a croaking drawling *croooaaak* or *cur-ruk* or metallic *tok*.

• **BEHAVIOR** Tame. Quick learner. Solitary or in pairs or small groups. Gregarious in winter, when it may occur in large foraging flocks and nightly communal roosts. Active forager, scavenger, and hunter. Omnivorous; eats wide variety of small invertebrates, from tadpoles and shellfish to worms and insects. Also takes many small vertebrates, including minnows, eggs and young of other birds, and rodents, as well as carrion and refuse. Elaborate courtship flight with great display of acrobatics and pair flying, male above female, wing-tip to wing-tip and heads touching.

• **BREEDING** Monogamous. Solitary; small, loose colonies in the North. Mates for life.

• **NESTING** Incubation 18–21 days by female. Altricial young stay in nest 38–44 days. Brooded by female. Fed by both sexes. 1 brood per year.

Similar Birds

AMERICAN CROW
Smaller; smaller bill; lacks shaggy throat feathers; fan-shaped tail; different call.

CHIHUAHUAN RAVEN
Smaller; shorter bill and wings; nasal bristles extend farther out on culmen; white-based neck and throat feathers.

• **POPULATION** Common. Expanding in California; also in Appalachians into areas where birds had been extirpated.

• **CONSERVATION** In past was shot, trapped, and poisoned for alleged damage to wild game and domesticated animals.

Flight Pattern

Strong flight, often rising in circles. Alternates deep wing beats with long glides or soaring on flat wings like a hawk. Soars on thermals and updrafts.

Nest Identification

Shape ___ ___   Location ___ ___ ___

Branches and sticks on outside; cup made of small sticks • lined with bark chips, animal hair, sheep's wool, lichens, moss, seaweed, and grass • on cliff near water, in mountains, or in fork of tree 13.5–24.5 m above ground • built by both sexes • 3–7 greenish or gray-green eggs with brown or olive spots; subelliptical to long oval, 5.1 x 3.6 cm.

Plumage Sexes similar	Habitat ___	Migration Nonmigratory	Weight 1.2 kg

DATE _____ TIME _____ LOCATION _____

Family ALAUDIDAE	Species *Alauda arvensis*	Length 18 cm	Wingspan 33 cm

SKY LARK

This European native was introduced to Vancouver Island, British Columbia, in the early 1900s. It has established a population there and in the open fields and meadows of nearby San Juan Island, Washington. Like most larks this bird seldom perches in trees but walks on the ground. Although it looks like just a small brown bird on the ground, its song-flight displays during courtship are spectacular. The male pursues the female to great heights in a towering flight, hovering or circling while singing a continuous eruption of warbles and trills in sustained runs.

small crest

buff eyebrows

slim pale bill

brown upperparts with heavy blackish brown streaking

blackish brown streaking on breast and sides

white outer tail feathers

buff-white underparts

pinkish legs and feet

- **SONG** Flies in circle or hovers high in air while singing an ongoing melody of complex gurgles, whistles, and trills. Ventriloquial. Call is gurgling bubbly *cherrup*.
- **BEHAVIOR** Solitary or in pairs. May form small flocks in winter. On ground has horizontal, head-down posture. Forages for food on ground by walking and running; does not hop. Eats mostly seeds, grains, and insects. Most often seen when flushed from roadside or grasses; rises with white tail edging and white secondary tips flashing. In courtship male runs around female, lifting his crest and tail and letting his wings fall limp.
- **BREEDING** Monogamous.
- **NESTING** Incubation 11–12 days by female. Altricial young stay in nest 9–10 days. Brooded by female. Fed by both sexes. 2 broods per year.
- **POPULATION** Vancouver Island population gradually declining. Common in Hawaii. Accidental in winter on Pacific Coast to northern California. Siberian race rare in migration on Aleutians.

Similar Birds

HORNED LARK
Juvenile lacks crest; white spots and streaking on upperparts; black tail with white outer feathers; lacks white trailing edge on secondaries.

AMERICAN PIPIT
Grayish upperparts; buff underparts with brownish streaking; black tail with white outer tail feathers; lacks crest and white secondary tips; bobs tail continuously.

Flight Pattern

Moderately swift flight with rapid wing beats. Hovers while skylarking in territory at great heights, then glides to ground.

Nest Identification

Shape —— ⌣ ⌢   Location ▬▬ ⚬⚬⚬

Lined with roots, grass, and occasionally hair • on ground in open field • built by female • 3–7 grayish white eggs with olive or brown blotches; subelliptical, 2.5 cm long.

Plumage Sexes similar	Habitat ___ ▲	Migration Nonmigratory	Weight 43 g

DATE _____ TIME_____ LOCATION _____

Family ALAUDIDAE	Species *Eremophila alpestris*	Length 18–20 cm	Wingspan 32–36 cm

HORNED LARK

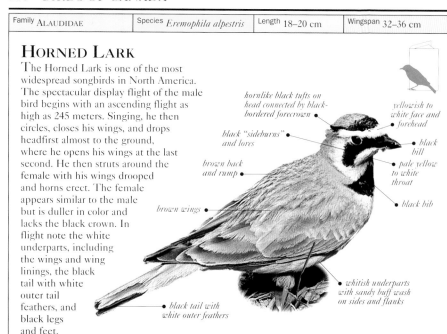

The Horned Lark is one of the most widespread songbirds in North America. The spectacular display flight of the male bird begins with an ascending flight as high as 245 meters. Singing, he then circles, closes his wings, and drops headfirst almost to the ground, where he opens his wings at the last second. He then struts around the female with his wings drooped and horns erect. The female appears similar to the male but is duller in color and lacks the black crown. In flight note the white underparts, including the wings and wing linings, the black tail with white outer tail feathers, and black legs and feet.

hornlike black tufts on head connected by black-bordered forecrown

yellowish to white face and forehead

black "sideburns" and lores

black bill

brown back and rump

pale yellow to white throat

brown wings

black bib

whitish underparts with sandy buff wash on sides and flanks

black tail with white outer feathers

• **SONG** Given from ground or in high, circling flight. Sings series of bell-like, tinkling notes *pit-wit, wee-pit, pit-wee.* Call is *tsee-tete* or *zeet.*

• **BEHAVIOR** Pairs; gregarious in winter, forming large flocks sometimes mixed with Snow Buntings and longspurs. Walks and runs rather than hops. Forages on ground, often in open fields with bare soil, pebbles, or short, sparse vegetation. Eats mostly seeds, grains, insects, and small mollusks. Often found in agricultural areas, to which it has adapted for nesting and foraging, on country roadways and farm roads standing and walking on pavement or gravel. This bird nests as early as February in the South. In courtship males perform display flights and skylark.

• **BREEDING** Monogamous. Solitary to gregarious.

• **NESTING** Incubation 11–12 days by female. Altricial young stay in nest 9–12 days. Brooded by female. Fed by both sexes. 1 brood per year in the North, 2 in the South.

• **POPULATION** Common. Has expanded eastern range since early 1800s because of agricultural development.

Similar Birds

AMERICAN PIPIT
Gray upperparts; brown-streaked whitish underparts; dark grayish brown tail with white outer tail feathers; bobs tail continuously; lacks horns, face pattern, and black bib • cinnamon-buff underparts in summer.

Flight Pattern

After each wing beat folds wing feathers close to body.

Nest Identification

Shape ⌣ ⌣   Location ▬ ⸬

Grass • lined with feathers and soft materials • in shallow depression, natural or dug by female, often near clumps of dirt or animal manure • built by female • 2–5 gray or greenish eggs dotted with browns; subelliptical, 2.0 x 1.5 cm.

Plumage Sexes differ	Habitat	Migration Migratory	Weight 31 g

Family HIRUNDINIDAE	Species *Progne subis*	Length 18–22 cm	Wingspan 39–43 cm

PURPLE MARTIN

Colonies once nested in holes in tall dead trees and saguaro cacti. Today the largest North American swallow usually nests in man-made multidwelling martin houses, sometimes with hundreds of pairs nesting together. Martin houses were inspired by the Native American custom of placing empty gourds on tall poles to attract the Purple Martin for aesthetic reasons and to reduce the insect population around villages and crops. Juvenile males have browner upperparts with whitish bellies and some purple sheen to their bodies. Juvenile females are brown overall with whitish bellies. A long-distant migrant, it winters from Venezuela to southeastern Brazil.

MALE

• dark iridescent purplish blue overall

FIRST SPRING MALE

• **SONG** A variety of rich low-pitched liquid gurgling notes and chirruping, mixed with cackling and varying in pitch. Songs often given predawn and in flight.

• **BEHAVIOR** In pairs or colonies. In fall, communal migratory and roosting flocks may number in the tens of thousands. Mostly catches and eats insects in flight, but also forages on ground. Nesting birds will eat broken eggshells placed for them. Frequents open country, rural agricultural areas, especially near water, and urban/suburban areas.

forked tail •

bluish gray upperparts •

grayish to whitish lower breast and belly •

• forked tail

• **BREEDING** Monogamous. Colonial.

• **NESTING** Incubation 15–18 days by female. Young altricial; brooded by female; stay in nest 26–31 days, fed by both sexes. 1–3 broods per year.

• **POPULATION** Common; declining, especially in the West.

FEMALE

Similar Birds

TREE SWALLOW
Smaller; entire underparts are bright white with no grayish tone; dark glossy blue-green upperparts • juveniles and first spring adults have browner upperparts.

GRAY-BREASTED MARTIN ♂
Smaller; gray-brown face, throat, and flanks; dusky gray-brown underparts; dark bluish upperparts; cleft tail • eastern range.

• **BIRDHOUSES** Man-made martin houses and gourds.

• **CONSERVATION** Neotropical migrant. National Audubon Society Blue List. Practice of removing dead cavity-filled trees, especially in riparian areas, has reduced nesting sites. Introduced European Starling and House Sparrow compete for nesting cavities.

Flight Pattern
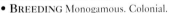
Strong graceful flight with few rapid wing beats followed by long glides. Often flies in circles while gliding.

Nest Identification	
Shape Location	Grasses, leaves, mud, feathers, and bits of debris • in martin houses, old woodpecker holes in trees and cacti, or in ridges in cliffs or large rocks • 1.5–6 m above ground • built by both sexes • 3–8 plain white eggs; oval to long oval, 2.4 x 1.7 cm.

Plumage Sexes differ	Habitat	Migration Migratory	Weight 48 g

DATE _____ TIME_____ LOCATION _____

Family HIRUNDINIDAE	Species *Tachycineta bicolor*	Length 15 cm	Wingspan 32 cm

TREE SWALLOW

The Tree Swallow is equally common in open fields, marshes, or towns. This bird's ability to adapt to its ever-changing environment has led to its abundant and widespread population. Migrating in huge flocks during the day, it is one of the first swallows to travel to its summer home in upper North America. Many winter on the southern Atlantic Coast, Gulf Coast, and in Florida. In flight it shows dark upperparts, white underparts, triangular wings with greenish underwing linings, and a notched tail. Juveniles have dusky brown upperparts and often a dusky wash on the breast.

• **SONG** Utters quick repetitious *silip* or *chi-veet*. In flight makes pleasant liquid gurgling chatter.

• **BEHAVIOR** Gregarious in migration and winter; often occurs in huge flocks. Feeds in mixed flocks with other swallow species. Catches insects in flight; sometimes forages on ground. Eats mainly flying insects but also may take small crustaceans and spiders. Often eats berries and seeds during cold snaps on wintering grounds or in spring migration. Inhabits open country and woodland edges near water. Male displays for female with series of aerial gymnastics.

• **BREEDING** Most often polygamous. Loose social colonies. Males may have 2 mates simultaneously and different mates each year.

• **NESTING** Incubation 13–16 days by female. Altricial young remain in nest 16–24 days. Fed by both sexes. 1 brood per year (rarely 2).

• **POPULATION** Abundant and increasing.

• **BIRDHOUSES** Uses man-made bird boxes and gourds.

• **CONSERVATION** Some are neotropical migrants. Forestry practice of removing dead trees eliminates many potential nesting sites.

white cheek patch stops below eye

dark iridescent greenish blue upperparts

white underparts

blackish flight feathers

slightly notched tail

JUVENILE

Similar Birds

VIOLET-GREEN SWALLOW
White rump patches extend onto sides of rump; white on cheek extends up to, behind, and above eye; purple-green gloss on upperparts • sympatric only in the West.

Flight Pattern

Swift graceful flight with slow deep wing beats alternated with long to short glides. Turns back sharply on insects it passes.

Nest Identification

Shape ☐² ☐ Location

Abandoned Nests

Dried stems and grass • lined with down and feathers • in tree cavity, abandoned nest, bird box, or other man-made structure • built by both sexes, but female does more • 4–6 white eggs; oval to long oval, 2.0 x 1.3 cm.

Plumage Sexes similar	Habitat	Migration Migratory	Weight 20 g

DATE _____ TIME_____ LOCATION _____

Family HIRUNDINIDAE	Species *Tachycineta thalassina*	Length 13 cm	Wingspan 28–30 cm

VIOLET-GREEN SWALLOW

The gloss of brilliant greens and purples that shows on its head, back, and rump in bright sunlight and the white patches on the sides of its rump that show in flight set this bird apart from its cousin, the Tree Swallow, with which it often closely associates. Its historical choice for nesting sites is in dead trees of partially cleared forests or abandoned woodpecker holes. Females show duller upperparts than males. Juveniles have gray-brown

white cheek marks extend above eye

notched greenish black tail

greenish black wings

white underparts

JUVENILE

upperparts without the green-purple gloss and grayish or mottled underparts.

• **SONG** Often makes series of slightly buzzing *chi-chit* notes. Male's courtship song is repetitive *tsip, tseet, tsip*, given in flight before daylight.

• **BEHAVIOR** Gregarious. Usually feeds in flocks and catches insects, its principal diet, in flight. Rarely takes insects from ground. Usually feeds by flying close to the ground or low over water; sometimes feeds at great heights on insects that have risen high in the air column. Defends nest cavities from other swallows. Has been documented helping feed Western Bluebird nestlings, then taking over the nesting cavity when they fledge. Often perches high in trees, on fences, or on utility wires.

• **BREEDING** Monogamous. Occasionally found in loose colonies of up to around 20 pairs.

• **NESTING** Incubation 13–14 days by female. Altricial young remain in nest 16–24 days. Fed by both sexes, but female does more. 1 brood per year.

• **POPULATION** Common in various woodland habitats in range, often found at higher elevations in mountains. Stable. Casual in the East.

• **BIRDHOUSES** Will nest in man-made bird boxes.

• **CONSERVATION** Neotropical migrant. Has declined where forestry practices include removal of dead trees.

Similar Birds

TREE SWALLOW
Snowy white underparts; steely blue-green upperparts, including cap to below eye; blue-green rump; • juvenile has brownish upperparts; white underparts.

WHITE-THROATED SWIFT
Black upperparts; white underparts with black side patches; longer more slender wings; long forked tail; more fluttering flight.

Flight Pattern

Swift graceful flight, alternating several rapid wing beats with long glides. Soars on thermals and updrafts along cliff faces and canyon walls.

Nest Identification

Shape

Location

Grass and weed stems • lined with feathers • in natural cavity, abandoned woodpecker hole, or crevice in dead tree; on rock ridges or in bird box • built by both sexes • 4–6 unmarked white eggs; oval, 2.0 x 1.4 cm.

Plumage Sexes similar	Habitat	Migration Migratory	Weight 17 g

Family HIRUNDINIDAE	Species *Stelgidopteryx serripennis*	Length 14 cm	Wingspan 28–30 cm

NORTHERN ROUGH-WINGED SWALLOW

This bird is named for the tiny hooks found on its outer primary feathers. Their function is unknown, but they may produce a sound during courtship display. The male and female use their feet to dig nesting burrows, some as long as 1.8 meters, depending on the nature of the soil, but most are 23 to 71 cm deep. Since it is highly adaptable this bird has a wide breeding range. Juveniles are similar to adults but show more cinnamon tones in their upperparts and have cinnamon wing bars.

short black bill

light gray-brown wash on chin, throat, and upper breast

medium brown upperparts

• **SONG** Usually remains silent, but sometimes utters harsh, buzzing *quiz-z-zeeitp* or *zzrrit*.

• **BEHAVIOR** Solitary or in pairs or small flocks. Gregarious during migration. Catches and consumes a variety of flying insects while in flight. Also occasionally takes insects from ground. Often feeds low over open landscapes or water and sometimes feeds along with other species of swallows. Quickly adapted nesting to utilize crevices in rock cuts along interstate highways. During courtship male chases female, flying with white undertail coverts spread along sides of tail.

dark brownish black wings and wing linings

dull white underparts

slightly forked dark brownish black tail

• **BREEDING** Monogamous. Solitary or in small colonies.

• **NESTING** Incubation 12 days by female. Altricial young remain in nest 19–21 days. Fed by both sexes. 1 brood per year.

• **POPULATION** Common and increasing.

• **BIRDHOUSES** Will nest in some types of man-made structures but has not been recorded to use nest boxes.

• **CONSERVATION** Neotropical migrant.

Similar Birds

BANK SWALLOW
Smaller; darker brown upperparts; dark brown breast band; snow-white underparts; faster wing beats with quick changes of direction.

Flight Pattern

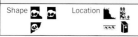

Swift graceful flight with several deep slow wing beats, pulling back wings after each stroke, then a short to long glide.

Nest Identification

Shape 🥚 🥚 🥚   Location 🏔 🪨 〰 🏚

No nest materials except a few bark chips, grass, and leaves • on bank, sides of rough cliff, highway/railroad rock cuts, or building or in abandoned burrows, drain pipes, or sewer pipes • dug by both sexes • 4–8 plain white eggs; long oval, 1.8 x 1.3 cm.

Plumage Sexes similar	Habitat ● 〰 ＿ ＿ ↓ ≈	Migration Migratory	Weight 17 g

DATE _____ TIME_____ LOCATION _____

Family HIRUNDINIDAE	Species *Riparia riparia*	Length 12 cm	Wingspan 25–28 cm

BANK SWALLOW

The smallest member of the North American swallow family is an aerial gymnast that twists and turns in the air over its breeding territory. Males and females take turns digging burrows into vertical banks with their bills. Once a hole is made, they use their feet to finish the tunnel, which sometimes is as long as 1.5 to 1.8 meters. The scientific name refers to their association with rivers during migration and their predilection for nesting along sandy gravelly river banks. The dark narrow breast band is difficult to see when the bird is in flight, but the combination of an erratic flight pattern, chocolate-brown upperparts, paler brown rump, dark brown wing linings, and snowy white underparts serve to identify this bird. Juvenile wing coverts and tertials are edged cinnamon and the throat and upper breast are washed pale cinnamon.

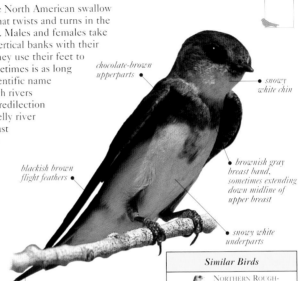

chocolate-brown upperparts

snowy white chin

blackish brown flight feathers

brownish gray breast band, sometimes extending down midline of upper breast

snowy white underparts

slightly forked tail

• **SONG** Dry chattering, *zzzrt orzzzrt, zzzrtt.*
• **BEHAVIOR** Gregarious. Often migrates and feeds with other swallows. Gathers in large premigratory and communal roosts. Catches insects while flying. Occasionally takes insects from ground or water's surface. Courtship includes dropping and catching feathers in the air, as if playing, by each member of pair; copulation in the nest burrow often follows such "play" and many feathers are used in the nest lining.
• **BREEDING** Monogamous. Colonial.
• **NESTING** Incubation 14–16 days by both sexes. Altricial young stay in nest 18–24 days, fed by both sexes. 1–2 broods per year.
• **POPULATION** Common and widespread; often near water. Numbers are stable overall, but species is declining in California due to river bank alteration for flood control.
• **CONSERVATION** Neotropical migrant.

Similar Birds

NORTHERN ROUGH-WINGED SWALLOW
Larger; paler brown upperparts; lacks brown chest band; dusky white underparts; light gray-brown wash on chin, throat, and upper breast; slower deeper wing beats.

TREE SWALLOW
Juvenile is larger; white underparts from chin to undertail coverts; often with dusky breast band; greenish blue upperparts.

Flight Pattern
Swift erratic fluttering flight on shallow wing beats; often alternates several rapid wing beats with short to long glides.

Nest Identification	
Shape [symbol] Location [symbol]	Lined with grass, rootlets, weed stems, horsehair, and feathers • in sandy or rocky bank, gravel pit, or man-made embankment, such as a highway road cut • dug by both sexes • 3–7 plain white eggs; oval to short oval, 1.8 x 1.3 cm.

Plumage Sexes similar	Habitat 〜〜 ⟂	Migration Migratory	Weight 14 g

DATE _____ TIME_____ LOCATION _____

| Family HIRUNDINIDAE | Species *Petrochelidon pyrrhonota* | Length 14 cm | Wingspan 30 cm |

CLIFF SWALLOW

Hundreds of gourd-shaped "mud jugs" plastered to the side of a barn or under a bridge or highway overpass are a typical nesting territory for these highly adaptable birds. Farmers heartily welcome this resident because it eats numerous flying insects that are harmful to crops. Nesting colonies may number from eight hundred to more than one thousand birds. Note the dark rusty brown throat, and in flight the brown underwing linings, cinnamon buff rump, square tail, dusky cinnamon undertail coverts with dark centers, and whitish buff edged feathers of back and tertials. Juveniles have dusky brown upperparts and paler underparts. This swallow has successfully expanded its range in the Southeast and the West. The southwestern race displays a cinnamon forehead similar to the Cave Swallow.

blue-black crown

whitish forehead

short black bill

black center patch on chestnut throat

chestnut sides of face extend to sides of nape

squared blackish tail with slight cleft

blue-black wings and back

whitish underparts with dusky gray-brown sides and flanks

JUVENILE

- **SONG** Utters a dry guttural *churr* or *zarp*. Alarm call is burry *keeer*. During breeding, a chattering, squeaking, sputtering warble.
- **BEHAVIOR** Gregarious. Catches food in flight; sometimes forages on ground. Eats variety of flying insects and some berries and fruit. Constructs one of the most complex swallow nests: a sphere of mud pellets with a tubular entrance on one side. Colonies are source of foraging information for other birds; birds follow members who are successfully feeding young back to food sources.
- **BREEDING** Monogamous. Large colonies.
- **NESTING** Incubation 14–16 days by both sexes. Altricial young in nest 21–24 days, fed by both sexes. 1–3 broods a year.
- **POPULATION** Common in open country, especially near water. Range is expanding and numbers are increasing.
- **CONSERVATION** Neotropical migrant. Previously listed as being of special concern, but successful adaptation to nesting on man-made structures such as buildings, highway bridges and overpasses, railroad bridges, dams, and other vertical walls has greatly expanded populations and range.

Similar Birds

CAVE SWALLOW
Pale cinnamon-buff
throat; cinnamon
forehead; richer
cinnamon-rust rump.

Flight Pattern

Swift graceful flight alternating several deep rapid wing beats with long elliptical glides with sharp sweeping upturns at the end. Soars on thermals and updrafts.

Nest Identification

Shape

Location

Pellets of clay or mud, with lining of grasses, down, and feathers • usually under eaves of buildings or under dams or bridges; sometimes on ridges of canyons; rarely on trunk of conifer tree under overhanging branch • built by both sexes • 3–6 white, cream, or pinkish eggs, marked with browns; oval to long oval, 2.0 x 1.3 cm.

| Plumage Sexes similar | Habitat | Migration Migratory | Weight 23 g |

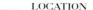

DATE _____ TIME_____ LOCATION _____

Family HIRUNDINIDAE	Species *Hirundo rustica*	Length 17–19 cm	Wingspan 32–34 cm

BARN SWALLOW

Since early colonial times this bird has been a welcome presence on farms because it eats many crop-destroying insects. Usually nesting inside of barns or other buildings, it is the only North American swallow with buffy to cinnamon underparts and underwing linings and a white-spotted deeply forked tail. The female is similar to the male but most often is duller in color. Juveniles have shorter forked tails and creamy white underparts. The most wide-ranging swallow in the world, it is cosmopolitan, found breeding or wintering on almost all continents.

rusty forehead

dark bluish black breast band

FEMALE

dark rusty brown throat

blackish flight feathers

dark iridescent blue-black upperparts

deeply forked blackish tail with white spots

JUVENILE

- **SONG** Utters a repetitive clipped *chi-dit, chi-dit* or *wit-wit*. Song is a prolonged twittering warble with liquid guttural notes interspersed.
- **BEHAVIOR** Gregarious. Often feeds close to ground or water. Eats a wide variety of flying insects, and follows farm machinery, even riding lawnmowers, to feed on stirred-up insects. Courtship flights may include pairs dropping and catching feathers in midair; upon landing pairs may engage in mutual preening. Individuals show strong site fidelity, and colonies may exist over long periods on the same site, with the same individuals sometimes building nests on the same site used the previous year. Has adapted to nesting in and on man-made structures.
- **BREEDING** Monogamous. Small colonies. During courtship, male chases female, flying over acres of land.
- **NESTING** Incubation 13–17 days by both sexes, but female does more. Young altricial; stay in nest 18–23 days, fed by both sexes. 2 broods per year.

Similar Birds

CLIFF SWALLOW
Blue-black upperparts; rusty cinnamon to buffy cinnamon rump; pale forehead; short squared tail without white spots.

CAVE SWALLOW
Blue-black upperparts; chestnut rump; short, squared tail without white spots.

- **POPULATION** Abundant and widespread in open country, agricultural lands, and savanna, especially near water. Increasing. Eurasian races are accidental to casual in Alaska.
- **CONSERVATION** Neotropical migrant.

Flight Pattern
Swift and graceful with deep wing beats and wing-tips pulled back at the end of each stroke; glides are short and infrequent.

Nest Identification	
Shape Location	Clay or mud, dried stems, grasses, and straw, with thick lining of horsehair, down, and feathers • inside barn or other building, in ridges of cliff, under bridge, under culvert, or attached to bank • built by both sexes • 4–7 white eggs, marked with browns; oval to long oval, 2.0 x 1.3 cm.

Plumage Sexes similar	Habitat	Migration Migratory	Weight 17 g

DATE _____ TIME_____ LOCATION _____

Family PARIDAE	Species *Poecile atricapilla*	Length 14 cm	Wingspan 19–22 cm

BLACK-CAPPED CHICKADEE

A common visitor at bird feeders in the northern US and Canada south of the tundra, this bird leaves its nesting grounds in woodland areas during autumn and visits bird feeders in suburban areas. The Black-capped Chickadee rarely moves beyond the southern edge of its breeding range, but occasionally it will irrupt southward in large numbers during autumn. It occasionally hybridizes with the Carolina Chickadee, in the overlapping zone, producing intergrades in size and song. It is the provincial bird of New Brunswick.

white cheeks

black cap

light gray upperparts

tertials and secondaries with broad whitish edges

short black bill

black bib

• **SONG** Lower huskier more drawn-out *chick-a-dee-dee-dee* than that of Carolina Chickadee. Song is clear fluted *fee-bee* or *fee-bee-be*.

white underparts with olive-buff wash on sides, flanks, lower belly, and crissum

blackish gray feet and legs

• **BEHAVIOR** Pairs; forms small groups after nesting season. Often joins mixed foraging flocks with other species. Tame. Forages among twigs and branches and under bark, often clinging upside down, for insects, and insect eggs. Eats seeds from conifers, bayberries, and other fruit. Holds large seeds between feet on perch and pounds seed coat open with beak. In winter eats mostly seeds. Incubating female hisses like a snake when nest cavity is disturbed.

long tail

• **BREEDING** Monogamous.
• **NESTING** Incubation 11–13 days by both sexes. Altricial young stay in nest 14–18 days. Brooded by female. Fed by both sexes. 1 brood per year.
• **POPULATION** Widespread and common in deciduous or mixed deciduous-conifer woodlands, often in riparian growth. Stable and possibly increasing.
• **FEEDERS AND BIRDHOUSES** Doughnuts, peanut butter–and-cornmeal mixture, and sunflower seeds. Will nest in birdhouses.

Similar Birds

CAROLINA CHICKADEE Smaller body; shorter tail; no broad white edges on greater wing coverts or secondaries (grayish); cleaner cut lower edge on shorter black bib; less olive in flanks; higher-pitched, faster *chick-a-dee-dee-dee* call; 4-note *fee-bee-fee-bay* whistled song.

BOREAL CHICKADEE Brown cap; gray-brown back and sides; more hoarse, drawling *chick-a-dee-deer* or *chick-chee-day-day* song.

Flight Pattern
Slow flitting short flights with rapid wing beats. On longer flights often folds wings to sides after several quick shallow strokes before repeating.

Nest Identification	
Shape ▨¹ ▨² Location ✿ ➤ 🌳 🐦 🏠	Lined with vegetation, moss, feathers, hair, and insect cocoons • in deciduous tree, conifer, snag, or nest box 1–12 m above ground • built by both sexes • 5–10 white eggs with fine reddish brown marks; oval to short oval, 1.5 x 1.1 cm.

Plumage Sexes similar	Habitat 🌲 🌳 🌿 🌊	Migration Nonmigratory	Weight 11 g

Family PARIDAE	Species *Poecile gambeli*	Length 14 cm	Wingspan 19 cm

MOUNTAIN CHICKADEE

Easily identified by its white eyebrow, the Mountain
Chickadee is a common inhabitant in mountainous
regions of the West from southern Yukon to California
and western Texas. During the fall months, some
Mountain Chickadees leave the higher
mountainous areas entering territory further
downslope and outside the mountains
that are normally inhabited by the
Black-capped Chickadee.
Birds of the Rocky
Mountain race are
washed with buff on
their grayish sides,
flanks, and back.
Although primarily
nonmigratory, some
birds wander in
winter outside the
breeding range.

black cap joins black postocular stripe

grayish upperparts

white eyebrow

short black bill

white cheeks and lores

black bib

paler gray underparts

pale gray or gray-buff sides and flanks

gray-black legs and feet

• **SONG** Call sounds like
a throaty *chick-adee-adee-adee.*
Song is a 3- or 4-note downward whistle
of *fee-bee-bay* or *fee-bee-fee-bee.*

• **BEHAVIOR** In pairs or small groups; joins mixed-species
feeding flocks after breeding season. Clings under branches and
pine cones when foraging and gleans food from trunk, branches,
and foliage; occasionally feeds on ground. Primary diet of insects
in breeding season and summer; conifer seeds, other plant
seeds, spiders, and insect or spider eggs are also taken
throughout year. Tame. When disturbed, incubating female
hisses like snake and lunges toward nest entrance.

• **BREEDING** Monogamous.

• **NESTING** Incubation 14 days by female. Young altricial;
brooded by female; stay in nest 21 days, fed by both sexes.
1–2 broods per year.

• **POPULATION** Common resident in coniferous and mixed
montane woodlands.

• **FEEDERS AND
BIRDHOUSES** Eats baby
chick scratch feed and
sunflower seeds. Will nest in
man-made birdhouses.

• **CONSERVATION**
Vulnerable to habitat loss due
to logging operations.

Similar Birds

BRIDLED TITMOUSE
Sharp pointed crest;
white face with black
line through eye,
outlining ear and
passing forward to
connect with black bib;
lacks black cap.

BLACK-CAPPED
CHICKADEE
Lacks white eyebrow;
lower edge of black bib
more ragged; olive-buff
wash on sides, flanks,
and crissum;
vocalizations differ.

Flight Pattern

Short slow weak flitting flights on rapidly
beating wings. Often folds wings to sides
after several quick wing beats; repeats.

Nest Identification

Shape [icons] Location [icons]

Moss-lined with animal fur, feathers, and shredded bark • 1–2.5 m above ground
in conifer, deciduous tree, nest box, or snag • built by both sexes, but female
does most • 5–12 white eggs, unmarked, with occasional reddish brown spots;
oval to short oval, 1.5 x 1.1 cm.

Plumage Sexes similar	Habitat [icons]	Migration Nonmigratory	Weight 11 g

DATE _____ TIME_____ LOCATION _____

Family PARIDAE	Species *Poecile rufescens*	Length 12 cm	Wingspan 13 cm

CHESTNUT-BACKED CHICKADEE

Known for its richly colored plumage, the Chestnut-backed Chickadee is a common resident of humid coniferous forests along the Pacific Coast. Pairs defend their individual nesting areas but typically reside near other pairs, forming a loose colony. They often feed high in the trees in pairs or small family groups. The race along the central California coast from San Francisco southward displays very little chestnut on the sides and flanks, and the underparts are mostly gray.

chestnut back and rump

gray wings edged white on tertials and secondaries

sooty brown cap

short black bill

white cheeks

black bib

whitish gray underparts

gray-black legs and feet

chestnut wash on flanks, sides, and crissum

• **SONG** Song not whistled like most other chickadees, rather a chipping sparrowlike *chip-chip-chip-chip*. Call is a gruff rapid *tseek-a-dee-dee*.

• **BEHAVIOR** Social, tame, and gregarious after the breeding season. Commonly observed high in treetops or on jumbled logs on the forest floor, looking for food. Eats primarily insects and their larvae, spiders and their eggs, and fruit pulp and seeds from conifers. Joins mixed-species feeding flocks after the breeding season. When disturbed on the nest, the incubating female makes hissing sounds like a snake and flutters her wings.

• **BREEDING** Monogamous. Loosely colonial.

• **NESTING** Breeding biology poorly known; incubation estimated at 11–14 days by female. Young altricial; brooded by female. Fledge nest at estimated 14–18 days, fed by both sexes. 1 brood per year.

• **POPULATION** Fairly common to common in humid conifer and mixed conifer forests. Has spread in Sierra Nevada and central California in recent decades.

• **FEEDERS** Baby chick scratch feed, sunflower seed, and suet.

• **CONSERVATION** Vulnerable to habitat loss caused by logging operations.

Similar Birds

BLACK-CAPPED CHICKADEE
Lacks bright chestnut back, rump, and sides; black cap; light gray upperparts; white underparts; buffy wash on sides, flanks, and crissum; voice differs.

MOUNTAIN CHICKADEE
Black cap; white eyebrow; gray back and rump; lacks chestnut on underparts; voice differs.

Flight Pattern

Slow fluttering weak flights of short duration on rapidly beating wings. Often folds wings to sides after several shallow wing strokes; repeated.

Nest Identification	
Shape	Location	Moss-lined with animal fur, feathers, and plant matter • usually 45 cm–3.5 m (but can be up to 25 m) above ground in snag or tree • 5–9 white eggs, with sparse reddish brown marks; oval to short oval, 1.5 x 1.1 cm.

Plumage Sexes similar	Habitat	Migration Nonmigratory	Weight 9.0 g

DATE _____ TIME_____ LOCATION _____

Family PARIDAE	Species *Poecile hudsonica*	Length 14 cm	Wingspan 20 cm

BOREAL CHICKADEE

In most of its range the Boreal Chickadee is the only chickadee with a brown cap. It is a calm tame little bird that prefers to nest among the conifer woodlands in the colder regions of North America, mostly north of the Canada-US border. Small flocks of these chickadees often are seen traveling in the company of Golden-crowned Kinglets, but they rarely associate with Black-capped Chickadees in their mixed-species foraging flocks in the winter season. In some winters in the eastern parts of North America, some individuals may appear as much as hundreds of kilometers south of their normal breeding range. Males and females are alike.

gray rear of face and sides of neck

brown cap

brownish upperparts

black bill

gray wings and tail

black bib

white cheeks restricted to small area graying posteriorly

brown sides, flanks, and crissum

whitish underparts

gray-black legs and feet

- **SONG** Song is short and warbled. Call is a drawling drawn-out lazy *chick-a-dee-dee-dee* or *chick-chee-day-day*.
- **BEHAVIOR** A highly tame and sociable bird. Pairs in breeding season may stay together all year; they travel in small to medium flocks of 4–20 birds in nonbreeding season. Gleans much of its food from branches and needles of conifers and by picking seeds out of cones. Eats variety of insects and their larvae and eggs.
- **BREEDING** Monogamous. Small colonies.
- **NESTING** Incubation 11–16 days by female. Young altricial; brooded by female; remain in nest 18 days, fed by both sexes. 1 brood per year.
- **POPULATION** Fairly common in boreal conifer forests and in mixed conifer-deciduous woodlands.
- **FEEDERS** In winter, Boreal Chickadees will come to a variety of feeders for a mixture of suet, peanut butter, cornmeal, and sunflower seeds.
- **CONSERVATION** Vulnerable to loss of habitat due to logging operations.

Similar Birds

GRAY-HEADED CHICKADEE
More extensive white cheeks; gray-brown cap; longer tail; paler flanks; gray-brown upperparts; pale edges on wing coverts; voice differs
- western range.

BLACK-CAPPED CHICKADEE
Black cap; light gray upperparts; large white cheek patch extending onto hindneck; white-edged tertials and secondaries; different livelier call.

Flight Pattern

Weak fluttering short flights on rapidly beating wings. Alternates pulling wings to body with several quick shallow strokes.

Nest Identification	
Shape	Filled with bark strips, mosses, plant down, lichen, and animal fur and hair • in live or dead conifer or used woodpecker hole • 30 cm–3 m above ground • built by female • 4–9 white eggs, with reddish brown specks; ovate to short ovate, some rather pointed, 1.5 x 1.1 cm.
Location	

Plumage Sexes similar	Habitat	Migration Nonmigratory	Weight 9.0 g

Family PARIDAE	Species *Poecile cincta*	Length 14 cm	Wingspan 20 cm

GRAY-HEADED CHICKADEE

Perhaps the hardiest of all chickadees, the Gray-headed Chickadee lives much farther north than the rest of its congeners, with only the Boreal Chickadee as a distant neighbor. This subarctic chickadee, formerly called the Siberian Tit, is a Eurasian native of Siberia and Alaska. Populations of the Gray-headed Chickadee are generally scarce and live primarily among scattered conifers and riparian willow and aspen thickets. The Gray-headed Chickadee is a permanent resident of the northern edges of the tree line and visits human habitations in winter, where it may dine on scraps of frozen meat.

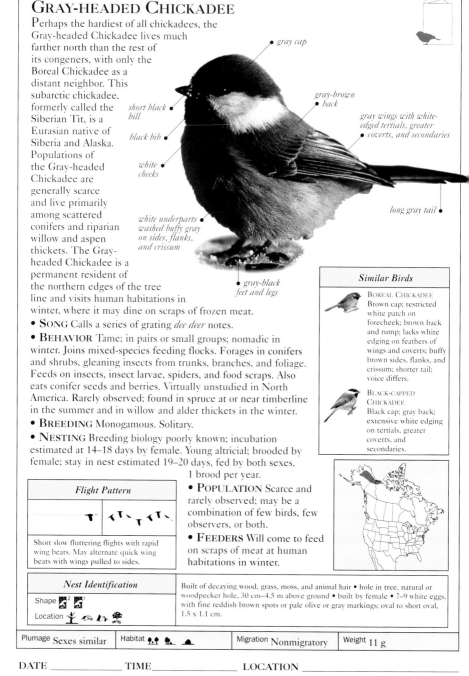

gray cap

gray-brown back

gray wings with white-edged tertials, greater coverts, and secondaries

short black bill

black bib

white cheeks

long gray tail

white underparts washed buffy gray on sides, flanks, and crissum

gray-black feet and legs

• **SONG** Calls a series of grating *dee deer* notes.
• **BEHAVIOR** Tame; in pairs or small groups; nomadic in winter. Joins mixed-species feeding flocks. Forages in conifers and shrubs, gleaning insects from trunks, branches, and foliage. Feeds on insects, insect larvae, spiders, and food scraps. Also eats conifer seeds and berries. Virtually unstudied in North America. Rarely observed; found in spruce at or near timberline in the summer and in willow and alder thickets in the winter.
• **BREEDING** Monogamous. Solitary.
• **NESTING** Breeding biology poorly known; incubation estimated at 14–18 days by female. Young altricial; brooded by female; stay in nest estimated 19–20 days, fed by both sexes. 1 brood per year.
• **POPULATION** Scarce and rarely observed; may be a combination of few birds, few observers, or both.
• **FEEDERS** Will come to feed on scraps of meat at human habitations in winter.

Similar Birds

BOREAL CHICKADEE Brown cap; restricted white patch on forecheek; brown back and rump; lacks white edging on feathers of wings and coverts; buffy brown sides, flanks, and crissum; shorter tail; voice differs.

BLACK-CAPPED CHICKADEE Black cap; gray back; extensive white edging on tertials, greater coverts, and secondaries.

Flight Pattern

Short slow fluttering flights with rapid wing beats. May alternate quick wing beats with wings pulled to sides.

Nest Identification

Shape

Location

Built of decaying wood, grass, moss, and animal hair • hole in tree, natural or woodpecker hole, 30 cm–4.5 m above ground • built by female • 7–9 white eggs, with fine reddish brown spots or pale olive or gray markings; oval to short oval, 1.5 x 1.1 cm.

Plumage Sexes similar	Habitat	Migration Nonmigratory	Weight 11 g

DATE _____ TIME _____ LOCATION _____

Family PARIDAE	Species *Baeolophus bicolor*	Length 17 cm	Wingspan 27 cm

TUFTED TITMOUSE

Undaunted by the presence of people, this lively bird sometimes will swoop down and pluck out a human hair to use for its nest. The largest titmouse, it will fly toward people making squeaking or pishing sounds to attract birds. It is intelligent and may learn to eat food out of a human hand. Often it can be seen digging in the ground, where it stores surplus sunflower seeds. Adapted to wooded residential areas with large shade trees and to bird feeders and nesting boxes, it has become a familiar yard bird with its jaunty crest and large black eyes set against gray plumage. The black-crested form in southern and western Texas was formerly considered a separate species, the Black-crested Titmouse.

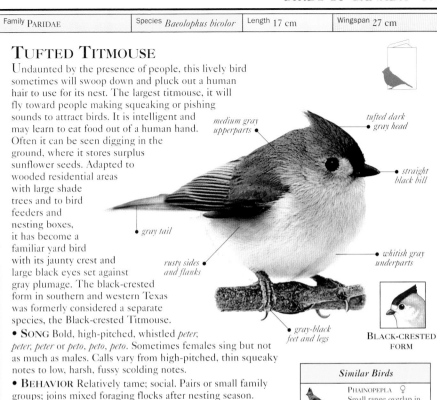

medium gray upperparts

tufted dark gray head

straight black bill

gray tail

rusty sides and flanks

whitish gray underparts

gray-black feet and legs

BLACK-CRESTED FORM

• **SONG** Bold, high-pitched, whistled *peter, peter, peter* or *peto, peto, peto*. Sometimes females sing but not as much as males. Calls vary from high-pitched, thin squeaky notes to low, harsh, fussy scolding notes.

• **BEHAVIOR** Relatively tame; social. Pairs or small family groups; joins mixed foraging flocks after nesting season. Inspects and forages in trees and shrubs for food, sometimes clinging upside down on trunk or branch tips. Uses bill to pound open nut, while anchoring it with feet. Eats insects and their larvae, spiders, snails, various berries, acorns and other nuts, and seeds. Male feeds female during courtship.

• **BREEDING** Monogamous. Solitary nester. Mates for life.

• **NESTING** Incubation 13–14 days by female. Altricial young stay in nest 15–18 days. Brooded by female. Fed by both sexes. 1 brood per year, 2 in the South.

Similar Birds
PHAINOPEPLA ♀ Small range overlap in Big Bend area of Texas with black-crested form • larger; medium sooty gray overall; crested; darker gray wing edges; white on wing coverts and tertials; whitish gray patch at base of primaries flashes in flight; long, rounded tail.

• **POPULATION** Abundant to common in forests, parks, and shaded suburbs.

• **FEEDERS AND BIRDHOUSES** Feeders with sunflower seeds, suet, cornmeal, and peanut butter. Will nest in man-made birdhouses.

Flight Pattern
Weak fluttering short flights with shallow rapid wing beats. Flitting flight with several quick wing beats alternating with wings drawn to sides, then repeated.

Nest Identification	
Shape	Location	Lined with bark, leaves, soft grass and moss, snakeskin, and bits of animal fur and hair • in natural cavity, bird box, or woodpecker hole 90 cm–27.5 m above ground • built by female • 4–8 white to creamy white eggs speckled with browns, occasionally wreathed; short subelliptical, 1.8 x 1.4 cm.

Plumage Sexes similar	Habitat	Migration Nonmigratory	Weight 23 g

DATE _____ TIME _____ LOCATION _____

Family AEGITHALIDAE	Species *Psaltriparus minimus*	Length 11 cm	Wingspan 18 cm

BUSHTIT

Often observed traveling in flocks, the Bushtit is
sociable toward other Bushtits and other birds,
often joining mixed-species flocks or letting
other groups of Bushtits forage through their
nesting territories. Females have cream to
yellowish eyes, distinguishing them from
male and juvenile birds, which have
dark brown eyes. Coastal birds
have brown crowns; interior
populations have gray
crowns and brown
cheeks. Southwest
populations, in
which some adult
males have black
masks, were formerly
considered a separate
species, the Black-eared
Bushtit. Some birds may
move downslope to lower
elevations during winter months.

brown crown (coastal species)

ashy gray upperparts

short black bill

long tail

whitish gray underparts sometimes washed buffy

blackish gray legs and feet

• **SONG** Call is high thin somewhat
buzzy excited twittering, given by
many members of flocks. Also a thin, trilled
sir-r-r-r-rrrrrr.

JUVENILE

• **BEHAVIOR** Gregarious, except when breeding. Forages in
groups of 6–30 or more, often with other species, among trees
and shrubs for food; gleans from foliage, branches, and twigs.
Eats insects, their larvae and eggs, and spiders; also some fruit
and berries. During the spring months, young often leave
territory to establish their own colonies. Groups huddle together
in tight mass on nightly roosts to conserve body heat and reduce
energy loss on cold desert nights. If pair is disturbed while
building nest or laying or incubating eggs, they often leave nest
site, sometimes changing mates, and build a new nest.

• **BREEDING** Monogamous. Solitary.

• **NESTING** Incubation 12 days by both sexes; both roost in
nest on eggs at night. Altricial
young brooded by female; stay
in nest 14–15 days, fed by both
sexes. 2 broods per year.

• **POPULATION** Common in
woodlands, scrub, chaparral,
suburbs, parks, and gardens.

Similar Birds

JUNIPER TITMOUSE
OAK TITMOUSE
Larger; head tufts;
larger bills; smaller
flocks; much less active.

VERDIN
Juvenile • shorter tail;
gray-brown upperparts;
gray-brown wash on
sides, flanks, and belly.

Flight Pattern

Weak fluttering flights of short duration,
with rapid wing strokes alternating with
wings pulled to sides; repeated.

Nest Identification

Shape 🐦   Location 🌳🌿

Jug-shaped hanging pouch • lined with vegetation, including flowers, grass,
twigs, moss, lichen, leaves, insect cocoons, hair, and feathers • often secured
by spider web • 1–7.5 m above ground in deciduous tree or shrub • built by
both sexes • 5–7 white eggs, unmarked; oval to short oval, 1.5 cm long.

Plumage Sexes similar	Habitat 🌳🌿 🦅 🌱 🌿	Migration Nonmigratory	Weight 6.0 g

DATE _____ TIME_____ LOCATION _____

Family SITTIDAE	Species *Sitta canadensis*	Length 11 cm	Wingspan 20 cm

RED-BREASTED NUTHATCH

This bird often will eat from the human hand. To protect young from predators, male and female smear pine pitch around the nest entrance. Females differ from males by the dark gray cap and nape and lighter underparts. The blue-gray tail spread in display or flight shows a white subterminal band. Winter range varies yearly, particularly in the East; this sedentary species remains in its breeding range as long as winter food supplies can support it.

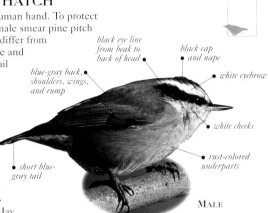

black eye line from beak to back of head

black cap and nape

blue-gray back, shoulders, wings, and rump

white eyebrow

white cheeks

rust-colored underparts

short blue-gray tail

MALE

• **SONG** Calls are nasal and high pitched, resembling the sound of a tiny tin horn, *ank*, *ink*, or *enk*, often repeated in a rapid series.

• **BEHAVIOR** Solitary or in pairs. May join mixed-species feeding flocks after breeding season. Climbs up and down tree trunks, often headfirst, and walks on the underside of limbs. Forages for conifer seeds, nuts, and some insects by gleaning them from bark or foliage; wedges food in tree bark crevices and pounds with bill to break shell or exoskeleton. Male courts female by feeding her, also by turning his back to her and lifting his head and tail, raising his back feathers and drooping his wings, swaying from side to side. Irruptive migrant.

blue-gray upperparts

dark gray crown and nape

FEMALE

lighter buff underparts are rustier on flank and crissum

• **BREEDING** Monogamous. Solitary.

• **NESTING** Incubation 12 days by female. Young altricial; brooded by female; stay in nest 14–21 days, fed by both sexes. 1 brood per year.

• **POPULATION** Fairly common to common in boreal and subalpine conifer forests and mixed conifer-deciduous northern montane forests. Stable. Eastern breeding range currently expanding southward.

• **FEEDERS** Sunflower seeds, peanut butter, and suet.

• **CONSERVATION** Vulnerable to habitat loss due to logging operations.

Similar Birds

WHITE-BREASTED NUTHATCH
Larger; white face lacks black eye line; white underparts with rusty wash on flanks and crissum; blue-gray tail with black outer tail feathers edged and tipped white; voice differs.

Flight Pattern

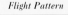

Somewhat weak fluttering flight of short duration, with rapid wing strokes followed by brief folding of wings to sides; repeated.

Nest Identification

Shape

Location

Lined with shredded bark, grass, and roots • usually 1.5–12 m above ground (but up to 36.5 m) in conifer • built by both sexes, but female does most of work • 4–7 white to pinkish white eggs, marked with reddish browns; oval to short oval, 1.5 x 1.2 cm.

Plumage Sexes differ	Habitat	Migration Some migrate	Weight 11 g

DATE _____ TIME_____ LOCATION _____

Family SITTIDAE	Species *Sitta carolinensis*	Length 13–15 cm	Wingspan 23–28 cm

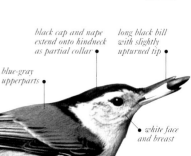

WHITE-BREASTED NUTHATCH

The largest and most widespread of the North American nuthatches, this nimble bird can balance upside down on tree trunks, catch a falling nut in midair, and rapidly hop down skinny branches. In winter it joins mixed-species flocks and often feeds together in the same tree with chickadees, Downy Woodpeckers, and Brown Creepers. It is quick to accept bird feeders, and will often attempt to intimidate other avian visitors by spreading its wings and tail and swaying back and forth. Females in the Northeast have dark blue-gray crowns.

black cap and nape extend onto hindneck as partial collar

long black bill with slightly upturned tip

blue-gray upperparts

blackish blue tertials, secondaries, primaries, and wing coverts with white edging

white face and breast

white patches in blue-black tail

white underparts with rusty wash on flanks, lower belly, and crissum

• **SONG** Sings an ascending *wee-wee-wee-wee-wee-wee-wee*. Call is a hoarse *yank-yank-yank*.

• **BEHAVIOR** Solitary or in pairs; sociable in nonbreeding season. Eats various nuts, seeds, spiders, and insects. Inspects trees with head pointed downward and circles around and underneath limb in search of food. Spends most of its time in trees. Roosts in tree cavities in the winter; often roosts in crevices of bark in summer, some sleeping in the head down, tail up position.

black feet and legs

• **BREEDING** Monogamous. Solitary. Sometimes known to form small colonies.

• **NESTING** Incubation 12 days by female. Young altricial; brooded by female; stay in nest 14 days, fed by both sexes. 1 brood per year.

• **POPULATION** Common in deciduous woodlots and in mixed coniferous-deciduous woods in the North and West.

Similar Birds

RED-BREASTED NUTHATCH Smaller; white face broken by long, black eye stripe; uniform rusty chestnut underparts; smaller bill; voice differs.

• **FEEDERS AND BIRDHOUSES** Comes to feeders for suet and/or seeds; will nest in nest boxes.

• **CONSERVATION** Vulnerable to habitat loss due to logging operations.

Flight Pattern
Weak fluttering flight of short duration; several rapid wing beats alternated with wings drawn to sides; repeated.

Nest Identification	
Shape Location	Lined with bark shreds, hair, and feathers • natural cavity, knothole, woodpecker's hole, or bird box, 3–18.5 m above ground • built by both sexes; female does more • 3–10 white to pinkish eggs, with brown, gray, purple, and red blotches; oval to short oval, 2.0 x 1.4 cm.

Plumage Sexes similar	Habitat	Migration Nonmigratory	Weight 20 g

DATE _____ TIME_____ LOCATION _____

Family SITTIDAE	Species *Sitta pygmaea*	Length 11 cm	Wingspan 20 cm

PYGMY NUTHATCH

In the fall and winter, these nuthatches work through the treetops in loud flocks along with chickadees and titmice. At night, groups of as many as 100 birds will roost in a single cavity. This is the smallest of the North American nuthatches, and like all birds in its genus, it has long toes with sharp claws, allowing it to cling to tree trunks. Its small size, gray-brown cap, and a white spot on its

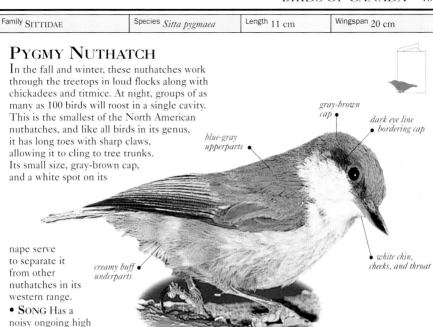

gray-brown cap

dark eye line bordering cap

blue-gray upperparts

white chin, cheeks, and throat

creamy buff underparts

nape serve to separate it from other nuthatches in its western range.

• **SONG** Has a noisy ongoing high rapid call of *tee-dee, tee-dee* and also a flutelike *wee-bee, wee-bee.*

• **BEHAVIOR** Social; gregarious. Often travels in small groups of 2–5, with some of the members being young unmated males that assist the mated pair with digging the nest cavity and feeding the young. Forages for food by climbing up, down, and around trunk and branches, often turning sideways and upside down. Gleans various insects, caterpillars, moths, and seeds of coniferous trees. Pairs bond long-term. Joins mixed-species feeding flocks after the nesting season. Roosts communally.

• **BREEDING** Monogamous. Cooperative.

• **NESTING** Incubation 15–16 days by female. Young altricial; brooded by female; stay in nest 20–22 days, fed by both parents and other birds. 1 brood per year.

• **POPULATION** Fairly common in pine forests and piñon-juniper woodlands. Accidental to the Midwest.

• **FEEDERS AND BIRDHOUSES** Nuts and seeds. Will nest in birdhouses.

• **CONSERVATION** Vulnerable to habitat loss due to logging activities.

Similar Birds

♂ ♀ RED-BREASTED NUTHATCH Larger; black cap; black eye line; white eyebrow; rusty chestnut underparts; voice differs.

Flight Pattern

Short flights, weak and fluttering, with several rapid wing beats, followed by wings pulled to sides; repeated.

Nest Identification

Shape

Location

Lined with leaves, shredded pinecones, plant down, fur, and feathers • in dead tree, old post, abandoned woodpecker hole, or nest box, 2.5–18.5 m above ground • built by both parents and other birds • 4–9 white eggs, sparsely flecked with reddish brown; oval to short oval, 1.5 x 1.1 cm.

Plumage Sexes similar	Habitat	Migration Nonmigratory	Weight 11 g

DATE _____ TIME_____ LOCATION _____

Family CERTHIIDAE	Species *Certhia americana*	Length 13 cm	Wingspan 18–20 cm

BROWN CREEPER

This tree-dwelling bird roosts by hanging onto a tree trunk or the side of a house with its sharp claws. Unlike the nuthatches, it does not move sideways or upside down when foraging for insects. Rather, it circles the tree in an upward direction, as if it were ascending a spiral staircase, or it takes a straighter path up, then drops to the base of a nearby tree and starts working its way up again. The long decurved bill is an efficient tool for picking insects out of bark crevices, and the stiff tail feathers prop the bird upright just as a woodpecker's tail does.

• **SONG** Call is a soft musical *see-see-titi-see*, similar to that of the Golden-crowned Kinglet, but thinner. Call note is a soft thin *see*.

• **BEHAVIOR** Solitary or in pairs. Tame. Often joins mixed-species foraging flocks in winter. Forages for food by spiraling up tree, but does not move down or sideways. Hops back occasionally, but then moves on up. Eats various insects, larvae, seeds, and some nuts. Well camouflaged and difficult to spot; often escapes predators by pressing its body tightly against tree, spreading wings and tail, and remaining motionless. Fledglings roost in tight circle with heads in center of ring.

• **BREEDING** Monogamous. Solitary nester.

• **NESTING** Incubation 13–17 days by female. Young altricial; brooded by female; stay in nest 13–16 days. Fed by both sexes. 1 brood per year.

• **POPULATION** Fairly common in pine, spruce-fir, mixed coniferous-deciduous, swampy forests; declining in some areas.

slender decurved pointed bill

white line over eyes

sharp claws

buff-streaked brown upperparts

white underparts

wings and coverts edged and tipped with buff and white

long rufous tail with stiff pointed tail feathers at end

• **FEEDERS** Will come to feeders for mixture of nuts, peanut butter, suet, and cornmeal. Mixture can be put directly on tree trunk.

• **CONSERVATION** Nesting area threatened due to cutting of forest habitat.

Flight Pattern
Strong direct flights of short duration with rapid shallow wing beats.

Nest Identification	Twigs, moss, conifer needles, pieces of bark, and silk, lined with shredded bark and feathers • in cavity of dead tree, or beneath piece of bark against tree, 1.5–15 m above ground • built by both sexes; female does more • 4–8 white eggs, sparsely flecked with reddish brown and often wreathed; oval to short oval, 1.5 x 1.2 cm.
Shape Location 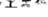	

Plumage Sexes similar	Habitat	Migration Migratory	Weight 9.0 g

DATE _____ TIME _____ LOCATION _____

Family TROGLODYTIDAE	Species *Salpinctes obsoletus*	Length 15 cm	Wingspan 23 cm

ROCK WREN

This bird frequents more arid and barren terrain than its cousin, the Canyon Wren. Its grayish brown color serves as a camouflage, but the male often can be spotted when he hops to the top of a boulder to sing or to admonish intruders. The nest is built in a rock crevice, but a trail of tiny rocks leading to the opening is a clue to its location.

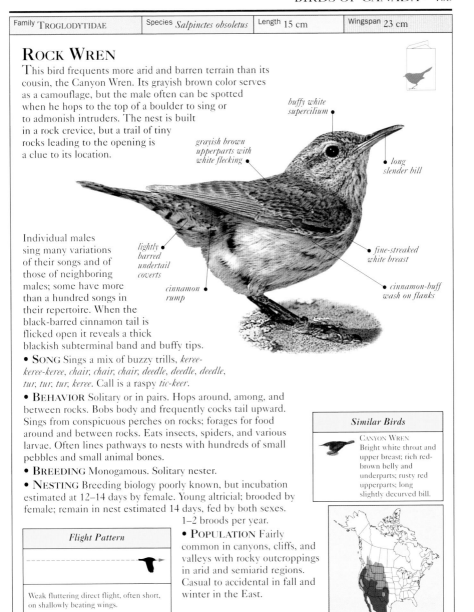

buffy white supercilium

grayish brown upperparts with white flecking

long slender bill

Individual males sing many variations of their songs and of those of neighboring males; some have more than a hundred songs in their repertoire. When the black-barred cinnamon tail is flicked open it reveals a thick blackish subterminal band and buffy tips.

lightly barred undertail coverts

cinnamon rump

fine-streaked white breast

cinnamon-buff wash on flanks

• **SONG** Sings a mix of buzzy trills, *keree-keree-keree, chair, chair, chair, deedle, deedle, deedle, tur, tur, tur, keree.* Call is a raspy *tic-keer.*

• **BEHAVIOR** Solitary or in pairs. Hops around, among, and between rocks. Bobs body and frequently cocks tail upward. Sings from conspicuous perches on rocks; forages for food around and between rocks. Eats insects, spiders, and various larvae. Often lines pathways to nests with hundreds of small pebbles and small animal bones.

• **BREEDING** Monogamous. Solitary nester.

• **NESTING** Breeding biology poorly known, but incubation estimated at 12–14 days by female. Young altricial; brooded by female; remain in nest estimated 14 days, fed by both sexes. 1–2 broods per year.

• **POPULATION** Fairly common in canyons, cliffs, and valleys with rocky outcroppings in arid and semiarid regions. Casual to accidental in fall and winter in the East.

Similar Birds

CANYON WREN
Bright white throat and upper breast; rich red-brown belly and underparts; rusty red upperparts; long slightly decurved bill.

Flight Pattern

Weak fluttering direct flight, often short, on shallowly beating wings.

Nest Identification

Shape

Location

Rootlets, grasses, and various stems, with lining of feathers, various hair, and fur • in ridges of rock, crevices, burrows, banks, or even buildings • usually hidden by pile of rocks • built by both sexes • 4–10 white eggs, lightly flecked with reddish brown; oval, 1.8 cm long.

Plumage Sexes similar	Habitat	Migration Migratory	Weight 17 g

DATE _____ TIME_____ LOCATION _____

| Family TROGLODYTIDAE | Species *Catherpes mexicanus* | Length 15 cm | Wingspan 19 cm |

CANYON WREN

True to its name, this energetic bird historically makes its home among the canyons, rocks, and caves in western North America. Adapting to man and his buildings, this wren now often builds its nest in or on them, especially those made of stone. Often staying hidden, its bold white breast showing through the crevices

reddish brown upperparts with dark barring and white flecking

long decurved bill

rusty chestnut tail with narrow black barring

bright white throat and upper breast

rusty chestnut underparts and belly

and ridges can be a clue to this bird's presence; but it is more often heard than seen, for the male's loud happy-sounding song cascades and bounces along canyon walls.

• **SONG** A descending gushing liquid rain of notes, *peup, peup, peup tew tew tew tew tew tew*, ending with a buzzy *mew*. Call is an abrasive nasal *jeet*.

• **BEHAVIOR** Solitary or in pairs. Thoroughly investigates rocks to look for food; hopping over, around, under, and between, then singing, it gleans food from rock surfaces and crevices. Often bobs body like a Rock Wren and cocks tail over back. Very tame; will enter houses and ranch buildings. Eats mainly spiders and insects.

• **BREEDING** Monogamous. Solitary nester.

• **NESTING** Incubation 12–18 days by female. Young altricial; brooded by female. Not known how long young stay in nest, but fed by both sexes. 2 broods per year; sometimes 3 in the South.

• **POPULATION** Common in arid and semiarid rocky canyons, rocky outcroppings, and cliffs, often near water; also around stone buildings and stone chimneys.

Similar Birds

ROCK WREN
Gray-brown upperparts barred dark brown and flecked white; cinnamon rump; barred tail with rufous-tipped corners and black subterminal band; dark streaking on white breast; whitish underparts washed buff; slender, shorter, barely curved bill.

Flight Pattern

Weak and fluttering direct flight, often of short duration, on shallowly beating wings.

Nest Identification

Shape ◗ ◖   Location ⌂ 🪨 🏠 🪹 🏚️

Sticks, leaves, mosses, and finer material, with lining of feathers and fur • hidden in ridges of rocks or crevice, under stones, in holes, or sometimes in buildings • built by both sexes • 4–7 white eggs, lightly flecked with reddish brown; oval, 1.8 cm long.

| Plumage Sexes similar | Habitat 🪨 ⛰️ | Migration Nonmigratory | Weight 14 g |

DATE _____ TIME_____ LOCATION _____

Family TROGLODYTIDAE	Species *Thryothorus ludovicianus*	Length 14 cm	Wingspan 20 cm

CAROLINA WREN

South Carolina's state bird is sensitive to cold weather. Mild winters allow Carolina Wrens to expand their range northwards but most will not survive the next hard winter. Energetic, loud, and conspicuous, the largest wren in eastern North America is equally at home in moist deciduous woodlots, on the farm, or in shaded suburbs. Pairs stay together on their territories all year, and the male may sing at any time of day, any day of the year. The female often responds with a quick "growl" of *t-shihrrr*.

bold white stripe above eye

rusty brown upperparts with dark brown bars on wings and tail

long slightly decurved bill

white chin, throat, and upper breast

rich buffy underparts

• **SONG** A bold clear *teakettle tea-kettle teakettle* or *cherry, cherry, cherry*. Each male has a repertoire of 25–40 or more songs that neighboring males match with a responding vocalization.

• **BEHAVIOR** Most often in pairs. Sings from exposed perch. Usually stays hidden in undergrowth, but will emerge if it hears squeaking noises. Pokes into every nook and cranny, hopping with tail cocked over back. Eats mostly insects, larvae, and insect eggs, but will take small vertebrates, snails, berries, and some fruits. Common around human habitation; enters open buildings to inspect dark recesses for insects or spiders. Builds its bulky nest in any container large enough to hold it, from coat pockets and boots to buckets, flower baskets, and mailboxes.

• **BREEDING** Monogamous. Solitary nester.

• **NESTING** Incubation 12–14 days by female. Altricial young brooded by female; stay in nest 12–14 days, fed by both sexes but often tended by the male while female begins another clutch. 2 broods per year, often 3 in the South.

• **POPULATION** Common. Numbers decrease in northern range after harsh winters, but overall population stable except in the Northeast and Midwest where it is recorded as declining.

• **FEEDERS AND BIRDHOUSES** Suet and peanut butter. Will use nest boxes, often filling several with dummy nests.

• **CONSERVATION** Declines are of some concern.

Similar Birds

BEWICK'S WREN Whitish underparts; long rounded tail edged with white spots; reddish brown to gray-brown upperparts; long white eye stripe; frequently flips long tail; voice differs.

MARSH WREN White-striped back; long white eye stripe; white underparts washed rufous-buff on sides and flanks; habitat and voice differ.

Flight Pattern
Direct flight somewhat weak and fluttering with shallow rapid wing beats.

Nest Identification	
Shape Location	Stems, leaves, grasses, bark pieces, mosses, feathers, and snakeskin • cavity of tree, stump, or bank; sometimes old woodpecker hole, rafter, mailbox, bird box, or almost any cavity • built by both sexes • 4–8 white or light pink eggs, marked with brown; oval, 2.0 x 1.5 cm.

Plumage Sexes similar	Habitat	Migration Nonmigratory	Weight 20 g

DATE _____ TIME_____ LOCATION _____

Family TROGLODYTIDAE	Species *Thryomanes bewickii*	Length 13 cm	Wingspan 18 cm

BEWICK'S WREN

This bird ranges across most of the western United States eastward to the Appalachians. It usually builds its nest in natural cavities, but also will nest in mailboxes, baskets, cow skulls, or almost anything that provides shelter. A tame bird, it often resides near farms, homes, and small towns. For reasons still largely unknown, the Bewick's Wren is now rare in areas where it was once common. Since at least the 1960s, populations have seriously declined east of the Mississippi River. Color varies geographically from mousy gray-brown in the West to rusty brown in the East.

fine, dark brown or black barring on tail

white eye stripe

reddish or grayish brown upperparts with barring on wings

long slightly decurved bill

long rounded tail, with white spots on tips of feathers

whitish to grayish underparts

• **SONG** Male sings *chip, chip, chip, de-da-ah, tee-dee*, similar to the pattern of a Song Sparrow, but high, thin, buzzing, and variable, often ending in a thin trill. Call is a flat *jipp.*

• **BEHAVIOR** Often in pairs. Noisy and conspicuous; rather tame and bold. Holds tail high above back as it hops, often flicking it from side to side. Sings with head thrown back and tail depressed downward. Feeds mostly on ground or gleans food from trees. Eats mostly insects, but takes some spiders. Male builds several "dummy" nests in his territory; female chooses one and helps construct it.

• **BREEDING** Monogamous. Solitary.

• **NESTING** Incubation 12–14 days by female. Young altricial; brooded by female; stay in nest 14 days, fed by both sexes. 1 brood per year; possibly 2 in the South.

• **POPULATION** Common in the West in open woodland, scrubland, and around farms and suburbs. Declining east of the Rocky Mountains with most dramatic reductions happening east of the Mississippi River.

• **BIRDHOUSES** Will accept nest boxes.

• **CONSERVATION** Of special concern, especially in the East.

Similar Birds

CAROLINA WREN
Larger; rusty brown upperparts; buff underparts; shorter tail without white tips; song differs.

MARSH WREN
White-streaked back; rich brown upperparts; buff-washed sides and flanks; tail lacks white tips; different habitat and song.

Flight Pattern

Somewhat weak fluttering direct flight on shallow wing beats; often of short duration.

Nest Identification

Shape ◣   Location 🏠🪹🪺🏚️🛖

Twigs, mosses, bits of snakeskin, and grass, lined with feathers • in cavity of almost anything; often tree, man-made structure, hollow log, post, basket, etc. • built by both sexes • 4–11 white eggs with flecks of purple, brown, and gray; oval, 1.8 x 1.3 cm.

Plumage Sexes similar	Habitat 🌳🌲🪴🔺✈	Migration Eastern birds migrate	Weight 11 g

DATE _____ TIME_____ LOCATION _____

Family TROGLODYTIDAE	Species *Troglodytes aedon*	Length 12 cm	Wingspan 15–18 cm

HOUSE WREN

This plain bird has a wide range, breeding from southern Canada to Mexico. However, even though its range spread southward in the East throughout most of the 20th century, it is not currently found nesting in southeastern states. Despite its size, the House Wren is highly competitive when searching for nesting territory. It often invades nests of other wrens and songbirds, puncturing their eggs and killing their young. When it comes to selecting a nesting site, the male begins building dummy nests in almost any available cavity in his territory, from natural cavities and nesting boxes to boots, cans, buckets, toolboxes, coat pockets, and mailboxes. Birds in southeastern Arizona mountains have a buff supercilium, throat, and breast.

narrow black barring on tail

narrow black barring on wings

grayish brown upperparts

pale streak above eyes

narrow pale eye ring

thin slightly decurved bill

pale gray underparts

narrow black barring on sides, lower belly, and crissum

- **SONG** Sings beautiful, trilling, energetic flutelike melody delivered in a gurgling outburst and repeated at short intervals. Call is rough scolding *cheh-cheh*, often run into a scolding chatter.
- **BEHAVIOR** Solitary or in pairs. Loud and conspicuous. Relatively tame and bold. Often cocks tail upward. Eats various insects, spiders, millipedes, and some snails. Male starts several dummy nests in territory as part of courtship, then female joins him to inspect them and selects one to complete for nest. Highly migratory except in extreme southwestern US.
- **BREEDING** Usually monogamous but sometimes polygamous. Males occasionally have 2 mates at same time.
- **NESTING** Incubation 13–15 days by female. Altricial young stay in nest 12–18 days. Brooded by female. Fed by both sexes or female only. 2–3 broods per year.
- **POPULATION** Common in open woodlands, shrubs, farmlands, suburbs, gardens, and parks.
- **FEEDERS** Will nest in man-made bird boxes.
- **CONSERVATION** Neotropical migrant. Nestlings sometimes are affected by bluebottle fly larvae and may die in nest.

Similar Birds

WINTER WREN
Smaller; darker; heavier black barring on tail, flanks, and underparts; shorter tail; different voice.

Flight Pattern
Weak fluttering direct flight with rapid shallow wing beats.

Nest Identification	
Shape Location	Base made of sticks • lined with hair, feathers, cocoons, and fine material • almost anywhere in cavity of tree, bird box, abandoned hole or nest, cow skull, pipes, watering cans, etc. • male builds platform; female lines • 5–9 white eggs with brown flecks, occasionally wreathed; short rounded ovate to oval, 1.5 x 1.3 cm.

Plumage Sexes similar	Habitat	Migration Most migrate	Weight 11 g

DATE _____ TIME_____ LOCATION _____

Family TROGLODYTIDAE	Species *Troglodytes troglodytes*	Length 10 cm	Wingspan 15 cm

WINTER WREN

One of the smallest songbirds in North America, this short-tailed wren nests primarily in the coniferous forests of Canada and the northern US, but it also resides along the Pacific Coast from central California to the Aleutians, and in the Appalachians south to northern Georgia. It usually hides in thick undergrowth, but when excited it will fly up, perch, bob its head up and down, and deliver an alarm call or a rapid, cascading song that may last six to seven seconds and contain more than a hundred notes. This is the only member of the wren family found in Europe.

gray to brown superciliary stripe

stubby tail

dark brown upperparts with faint barring

• **SONG** Male sings warbling melody of varied up-and-down notes with rapid trills; some notes high, thin, and silvery. Also has whisper song. Call is abrasive *chirrr* or *tik-tik-tik*.

• **BEHAVIOR** Often solitary; pairs in breeding season. Scampers on ground and in low trees while foraging, ducking in and out of root wads, in and around logs, into brush piles, and any opening or cranny large enough. Gleans food from surfaces, mostly insects, caterpillars, and berries. Sometimes will approach humans for bread crumbs. Bobs head and body and flicks tail, which is often cocked over back. Frequents habitats near water.

dark brown underparts

heavy, dark brownish black barring on flanks, underparts, and tail

• **BREEDING** Polygamous.

• **NESTING** Incubation 12–16 days by female. Altricial young stay in nest 16–19 days, fed by female or both sexes. 1–2 broods per year.

• **POPULATION** Abundant. West Coast, northwest montane, and southern Appalachian populations permanent; others highly migratory.

• **BIRDHOUSES** Will roost in bird box.

• **CONSERVATION** Vulnerable to habitat loss caused by logging operations.

Similar Birds

HOUSE WREN
Larger; longer tail; less prominent barring on belly, sides, and flanks; faint eye stripe; voice differs.

Flight Pattern

Weak fluttering flights of short duration on rapidly beating wings.

Nest Identification

Shape

Location

Cavity filled with platform of sticks, covered with moss and grass, lined with hair and feathers • in cavity of log or stump, under tree roots, and sometimes in building • 0–2 m above ground • male builds 1–5 nests; female chooses • 4–7 white eggs with brown flecks concentrated at large end; oval, 1.7 x 1.3 cm.

Plumage Sexes similar	Habitat	Migration Most migrate	Weight 9.0 g

DATE _____ TIME_____ LOCATION _____

Family TROGLODYTIDAE	Species *Cistothorus platensis*	Length 11 cm	Wingspan 14–15 cm

SEDGE WREN

Camouflaged by its plumage, this wren stays hidden in dense marsh grasses, except when it perches to sing, which it sometimes does at night. The female chooses one of several rather well-concealed nests built by the male, then lines it with materials of her choice. This wren ranges over much of the grasslands and marshlands of the central and north-central United States and south-central Canada, often going where the habitat is most suitable and often changing nesting areas from year to year.

brownish black streaking on crown

brown upperparts

short slender bill

whitish eyebrow

brownish black and white streaking on back and scapulars

buff to whitish underparts

short barred tail

• **SONG** Sings a bold melody of single disconnected notes, followed by a rapid chatter of dry notes. Has call of *chip-chip*.

• **BEHAVIOR** Solitary on wintering grounds; often in pairs in small habitats; in small colonies in larger more favorable habitats. Secretive, staying down in the foliage except while singing, when it often ascends to a more exposed perch. Scampers on ground in wet meadows and in low brush, foraging for food. Eats mostly insects and spiders. Male builds several dummy nests and female chooses one; males will often destroy other bird's eggs when they discover them, including those of other Sedge Wrens.

• **BREEDING** Polygamous.

• **NESTING** Incubation 12–16 days by female. Young altricial; stay in nest 12–14 days. Fed by both sexes, but female does more. 2 broods per year.

• **POPULATION** Common in range but often very local; numbers may change from year to year. Rare in winter in New Mexico and casual to California in fall migration.

• **CONSERVATION** Neotropical migrant with some birds wintering in northeast Mexico. Vulnerable to habitat loss caused by agriculture.

Similar Birds

MARSH WREN
Larger; longer bill; dark crown; darker and more brown overall; unbarred rufous rump • western birds have duller, paler plumage with less distinct white streaking on back • eastern birds have richer browns and distinct back streaking.

Flight Pattern

Weak fluttering flight with shallow, rapid wing beats; alternating several wing strokes with wings being drawn to sides; repeated.

Nest Identification	
Shape ⬡ Location 🌾 🌿 🌱	Stems, grasses, and sedges • lined with plant down, feathers, and fur • on grasses or reeds, usually near water or marshy area • 0–60 cm above ground in grass • male builds several nests; female selects one and lines • 4–8 white eggs; oval to pyriform, 1.5 x 1.2 cm.

Plumage Sexes similar	Habitat	Migration Migratory	Weight 9.0 g

DATE _____ TIME _____ LOCATION _____

Family TROGLODYTIDAE	Species *Cistothorus palustris*	Length 11–13 cm	Wingspan 14–18 cm

MARSH WREN

This bird usually stays hidden, but its song can be heard over the reeds and cattails of the marshlands. The male builds several intricate globular-shaped nests, which have side doors; the female chooses one and adds the lining of shredded plants and feathers. The male often roosts in one of the dummy nests. Some males have more than one mate, with each one occupying a small section of his territory. The black-and-white streaking on the back of the Marsh Wren is less distinct in western birds.

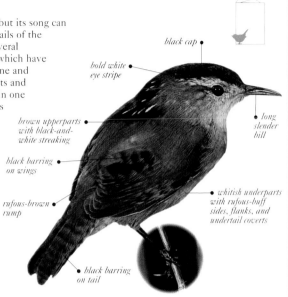

black cap

bold white eye stripe

brown upperparts with black-and-white streaking

black barring on wings

rufous-brown rump

long slender bill

whitish underparts with rufous-buff sides, flanks, and undertail coverts

black barring on tail

• **SONG** Sings a gurgling trilling melody, with western birds singing a harsher song than eastern birds. Call is an abrasive *te-suk-te-suk*. Western birds may have more than 200 songs in their varied repertoire, while eastern males may have only around 70.

• **BEHAVIOR** Solitary; in pairs or small colonies, depending on the size and quality of the habitat. Often secretive, foraging for food in tall marsh grasses and reeds, where it gleans aquatic insects, larvae, caterpillars, snails, and sometimes other bird's eggs. Males often sing from exposed perches or even skylark before dropping back into the cover of the thick vegetation; sometimes sing at night. Often enters the nests of other birds and destroys their eggs, sometimes having its own eggs destroyed in turn.

• **BREEDING** Polygamous. Colonial.

• **NESTING** Incubation 12–16 days by female. Young altricial; stay in nest 11–16 days, fed by both sexes, but female does more. 2 broods per year.

• **POPULATION** Common despite loss of freshwater wetlands. Most populations are migratory, but some in the West and on the coasts, are nonmigratory year round residents.

• **CONSERVATION** Neotropical migrant; vulnerable to habitat lost to development, agriculture, wetland drainage.

Similar Birds
SEDGE WREN Smaller; shorter bill; buffy brown head and upperparts; dark streaking on cinnamon rump; less distinct eye stripe; voice differs.

Flight Pattern
Weak fluttering flights, often of short duration; alternates several quick wing beats with brief pause and wings at sides.

Nest Identification	Reeds, grass, sedge, bulrushes for outer layer; grasses, reeds, and cattails for central cavity, lined with shredded soft materials • about 30–90 cm above water (but up to 4.5 m) • male builds several nests, female selects and completes • 3–10 brown eggs, flecked with darker brown and sometimes wreathed; usually ovate, 1.8 x 1.4 cm.
Shape Location	

Plumage Sexes similar	Habitat	Migration Migratory	Weight 11 g

DATE _____ TIME_____ LOCATION _____

Family CINCLIDAE	Species *Cinclus mexicanus*	Length 19 cm	Wingspan 23 cm

AMERICAN DIPPER

The American Dipper frequents habitat in western mountains or canyons near streams fed by melting snow, glaciers, and coastal rains. A notable characteristic of the American Dipper is its ability to fly straight into the air from underwater. Penguinlike, it uses its wings to "fly" underwater to depths of more than 6 meters. It may even walk on the bottom as it forages. This bird usually builds its nests just above the water level on cliffs, midstream boulders, or bridges, and often hidden behind waterfalls. Some of its behavior is similar to that of a wren, and it often bobs its body up and down as it stands above the water. Juveniles are similar to adults but have a pinkish bill and are paler gray, especially on the underparts.

smoky black head

straight black bill

slaty gray-black overall

pink legs and feet

- **SONG** Long series of rich warbles, buzzes, and trills, somewhat like a mimic thrush. Calls are a shrill loud *zzeip, zzreip,* or *rreip.*
- **BEHAVIOR** Solitary; in pairs only during breeding season. Wading, diving, or swimming to stream bottoms, this bird feeds on aquatic insects, their larvae, clams, snails, small fish, and crustaceans. Sometimes catches insects floating on water surfaces or gleans them from rocks and logs along the shoreline. The dipping and bobbing of its body may be a visual signal to its mate when the noise of a mountain stream would drown out any vocalization. Ranges as high as 3,500 meters in summer and moves to lower elevations in winter instead of migrating. Territories are linear, following a stream for up to a 1.5 km.

JUVENILE

- **BREEDING** Monogamous. Sometimes polygamous.
- **NESTING** Incubation 13–17 days by female. Young altricial; stay in nest 18–25 days, fed by both sexes, but female does more. Young able to swim and dive upon departing the nest. 2 broods per year.
- **POPULATION** Fairly common but local.
- **CONSERVATION** Vulnerable to habitat loss caused by the damming and pollution of streams.

Similar Birds

No other songbird in North America is similar in appearance and habits.

Flight Pattern
Strong swift direct flight on rapidly beating wings.

Nest Identification	
Shape ⬤ Location 🪨 🌲 〰〰	Mosses • 0–2.5 m above the stream • built by female • 3–6 white eggs, unmarked; subelliptical, 2.5 cm long.

Plumage Sexes similar	Habitat 〰 ▲ 〰〰	Migration Nonmigratory	Weight 6.0 g

Family REGULIDAE	Species *Regulus satrapa*	Length 10 cm	Wingspan 17–18 cm

GOLDEN-CROWNED KINGLET

Living in dense coniferous forests, this tiny bird's baseball-sized sphere-shaped nest is so small that its clutch of tiny eggs must be laid in two layers. A tame bird, it will sometimes enter human habitations and not try to escape if held. It often feeds in mixed-species foraging flocks with woodpeckers, creepers, chickadees, nuthatches, and others. Females and juveniles have a yellow crown bordered by black.

orange patch on crown bordered by yellow

broad whitish stripe above eye

olive-green upperparts

black yellowish-edged tertials and secondaries

short straight black bill

2 whitish wing bars

pale buff to whitish underparts

MALE

- **SONG** Sings a song beginning with 3–4 high-pitched *tsee, tsee, tsee* notes, followed by a rapid trill. Call is a series of 3–4 high-pitched *tsee* notes.
- **BEHAVIOR** Solitary or in pairs. Tame. Flits wings as it hops along branches. Forages through dense foliage of trees to pick off food. Eats mainly insects, their eggs, and larvae; takes some seeds. Drinks tree sap, sometimes taking it from sapsucker drill wells. May hawk insects or hover briefly to glean them from trunk, branch, or foliage.
- **BREEDING** Monogamous. Solitary nester.
- **NESTING** Incubation 14–15 days by female. Young altricial; stay in nest 14–19 days, fed by both sexes. 1–2 broods per year.
- **POPULATION** Common in coniferous woodlands. Populations may drop after harsh cold seasons on winter range;

yellow crown patch bordered by black

FEMALE

Similar Birds

RUBY-CROWNED KINGLET
White eye ring instead of white stripe over eye; underparts are darker, dusky greenish yellow; olive-green crown and upperparts; different call • only male has concealed red crown patch.

long-term stable, with range expanding to northeast. Many populations nonmigratory.
- **CONSERVATION** Neotropical migrant. Vulnerable to habitat loss caused by logging, especially of mature coniferous forests.

Flight Pattern

Weak fluttering flight, alternating rapid shallow wing strokes with a brief pull of wings to sides. Hovers over food before dipping down to pick it up with beak.

Nest Identification	
Shape 🥚 🦅 Location	Lichen and moss, with lining of bark chips, rootlets, and feathers • in branch of conifer, 9–18.5 m above ground • built by female • 5–11 creamy white to muddy cream eggs splotched brown or gray, usually wreathed; elliptical ovate, 1.3 cm long.

Plumage Sexes differ	Habitat 🌲 🌾	Migration Migratory	Weight 6.0 g

Family REGULIDAE	Species *Regulus calendula*	Length 11 cm	Wingspan 17–19 cm

RUBY-CROWNED KINGLET

This small bird often is seen in mixed-species foraging flocks with creepers, nuthatches, titmice, warblers, and other kinglets. The red patch on the male's crown usually is not visible, unless he becomes excited, at which time he flashes it open and the whole crown seems to be gushing blood. The female and juvenile are similar to the male but lack the red patch. This species is widely distributed in the boreal zone across northern and western North America as a breeding bird, it is highly migratory.

small, often concealed, red patch on crown

white eye ring

short black bill

dusky buff to whitish underparts

olive-green upperparts

MALE

• **SONG** Series of high-pitched *tsee, tsee* notes, followed by several *tew* notes, followed by a 3-note trill of *liberty-liberty-liberty;* an impressively long and loud song for such a small bird. Calls are emphatic *je-ditt* and *cack-cack.*

• **BEHAVIOR** Solitary or in pairs. Tame and active. Picks food off tree trunks, branches, and dense foliage; may hawk or hover to take food. Eats mainly insects, their eggs, and larvae. Also eats some fruits and seeds. Drinks tree sap, especially from the drill wells of sapsuckers. Has "nervous" habit of flicking wings when foraging, perhaps to startle insects into flinching and revealing themselves.

2 white wing bars

yellowish edged secondaries and tertials

FEMALE

• **BREEDING** Monogamous. Solitary nester.

• **NESTING** Incubation 12–14 days by female. Altricial young leave nest at 10–16 days, fed by both sexes. 1 brood per year.

• **POPULATION** Common and widespread in coniferous and mixed conifer-deciduous forests. Studies indicate that populations may be regulated by conditions on the wintering grounds.

• **CONSERVATION** Neotropical migrant. Vulnerable to habitat lost to logging operations. Rare cowbird host.

Similar Birds

GOLDEN-CROWNED KINGLET
White stripe above eye; paler underparts; song differs • male has orange crown patch with yellow and black border • females and juveniles have yellow crown patch with black border.

HUTTON'S VIREO
Stockier; larger head; stout bill; pale lores; olive-gray upperparts; secondaries and tertials lack yellow edging; does not flick wings; white eye ring broken above eyes; voice differs • western range.

Flight Pattern	

Weak fluttering flight with shallow wing beats, alternating several quick strokes with brief periods of wings folded to sides. Hovers over branches to pick off food.

Nest Identification	
Shape 〇 ▮ Location 🜊	Moss, lichen, down, twigs, and dead leaves, lined with finer materials, including feathers • hanging from tree branch, 60 cm–30.5 m above ground • built by female • 5–11 creamy white to muddy cream eggs, splotched with brown or gray, usually wreathed; elliptical ovate to oval, 1.3 cm long.

Plumage Sexes differ	Habitat 🌲🌿	Migration Migratory	Weight 6.0 g

DATE _____ TIME_____ LOCATION _____

Family SYLVIIDAE	Species *Polioptila caerulea*	Length 11 cm	Wingspan 15–17 cm

BLUE-GRAY GNATCATCHER

This slender bird can be seen in the East foraging in the foliage of tall trees; in the West it can be seen in thickets or chaparral. Females are similar to males but have less blue in their plumage and, like the juvenile male, lack the black line on the sides of the crown. The high thin *speee, speee, speee* notes, sounding like the calls of a baby bird, may attract attention before the tiny bird is seen.

• **SONG** Sings a low-pitched trilling *zee-you, zee-you,* heard infrequently. Its call, which is given often, is a *pwee* or *speee,* inflected like a question.

• **BEHAVIOR** Solitary or in pairs. Forages in trees, shrubs, or thickets. Eats insects, their eggs, and larvae. Flicks long tail open and from side to side. Forages near branch tips. Catches insects in flight. May hover briefly above food before taking it in its bill. Disturbance of the nest early in nest building may cause the pair to dismantle it and rebuild on another site.

• **BREEDING** Monogamous. Solitary nester.

• **NESTING** Incubation 13 days by both sexes. Young altricial; brooded by female; stay in nest 10–12 days, fed by both sexes. 1 brood per year; 2 in far south.

• **POPULATION** Common. Population increasing and range expanding northeasterly.

• **CONSERVATION** Neotropical migrant. Common victim of cowbird parasitism.

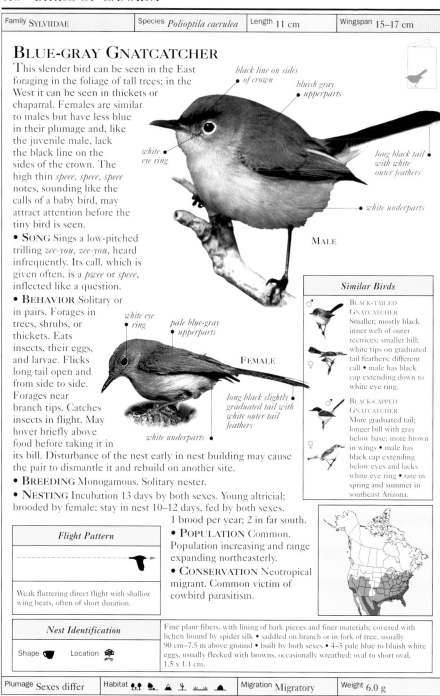

black line on sides of crown

bluish gray upperparts

white eye ring

long black tail with white outer feathers

white underparts

MALE

Similar Birds

BLACK-TAILED GNATCATCHER
Smaller; mostly black inner web of outer rectrices; smaller bill; white tips on graduated tail feathers; different call • male has black cap extending down to white eye ring.

BLACK-CAPPED GNATCATCHER
More graduated tail; longer bill with gray below base; more brown in wings • male has black cap extending below eyes and lacks white eye ring • rare in spring and summer in southeast Arizona.

white eye ring

pale blue-gray upperparts

FEMALE

long black slightly graduated tail with white outer tail feathers

white underparts

Flight Pattern

Weak fluttering direct flight with shallow wing beats, often of short duration.

Nest Identification

Shape • Location •

Fine plant fibers, with lining of bark pieces and finer materials; covered with lichen bound by spider silk • saddled on branch or in fork of tree, usually 90 cm–7.5 m above ground • built by both sexes • 4–5 pale blue to bluish white eggs, usually flecked with browns, occasionally wreathed; oval to short oval, 1.5 x 1.1 cm.

Plumage Sexes differ	Habitat	Migration Migratory	Weight 6.0 g

DATE _____ TIME_____ LOCATION _____

Family TURDIDAE	Species *Luscinia svecica*	Length 14 cm	Wingspan 23 cm

BLUETHROAT

This Eurasian bird has successfully established a breeding population in North America on the tundra of northern Alaska, and it is a regular migrant on St. Lawrence Island. It usually hides on the ground under dense thickets and trees, except when the male skylarks or flies to a high perch to sing. Females and juveniles have a pale throat with a black border. In all plumages, the bird can be identified in flight by the rufous patches at the base of the tail in combination with its dark brown terminal band.

• **SONG** Has clear bell-like *ting-ting-ting* at the beginning of its varied, melodious song, which often includes imitations of other birds. Sings day or night. Call is a *buyt-tock*.

• **BEHAVIOR** Furtive. Frequents overgrown thickets, especially near water. Forages on ground or in low bushes for food. Often runs on ground and holds its tail erect. Eats mostly insects, small snails, earthworms, seeds, and some berries.

• **BREEDING** Monogamous. Males have intricate display flight. Male sings while moving around female with his wings drooped, tail cocked, and head thrown back.

• **NESTING** Incubation 14 days by female. Altricial young brooded by female; stay in nest 14 days, fed by both sexes. 1 brood per year.

• **POPULATION** Uncommon. Small Alaskan population stable or possibly increasing. Casual to regular migrant on outer islands in Bering Sea.

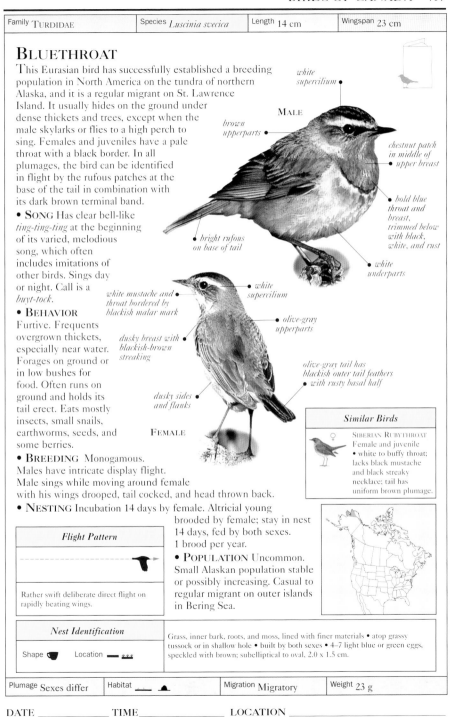

white supercilium

MALE

brown upperparts

chestnut patch in middle of upper breast

bold blue throat and breast, trimmed below with black, white, and rust

bright rufous on base of tail

white underparts

white mustache and throat bordered by blackish malar mark

white supercilium

olive-gray upperparts

dusky breast with blackish-brown streaking

olive-gray tail has blackish outer tail feathers with rusty basal half

dusky sides and flanks

FEMALE

Similar Birds

♀ SIBERIAN RUBYTHROAT Female and juvenile • white to buffy throat; lacks black mustache and black streaky necklace; tail has uniform brown plumage.

Flight Pattern
Rather swift deliberate direct flight on rapidly beating wings.

Nest Identification	
Shape	Location

Grass, inner bark, roots, and moss, lined with finer materials • atop grassy tussock or in shallow hole • built by both sexes • 4–7 light blue or green eggs, speckled with brown; subelliptical to oval, 2.0 x 1.5 cm.

Plumage Sexes differ	Habitat	Migration Migratory	Weight 23 g

DATE _____ TIME_____ LOCATION _____

Family TURDIDAE	Species *Oenanthe oenanthe*	Length 14–15 cm	Wingspan 27–28 cm

NORTHERN WHEATEAR

This long-distance flier begins its migratory route near Greenland and eventually reaches West Africa. During its courtship display, the male sings while flying upward, continues to sing while hovering, then sings with tail spread toward the female as it is gliding back down. Females and nonbreeding males are similar and show a white rump and tail base in flight.

- **SONG** Utters bossy *chack-chack* and whistled *hweet*. Song is often given in flight and imitates songs of other birds, combining call notes into a scratchy jumble of warbled notes.

- **BEHAVIOR** Solitary or in pairs. Bobs tail. Active; often nervously restless when foraging. Often makes short flights to hawk insects in air near ground. Picks food off trees and shrubs and forages on ground. Eats various insects, fruit, seeds, and small bulbs. Inhabits open, dry areas of tundra and mountain slopes, often near rocky areas. Often perches on rocks, trees, or posts.

- **BREEDING** Monogamous. Solitary nester.

- **NESTING** Incubation 14 days by both sexes, but female does more. Altricial young stay in nest 15–16 days; brooded by female; fed by both sexes. 1–2 broods per year.

- **POPULATION** Rare on Atlantic Coast primarily in autumn migration. Accidental elsewhere. Fairly common breeding bird in Greenland, Siberia, and arctic regions of Alaska and both eastern and western Canada.

dark gray cap

white supercilium

dark gray back and nape

black wings

black terminal half of tail

white tail base

black eye line and cheeks

buff wash on throat, breast, and flanks

white underparts

MALE

rusty wash on throat and breast

brown upperparts

white belly

FEMALE

Flight Pattern	
Relatively slow direct flight with shallow wing beats. Sallies from ground and hawks insects in air.	

Nest Identification	
Shape	Grass, roots, and moss • lined with finer materials • in rock crevice or wood pile or on ground or cliff ridge • built by both sexes • 3–8 pale blue eggs usually flecked with red-brown; subelliptical, 2.0 x 1.5 cm.
Location	

Plumage Sexes differ	Habitat	Migration Migratory	Weight 14 g

DATE _____ TIME _____ LOCATION _____

Family TURDIDAE	Species *Sialia sialis*	Length 18–20 cm	Wingspan 29–33 cm

EASTERN BLUEBIRD

This brightly colored bird inhabits open woodlands, meadows, and fields. Its population has been in serious decline due to competition from other birds for its nesting holes, as well as occasional severe snowstorms in the South that kill them in great numbers. Juveniles show gray-brown upperparts with white spotting on the back, a brownish chest with white scalloping, a white belly and crissum, a white eye ring, and a bluish tail and wings.

- **SONG** Sings melodic *chur chur-lee chur-lee.* Male gives call of *true-a-ly, true-a-ly.*
- **BEHAVIOR** Pairs, family groups, or small flocks. Gregarious in winter, often forming large flocks and roosting communally in natural cavities or nest boxes at night. Forages in open from low perches. Flies from perch to ground and forages for food. Eats mostly insects, earthworms, and spiders but also takes snails, lizards, and frogs. In winter eats mostly berries and seeds.
- **BREEDING** Monogamous. In pairs and small groups.
- **NESTING** Incubation 12–14 days by female. Altricial young stay in nest 15–20 days; brooded by female, fed by both sexes. 2–3 broods per year.
- **POPULATION** Fairly common, but declined by more than 90 percent in 20th century. Adversely affected by severe winters.
- **FEEDERS AND BIRDHOUSES** Peanut butter–cornmeal mixture and commercial bluebird food. Nests in man-made bird boxes.
- **CONSERVATION** European Starling, House Sparrow, and other's intrude on nesting sites. Many nesting sites lost to cutting cavity trees. Bird boxes have helped recovery, especially those with proper hole sizes and predator guards.

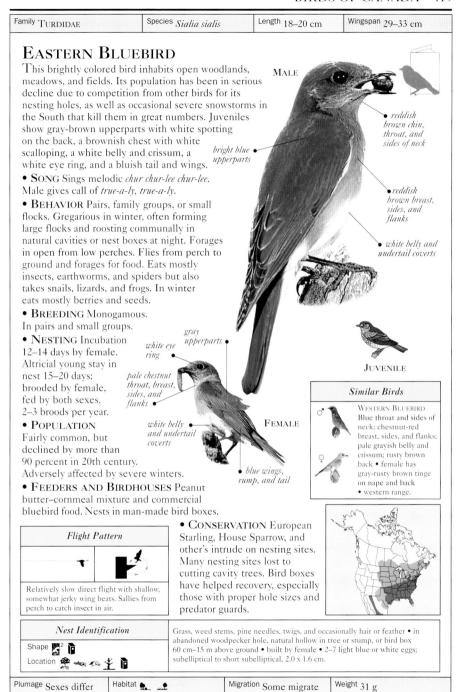

MALE

- *reddish brown chin, throat, and sides of neck*
- *bright blue upperparts*
- *reddish brown breast, sides, and flanks*
- *white belly and undertail coverts*

JUVENILE

gray upperparts
white eye ring
pale chestnut throat, breast, sides, and flanks
white belly and undertail coverts

FEMALE

blue wings, rump, and tail

Similar Birds

WESTERN BLUEBIRD Blue throat and sides of neck; chestnut-red breast, sides, and flanks; pale grayish belly and crissum; rusty brown back • female has gray-rusty brown tinge on nape and back • western range.

Flight Pattern

Relatively slow direct flight with shallow, somewhat jerky wing beats. Sallies from perch to catch insect in air.

Nest Identification	
Shape	Grass, weed stems, pine needles, twigs, and occasionally hair or feather • in abandoned woodpecker hole, natural hollow in tree or stump, or bird box 60 cm–15 m above ground • built by female • 2–7 light blue or white eggs; subelliptical to short subelliptical, 2.0 x 1.6 cm.
Location	

Plumage Sexes differ	Habitat	Migration Some migrate	Weight 31 g

DATE _____ TIME _____ LOCATION _____

Family TURDIDAE	Species *Sialia mexicana*	Length 18–20 cm	Wingspan 29–33 cm

WESTERN BLUEBIRD

The Western Bluebird's brilliant blue throat distinguishes it from the Eastern Bluebird, and its chestnut-red underparts distinguish it from the Mountain Bluebird. In recent years its population has declined due to loss of habitat, especially large old trees, which it uses for nesting cavities. Bird boxes have been helpful but have not kept up with the loss of trees. Juveniles are brownish gray with white-spotted upperparts and underparts and bluish wings and tails.

• **SONG** Male's song is *f-few, f-few, faweee.* Also calls *pa-wee* or *mew.*

• **BEHAVIOR** In pairs or small family groups. More gregarious in winter. Often hunts from low perches from which it drops down on prey or hawks insects. Forages for food on ground and catches insects in flight. Eats insects, earthworms, spiders, and snails; in winter, principally feeds on various berries. Defends nesting cavity from other birds. Often roosts communally in winter, with many individuals sharing the same cavity for the night.

• **BREEDING** Monogamous. Solitary or small colonies.

• **NESTING** Incubation 13–14 days by female. Young altricial; brooded by female; leave nest in 15–22 days, fed by both sexes. 2 broods per year.

• **POPULATION** Common in open woodlands, riparian woodlands, cut-over woodlands, and farmlands; common in winter in deserts and semideserts.

• **FEEDERS AND BIRDHOUSES** Mealworms, peanut butter and suet mixture, cornmeal mixes, and commercial bluebird mixes. Currents, raisins, and soaked raisins are also favorites. Will nest in bird boxes.

• **CONSERVATION** Population declining due to loss of habitat and nesting sites because of competition from other songbirds.

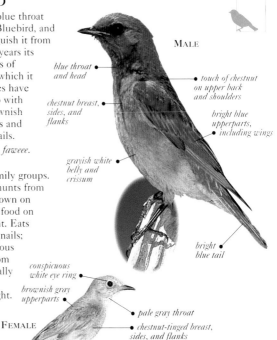

MALE

blue throat and head

touch of chestnut on upper back and shoulders

chestnut breast, sides, and flanks

bright blue upperparts, including wings

grayish white belly and crissum

bright blue tail

conspicuous white eye ring

brownish gray upperparts

pale gray throat

chestnut-tinged breast, sides, and flanks

grayish white belly and crissum

FEMALE

Similar Birds

♂ EASTERN BLUEBIRD Reddish brown throat and breast; white belly and undertail coverts;
♀ blue back.

Flight Pattern

Relatively slow flight with shallow wing beats and somewhat jerky motion. Sallies forth to take insects in flight, returning to perch; sometimes hovers briefly over prey.

Nest Identification	
Shape	Grass, weeds, stems, pine needles, and twigs, occasionally with hair or feathers • in natural cavity of tree or in bird box • 60 cm–15 m above ground • built by both sexes • 3–8 pale blue to bluish white eggs; oval to short oval, 2.0 x 1.6 cm.
Location	

Plumage Sexes differ	Habitat	Migration Northern birds migrate	Weight 28 g

DATE _____ TIME_____ LOCATION _____

Family TURDIDAE	Species *Sialia currucoides*	Length 18 cm	Wingspan 28–32 cm

MOUNTAIN BLUEBIRD

The overall brilliant blue coloring of the male sets it apart from other birds in its genus. Most often making its home in the tree-covered mountains and open landscapes of western North America, generally above two kilometers, it is considered to be at risk by conservationists due to its declining nesting habitat. In winter it descends to open lowlands and deserts. Juveniles are similar to females but with pale whitish streaking and spotting on the breast and sides.

- **SONG** Often silent. A low warbling *tru-lee.* Call is a *phew.*
- **BEHAVIOR** Solitary or in pairs or small family groups. Hovers more than other bluebirds, dropping on prey from above or pouncing on it from low perches. Catches insects in flight and forages on ground. Eats insects, caterpillars, and some fruits and berries. Eats mostly insects in summer.
- **BREEDING** Monogamous. Solitary nester.
- **NESTING** Incubation 13–14 days by female. Altricial young brooded by female first 6 days; stay in nest 22–23 days, fed by both sexes. 2 broods per year.
- **POPULATION** Fairly common but declined over much of its range in the 1900s due to loss of nesting cavities to other species. Casual in the East during migration and winter to north Atlantic seaboard.
- **BIRDHOUSES** Will nest in bird boxes.
- **CONSERVATION** Habitat loss is a concern.

turquoise-blue overall

MALE

pale blue underparts

white eye ring

white belly and undertail coverts

white-edged wing coverts, tertials, and secondaries

FEMALE

dull brownish gray overall

white undertail coverts and belly

Similar Birds

WESTERN BLUEBIRD Male is darker blue-purple with chestnut-red breast, sides, and flanks; pale grayish belly and crissum; rusty brown back • female is tinged gray-rusty brown on nape and back; chestnut-red on breast, sides, and flanks • western range.

Flight Pattern

Relatively slow direct flight with shallow, somewhat jerky wing beats. Often hovers over prey before dipping down to seize it.

Nest Identification

Shape

Location

Grass, weed stems, pine needles, and twigs, occasionally with hair or feathers • in natural tree cavity, ridges of buildings, abandoned nest of swallow, or nest box • built by both sexes • 4–8 pale blue to bluish white eggs, rarely white; subelliptical to oval, 2.0 x 1.6 cm.

Plumage Sexes differ	Habitat	Migration Migratory	Weight 31 g

DATE _____ TIME_____ LOCATION _____

Family TURDIDAE	Species *Myadestes townsendi*	Length 22–23 cm	Wingspan 33–37 cm

TOWNSEND'S SOLITAIRE

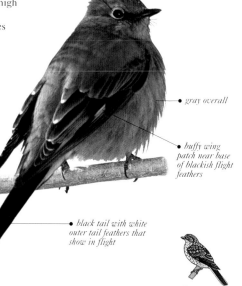

white eye ring

gray overall

buffy wing patch near base of blackish flight feathers

black tail with white outer tail feathers that show in flight

Its beautiful prolonged song, given from high up in the trees, is in marked contrast with the rather plain-looking plumage of this gray bird. Although it makes its home in the high mountains most of the year, during the winter season Townsend's Solitaire moves into the canyons, where it maintains a winter territory and protects a critical food supply. In flight the white outer tail feathers contrast with the inner black ones, and the bird shows white axillaries and a long buffy wing patch. Juveniles are dark brownish gray, with buffy and white scalloping on both the upperparts and underparts, as well as a buffy crissum and wing patch.

• **SONG** A pleasant trilling and rich warble. Often sings in flight. Call is a squeaking *eek* or a plaintive whistled *whee*.

• **BEHAVIOR** Solitary or in pairs. Forms small groups in winter. Perches upright and remains still for long periods of time, thus is easily overlooked. Perches on exposed branch to spot insect, then sallies out to catch in midair and returns to perch. Also forages on ground. Feeds on various insects, worms, and caterpillars in summer; winter diet consists principally of juniper berries. In summer, frequents mountainous coniferous forests around 900 meters below the timberline; in winter, descends to canyons with open juniper forests on lower slopes.

• **BREEDING** Monogamous. Solitary or small family groups.

• **NESTING** Incubation 14 days by both sexes, but female does more. Altricial young brooded by female; remain in nest 15–16 days, fed by both sexes. 1 brood per year (possibly 2 broods in the South).

• **POPULATION** Fairly common in montane coniferous forests. Casual to rare in winter in eastern North America.

JUVENILE

Similar Birds

NORTHERN MOCKINGBIRD
Superficial resemblance • paler gray overall; 2 whitish wing bars; white wing patch; faint eye stripe; longer bill.

Flight Pattern	

Rather slow flight; several slow wing beats followed by short glides. Often irregular in flight pattern, changing directions quickly. Sallies from perch to snatch insects in air.

Nest Identification	
Shape	Location	Grass, roots, and moss, lined with fine materials • on ground, sheltered by overhanging branches, rocks, or natural overhang • built by both sexes • 3–8 pale blue eggs, usually unmarked, occasionally flecked with red-brown; oval, varying from short oval to long oval, 2.0 x 1.6 cm.

Plumage Sexes similar	Habitat	Migration Migratory	Weight 34 g

DATE _____ TIME_____ LOCATION _____

Family TURDIDAE	Species *Catharus fuscescens*	Length 18–20 cm	Wingspan 28–29 cm

VEERY

This bird is named for the lovely ethereal downward-slurring song of the male, which is heard at sunset, a repeated *veer-u*. It is one of the most splendid songs of any bird in North America. Its tawny and buff plumage serves as camouflage in the forest it calls home. The Veery is the least spotted of North America's brown-backed thrushes, with the western populations slightly more spotted than the eastern ones. This bird haunts shaded moist woodlands with dense to scattered understory.

tawny reddish brown upperparts

indistinct grayish eye ring

black upper mandible

creamy pink lower mandible with black tip

buff breast with pale tawny brown spotting

white underparts

creamy pink legs and feet

- **SONG** Sings pleasant liquid descending *veer-u, veer-u, veer-u*, with each note sung lower, repeated frequently with variation in phrasing. Call is harsh down-slurred *veer*. Summer evenings, woodlots and forests fill with the song of one singer cascading into that of another; the chorus at twilight is one of the truly beautiful sounds of nature in the Northwoods.
- **BEHAVIOR** Solitary or in pairs. Somewhat shy and retiring. Forages on ground and in trees; swoops from low perch to take prey on ground, or gleans food from branches, foliage, or ground. Eats various insects, caterpillars, spiders, berries, and fruit. Agitated birds flick wings and raise small crest. Both sexes guard and defend young.
- **BREEDING** Monogamous. Solitary nester.
- **NESTING** Incubation 10–12 days by female. Young altricial; brooded by female; remain in nest 10 days, fed by both sexes. 1 brood per year (sometimes 2 in the South).
- **POPULATION** Fairly common but numbers declining due to habitat loss on breeding and wintering grounds.
- **CONSERVATION** Neotropical migrant. Common nest host to Brown-headed Cowbird. Vulnerable to habitat loss due to deforestation.

Similar Birds

WOOD THRUSH Larger; dark spotting on breast, sides, and upper belly; rufous on upperparts, brightest on nape and crown; black streaking on face; white eye ring.

HERMIT THRUSH Olive- to russet-brown upperparts; pale grayish white underparts with blackish brown spots and speckles; reddish brown tail and rump; white eye ring.

Flight Pattern
Relatively swift direct flight with somewhat hesitant motion on rapidly beating wings.

Nest Identification	Grass, bark strips, weed stems, twigs, and moss, with lining of soft bark and dry leaves • atop platform on dry ground, sheltered by shrubs, grasses, or weeds; sometimes in low tree or shrub, 0–2 m above ground • built by female • 3–5 pale blue eggs, usually unmarked; subelliptical to short subelliptical, 2.3 x 1.7 cm.
Shape ⌒ ◗ Location ━ ◆ ❀	

Plumage Sexes similar	Habitat 🌱 🌳	Migration Migratory	Weight 31 g

DATE _____ TIME_____ LOCATION _____

Family TURDIDAE	Species *Catharus minimus*	Length 18–20 cm	Wingspan 29–34 cm

GRAY-CHEEKED THRUSH

This bird is a truly long-distance migrant. Each spring some of its population fly from southern Brazil to Alaska, across the Bering Strait, and on to their nesting grounds in eastern Siberia. Others spread across the arctic tundra and northern taiga from Alaska to Newfoundland. It has the most northern nesting range of any spotted thrush. In migration it can be found in almost any habitat from woodlots to city parks. The Newfoundland race has warmer-toned upperparts with a sepia back.

inconspicuous gray eye ring

black upper mandible

olive-gray brown upperparts

black lower mandible with yellowish pink base

gray cheeks

pale buff wash on breast and throat, with black-brown spots

• **SONG** Male sings thin oboelike phrases, somewhat like the Veery, but middle phrases rise and first and last ones drop, *wheeoo-titi-wheeoo*. Call is a thin high abrasive *phreu*. Vocal at dawn and especially at dusk.

grayish white underparts

pink legs and feet

• **BEHAVIOR** Solitary or in pairs. Shy and retiring, often staying in the dense understory and thickets. More heard than seen. Feeds on spiders, caterpillars, earthworms, various insects, and even small crayfish. In fall migration, feeds more on berries and some fruits.

• **BREEDING** Monogamous. Solitary nester.

• **NESTING** Incubation 13–14 days by female. Young altricial; brooded by female; stay in nest 11–13 days. Fed by female. 1–2 broods per year.

• **POPULATION** Common; southern breeding populations declining due to loss of habitat.

• **CONSERVATION** Neotropical migrant. Vulnerable on both breeding grounds and wintering areas to habitat loss from logging operations and forest fragmentation.

Similar Birds

SWAINSON'S THRUSH Conspicuous eye ring; browner upperparts; buffy lores, cheeks, throat, and upper breast; buffy underwing linings; different voice.

BICKNELL'S THRUSH Formerly considered subspecies of Gray-cheeked Thrush • smaller; warmer brown tones on upperparts, especially on tail and rump; more extensive yellow on lower mandible • limited range in extreme northeast US • best separated by voice.

Flight Pattern

Relatively swift direct flight with somewhat jerky wing strokes.

Nest Identification

Shape 🥣   Location 🌿 🌳 🌲

Grass, sedge, bark, weed stems, twigs, and moss, with lining of grass, leaves, and fine rootlets • on low branch of tree or shrub, usually 0–3 m above ground (but as high as 6 m) • built by female • 3–6 greenish blue to pale blue eggs, most often speckled brown; oval to short oval, 2.3 x 1.7 cm.

Plumage Sexes similar	Habitat 🌾 🌱 🌳	Migration Migratory	Weight 34 g

DATE _____ TIME_____ LOCATION _____

Family TURDIDAE	Species *Catharus bicknelli*	Length 16 cm	Wingspan 25–28 cm

BICKNELL'S THRUSH

Except when the male perches at the top of a tree to sing, this shy bird remains hidden in trees and bushes. It is a long-distance migrant that until recently was considered a subspecies of the Gray-cheeked Thrush, from which it is difficult to separate in the field. Its eastern breeding range in the northeastern US, southeastern Canada, and the Maritimes helps to isolate it for identification purposes from the more northern and widespread Gray-cheeked Thrush.

olive-brown head and back

indistinct grayish eye ring

olive-brown wings

grayish wash on flanks

sepia-tinged tail and rump

blackish upper mandible with pale base

yellowish lower mandible with black tip

buffy breast with brown speckles and spots

whitish to buff belly and undertail coverts

• **SONG** A raspy thin nasal whistled descending series of trilling phrases, somewhat like a Veery, in 3 parts, with the first and last parts rising. Call is a 2-syllabled down-slurred *vee-ah*.

• **BEHAVIOR** Solitary or in pairs. Shy and retiring, often retreating to dense cover when approached. Feeds primarily on ground or low in understory or trees. Eats mainly insects, their larvae, spiders, and earthworms, which it picks from the ground or gleans from branches and foliage. In fall, eats more berries and fruit.

• **BREEDING** Monogamous. Solitary.

• **NESTING** Incubation 13–14 days by female. Young altricial; brooded by female; first flight at 11–13 days, fed by both sexes. 1 brood per year.

• **CONSERVATION** Neotropical migrant. Vulnerable on both breeding and wintering grounds to habitat loss due to timbering operations and forest fragmentation. Host to nest parasitism by cowbirds.

Similar Birds

GRAY-CHEEKED THRUSH
Larger; olive-gray upperparts; olive-brown tail; gray cheeks; gray wash on breast, sides, and flanks; yellow on lower mandible less extensive; voice differs.

SWAINSON'S THRUSH
Conspicuous eye ring; browner upperparts; buffy lores, cheeks, throat, and upper breast; buffy underwing linings; yellow on lower mandible is less extensive; voice differs.

Flight Pattern
Relatively swift direct flight with somewhat jerky wing strokes.

Nest Identification	
Shape	Location	Grasses, leaves, bark, mud, and mosses, with no lining or a few leaves • in tree, about 1–6 m above ground • built by female • 3–6 greenish blue to pale blue eggs, with faint blotches of brown; oval to short oval, 2.0 x 1.5 cm.

Plumage Sexes similar	Habitat	Migration Migratory	Weight Undetermined

DATE _____ TIME_____ LOCATION _____

Family TURDIDAE	Species *Catharus ustulatus*	Length 18 cm	Wingspan 29 cm

SWAINSON'S THRUSH

Named for 19th-century British ornithologist William Swainson, this bird migrates through North America from its nesting grounds in Canada and mountainous eastern and western US to its winter home in the tropics. Migrating at night, flocks of these birds give plaintive, Spring Peeper-like calls in the darkness as they pass overhead. It often travels in mixed flocks with other thrushes, vireos, and wood warblers. In flight these birds show buff underwing linings.

prominent buff eye ring

buff-olive-brown upperparts

black bill with pinkish yellow base to lower mandible

buff chin, cheeks, and throat

buff breast with brownish spots

whitish gray underparts

pink legs and feet

• **SONG** Sings upward series of thin, musical, varied whistling notes repeated at intervals without change. Call is liquid *whit* similar to the dripping sound of a leaky faucet.

• **BEHAVIOR** Solitary or in pairs. Shy and retiring. Feeds more in trees than other spotted brown thrushes. Picks food off leaves, catches some insects in air, and forages for food on ground. Eats insects, snails, and earthworms. In fall migration eats more fruits and berries. A habitat generalist during migration; prefers conifers and mixed conifer-deciduous forests for nesting. In agonistic displays flicks wings and raises crest. More often heard than seen.

• **BREEDING** Monogamous. Solitary nester.

• **NESTING** Incubation 12–14 days by female. Altricial young stay in nest 10–13 days. Brooded by female. Fed by both sexes. 1 brood per year.

• **POPULATION** Fairly common in most woodlands as well as coniferous forests. Abundant in boreal forests.

• **CONSERVATION** Neotropical migrant. Vulnerable to habitat loss from logging and deforestation on breeding and wintering grounds.

Similar Birds

GRAY-CHEEKED THRUSH Larger; gray cheeks; buff-gray wash on spotted breast; gray wash on sides and flanks; olive-gray upperparts; indistinct eye ring; different voice.

BICKNELL'S THRUSH Smaller; more brown upperparts; tawny brown on rump and tail; more extensive yellow on lower mandible; different voice • northeastern range.

Flight Pattern
Relatively swift direct flight with rapid wing beats.

Nest Identification	Sticks, moss, leaves, plant fibers, and bark with occasional middle layer of mud • lined with lichens, dried leaves, and rootlets • on branch close to trunk of conifer, or occasionally in other trees or shrubs, 0–12 m (usually 1–6 m) above ground • built by female • 3–5 pale blue eggs usually flecked with browns; oval to short oval, 2.0 x 1.5 cm.
Shape 🐦 Location 🌲🌳🌿	

Plumage Sexes similar	Habitat 🌿 🌱 🌳 🌲	Migration Migratory	Weight 31 g

DATE _____ TIME_____ LOCATION _____
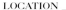

Family TURDIDAE	Species *Catharus guttatus*	Length 17 cm	Wingspan 29 cm

HERMIT THRUSH

Often considered to have one of the most beautiful songs of all North American birds, the Hermit Thrush lives in habitats with coniferous and deciduous trees and along forest edges. It is Vermont's state bird and the only brown-backed spotted thrush to winter in the US. Color variations exist across its broad breeding range: northern Pacific Coast races are smaller and darker with gray flanks; western mountain races are larger and paler also with gray flanks; and eastern races are brownish gray with buff-brown flanks.

distinct white eye ring

blackish upper mandible

olive-brown to russet-brown upperparts

black-tipped lower mandible with pinkish yellow at base

buff wash on breast and throat

reddish brown tail and rump

pale grayish white underparts with blackish brown spots and speckles

pinkish legs and feet

- **SONG** Song begins with long clear low flutelike note and then rises with delicate ringing tones ending in thin, silvery notes; each phrase is repeated, and the pitch differs from that of the previous song. Call note is *chuck*, often doubled; also gives upslurred *whee*.

- **BEHAVIOR** Solitary or in pairs. Often curious and approachable. Responds to pishing sound or imitations of Eastern Screech-Owl by coming close, flicking wings, raising crest, and raising and lowering tail. Often slightly raises and lowers tail upon landing. Sometimes hovers above food on branch or foliage and picks it off with beak. Forages on ground for various insects, insect larvae, and other small invertebrates, including earthworms and snails. Also eats berries and some fruit, especially in autumn migration and winter.

- **BREEDING** Monogamous. Solitary nester.

- **NESTING** Incubation 12–13 days by female. Altricial young remain in nest 12 days; brooded by female, fed by both sexes. 2–3 broods per year.

- **POPULATION** Fairly common. Breeding range is extending southward in southern Appalachians.

- **CONSERVATION** Neotropical migrant. Uncommon host to cowbirds.

Similar Birds

VEERY
Reddish brown upperparts; lacks dark spotting on breast; inconspicuous eye ring; different voice.

WOOD THRUSH
Reddish brown upperparts; brightest on crown and nape; heavy black spotting on underparts; different voice.

Flight Pattern

Rather swift direct flight with rapid wing beats. Sometimes hovers briefly over prey before dipping to pick it up.

Nest Identification	
Shape 🥄 Location ➝ 🌿 🌳	Weeds, rotted wood, twigs, mud, and other fine materials • lined with moss and grass • on ground or low on branch of tree 0–2.5 m above ground • occasionally nests in rafters of mountain buildings • built by female • 3–6 greenish blue eggs usually unmarked but sometimes with black flecks; oval to short oval, 2.0 x 1.5 cm.

Plumage Sexes similar	Habitat 🌲 🌿 🐾	Migration Most migrate	Weight 31 g

DATE _____ TIME_____ LOCATION _____

Family TURDIDAE	Species *Hylocichla mustelina*	Length 20 cm	Wingspan 33–36 cm

WOOD THRUSH

In early spring, the peaceful flutelike songs of the males are heard throughout the nesting territory, announcing their arrival. It frequents moist forests or large woodlots, but also can be seen in parks, towns, and country gardens. When this heavy-bodied big-eyed short-tailed thrush is agitated, it lifts the feathers on its head like a crest. The song, one of the most beautiful thrush songs, is given before daybreak, but is most prolonged at dusk, when the singer perches high above ground and delivers it in leisurely fashion, rising and falling, until darkness silences him.

white eye ring surrounds large dark eye

bright russet nape and crown

black bill with creamy pink base to lower mandible

reddish brown upperparts

black streaking on white face

large black spots on breast, sides, and flanks

creamy pink legs and feet

• **SONG** A serene flutelike series of triple phrases, the middle note lower than the first, the last note highest and trilled, *ee-o-lee, ee-o-lay.* Call is an abrasive *quirt* or rapid *pit, pit, pit.*

• **BEHAVIOR** Solitary or in pairs. Somewhat shy and retiring but may feed in the open on wooded lawns. Feeds on ground or in trees close to ground, gleaning food from ground or from branches and foliage. Eats various insects, spiders, and fruits; feeds largely on fruits and berries in fall migration. In courtship, male chases female in series of fast twisting circling flights within the male's territory. Territorial in winter.

• **BREEDING** Monogamous. Solitary.

• **NESTING** Incubation 13–14 days by female. Young altricial; brooded by female; remain in nest 12 days, fed by both sexes. 1–2 broods per year.

• **POPULATION** Common in moist deciduous or mixed deciduous-conifer woodlands, often near water. Casual in the West during migration.

• **CONSERVATION** Neotropical migrant. Population declining in recent decades due to nest parasitism by cowbirds, forest fragmentation on breeding grounds, and habitat loss on wintering grounds in Central America.

Similar Birds

VEERY
Smaller; uniform reddish brown upperparts; lacks black spotting of underparts; longer tail; voice differs.

HERMIT THRUSH
Smaller; rich brown to gray-brown upperparts; buff wash on breast; dark spotting confined to throat and upper breast; rufous rump and tail; voice differs.

Flight Pattern
Relatively swift direct flight on rapidly beating wings. Flights in woodlots often of short duration.

Nest Identification
Shape 🐦   Location 🌿 🌳 🐦

Moss, mud, and dried leaves, with lining of fine rootlets • in fork of tree or shrub, usually 2–15 m above ground (but generally 2–4 m) • built by female • 2–5 unmarked pale blue or bluish green eggs; short oval to short subelliptical, slightly pointed at end, 2.5 x 1.9 cm.

Plumage Sexes similar	Habitat 🌳 🌿 🏞	Migration Migratory	Weight 48 g

DATE _____ TIME_____ LOCATION _____

Family TURDIDAE	Species *Turdus merula*	Length 25–27 cm	Wingspan 38–41 cm

EURASIAN BLACKBIRD

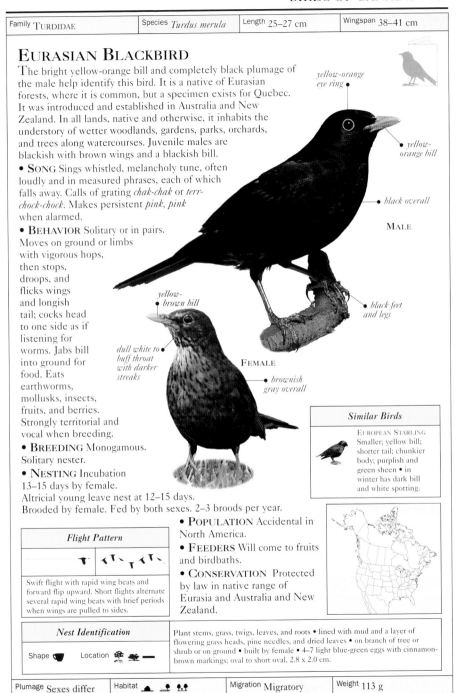

The bright yellow-orange bill and completely black plumage of the male help identify this bird. It is a native of Eurasian forests, where it is common, but a specimen exists for Quebec. It was introduced and established in Australia and New Zealand. In all lands, native and otherwise, it inhabits the understory of wetter woodlands, gardens, parks, orchards, and trees along watercourses. Juvenile males are blackish with brown wings and a blackish bill.

- **SONG** Sings whistled, melancholy tune, often loudly and in measured phrases, each of which falls away. Calls of grating *chak-chak* or *terr-chock-chock*. Makes persistent *pink, pink* when alarmed.
- **BEHAVIOR** Solitary or in pairs. Moves on ground or limbs with vigorous hops, then stops, droops, and flicks wings and longish tail; cocks head to one side as if listening for worms. Jabs bill into ground for food. Eats earthworms, mollusks, insects, fruits, and berries. Strongly territorial and vocal when breeding.
- **BREEDING** Monogamous. Solitary nester.
- **NESTING** Incubation 13–15 days by female. Altricial young leave nest at 12–15 days. Brooded by female. Fed by both sexes. 2–3 broods per year.
- **POPULATION** Accidental in North America.
- **FEEDERS** Will come to fruits and birdbaths.
- **CONSERVATION** Protected by law in native range of Eurasia and Australia and New Zealand.

yellow-orange eye ring

yellow-orange bill

black overall

MALE

yellow-brown bill

dull white to buff throat with darker streaks

FEMALE

brownish gray overall

black feet and legs

Similar Birds

EUROPEAN STARLING Smaller; yellow bill; shorter tail; chunkier body; purplish and green sheen • in winter has dark bill and white spotting.

Flight Pattern

Swift flight with rapid wing beats and forward flip upward. Short flights alternate several rapid wing beats with brief periods when wings are pulled to sides.

Nest Identification

Shape   Location

Plant stems, grass, twigs, leaves, and roots • lined with mud and a layer of flowering grass heads, pine needles, and dried leaves • on branch of tree or shrub or on ground • built by female • 4–7 light blue-green eggs with cinnamon-brown markings; oval to short oval, 2.8 x 2.0 cm.

Plumage Sexes differ	Habitat	Migration Migratory	Weight 113 g

DATE _____ TIME_____ LOCATION _____

Family TURDIDAE	Species *Turdus naumanni*	Length 24 cm	Wingspan 37–42 cm

DUSKY THRUSH

The most likely place to spot this Asian native in North America is off the coast of Alaska in the western Aleutian Islands or St. Lawrence Island, but it has been recorded in coastal Alaska and coastal British Columbia. Like the American Robin, this bird spends time in suburban areas where it may frequent lawns and ornamental fruit-bearing shrubs and trees. The female and juvenile male are similar to the adult male but have duller coloring. In flight nearly the entire underwing shows rufous, as does the rump.

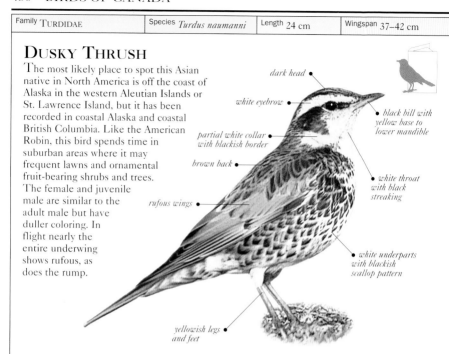

dark head

white eyebrow

black bill with yellow base to lower mandible

partial white collar with blackish border

brown back

rufous wings

white throat with black streaking

white underparts with blackish scallop pattern

yellowish legs and feet

It inhabits cultivated fields, open woods, riverbanks, city parks, and gardens.

- **SONG** A series of melodious whistles. Call is harsh *shack-shack-shack*. Also a piecing *shreee*.
- **BEHAVIOR** Solitary or in pairs. Gregarious and often conspicuous. May form small foraging parties to large flocks on wintering grounds. Forages for food by hopping on ground with frequent pauses between hops to scan for food. Eats insects, earthworms, berries, and fruits.
- **BREEDING** Monogamous. Solitary nester.
- **NESTING** Incubation 13–15 days by female. Altricial young remain in nest 13–15 days; brooded by female, fed by both sexes. 1–2 broods per year.
- **POPULATION** Casual in Alaska in spring migration. Rare to accidental in coastal Alaska and coastal British Columbia in winter. Fairly common to common in Siberia.

Similar Birds

EYEBROWED THRUSH ♀ Brown upperwings; rufous wash on belly; gray upper breast; white chin and white throat with black streaking; white eye stripe; white spot from eye to chin; lacks black scalloping on underparts.

Flight Pattern
Rather swift direct flight with rapid wing beats. Short flights alternate wing beats with wings pulled briefly to sides.

Nest Identification	
Shape 🍵 Location 🌿 🪴 🌳 ━ 🦅 🪨	Grass, rootlets, and twigs • lined with clay • on tree branch, in stump, and sometimes on ground or cliff ledge • built by female • 4–6 light bluish green eggs with brown blotches; oval to short oval, 2.0 x 1.5 cm.

Plumage Sexes similar	Habitat 🌿 🌱 ⛰	Migration Migratory	Weight 71 g

DATE _____ TIME_____ LOCATION _____

Family TURDIDAE	Species *Turdus iliacus*	Length 21 cm	Wingspan 34–36 cm

REDWING

The combination of its rufous-red flanks, streaked and spotted throat, breast, and sides, and its distinctive buff eyebrows sets this bird apart from the native North American thrushes. A native of Eurasia, the Redwing strays occasionally to visit Newfoundland and is accidental to Long Island, New York, in the winter season. In flight this thrush's underwing linings are a deep orange-rufous. The adult also has white underparts. Juvenile Redwings are similar to adults but they have paler upperparts and also washed-out rufous on their flanks as well as on their underwings.

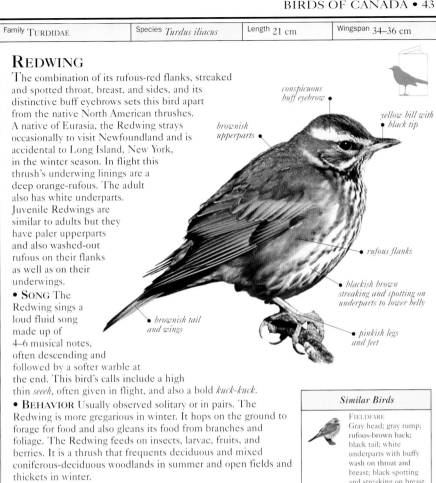

conspicuous buff eyebrow

yellow bill with black tip

brownish upperparts

rufous flanks

blackish brown streaking and spotting on underparts to lower belly

brownish tail and wings

pinkish legs and feet

• **SONG** The Redwing sings a loud fluid song made up of 4–6 musical notes, often descending and followed by a softer warble at the end. This bird's calls include a high thin *seeeh*, often given in flight, and also a bold *kuck-kuck*.

• **BEHAVIOR** Usually observed solitary or in pairs. The Redwing is more gregarious in winter. It hops on the ground to forage for food and also gleans its food from branches and foliage. The Redwing feeds on insects, larvae, fruits, and berries. It is a thrush that frequents deciduous and mixed coniferous-deciduous woodlands in summer and open fields and thickets in winter.

• **BREEDING** Monogamous. Solitary nester.

• **NESTING** Incubation 12–14 days by female. Young altricial; brooded by female; stay in nest 12–15 days, fed by both sexes. 2 broods per year.

• **POPULATION** The Redwing is casual to accidental in the Maritimes and north Atlantic Coast of the US. It is uncommon to fairly common in western Europe.

Similar Birds

FIELDFARE
Gray head; gray rump; rufous-brown back; black tail; white underparts with buffy wash on throat and breast; black spotting and streaking on breast, sides, and flanks; white underwing linings.

Flight Pattern
Rather swift strong direct flight on rapidly beating wings.

Nest Identification	
Shape 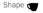 Location	Grasses, mud, and twigs • in shrub or branch of tree, 1–9 m above ground • built by female • 5–6 bluish green eggs, spotted with red-brown; oval to short oval, 2.0 x 1.5 cm.

Plumage Sexes similar	Habitat	Migration Migratory	Weight 62 g

Family TURDIDAE	Species *Turdus migratorius*	Length 25 cm	Wingspan 36–41 cm

AMERICAN ROBIN

In many areas this bird is considered a sign of spring, though it is a year-round resident in most of its US range. It is among the most common, widely distributed, and most well-known birds in North America. Juveniles are similar to adults but have heavily spotted underparts and white spotting and edging on the back and shoulders.

- **SONG** A bold gurgling leisurely *sing-song cheerily cheer-up cheerio*, with phrases often repeated. Has rapid call of *tut-tut-tut* or *hip-hip-hip*.

- **BEHAVIOR** Solitary or in pairs. Gregarious after breeding season; in winter often in flocks and roosts communally with other species. Eats earthworms, insects, and berries. Berries and fruits are principal diet in winter. Defensive of nest site and young. Adapted to human disturbance, especially agricultural areas and the combination of shade trees and lawns. Running-stopping foraging style in fields and lawns.

- **BREEDING** Monogamous. Solitary. Sometimes observed in loose colonies.

- **NESTING** Incubation 12–14 days by female. Altricial young brooded by female; stay in nest 14–16 days; female does more feeding. Male often tends first brood while female begins to incubate second clutch. 2–3 broods per year in south; fewer in north.

- **POPULATION** Abundant and widespread in variety of habitats, including forests, woodlands, gardens, and parks.

- **FEEDERS AND BIRDHOUSES** Will come to feeders for breadcrumbs. Attracted to birdbaths. Uses nesting shelves.

- **CONSERVATION** Neotropical migrant. Becoming more common in the Midwest and onto the Great Plains with planting of shelter belt trees and irrigation. Vulnerable to pesticide poisoning in the food chain.

blackish head

broken white eye ring

dark brownish gray upperparts

yellow bill

white throat with black striping

brick red breast

MALE

white lower belly and undertail coverts

blackish tail has white outer corners

dark brownish gray head

dark brownish gray upperparts

yellow bill

chestnut-orange breast

JUVENILE

FEMALE

Similar Birds

RUFOUS-BACKED ROBIN Rufous chest, back, and wing coverts; gray head and tail; heavy streaking on throat; yellow bill; yellow eye ring • southwestern range.

Flight Pattern

Swift rapid direct flight on strongly beating wings.

Nest Identification

Shape   Location

Grasses and mud, with lining of fine grass • in all areas of tree, but with shelter from rain, or in building or nest shelf • female does more building • 3–7 pale blue eggs, occasionally white, usually unmarked, but occasionally flecked with brown; oval to short oval, 2.8 x 2.0 cm.

Plumage Sexes differ	Habitat	Migration Migratory	Weight 77 g

DATE _____ TIME_____ LOCATION _____

Family TURDIDAE	Species *Ixoreus naevius*	Length 24 cm	Wingspan 36–41 cm

VARIED THRUSH

This uniquely colored thrush, unlike the American Robin, frequents dense damp coniferous and deciduous forests and undergrowth as well as suburban lawns. It usually feeds and spends time on the ground, except when the male perches to sing his somewhat eerie song. One of the most strikingly colored thrushes, it has orange underparts, wing bars, and eyebrows. Females have a dusky brown cast to the upperparts and a dusky brown breast band. Juveniles are similar to the female but have a scaly appearance to the neck and breast and have white underparts.

orange eyebrow

bluish gray upperparts, nape, and crown

MALE

white undertail coverts

black ear patch

wide black necklace

rusty orange breast and throat

rusty orange wing bars

- **SONG** A slow whistled mysterious-sounding caroling melody followed by fast prolonged warbling, first high, then low, and fading at the end. Has a soft low call of *chup*.
- **BEHAVIOR** Solitary or in pairs. Forages for food on ground and low in trees. Often remains hidden. Eats insects, caterpillars, berries, acorns, and sometimes seeds. Defensive of nest site and young. Responds readily to squeaking by birders.
- **BREEDING** Monogamous. Solitary.
- **NESTING** Breeding biology poorly known. Incubation estimated at 12–14 days by female. Young altricial; brooded by female; leave nest at 13–15 days, fed by both sexes. 1–2 broods per year.

orange eyebrow

brownish gray upperparts and head

orange breast and throat

FEMALE

Similar Birds

♂ **AMERICAN ROBIN** Broken white eye ring; solid gray wings without wing bars; white throat with black striping; chestnut-orange underparts without breast band or scalloping; yellow bill; lacks orange eyebrow.

- **POPULATION** Common to fairly common in dense moist woodlands, particularly conifers. Rare winter visitor in the East to the Atlantic coast.
- **FEEDERS** Comes to feeders.
- **CONSERVATION** Vulnerable to loss of habitat and forest fragmentation due to logging and development.

Flight Pattern
Swift rapid direct flight on rapidly beating wings.

Nest Identification	
Shape	Location	Dried leaves, inner bark strips, and soft moss, reinforced with twigs, lined with grass and rootlets • on branch or fork of tree, usually 3–5 m above ground (but up to 8 m) • built by female • 2–5 pale blue eggs, flecked with browns; oval to long oval, 3.0 x 2.3 cm.

Plumage Sexes differ	Habitat	Migration Migratory	Weight Undetermined

DATE _____ TIME_____ LOCATION _____

| Family MIMIDAE | Species *Dumetella carolinensis* | Length 22–23 cm | Wingspan 28–30 cm |

GRAY CATBIRD

Its black cap, long tail, and gentle mewing calls are helpful in identifying this tame gray bird. Frequenting thick undergrowth and bushes, it will reside in summer in the ornamental shrubs, thickets, and hedges in farmyards and towns. An accomplished songster with the quality of the other members of the mimic thrush family, it patterns its song with phrases, some squeaky, some melodious, but none repeated. The song is often interrupted with catlike mewing notes. This bird migrates at night. Although primarily migratory, birds on the coastal plain are nonmigratory.

slate-gray upperparts

black tail

black cap

short dark bill

reddish chestnut undertail coverts

• **SONG** A mixture of sweet to melodious, thin to squeaky, and sometimes abrasive phrases mixed with pauses. Does not repeat phrases like other eastern mimic thrushes. Some individuals mimic sounds

pale gray underparts

of other birds, amphibians, and machinery, and incorporate them into their song. Distinctive *mew* notes often included in the phrases. Has call of quiet *mew*. Also a harsh *quit* or *chack*.

• **BEHAVIOR** Solitary or in pairs. Often stays low in thick bush and is easily overlooked. Relatively tame, frequently allowing a close approach. Sings from an exposed perch; sometimes sings at night. Often cocks tail upward and flicks from side to side. Gleans food from branches and foliage and picks it from ground. Eats mostly insects, spiders, berries, and fruits. Strongly defends nest and nestlings from predators and intruders. Uncommon cowbird host; recognizes their eggs and ejects them from nest. Often in loose flocks with other species in winter.

• **BREEDING** Monogamous. Solitary nester.

• **NESTING** Incubation 12–13 days by female. Young altricial; brooded by female; stay in nest 10–11 days, fed by both sexes but more by male. 2 broods per year.

Similar Birds
No other bird in its range is slate gray above and below with a long tail.

• **POPULATION** Common.

Flight Pattern
Swift direct flight on rapid wing beats over some distance; short flights often with several rapid wing beats and a short period with wings pulled to sides.

• **FEEDERS** Cheese, bread, raisins, cornflakes, milk, cream, currants, peanuts, and crackers.

• **CONSERVATION** Neotropical migrant. Uncommon cowbird host.

Nest Identification	
Shape ⬤ Location 🪹 🌿	Grass, stems, twigs, and leaves, lined with fine materials • in shrub or tree, 1–3 m above ground (as high as 15 m) • built by both sexes but female does more • 2–6 dark blue-green eggs; subelliptical, 2.3 x 1.8 cm.

| Plumage Sexes similar | Habitat 🪨 ▲ 🌱 | Migration Most migrate | Weight 37 g |

DATE _____ TIME_____ LOCATION _____

Family MIMIDAE	Species *Mimus polyglottos*	Length 25 cm	Wingspan 33–38 cm

NORTHERN MOCKINGBIRD

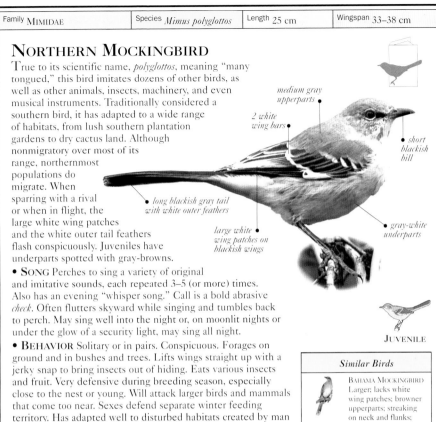

True to its scientific name, *polyglottos*, meaning "many tongued," this bird imitates dozens of other birds, as well as other animals, insects, machinery, and even musical instruments. Traditionally considered a southern bird, it has adapted to a wide range of habitats, from lush southern plantation gardens to dry cactus land. Although nonmigratory over most of its range, northernmost populations do migrate. When sparring with a rival or when in flight, the large white wing patches and the white outer tail feathers flash conspicuously. Juveniles have underparts spotted with gray-browns.

medium gray upperparts

2 white wing bars

short blackish bill

long blackish gray tail with white outer feathers

large white wing patches on blackish wings

gray-white underparts

- **SONG** Perches to sing a variety of original and imitative sounds, each repeated 3–5 (or more) times. Also has an evening "whisper song." Call is a bold abrasive *check*. Often flutters skyward while singing and tumbles back to perch. May sing well into the night or, on moonlit nights or under the glow of a security light, may sing all night.

JUVENILE

- **BEHAVIOR** Solitary or in pairs. Conspicuous. Forages on ground and in bushes and trees. Lifts wings straight up with a jerky snap to bring insects out of hiding. Eats various insects and fruit. Very defensive during breeding season, especially close to the nest or young. Will attack larger birds and mammals that come too near. Sexes defend separate winter feeding territory. Has adapted well to disturbed habitats created by man and thrives in suburbs, towns, villages, and farmlands.
- **BREEDING** Monogamous. Solitary nester. Long-term pair bonds. Males perform display where they face one another and hop sideways, trying to keep other birds out of territory.
- **NESTING** Incubation 12–13 days by female. Young altricial; brooded by female; stay in nest 11–13 days, fed by both sexes. 2–3 broods per year.

Similar Birds

BAHAMA MOCKINGBIRD Larger; lacks white wing patches; browner upperparts; streaking on neck and flanks; white-tipped tail • eastern range.

TOWNSEND'S SOLITAIRE Darker gray; white eye ring; buff wing patches; shorter bill; white outer tail feathers.

- **POPULATION** Common in the United States. Range is expanding north, particularly to the Northeast. Casual north of the mapped distribution range, sometimes as far north as Alaska.
- **FEEDERS** Will come for bread, suet, and raisins.

Flight Pattern
Long flight is swift and strong on steadily beating wings. Shorter flights with several quick wing strokes alternated with wings pulled to sides; repeated.

Nest Identification	
Shape Location	Sticks, stems, bits of fabric, dead leaves, and string, lined with finer materials • set in fork on branch of tree or shrub, usually 1–3 m above ground • built by both sexes • 2–6 blue-green eggs, with splotches of brown; oval to short oval, occasionally short subelliptical, 2.5 x 2.0 cm.

Plumage Sexes similar	Habitat	Migration Nonmigratory	Weight 48 g

DATE _____ TIME_____ LOCATION _____

Family MIMIDAE	Species *Oreoscoptes montanus*	Length 22 cm	Wingspan 29 cm

SAGE THRASHER

At dawn the male Sage Thrasher flies to a high perch and sings its pleasant song over the sagebrush plains. Slightly smaller than a robin, its short bill, ashy brown upperparts, and striped breast set it apart from other thrashers in its range. This shy bird quickly flies away when approached and slips into the thick sagebrush or runs off on the ground. Its streaking may be very faded and faint on individuals with worn plumage. The juvenile has a streaked head and back.

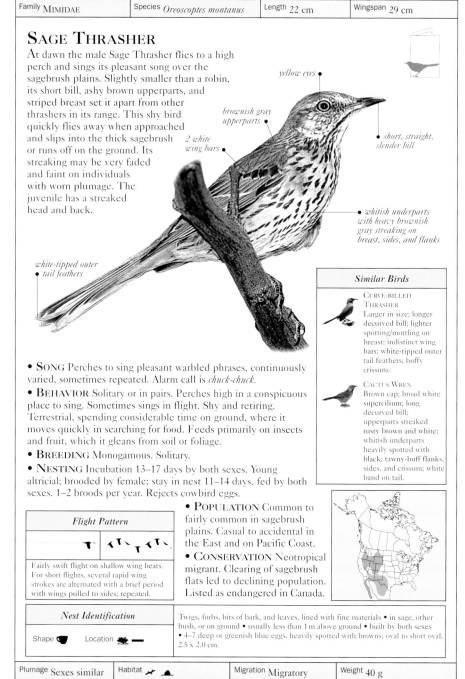

yellow eyes

brownish gray upperparts

short, straight, slender bill

2 white wing bars

whitish underparts with heavy brownish gray streaking on breast, sides, and flanks

white-tipped outer tail feathers

• **SONG** Perches to sing pleasant warbled phrases, continuously varied, sometimes repeated. Alarm call is *chuck-chuck*.
• **BEHAVIOR** Solitary or in pairs. Perches high in a conspicuous place to sing. Sometimes sings in flight. Shy and retiring. Terrestrial, spending considerable time on ground, where it moves quickly in searching for food. Feeds primarily on insects and fruit, which it gleans from soil or foliage.
• **BREEDING** Monogamous. Solitary.
• **NESTING** Incubation 13–17 days by both sexes. Young altricial; brooded by female; stay in nest 11–14 days, fed by both sexes. 1–2 broods per year. Rejects cowbird eggs.

Similar Birds

CURVE-BILLED THRASHER
Larger in size; longer decurved bill; lighter spotting/mottling on breast; indistinct wing bars; white-tipped outer tail feathers; buffy crissum.

CACTUS WREN
Brown cap; broad white supercilium; long decurved bill; upperparts streaked rusty brown and white; whitish underparts heavily spotted with black; tawny-buff flanks, sides, and crissum; white band on tail.

• **POPULATION** Common to fairly common in sagebrush plains. Casual to accidental in the East and on Pacific Coast.
• **CONSERVATION** Neotropical migrant. Clearing of sagebrush flats led to declining population. Listed as endangered in Canada.

Flight Pattern

Fairly swift flight on shallow wing beats. For short flights, several rapid wing strokes are alternated with a brief period with wings pulled to sides; repeated.

Nest Identification

Shape [icon]   Location [icons]

Twigs, forbs, bits of bark, and leaves, lined with fine materials • in sage, other bush, or on ground • usually less than 1 m above ground • built by both sexes • 4–7 deep or greenish blue eggs, heavily spotted with browns; oval to short oval, 2.5 x 2.0 cm.

Plumage Sexes similar	Habitat [icons]	Migration Migratory	Weight 40 g

DATE _____ TIME_____ LOCATION _____

Family MIMIDAE	Species *Toxostoma rufum*	Length 29 cm	Wingspan 32–36 cm

BROWN THRASHER

This shy bird becomes highly aggressive when defending its young, often charging toward the head of any intruder. The male bird sings from an exposed perch, sometimes quite high. It is able to imitate other birds but most often sings its own song, which is a curious mixture of musical phrases. Its bright rufous upperparts and heavily streaked underparts distinguish this species from all other thrashers in its range. Although primarily migratory, birds in the South do not migrate.

long decurved brownish black bill with paler base to lower mandible

deep yellow eyes

reddish brown upperparts

• **SONG** Male sings conversation-like phrases of *hello, hello, yes, yes, who is this? Who is this? I should say, I should say,* with the varied phrases being given in two's and three's. Reported to have the largest song repertoire of all North American birds with more than 1,100 song types recorded. Call is a bold *smack* or *churr*.

2 white wing bars

pale buff to white underparts with heavy streaking

• **BEHAVIOR** Solitary or in pairs. Highly terrestrial; forages on or near ground for food. Finds insects by digging with bill. Eats mainly insects, small amphibians, fruit, and some grains. Runs quickly on ground; turns over leaves and moves debris with bill. Frequents dense brush, early successional stage woodlots, and forest edges. Has adapted to living in shrubby ornamental vegetation of suburbs and gardens.

long reddish brown tail

Similar Birds

LONG-BILLED THRASHER More brownish gray upperparts; darker streaking on creamy white underparts; 2 white wing bars; longer, more decurved bill; reddish orange eye; long gray-brown tail.

• **BREEDING** Monogamous. Solitary nester.
• **NESTING** Incubation 11–14 days by both sexes. Young altricial; brooded by female; stay in nest 9–13 days, fed by both sexes. 2–3 broods per year.

• **POPULATION** Common to fairly common. Rare in the Maritimes and in the West.
• **FEEDERS** Will sometimes tend feeders for raisins, suet, and bread.

Flight Pattern

Rather fast flight on shallow wing beats. Short flights are made with several rapid wing beats alternated with brief periods with wings pulled to sides; repeated.

Nest Identification

Shape ◗   Location 🐦 — 🐦 🪶

Sticks, grasses, and dried leaves, lined with fine grasses • in bush, on ground, or in low tree, usually 30 cm–3 m above ground • built by both sexes • 2–6 pale bluish white or white eggs, with pale brown specks, occasionally wreathed; oval to short oval, 2.5 x 2.0 cm.

Plumage Sexes similar	Habitat 🪴 🌳 🌲	Migration Migratory	Weight 68 g

DATE _____ TIME_____ LOCATION _____

Family STURNIDAE	Species *Sturnus vulgaris*	Length 22 cm	Wingspan 39 cm

EUROPEAN STARLING

This chunky Eurasian species was introduced to North America in 1890 in New York City's Central Park and has become so well established that large flocks have in some cases become a nuisance, roosting in cities and towns from coast to coast and north into Canada to the tree line. Tenacious in nature, this bird competes with native species such as woodpeckers, flycatchers, and bluebirds for nesting holes. This bird's winter plumage shows white specks and its yellow bill becomes a dull gray. Juveniles are sooty gray-brown overall with pale streaking on the underparts and a dull brown bill.

buffy tips and edging to mantle feathers

short tail

long pointed yellow bill

black overall with iridescent sheen of green and purple

• **SONG** Sings various trilling melodies, clear whistles, clatters, and twitters in groups. Imitates songs of other birds, including Eastern Wood-Pewee and Northern Bobwhite, as well as mechanical sounds. Also has a flutelike *pheeEW*. Singing male often stands erect and flaps wings vigorously in display.

• **BEHAVIOR** Solitary or in pairs in breeding season. Juveniles form foraging flocks. Gregarious after breeding season, forming flocks with juveniles for foraging and roosting. Joins other species in winter roosts, which may number more than a million birds. Most often feeds in open areas, primarily on the ground. Eats various insects, fruits, and grains. The muscles that open its bill are stronger than those that close it, a unique trait that allows this bird to insert its bill in vegetation or into the ground and then pry it open to reveal food.

JUVENILE

• **BREEDING** Monogamous. Often forms loose colonies. Some individual males polygynous. Aggressive in claiming nesting chambers.

• **NESTING** Incubation 12–14 days by both sexes, but female does more. Young altricial; brooded by female; stay in nest 18–21 days, fed by both sexes. First flight at about 26 days. 2–3 broods per year.

Similar Birds
No native species of blackbird has yellow bill; short tail; chunky body; buffy streaking on back and wing coverts; and a notched tail.

• **POPULATION** Common. Stable over most of continent; perhaps still expanding range north and south.

• **FEEDERS AND BIRDHOUSES** Bread, peanut butter, suet, and small seeds. Uses bluebird-sized or larger nest boxes.

• **CONSERVATION** Canadian and US laws do not protect nongame, non-native species.

Flight Pattern
Strong swift direct flight on rapidly beating wings.

Nest Identification	Grass, twigs, forbs, rootlets, and straw • in natural hollow of tree, bird box, crevice in man-made structure, or abandoned woodpecker hole, 3–8 m above ground (but up to 18 m) • built by both sexes • 4–8 pale bluish or greenish white eggs, usually unmarked, but sometimes marked with browns; short oval to long oval, 3.0 x 2.0 cm.
Shape	
Location	

Plumage Sexes similar	Habitat	Migration Northern birds migrate	Weight 85 g

DATE _____ TIME_____ LOCATION _____

Family STURNIDAE	Species *Acridotheres cristatellus*	Length 25–27 cm	Wingspan 41–46 cm

CRESTED MYNA

Originally a native of Southeast Asia, this bird was introduced in Vancouver, British Columbia, in 1897, and its population rose to a few thousand birds in the 1920s. Today, it has declined to only a few hundred birds, perhaps due to the unsuitable climate and competition for nesting holes with recently arrived and expanding populations of the European Starling. The Crested Myna is a short-tailed starling with a stocky body set off by a white wing patch and short brushy crest. In flight the large white wing patches show in bold contrast to the glossy black body.

short ragged crest

yellow bill

yellow eyes

glossy black overall

white wing patch

yellow legs and feet

white mottling on undertail coverts

white band on tip of tail

- **SONG** Chattering followed by a warbling melody, somewhat like the European Starling. Imitates calls of other birds.

- **BEHAVIOR** Usually in pairs during breeding season. Otherwise gregarious, often in foraging and roosting flocks. Often walks on ground, foraging for food. Follows farm equipment and picks insects off livestock; picks insects and fly larvae from manure. Also eats insects, fruit, grains, and the eggs and young of other birds, as well as refuse. In winter, flocks sometimes roost on top of buildings or in trees. Competes with other hole-nesting birds for nesting cavities and often loses out to the more aggressive European Starling. Sedentary, urban.

- **BREEDING** Monogamous. Social.

- **NESTING** Incubation 14–15 days by both sexes. Young altricial; brooded by female; remain in nest about 27 days, fed by both sexes. 1 brood per year.

- **POPULATION** Introduced; rare and local. Has never spread far from point of introduction. Numbers are declining. Some escaped caged birds in southern Florida may become established.

- **FEEDERS AND BIRDHOUSES** Will come to bird feeders and nest in bird boxes.

- **CONSERVATION** Introduced species without the protections given to native species. Losing nesting cavities to other introduced species.

Flight Pattern
Swift direct flight with powerful rapid wing strokes.

Nest Identification	Grass, forbs, rootlets, paper, and snakeskin • in cavity of tree, bird box, or under eave of building • built by both sexes • 4–7 shiny greenish blue eggs; short oval to long oval, 3.0 cm long.
Shape Location	

Plumage Sexes similar	Habitat	Migration Nonmigratory	Weight 113 g

DATE _____ TIME_____ LOCATION _____

| Family PRUNELLIDAE | Species *Prunella montanella* | Length 14 cm | Wingspan 23 cm |

SIBERIAN ACCENTOR

Strays of this Eurasian species sometimes can be spotted in Alaska or along the northern Pacific coast of North America, usually in fall or winter. A shy bird, it stays hidden among dense coniferous trees and shrubs in the mountains, where it feeds on the ground. Note the rusty brown upperparts, grayish rump, and the tawny buff underparts

dark crown with central gray stripe

ocher-buff eyebrow

blackish brown ear patches

rusty brown upperparts with brown streaks

short thin black bill

white wing bar

gray collar on sides of neck and nape

notched tail

bright ocher-buff throat and breast

on this sparrow-sized, straight-tailed bird. The crown and cheeks are blackish, the crown being broken by a gray median stripe, and a buffy eyebrow that broadens behind the eye.

brownish streaking on sides and flanks

tawny buff underparts

• **SONG** Sings bold warbling trills. Also has a high-pitched nasal *see-see-see*.

pink feet and legs

• **BEHAVIOR** Solitary or in pairs or small flocks. Territorial male sings from treetops. Forages on ground and in low bushes. Eats mostly small invertebrates and seeds, feeding more on seeds in winter. Stays hidden in thickest part of overgrown thickets in coniferous forests, especially in riparian growth along river valleys.

• **BREEDING** Monogamous. Solitary nester.

Similar Birds

No other North American species in the range has similar color and pattern.

Flight Pattern

Short flights on rapidly beating wings, alternated with brief period of wings pulled to sides; repeated.

• **NESTING** Incubation 12–15 days by both sexes. Altricial young brooded by female. Young stay in nest 11–12 days, fed by both sexes. 1–2 broods per year.

• **POPULATION** Casual in Alaska and Pacific Northwest.

Nest Identification

Shape 🥄   Location 🐦 🌿

Sticks, grasses, and finer materials • in low tree or shrub • undetermined which sex builds nest • 4 pale blue eggs; elliptical to short oval, 2.3 x 1.8 cm.

| Plumage Sexes similar | Habitat 🌳 🌿 🌲 ⛰ | Migration Migratory | Weight 23 g |

DATE _____ TIME_____ LOCATION _____

Family MOTACILLIDAE	Species *Motacilla flava*	Length 17 cm	Wingspan 23 cm

YELLOW WAGTAIL

Primarily a Eurasian species, this bird is one of two wagtails that summer and nest in North America. It is a small sparrow-sized bird with a long tail, which it pumps up and down as it walks, and it frequents wet meadows and river banks, where it often perches on grass stems or trees. The white outer tail feathers are obvious in flight, as is the inner white bar on the wing. The female is similar to the male but duller in color. The juvenile has brownish upperparts and ocher-white underparts with a blackish brown breast band and malar marks.

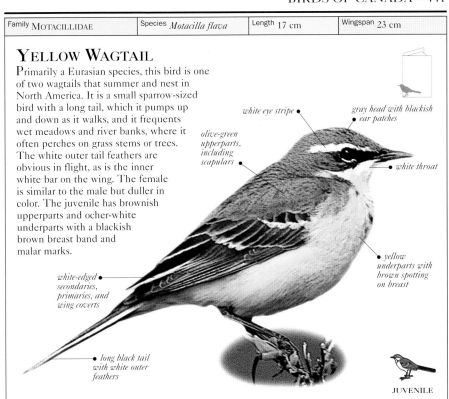

white eye stripe

gray head with blackish ear patches

olive-green upperparts, including scapulars

white throat

yellow underparts with brown spotting on breast

white-edged secondaries, primaries, and wing coverts

long black tail with white outer feathers

JUVENILE

- **SONG** Call is a bold *tsweep* or *jijit-jijit*, reminiscent of the call of an Eastern Kingbird. Song is a short trilling *chip-chip-chip* or quiet *pee-weet, pee-weet*.
- **BEHAVIOR** Solitary or in pairs or small flocks. Forages for food on ground. Eats mostly insects, worms, snails, and sometimes seeds or fruit. Moves tail up and down as it walks and runs on ground.
- **BREEDING** Monogamous. Solitary.
- **NESTING** Incubation 10–13 days by both sexes, but mostly by female. Young altricial; brooded by female; stay in nest 15–16 days, fed by both sexes. 2 broods per year.
- **POPULATION** Common in Alaska on wet meadows, river banks, and lake shores. Casual south to California.

Similar Birds

GRAY WAGTAIL ♂ Longer tail; gray back; wing coverts and flight feathers not edged white; more extensive white on tail • black throat during the breeding season.

Flight Pattern

Several rapid wing beats followed by wings tucked to sides; repeated.

Nest Identification	Grass, forbs, leaves, and mosses, lined with hair and feathers • on ground, sheltered by hummock of grass, overhang, or tree roots • built by female • 4–7 buff to off-white eggs, with brown, buff, or gray markings; subelliptical, 2.0 x 1.5 cm.
Shape 🥄 Location ▬	

Plumage Sexes similar	Habitat	Migration Migratory	Weight 23 g

DATE _____ TIME_____ LOCATION _____

Family MOTACILLIDAE	Species *Motacilla alba*	Length 17–18 cm	Wingspan 22–25 cm

WHITE WAGTAIL

This Eurasian bird has a small but stable nesting population in Alaska and Greenland. Like most wagtails, it wags its long black tail, with white outer tail feathers, up and down and bobs its head while walking. Highly adaptable, it will nest under eaves of houses, on bridges, and ivy-covered walls, as well as natural cavities of cliffs and banks. The adult female is similar to the male. Wintering adults have less extensive black on the chin, throat, and breast, and juveniles have mostly white underparts.

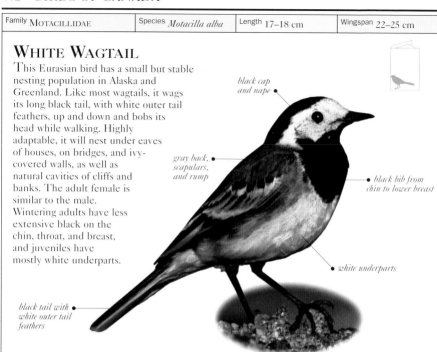

black cap and nape

gray back, scapulars, and rump

black bib from chin to lower breast

white underparts

black tail with white outer tail feathers

• **SONG** Sings an energetic trilling twitter with notes similar to its call notes, which sound like *chizzik-chizzik*.

• **BEHAVIOR** Solitary or in pairs; in flocks in migration and winter. Forages for food on ground, on and around rocks, and in shallow water. Eats mostly insects and snails. Frequents wetlands, shores of lakes, ponds, rivers, and inhabited areas, including agricultural areas.

• **BREEDING** Monogamous. Solitary. Courting male chases female until she notices him, then he shows off his shining black neck.

• **NESTING** Incubation 12–14 days by both sexes, but female does more. Young altricial; brooded by female; stay in nest 14–16 days, fed by both sexes. 1–2 broods per year.

• **POPULATION** Small Alaskan population is fairly common and stable. Casual in North America on the West Coast; accidental in the East.

Similar Birds

BLACK-BACKED WAGTAIL
In flight, shows mostly white wings with black tips to outer primaries • breeding adult has black back • winter adult has black U-shaped patch encircling breast from side of head.

Flight Pattern
Several rapid wing beats alternated with wings drawn to sides.

Nest Identification	
Shape ⬛ Location 🏔 🏚 🏠	Grass, forbs, leaves, roots, twigs, lichen, and moss, lined with grass, hair, and feathers • in cavity or ridge of cliff, bank, bridge, or building, 1–3 m above ground • sometimes on ground sheltered by grassy tussock or tree roots • built by female • 4–8 grayish or bluish white eggs, with gray or brown speckles; subelliptical, 2.0 x 1.5 cm.

Plumage Sexes similar	Habitat 🪶 🌾 ___ 〰	Migration Migratory	Weight 20 g

DATE _____ TIME_____ LOCATION _____

Family MOTACILLIDAE	Species *Motacilla lugens*	Length 18 cm	Wingspan 25 cm

BLACK-BACKED WAGTAIL

This slender long-tailed native of Asia reaches the Western Hemisphere by making regular spring and summer visits to the western Aleutian Islands. Occasionally these birds also nest in the Aleutians. Although the Black-backed Wagtail is very similar to the White Wagtail in appearance, its upperparts are black instead of gray when the bird is in breeding plumage. The long tail is black with white outer tail feathers, which is conspicuous in flight, as are the almost entirely white wings. Winter plumage shows a white throat with a black necklace. Juveniles resemble adults but are gray without black markings on head, upperparts, or breast. This bird frequents wetlands, river banks, and lake shores.

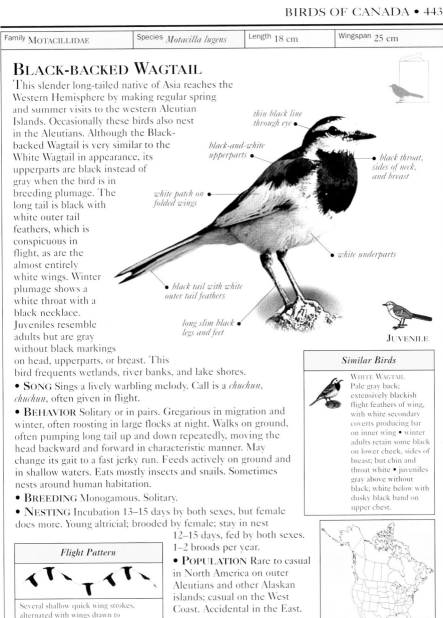

thin black line through eye

black-and-white upperparts

black throat, sides of neck, and breast

white patch on folded wings

white underparts

black tail with white outer tail feathers

white underparts

long slim black legs and feet

JUVENILE

- **SONG** Sings a lively warbling melody. Call is a *chuchun, chuchun*, often given in flight.
- **BEHAVIOR** Solitary or in pairs. Gregarious in migration and winter, often roosting in large flocks at night. Walks on ground, often pumping long tail up and down repeatedly, moving the head backward and forward in characteristic manner. May change its gait to a fast jerky run. Feeds actively on ground and in shallow waters. Eats mostly insects and snails. Sometimes nests around human habitation.
- **BREEDING** Monogamous. Solitary.
- **NESTING** Incubation 13–15 days by both sexes, but female does more. Young altricial; brooded by female; stay in nest 12–15 days, fed by both sexes. 1–2 broods per year.
- **POPULATION** Rare to casual in North America on outer Aleutians and other Alaskan islands; casual on the West Coast. Accidental in the East.

Similar Birds

WHITE WAGTAIL
Pale gray back; extensively blackish flight feathers of wing, with white secondary coverts producing bar on inner wing • winter adults retain some black on lower cheek, sides of breast; but chin and throat white • juveniles gray above without black; white below with dusky black band on upper chest.

Flight Pattern

Several shallow quick wing strokes, alternated with wings drawn to sides; repeated.

Nest Identification

Shape ⌣ 🪹   Location 🪨 🏔️

Grass, forbs, leaves, roots, and twigs, lined with grass, hair, and feathers • in ridges of cliff or hollow in bank; sometimes on ground • built by female • 4–6 grayish or bluish white eggs, with brown speckles; subelliptical, 2.0 x 1.5 cmß.

Plumage Sexes similar	Habitat 🦆 🪿 ___ ≈≈	Migration Migratory	Weight Undetermined

Family MOTACILLIDAE	Species *Anthus cervinus*	Length 15 cm	Wingspan 25 cm

RED-THROATED PIPIT

This bird takes its name from its reddish head, throat, and breast in breeding season. A mainly Eurasian species, it breeds in extreme western Alaska and off-shore islands and occurs rarely as a migrant in California. The head and breast of both the female and nonbreeding male are duller in color. Juveniles and some adult females show no red and have heavily streaked and spotted underparts. Winter males usually retain some reddish pink on their cheeks.

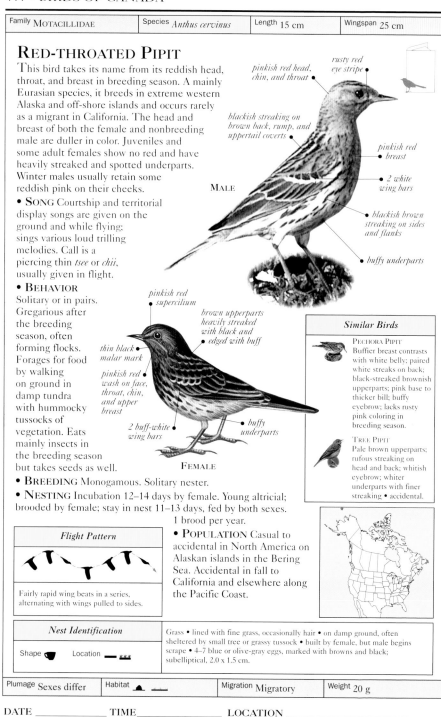

pinkish red head, chin, and throat

rusty red eye stripe

blackish streaking on brown back, rump, and uppertail coverts

pinkish red breast

2 white wing bars

blackish brown streaking on sides and flanks

buffy underparts

MALE

• **SONG** Courtship and territorial display songs are given on the ground and while flying; sings various loud trilling melodies. Call is a piercing thin *tsee* or *chii*, usually given in flight.

• **BEHAVIOR** Solitary or in pairs. Gregarious after the breeding season, often forming flocks. Forages for food by walking on ground in damp tundra with hummocky tussocks of vegetation. Eats mainly insects in the breeding season but takes seeds as well.

pinkish red supercilium

brown upperparts heavily streaked with black and edged with buff

thin black malar mark

pinkish red wash on face, throat, chin, and upper breast

2 buff-white wing bars

buffy underparts

FEMALE

Similar Birds

PECHORA PIPIT
Buffier breast contrasts with white belly; paired white streaks on back; black-streaked brownish upperparts; pink base to thicker bill; buffy eyebrow; lacks rusty pink coloring in breeding season.

TREE PIPIT
Pale brown upperparts; rufous streaking on head and back; whitish eyebrow; whiter underparts with finer streaking • accidental.

• **BREEDING** Monogamous. Solitary nester.

• **NESTING** Incubation 12–14 days by female. Young altricial; brooded by female; stay in nest 11–13 days, fed by both sexes. 1 brood per year.

• **POPULATION** Casual to accidental in North America on Alaskan islands in the Bering Sea. Accidental in fall to California and elsewhere along the Pacific Coast.

Flight Pattern

Fairly rapid wing beats in a series, alternating with wings pulled to sides.

Nest Identification

Shape   Location

Grass • lined with fine grass, occasionally hair • on damp ground, often sheltered by small tree or grassy tussock • built by female, but male begins scrape • 4–7 blue or olive-gray eggs, marked with browns and black; subelliptical, 2.0 x 1.5 cm.

Plumage Sexes differ	Habitat	Migration Migratory	Weight 20 g

DATE _____ TIME_____ LOCATION _____

Family MOTACILLIDAE	Species *Anthus rubescens*	Length 17 cm	Wingspan 25–28 cm

AMERICAN PIPIT

This sparrow-sized bird spends most of its time on the open ground, where it runs and walks, rather than hops. Like many of the pipits, the male has a dramatic song flight in which he flies to a height of 15 to 61 meters then floats down with feet dangling below and tail cocked upward, all the while continuing to sing. The American Pipit's breeding ranges extend from alpine tundra in the high mountains of the western US to arctic tundra across the top of the continent. Winter birds have browner upperparts and they have more heavily streaked underparts.

slim blackish bill

grayish brown upperparts

buffy wing bars on dark gray wings

buff underparts with faint brown streaking

- **SONG** A repetitive rapid series of notes, *chee-chee-chee* or *cheedal-cheedal-cheedal*. Call sounds like *wit, wit* or *pip-pit* and is most often given in flight.

- **BEHAVIOR** Solitary or in pairs; gregarious after breeding season, forming flocks that may be very large and mixed with other species, including Horned Larks and longspurs. Walks on ground, often bobbing its head while pumping tail up and down or wagging it. Forages in foliage, grass, and soil. Also wades into shallow waters to pick food from surface. Eats insects and their larvae, seeds, small mollusks, and crustaceans. Alpine species may escape severe weather by moving down mountain slopes to warmer valleys.

white outer tail feathers

black legs and feet

- **BREEDING** Monogamous. Solitary nester. Male has courtship song flight.

- **NESTING** Incubation 13–15 days by female. Young altricial; brooded by female; stay in nest 13–15 days, when they can make short flight. Fed by both sexes. 1 brood per year.

- **POPULATION** Common and widespread in tundra and alpine tundra; in winter, in fields and on beaches.

- **CONSERVATION** Neotropical migrant. Vulnerable to habitat loss on wintering grounds as well as foraging areas used during migration.

Similar Birds

SPRAGUE'S PIPIT
Buff- and blackish-streaked upperparts; dark eye on pale buff face with pale eye ring; pinkish to yellow legs and feet; slender yellowish bill; white underparts with deeper buff on lightly streaked breast; does not pump tail.

Flight Pattern

Swift flight on series of rapidly beating wings, alternated with wings pulled to sides; repeated.

Nest Identification

Shape Location

Often no nest materials; sometimes sticks and grass, occasionally with lining of small amount of mammal hair • sheltered by bank, rocks, or hillock • built by female • 3–7 grayish white eggs, with brown splotches; subelliptical, 2.0 x 1.5 cm.

Plumage Sexes similar	Habitat	Migration Migratory	Weight 23 g

Family MOTACILLIDAE	Species *Anthus spragueii*	Length 17 cm	Wingspan 25–28 cm

SPRAGUE'S PIPIT

Because its plumage serves as camouflage in the prairie grasses, this bird is hard to spot. When frightened, it often chooses to run or freeze, rather than fly. Olive-tan upperparts are edged with buff on the coverts, flight feathers, and back, creating a scaly appearance. Dark eyes encircled by thin eye rings stand out in sharp contrast to a buffy face. In flight, white outer feathers are evident on the mostly black tail. Unlike the American Pipit, it does not bob or wag its tail when it walks.

buff- and black-streaked upperparts

dark eyes

thin pale bill

pale buff face

buff to whitish underparts with dark streaking

white outer tail feathers

creamy pink to yellowish feet and legs

• **SONG** In display flight sings tinkling downward series of clear musical notes, *tzee, tzee-a.* Call is high-pitched *squeet-squeet-squeet,* mostly given in flight.

• **BEHAVIOR** Solitary or in pairs; gregarious after breeding season, forming flocks, often with other species. Secretive. Walks and runs on ground as it forages in tall grasses and grain fields. Eats insects and seeds. When flushed, flies an extended erratic pattern before dropping back into the grasses. Female sits tightly on the nest; she often flies up to meet the male as he descends from his aerial courtship flight.

• **BREEDING** Monogamous. Solitary. Courting male flies in spirals as high as 152 meters, circles and sings, then closes his wings and falls earthward, opening his wings just above ground.

• **NESTING** Incubation unknown but estimated at 12–14 days by female. Altricial young brooded by female; stay in nest 10–11 days, fed by female. 1–2 broods per year.

• **POPULATION** Uncommon in short-grass prairies and grassy agricultural fields. Rare in fall and winter in California; accidental in East.

• **CONSERVATION** Neotropical migrant. Declining due to habitat loss on breeding and perhaps wintering ranges.

Similar Birds

AMERICAN PIPIT
Darker and grayer back without stripes; deeper buff breast; brown to black legs and feet; dark bill; buffy wing bars; dark grayish face; bobs and wags tail continuously.

VESPER SPARROW
Stockier; short conical bill; less extensive white on outer tail feathers; white-bordered dark ear patch; chestnut patch in bend of wing.

Flight Pattern

Swift flight on series of rapidly beating wing strokes, alternated with wings pulled in to body.

Nest Identification

Shape ◖   Location ▬ ✶✶✶

Grasses • on ground, sometimes on grassy tussock • built by female • 4–6 pale buff or grayish white eggs, splotched with browns or gray, often with fine dark brown lines at larger end; subelliptical, 2.0 x 1.5 cm.

Plumage Sexes similar	Habitat ♠ ▬▬	Migration Migratory	Weight 26 g

DATE _____ TIME_____ LOCATION _____

Family BOMBYCILLIDAE	Species *Bombycilla garrulus*	Length 21 cm	Wingspan 33–36 cm

BOHEMIAN WAXWING

True to its name, this bird is highly nomadic and travels in flocks over a wide range in search of abundant food sources, particularly berries, which make up its principal diet. In winter it often is attracted to berries and fruits produced by ornamental plantings in towns and residential areas, and flocks may appear as if from nowhere, lingering until the larder is stripped. Gray underparts with cinnamon undertail coverts distinguish it from the smaller Cedar Waxwing. Like that more widespread relative its tail is yellow tipped. In flight it shows a white patch at the base of the primaries. Juveniles have heavily streaked underparts and whitish throats.

long grayish cinnamon crest

narrow black mask with white lower border

grayish upperparts with more brown on the back and head

black chin

usually waxy red tips on secondaries

gray underparts

white markings on grayish wings with red and yellow borders

cinnamon undertail coverts

blackish gray tail with yellow trim

JUVENILE

• **SONG** While flying, utters continuous twittering and chatter. Call is an abrasive *scree* or *zirrrr.*

• **BEHAVIOR** In pairs or small groups during breeding season; gregarious rest of year, forming flocks. Usually feeds close to other birds on ground and in trees. Perches to spot insects, then hawks them in flight. Eats fruit, berries, and insects. Drinks sap. Very tame. Southward eruptions are unpredictable and varied, often tied to crashes in food sources in breeding range.

• **BREEDING** Monogamous. Colonial.

• **NESTING** Incubation 14–15 days by female. Young altricial; brooded by female; stay in nest 13–18 days, fed by both sexes. 1 brood per year.

• **POPULATION** Fairly common to uncommon in mixed conifer and open coniferous woodlands and muskeg; widespread in range during winter.

• **FEEDERS** Comes to feeders for dried fruits and berries.

• **CONSERVATION** Vulnerable to habitat loss due to logging in coniferous forests.

Similar Birds

CEDAR WAXWING
Smaller; browner upperparts; yellow on belly; white undertail coverts; lacks yellow and white bars and spots on wings.

Flight Pattern

Strong rapid flight with a series of rapid wing beats alternating with wings pulled briefly to sides. Hawks for insects.

Nest Identification	
Shape Location	Sticks, lichen, stems, and grass; lined with mosses and fine materials • far out on horizontal limb, 1–15 m above ground • built by both sexes • 2–6 pale bluish gray eggs, splotched and marked with black, especially at larger end; oval, 2.5 x 1.8 cm.

Plumage Sexes similar	Habitat	Migration Migratory	Weight 57 g

Family BOMBYCILLIDAE	Species *Bombycilla cedrorum*	Length 18 cm	Wingspan 28–31 cm

CEDAR WAXWING

Named for the red waxlike tips on its secondaries, this social bird travels in large flocks in the nonbreeding season and may even nest in loose colonies. The purpose of the "red wax" is long-debated, but younger birds do not have it and the older birds that do often choose each other as mates and produce more young than the younger pairs. At times this bird may become so intoxicated on overripe fruit that it cannot fly. Females are similar to males but show a brownish rather than a blackish throat (a difficult field mark that can be observed only at close range). Juveniles have streaked upperparts and underparts.

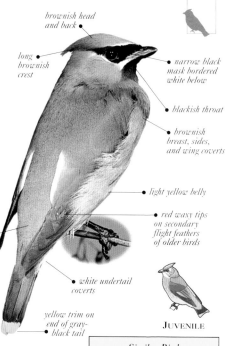

brownish head and back

long brownish crest

narrow black mask bordered white below

blackish throat

brownish breast, sides, and wing coverts

light yellow belly

red waxy tips on secondary flight feathers of older birds

gray rump and uppertail coverts

white undertail coverts

yellow trim on end of gray-black tail

JUVENILE

- **SONG** Call is thin, high-pitched warbled *zeeee* or *zeeeet*, more protracted just before leaving perch; may call constantly in flight.
- **BEHAVIOR** In pairs or in small to large flocks. Gregarious, especially in migration and winter. Tame and sociable. Feeds close to other birds in trees or on ground. Eats fruit, flower petals, and insects; drinks sap. Several may sit on a wire or branch and pass a piece of fruit back and forth, beak to beak. Hawks insects, particularly mayfly hatches and those of similar species, especially along streams.
- **BREEDING** Monogamous. Solitary to colonial. During courtship, male and female will sit together and pass flower petals back and forth, share food, and rub bills.
- **NESTING** Incubation 12–16 days by both sexes. Young altricial; brooded by female; stay in nest 14–18 days, fed by both sexes. 1–2 broods per year.
- **POPULATION** Fairly common to uncommon in woodland, forest edge, farmlands with fruit trees, towns, and suburbs.
- **FEEDERS** Raisins and berries; attracted to birdbaths.
- **CONSERVATION** Neotropical migrant. Not a common cowbird host; often rejects or damages its eggs.

Similar Birds

BOHEMIAN WAXWING Larger; grayer; cinnamon undertail coverts; white and yellow spots and bars on wings; white bar at base of primaries on folded wing shows as white patch in flight.

Flight Pattern

Strong rapid flight with several quick wing strokes alternating with brief periods of wings pulled to sides.

Nest Identification

Shape ◗ ▆   Location ▲ ♣

Sticks, mosses, and grass, lined with fine grass, moss, rootlets, hair, and pine needles • on limb or in fork of conifer or deciduous tree, 2–18 m above ground • built by both sexes • 2–6 pale bluish gray eggs, dotted with black and brown; oval, 2.0 x 1.5 cm.

Plumage Sexes similar	Habitat 🌿 🌳	Migration Migratory	Weight 31 g

DATE _____ TIME_____ LOCATION _____

Family PARULIDAE	Species *Vermivora pinus*	Length 12 cm	Wingspan 17–19 cm

BLUE-WINGED WARBLER

Except when the male perches high to sing, this unobtrusive, deliberate bird usually forages low, amid brushy overgrown fields and thickets. It often interbreeds with the Golden-winged Warbler, producing the fertile hybrids known as Lawrence's Warbler and Brewster's Warbler. The female is similar to the male but duller in color and has less yellow on her crown. When its range overlaps that of the Golden-winged Warbler, it tends to displace it.

black eye line

olive-green upperparts

bold yellow crown

blue-gray wings with 2 white wing bars

yellowish to white undertail coverts and white underside of tail

long slim bill

bold yellow underparts

• **SONG** Sings a breathy descending *beeee-buzzzz*. A dry *buzz* followed by a lower *buzz* is the typical song. The alternate song sounds similar to that of the Golden-winged Warbler's *beee-buzz, buzz, buzz*. Call note is a sharp *tisk*.

• **BEHAVIOR** Solitary or in pairs. Somewhat tame, but also somewhat inconspicuous. Feeds low in trees and close to ground, often hanging upside down in the manner of a chickadee. Often probes into curled dead leaves with long bill. Eats insects and spiders. Sometimes hover gleans. More generalized in habitat requirements than Golden-winged Warbler, it lives in a wide variety of early successional stages from old fields to young clear-cuts to power line right-of-ways.

• **BREEDING** Monogamous. Solitary or small loose colonies.

• **NESTING** Incubation 10–12 days by female. Young altricial; brooded by female; stay in nest 8–11 days, fed by both sexes. 1–2 broods per year.

• **POPULATION** Uncommon to fairly common in second growth and early successional habitat. Expanding in northern and northeastern portions of range. Casual in West on migration.

• **CONSERVATION** Neotropical migrant. Host to cowbird parasitism. Decreasing in the Midwest due to habitat lost to agriculture.

Similar Birds

YELLOW WARBLER
Female and juvenile • yellow wing bars, tail spots, and undertail coverts; lacks bluish wings, black eye stripe.

PROTHONOTARY WARBLER
Golden yellow head, neck, and underparts; white undertail coverts; blue-gray wings and tail; large white tail patches; olive green back; long black bill; no wing bars or eyeline.

BREWSTER'S WARBLER
Blue-winged/Golden-winged hybrid • yellow or whitish underparts tinged with yellow; whitish to yellowish wing bars.

Flight Pattern

Weak fluttering flight with wings briefly pulled to sides; repeated. Sometimes hovers to glean insects from foliage or branches.

Nest Identification

Shape   Location ━ ✸✸✸

Grasses, dried leaves, and bits of bark, with lining of fine grasses, vines, and hair • on ground, usually in vines or grasses and sheltered by shrub • built by female, perhaps aided by male • 4–7 white eggs, with flecks of brown and gray; oval to short oval, 1.5 x 1.3 cm.

Plumage Sexes similar	Habitat	Migration Migratory	Weight 9.0 g

DATE _____ TIME_____ LOCATION _____

Family PARULIDAE	Species *Vermivora chrysoptera*	Length 12–13 cm	Wingspan 20–21 cm

GOLDEN-WINGED WARBLER

This bird feeds chickadee-style, often hanging upside down, to find its favorite food, leaf-eating caterpillars. Its combination of a yellow wing patch and a black throat sets it apart from other similar warblers. The female is similar to the male but is duller in color, and her throat and eye patch are gray. The Golden-winged Warbler hybridizes with the Blue-winged Warbler, producing two hybrid forms known as Brewster's Warbler and the very rare Lawrence's Warbler. The hybrids generally cross back with the parent species.

bright yellow crown

white supercilium

black patch through eyes

pearl gray upperparts

black throat

white malar mark

blackish wings

white underparts washed gray on flanks

BREWSTER'S WARBLER

blackish tail

• **SONG** Primary song is an insectlike *bee-buz-buz-buz*; gives second song of *bee-buzzz*, similar to that of Blue-winged Warbler.

• **BEHAVIOR** Solitary or in pairs. Energetic feeder. Inspects all sides of branches and foliage. Eats mainly caterpillars and spiders. Commonly probes leaves for larvae. Forages in dead leaves in fall and winter. A habitat specialist, using early successional stages of old fields and woodland borders.

• **BREEDING** Monogamous. Solitary nester.

• **NESTING** Incubation 10 days by female. Young altricial; brooded by female; stay in nest 9–10 days, fed by both sexes. 1 brood per year.

• **POPULATION** Uncommon to rare. Numbers are declining.

• **CONSERVATION** Neotropical migrant. Declining with loss of habitat primarily due to later stages of succession and to competition with increasing Blue-winged Warbler, which displaces it when ranges are sympatric. Vulnerable to nest parasitism by Brown-headed Cowbird.

Flight Pattern
Weak fluttering flight with rapid wing beats, alternating with brief periods of wings drawn to sides; repeated.

Nest Identification	Bark pieces and grass, lined with hair and a few bark chips • on ground at base of shrub or tree or hidden in tall grass; sometimes set on pile of stems • built by female • 4–7 white or cream-white eggs, with brown splotches and dots; oval to short oval; 1.8 x 1.3 cm.
Shape ◣ Location ▬ ▰▰▰	

Plumage Sexes similar	Habitat ▲ ▲ ▲	Migration Migratory	Weight 9.0 g

DATE _____ TIME_____ LOCATION _____

Family PARULIDAE	Species *Vermivora peregrina*	Length 12 cm	Wingspan 19–20 cm

TENNESSEE WARBLER

Despite its name, this short-tailed plump-bodied warbler nests almost entirely in Canada and is found in Tennessee only during migration. Fall adults and juveniles are similar to females but have a yellowish wash on the underparts, except for the undertail coverts, which are almost always white.

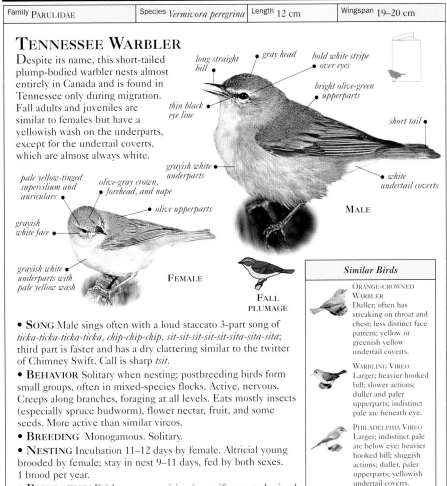

long straight bill
gray head
bold white stripe over eyes
bright olive-green upperparts
thin black eye line
short tail
grayish white underparts
white undertail coverts

MALE

pale yellow-tinged supercilium and auriculars
olive-gray crown, forehead, and nape
olive upperparts
grayish white face
grayish white underparts with pale yellow wash

FEMALE

FALL PLUMAGE

Similar Birds

ORANGE-CROWNED WARBLER Duller; often has streaking on throat and chest; less distinct face pattern; yellow or greenish yellow undertail coverts.

WARBLING VIREO Larger; heavier hooked bill; slower actions; duller and paler upperparts; indistinct pale arc beneath eye.

PHILADELPHIA VIREO Larger; indistinct pale arc below eye; heavier hooked bill; sluggish actions; duller, paler upperparts; yellowish undertail coverts.

• **SONG** Male sings often with a loud staccato 3-part song of *ticka-ticka-ticka-ticka, chip-chip-chip, sit-sit-sit-sit-sit-sita-sita-sita*; third part is faster and has a dry clattering similar to the twitter of Chimney Swift. Call is sharp *tsit*.

• **BEHAVIOR** Solitary when nesting; postbreeding birds form small groups, often in mixed-species flocks. Active, nervous. Creeps along branches, foraging at all levels. Eats mostly insects (especially spruce budworm), flower nectar, fruit, and some seeds. More active than similar vireos.

• **BREEDING** Monogamous. Solitary.

• **NESTING** Incubation 11–12 days by female. Altricial young brooded by female; stay in nest 9–11 days, fed by both sexes. 1 brood per year.

• **POPULATION** Fairly common; rising in coniferous and mixed deciduous-coniferous woodlands. Uncommon in West in fall. Rare in winter in California.

• **FEEDERS** Mixture of suet, peanut butter, and ripe banana.

• **CONSERVATION** Neotropical migrant. Rare cowbird host. Vulnerable to habitat loss.

Flight Pattern

Weak, somewhat fluttering flight with brief periods of wings pulled to sides.

Nest Identification	
Shape	Dried grasses and moss, with lining of fine grasses, stems, and hair • above bog in moss, on ground, or in base of shrub • built by female • 4–7 white or creamy white eggs, with brown splotches; ovate to short ovate, subelliptical to short subelliptical, 1.6 x 1.2 cm.
Location	

Plumage Sexes differ	Habitat	Migration Migratory	Weight 11 g

DATE _____ TIME_____ LOCATION _____

Family PARULIDAE	Species *Vermivora celata*	Length 12–13 cm	Wingspan 18–20 cm

ORANGE-CROWNED WARBLER

The brownish orange head patch for which this warbler is named is rarely noticeable unless the bird is frightened or agitated. It most often lives and nests in thick foliage close to the ground, but the male perches at the tops of tall trees to sing. Considerable color variation in this widely distributed species ranges from dull greenish birds in the East to brighter yellow birds in the West. The female

pale yellowish supercilium

indistinct dark eye line

thin slightly decurved bill

olive-green upperparts

faint streaking on sides of breast

small yellowish patch on marginal wing coverts

paler yellowish green underparts

yellow undertail coverts

sometimes lacks the crown patch. Juveniles are similar to adults but may show indistinct wing bars.

• **SONG** Male sings a high-pitched abrupt trill, which changes pitch toward the end, often slowing and dropping, *chip-ee, chip-ee, chip-ee*. Call note is a rough *stic*.

• **BEHAVIOR** Solitary. Vocal. Slow deliberate actions. Forages for food along branches and in foliage low in trees, shrubs, and grasses. Probes curled dead leaves. Eats mainly insects, flower nectar, and some fruits. Feeds from sapsucker drill wells. Hardy species, wintering farther north than most other warblers. Inquisitive; will respond to pishing and squeaking by birders.

• **BREEDING** Monogamous. Solitary.

• **NESTING** Incubation 12–14 days by female. Young altricial; brooded by female; stay in nest 8–10 days, fed by both sexes. 1 brood per year.

Similar Birds

YELLOW WARBLER ♀
Female and juvenile • pale edging to tertials, flight feathers, and wing coverts; yellow tail spots; dark eye on pale face.

NASHVILLE WARBLER
Clear yellow underparts with no streaking; clear white eye ring; shorter tail.

TENNESSEE WARBLER
Fall plumage • greener upperparts; shorter tail; unstreaked underparts; white undertail coverts.

• **POPULATION** Common in the West; rarer in the East.

• **FEEDERS** Mixture of peanut butter and suet. Also eats doughnuts.

• **CONSERVATION** Neotropical migrant. Rare cowbird host.

Flight Pattern

Somewhat weak flight with series of wing beats followed by brief period of wings pulled to sides.

Nest Identification

Shape ◖   Location ▬ ▪▪▪ ⩎⩎

Bark pieces, grass, leaves, and plant fibers, with lining of hair, feathers, and grass • on ground, usually sheltered by shrub or grasses • built by female • 3–6 white eggs, with dark red and brown blotches; short ovate, 1.7 x 1.3 cm.

Plumage Sexes similar	Habitat 🌲 🌿 〰	Migration Migratory	Weight 9.0 g

Family PARULIDAE	Species *Vermivora ruficapilla*	Length 12 cm	Wingspan 18–20 cm

NASHVILLE WARBLER

First collected while migrating near Nashville, Tennessee, this is the only North American warbler with a yellow throat, no wing bars, a white eye ring, and a blue-gray head. It also has a chestnut crown that is rarely noticeable. It has two breeding populations: one in the Pacific Coast states that often wags its tail, and another in northeastern and midwestern North America that does not wag its tail. The female is similar to the male but is duller in color and often lacks the chestnut crown.

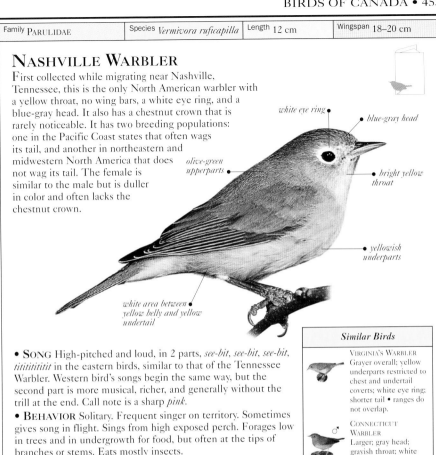

white eye ring

blue-gray head

bright yellow throat

olive-green upperparts

yellowish underparts

white area between yellow belly and yellow undertail

- **SONG** High-pitched and loud, in 2 parts, *see-bit, see-bit, see-bit, titititititit* in the eastern birds, similar to that of the Tennessee Warbler. Western bird's songs begin the same way, but the second part is more musical, richer, and generally without the trill at the end. Call note is a sharp *pink*.
- **BEHAVIOR** Solitary. Frequent singer on territory. Sometimes gives song in flight. Sings from high exposed perch. Forages low in trees and in undergrowth for food, but often at the tips of branches or stems. Eats mostly insects.
- **BREEDING** Monogamous. Solitary.
- **NESTING** Incubation 11–12 days by both sexes; female does more. Young altricial; brooded by female; stay in nest 11 days, fed by both sexes but mostly by female. 1 brood per year.
- **POPULATION** Common to fairly common in riparian woodlands and bogs, deciduous or coniferous woodlands, and thickets.
- **CONSERVATION** Neotropical migrant. Rare cowbird host. Vulnerable to habitat loss.

Similar Birds

VIRGINIA'S WARBLER Grayer overall; yellow underparts restricted to chest and undertail coverts; white eye ring; shorter tail • ranges do not overlap.

CONNECTICUT WARBLER Larger; gray head; grayish throat; white eye ring; pink legs and feet; yellow underparts, including belly; sluggish behavior walking on limbs and on ground.

Flight Pattern
Rather weak flight with series of rapid wing strokes alternating with brief periods of wings pulled to sides.

Nest Identification	
Shape 🐦 Location ▬ •••	Plant stems, pine needles, mosses, and rabbit fur, with lining of finer materials • on ground, sheltered by shrub or small tree, or sometimes placed on grassy or mossy tussock • built by female • 4–5 white or cream-white eggs, with fine dots of brown; ovate to short ovate, 1.5 x 1.2 cm.

Plumage Sexes similar	Habitat 🌳 🌿 🌲 〰	Migration Migratory	Weight 9.0 g

DATE _____ TIME_____ LOCATION _____

| Family PARULIDAE | Species *Parula americana* | Length 11 cm | Wingspan 18 cm |

NORTHERN PARULA

The male often can be heard singing its buzzy song during migration and from the tops of tall trees on its nesting ground. Nesting in the Deep South, it most often is associated with Spanish moss-covered trees, while more northern nests are in trees laced with the lichen *Usnea*. Both are important for construction of the nest. Females lack the chestnut/slate breast bands.

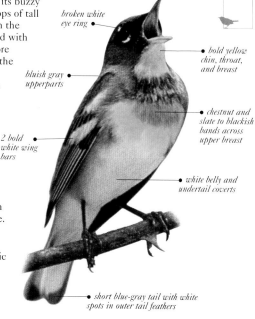

broken white eye ring

bold yellow chin, throat, and breast

bluish gray upperparts

chestnut and slate to blackish bands across upper breast

2 bold white wing bars

white belly and undertail coverts

- **SONG** Ascending insectlike buzzy trill of *zeeeeeeee-yip*, which rises and trips over the top; the equivalent of the bird filling a cup with its song and running it over the rim. Secondary song is series of slow rising buzzy notes ending in a trill, reminiscent of the Cerulean Warbler. Regional variation; western birds often lack the abrupt downward ending note. Call note is a sharp *chip*.
- **BEHAVIOR** Solitary or in pairs. Allows close approach. Active, acrobatic forager; sometimes upside down to hunt for insects on trunk, cluster of leaves, or branch tip; hover gleans and hawks flying insects. Eats insects, caterpillars and larvae, and spiders. One of the smallest warblers, often dominated by other birds, including other warbler species.

short blue-gray tail with white spots in outer tail feathers

- **BREEDING** Monogamous. Solitary.
- **NESTING** Incubation 12–14 days by both sexes; more by female. Altricial young brooded by and fed mostly by female. 1–2 broods per year.
- **POPULATION** Common in boreal forest, mixed hardwoods, bottomland forests, riparian corridors, and swamps. Rare in the West in migration.
- **CONSERVATION** Neotropical migrant. Rare cowbird host. Vulnerable to habitat loss due to logging, clearing of bottomland hardwoods for agriculture. Declining in Great Lakes region and on Atlantic Coast due to loss of *Usnea* lichen as a result of air pollutants.

Similar Birds

TROPICAL PARULA
More extensive yellow on underparts; orange wash on breast; lacks chestnut and gray-black chest bands; lacks white eye ring; often has dark mask.

Flight Pattern	

Relatively swift flight of short duration on rapidly beating wings. Sallies forth to take insects in midair, returning to perch.

Nest Identification	
Shape 🪹	Location 🌳

Lined with fine grasses, moss, and plant down • in Spanish moss, *Usnea* lichen, or tangled vine, hanging from tree, 0–17 m above ground • built by female • 3–7 white to creamy white eggs, splotched and flecked with browns; subelliptical to short subelliptical, 1.6 x 1.2 cm.

| Plumage Sexes differ | Habitat 🌳 🌾 🪨 〰️ 〰️ | Migration Migratory | Weight 9.0 g |

DATE _____ TIME_____ LOCATION _____

Family PARULIDAE	Species *Dendroica petechia*	Length 13 cm	Wingspan 20 cm

YELLOW WARBLER

This plump-bodied bird has a wider range than any other North American warbler, nesting from Canada to Mexico and from the Pacific to the Atlantic Coasts. A habitat generalist, like many warblers, it feeds harmful leaf-eating caterpillars to its nestlings. When a cowbird invades and lays eggs in this warbler's nest, the female builds a roof over all of the eggs, both hers and the brood parasite's, and often lays a new set on the "new" nest floor. As many as six stories have been found in a single nest, each floor containing entombed cowbird eggs. Bright red streaking on the male's underparts distinguishes him from the female and all other North American warblers. Females may have faint reddish streaking on their underparts. Juveniles resemble adult females.

bright yellow head

dark eye contrasts with yellow face

short tail with yellow edging on feathers

yellowish overall

MALE

bright yellow underparts with reddish streaking

- **SONG** Sings a swift warbling *sweet-sweet*, *I'm-so-sweet* or *tseet-tseet-tseet-titi-deet*, bouncy and variable. Similar to some songs of Chestnut-sided Warbler and American Redstart.
- **BEHAVIOR** Solitary or in pairs. Tame and conspicuous. Active. Forages in bushes, shrubs, or trees. Gleans food from branches and foliage; sometimes hawks insects. Eats mostly insects, larvae, and some fruit.
- **BREEDING** Monogamous. Solitary.
- **NESTING** Incubation 11–12 days by female. Altricial young brooded by female; stay in nest 9–12 days, fed by both sexes. 1–2 broods per year.
- **POPULATION** Common and widespread in riparian thickets, second-growth woodlands, gardens, orchards, and wetlands.

yellowish olive back, wings, and tail

yellow wing bars and edging

FEMALE

Similar Birds

WILSON'S WARBLER ♀
Female and juvenile
- longer darker tail; lacks yellow tail spots; more uniform olive-green coloring on upperparts; no wing bars; female may show trace of dark cap.

ORANGE-CROWNED WARBLER
Olive-green overall; paler underparts with dusky streaking; uniform dark tail without pale edging or spots; lacks wing bars.

- **CONSERVATION** Neotropical migrant. Common host to cowbird parasitism. Vulnerable to habitat loss, especially in riparian areas, and to herbicide spraying of willow thickets for grazing.

Flight Pattern

Weak, fluttering flight with brief periods of wings drawn to sides. Sallies out to snatch insects in air and returns to perch.

Nest Identification	
Shape ◗ Location 🐦🌳	Strongly built from plant material, grasses, moss, lichen, and fur, bound with spider's silk and cocoon material; lined with fine materials • in fork of tree or bush, 2–4 m high (but up to 18 m) • built mostly by female; male watches • 3–6 grayish, green, or bluish white eggs, splotched with grays, olives, and browns, wreathed at large end; oval to short oval, 1.8 x 1.3 cm.

Plumage Sexes differ	Habitat 🏙️ ⛰️ 🌿	Migration Migratory	Weight 9.0 g

DATE _____ TIME_____ LOCATION _____

Family PARULIDAE	Species *Dendroica pensylvanica*	Length 13 cm	Wingspan 20–21 cm

CHESTNUT-SIDED WARBLER

The only North American warbler with pure white underparts in all seasons, this bird most often lives in second-growth deciduous woodlands. An active feeder, it often cocks its tail high above its back, exposing a white crissum. Birds in fall plumage have a white eye ring on a gray face, a green crown, and creamy yellow wing bars; males have chestnut on the sides and black streaking on a green back.

- **SONG** High-pitched *please-please-pleased-to-meetcha.* Alternate or "second" song lacks strong up-and-down slurred notes at the end and is similar to that of the Yellow Warbler, *deet-deet-deet-titi-deet.* Call is a husky slurred *chip.*

- **BEHAVIOR** Solitary or in pairs. Tame and active. Singing male is conspicuous on territory. Eats insects, caterpillars, seeds, and berries. Picks food off leaves of trees and forages on ground. Catches insects in flight.

- **BREEDING** Monogamous. Solitary.

- **NESTING** Incubation 11–13 days by female. Altricial young brooded by female; remain in nest 10–12 days, fed by both sexes. 1–2 broods per year.

- **POPULATION** Fairly common to common in brushy thickets, second-growth deciduous woodlands, brushy old fields, and young clear-cuts. Rare migrant in West.

- **CONSERVATION** Neotropical migrant. Vulnerable to habitat loss through natural succession processes. Rare in the early 1800s, but became increasingly common as eastern forests were cut, and brushy, early succession-stage woody habitats emerged. Declining in some areas as current forests mature.

light olive-green upperparts with black streaking

yellow crown

black lores and eye stripe

2 pale yellow wing bars

black malar mark

rich chestnut sides

MALE

slate-blue legs and feet

white underparts

2 yellowish white wing bars

greenish upperparts with black streaking

yellow-green crown and forehead

FALL PLUMAGE

FEMALE

less chestnut on sides

blackish gray lores, malar, and postocular stripe

Similar Birds

All plumages are distinctive and if seen well are not likely to be confused with any other warbler.

Flight Pattern

Weak fluttering flight with brief periods of wings drawn to sides. Sallies forth to snatch insects in air, returning to perch.

Nest Identification

Shape | Location

Bark chips, vines, and plant material, with lining of animal hair and grasses • in fork of small tree or shrub, or in blackberry thicket, 30–122 cm above ground • built by female • 3–5 white to greenish white or creamy white eggs, with purple and brown blotches; oval to short oval, 1.7 x 1.3 cm.

Plumage Sexes differ	Habitat	Migration Migratory	Weight 11 g

DATE _____ TIME_____ LOCATION _____

Family PARULIDAE	Species *Dendroica magnolia*	Length 13 cm	Wingspan 20 cm

MAGNOLIA WARBLER

Often fanning its tail to show its broad white subterminal band and yellow rump, this bird nests in damp coniferous forests. The tail from below is white at the base with a black terminal band. From above, the white band is interrupted in the middle. Females are similar but show two white wing bars and sometimes a white eye ring during their first spring; a black loral mask may extend onto auriculars. Juveniles and fall-plumaged birds have gray heads with white eye rings, greenish gray upperparts with black streaking on the males, black streaking on the sides and flanks of males, and faint streaking on the flanks of females.

- **SONG** Brief high-pitched *wee-o, wee-o, wee-chew* or *weety-weety-weeteeo*, 2 or 3 slurred phrases with an ending note higher in pitch, emphatic and down-slurred. Call is distinctive nasal dry chip *tzek*.

- **BEHAVIOR** Solitary or in pairs. Tame and active. Males sing from conspicuous perches or while foraging. Often spreading tail, busily gleans insects from branches and foliage; occasionally hawks them in flight. Eats insects, larvae, caterpillars, and spiders.

- **BREEDING** Monogamous. Solitary.

- **NESTING** Incubation 11–13 days by female. Altricial young brooded by female; stay in nest 8–10 days, fed by both sexes. 1 brood per year.

- **POPULATION** Fairly common to common; slight decline in parts of Appalachians, increase in southern Appalachians and in New England. Casual in winter in Florida. Rare migrant in West.

- **CONSERVATION** Neotropical migrant. Vulnerable to habitat loss. The loss of eastern spruce-fir forests to adelgids and air pollution is causing a decline in numbers.

Labels on male illustration:
- blackish upperparts
- white wing patch
- broad white eyebrow
- broken white eye ring
- dark blackish streaking on breast, sides, and flanks
- yellow underparts
- **MALE**

Labels on first spring female illustration:
- olive-tinged gray crown and hindneck
- white supercilium and eye ring
- black-spotted yellow-olive back
- gray wings with 2 white wing bars
- yellow underparts with black streaking
- white undertail coverts
- **FIRST SPRING FEMALE**

FALL PLUMAGE

Similar Birds

PRAIRIE WARBLER Fall • yellowish supercilium; has only arc beneath eye; olive-green rump; uniform olive-green tail; lacks grayish white breast band; pumps tail.

Flight Pattern
Weak fluttering flight with brief periods of wings drawn to sides. Sallies forth to take insects in flight, returning to perch.

Nest Identification	
Shape ☙ Location 🌿 🌲	Grasses and sticks, lined with rootlets • on horizontal branch, usually 30 cm–5 m above ground • built by both sexes • 3–5 white, creamy white, or greenish white eggs, with brown dots or splotches, sometimes wreathed at larger end; subelliptical to short subelliptical. 1.6 x 1.2 cm.

Plumage Sexes differ	Habitat 🌿🌿 🌲	Migration Migratory	Weight 9.0 g

DATE _____ TIME_____ LOCATION _____

Family PARULIDAE	Species *Dendroica tigrina*	Length 12 cm	Wingspan 18 cm

CAPE MAY WARBLER

Identifiable by its chestnut cheek patches, this bird is named after Cape May, New Jersey, where it was discovered in 1811. This fairly common inhabitant of northern spruce forests is known for its aggressive behavior of chasing other birds from treetop foraging areas. Females are duller but are easily identified by the yellow rump and patches on the side of the neck. Juveniles and fall-plumaged birds are similar to females, but many have faint gray streaking on pale yellow to whitish underparts.

• **SONG** Sounds like *seet seet seet seet*, high-pitched, wiry, and upslurred, usually in series of 5–6 notes. Call is high thin *seet*.

• **BEHAVIOR** Solitary or in pairs. Forages in thickets or high in trees, particularly in conifers on breeding grounds. Hawks insects and spruce budworms. Sometimes drinks tree sap, juice from grapes, and flower nectar.

• **BREEDING** Monogamous. Solitary.

• **NESTING** Breeding biology poorly known. Incubation about 11–13 days by female. Altricial young brooded by female; fed by both sexes; stay in nest estimated 10–12 days. 1 brood per year.

• **POPULATION** Uncommon in spruce fir forests; may become locally common during spruce budworm outbreaks. Declining short-term populations. Very rare to casual in West during migration.

• **CONSERVATION** Neotropical migrant. Vulnerable to loss of breeding and wintering grounds due to deforestation and forest fragmentation.

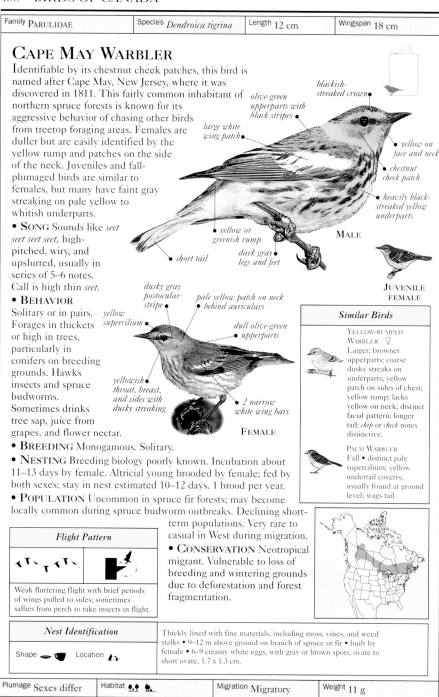

olive-green upperparts with black stripes
blackish-streaked crown
large white wing patch
yellow on face and neck
chestnut cheek patch
heavily black-streaked yellow underparts
yellow or greenish rump
short tail
dark gray legs and feet
MALE

JUVENILE FEMALE

dusky gray postocular stripe
pale yellow patch on neck behind auriculars
dull olive-green upperparts
yellow supercilium
yellowish throat, breast, and sides with dusky streaking
2 narrow white wing bars
FEMALE

Similar Birds

YELLOW-RUMPED WARBLER ♀
Larger; browner upperparts; coarse dusky streaks on underparts; yellow patch on sides of chest; yellow rump; lacks yellow on neck; distinct facial pattern; longer tail; *chip* or *check* notes distinctive.

PALM WARBLER
Fall • distinct pale supercilium; yellow undertail coverts; usually found at ground level; wags tail.

Flight Pattern

Weak fluttering flight with brief periods of wings pulled to sides; sometimes sallies from perch to take insects in flight.

Nest Identification

Shape ⌣🥣   Location 🐾

Thickly lined with fine materials, including moss, vines, and weed stalks • 9–12 m above ground on branch of spruce or fir • built by female • 6–9 creamy white eggs, with gray or brown spots; ovate to short ovate, 1.7 x 1.3 cm.

Plumage Sexes differ	Habitat 🌳 🌲	Migration Migratory	Weight 11 g

DATE _____ TIME_____ LOCATION _____

Family PARULIDAE	Species *Dendroica caerulescens*	Length 13 cm	Wingspan 18–20 cm

BLACK-THROATED BLUE WARBLER

Easily identified by its deep blue-gray back, white underparts, and white wing patch, this common migratory bird can be seen across eastern North America every spring and fall. Its nesting ranges from southern Canada through the Appalachians to northern Georgia. Females differ from their mates more than any of the wood warblers, with brownish olive to gray upperparts, whitish supercilium, and small white patch at the base of the primaries. Juvenile females sometimes lack the white patch.

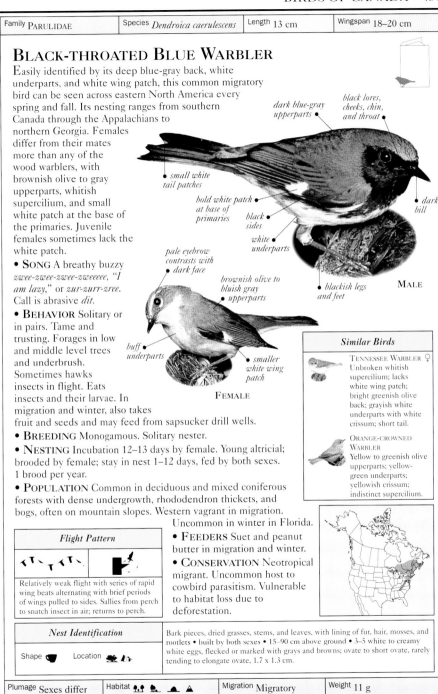

dark blue-gray upperparts

black lores, cheeks, chin, and throat

small white tail patches

bold white patch at base of primaries

black sides

white underparts

dark bill

blackish legs and feet

MALE

pale eyebrow contrasts with dark face

brownish olive to bluish gray upperparts

buff underparts

smaller white wing patch

FEMALE

- **SONG** A breathy buzzy *zwee-zwee-zwee-zweeeee*, "*I am lazy*," or *zur-zurr-zree*. Call is abrasive *dit*.
- **BEHAVIOR** Solitary or in pairs. Tame and trusting. Forages in low and middle level trees and underbrush. Sometimes hawks insects in flight. Eats insects and their larvae. In migration and winter, also takes fruit and seeds and may feed from sapsucker drill wells.
- **BREEDING** Monogamous. Solitary nester.
- **NESTING** Incubation 12–13 days by female. Young altricial; brooded by female; stay in nest 1–12 days, fed by both sexes. 1 brood per year.
- **POPULATION** Common in deciduous and mixed coniferous forests with dense undergrowth, rhododendron thickets, and bogs, often on mountain slopes. Western vagrant in migration. Uncommon in winter in Florida.
- **FEEDERS** Suet and peanut butter in migration and winter.
- **CONSERVATION** Neotropical migrant. Uncommon host to cowbird parasitism. Vulnerable to habitat loss due to deforestation.

Similar Birds

TENNESSEE WARBLER ♀
Unbroken whitish supercilium; lacks white wing patch; bright greenish olive back; grayish white underparts with white crissum; short tail.

ORANGE-CROWNED WARBLER
Yellow to greenish olive upperparts; yellow-green underparts; yellowish crissum; indistinct supercilium.

Flight Pattern
Relatively weak flight with series of rapid wing beats alternating with brief periods of wings pulled to sides. Sallies from perch to snatch insect in air; returns to perch.

Nest Identification	
Shape / Location	Bark pieces, dried grasses, stems, and leaves, with lining of fur, hair, mosses, and rootlets • built by both sexes • 15–90 cm above ground • 3–5 white to creamy white eggs, flecked or marked with grays and browns; ovate to short ovate, rarely tending to elongate ovate, 1.7 x 1.3 cm.

Plumage Sexes differ	Habitat	Migration Migratory	Weight 11 g

DATE _____ TIME _____ LOCATION _____

Family PARULIDAE	Species *Dendroica coronata*	Length 14 cm	Wingspan 22 cm

YELLOW-RUMPED WARBLER

In the East this is the most prevalent migrating warbler, and in winter it is the most abundant in North America. Plumage varies with geography. In the West the group known as Audubon's Warbler has a yellow throat and broken white eye ring. The northern and eastern group known as the Myrtle Warbler has white eyebrows, a white arc beneath the eye, and white on the throat and both sides of the neck. Until recently these groups were considered two species, but they interbreed where their ranges overlap and have been classified as geographic races of one species. Juveniles are similar to winter adults.

black auricular patch
yellow crown patch
gray upperparts
2 white wing bars
yellow rump
black streaking on breast, sides, and flanks

MALE MYRTLE WARBLER

white underparts

• **SONG** Variable slow warble that often slows in the middle then speeds up and ends on rising or falling notes. Some have musical trill. Call is loud *check, chup,* or *chip.*

black-streaked gray-brown upperparts
gray-brown wings
white arc below eye

FEMALE MYRTLE WARBLER

yellow side patches

AUDUBON'S BREEDING MALE

WINTER PLUMAGE
FALL MYRTLE

white underparts with gray streaks on breast and sides

• **BEHAVIOR** Solitary or in pairs. Gregarious in winter, often joins mixed feeding flocks. Gleans or hover-gleans on ground and in bushes and trees; also hawks. Able to live for long periods on berries and seeds. Also eats insects and spiders, and drinks tree sap and juice from fallen oranges.
• **BREEDING** Monogamous. Solitary.
• **NESTING** Incubation 12–13 days by female. Altricial young brooded by female; stay in nest 10–12 days, fed by both sexes. 2 broods per year.
• **POPULATION** Abundant in coniferous or mixed forests; wooded and brushy habitats in winter. In winter Myrtle form common in East, fairly common on West Coast; Audubon's form casual in East in winter.
• **FEEDERS** Suet, doughnuts, and peanut butter.
• **CONSERVATION** Neotropical migrant. Myrtles are common cowbird hosts.

Similar Birds

PALM WARBLER
Juvenile • yellow undertail coverts; white spots in tail corners; pumps tail.

CAPE MAY WARBLER
Juvenile • smaller; yellow on sides of neck; shorter tail; dull green rump; pale yellow wash on center of breast.

Flight Pattern

Fairly rapid flight with quick wing strokes, alternating with brief periods of wings pulled to sides. Sallies forth and takes insects in flight, returning to perch.

Nest Identification

Shape ⬤   Location 🪹

Shredded bark, weed stalks, twigs, and roots, lined with feathers • 1–15 m above ground in conifer • built by female • 3–5 white to creamy eggs, with brown and gray markings, occasionally wreathed; oval to short oval, 1.8 x 1.3 cm.

Plumage Sexes differ	Habitat 🌲🌲	Migration Migratory	Weight 14 g

DATE _____ TIME_____ LOCATION _____

| Family PARULIDAE | Species *Dendroica nigrescens* | Length 12–13 cm | Wingspan 19–20 cm |

BLACK-THROATED GRAY WARBLER

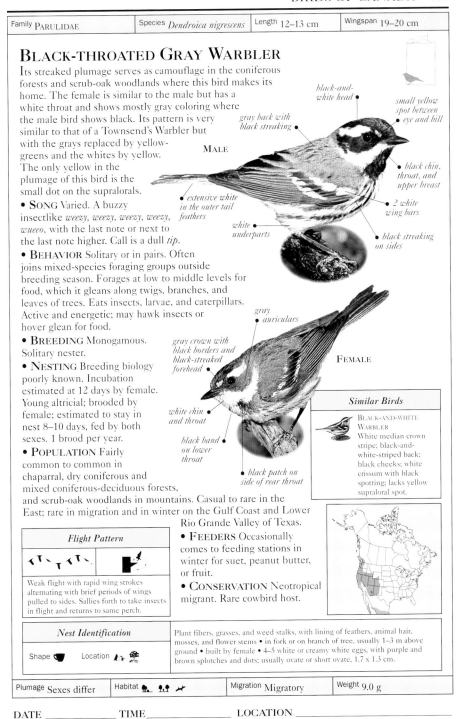

Its streaked plumage serves as camouflage in the coniferous forests and scrub-oak woodlands where this bird makes its home. The female is similar to the male but has a white throat and shows mostly gray coloring where the male bird shows black. Its pattern is very similar to that of a Townsend's Warbler but with the grays replaced by yellow-greens and the whites by yellow. The only yellow in the plumage of this bird is the small dot on the supralorals.

- **SONG** Varied. A buzzy insectlike *weezy, weezy, weezy, weezy, wueeo*, with the last note or next to the last note higher. Call is a dull *tip*.
- **BEHAVIOR** Solitary or in pairs. Often joins mixed-species foraging groups outside breeding season. Forages at low to middle levels for food, which it gleans along twigs, branches, and leaves of trees. Eats insects, larvae, and caterpillars. Active and energetic; may hawk insects or hover glean for food.
- **BREEDING** Monogamous. Solitary nester.
- **NESTING** Breeding biology poorly known. Incubation estimated at 12 days by female. Young altricial; brooded by female; estimated to stay in nest 8–10 days, fed by both sexes. 1 brood per year.
- **POPULATION** Fairly common to common in chaparral, dry coniferous and mixed coniferous-deciduous forests, and scrub-oak woodlands in mountains. Casual to rare in the East; rare in migration and in winter on the Gulf Coast and Lower Rio Grande Valley of Texas.
- **FEEDERS** Occasionally comes to feeding stations in winter for suet, peanut butter, or fruit.
- **CONSERVATION** Neotropical migrant. Rare cowbird host.

black-and-white head

small yellow spot between eye and bill

gray back with black streaking

MALE

black chin, throat, and upper breast

extensive white in the outer tail feathers

2 white wing bars

white underparts

black streaking on sides

gray auriculars

gray crown with black borders and black-streaked forehead

FEMALE

white chin and throat

black band on lower throat

black patch on side of rear throat

Similar Birds

BLACK-AND-WHITE WARBLER
White median crown stripe; black-and-white-striped back; black cheeks; white crissum with black spotting; lacks yellow supraloral spot.

Flight Pattern	

Weak flight with rapid wing strokes alternating with brief periods of wings pulled to sides. Sallies forth to take insects in flight and returns to same perch.

Nest Identification	
Shape [icon] Location [icons]	Plant fibers, grasses, and weed stalks, with lining of feathers, animal hair, mosses, and flower stems • in fork or on branch of tree, usually 1–3 m above ground • built by female • 4–5 white or creamy white eggs, with purple and brown splotches and dots; usually ovate or short ovate, 1.7 x 1.3 cm.

| Plumage Sexes differ | Habitat [icons] | Migration Migratory | Weight 9.0 g |

DATE _____ TIME_____ LOCATION _____

Family PARULIDAE	Species *Dendroica virens*	Length 12–13 cm	Wingspan 19–20 cm

BLACK-THROATED GREEN WARBLER

Like many in its family, the individual Black-throated Green Warbler sings two different songs, but in two different contexts: one in the vicinity of the female and nest and the other near the territorial boundaries or when stimulated by another male. It is the only warbler in eastern North America with bold yellow cheeks. The female is similar to the male but shows fewer black streaks on the sides of her body, less black on her throat, and has a yellowish chin and upper throat. The juvenile is similar to the female but has a white throat and lacks the black on its breast.

olive-green auricular patch •

yellow- and olive-green upperparts with black • streaking on back

MALE

bright yellow forehead and sides of face •

• yellow wash on flanks

black chin, throat, and upper breast •

• 2 white wing bars

white underparts •

• black streaking on flanks and sides

FEMALE

yellowish chin •

black throat veiled with whitish feather tips

• **SONG** A throaty *trees-trees-whispering-trees* (the territorial/male interaction song) and a hoarse *zay-zay-zay-zoo-zeee* (the pair bonding/nest vicinity song). Call is a flat soft *tsip*.

• **BEHAVIOR** Solitary or in pairs. Forages at mid-level in vegetation and in the interior of branches, usually not at the tips. Gleans from twigs and foliage; hover-gleans and may hawk flying prey. Eats adult insects, caterpillars, larvae, and some berries, particularly in migration.

• **BREEDING** Monogamous. Solitary.

• **NESTING** Incubation 12 days by female. Young altricial; brooded by female; remain in nest 8–10 days, fed by both sexes, but female does more. 1–2 broods per year.

• **POPULATION** Fairly common in a variety of habitats of conifer, mixed deciduous-conifer, and deciduous woodlands. Some winter regularly in southern Florida; casual to accidental in the West. Numbers decreasing in the Great Lakes areas and in parts of New England.

• **CONSERVATION** Neotropical migrant. Vulnerable to habitat loss. Rare host to cowbird parasitism.

Similar Birds

♂ ♀

GOLDEN-CHEEKED WARBLER
Gray to black upperparts with black streaking; black or black-streaked crown; yellow face; black eye line connected to the dark color of nape; black ear patch; white crissum • restricted range in Texas.

Flight Pattern

Somewhat weak flight with rapid wing strokes, alternating with brief periods of wings pulled to sides. Sallies from perch, takes insect in air, and returns to perch.

Nest Identification

Shape   Location

Dead grasses, plant fibers, and stems, with lining of animal hair, flower stems, and feathers • usually in crotch of small or large evergreen or in hardwood tree on horizontal branch, 1–24 m above ground • built by both sexes • 3–5 gray-white or creamy white eggs, with brown and purple dots and blotches, often wreathed; oval to short oval, 1.7 x 1.3 cm.

Plumage Sexes differ	Habitat	Migration Migratory	Weight 9.0 g

DATE _____ TIME_____ LOCATION _____

Family PARULIDAE	Species *Dendroica townsendi*	Length 12–13 cm	Wingspan 19–20 cm

TOWNSEND'S WARBLER

The western counterpart of the Black-throated Green Warbler nests in high pines and spruces of the Pacific Northwest. The bright yellow underparts and yellow face with black cheek patch are difficult to see because the bird forages and sings in the tops of the mature conifers. Townsend's Warbler often hybridizes with the Hermit Warbler where ranges overlap.

blackish ear patch with wide yellow trim

olive-green upperparts with black streaks

dark blackish crown

2 white wing bars

black chin, throat, and upper breast

white in outer 2–3 tail feathers

yellow breast

white belly

yellowish sides with black streaking

MALE

olive crown with black streaking

narrow black streaking on back

2 thin white wing bars

yellow chin and throat

olive cheeks

necklace of black streaks on lower throat

thin black streaks on sides and flanks

FEMALE

- **SONG** Variable. Raspy high *weezy, weezy, weezy, tweea*, rising in pitch but dropping at the end. Call is high sharp *tsik*.
- **BEHAVIOR** Solitary or in pairs. Gregarious after breeding season; joins mixed-species foraging flocks. Aggressive toward other species. Sometimes hover-gleans from branches and foliage. Eats insects, caterpillars, and spiders.
- **BREEDING** Monogamous. Solitary.
- **NESTING** Breeding biology poorly known. Incubation estimated at 12 days by female. Altricial young brooded by female; stay in nest estimated 8–12 days. Fed by both sexes; female may do more. 1 brood per year.
- **POPULATION** Fairly common in coniferous and mixed coniferous-deciduous forests. Casual to accidental in winter and in migration in the East. May be increasing slightly and expanding range southward in Washington and Oregon.
- **FEEDERS** Mixture of peanut butter, marshmallows, and cheese.
- **CONSERVATION** Neotropical migrant. Degree of cowbird parasitism unknown. Subject to forest fragmentation by logging.

Similar Birds

BLACK-THROATED GREEN WARBLER Yellow cheeks and face without dark ear patches; whitish chest; olive back with black streaking; yellowish wash on undertail coverts • eastern breeding range has almost no overlap.

HERMIT WARBLER Lacks black cheeks and crown; yellow restricted to breast and sides; fine black streaking on sides and flanks.

Flight Pattern

Relatively weak flight on rapidly beating wings, alternating with brief periods of wings pulled to sides.

Nest Identification

Shape ⌒   Location 🌲

Bark pieces, plant fibers, lichens, grasses, and cocoon materials, with lining of feathers and animal hair • across limb of conifer, high above ground • built by both sexes • 3–5 white eggs, with fine dots of brown; short ovate, 1.8 x 1.3 cm.

Plumage Sexes differ	Habitat 🌿 🌳	Migration Migratory	Weight 9.0 g

DATE _____ TIME_____ LOCATION _____

Family PARULIDAE	Species *Dendroica fusca*	Length 13 cm	Wingspan 20 cm

BLACKBURNIAN WARBLER

Head and throat glowing like embers, the males are unmistakable. Juveniles and fall males are similar. It frequents coniferous or mixed deciduous-conifer forests in most of its breeding range; in the Appalachians, it is also found in lower drier forests of pine-oak-hickory.

• **SONG** Thin high-pitched ascending trill in 2–3 parts, ending with upslurred note that some people cannot hear: *seep seep seep seep titi zeeeeee.* Call is rich *tsip.*

• **BEHAVIOR** Solitary or in pairs. May join mixed foraging flocks after breeding. Gleans prey from branches, twigs, and foliage in treetops. Sometimes catches insects in flight. Eats insects, caterpillars, and some berries.

brilliant orange head, throat, and upper breast

black nape and sides of crown

black triangular ear patch

black back with white streaking

black wings with large white patches

MALE

white breast with pale ocher wash

black streaking on sides

buff-white belly, flanks, and undertail coverts

white patches in outer tail feathers

dark gray-olive upperparts

JUVENILE

pale orange-ocher supercilium and sides of head behind ear patch

FEMALE

pale orange to ocher throat and upper breast

2 broad white wing bars

white underparts with black streaks on sides and flanks

• **BREEDING** Monogamous. Solitary nester.

• **NESTING** Incubation 11–12 days by female. Altricial young brooded by female; stay in nest estimated 9–12 days, fed by both sexes. 1 brood per year.

• **POPULATION** Fairly common in coniferous and mixed deciduous-conifer forests; stable. Strays to California in fall migration. Can be numerous in areas where there are spruce budworm outbreaks.

• **CONSERVATION** Neotropical migrant. Infrequent cowbird host. Vulnerable to loss of habitat due to land clearing. Hemlock infestations by insect pests could negatively impact.

Similar Birds

TOWNSEND'S WARBLER Juvenile female • yellow throat and chest; olive crown and upperparts; entirely dark bill; more distinct dark streaking on sides.

CERULEAN WARBLER Female and juvenile male • supercilium broadens behind eye; less distinct rounded ear patch; white or buff underparts; pale lines on back; dark streaks across back; shorter tail • eastern range.

Flight Pattern	

Fairly swift direct flight on rapidly beating wings. Sallies forth from perch, taking insects in midair and returning to perch.

Nest Identification	
Shape	Location	Small sticks, lichen, and plant down • lined with hair, bark pieces, and small roots • on horizontal branch, 6–15 m above ground (but as high as 24 m) • built by female • 4–5 white or greenish white eggs, with brown dots and splotches; oval to short oval, 1.7 x 1.2 cm.

Plumage Sexes differ	Habitat	Migration Migratory	Weight 11 g

Family PARULIDAE	Species *Dendroica pinus*	Length 13 cm	Wingspan 22 cm

PINE WARBLER

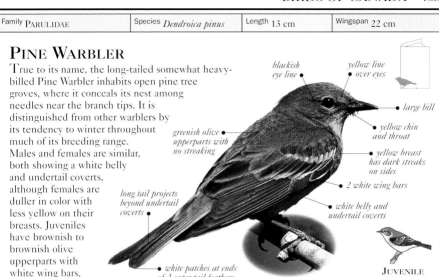

True to its name, the long-tailed somewhat heavy-billed Pine Warbler inhabits open pine tree groves, where it conceals its nest among needles near the branch tips. It is distinguished from other warblers by its tendency to winter throughout much of its breeding range. Males and females are similar, both showing a white belly and undertail coverts, although females are duller in color with less yellow on their breasts. Juveniles have brownish to brownish olive upperparts with white wing bars, and underparts varying from white to yellowish with a brownish wash on the flanks.

blackish eye line
yellow line over eyes
large bill
greenish olive upperparts with no streaking
yellow chin and throat
yellow breast has dark streaks on sides
2 white wing bars
long tail projects beyond undertail coverts
white belly and undertail coverts
white patches at ends of 2 outer tail feathers

JUVENILE FEMALE

- **SONG** Twittering musical trill similar to Chipping Sparrow but varying in speed, loudness, and pitch. Call is slurred *tsup*.
- **BEHAVIOR** Solitary or in pairs. Very vocal. Gregarious in winter; often joins mixed feeding flocks. Gleans food by creeping slowly and deliberately along branches, usually high in trees, but sometimes lower, even on ground. Often flies from tree to tree, diving for passing insects. Eats insects, caterpillars, and spiders. Also eats seeds, wild grapes, and some berries. Aggressive toward other species sharing same pine habitat.
- **BREEDING** Monogamous. Solitary.
- **NESTING** Incubation 10 days by both sexes. Young altricial; brooded by female; leave nest within 10 days, fed by both sexes. 2–3 broods per year in the South, 1 brood per year in the North.
- **POPULATION** Fairly common to common. Stable or increasing slightly, but some decline in coastal New England and Great Lakes region due to clearing of pines. Subject to loss in severe winters. Increases occur as pines mature. Casual in West.
- **FEEDERS** Peanut butter and cornmeal mixture.
- **CONSERVATION** Neotropical migrant. Infrequent host to cowbird parasitism. Vulnerable to fragmentation and clearing of pine forests.

Similar Birds

YELLOW-THROATED VIREO
Heavier hooked bill; yellow spectacles; white belly and flanks; no streaking on sides or breast; gray rump and crissum; no white in tail corners; sluggish.

BAY-BREASTED WARBLER ♂
BLACKPOLL WARBLER ♀
Basic plumage • black streaking on back; much less white in tail corners; shorter tails with less extension from undertail coverts; paler cheeks contrast less with throat color.

Flight Pattern	
Weak flight, rapid wing beats alternated with brief period of wings pulled to sides. Sallies out to take flying insects, returns.	

Nest Identification	
Shape ⬤ 🐦 Location 🌿	Lined with feathers, weeds, grass, bark, pine needles, twigs, and spider webs • built on or near end of limb, 3–41 m above ground • built by female • 3–5 off-white eggs, with brown specks near larger end; oval to short oval, 1.8 x 1.3 cm.

Plumage Sexes similar	Habitat 🌲🌲	Migration Northern birds migrate	Weight 11 g

DATE _____ TIME_____ LOCATION _____

Family PARULIDAE	Species *Dendroica discolor*	Length 12 cm	Wingspan 19 cm

PRAIRIE WARBLER

Rather than the prairies as its name might imply, this bird can be found in brushy old fields, open pine stands, and sometimes in coastal mangroves in eastern and southern North America. Like many warblers, the male sings from an exposed perch at the tops of tall trees. Females are similar to males but duller in color. Juvenile females are duller still, with grayish olive upperparts, pale supercilium, and broken eye rings.

yellow sides of face with black streak through eyes, outlining ear patch

bright yellow eyebrow

olive-green upperparts with chestnut markings on back

2 light yellow wing bars

black streaking on sides

white patches on outer tail feathers

bright yellow underparts

- **SONG** An ascending trilling *zzee-zzee-zzee-zzee-zzee-zzee-zzee*, starting at one pitch and rising sharply over the last half of song. Call note is a rich smacking *tchick*.
- **BEHAVIOR** Solitary or in pairs. Joins mixed feeding flocks after breeding season. Tame. Active and restless. Constantly pumps or wags tail while feeding. Forages in low branches of trees and bushes and sometimes on ground. Catches some insects in flight but primarily gleans from foliage; sometimes hover-gleans. Eats mostly insects and spiders.
- **BREEDING** Monogamous; some males polygynous in midnesting season. Solitary nester.
- **NESTING** Incubation 11–14 days by female. Young altricial; brooded by female; stay in nest 8–11 days, fed by both sexes. Both sexes tend for additional 40–50 days. 2 broods per year.
- **POPULATION** Common but is declining.
- **CONSERVATION** Neotropical migrant. Frequently host to cowbird parasitism. Vulnerable to habitat loss that occurs with maturation of forests.

Similar Birds

PINE WARBLER Yellow-green face; indistinct yellowish eye ring and supercilium; olive-green back without streaking; yellowish underparts with indistinct dusky streaking; extensive white tail spots; bobs tail but not as strongly.

Flight Pattern

Fairly fast flight with rapidly beating wings, alternating with brief periods of wings pulled to sides. May sally forth and take insects in flight.

Nest Identification	
Shape ☕ Location 🌿 🌳 🌾	Grasses, stems, bark pieces, plant down, and leaves, bound with spider's silk and lined with feathers and mammal hair • hidden in tree or bush, usually 3–5 m above ground (but ranges from 30 cm–14 m) • built by female • 4–5 white, creamy white, or greenish white eggs, with fine and large dots of brown, concentrated on larger end; oval to short oval, 1.5 x 1.2 cm.

Plumage Sexes differ	Habitat 🌿🌾 🌲 🌱🌿 🌳	Migration Migratory	Weight 9.0 g

Family PARULIDAE	Species *Dendroica palmarum*	Length 13 cm	Wingspan 22 cm

PALM WARBLER

This inhabitant of northern bogs pumps its tail up and down more than any other warbler. Two subspecies occur: the eastern form with strongly washed yellow underparts and the western form with whitish underparts with stronger streaking. Both nest on knolls of moss at the foot of small spruce or pine trees. A medium-distance migrant, the Palm Warbler winters in the South and frequents open habitats such as cultivated fields, marshes, pastures, parks, and gardens. Some winter in open pine woods or along their edges. The species is associated with palms only on some of its wintering areas and shows no inclination to seek them out. Fall adults and juveniles are drab, washed out, and lack the chestnut cap.

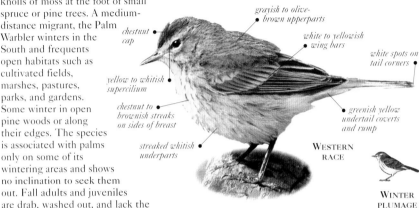

grayish to olive-brown upperparts

white to yellowish wing bars

white spots on tail corners

chestnut cap

yellow to whitish supercilium

chestnut to brownish streaks on sides of breast

streaked whitish underparts

greenish yellow undertail coverts and rump

WESTERN RACE

WINTER PLUMAGE

- **SONG** Monotone buzzlike fast trill, often stronger in middle, *swee-swee-swee-swee-swee-swee*. Call is forceful slurred *tsik*.
- **BEHAVIOR** Solitary or in pairs. Gregarious after breeding season, forming flocks and often mixing in foraging flocks with other species. Terrestrial; searches for food on ground or along beaches during migration, particularly among twigs and cones from conifers. Also foliage-gleans and hover-gleans in shrubs and trees; sometimes hawks prey in flight. Eats insects and caterpillars, also bayberries and raspberries.
- **BREEDING** Monogamous. Solitary.
- **NESTING** Incubation 12 days by both sexes. Young altricial; brooded by female; stay in nest 12 days, fed by both sexes. 2 broods per year.
- **POPULATION** Fairly common to common. Stable with some decline noted in wintering numbers in Florida.
- **CONSERVATION** Neotropical migrant. Rare cowbird host; buries eggs of parasite in floor of nest. Vulnerable to loss of habitat due to forest fragmentation.

Similar Birds

CAPE MAY WARBLER ♀
Pale lemon supercilium; white undertail coverts; does not wag short tail.

YELLOW-RUMPED WARBLER
Myrtle form, basic plumage • brown to gray upperparts with black streaking on back; white supercilium; bright yellow rump; streaked underparts; does not pump tail.

Flight Pattern

Weak flight; rapid wing beats alternate with brief periods of wings pulled to sides. Sallies from perch to take insects in air.

Nest Identification

Shape   Location ▬ ▲▶

Grass and shredded bark, lined with feathers • built on or near ground or up to 122 cm above ground in coniferous tree • built by female • 4–5 white to creamy eggs, with brown markings; ovate, short ovate, or elongated ovate, 1.8 x 1.3 cm.

Plumage Sexes similar	Habitat 🌾🐦 🏞️	Migration Migratory	Weight 11 g

DATE _____ TIME_____ LOCATION _____

Family PARULIDAE	Species *Dendroica castanea*	Length 14 cm	Wingspan 22 cm

BAY-BREASTED WARBLER

The male's warm chestnut and creamy markings help identify this native of northern coniferous forests. It is one of the largest warblers. Females are duller and have a gray rump. Juveniles and winter adults have olive upperparts with streaking

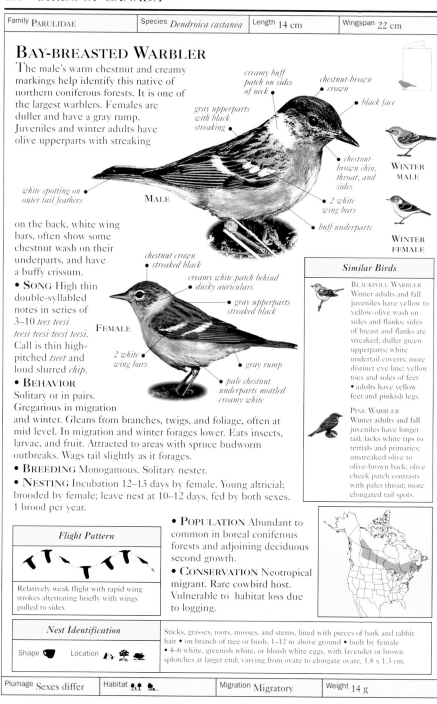

creamy buff patch on sides of neck

chestnut-brown crown

gray upperparts with black streaking

black face

white spotting on outer tail feathers

MALE

chestnut-brown chin, throat, and sides

WINTER MALE

2 white wing bars

buff underparts

WINTER FEMALE

on the back, white wing bars, often show some chestnut wash on their underparts, and have a buffy crissum.

chestnut crown streaked black

creamy white patch behind dusky auriculars

gray upperparts streaked black

FEMALE

2 white wing bars

gray rump

pale chestnut underparts mottled creamy white

- **SONG** High thin double-syllabled notes in series of 3–10 *tees teesi teesi teesi teesi teesi.* Call is thin high-pitched *tseet* and loud slurred *chip.*

- **BEHAVIOR** Solitary or in pairs. Gregarious in migration and winter. Gleans from branches, twigs, and foliage, often at mid level. In migration and winter forages lower. Eats insects, larvae, and fruit. Attracted to areas with spruce budworm outbreaks. Wags tail slightly as it forages.

- **BREEDING** Monogamous. Solitary nester.

- **NESTING** Incubation 12–13 days by female. Young altricial; brooded by female; leave nest at 10–12 days, fed by both sexes. 1 brood per year.

Similar Birds

BLACKPOLL WARBLER
Winter adults and fall juveniles have yellow to yellow-olive wash on sides and flanks; sides of breast and flanks are streaked; duller green upperparts; white undertail coverts; more distinct eye line; yellow toes and soles of feet
- adults have yellow feet and pinkish legs.

PINE WARBLER
Winter adults and fall juveniles have longer tail; lacks white tips to tertials and primaries; unstreaked olive to olive-brown back; olive cheek patch contrasts with paler throat; more elongated tail spots.

- **POPULATION** Abundant to common in boreal coniferous forests and adjoining deciduous second growth.

- **CONSERVATION** Neotropical migrant. Rare cowbird host. Vulnerable to habitat loss due to logging.

Flight Pattern

Relatively weak flight with rapid wing strokes alternating briefly with wings pulled to sides.

Nest Identification

Shape   Location

Sticks, grasses, roots, mosses, and stems, lined with pieces of bark and rabbit hair • on branch of tree or bush, 1–12 m above ground • built by female • 4–6 white, greenish white, or bluish white eggs, with lavender or brown splotches at larger end; varying from ovate to elongate ovate, 1.8 x 1.3 cm.

Plumage Sexes differ	Habitat	Migration Migratory	Weight 14 g

DATE _____ TIME_____ LOCATION _____

Family PARULIDAE	Species *Dendroica striata*	Length 13 cm	Wingspan 22 cm

BLACKPOLL WARBLER

This summer resident of Canadian boreal forests migrates more than 4,000 km in the fall, flying nonstop over water to winter in northern South America. Juveniles and fall adults have streaked greenish upperparts; a pale greenish yellow wash on the face, throat, and breast; a white belly and crissum; legs that are pale pinkish on the front and back but dark on the sides; and yellow soles.

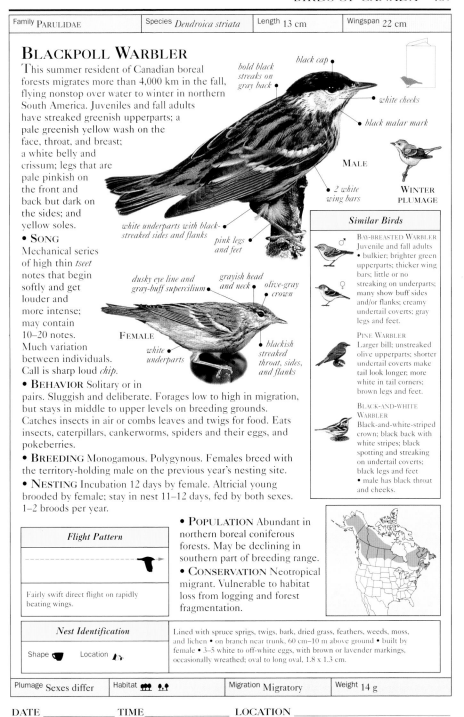

black cap

bold black streaks on gray back

white cheeks

black malar mark

MALE

2 white wing bars

WINTER PLUMAGE

white underparts with black-streaked sides and flanks

pink legs and feet

dusky eye line and gray-buff supercilium

grayish head and neck

olive-gray crown

FEMALE

white underparts

blackish streaked throat, sides, and flanks

• **SONG** Mechanical series of high thin *tseet* notes that begin softly and get louder and more intense; may contain 10–20 notes. Much variation between individuals. Call is sharp loud *chip*.

• **BEHAVIOR** Solitary or in pairs. Sluggish and deliberate. Forages low to high in migration, but stays in middle to upper levels on breeding grounds. Catches insects in air or combs leaves and twigs for food. Eats insects, caterpillars, cankerworms, spiders and their eggs, and pokeberries.

• **BREEDING** Monogamous. Polygynous. Females breed with the territory-holding male on the previous year's nesting site.

• **NESTING** Incubation 12 days by female. Altricial young brooded by female; stay in nest 11–12 days, fed by both sexes. 1–2 broods per year.

Similar Birds

♂ BAY-BREASTED WARBLER Juvenile and fall adults • bulkier; brighter green upperparts; thicker wing bars; little or no streaking on underparts; many show buff sides and/or flanks; creamy undertail coverts; gray legs and feet.

PINE WARBLER Larger bill; unstreaked olive upperparts; shorter undertail coverts make tail look longer; more white in tail corners; brown legs and feet.

BLACK-AND-WHITE WARBLER Black-and-white-striped crown; black back with white stripes; black spotting and streaking on undertail coverts; black legs and feet • male has black throat and cheeks.

• **POPULATION** Abundant in northern boreal coniferous forests. May be declining in southern part of breeding range.

• **CONSERVATION** Neotropical migrant. Vulnerable to habitat loss from logging and forest fragmentation.

Flight Pattern
Fairly swift direct flight on rapidly beating wings.

Nest Identification	
Shape 🪶 Location 🪹	Lined with spruce sprigs, twigs, bark, dried grass, feathers, weeds, moss, and lichen • on branch near trunk, 60 cm–10 m above ground • built by female • 3–5 white to off-white eggs, with brown or lavender markings, occasionally wreathed; oval to long oval, 1.8 x 1.3 cm.

Plumage Sexes differ	Habitat 🌱 🌿	Migration Migratory	Weight 14 g

DATE _____ TIME_____ LOCATION _____

Family PARULIDAE	Species *Dendroica cerulea*	Length 11 cm	Wingspan 18 cm

CERULEAN WARBLER

Although its buzzy song can be heard from dawn until dusk, this bird, one of the smallest warblers, is difficult to spot, as it stays hidden in dense foliage in the crowns of tall deciduous trees. This habit of remaining high in mature trees has made studies of its natural history difficult, and its breeding biology and feeding habits are poorly known. Juveniles are similar to females.

- **SONG** A series of accelerating buzzy notes on the same or slightly ascending pitch, ending in a drawn-out buzz, *zray, zray, zray, zray, zeeeeeee*, reminiscent of the slower second song of the Northern Parula. Call is a slurred *chip*.
- **BEHAVIOR** Solitary or in pairs. Vigorous and persistent singer on breeding grounds. Eats mainly insects, larvae, and spiders. Very active and acrobatic forager but sometimes moves sluggishly, gleaning food off leaves and branches while staying hidden in trees. Also catches insects in flight.
- **BREEDING** Monogamous. Solitary nester.
- **NESTING** Incubation about 12–13 days by female. Altricial young brooded by female; stay in nest estimated 8–10 days, fed by both sexes. 1–2 broods per year.
- **POPULATION** Fairly common to uncommon in mature deciduous forest. Declining dramatically, particularly in the heart of range, but range is expanding north and northeast, on the

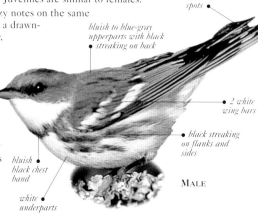

white tail spots

bluish to blue-gray upperparts with black streaking on back

2 white wing bars

black streaking on flanks and sides

bluish black chest band

white underparts

MALE

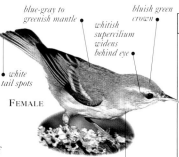

blue-gray to greenish mantle

bluish green crown

whitish supercilium widens behind eye

white tail spots

FEMALE

pale yellowish buff breast and throat

Similar Birds

The small and short-tailed male is the only warbler with a blue back, black necklace, and white throat.

♀ BLACKBURNIAN WARBLER
Female and juvenile
- pale orange supercilium broadens behind eye; white or buff underparts; longer tail; triangular cheek patch; pale lines and dark streaking on back.

Atlantic coastal plain, and the Piedmont.
- **CONSERVATION** Neotropical migrant. Moderate host to cowbird parasitism. Vulnerable to habitat loss and forest fragmentation.

Flight Pattern

Relatively weak flight with quick wing strokes alternating with brief periods of wings pull to sides; repeated.

Nest Identification

Shape ⌒ Location 🌲

Stems, grasses, mosses, bark pieces, and spider's silk, with lining of mammal hair and mosses • far out on branch of tree, usually 9–18 m above ground • built by female • 3–5 grayish or creamy white eggs, with fine dots or splotches of brown, usually loosely wreathed; oval to short oval, 1.8 x 1.3 cm.

Plumage Sexes differ	Habitat 🌳 🌿 🪴	Migration Migratory	Weight 9.0 g

DATE _____ TIME _____ LOCATION _____

Family PARULIDAE	Species *Mniotilta varia*	Length 13 cm	Wingspan 22–23 cm

BLACK-AND-WHITE WARBLER

This mostly black-and-white striped bird feeds nuthatch-style, moving up and down the trunks of trees and crawling over and under branches, a foraging behavior unlike any other warbler. It is one of the earliest warblers to return to the breeding grounds in early spring, because its bark-gleaning foraging habit does not require it to linger on wintering grounds until the leaves begin to develop. Females are similar to males but have cream-colored flanks and creamy whitish rather than black cheeks. Juveniles are similar to females.

bold black-and-white stripes on head and most of body

distinctive white stripe over and under each eye

slightly curved slim bill

black cheeks and throat

2 white wing bars

white belly

JUVENILE

• **SONG** Repetitive thin high-pitched series of 6–10 *wee-sea*, *wee-sea* notes like the sound of a turning squeaky wheel. Sometimes a trill is added as an ending to the cadence. Has call of an abrasive *chip* or *tink*, and a *seap*.

• **BEHAVIOR** Solitary or in pairs. Probes into bark crevices with long bill; does not prop body on tree with tail as do woodpeckers and creepers. Eats adult insects, caterpillars, and spiders. Occasionally hawks and hover-gleans. If flushed from ground nest, female performs distraction display, dragging wings with tail spread.

• **BREEDING** Monogamous. Solitary.

• **NESTING** Incubation 10–12 days by female. Young altricial; brooded by female; remain in nest 8–12 days but still not able to fly well; fed by both sexes. 1–2 broods per year.

• **POPULATION** Widespread in mature and second-growth deciduous or mixed deciduous-conifer woodlands with large trees. Declining in the Midwest and Great Lakes region because of habitat loss and cowbird parasitism. Vagrant in the West during migration as far north as Alaska.

• **CONSERVATION** Neotropical migrant. Common host to cowbird eggs. Vulnerable to forest fragmentation and habitat loss due to logging operations in mature forests.

Similar Birds

BLACK-THROATED GRAY WARBLER ♂ Small yellow spot between eye and bill; blackish crown; gray back with black streaking; white undertail coverts; lacks central crown stripe.

BLACKPOLL WARBLER ♂ Black crown; white cheeks; gray back with black streaking; white throat; white undertail coverts.

Flight Pattern

Relatively weak flight with rapid wing strokes alternating with brief periods of wings pulled to sides; repeated.

Nest Identification

Shape _____ Location _____

Grasses, bark pieces, dead leaves, rootlets, and pine needles, lined with moss and mammal hair • on ground, near base of tree or bush, or in small hollow of rock, stump, or log • built by female • 4–6 creamy white or white eggs, flecked with brown; short subelliptical to subelliptical, 1.7 x 1.3 cm.

Plumage Sexes similar	Habitat	Migration Migratory	Weight 11 g

DATE _____ TIME _____ LOCATION _____

Family PARULIDAE	Species *Setophaga ruticilla*	Length 13 cm	Wingspan 20 cm

AMERICAN REDSTART

Birders enjoy watching this vivacious bird as it flits to catch insects or sits on a perch, partially spreading and drooping its wings and spreading its tail. Other warblers pump or flick their tails, but this bird fans its tail and holds it there for a second. The male's tail can be either orange and black or yellow and dusky olive-gray. This woodland inhabitant is one of the most common warblers nesting in North America. Juvenile males look like females but with an orange wash on the sides.

glossy black overall

orange patches on wings, sides, and tail

white belly and undertail coverts

MALE

FEMALE

thin white supercilium and eye ring

grayish olive upperparts

whitish underparts from chin to tip of undertail coverts

yellow patches on sides, wings, and tail

- **SONG** Variable. Sings often and through the heat of midday. Basic song is 4–8 high-pitched, somewhat coarse notes, with explosive accented lower-ending *zeet-zeet-zeet-zeet-zeeeah*. Other songs have unaccented ending. Some are reminiscent of the Yellow, Chestnut-sided, and Black-and-white Warblers. Territorial males have repertoire of several songs. Call is slurred thin *chip*.
- **BEHAVIOR** Solitary or in pairs. Tame. Conspicuous. Sings often. Responds to squeaking or pishing by birders. Sallies into air to catch insects, perching between hawking events like a small flycatcher. Gleans food from branches and foliage; hover-gleans. Eats insects, caterpillars, spiders, berries, fruit, and seeds.
- **BREEDING** Monogamous. Solitary nester.
- **NESTING** Incubation 11–12 days by female. Altricial young brooded by female; stay in nest 9 days, fed by both sexes. 1–2 broods per year.
- **POPULATION** Common to fairly common in wet deciduous and mixed conifer-deciduous woodlands with understory, woodland edges, riparian woodlands, and second growth. Widespread but declining in the Midwest, Great Lakes, the Northeast, and the Maritime Provinces. Rare to uncommon migrant in the West to California.

FIRST SPRING MALE

Similar Birds
None in range.

- **CONSERVATION** Neotropical migrant. Common cowbird host. Vulnerable to habitat loss caused by deforestation or maturation of second-growth forests.

Flight Pattern
Somewhat weak flight on rapidly beating wings, alternating with brief periods of wings pulled to sides. Flies into air from perch to take flying insects, and returns.

Nest Identification	Grasses, pieces of bark, rootlets, and plant down, decorated with lichens, birch bark, and spider's silk, and lined with feathers • in fork of tree or bush, usually 3–6 m above ground (but ranges from 4–21 m) • built by female • 2–5 off-white, greenish white, or white eggs, flecked and dotted with browns or grays; ovate, occasionally short ovate, 1.6 x 1.2 cm.
Shape 🍵 Location 🌳🌳	

Plumage Sexes differ	Habitat 🌿 〰 🐾	Migration Migratory	Weight 9.0 g

DATE _____ TIME_____ LOCATION _____

Family PARULIDAE	Species *Protonotaria citrea*	Length 13 cm	Wingspan 22 cm

PROTHONOTARY WARBLER

The male builds several nests, then sings continuously until the female arrives to choose a nest and complete it. This is the only eastern warbler that nests in tree hollows, a trait it shares with just one other North American warbler, the western Lucy's Warbler. It was once called the "Golden Swamp Warbler," describing the bird and its dark backwater haunts.

- **SONG** A bold ringing repetitive *zweet*, slightly up-slurred as *sweet, sweet, sweet, sweet*. Call is loud *chip-chip*.
- **BEHAVIOR** Solitary or in pairs. Gregarious in winter, roosting communally. Tame, noisy, and conspicuous. Deliberate in its feeding, gleaning food and probing crevices with its bill. Picks food off floating logs and branches and out of water. Also forages in trees while grasping trunk like a nuthatch. Eats insects, spiders, larvae, and snails. Takes small crustaceans and snails. Inquisitive; will come to squeaking and pishing by birders.
- **BREEDING** Monogamous. Solitary nester.
- **NESTING** Incubation 12–14 days by female. Altricial young brooded by female, fed by both sexes; first flight at 11 days. 2 broods per year in the South.
- **POPULATION** Fairly common in swampy lowland forest, river-bottom woodlands subject to flooding, and riparian corridors along streams. Accidental to rare in the West.
- **BIRDHOUSES** Nest boxes.

golden yellow head, neck, and underparts

large dark eyes

olive-green back

long black bill

blue-gray wings

chunky body

short blue-gray tail with large white patches

white undertail coverts

MALE

greenish yellow crown and nape

greenish back

bright yellow throat, face, and breast

gray wings, rump, uppertail coverts, and tail

FEMALE

white belly and undertail coverts

white spots on inner web of tail feathers

Similar Birds

YELLOW WARBLER Bright yellow underparts; orange-yellow forehead and front of crown; reddish streaking on underparts; yellow-olive wings; yellow spots in tail • appears completely yellow from a distance.

BLUE-WINGED WARBLER Blue-gray wings with 2 white wing bars; black eye line; shorter bill; yellow head and underparts; olive back; no white spots in tail.

- **CONSERVATION** Neotropical migrant. Common cowbird host. Destruction of mangrove swamps and wetland drainage reduce populations. Competition from other cavity nesters that destroy eggs or usurp cavities. Listed as endangered in Canada.

Flight Pattern
Rapid direct flight, often low over water, on quickly beating wings.

Nest Identification	
Shape	Grasses, moss, leaves, and sticks, lined with feathers and rootlets • in natural hollow or woodpecker cavity in snag, tree, post, or nest box, near water and usually 1.5–3 m above ground (but range from 60 cm–10 m) • male builds dummy nests; female selects and completes one • 4–6 pinkish or cream eggs, with brown and gray dots; short elliptical to elliptical, 2.0 x 1.4 cm.
Location	

Plumage Sexes differ	Habitat	Migration Migratory	Weight 14 g

DATE _____ TIME_____ LOCATION _____

Family PARULIDAE	Species *Helmitheros vermivorus*	Length 13 cm	Wingspan 22 cm

WORM-EATING WARBLER

Similar to a sparrow in color, size, and habits, the Worm-eating Warbler's steady diet of moth caterpillars and worms has earned this bird its name. An inhabitant of deciduous forests, it seldom is observed combing the forest floor for food; rather, it usually forages in the understory vegetation, where it often probes for food in clusters of dead leaves. While primarily a solitary bird, the Worm-eating Warbler sometimes is known to associate loosely with foraging flocks of mixed bird species.

buff-colored head with 2 pairs of bold dark stripes

long spikelike bill

brownish olive upperparts

buff-colored underparts

• **SONG** A buzzy insectlike fricative trill, often beginning softly and fading away at the end with a series of *chip* notes. Song is similar to the Chipping Sparrow's but more rapid and given in a thick shaded wooded habitat. Call is a *zit-zit*.

• **BEHAVIOR** Solitary or in pairs. More often heard than seen in the breeding season. Most often observed foraging alone for insects, spiders, and some worms. Gleans food by moving along branches like a Black-and-white Warbler, but specializes in probing clusters of dead leaves for food. Usually forages in low to middle levels, but sometimes in treetops; rarely in leaf litter on ground. Frequents deciduous woodlots on slopes, along ravines, or mountain sides. When flushed from nest, female drags wings and spreads tail, running on ground in distraction display. Mixed flocks postbreeding season.

• **BREEDING** Monogamous. Solitary.

• **NESTING** Incubation 13 days by female. Young altricial; brooded by female; stay in nest 10 days, fed by both sexes. 1–2 broods per year.

• **POPULATION** Fairly common to common in ravines, hillsides, and mountainsides in thick deciduous woodlands. Stable in most of its range but regional declines noted. Casual to rare vagrant in migration in the West to California.

• **CONSERVATION** Neotropical migrant. Frequent host to cowbird parasitism. Vulnerable to habitat loss due to forest fragmentation.

Similar Birds

SWAINSON'S WARBLER
Larger; longer bill; browner upperparts; grayish buff underparts; brown cap without stripes; pale supercilium; thin dark eye line.

Flight Pattern
Fairly fast direct flight on rapidly beating wings.

Nest Identification	
Shape ◥ Location ▬	Lined with dead leaves, animal hair, fungus, moss, and tree stems • often built on sloping ground near base of deciduous shrubs or saplings or on ridges of leaves on forest floor • built by female • 4–6 white eggs, with brown spots or blotches, often wreathed; short ovate, 1.8 x 1.4 cm.

Plumage Sexes similar	Habitat ♣♣♣	Migration Migratory	Weight 20 g

DATE _____ TIME_____ LOCATION _____

Family PARULIDAE	Species *Seiurus aurocapillus*	Length 15 cm	Wingspan 23 cm

OVENBIRD

In the leaf litter under tall deciduous trees, the female bird builds a small oven-shaped nest with a side entrance. Unlike many warblers, it does not often forage in live vegetation; instead it walks on the ground, foraging among the leaf litter and twigs, its wings partially drooped and its tail cocked upward and sometimes quickly raised and slowly lowered. It is sometimes called the Wood Wagtail because it moves its tail up and down. Most singing is done from an elevated perch, and the song of one territorial male initiates a response song from each neighbor, which in turn stimulates another to do so, until a wave of Ovenbird songs sweeps across the woodlot.

brownish orange stripe, edged in black, over head from bill to nape

white eye ring

olive-brown upperparts

• **SONG** More often heard than seen. Sings a loud and repetitive *TEAcher-TEAcher-TEAcher*, rising and becoming more emphatic. There is regional variation, with some birds singing *teach-teach-teach-teACH!* From a distance the song sounds like two stones being tapped together harder and harder. Call note is a loud sharp *tsick*.

pale pink legs and feet

white underparts with dark brown splotching

• **BEHAVIOR** Solitary or in pairs. Tame. Eats adult insects, caterpillars, snails, slugs, earthworms, small amphibians, seeds, berries, and fruit. When flushed, usually flies up to perch. Walks on limbs in interior of trees.

• **BREEDING** Monogamous. Solitary nester.

• **NESTING** Incubation 11–14 days by female. Young altricial; brooded by female; remain in nest 8–11 days, fed by both sexes. 1–2 broods per year (occasionally 3 in regions with spruce budworm outbreaks).

• **POPULATION** Common to fairly common in mature deciduous forests; rarely in pine forests. Rare in the west of the Rockies in migration; rare to casual on southern Atlantic Coast and Gulf Coast in winter.

Similar Birds

LOUISIANA WATERTHRUSH NORTHERN WATERTHRUSH White to yellowish supercilium; lack eye ring and black border to crown; brownish upperparts; usually near water; habitual tail bobbing.

• **CONSERVATION** Neotropical migrant. Host to cowbird parasitism. Significant declines documented in the northeast beginning in the 1970s but now increasing in much of its range.

Flight Pattern
Relatively swift, short direct flight on rapidly beating wings.

Nest Identification	
Shape ⬨ Location ▬	Leaves, grasses, stems, rootlets, mosses, and hair • in slight hollow on ground of forest, concealed by leaves on top of nest, creating a dome • built by female • 3–6 white eggs, with gray or brown flecks; subelliptical to short subelliptical, 2.0 x 1.5 cm.

Plumage Sexes similar	Habitat 🌿 🌱	Migration Migratory	Weight 20 g

DATE _____ TIME_____ LOCATION _____

Family PARULIDAE	Species *Seiurus noveboracensis*	Length 15 cm	Wingspan 22 cm

NORTHERN WATERTHRUSH

Northern lakeshores, slow-running streams, and bogs are
the most common habitats of the Northern Waterthrush.
Walking, rather than hopping, along the ground,
the Northern Waterthrush often is observed
repeatedly bobbing the rear part of its body
and its tail while searching for food. An early
migrant, the Northern Waterthrush
generally begins traveling
southward by mid-July.

*pale yellow to
whitish supercilium*

*olive-brown to
gray-brown
upperparts*

*heavily
streaked throat,
upper breast,
and sides*

*pale yellow to
whitish underparts*

• **SONG** Begins
with loud
insistent notes,
tapering to
rapidly whistled
lower tones, *twit twit twit twit
sweet sweet sweet chew chew chew*, with the
individual notes grouped in series of 3's and
4's. Call is a very loud ringing metallic *chink*.

• **BEHAVIOR** Solitary or in pairs. Terrestrial
but often sings from elevated perches and walks,
bobbing, on branches. Forages on ground by
picking up leaves with its bill and tossing them
aside or turning them over. Eats aquatic and terrestrial adult
insects, caterpillars, and case worms; also sometimes slugs,
mollusks, crustaceans, and small fish. Frequents areas with
dense shrub and slowly moving or still water.

• **BREEDING** Monogamous. Solitary.

• **NESTING** Breeding biology poorly known. Estimated
incubation 13 days by female. Young altricial; brooded by
female; stay in nest estimated 10 days, fed by both sexes.
1 brood per year.

• **POPULATION** Generally common in wooded swamps, forests
with standing water, bogs, and thickets with slowly running or
standing water. Rare to uncommon in migration in the
Southwest to California. Rare to casual in winter in the US,
except for southern Florida where it is uncommon.

• **CONSERVATION** Neotropical migrant. Uncommon host to
cowbird parasitism. Some
declines in southern portions of
breeding range and increases in
New England portions.
Vulnerable to habitat loss due to
deforestation and drainage.

Similar Birds

LOUISIANA
WATERTHRUSH
Longer stouter bill;
white supercilium
broadens behind eye;
fewer and less-
contrasting streaks on
underparts; unmarked
white throat; contrasting
pinkish buff wash on
flanks; bright pink legs
and feet; more
deliberate and
exaggerated tail bobbing
with a circular body
motion; song differs.

Flight Pattern

Fairly swift direct flight for short distances
on rapidly beating wings.

Nest Identification

Shape ▬ Location ▬

Lined with grass, animal hair, moss, twigs, pine needles, bark strips, and roots
• often built in moss-covered stumps near water • 0–60 cm above ground • built
by female • 3–6 cream or buff-white eggs, with brown or gray spots or speckles;
ovate to short ovate, 2.0 x 1.4 cm.

Plumage Sexes similar	Habitat	Migration Migratory	Weight 23 g

DATE _____ TIME_____ LOCATION _____

Family PARULIDAE	Species *Seiurus motacilla*	Length 15 cm	Wingspan 23 cm

LOUISIANA WATERTHRUSH

The less common of the two waterthrush species frequents fast-running streams and floodplain river swamps, where it hides its nests on streamside banks, under tree roots, or in rock crevices. This bird has a nesting range from Minnesota to New England and as far south as Texas and Georgia. In spring it is one of the earliest warblers to arrive on the nesting grounds and one of the first to depart in late summer and early fall.

darker crown

long stout bill

broad gray-buff stripe broadens behind eye and becomes white

olive-gray to olive-brown upperparts

unstreaked white throat and chin

olive-striped breast, sides, and flanks

white or buff-white underparts

pinkish buff flanks contrast with white underparts

bright pink legs and feet

- **SONG** Loud and clear, beginning with 3–4 high-pitched downslurred notes, followed by a brief rapid medley of jumbled notes that cascade up and down prior to fading away, *SWEER SWEER SWEER chee chi-wit-it chit swee-yuu*. The combination of slurred opening notes and ending twittering is diagnostic. Call is a loud bright *chik*.

- **BEHAVIOR** Solitary or in pairs. Sings on ground or from elevated perch in trees. Bobs rear and tail while walking. Terrestrial, primarily foraging on ground, along stream banks, on rocks and logs in water, and in the stream shallows. Bobs up and down while foraging, much like a sandpiper, with a slow circular exaggerated motion. Dines on adult aquatic and terrestrial insects, caterpillars, mollusks, snails, and small fish. Territories are linear along stream.

- **BREEDING** Monogamous. Solitary.

- **NESTING** Incubation 12–14 days by female. Young altricial; brooded by female; remain in nest 9–10 days, fed by both sexes. 1 brood per year.

- **POPULATION** Uncommon to fairly common in eastern United States. Rare in southeastern Canada. Restricted habitat specialist along fast-flowing streams within woodlands, often in mountains or hilly terrain, or in floodplain forests and swamps in lower country. Casual in the West during migration.

- **CONSERVATION** Neotropical migrant. Frequent host to cowbird parasitism. Deforestation and stream siltation negatively impact both breeding and wintering areas.

Similar Birds

NORTHERN WATERTHRUSH Narrow buff to white eye stripes of uniform color and width; smaller bill; streaked and spotted throat; pale yellow to white underparts with darker, more uniform streaking; olive-brown to gray-brown upperparts; dull pink legs and feet; different voice.

Flight Pattern	
Swift short direct flights on rapidly beating wings.	

Nest Identification	
Shape 🦴 Location ▬ 🪨	Lined with roots, fern stems, grass, animal fur, dead leaves, moss, and twigs • 0–60 cm above ground, on bank, rock crevice, or roots of tree, no further than 1–2 m from water • built by both sexes, but female does more • 4–6 white or cream-colored eggs, with brown and gray specks or blotches; oval to short oval, 2.0 x 1.5 cm.

Plumage Sexes similar	Habitat 🌳 🪨 🌿 ▲ 〰	Migration Migratory	Weight 20 g

DATE _____ TIME_____ LOCATION _____

Family PARULIDAE	Species *Oporornis agilis*	Length 14 cm	Wingspan 22 cm

CONNECTICUT WARBLER

Although this large chunky short-tailed shy bird does not nest in Connecticut, it was first seen in that state and is a regular autumn visitor. Its secretive habits make this a poorly known species. Its wintering grounds in South America are not clearly defined, and as one of the year's latest migrants, taking vastly different spring and fall routes, it often is not seen. Males and females have long yellowish undertail coverts.

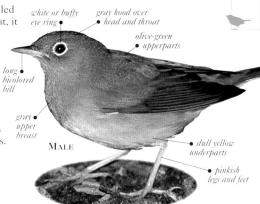

white or buffy eye ring

gray hood over head and throat

olive-green upperparts

long bicolored bill

gray upper breast

MALE

dull yellow underparts

pinkish legs and feet

• **SONG** Bold rocking jerky *whipity-whipity-whipity* or *beacher, beacher, beacher*. Call is *plink* or *chimp*.

• **BEHAVIOR** Solitary or in pairs. Secretive. Terrestrial; also forages low in vegetation. Singing males may move higher in trees. Female lands 9–18 meters from nest and walks to conceal location. Walks with slight bobbing of tail instead of hopping. Walks on logs and branches. Gleans insects and spiders; also snails, berries, and seeds. When flushed, flies up to perch and may sit still for several minutes, thrushlike.

brownish olive hood

olive-green upperparts

FEMALE

white or buffy eye ring

grayish chest and face

dull pale yellow underparts

JUVENILE

Similar Birds

MOURNING WARBLER
Smaller; thinner; thin broken grayish white eye ring; shorter undertail coverts; richer yellow underparts; hops rather than walks
• juvenile has paler throat.

NASHVILLE WARBLER
Smaller; thinner; white eye ring with pale lores; short undertail coverts; yellow throat; dark legs; short bill.

• **BREEDING** Monogamous. Solitary nester.

• **NESTING** Breeding biology poorly known. Estimated incubation 11–12 days by female. Young altricial; brooded by female; stay in nest estimated 8–9 days, fed by both sexes. 1 brood per year.

• **POPULATION** Uncommon in most woodlands. Fall migrants uncommon in East.

• **CONSERVATION** Neotropical migrant. Infrequent host to cowbirds. Species may be declining; reasons unknown.

Flight Pattern
Rather swift direct flight for short distances on rapidly beating wings.

Nest Identification	
Shape ☕ Location ▬	Bark pieces and grass, with lining of fine plant materials and mammal hair • on small hillock of moss or sheltered by reeds and grasses • may be built by both sexes • 3–5 creamy white eggs, splotched and flecked with lavender, browns, and black; short ovate, 1.9 x 1.4 cm.

Plumage Sexes differ	Habitat	Migration Migratory	Weight 14 g

DATE _____ TIME_____ LOCATION _____

Family PARULIDAE	Species *Oporornis philadelphia*	Length 13 cm	Wingspan 21 cm

MOURNING WARBLER

The eastern counterpart to MacGillivray's Warbler was named for the way its black breast and gray hood resemble a person in mourning. Usually skulking in the undergrowth of damp woodlands, the male will fly up from the bushes to sing and is more often heard than seen. The female is similar to the male but has a paler dusky hood, light grayish throat, and a more distinct eye ring. Juveniles have pale yellowish throats and broken thin white eye rings. Traveling over eastern Mexico, this bird circumnavigates the western Gulf of Mexico, making it one of the latest spring migrants of all North American warblers.

• **SONG** Typically a 2-part song, with the second part lower in pitch, *cherrie, cherrie, chorrie, chorrie*. Individual and regional variations exist. Call is a sharp raspy *chit*, sometimes given in a series.

• **BEHAVIOR** Solitary or in pairs. Secretive. Sings often in migration and on breeding grounds. Will respond to pishing by birders. Terrestrial, forages low in vegetation hidden in undergrowth. Hops and flicks wings and tail. Gleans insects and spiders.

• **BREEDING** Monogamous. Solitary nester.

• **NESTING** Incubation 12 days by female. Altricial young brooded by female; remain in nest 7–9 days, fed by both sexes. 1 brood per year.

• **POPULATION** Fairly common in dense shrubbery in open deciduous woodlands, dense second growth, bog, and marsh edges.

• **CONSERVATION** Neotropical migrant. Infrequent host to cowbirds.

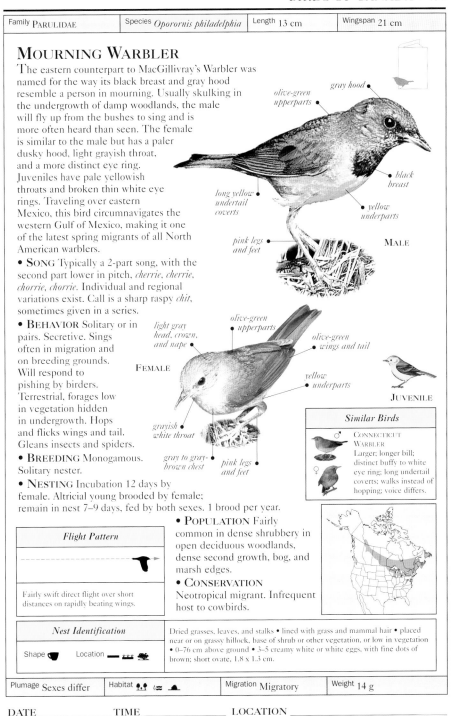

olive-green upperparts
gray hood
black breast
yellow underparts
long yellow undertail coverts
pink legs and feet
MALE

olive-green upperparts
olive-green wings and tail
light gray head, crown, and nape
FEMALE
yellow underparts
grayish white throat
gray to gray-brown chest
pink legs and feet

JUVENILE

Similar Birds

♂ CONNECTICUT WARBLER
♀ Larger; longer bill; distinct buffy to white eye ring; long undertail coverts; walks instead of hopping; voice differs.

Flight Pattern
Fairly swift direct flight over short distances on rapidly beating wings.

Nest Identification	
Shape ⬤ Location ▬ ••• 🌳	Dried grasses, leaves, and stalks • lined with grass and mammal hair • placed near or on grassy hillock, base of shrub or other vegetation, or low in vegetation • 0–76 cm above ground • 3–5 creamy white or white eggs, with fine dots of brown; short ovate, 1.8 x 1.3 cm.

Plumage Sexes differ	Habitat 🐦 〰 ▲	Migration Migratory	Weight 14 g

DATE _____ TIME_____ LOCATION _____

| Family PARULIDAE | Species *Oporornis tolmiei* | Length 13 cm | Wingspan 21 cm |

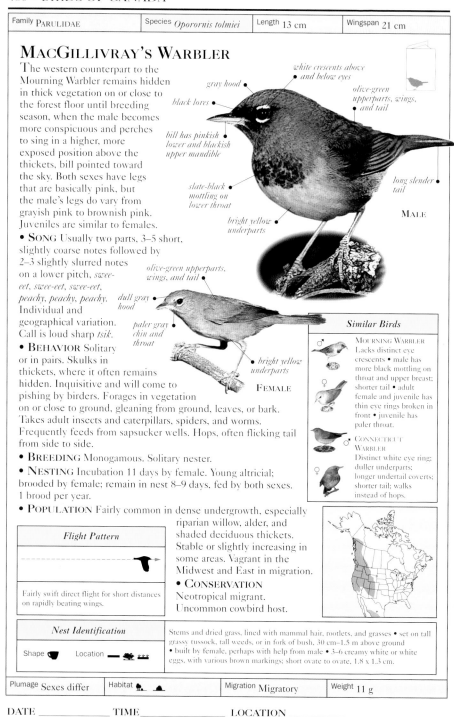

MACGILLIVRAY'S WARBLER

The western counterpart to the Mourning Warbler remains hidden in thick vegetation on or close to the forest floor until breeding season, when the male becomes more conspicuous and perches to sing in a higher, more exposed position above the thickets, bill pointed toward the sky. Both sexes have legs that are basically pink, but the male's legs do vary from grayish pink to brownish pink. Juveniles are similar to females.

- **SONG** Usually two parts, 3–5 short, slightly coarse notes followed by 2–3 slightly slurred notes on a lower pitch, *swee-eet, swee-eet, swee-eet, peachy, peachy, peachy*. Individual and geographical variation. Call is loud sharp *tsik*.

- **BEHAVIOR** Solitary or in pairs. Skulks in thickets, where it often remains hidden. Inquisitive and will come to pishing by birders. Forages in vegetation on or close to ground, gleaning from ground, leaves, or bark. Takes adult insects and caterpillars, spiders, and worms. Frequently feeds from sapsucker wells. Hops, often flicking tail from side to side.

- **BREEDING** Monogamous. Solitary nester.

- **NESTING** Incubation 11 days by female. Young altricial; brooded by female; remain in nest 8–9 days, fed by both sexes. 1 brood per year.

- **POPULATION** Fairly common in dense undergrowth, especially riparian willow, alder, and shaded deciduous thickets. Stable or slightly increasing in some areas. Vagrant in the Midwest and East in migration.

- **CONSERVATION** Neotropical migrant. Uncommon cowbird host.

white crescents above and below eyes
gray hood
black lores
olive-green upperparts, wings, and tail
bill has pinkish lower and blackish upper mandible
slate-black mottling on lower throat
long slender tail
bright yellow underparts
MALE

olive-green upperparts, wings, and tail
dull gray hood
paler gray chin and throat
bright yellow underparts
FEMALE

Similar Birds

MOURNING WARBLER
Lacks distinct eye crescents • male has more black mottling on throat and upper breast; shorter tail • adult female and juvenile has thin eye rings broken in front • juvenile has paler throat.

CONNECTICUT WARBLER
Distinct white eye ring; duller underparts; longer undertail coverts; shorter tail; walks instead of hops.

Flight Pattern

Fairly swift direct flight for short distances on rapidly beating wings.

Nest Identification

Shape ◗   Location ━ 🌳 🌿

Stems and dried grass, lined with mammal hair, rootlets, and grasses • set on tall grassy tussock, tall weeds, or in fork of bush, 30 cm–1.5 m above ground • built by female, perhaps with help from male • 3–6 creamy white or white eggs, with various brown markings; short ovate to ovate, 1.8 x 1.3 cm.

| Plumage Sexes differ | Habitat 🌿 🔺 | Migration Migratory | Weight 11 g |

DATE _____ TIME _____ LOCATION _____

Family PARULIDAE	Species *Geothlypis trichas*	Length 13 cm	Wingspan 20 cm

COMMON YELLOWTHROAT

One of the most numerous and widespread warblers usually stays close to the ground, concealed in vegetation. The amount of yellow on the underparts, the shade of olive on the upperparts, and the color of the pale border between the mask and crown all vary with geography.

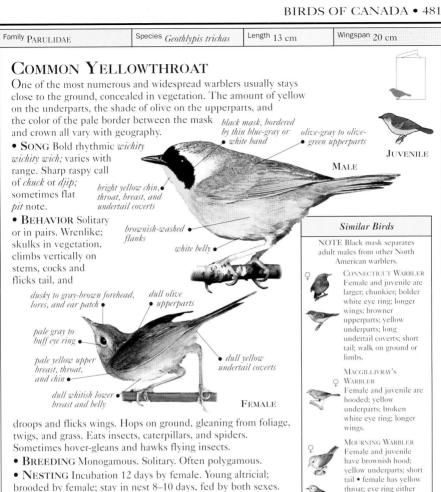

black mask, bordered by thin blue-gray or white band

olive-gray to olive-green upperparts

JUVENILE

MALE

bright yellow chin, throat, breast, and undertail coverts

brownish-washed flanks

white belly

dusky to gray-brown forehead, lores, and ear patch

dull olive upperparts

pale gray to buff eye ring

pale yellow upper breast, throat, and chin

dull yellow undertail coverts

dull whitish lower breast and belly

FEMALE

- **SONG** Bold rhythmic *wichity wichity wich;* varies with range. Sharp raspy call of *chuck* or *djip;* sometimes flat *pit* note.
- **BEHAVIOR** Solitary or in pairs. Wrenlike; skulks in vegetation, climbs vertically on stems, cocks and flicks tail, and droops and flicks wings. Hops on ground, gleaning from foliage, twigs, and grass. Eats insects, caterpillars, and spiders. Sometimes hover-gleans and hawks flying insects.
- **BREEDING** Monogamous. Solitary. Often polygamous.
- **NESTING** Incubation 12 days by female. Young altricial; brooded by female; stay in nest 8–10 days, fed by both sexes. 2 broods with single female per year; more if polygamous.
- **POPULATION** Common to abundant in marshes, brushy fields, hedgerows, woodland edges, and second growth brush. Some decline in the South, Texas, and San Francisco Bay.
- **CONSERVATION** Neotropical migrant. Frequent cowbird host. Vulnerable to habitat loss caused by wetland drainage and stream channelization.

Similar Birds

NOTE Black mask separates adult males from other North American warblers.

CONNECTICUT WARBLER ♀ Female and juvenile are larger; chunkier; bolder white eye ring; longer wings; browner upperparts; yellow underparts; long undertail coverts; short tail; walk on ground or limbs.

MACGILLIVRAY'S WARBLER ♀ Female and juvenile are hooded; yellow underparts; broken white eye ring; longer wings.

MOURNING WARBLER ♀ Female and juvenile have brownish hood; yellow underparts; short tail • female has yellow throat; eye ring either complete or broken.

Flight Pattern

Slow weak jerky flight with rapid wing beats, alternating with brief periods of wings pulled to sides. Sallies from perch to take insects in midair, returning to perch.

Nest Identification

Shape ▭ Location ☀☀☀ ▬ ⱲⱲ ☘

Dried grasses, dried leaves, stems, bark chips, and sedges • lined with fine grasses, hair, and bark fibers • atop small pile of weeds or grass or atop cattails, sometimes in small shrub, less than 1 m above ground • built by female • 3–6 creamy white or white eggs, flecked with black, grays, and browns, mostly at larger end; oval to short oval, 1.8 x 1.3 cm.

Plumage Sexes differ	Habitat 〰 — ▲ 🌳	Migration Migratory	Weight 11 g

DATE _____ TIME_____ LOCATION _____

Family PARULIDAE	Species *Wilsonia citrina*	Length 13 cm	Wingspan 20 cm

HOODED WARBLER

This bird resides in the thick foliage of the understory beneath tall deciduous trees. When the male sings from his high perch, often concealed, he may sit almost motionless as he delivers his ringing song. The juvenile female lacks the black on her crown but has dusky lores and white tail spots.

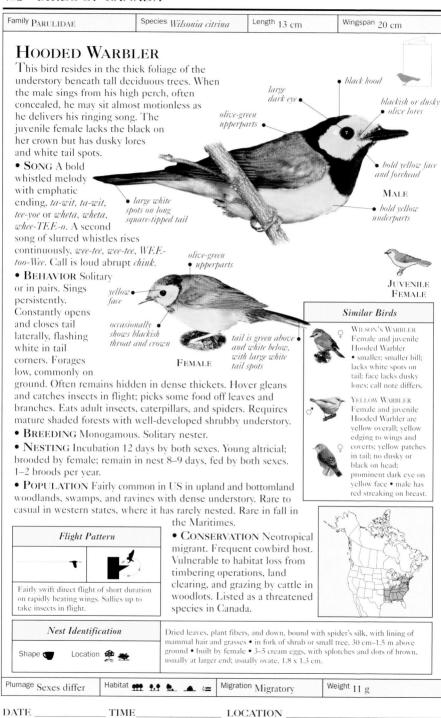

large dark eye

olive-green upperparts

olive-green uppparts

black hood

blackish or dusky olive lores

bold yellow face and forehead

MALE

bold yellow underparts

large white spots on long square-tipped tail

yellow face

occasionally shows blackish throat and crown

tail is green above and white below, with large white tail spots

FEMALE

JUVENILE FEMALE

- **SONG** A bold whistled melody with emphatic ending, *ta-wit, ta-wit, tee-yoe* or *wheta, wheta, whee-TEE-o*. A second song of slurred whistles rises continuously, *wee-tee, wee-tee, WEE-too-Wee*. Call is loud abrupt *chink*.

- **BEHAVIOR** Solitary or in pairs. Sings persistently. Constantly opens and closes tail laterally, flashing white in tail corners. Forages low, commonly on ground. Often remains hidden in dense thickets. Hover gleans and catches insects in flight; picks some food off leaves and branches. Eats adult insects, caterpillars, and spiders. Requires mature shaded forests with well-developed shrubby understory.

- **BREEDING** Monogamous. Solitary nester.

- **NESTING** Incubation 12 days by both sexes. Young altricial; brooded by female; remain in nest 8–9 days, fed by both sexes. 1–2 broods per year.

- **POPULATION** Fairly common in US in upland and bottomland woodlands, swamps, and ravines with dense understory. Rare to casual in western states, where it has rarely nested. Rare in fall in the Maritimes.

- **CONSERVATION** Neotropical migrant. Frequent cowbird host. Vulnerable to habitat loss from timbering operations, land clearing, and grazing by cattle in woodlots. Listed as a threatened species in Canada.

Similar Birds

WILSON'S WARBLER Female and juvenile Hooded Warbler • smaller; smaller bill; lacks white spots on tail; face lacks dusky lores; call note differs.

YELLOW WARBLER Female and juvenile Hooded Warbler are yellow overall; yellow edging to wings and coverts; yellow patches in tail; no dusky or black on head; prominent dark eye on yellow face • male has red streaking on breast.

Flight Pattern
Fairly swift direct flight of short duration on rapidly beating wings. Sallies up to take insects in flight.

Nest Identification	
Shape Location	Dried leaves, plant fibers, and down, bound with spider's silk, with lining of mammal hair and grasses • in fork of shrub or small tree, 30 cm–1.5 m above ground • built by female • 3–5 cream eggs, with splotches and dots of brown, usually at larger end; usually ovate, 1.8 x 1.3 cm.

Plumage Sexes differ	Habitat	Migration Migratory	Weight 11 g

DATE _____ TIME _____ LOCATION _____

Family PARULIDAE	Species *Wilsonia pusilla*	Length 12 cm	Wingspan 19 cm

WILSON'S WARBLER

Making its home in the thick damp woodlands and bogs of western North America, this active warbler has a wide nesting range, from Alaska to New Mexico, in the boreal forest from the Pacific to the Atlantic coast in Canada, and south into the New England states. The female is similar to the male but lacks the black cap or has only a light gray-black wash on her crown. Juvenile females lack the black crown altogether.

olive-green upperparts

black cap

MALE

long brownish olive tail

bright yellow face and lores

bold yellow to greenish yellow underparts

- **SONG** Quick series of slurred *chee-chee-chee* notes, dropping in pitch at the end. Subject to much individual and regional variation. Call is abrasive nasal *chimp*.
- **BEHAVIOR** Solitary or in pairs. Tame and inquisitive; responds to pishing by birders. Energetic. Moves tail up and down or in a circular fashion, similar to a gnatcatcher, as it picks food off foliage by gleaning and hover-gleaning. Also catches insects in flight. Eats spiders, insects, and berries.
- **BREEDING** Monogamous. Solitary in coastal areas. Forms loose colonies and is polygynous at high elevations.
- **NESTING** Incubation 10–13 days by female. Young altricial; brooded by female; stay in nest 8–11 days, fed by both sexes. 1 brood per year.
- **POPULATION** Common to fairly common in dense moist woodlands, willow and alder bogs, riparian corridors, and dense brushy ground cover in moist situations. Much more numerous in the West than in the East.

olive to grayish crown

dusky yellow ear patch

FEMALE

Similar Birds

HOODED WARBLER White spots on tail, which it constantly flicks open and closed; longer bill; dark dusky lores; black hood in males, with suggestion of hood in many females.

YELLOW WARBLER ♀ Female and juvenile • yellow edging to wings and wing coverts; yellow spots in tail; short tail with undertail coverts reaching closer to tip; more subdued tail wag.

- **CONSERVATION** Neotropical migrant. Uncommon cowbird host, except in the coastal lowlands of California. Vulnerable to habitat loss from destruction of lowland riparian thickets.

Flight Pattern
Swift flight of short duration on rapidly beating wings. Sallies forth from perch to take insects in midair before returning.

Nest Identification	
Shape Location ▬ ▰▰▰ ▦	Dried leaves, stalks, moss, and grass, with lining of fine grasses • atop grassy tussock, pile of moss, or sedges, or set at base of tree or bush, or in low shrub • 0–1 m above ground • built by female • 4–7 creamy white or white eggs, with flecks of brown, sometimes wreathed; oval to short oval, 1.5 cm long.

Plumage Sexes differ	Habitat 🐦 🐦 🐦 🐦	Migration Migratory	Weight 9.0 g

DATE _____ TIME_____ LOCATION _____

Family PARULIDAE	Species *Wilsonia canadensis*	Length 13–15 cm	Wingspan 19–22 cm

CANADA WARBLER

This bird sings frequently from the dense forest undergrowth it favors, or from an exposed perch just above it, with a jumbled warbling song that defies a fitting mnemonic. It actively forages for insects by flushing them from the foliage and chasing them. Males have been observed in "anticipatory feeding," offering insects to the unhatched eggs in the well-concealed nest on the ground. Canada Warblers are more often seen than heard on the breeding grounds, but a bird often will reveal itself, coming close to squeaking and pishing sounds made by birders. This early fall migrant heads southward before many other warblers begin their migrations. During migration they are often seen in pairs, and may be traveling with their mate of the season.

yellow supraloreal stripe

whitish eye ring forms spectacles

black necklace on breast

lacks wing bars

MALE

- **SONG** *Chip* followed by explosive staccato series of short notes ending with 3-note phrase, the last note rising in pitch. Song carries well and is given often on breeding grounds.
- **BEHAVIOR** Skulks in the undergrowth; often concealed when perched. Frequently found in low, dense, luxuriant undergrowth under mixed hardwoods. Gleans insects from foliage, stems, and ground; sometimes flycatches.
- **BREEDING** Solitary nester.
- **NESTING** Incubation 12 days by female. Altricial young fledge at 10–12 days. Probably 1 brood per year.
- **POPULATION** Common to fairly common in breeding range and in migration in the East; casual to accidental elsewhere. Declining.

pinkish legs and feet

black lores

spectacles

gray upperparts, wings, and tail

yellow underparts with faint gray streaking on breast

pinkish legs and feet

white undertail coverts

FEMALE

Similar Birds

MAGNOLIA WARBLER Black streaking extends onto sides; yellow rump; white wing patch or bars; white patches in tail; white supercilium; black lores and cheeks.

- **CONSERVATION** Neotropical migrant. Host to Brown-headed Cowbirds. Vulnerable to disturbance of mature forest on wintering ground. Habitat loss and forest fragmentation negatively affecting populations.

Flight Pattern
Direct flight with rapid somewhat fluttering wing beats.

Nest Identification	
Shape 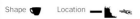 Location	Generally on the ground • bulky cup of dead leaves, grasses, dried plants, and ferns • lined with finer grasses and rootlets • on a bank, upturned tree roots, or mossy hummocks • built by female • 3–5 brown, buff, or creamy white eggs with speckled dots and small blotches of various shades of brown, gray, and purple; oval to short oval, 1.7 x 1.3 cm.

Plumage Sexes differ	Habitat	Migration Migratory	Weight 11 g

DATE _____ TIME_____ LOCATION _____

Family PARULIDAE	Species *Icteria virens*	Length 18 cm	Wingspan 23–25 cm

YELLOW-BREASTED CHAT

The largest North American warbler is named for its song, which resembles bizarre loud chattering. The large size, stocky body, thick bill, and long tail are unusual for a warbler, yet DNA studies confirm its taxonomic placement within this family. Unlike other warblers, it often sings at night in addition to its daytime vocalizations, a trait shared with some of the mimic thrushes. The female is similar to the male but has gray lores.

- **SONG** A clashing mixture of prattles, whistles, catlike sounds, clucking, screeching, and *caw* notes, both musical and harsh. Pacing is slow, hesitant, and unwarbler-like, more like a mockingbird or thrasher. Has the lowest voice of any American wood warbler. Some songs given in hovering mothlike display flights. Call notes are harsh *cheow* or nasal *hair.*

olive-green to olive-gray upperparts

blackish auriculars

white spectacles

thick curved bill

long graduated tail

white belly and crissum

black lores

white malar mark

bright yellow throat and breast

- **BEHAVIOR** Solitary or in pairs. Acts more like a mockingbird than a warbler. Shy, skulking, and secretive. Often remains hidden in thick foliage. Best seen when male sings from an exposed perch or is displaying. Display flight lasts several seconds, head held high, tail pumping, legs dangling, and singing all the while. Forages low in dense brushy shrubbery and sometimes on the ground, gleaning insects, larvae, berries, and fruits. The only warbler known to hold food in its feet.

- **BREEDING** Monogamous. Solitary nester or small colonies.

- **NESTING** Incubation 11–12 days by female. Altricial young brooded by female; stay in nest 8–11 days, fed by both sexes. 2 broods per year.

- **POPULATION** Common in dense thickets, brush, or scrub, especially along swamp margins and streams. Significant decline over much of its eastern range.

- **CONSERVATION** Neotropical migrant. Common host to Brown-headed Cowbird. Vulnerable to habitat loss due to land development and clearing, urbanization, and natural succession from old fields to maturation of forests. Federally listed as endangered in British Columbia.

Similar Birds
No similar species in North America.

Flight Pattern
Weak direct flights of short duration. In singing display, flies with legs dangling and wings flapping limply.

Nest Identification	
Shape 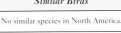 Location	Dried stems, leaves, grasses, and bark pieces, lined with soft grasses, stems, and leaves • in bush, vines, or thorny shrub, 60 cm–2.5 m above ground • built by female • 3–6 white or creamy white eggs, with flecks of rust or violet, concentrated at larger end; oval, 2.2 x 1.7 cm.

Plumage Sexes similar	Habitat	Migration Migratory	Weight 26 g

DATE _____ TIME _____ LOCATION _____

Family THRAUPIDAE	Species *Piranga olivacea*	Length 18 cm	Wingspan 28–30 cm

SCARLET TANAGER

No other bird in North America has the breeding male's unique plumage of a rich scarlet body with black wings and tail. When the male arrives on the breeding grounds, he perches at the tops of tall trees and sings to defend his territory and attract a mate. In the molt following the breeding season, the male retains his black wings and tail, but his plumage becomes a mixture of green, yellow, and red patches, later becoming dull green and yellow, appearing similar to the female bird. Juveniles and first fall males are similar in appearance to the adult female.

bright scarlet overall

black wings and tail

tan to creamy pink bill with blackish culmen

MALE

• **SONG** A breathy, coarse series of 4–5 notes, somewhat rapidly delivered, *querit-queer-query-querit-queer*. Pattern is sing-song and back-and-forth, somewhat like a robin with a sore throat. Has call of *chip-burrr.*

• **BEHAVIOR** Solitary or in pairs. May forage for food on ground but more often high in tops of trees. Eats insects, including wasps, bees, and caterpillars. Also takes berries and fruit. Gleans food from branches and foliage and frequently hawks insects. Frequents drier forests, often pine and pine-oak.

pale broken eye ring

dull green upperparts

blackish wings and tail

FALL MALE

lemon-yellow underparts

FEMALE

• **BREEDING** Monogamous; solitary or in pairs. Male displays by perching below female, opening his wings and showing off his scarlet back.

• **NESTING** Incubation 13–14 days by female. Young altricial; brooded by female; stay in nest 9–11 days, fed by both sexes. 1 brood per year.

• **POPULATION** Fairly common in deciduous and mixed conifer-hardwood forests. Some recent declines. Casual in West.

• **FEEDERS** Will come to feeders for mixture of bread crumbs, cornmeal, and peanut butter.

Similar Birds	
♂	WESTERN TANAGER Male has additional yellow upper wing bar • females and winter males are similar to their counterparts but have white wing bars.
♀	

• **CONSERVATION** Neotropical migrant. Vulnerable to loss of habitat and forest fragmentation, as it requires large areas of forest for breeding. Fairly common host to cowbird parasitism.

Flight Pattern
Swift rapid flight with quick wing strokes. Sallies forth to take insects in flight.

Nest Identification	
Shape ⬷ Location 🐝 🌿	Forbs, grasses, sticks, rootlets, and twigs, with lining of soft grasses and conifer needles • far out on limb, 1.5–21 m above ground • built by female • 2–5 bluish greenish eggs, marked with brown, often wreathed; oval to short oval, 2.3 x 1.8 cm.

Plumage Sexes differ	Habitat 🌲🌲 🌳	Migration Migratory	Weight 28 g

DATE _____ TIME_____ LOCATION _____

| Family THRAUPIDAE | Species *Piranga ludoviciana* | Length 18 cm | Wingspan 28–30 cm |

WESTERN TANAGER

One of only two North American tanagers with distinct wing bars, this bird frequents the coniferous forests of the western mountain region, where it is one of the most colorful species present. It has on rare occasions hybridized with its close cousin, the Scarlet Tanager. In the molt after the breeding season, the male's red head fades to a yellowish color with fine streaking on the crown. The female's olive-gray back contrasts sharply with the yellow-green rump, uppertail coverts, and nape. Juveniles resemble females but with head and body streaked dark brown.

yellow uppertail coverts, rump, and lower back

red head, throat, and upper breast

creamy pinkish orange bill with dark culmen

upper yellow and lower white wing bars

yellow underparts

MALE

black tail

WINTER MALE

- **SONG** A hoarse vireo-like series of 3–4 phrases, *che-ree, che-ree, che-weeu, cheweeu.* Call is *pit-ick, pri-tick-tick.*

- **BEHAVIOR** Solitary or in pairs. Forages in trees and on ground, gleaning food from bark, limbs, foliage, and soil. Eats fruit and insects, including wasps and bees. Hawks insects in flight. Bathes in birdbaths. Frequent singer often first detected by vocalizations. In postbreeding season, often joins mixed-species foraging flocks.

yellow-olive head

olive-gray back, shoulders, and wing coverts

FEMALE

pale broken eye ring

thin yellow and white wing bars

yellowish underparts

- **BREEDING** Monogamous. Solitary.

- **NESTING** Incubation 13 days by female. Altricial young brooded by female; stay in nest 13–15 days, fed by both sexes. 1 brood per year.

- **POPULATION** Fairly common in coniferous and pine-oak forests, particularly in mountain canyons. Casual in East in winter.

Similar Birds

FLAME-COLORED TANAGER ♀ Dark bill; dusky auriculars; bolder whitish wing bars; white tail corners; darkly streaked back.

♂ SCARLET TANAGER Females and winter males are similar to their counterparts but ♀ have olive backs and lack the wing bars.

- **FEEDERS** Fresh oranges, dried fruit, bread crumbs.

- **CONSERVATION** Neotropical migrant. Uncommon cowbird host. Vulnerable to loss of habitat and forest fragmentation.

Flight Pattern
Swift direct flight on rapidly beating wings. Sallies forth from perch to take insects in flight.

Nest Identification	
Shape ⬗ Location 🪹🌳	Rootlets, sticks, and moss, with lining of plant down and mammal hair • far out on branch, 1.5–20 m above ground • built mostly by female • 3–5 bluish eggs, marked with browns, often wreathed; oval to short subelliptical, 2.3 x 1.7 cm.

| Plumage Sexes differ | Habitat 🌳 ⛰ | Migration Migratory | Weight 28 g |

DATE _____ TIME _____ LOCATION _____

Family EMBERIZIDAE	Species *Pipilo maculatus*	Length 18–20 cm	Wingspan 25–28 cm

SPOTTED TOWHEE

This bird is the western counterpart of the Eastern Towhee, and until recently they were considered one species, the Rufous-sided Towhee. The white spotting on the upperparts, wings, and tail shows geographical variation. The white on the undersides of the tail corners flash in flight. Juveniles are brown with two white wing bars and darker brown streaking on the upperparts and underparts.

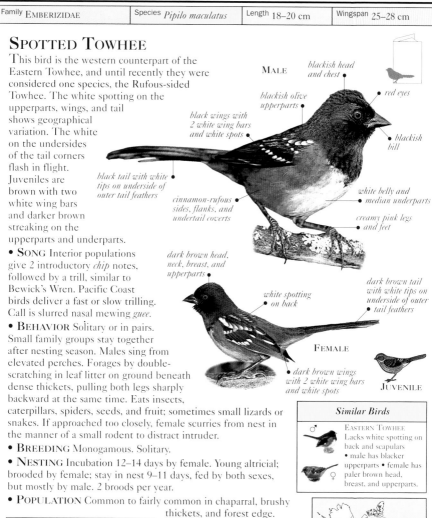

MALE

blackish head and chest

blackish olive upperparts

black wings with 2 white wing bars and white spots

red eyes

blackish bill

black tail with white tips on underside of outer tail feathers

cinnamon-rufous sides, flanks, and undertail coverts

white belly and median underparts

creamy pink legs and feet

dark brown head, neck, breast, and upperparts

white spotting on back

dark brown tail with white tips on underside of outer tail feathers

FEMALE

dark brown wings with 2 white wing bars and white spots

JUVENILE

• **SONG** Interior populations give 2 introductory *chip* notes, followed by a trill, similar to Bewick's Wren. Pacific Coast birds deliver a fast or slow trilling. Call is slurred nasal mewing *guee*.

• **BEHAVIOR** Solitary or in pairs. Small family groups stay together after nesting season. Males sing from elevated perches. Forages by double-scratching in leaf litter on ground beneath dense thickets, pulling both legs sharply backward at the same time. Eats insects, caterpillars, spiders, seeds, and fruit; sometimes small lizards or snakes. If approached too closely, female scurries from nest in the manner of a small rodent to distract intruder.

• **BREEDING** Monogamous. Solitary.

• **NESTING** Incubation 12–14 days by female. Young altricial; brooded by female; stay in nest 9–11 days, fed by both sexes, but mostly by male. 2 broods per year.

• **POPULATION** Common to fairly common in chaparral, brushy thickets, and forest edge.

• **FEEDERS** Mixture of oats, suet, and flax seeds.

• **CONSERVATION** Vulnerable to loss of habitat due to land clearing, grazing, and development. Fairly common host to cowbird parasitism.

Similar Birds

♂ EASTERN TOWHEE Lacks white spotting on back and scapulars • male has blacker upperparts • female has paler brown head, ♀ breast, and upperparts.

Flight Pattern

Short bounding flights with several rapid wing strokes followed by wings pulled to sides.

Nest Identification

Shape 🍵   Location ━ 🌿 🌳

Twigs, leaves, rootlets, grass, and bark • lined with grasses • on ground, sheltered by bush or grassy tussock, occasionally in low shrub or tree • built by female • 2–6 gray-brown or creamy white eggs, flecked and dotted with purple, red-brown, and gray; ovate, 2.4 x 1.8 cm.

Plumage Sexes differ	Habitat 🌿 🌲 ✈	Migration Some migrate	Weight Undetermined

DATE _____ TIME_____ LOCATION _____

Family EMBERIZIDAE	Species *Pipilo erythrophthalmus*	Length 18–20 cm	Wingspan 25–28 cm

EASTERN TOWHEE

Sometimes called a Ground Robin in the South, this is the eastern counterpart of the Spotted Towhee. Until recently these birds were classified as one species, the Rufous-sided Towhee. The two species hybridize where their ranges overlap along rivers in the Great Plains. The smaller Florida race has whitish eyes instead of red like most other races. In flight the white undertail corners flash conspicuously. Juveniles are brown overall with pale chins and dark streaking on underparts and upperparts.

• **SONG** A clear whistled *drink-your-teeeaaa*, with the "tea" trilled. Much individual variation, with some birds leaving off the introductory note and some omitting the ending trill. Has calls of *toe-WHEE* and *che-wink* or *wank*.

• **BEHAVIOR** Solitary or in pairs. Secretive; stays low in underbrush and on ground. Frequents brushy thickets, woodland edges, and riparian areas. Males are conspicuous when singing, often choosing an exposed perch. Usually detected by the rustle of dry leaves on ground; forages by double-scratching, pulling both legs sharply backward at once. Eats insects, caterpillars, small salamanders, fruits, and seeds.

• **BREEDING** Monogamous. Solitary. Courting male chases female and fans tail to show off white spots on outer feathers.

• **NESTING** Incubation 12–13 days by female. Young altricial; brooded by female; stay in nest 10–12 days, fed by both sexes, more by male. 2–3 broods per year.

• **POPULATION** Common to fairly common. Major decline in Northeast in last half of 20th century.

• **FEEDERS** Mixture of oats, suet, and seeds.

• **CONSERVATION** Declines in Northeast poorly understood; vulnerable to loss of habitat, clearing of land, development, and pesticides in food chain. Frequent cowbird host.

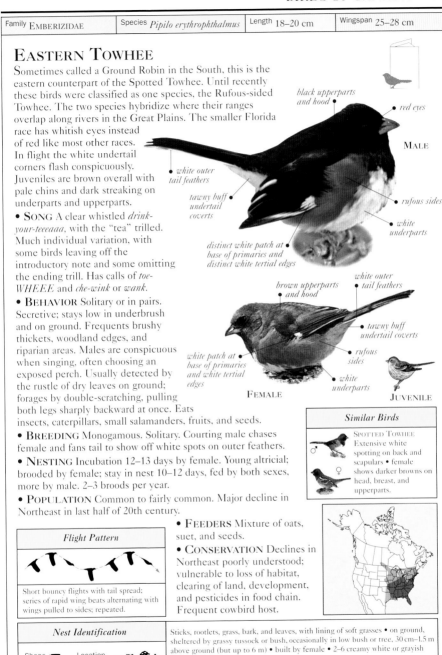

black upperparts and hood

red eyes

MALE

white outer tail feathers

tawny buff undertail coverts

rufous sides

white underparts

distinct white patch at base of primaries and distinct white tertial edges

white outer tail feathers

brown upperparts and hood

tawny buff undertail coverts

white patch at base of primaries and white tertial edges

rufous sides

white underparts

FEMALE

JUVENILE

Similar Birds

SPOTTED TOWHEE Extensive white spotting on back and scapulars • female shows darker browns on head, breast, and upperparts.

Flight Pattern

Short bouncy flights with tail spread; series of rapid wing beats alternating with wings pulled to sides; repeated.

Nest Identification

Shape

Location

Sticks, rootlets, grass, bark, and leaves, with lining of soft grasses • on ground, sheltered by grassy tussock or bush, occasionally in low bush or tree, 30 cm–1.5 m above ground (but up to 6 m) • built by female • 2–6 creamy white or grayish eggs; oval, 2.3 x 1.7 cm.

Plumage Sexes differ	Habitat	Migration Northern birds migrate	Weight 43 g

DATE _____ TIME_____ LOCATION _____

Family EMBERIZIDAE	Species *Spizella arborea*	Length 16 cm	Wingspan 25 cm

AMERICAN TREE SPARROW

After nesting near the frigid tundra regions, flocks of these sparrows migrate south and can be found primarily in the United States during the winter. Sometimes traveling in flocks of thirty-five to forty birds, but often smaller, they scout out food supplies and willingly come to outdoor feeders. Males often winter farther north than females and juveniles. Males sing during courtship and also to claim territory.

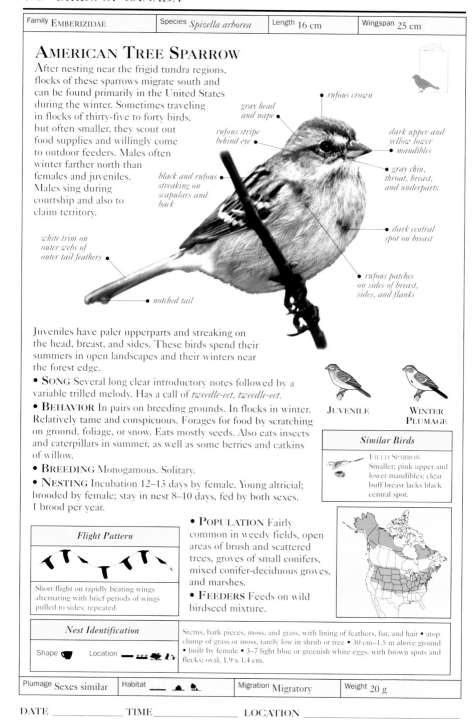

gray head and nape

rufous stripe behind eye

rufous crown

dark upper and yellow lower mandibles

gray chin, throat, breast, and underparts

black and rufous streaking on scapulars and back

dark central spot on breast

white trim on outer webs of outer tail feathers

rufous patches on sides of breast, sides, and flanks

notched tail

Juveniles have paler upperparts and streaking on the head, breast, and sides. These birds spend their summers in open landscapes and their winters near the forest edge.

- **SONG** Several long clear introductory notes followed by a variable trilled melody. Has a call of *tweedle-eet, tweedle-eet*.
- **BEHAVIOR** In pairs on breeding grounds. In flocks in winter. Relatively tame and conspicuous. Forages for food by scratching on ground, foliage, or snow. Eats mostly seeds. Also eats insects and caterpillars in summer, as well as some berries and catkins of willow.
- **BREEDING** Monogamous. Solitary.
- **NESTING** Incubation 12–13 days by female. Young altricial; brooded by female; stay in nest 8–10 days, fed by both sexes. 1 brood per year.

JUVENILE

WINTER PLUMAGE

Similar Birds

FIELD SPARROW Smaller; pink upper and lower mandibles; clear buff breast lacks black central spot.

- **POPULATION** Fairly common in weedy fields, open areas of brush and scattered trees, groves of small conifers, mixed conifer-deciduous groves, and marshes.
- **FEEDERS** Feeds on wild birdseed mixture.

Flight Pattern

Short flight on rapidly beating wings alternating with brief periods of wings pulled to sides; repeated.

Nest Identification	
Shape	Location	Stems, bark pieces, moss, and grass, with lining of feathers, fur, and hair • atop clump of grass or moss, rarely low in shrub or tree • 30 cm–1.5 m above ground • built by female • 3–7 light blue or greenish white eggs, with brown spots and flecks; oval, 1.9 x 1.4 cm.

Plumage Sexes similar	Habitat	Migration Migratory	Weight 20 g

Family EMBERIZIDAE	Species *Spizella passerina*	Length 14 cm	Wingspan 20–23 cm

CHIPPING SPARROW

Its bold chestnut cap, bordered by a long white superciliary stripe during breeding season, helps identify this tiny sparrow. Named for its song and call, it sings from its high perch during the day, and sometimes even at night, or calls as it forages for food in trees, gardens, and backyards. One of the tamest sparrows, it will take food from human hands. Juveniles lack the white eyebrow and

gray nape and cheeks

light brown upperparts with black or brown streaking

long slightly notched tail

chestnut cap

white supercilium

black bill

black line extends from bill through eye to ear

2 white wing bars

gray underparts

JUVENILE

WINTER PLUMAGE

chestnut cap but have a streaked crown and nape, streaked underparts, and buffy wing bars. Winter birds have brown-streaked crowns, brown faces, and dark lores.

- **SONG** A repetitive series of trilled chip notes, *chip-chip-chip-chip-chip-chip-chip*, all the same pitch. Has a call of *seek*.
- **BEHAVIOR** Solitary or in pairs. In small family groups after breeding season. May join mixed-species foraging flocks in winter. Forages on ground and picks off foliage. Eats seeds, insects, their caterpillars, and spiders.
- **BREEDING** Monogamous. Solitary. A few males polygynous.
- **NESTING** Incubation 11–14 days by female. Young altricial; brooded by female; stay in nest 8–12 days, fed by both sexes. 2 broods per year.
- **POPULATION** Common and widespread in open mixed coniferous-deciduous forests, forest edges, gardens, lawns, and short-grass fields.
- **FEEDERS** Comes to feeders for breadcrumbs and seeds.
- **CONSERVATION** Neotropical migrant. Common host to cowbird parasitism.

Similar Birds

CLAY-COLORED SPARROW
Black-streaked brown crown with gray center stripe; buffy brown cheek patch bordered by dark postocular stripe and dark mustache mark; pale grayish eyebrow; whitish chin and submustachial stripe separated by buffy malar mark; whitish underparts with buffy wash on breast.

Flight Pattern

Typically, short flights with rapidly beating wings alternating with brief periods of wings pulled to sides; repeated.

Nest Identification

Shape   Location

Grass, forbs, weed stalks, and rootlets, with lining of mammal hair and grass • on branch or vine tangle, rarely on ground • most often 90 cm–3.5 m above ground (but up to 18 m) • built by female • 2–5 bluish green eggs, marked with dark browns, blues, and blacks, often wreathed; subelliptical to short subelliptical, 1.8 x 1.3 cm.

Plumage Sexes similar	Habitat	Migration Migratory	Weight 11 g

DATE _____ TIME_____ LOCATION _____

| Family EMBERIZIDAE | Species *Spizella pallida* | Length 14 cm | Wingspan 20 cm |

CLAY-COLORED SPARROW

The male bird perches to claim its territory while singing its buzzy insectlike song across the grasslands. Wintering primarily in the highlands of central Mexico, this tiny bird flies north to summer in the prairies of Canada and the northern United States. In flight this frequent visitor to backyard feeders shows a dark buff rump. Juveniles have a gray nape, buffy brown cheek patch, and streaked underparts.

white supercilium

brown crown with black streaks

whitish stripe in middle of crown

white malar stripe

dark mustache stripe

brown ear patches

pale gray-white underparts with buffy wash on breast

dark stripe from behind eye

light brown back with dark streaks

JUVENILE

2 white wing bars

- **SONG** Insectlike repetitive *bzzz-bzzzz-zeee-zeee*. Has a call of *chip* or *sip*.
- **BEHAVIOR** In pairs during breeding season. Small family groups prior to fall migration. Males vigorously defend small territory. Sings often and well into the heat of July. Forages on ground or low in trees. Eats seeds and insects. May join mixed-species feeding flocks with other sparrows in winter.
- **BREEDING** Monogamous. Solitary.
- **NESTING** Incubation 10–12 days by both sexes, but female does more. Young altricial; brooded by female; stay in nest 8–9 days, fed by both sexes. 1–2 broods per year.
- **POPULATION** Fairly common in brushy weedy fields, riparian thickets, and forest edges. Slight decline over recent decades due to loss of habitat after human populations increased in the North and East. Rare to casual visitor in migration and winter on both coasts, the Southwest, and southern Florida.
- **FEEDERS** Will come to feeding stations for breadcrumbs, cracked corn, sunflower seeds, and millet.

Similar Birds

CHIPPING SPARROW Winter adults have gray rump; brown crown with black streaking and whitish central crown stripe; gray underparts • first winter birds have buffy underparts.

BREWER'S SPARROW Lacks whitish crown stripe; blacker streaking on upperparts; paler brown ear patch lacks black outline; whitish eye ring.

- **CONSERVATION** Neotropical migrant. Common host to cowbird parasitism. Vulnerable to habitat loss due to development and land clearing for agriculture.

Flight Pattern

Typically, short flight on rapidly beating wings alternating with brief periods of wings pulled to sides.

Nest Identification

Shape ☕   Location ▬ 🐦 🐦

Sticks, grass, forbs, and rootlets, with lining of mammal hair and rootlets • atop grassy tussock, on ground sheltered by bush, or low in branch of shrub or tree • less than 1.5 m above ground • built by female • 3–5 bluish green eggs, marked with dark browns and blacks, often wreathed; ovate, 1.7 x 1.3 cm.

| Plumage Sexes similar | Habitat 🌾 ▬ 🌿 🌲 | Migration Migratory | Weight 11 g |

| Family EMBERIZIDAE | Species *Spizella breweri* | Length 14 cm | Wingspan 20 cm |

BREWER'S SPARROW

At sunrise and just before sunset, countless territorial males sing continuous choruses, their buzzing trill spreading across the Great Basin of the western United States. The Timberline Sparrow, an isolated subspecies that nests above the timberline in the subalpine

brown crown with fine black streaking

pale brown ear patch with dark borders

brown upperparts with black streaking

grayish white eyebrow

pale lores

whitish eye ring

dark malar stripe

grayish white throat and underparts

dark brown wings with buff wing bars

JUVENILE

zone of the Canadian Rockies north into southeastern Alaska, may be a separate species. Shy and wary on the nesting grounds, this sparrow is tame during other times of the year and often visits gardens and outdoor feeders. Juveniles are similar to adults but are buffier overall with streaked underparts; both juveniles and adults show a buffy brown rump.

- **SONG** An insectlike long-continuing buzzing trill, with each sequence of the song given on different pitches, one sequence following another in long sessions without pauses. Call is *tsip*.
- **BEHAVIOR** Solitary or in pairs. In small family groups after breeding season. In winter, may join mixed-species foraging flocks with other sparrows and buntings. Forages on or near ground for food. Eats mostly insects in spring and summer. In fall and winter, eats mostly seeds. Found almost anywhere that sagebrush occurs. When disturbed by intruder, incubating or brooding female often runs rather than flies from nest.
- **BREEDING** Monogamous. Solitary.
- **NESTING** Incubation 11–13 days, mostly by female, but some by male. Young altricial; brooded by female; stay in nest 8–9 days, fed by both sexes. 1–2 broods per year.
- **POPULATION** Common in arid brushland, sagebrush flats, mountain meadows, and also in thickets. Accidental in the East.
- **FEEDERS** Will come for baby chick scratch feed.
- **CONSERVATION** Neotropical migrant. Infrequent host to cowbird parasitism.

Similar Birds

CHIPPING SPARROW
Winter • dark streaking on rufous crown; gray rump; bold white wing bars; less contrasting eyebrow stripe; lacks white eye ring and dark malar mark.

CLAY-COLORED SPARROW
Whitish or buffy white central stripe; buffier streaking on upperparts; buffier washes on underparts; gray nape; buffier cheek patch; lacks white eye ring.

Flight Pattern

Short flights with rapid wing beats alternating with brief periods of wings pulled to sides; repeated.

Nest Identification

Shape   Location

Forbs and dried grasses, with lining of rootlets and mammal hair • in bush or cactus • usually less than 1 m above ground • built by female • 3–5 bluish green eggs, with dark brown dots and specks; subelliptical to ovate, 1.8 x 1.3 cm.

| Plumage Sexes similar | Habitat | Migration Migratory | Weight 14 g |

DATE _____ TIME_____ LOCATION _____

| Family EMBERIZIDAE | Species *Spizella pusilla* | Length 15 cm | Wingspan 22 cm |

FIELD SPARROW

This sparrow stays near the ground in fields and open woodlands. When defending its nest, the male flies from tree to tree singing a melody that accelerates like the bouncing of a dropped rubber ball. The clearing of the primeval eastern forest provided thousands of hectares of habitat ideally suited for

rusty back with dark streaking

rusty cap

buffy white eye ring

pink bill

gray sides of head

brown streak behind each eye

buff breast, sides, and flanks

grayish brown rump

rusty brown wings

2 wing bars

pink legs and feet

JUVENILE

this small sparrow. Now, as the old farms become suburbs or succumb to the woodlots brought on by ecological succession, this bird is declining in this range.

• **SONG** A pleasant *seea-seea-seea-wee-wee-wee*, which begins with separate clear whistled notes and accelerates, either ascending, descending, or staying on the same pitch. Call is abrasive *chip*.

• **BEHAVIOR** Solitary or in pairs in breeding season. In small family flocks after nesting. In winter, forms flocks that may join mixed-species foraging flocks. Forages on ground or low in shrubbery for insects, caterpillars, seeds, and spiders. Tame and curious; responds to squeaking and pishing by birders.

• **BREEDING** Monogamous. Solitary.

• **NESTING** Incubation 10–17 days by female. Young altricial; brooded by female; stay in nest 7–8 days, fed by both sexes. Male tends and feeds fledglings while female incubates second clutch. 2–3 broods per year.

• **POPULATION** Fairly common in old fields, open brushy woodlands, thorn scrub, and forest edge. Casual in West. Uncommon in the Maritimes.

• **FEEDERS** Small grain.

• **CONSERVATION** Common host to cowbird parasitism.

Similar Birds

CLAY-COLORED SPARROW
Brown crown with central stripe; buffy cheek patch; buffy brown malar mark; gray nape; buffy edges and streaks on upperparts; whitish underparts with buffy wash on chest and flanks; 2 buffy wing bars.

Flight Pattern

Short flights with rapid wing beats alternating with brief periods of wings pulled to sides; repeated.

Nest Identification

Shape ☕   Location ▬ ▬ ✿✿✿ ⟋

Fine grasses, leaves, and dried grass, with lining of mammal hair and rootlets • atop grassy tussock or clump of vegetation, sometimes in vine or bush • less than 1 m above ground • built by female • 2–6 creamy pale greenish bluish white eggs, marked with browns, occasionally wreathed; short subelliptical, 1.8 x 1.3 cm.

| Plumage Sexes similar | Habitat 🌿 ▬ ⛰ | Migration Northern birds migrate | Weight 11 g |

DATE _____ TIME_____ LOCATION _____

Family EMBERIZIDAE	Species *Pooecetes gramineus*	Length 14–17 cm	Wingspan 25–29 cm

VESPER SPARROW

This bird is named for the time of day it usually sings its best and most continuous choruses, which is at twilight when many other songbirds have become silent. Its song is not limited to the vespers hour, however, for during nesting season, it sings throughout the day from the highest perch available in its territory. This sparrow, with chestnut lesser coverts on its shoulder and white outer tail feathers, has a vast geographical distribution, its home habitats ranging from dry grasslands and farmlands to sagebrush flats. Juveniles resemble adults but have more extensive streaking on the underparts.

brown ear patch bordered behind and below with white

upperparts streaked gray-brown

chestnut patch at bend of wing, with row of black spots beneath

white eye ring

grayish brown streaking on breast, throat, and sides

white underparts

white outer tail feathers

long notched tail

• **SONG** Two drawled clear notes followed by two higher notes, then a short descending trill. Call is a high thin *tssit*.
• **BEHAVIOR** Solitary or in pairs. May form small family groups after breeding season. May join loose flocks in winter. Walks on ground. Runs from danger instead of flying. Forages on ground, in grasses, and in low shrubbery for insects and seeds. Very fond of dust baths. Neither bathes in nor drinks water, meeting all internal water needs through diet.
• **BREEDING** Monogamous. Solitary or loose colonies.
• **NESTING** Incubation 11–13 days by both sexes, but female does more. Young altricial; brooded by female; stay in nest 7–14 days, fed by both sexes. Fledglings tended and fed by male while female starts another nest. 1–3 broods per year.
• **POPULATION** Uncommon to fairly common. Numbers declining in the East as habitat is lost to development and because logged areas become older and less suitable for nesting.
• **CONSERVATION** Neotropical migrant. Common host to cowbird parasitism. Nesting sites are being lost due to agricultural mowing and other operations.

Similar Birds

SAVANNAH SPARROW Shorter tail; yellow supercilium; pale central crown stripe; central "stickpin" spot on chest; lacks chestnut lesser coverts; lacks white eye ring and outer tail feathers.

Flight Pattern
Short flights on rapidly beating wings alternating with brief periods of wings pulled to sides; repeated.

Nest Identification	
Shape ◣ Location ▬ ⚘⚘⚘	Dry grasses, weed stalks, and rootlets, lined with finer grasses and animal hair • in scraped-out depression on ground • hidden under vegetation, in field, near tall grass clump, on sand or dirt • built by female • 2–6 creamy white or pale greenish white eggs with brown markings; oval, 2.0 x 1.5 cm.

Plumage Sexes similar	Habitat ⚘ ▬ ⚘	Migration Migratory	Weight 28 g

DATE _____ TIME_____ LOCATION _____

Family EMBERIZIDAE	Species *Chondestes grammacus*	Length 15–17 cm	Wingspan 27–28 cm

LARK SPARROW

This sparrow, with its harlequin head pattern, has a lovely voice and sings from the ground, a perch, or while flying, sometimes even at night. Frequenting the open prairies and other open habitats, mostly west of the Mississippi River, it can be identified by the dark spot in the center of its breast and the long rounded tail with extensive white edging. Juveniles are similar to adults but more washed-out with an ill-defined head pattern, buffier coloration, dark brown streaking on the white throat, and white underparts with a buffy wash on the sides of the breast.

black, white, and chestnut-brown stripes on head

chestnut ear patches

white mustache

black malar mark

brown and black streaking on back

whitish underparts with buff wash on flanks

long rounded black tail with white edging

- **SONG** Long, pleasant bubbling melody, beginning with 2 loud clear notes followed by series of chips, buzzes, and trills. Call is repetitive sharp metallic *tik*, often given in flight.

- **BEHAVIOR** Solitary or in pairs. Gregarious. Feeds in flocks, even during breeding season. Forages for food on ground and low in trees and shrubs. Eats seeds, insects, and caterpillars. Females on nest perform distraction display when disturbed, scurrying away with wings fluttering and tail spread. Prior to copulating, male often passes to female a twig or grass stem, which she holds.

- **BREEDING** Monogamous. Occasionally polygamous. Often in loose colonies. Male displays while swaggering on the ground in front of female, his tail spread, showing off its white feathers.

- **NESTING** Incubation 11–12 days by female. Young altricial; brooded by female; remain in nest 9–10 days, fed by both sexes. 1 brood per year.

- **POPULATION** Common in cultivated areas, fields, pastures, grassland, prairie, and savanna. Range has declined east of the Mississippi River due to loss of habitat. Casual to East Coast.

JUVENILE

Similar Birds

Head pattern is distinctive; not likely to be confused with other sparrows.

- **FEEDERS** Small grains.

- **CONSERVATION** Neotropical migrant. Uncommon cowbird host. Vulnerable to habitat loss due to land clearing, development, overgrazing, and nest losses resulting from agricultural operations.

Flight Pattern

Short fluttering flight on rapidly beating wings alternating with brief periods of wings pulled to sides.

Nest Identification

Shape [cup]   Location

Sticks, grass, and forbs • lined with rootlets and grasses • atop grassy tussock shaded by bush, or low in tree, sometimes in shrub or bush or in abandoned nest • 1–9 m above ground • built by female • 3–6 creamy to grayish white eggs, marked with dark browns and blacks, often wreathed; oval, 2.0 x 1.6 cm.

Plumage Sexes similar	Habitat	Migration Migratory	Weight 28 g

DATE _____ TIME_____ LOCATION _____

Family EMBERIZIDAE	Species *Calamospiza melanocorys*	Length 18 cm	Wingspan 28 cm

LARK BUNTING

In the spring hundreds of these birds fly in choreographed circles and shapes like a rolling wheel of birds. As they move across the prairie, birds from the rear fly to the front over birds settling into vegetation. They remain in flocks as they return to their nesting grounds on the sagebrush plains. Males and females have similar winter plumage, but males show black primaries. Juveniles are similar to winter adults. This is the state bird of Colorado.

black or slate-gray overall

bluish gray bill

large white wing patches

MALE

- **SONG** Flutelike warbling melody of full whistles and trills. Often sings in groups. Call is *hoo-ee*.
- **BEHAVIOR** In pairs or flocks. Gregarious; in flocks most of year. Forages on ground and in low vegetation. Eats insects, caterpillars, and seeds. Territorial males ascend 6–9 meters with white wing patches flashing, pour out song, and descend with jerky butterfly movements to ground. Neighboring males often join in display flights.

short tail with white tips on all but central tail feathers

bluish gray bill

streaked gray-brown upperparts

FEMALE

white wing patch with hint of buff

short tail

WINTER PLUMAGE

- **BREEDING** Monogamous. Some are polygynous. Loose colonies. Displaying male fluffs out feathers and crest and sings.
- **NESTING** Incubation 11–12 days by female; some males help. Altricial young brooded by female; stay in nest 8–9 days, fed by both sexes. 2 broods per year.

unstreaked belly

white underparts with dusky streaking

Similar Birds

BOBOLINK ♂
White on back, rump, uppertail coverts, and wings; buffy ocher hindneck.

- **POPULATION** Common in grasslands, dry plains, prairies, sagebrush flats, and meadows. Rare to casual on Pacific Coast in fall and winter. Casual in the East in fall and winter.
- **FEEDERS** Occasionally attends feeders that supply small grains and seeds.

- **CONSERVATION** Neotropical migrant. Uncommon host to cowbird parasitism. Historical population declines in northern and eastern parts of breeding range caused by loss of the bird's prairie habitat.

Flight Pattern
Strong flight with shallow wing beats alternating with brief periods of wings pulled to sides.

Nest Identification	
Shape	Location	Grass, forbs, and fine roots • lined with hair and plant down • in grassy depression • built by female • 3–7 pale blue or greenish blue eggs, occasionally spotted with reddish browns; oval, 2.3 cm long.

Plumage Sexes differ	Habitat	Migration Migratory	Weight 31 g

DATE _____ TIME_____ LOCATION _____

Family EMBERIZIDAE	Species *Passerculus sandwichensis*	Length 13–16 cm	Wingspan 20–24 cm

SAVANNAH SPARROW

Named for the city in Georgia where it was first spotted, this bird has a wide range, living in grassy marshes and wet meadows to grasslands and cultivated grass to tundra. It also has considerable variation between the many races that make up the species. Like many sparrows, it spends most of its time on the ground; when disturbed, it scurries through the grasses, running mouselike rather than flying away. But if hard-pressed it flies up a short distance then drops back into the grasses.

whitish or pale median crown stripe

yellow or whitish supercilium

dark brown-streaked upperparts

central "stickpin" on chest

pinkish legs and feet

buff to white underparts with brown streaking

IPSWICH FORM

• **SONG** Begins with 2–3 *chip* notes followed by 2 buzzy insectlike trills, *tip-tip-seeeee-saaaay*. Call note is *seeep*.

short notched tail

• **BEHAVIOR** Solitary or in pairs. May form small family groups after breeding season. Gregarious; forms flocks in migration and winter. Forages for food on ground, sometimes scratching in dirt and foliage. Eats seeds, insects, spiders, and sometimes snails. Roosts in small tight groups on the ground.

• **BREEDING** Monogamous. Solitary. Some marsh-dwelling populations tend to be polygynous. Sometimes loose colonies.

• **NESTING** Incubation 10–13 days by both sexes, but female does most. Young altricial; brooded by female; stay in nest 7–14 days; fed by both sexes. 1–2 broods per year.

Similar Birds

SONG SPARROW
Longer rounded tail without notch; heavier streaking on the underparts; large central "stickpin" on chest in most races; lacks yellow in lores and supercilium.

VESPER SPARROW
Gray-brown streaking on upperparts, throat, breast, and sides; wing has chestnut patch at bend; white outer tail feathers; white eye ring; brown ear patch.

• **POPULATION** Abundant and widespread in open grassy landscapes and tundra. May be extending range farther south in the southern Appalachians.

• **CONSERVATION** Neotropical migrant. Uncommon cowbird host.

Flight Pattern
Short flights with rapidly beating wings alternating with brief periods of wings pulled to sides.

Nest Identification	
Shape 🍵 Location ▬ ▬ ***	Moss and dried grasses • lined with fine hair, fine grasses, and roots • in depression or scrape, sheltered by vines, grasses, or dune • built by female • 2–6 pale greenish blue or whitish eggs, marked with brown, sometimes wreathed; ovate to short ovate, 2.0 x 1.4 cm.

Plumage Sexes similar	Habitat ▬ ⚘ 〰	Migration Migratory	Weight 23 g

DATE _____ TIME _____ LOCATION _____

Family EMBERIZIDAE	Species *Ammodramus savannarum*	Length 12–14 cm	Wingspan 20–22 cm

GRASSHOPPER SPARROW

These birds are named for their insectlike song. The male claims his territory by singing from a low exposed perch during the day. Hidden in tall grasses, this bird runs rather than flies from danger. Because it nests on the ground in cultivated grasslands, lives are lost when the crop is mowed; after mowing, predators take eggs, young, and adults.

dark crown with pale stripe through center

yellow lore

white eye ring

gray-brown streaking on upperparts

buff breast, sides, flanks, and undertail coverts

yellow at bend of wings

white belly

JUVENILE

• **SONG** High thin insectlike buzzing with 2 notes then a trill, *pit-tuck, zeeeeeeeeeeee*. At dusk may sing with more squeaky buzzy notes and trills. Call is soft insectlike *tisk*.

• **BEHAVIOR** Solitary or in pairs. May form small family groups after breeding season. Forages on ground and from low vegetation. Eats insects, worms, snails, seeds, and grains. Males sing from any exposed perch. When disturbed on nest, female flutters away in distraction display.

short notched tail

Similar Birds

BAIRD'S SPARROW Buffy orange crown and supercilium; dark spot in each rear corner of ear patch; blackish malar mark; necklace of dark brown streaks on breast; chestnut scapulars with pale edging forming scaly appearance on upperparts.

HENSLOW'S SPARROW Greenish buff head and nape; blackish crown stripes; black-bordered ear patch; rusty brown upperparts edged whitish and streaked black; dark brown streaking on breast, sides, and flanks • juvenile is paler and more washed with buffy head, nape, upperparts, and underparts; faint dusky streaking on sides • eastern range.

• **BREEDING** Monogamous Loose colonies.

• **NESTING** Incubation 11–12 days by female. Young altricial; brooded by female; stay in nest 9 days, fed by both sexes. 2–3 broods per year.

• **POPULATION** Common in cultivated fields, grasslands, prairies, savanna, and palmetto scrub. Declining in eastern part of its range.

• **CONSERVATION** Neotropical migrant. Uncommon host to cowbird parasitism. Declining due to changes in grasses grown and losses to agricultural operations. Threatened or endangered in Florida and parts of the Appalachian Mountains.

Flight Pattern
Flies close to the ground with a fluttering rapid undulating flight, similar to a wren.

Nest Identification	Dried grass with lining of rootlets, hair, and grass, partially domed on one side • in slight hollow on ground, sheltered by tall grasses • built by female • 3–6 creamy white eggs with flecks and dots of reddish brown, occasionally wreathed; ovate, 2.0 x 1.4 cm.
Shape ◖ Location ▬	

Plumage Sexes similar	Habitat	Migration Migratory	Weight 23 g

DATE _____ TIME_____ LOCATION _____

Family EMBERIZIDAE	Species *Ammodramus bairdii*	Length 14 cm	Wingspan 22 cm

BAIRD'S SPARROW

On nesting grounds males establish territories by perching on a tussock or shrub and singing. In the 1870s this bird was one of the most abundant in the prairies of its region, but remnant populations now cling to the habitat remains. When frightened it scurries mouselike through the grass and hides. The best field marks on this elusive sparrow are the broad buff-ocher central crown stripe and the necklace of brownish black streaks across the chest.

short spiky tail with pale edges

dark spot at each rear corner of auriculars

flat ocherous crown with black stripes and wide ocher center stripe

large bill

black mustache

buffy brown, rufous, and black upperparts

buffy wash on streaked sides and flanks

band of fine black streaks on breast

Underparts are white. Juveniles are more washed out and paler with less streaking on the underparts.

- **SONG** Silvery tinkling bell-like 2–3 notes, then lone warbled note, then trilling *zip-zip-zip-zr-r-rrrrrrrr*. Call is abrasive *chip*.
- **BEHAVIOR** Solitary or in pairs. Difficult to observe unless singing. Flushed birds fly up and drop, running to hide. Forages on ground. Eats seeds, insects, and spiders.
- **BREEDING** Monogamous. Loose colonies.
- **NESTING** Incubation 11–12 days by female. Young altricial; brooded by female; stay in nest 8–10 days, fed by both sexes. 1 brood per year.
- **POPULATION** Uncommon and local on short-grass prairie and grasslands. Declining. Accidental on both coasts.
- **CONSERVATION** Neotropical migrant. Vulnerable to loss of prairie habitat.

Similar Birds

GRASSHOPPER SPARROW Plain buff face and chest; pale narrow central crown stripe; dark postocular stripe; auriculars outlined above and on rear with dark border • juvenile has buffy wash on streaked breast and sides.

SAVANNAH SPARROW More extensive streaking on underparts; large central "stickpin" on chest (typically); conspicuous white to yellow narrow crown stripe; yellowish to white supercilium.

Flight Pattern
Short flights low over grasses with rapid wing beats alternating with brief periods of wings pulled to sides.

Nest Identification	
Shape Location ▬ ✱✱✱	Dried grass and forbs, with lining of mammal hair and soft grass • in slight depression, set in tall grasses or near bush • built by female • 3–6 white to grayish white eggs, with lilac and reddish brown markings; oval, 2.0 cm long.

Plumage Sexes similar	Habitat ▬ ●	Migration Migratory	Weight 23 g

Family EMBERIZIDAE	Species *Ammodramus henslowii*	Length 12–13 cm	Wingspan 18–20 cm

HENSLOW'S SPARROW

Upon arrival at the nesting grounds, the male begins singing day or night, rain or shine, perched or concealed. He cocks his tail down, elevates his head, and expels with a bodily shudder one of the shortest songs of any songbird. Occasionally, these sparrows battle one another in defense of territory. Their plumage serves as camouflage in the marshes and meadows. Juveniles resemble adults but are buffier and paler and have only faint streaking on their underparts.

flat greenish ocherous head with black stripes

green wash on neck and nape

large grayish bill

reddish back and wings with black streaking and white to buff edging

buff-green mustache, bordered black on both sides

conspicuous streaking on breast and sides

• **SONG** Sings *flee-LICK*, like an explosive bird hiccup, with emphasis on the second note. Call is a thin high *tsip*.

whitish underparts with buff wash on chest, sides, and flanks

short notched tail

JUVENILE

• **BEHAVIOR** Solitary or in pairs. Unobtrusive, secretive, and easily overlooked, except for the persistent song of the male, from low concealed or higher exposed perches. Singing males allow reasonably close approach. Forages and skulks on ground among vegetation. Eats insects, caterpillars, and seeds.

• **BREEDING** Monogamous. Loose colonies.

• **NESTING** Incubation 11 days by female. Young altricial; brooded by female; stay in nest 9–10 days, fed by both sexes. 2 broods per year.

• **POPULATION** Uncommon in weedy meadows, grassy fields (especially wet), and reclaimed strip mine benches in pine-grass savannas in the West. Declining, particularly in the Northeast.

Similar Birds

GRASSHOPPER SPARROW Brown to buffy head; pale central crown stripe; dark postocular stripe; buffy wash on white underparts, particularly on chest, sides, flanks, and crissum; lacks streaking on underparts.

• **CONSERVATION** Listed as endangered in Canada. Vulnerable to habitat loss due to grazing, agricultural mowing operations, land clearing, and development. Uncommon host to cowbird parasitism.

Flight Pattern

Weak fluttering flight with jerking of tail, low over vegetation. Alternates rapid series of wing beats with brief periods of wings pulled to sides.

Nest Identification

Shape   Location ▬ ⚫⚫⚫

Grass and forbs, with lining of fine grass and hair • on ground in slight hollow or sheltered by grassy clump or weeds • built by female • 3–5 creamy or pale greenish white eggs, marked with reddish browns, often wreathed; oval, 1.8 x 1.4 cm.

Plumage Sexes similar	Habitat ▬ ⚫	Migration Migratory	Weight 14 g

DATE _____ TIME_____ LOCATION _____

Family EMBERIZIDAE	Species *Ammodramus leconteii*	Length 11–13 cm	Wingspan 17–18 cm

LE CONTE'S SPARROW

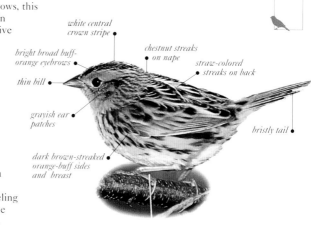

white central crown stripe

bright broad buff-orange eyebrows

thin bill

grayish ear patches

dark brown-streaked orange-buff sides and breast

chestnut streaks on nape

straw-colored streaks on back

bristly tail

One of the smallest sparrows, this bird is most often found in prairie wetlands. A secretive bird, Le Conte's Sparrow often scurries mouselike in thick cover when flushed, rarely flying, and only a meter or so at a time when it does. The species has declined in some parts of its range with the disappearance of damp fields and other similar habitats. This sparrow is a casual migrant in the Northeast and West, traveling only short distances off the main migration pathways. Juveniles are buffier overall and are heavily streaked on their underparts.

• **SONG** Call resembles a short shrill grasshopper-like *buzz*. High-pitched and thin, it has a short squeaky introductory note followed by a buzzy trill and ending with a final *chip* note. Call note is a thin *tsip*.

• **BEHAVIOR** Solitary or in pairs. Secretive. Skulking. Walks and runs on ground to forage within matted vegetation, often in wet grasslands and bogs. In winter months, combs ground for seeds from grass and weeds. During summer, eats wide variety of insects, seeds, and spiders. Territorial male sings from exposed perch, with head pulled back and bill pointed skyward.

• **BREEDING** Monogamous. Solitary.

• **NESTING** Incubation 12–13 days by female. Young altricial; brooded by female; stay in nest estimated 8–10 days, fed by both sexes. 1–2 broods per year.

• **POPULATION** Fairly common and somewhat local in wet meadows, bog, and marsh edges. Declining in parts of range.

• **CONSERVATION** Uncommon host to cowbird parasitism. Vulnerable to loss of habitat due to draining of wetlands and development of habitat for agriculture.

Similar Birds

NELSON'S SHARP-TAILED SPARROW
Broad blue-gray crown stripe; unstreaked blue-gray nape; less color contrast on upperparts; olive-brown body with whitish streaks; frequents marsh habitat.

GRASSHOPPER SPARROW
Whitish to buff eyebrows; brown, black, and buff nape; brown auricular patch with dark borders; whitish underparts with buffy wash on chest and sides; lacks streaks on breast and sides.

Flight Pattern

Alternates of rapid wing beats with brief periods of wings pulled to sides; flies short distances before dropping back into grass.

Nest Identification

Shape ◣   Location ▬ ⁘

Grass, rushes, and stems, lined with fine materials • usually on or near ground • built by female • 3–5 grayish white eggs with brown spots; ovate. 1.8 x 1.3 cm.

Plumage Sexes similar	Habitat ▲ ≋	Migration Migratory	Weight 14 g

DATE _____ TIME_____ LOCATION _____

Family EMBERIZIDAE	Species *Ammodramus nelsoni*	Length 12 cm	Wingspan 18 cm

NELSON'S SHARP-TAILED SPARROW

Its streaked plumage serves as camouflage in the dense freshwater marsh grasses it inhabits in Canada, the northern prairie marshes of the US, and parts of Maine. When frightened, it scampers mouselike, with its head held low, and does not fly. It recently was determined to be a separate species from the Saltmarsh Sharp-tailed Sparrow; both were formerly lumped together under the name Sharp-tailed Sparrow. Adults show whitish or gray streaking on scapulars. Juveniles have buffier underparts and buffy heads without the gray auriculars and nape and lack streaking on the breast and flanks.

gray median crown stripe

plain gray nape and ear patch

buff to light brownish upperparts with blackish streaking

ocherous orange on face

gray to dark-brown streaked ocherous buff breast, sides, and flanks

white belly

JUVENILE

- **SONG** An explosive wheezy descending *p-tssssshh-uk*, like the sound of cold water tossed on hot metal.

- **BEHAVIOR** In pairs or small groups. Secretive. Difficult to observe unless male is singing, which it does from conspicuous perches. Curious, and will come up in vegetation and draw closer to pishing and squeaking by birders. Walks around on ground and picks up food or gleans from vegetation. Eats insects, their caterpillars, various seeds, and small snails. Males loosely territorial or nonterritorial. Flushed birds usually fly short distance before dropping back down into dense cover.

- **BREEDING** Polygamous. Loose colonies.

- **NESTING** Incubation 11 days by female. Young altricial; brooded by female; stay in nest 10 days, fed mostly by female. 1 brood per year.

- **POPULATION** Fairly common in wet meadows, freshwater marshes, and tule beds. Numbers decline with habitat drainage.

Similar Birds

LE CONTE'S SPARROW Bold dark brown stripes on sides; white median crown stripe; gray nape with chestnut streaking; straw-colored streaking on back and scapulars; lives in prairies
- juveniles have heavily streaked underparts.

SALTMARSH SHARP-TAILED SPARROW Larger orange-buff facial triangle contrasts sharply with body; larger bill; black-streaked supercilium behind eye
- juveniles have heavily streaked underparts
- eastern range.

- **CONSERVATION** Rare host to cowbird parasitism. Vulnerable to loss of habitat due to marsh draining and agricultural practices, including cattle grazing.

Flight Pattern

Short flights low over vegetation, with rapid wing beats alternating with brief periods of wings pulled to sides; repeated.

Nest Identification

Shape ◗   Location ▬ ⩜ ⁂

Dried grasses and stems • atop grassy tussock or on pile of reeds • built by female • 3–7 light green eggs, with heavy brown spotting; oval, 1.9 x 1.4 cm.

Plumage Sexes similar	Habitat	Migration Migratory	Weight Undetermined

DATE _____ TIME_____ LOCATION _____

Family EMBERIZIDAE	Species *Passerella iliaca*	Length 17–19 cm	Wingspan 27–30 cm

FOX SPARROW

Named for its rufous coloring, particularly on the rump and tail, the Fox Sparrow is one of the largest of all sparrows. There is much variation in size and coloration over the wide breeding range. The most richly plumaged birds breed in the boreal forests from Alaska to Newfoundland and are the forms seen in winter in the southeastern US, such as the *P. i. zaboria* pictured here. In the western mountain races, birds have gray heads and backs, while northwestern Pacific coastal races are sooty brown with dark brown rumps and tails. While mostly solitary, this sparrow sometimes is observed associating with other sparrows. Migrates in late March and early November, generally traveling at night.

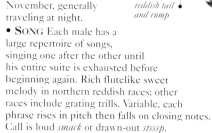

stout conical bill with darker upper mandible

grayish nape and upper back

reddish wings

large rufous to brown spot on central breast

reddish tail and rump

underparts heavily marked with triangular spots

• **SONG** Each male has a large repertoire of songs, singing one after the other until his entire suite is exhausted before beginning again. Rich flutelike sweet melody in northern reddish races; other races include grating trills. Variable, each phrase rises in pitch then falls on closing notes. Call is loud *smack* or drawn-out *stsssp*.

• **BEHAVIOR** Solitary or in pairs in breeding season. Small flocks in migration and on wintering grounds. Forages by double-scratching, towheelike, on ground and digging small holes by kicking backward with claws. Eats weed seeds, wild fruits and berries, insects, spiders, millipedes, and small snails.

• **BREEDING** Monogamous. Solitary.

• **NESTING** Incubation 12–14 days by female. Young altricial; brooded by female; stay in nest 9–11 days, fed by both sexes. 2 broods per year.

• **POPULATION** Uncommon to common in deciduous or conifer forest, undergrowth, chaparral, montane thicket, and riparian woodland. Declining in East.

• **FEEDERS** Birdseed and breadcrumbs attract it to ground underneath feeders.

• **CONSERVATION** Rare cowbird host. Vulnerable to habitat loss due to logging operations and development.

Similar Birds

HERMIT THRUSH Reddish tail; lacks streaking on brownish back; brown to gray-brown upperparts; whitish gray underparts; thin bicolored bill with dark tip and creamy pinkish yellow base; spotted breast, sides, and flanks.

Flight Pattern

Short flights on rapidly beating wings alternating with brief periods of wings pulled to sides.

Nest Identification	
Shape ⬛ Location ▬ 🌿 🌿 🌿	Lichen, roots, bark, leaves, twigs, grass, feathers, and animal fur • lined with grass and moss • on ground or in shrub, rarely on branch of tree • 0–1 m above ground (rarely up to 6 m) • built by female • 2–5 pale green to greenish white eggs, with reddish brown markings; oval, 2.3 cm long.

Plumage Sexes similar	Habitat 🐦 🌾 ⛰ 🌲 🌳	Migration Migratory	Weight 31 g

DATE _____ TIME_____ LOCATION _____

Family EMBERIZIDAE	Species *Melospiza melodia*	Length 15–19 cm	Wingspan 21–32 cm

SONG SPARROW

Even with its drab plumage, this bold songbird is so easy to spot when it perches in the open, trilling its pleasant melody. In flight it pumps its tail up and down. Inhabiting a wide range, this bird is found throughout most of North America and is perhaps the continent's most variable species, with approximately thirty-one subspecies recognized. The Aleutian race, *M. m. maxima*, is so large and dark it looks like a different species. Because of the work of Ohio bird biologist Margaret Morse Nice, the biology of this bird may be the best-known of any songbird on the continent. Juveniles are similar to adults but appear buffier overall with finer streaking.

dark malar stripe borders white throat

broad grayish eyebrow

brownish, grayish, or brownish gray upperparts, usually streaked

streaking on sides and breast meet in center and form "stickpin"

whitish underparts

pinkish legs and feet

long rounded tail

ALEUTIAN RACE

- **SONG** Whistles 2–3 clear introductory notes, followed by a trill. Much variation in each individual's song and between individuals. Call is *chimp* or *what* and a high thin *ssst*.

- **BEHAVIOR** Solitary or in pairs. May be in small loose flocks in winter, often with other species of sparrows. Forages in trees, bushes, and on ground by picking food off foliage, grass, and soil; also scratches on ground. Eats insects, larvae, grains, seeds, berries, and some fruits. Coastal species take small mollusks and crustaceans. Males sing from exposed perches to claim territory.

- **BREEDING** Monogamous. Polygynous in some cases. Male vigorously defends territory and battles with other males. Often chases invading birds from territory.

- **NESTING** Incubation 12–14 days by female. Young altricial; brooded by female; stay in nest 9–16 days, fed by both sexes. 2–3 broods per year (occasionally 4 in southern parts of range).

- **POPULATION** Widespread and abundant to common in brushy areas, thickets, riparian scrub, weedy fields, urban/suburban lawns, and forest edge.

- **FEEDERS** Birdseed.

- **CONSERVATION** Species is one of the most frequent victims of parasitism by the Brown-headed Cowbird.

Similar Birds

SAVANNAH SPARROW
Yellowish above eye; shorter notched tail; pinker legs; finer streaking on upperparts; central "stickpin" on chest.

LINCOLN'S SPARROW
Smaller; buff wash on chest; more distinct markings; finer streaking on throat, breast, sides, and flanks; lacks central "stickpin" on chest.

Flight Pattern

Short flights close to ground, tail pumping up and down. Alternates rapid wing beats with brief periods of wings pulled to sides.

Nest Identification

Shape — Location

Grass, forbs, leaves, and bark strips, with lining of fine materials • usually on ground, sheltered by grassy tussock or reeds • sometimes in bush or tree, 60 cm–1 m above ground (but up to 3.5 m) • built by female • 2–6 greenish white eggs, marked with reddish browns; oval to short oval, 2.0 x 1.5 cm.

Plumage Sexes similar	Habitat	Migration Northern birds migrate	Weight 20 g

DATE _____ TIME_____ LOCATION _____

Family EMBERIZIDAE	Species *Melospiza lincolnii*	Length 13–15 cm	Wingspan 18–22 cm

LINCOLN'S SPARROW

This inhabitant of northern bogs and mountain meadowlands is skittish, often raising its slight crest when disturbed. It is sometimes overlooked because of its furtive habits and similarity to the Song Sparrow, with which it may compete when nesting territories overlap. This sparrow can be distinguished by its sweet gurgling melody that sounds similar to that of a House Wren or Purple Finch, and by the buffy band crossing the chest and separating the white chin and throat from the white lower breast and belly. Juveniles are paler and buffier overall with more streaking on their underparts.

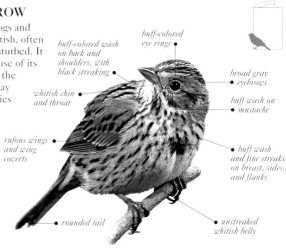

buff-colored wash on back and shoulders, with black streaking

buff-colored eye rings

broad gray eyebrows

buff wash on mustache

whitish chin and throat

rufous wings and wing coverts

buff wash and fine streaks on breast, sides, and flanks

rounded tail

unstreaked whitish belly

• **SONG** Features rapid bubbling trilled notes, with last notes harsher, louder, and lower in pitch, *chur-chur-chur-wee-wee-wee-wee-wah.* Alarm call is a flat-toned repetitious *tschup.* Calls also include a sharp buzzlike *zeee.*

• **BEHAVIOR** Solitary or in pairs. Sometimes joins mixed-species foraging flocks on wintering grounds. Secretive. Skulks low in thickets or on ground. Kicks backward with both feet like a towhee as it scratches among leaves on the ground; feeds on insects and small grains, as well as seeds from weeds and grasses. In migration, often found in brushy tangles near water. Often sings from a concealed perch during spring migration.

• **BREEDING** Monogamous. Solitary.

• **NESTING** Incubation 12–14 days by female. Young altricial; brooded by female; stay in nest 9–12 days, fed by both sexes. 1–2 broods per year.

• **POPULATION** Uncommon to fairly common in bogs, wet meadows, riparian thickets, and mountain meadows. Uncommon to fairly common in thickets and weedy fields in winter.

• **FEEDERS** Attracted by seed, particularly in migration.

• **CONSERVATION** Neotropical migrant. Rare host to cowbird parasitism. Vulnerable to loss of habitat because of logging operations and development.

Similar Birds

SONG SPARROW
Longer tail; thicker bill; thicker malar stripe; heavier streaking on underparts; central "stickpin" on chest; white underparts lack buffy wash on chest; brown upperparts with rufous and black streaking.

SWAMP SPARROW
Duller breast with thinner blurry streaks; gray head; rufous-brown crown with gray central stripe; unstreaked white throat; rufous wings and primary coverts.

Flight Pattern

Short flights with rapid wing beats alternating with brief periods of wings pulled to sides; repeated.

Nest Identification

Shape ◖   Location ⋯ ▬

Grass or sedge lined, sometimes with hair • often built in grass, hollow depressions, or moss • built by female • 3–6 pale green to greenish white eggs, with reddish brown markings; oval to short oval, 2.0 x 1.5 cm.

Plumage Sexes similar	Habitat ▲ ▲ ⬥ ⩲	Migration Migratory	Weight 23 g

Family EMBERIZIDAE	Species *Melospiza georgiana*	Length 12–15 cm	Wingspan 19–20 cm

SWAMP SPARROW

reddish crown

deep rufous upperparts with black streaking

deep rufous wings

gray face

whitish throat

gray breast

whitish belly

This small stocky sparrow will nest anywhere within its range where there is sufficient emergent dense vegetation in marshes, bogs, wet meadows, or sluggish streams. As nestlings learn to fly, they must stay above the water, so as not to be eaten by turtles, frogs, or fish. Adult females are similar to males but have brown-striped crowns. Juveniles are buffy with reddish wings and tails and heavily streaked underparts. Immatures resemble winter adults with rich buff sides, gray central crown stripe, and buffy wash overall.

JUVENILE   WINTER PLUMAGE

- **SONG** A bold slow melodious musical trill of either sharp single-note or slurred double-note phrases, *peat-peat-peat-peat-peat-peat-peat*. Has a call of *zeee* or *chip*.
- **BEHAVIOR** Solitary or in pairs in breeding season. May form loose flocks in winter. Secretive and skulking in dense vegetation or on ground. Curious, it will come to pishing or squeaking by birders. Forages by wading in water and picking up food with bill or by gleaning prey from vegetation or ground. Eats insects and seeds. Male sings to claim territory.
- **BREEDING** Monogamous. Loose colonies. Male often feeds incubating or brooding female while on nest.
- **NESTING** Incubation 12–15 days by female. Young altricial; brooded by female; stay in nest 11–13 days, fed by both sexes. 2 broods per year.
- **POPULATION** Common in marshes, bogs, and riparian stands of reeds, cattails, and sedges. Rare in the West. Some population declines due to loss of marsh habitat.
- **CONSERVATION** Neotropical migrant. Common host to cowbird parasitism. Vulnerable to habitat loss due to draining of wetlands, livestock overgrazing, and development.

Similar Birds

WHITE-THROATED SPARROW Stockier; larger; yellow supraloral spot; whitish or buff supercilium; two whitish wing bars; gray underparts; white-and-black- or brown-and-tan-striped crown.

LINCOLN'S SPARROW Buffy back and shoulders with black streaking; buffy breast band, sides, and flanks; black streaking on throat, breast, sides, and flanks; broad gray supercilium; brown crown with black streaks; buffy eye ring.

Flight Pattern
Short flights low over vegetation on rapidly beating wings alternating with brief periods of wings pulled to sides.

Nest Identification	
Shape Location 🌿🐚	Dry thick grasses with lining of finer grasses • set in reeds, usually 0–1.5 m above water • in some areas, in bush near water, 30 cm–2 m above ground • built by female • 3–6 greenish white eggs, marked with reddish browns; short subelliptical, 2.0 x 1.4 cm.

Plumage Sexes differ	Habitat 〰️ ▬▬	Migration Migratory	Weight 23 g

DATE _____ TIME_____ LOCATION _____

Family EMBERIZIDAE	Species *Zonotrichia albicollis*	Length 16–19 cm	Wingspan 22–25 cm

WHITE-THROATED SPARROW

The song of the White-throated Sparrow is heard in the Canadian wilderness and in the northeastern US where it breeds in woodland undergrowth, clearings, and gardens. Distinguishing marks include a broad yellow eyebrow, or supraloral stripe in the front of the eye, which tapers to either white or tan, and a sharply outlined white throat. Although it is common and widespread, sightings of this bird are rare in the West.

black or brown borders crown stripes and eye line

rusty brown upperparts

yellow supraloral stripe

dark bill

white throat

2 white wing bars

grayish underparts with diffuse streaking

• **SONG** A thin whistle, starting with 2 single notes followed by 3 triple notes: *poor-sam-peabody, peabody, peabody* or *pure-sweet-Canada, Canada, Canada.* Calls include a grating *pink* and a drawled lisping *tseep.* Territorial birds often sing at night. Some black-and-white-striped females sing.

JUVENILE

TAN-STRIPED

• **BEHAVIOR** Solitary or in pairs. In winter joins flocks of other White-throats and mixed species. Hops on ground or forages in shrubs and trees. Scratches among leaves for food. Eats mostly weed seeds, fruit from trees, tree buds, and insects. May hawk insects in midair. Attracted by pishing and squeaking by birders. Two adult color morphs are based on head striping: black-and-white-striped and brown-and-tan-striped. Field studies show that white-striped males tend to mate with tan-striped females, and tan-striped males tend to mate with white-striped females.

• **BREEDING** Monogamous. Solitary.

• **NESTING** Incubation 11–14 days by female. Young altricial; brooded by female; stay in nest 7–12 days, fed by both sexes. 1–2 broods per year.

• **POPULATION** Common and widespread in conifer and mixed-conifer forest, forest edge and clearings, and thickets. Rare in the West.

• **FEEDERS** Seeds and grains.

• **CONSERVATION** Uncommon host to cowbird parasitism. Vulnerable to habitat loss due to logging operations.

Similar Birds

WHITE-CROWNED SPARROW Black-and-white-striped crown; pink bill; lacks whitish throat contrasting with gray breast; lacks yellow supraloral spot; tertials lack bright rufous coloring.

HARRIS'S SPARROW Winter adult and juvenile • slightly larger; pink bill; crown varies from tan with black stippling, to black with white spotting, to black; face buffy tan; chin varies from white to blackish; throat white, black-and-white, or black; blackish band crossing upper breast.

Flight Pattern

Relatively short flights with rapid wing beats alternating with brief periods of wings pulled to sides; repeated.

Nest Identification	Lined with coarse grass, wood chips, twigs, pine needles, roots, and other fine materials • often found at edge of clearing • 0–90 cm above ground • built by female • 3–6 greenish, bluish, or cream-white eggs with reddish brown markings; subelliptical or long elliptical, 2.0 x 1.5 cm.
Shape ◥ Location 🐦 ▬	

Plumage Sexes similar	Habitat 🌳 🌿 🪨 🌳	Migration Migratory	Weight 26 g

Family EMBERIZIDAE	Species *Zonotrichia querula*	Length 17–20 cm	Wingspan 26–30 cm

HARRIS'S SPARROW

This large sparrow is named after Edward Harris, one of John James Audubon's expedition partners. Where it nested was one of the great ornithological mysteries of the early 20th century. The nest was seen and documented in 1931, making this the last songbird to have its nesting information recorded. In winter, breeding plumage is replaced by a buffy face, all or mostly black crown, black chin, and throat that varies from all black to having a white band through it. The amount of black on the winter bird is under hormonal control and signals social dominance; the more black the higher its rank in the pecking order of the flock. Juveniles are similar to winter adults but show less black on the crown and upper breast and have a white throat bordered by a black malar mark.

black crown, face, and bib
black auricular spot
brown back and sides, streaked blackish brown
2 buffy to white wing bars
pink-orange bill
pale gray cheeks and nape
white underparts

- **SONG** Repeated clear tremulous whistles in 1 pitch, followed at an interval by several clear notes in another pitch. Calls sound like a loud metallic *spink* and a drawn-out *tseep*.
- **BEHAVIOR** Solitary or in pairs. Shows faithfulness to wintering territories. Forages on ground by kicking and scratching among leaf litter and dry weed stalks. Bulk of diet is wild fruits, grains, and seeds from grass and weeds; also eats insects, spiders, and snails. Breeds among stunted trees and shrubs in taiga-tundra ecotone.
- **BREEDING** Monogamous. Solitary.
- **NESTING** Incubation 12–15 days by female. Altricial young brooded by female; stay in nest estimated 7–12 days, fed by both sexes. 1 brood per year.
- **POPULATION** Common to fairly common on restricted breeding and wintering grounds. Rare to casual in winter elsewhere.
- **FEEDERS** Grains, mixed birdseed, suet, breadcrumbs.

JUVENILE

WINTER PLUMAGE

Similar Birds

WHITE-CROWNED SPARROW Black-and-white-striped crown; pink bill; mostly gray underparts; brown upperparts with blackish brown streaks on back and shoulders; 2 white wing bars; brown rump • juvenile similar to adult but with gray-and-brown-striped head.

WHITE-THROATED SPARROW Distinctly outlined white throat; dark bill; black-and-white- or brown-and-tan-striped crown; broad eyebrow yellow in front of eye, remainder is white or tan; 2 white wing bars.

Flight Pattern

Series of rapid wing beats alternating with brief periods of wings pulled to sides; repeated.

Nest Identification

Shape ⌒   Location ▬

Lined with grass and coarse roots • in depression on ground under stunted woody vegetation or moss hummock • built by female • 3–5 white to greenish white eggs with brown markings; ovate to elliptical ovate, 2.3 x 1.8 cm.

Plumage Sexes similar	Habitat 🐾 ▲ ⌂	Migration Migratory	Weight 40 g

DATE _____ TIME_____ LOCATION _____

Family EMBERIZIDAE	Species *Zonotrichia leucophrys*	Length 17–19 cm	Wingspan 23–26 cm

WHITE-CROWNED SPARROW

This bold bird is easy to identify, with conspicuous black stripes on its white crown, a pink to dull yellow bill, and a pale gray throat. Like many sparrows, the male sings to claim its territory and duels to defend its ground. His songs may even continue into the night. As is usual with a wide geographical range, there is morphological and behavioral variation. The most striking subspecies differences include bill color and white versus black supraloras. Juveniles have heavily streaked underparts and a brown-and-buff-streaked head. Immatures have a brown-and-tan-striped head and unstreaked underparts.

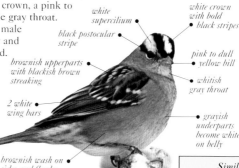

white supercilium

black postocular stripe

brownish upperparts with blackish brown streaking

2 white wing bars

brownish wash on sides and flanks

white crown with bold black stripes

pink to dull yellow bill

whitish gray throat

grayish underparts become white on belly

JUVENILE

FIRST WINTER

- **SONG** A melancholy whistled *poor-wet-wetter-chee-zee*. Has call note of *pink* or sharp *tseek*.

- **BEHAVIOR** Solitary or in pairs. In small family groups after breeding season. Forms flocks in winter. Males sing from exposed perches; sometimes in spring on wintering grounds. Gleans food from vegetation; hops on ground and forages by scratching. Eats seeds, insects, caterpillars, and parts of plants.

- **BREEDING** Monogamous. Individuals in some nonmigratory populations may pair for life. Some polygynous.

- **NESTING** Incubation 11–14 days by female. Young altricial; brooded by female; stay in nest 7–12 days, fed by both sexes. Male continues to feed young while female starts another nest. 2–4 broods per year (largest number of broods in southern populations; 1 brood in far north).

- **POPULATION** Common to fairly common in woodlands, thickets, wet meadows, and chaparral.

Similar Birds

WHITE-THROATED SPARROW
More rufous-brown upperparts; mostly dark bill; well-defined white throat patch; yellow spot between eye and bill; gray underparts; two white wing bars; black-and-white- or brown-and-tan-striped cap.

HARRIS'S SPARROW
Winter adult and juvenile • slightly larger; pink bill; crown varies from tan with black stippling, to black with white spotting, to black; face buffy tan; chin varies from white to blackish; throat white, black-and-white, or black; blackish band crossing upper breast.

- **FEEDERS** Baby chick scratch and seeds.

- **CONSERVATION** Neotropical migrant. Uncommon host to cowbird parasitism. Vulnerable in the West to habitat loss because of land development and logging.

Flight Pattern

Short flights on rapidly beating wings alternating with brief periods of wings pulled to sides; repeated.

Nest Identification

Shape ◗   Location ━ ⋆⋆⋆ ⋏

Grass, sticks, rootlets, and forbs • lined with soft grasses, feathers, and hair • on clump of grass or moss, sheltered by bush, or in small tree • 0–1.5 m above ground (but up to 9 m) • built by female • 2–6 light blue or green eggs marked with reddish browns; ovate to short ovate or long ovate. 2.0 x 1.5 cm.

Plumage Sexes similar	Habitat 🌱 🏘 🌲 ⛰	Migration Northern birds migrate	Weight 28 g

DATE _____ TIME_____ LOCATION _____

Family EMBERIZIDAE	Species *Zonotrichia atricapilla*	Length 18 cm	Wingspan 25 cm

GOLDEN-CROWNED SPARROW

When miners worked along the Alaskan gold trails, this Pacific Coast sparrow was known as "Weary Willie" because of its song, which sounded to them like *I'm so weary*. The yellow patch on the dark-bordered crown is present all year. In the winter, it often flocks with its close cousin, the White-crowned Sparrow. Winter adults have browner faces, are paler and more washed-out overall, and show varying amounts of black on the crown. The juvenile has a yellow wash on its streaked crown, dark brown-streaked underparts, and is similar to the winter adult but has fainter yellow steaking on the forecrown.

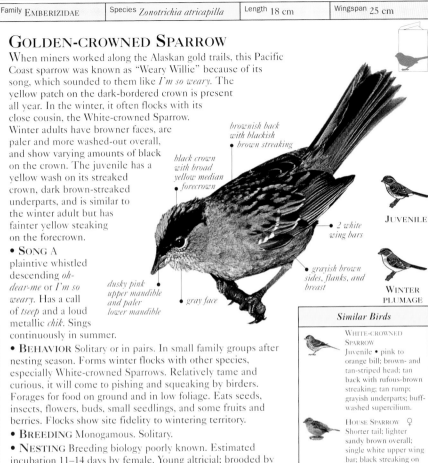

brownish back with blackish brown streaking

black crown with broad yellow median forecrown

2 white wing bars

JUVENILE

grayish brown sides, flanks, and breast

WINTER PLUMAGE

dusky pink upper mandible and paler lower mandible

gray face

- **SONG** A plaintive whistled descending *oh-dear-me* or *I'm so weary*. Has a call of *tseep* and a loud metallic *chik*. Sings continuously in summer.
- **BEHAVIOR** Solitary or in pairs. In small family groups after nesting season. Forms winter flocks with other species, especially White-crowned Sparrows. Relatively tame and curious, it will come to pishing and squeaking by birders. Forages for food on ground and in low foliage. Eats seeds, insects, flowers, buds, small seedlings, and some fruits and berries. Flocks show site fidelity to wintering territory.
- **BREEDING** Monogamous. Solitary.
- **NESTING** Breeding biology poorly known. Estimated incubation 11–14 days by female. Young altricial; brooded by female; stay in nest estimated 7–12 days, fed by both sexes. 1 brood per year.
- **POPULATION** Fairly common in montane thickets, boreal bogs, dwarf conifers, and brushy canyons. Winters in brushy thickets and woodland tangles. Casual in the East in winter.
- **FEEDERS** Will attend feeders for seeds.

Similar Birds

WHITE-CROWNED SPARROW
Juvenile • pink to orange bill; brown- and tan-striped head; tan back with rufous-brown streaking; tan rump; grayish underparts; buff-washed supercilium.

HOUSE SPARROW ♀
Shorter tail; lighter sandy brown overall; single white upper wing bar; black streaking on back; buffy eyebrow; no yellow crown patch.

Flight Pattern

Short flights with rapid wing beats alternating with brief periods of wings pulled to sides; repeated.

Nest Identification

Shape ◖ Location ▬ ▲🌳 🌿

Sticks, rootlets, moss, grass, leaves, and bark • lined with feathers, grass, and mammal hair • on ground, hidden in foliage and vines, sometimes on branch of small tree or bush • 0–90 cm above ground • built by female • 3–5 creamy or pale bluish white eggs, with brown splotches; subelliptical to long subelliptical, 2.3 x 1.8 cm.

Plumage Sexes similar	Habitat ▲ 🏠 ▲	Migration Migratory	Weight 31 g

DATE _____ TIME_____ LOCATION _____

Family EMBERIZIDAE	Species *Junco hyemalis*	Length 15–17 cm	Wingspan 23–25 cm

DARK-EYED JUNCO

In 1973 the American Ornithologists' Union grouped under one heading what was once considered five different junco species. Thus, the Dark-eyed Junco is composed of geographic races that differ in color and range but are closely related and have similar habits. All races of the species complex have white outer tail feathers; a black, gray, or brown hood; and white lower breast, belly, and undertail coverts. All have similar songs; all but one have a pink bill. Females tend to be paler and sometimes browner on the back. Juveniles have streaked upperparts and underparts.

gray upperparts

dark gray hood

SLATE-COLORED MALE

white outer tail feathers

SLATE-COLORED JUVENILE

• **SONG** Melodic trill, varied in pitch and tempo and from dry *chip* notes to tinkling bell-like sounds, similar to Chipping Sparrow. Call is abrasive *dit* produced with sucking smack. Twitters in flight.

brownish gray hood

brownish gray upperparts

SLATE-COLORED FEMALE

OREGON MALE

PINK-SIDED MALE

WHITE-WINGED MALE

GRAY-HEADED MALE

• **BEHAVIOR** Solitary or in pairs. In small family groups after breeding season. In spring and fall may join mixed-species foraging flocks; forms flocks in winter. Forages by gleaning from vegetation and scratching on ground. Hops. Eats seeds, grains, berries, insects, caterpillars, and some fruits; occasionally hawks flying insects. The larger males often winter farther north or at higher elevations than juveniles and females.

• **BREEDING** Monogamous. Solitary.

• **NESTING** Incubation 11–13 days by female. Altricial young brooded by female; leave nest at 9–13 days, fed by both sexes. 1–3 broods per year.

• **POPULATION** Common to fairly common in coniferous and mixed conifer-deciduous forests and bogs; winter habitats vary.

• **FEEDERS** Breadcrumbs, nuts, and seeds.

• **CONSERVATION** Uncommon cowbird host. Vulnerable to habitat loss due to logging operations.

Similar Birds

YELLOW-EYED JUNCO Yellow eyes; black lores; rufous-trimmed greater coverts and tertials; gray head and nape; gray throat and underparts paler than head; white belly
• limited southwest range.

Flight Pattern

Short flights with white outer tail feathers flashing conspicuously. Alternates several rapid wing beats with brief periods of wings pulled to sides.

Nest Identification	
Shape	Location	Grass, weeds, and leaves, with lining of fine grass, hair, and feathers • on ground, sometimes in cavity, sheltered by bush, tree roots, log, occasionally in shrub or tree, 0–6 m above ground • male gathers materials and female builds • 3–6 whitish to bluish white eggs, with markings of brown and gray, sometimes concentrated at larger end; oval to short or long oval, 2.0 x 1.4 cm.

Plumage Sexes differ	Habitat	Migration Northern birds migrate	Weight 20 g

DATE _____ TIME_____ LOCATION _____

Family EMBERIZIDAE	Species *Calcarius mccownii*	Length 15 cm	Wingspan 25 cm

McCown's Longspur

During years of heavy rainfall, this inhabitant of arid short-grass plains will desert its nesting grounds. A monogamous species, males and females are often together, walking side by side. Winter males are similar to breeding females but show deeper chestnut in the median coverts and more black in the breast band. Winter females are buffy with broad buffy eyebrows. Juveniles are paler with a scaly-backed look and streaked heads and underparts. All plumages show a white tail with a black inverted T-shaped pattern.

• **SONG** High-spirited warbling and twittering on breeding grounds. Call sounds like dry rattle or double-noted *churrip-churrip.*

• **BEHAVIOR** In pairs on breeding grounds. Forms large flocks in winter. Forages on ground and makes daily visits to water, including irrigation reservoirs, with other species. Eats weed seeds, variety of insects, and caterpillars. This species frequents drier prairies and stubble fields than other longspurs.

• **BREEDING** Monogamous. Solitary.

• **NESTING** Incubation 12 days by female. Altricial young brooded by both sexes; stay in nest 10–12 days, fed by both sexes; remain with parents 3 more weeks. 2 broods per year.

• **POPULATION** Fairly common locally. Stable with increase possible on dry short-grass prairies. Ranges have shrunk since 1800s. Casual to California coast and southern Oregon. Accidental to East Coast. Rare in interior California and Nevada.

• **CONSERVATION** Uncommon cowbird host. Vulnerable to habitat loss.

MALE
- black crown
- buff- and brown-streaked upperparts
- stout thick bill
- white face and throat
- black malar stripe
- black crescent on breast
- chestnut wing bar
- gray sides and nape
- white underparts

WINTER MALE

FEMALE
- white face with tan auriculars
- tawny upper wing bar
- buff-tipped feathers produce scalloped effect on brown breast
- white tail marked with dark inverted T shape

WINTER FEMALE

Similar Birds

CHESTNUT-COLLARED LONGSPUR White tail with black triangle • breeding male has black belly and chestnut collar • winter birds buffy overall; male with black mottling on breast and white spot on shoulder.

Flight Pattern

Series of rapid wing beats alternating with brief periods of wings pulled to sides; repeated.

Nest Identification

Shape ▐ Location ▬ ∗∗∗

Grass lined with occasional weeds, roots, and lichen • in scrape on ground • scratched out by both and built by female • 2–4 white to pale olive eggs, with brown and lavender markings; oval, elliptical, or pyriform; 2.0 x 1.5 cm.

Plumage Sexes differ	Habitat ▬▬	Migration Migratory	Weight 23 g

DATE _____ TIME_____ LOCATION _____

Family EMBERIZIDAE	Species *Calcarius lapponicus*	Length 15–18 cm	Wingspan 27–30 cm

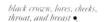

LAPLAND LONGSPUR

In winter this bird is commonly in the company of Horned Larks, Snow Buntings, and other longspurs on barren snow-swept fields throughout southern Canada and the north and central US, sometimes in large flocks. Resembling a House Sparrow, it is seen often. In all plumages the outer two tail feathers are partly white and partly black. Females are duller in color with rufous greater wing coverts and edging on the tertials, and a bold dark triangle outlines buff ear patches. Juveniles are similar to females but with heavy streaking on the head, back, and underparts.

black crown, lores, cheeks, throat, and breast

reddish brown nape

broad white stripe extends from eye to sides of breast

white underparts with black streaking on sides and flanks

MALE

• **SONG** Liquid warbling Bobolink-like song given in flight. Call is melodious *tee-lee-oo* or *tee-dle* or dry rattling *drit-ri-it.*

• **BEHAVIOR** In pairs or small family groups in summer. Forages on ground for insects and spiders; also eats seeds from grass and sedges; mostly weed seeds in winter. Migrates in flocks in late fall and early spring. Flocks number in the thousands on US wintering grounds. Courting tundra male may sing while chasing female on ground; gives skylarking flight song, rising from ground in front of female, singing above her, and gliding back down with tail and wings spread.

blackish brown crown

tan auriculars bordered blackish

broad white supercilium

chestnut nape with blackish streaking

WINTER MALE   **WINTER FEMALE**

FEMALE

Similar Birds

♂ SMITH'S LONGSPUR
Winter • rich buff nape and underparts; thin dusky streaking on underparts; white shoulder patch, often hidden; 2 white outer tail feathers tipped black on distal third of outer web; small thin bill; buffy supercilium.

♀

• **BREEDING** Monogamous. Solitary.

• **NESTING** Incubation 10–14 days by female. Young altricial; brooded by female; stay in nest 8–10 days, fed by both sexes. Fledglings are divided equally between the sexes; each tends its half of the brood. 1 brood per year.

• **POPULATION** Common to abundant on arctic tundra in summer; prairies, grassy fields, stubble fields, and dune areas along shorelines. Widespread.

Flight Pattern
Rapid wing beats alternating with brief periods of wings pulled to sides.

Nest Identification	
Shape 🦴 Location ▬	Fine grass and feathers • lined with grass and moss • in scrape or shallow depression • built by female • 4–7 greenish white to pale gray-green eggs, with brown and black markings; elliptical to oval, 2.0 x 1.5 cm.

Plumage Sexes differ	Habitat ___ 🌱 🌾	Migration Migratory	Weight 28 g

DATE _____ TIME_____ LOCATION _____

Family EMBERIZIDAE	Species *Calcarius pictus*	Length 15–17 cm	Wingspan 25–28 cm

SMITH'S LONGSPUR

This bird is most often observed during winter months, foraging in pastures and other open areas, including airports, in the Midwest and farther south. Winter flocks often do not closely associate with other foraging longspurs, pipits, or Horned Larks. Smith's Longspur is not wary and allows close approach, but if pushed to flight the birds fly up in a zigzag, giving clicking call notes. The white outer tail feathers bordering the black tail are conspicuous in flight.

- **SONG** Generally heard in spring migration and around breeding grounds. Series of rapid sweet melodious warbles ending in *wee-chew!*, like the ending of a Chestnut-sided Warbler's song. Call sounds like a dry tickling rattle.

- **BEHAVIOR** In pairs on breeding grounds in arctic tundra. In small flocks, pairs, or as individuals on wintering grounds. Somewhat secretive but tame and easily approached. On tundra, eats seeds, insects, and spiders. Feeds mostly on seeds in winter. Seldom seen by biologists or birders due to high arctic breeding range and inconspicuous flock size, so its biology is poorly known.

- **BREEDING** Monogamous. Solitary.

- **NESTING** Incubation 11–13 days by female. Young altricial; brooded by female; leave nest at 7–9 days, with flight 14 days later, fed by both sexes. 1 brood per year.

- **POPULATION** Generally uncommon, especially in migration and winter. Casual vagrant to the Atlantic Coast. Casual to California.

black-and-white head with white ear patch entirely bordered by black

buff-colored nape and underparts

thin bill

MALE

white shoulder patch

yellowish legs and feet

black tail bordered by 2 mostly white outermost tail feathers

brown-streaked tawny crown

broad buffy supercilium

thin brown malar mark

dusky auriculars bordered dark brown

buffy underparts with thin dark brown streaking

FEMALE

WINTER MALE

WINTER FEMALE

Similar Birds

LAPLAND LONGSPUR ♂ Winter plumage • white underparts; black legs and feet; thick pinkish bill with black tip; rufous greater coverts; outer 2 tail feathers black-and-white ♀ • winter male has scalloped blackish bib; streaked black crown.

Flight Pattern

Swift erratic zigzag flight when flushed, then undulating flight with series of rapid wing beats alternating with brief periods of wings pulled to sides.

Nest Identification

Shape   Location ▬

Lichen, animal hair, and feathers • lined with grass and sedge • on ground in shallow depression • built by female • 4–6 pale tan to pale green eggs, with lavender and dark brown markings, or grayish eggs, marked with dark brown and lavender; subelliptical to short subelliptical, 2.0 x 1.5 cm.

Plumage Sexes differ	Habitat ▬	Migration Migratory	Weight 28 g

DATE _____ TIME_____ LOCATION _____

Family EMBERIZIDAE	Species *Calcarius ornatus*	Length 15–17 cm	Wingspan 25–27 cm

CHESTNUT-COLLARED LONGSPUR

All the longspurs are named for the long claw on their hind toe. The male is conspicuous as it rises from the ground, circles and sings above its territory, then glides down on rapidly beating wings, hanging as if to land with wings extended above its back. Males may repeat this several times before landing. In flight the white tail with its black terminal triangle is distinctive.

- **SONG** Soft sweet tumbling warble, similar to song of Western Meadowlark, given only on breeding grounds. Call is nasal *kit-tal, kit-tal.*

- **BEHAVIOR** In pairs or small family groups in summer. Flocks can number more than 100 birds in winter, often including pipits and Horned Larks. Eats weed seeds and insects. Males may attack other birds and ground squirrels that approach the nest. Female has unique distraction display when intruders close to nest, fluttering 60–90 cm into air in aerial "jumps."

- **BREEDING** Monogamous. Solitary.

- **NESTING** Incubation 10–13 days by female. Young altricial; brooded by female; stay in nest 10 days, first flight at 9–14 days, fed by both sexes. 2 broods per year.

- **POPULATION** Fairly common in moist upland prairies; winters in grassy and stubble fields. In migration, casual east and west of range.

- **CONSERVATION** Uncommon host to cowbird parasitism. Vulnerable to habitat loss due to agriculture and development.

black-and-white head

buffy yellow face

chestnut collar

bold black breast and upper belly

upperparts streaked with black, buff, and brown

single white wing bar

very short primary projection

MALE

whitish lower belly and undertail coverts

white tail with blackish triangle

WINTER MALE

WINTER FEMALE

chestnut wash on nape

buff upperparts with brownish streaking

whitish buff underparts with faint streaking

FEMALE

Similar Birds

♂ MCCOWN'S LONGSPUR Gray hindneck; white face with black malar mark; black crescent on chest; white underparts; chestnut wing bar; white tail with inverted black T; larger heavy pink bill; longer primary projection • females and winter-plumaged birds have tail pattern of breeding male; white underparts without streaking; buffy wash on sides and flanks • winter male has mottled blackish chest.

♀

Flight Pattern
Swift flight on rapidly beating wings alternating with brief periods of wings pulled to sides.

Nest Identification	Grass • lined with finer grass and sometimes with feathers and hair • in hollow on ground, usually hidden in grasses • built by female • 4–5 whitish eggs, marked with brown, black, and purple, occasionally wreathed; oval, 2.0 x 1.5 cm.
Shape ⬛ Location ▬ ⚥	

Plumage Sexes differ	Habitat	Migration Migratory	Weight 20 g

DATE _____ TIME_____ LOCATION _____

Family EMBERIZIDAE	Species *Emberiza rustica*	Length 15 cm	Wingspan 23–24 cm

RUSTIC BUNTING

This bird is a native of Eurasia and visits the Aleutians and other islands in the Bering Sea regularly during migration. It is casual along the Pacific Coast to California. Females and winter males are similar to breeding males but have a chestnut rump, brown crown, brown cheeks, a pale spot at the end of the ear patch, and white underparts streaked with brown. Juveniles are similar to females but are duller overall and have darker brown streaking.

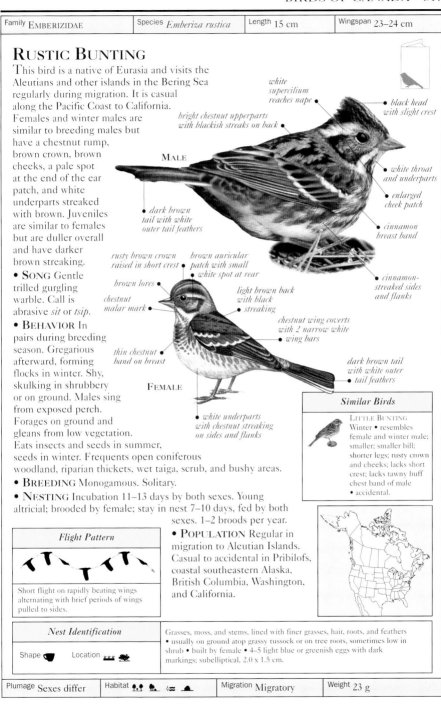

white supercilium reaches nape

black head with slight crest

bright chestnut upperparts with blackish streaks on back

MALE

white throat and underparts

enlarged cheek patch

dark brown tail with white outer tail feathers

cinnamon breast band

cinnamon-streaked sides and flanks

rusty brown crown raised in short crest

brown auricular patch with small white spot at rear

brown lores

light brown back with black streaking

chestnut malar mark

chestnut wing coverts with 2 narrow white wing bars

thin chestnut band on breast

FEMALE

dark brown tail with white outer tail feathers

white underparts with chestnut streaking on sides and flanks

- **SONG** Gentle trilled gurgling warble. Call is abrasive *sit* or *tsip*.
- **BEHAVIOR** In pairs during breeding season. Gregarious afterward, forming flocks in winter. Shy, skulking in shrubbery or on ground. Males sing from exposed perch. Forages on ground and gleans from low vegetation. Eats insects and seeds in summer, seeds in winter. Frequents open coniferous woodland, riparian thickets, wet taiga, scrub, and bushy areas.
- **BREEDING** Monogamous. Solitary.
- **NESTING** Incubation 11–13 days by both sexes. Young altricial; brooded by female; stay in nest 7–10 days, fed by both sexes. 1–2 broods per year.
- **POPULATION** Regular in migration to Aleutian Islands. Casual to accidental in Pribilofs, coastal southeastern Alaska, British Columbia, Washington, and California.

Similar Birds

LITTLE BUNTING
Winter • resembles female and winter male; smaller; smaller bill; shorter legs; rusty crown and cheeks; lacks short crest; lacks tawny buff chest band of male • accidental.

Flight Pattern

Short flight on rapidly beating wings alternating with brief periods of wings pulled to sides.

Nest Identification

Shape   Location

Grasses, moss, and stems, lined with finer grasses, hair, roots, and feathers • usually on ground atop grassy tussock or on tree roots, sometimes low in shrub • built by female • 4–5 light blue or greenish eggs with dark markings; subelliptical, 2.0 x 1.5 cm.

Plumage Sexes differ	Habitat	Migration Migratory	Weight 23 g

DATE _____ TIME_____ LOCATION _____

Family EMBERIZIDAE	Species *Plectrophenax nivalis*	Length 16–18 cm	Wingspan 30–33 cm

SNOW BUNTING

This bird can survive temperatures as low as fifty degrees Celsius below zero and often tunnels in the snow in the shelter of grass tussocks or shrubs to keep warm. When seen in flight from below, it often appears completely white, like a large snowflake. Males have a white rump. Nonbreeding females have a cinnamon rump and shoulders.

white head and shoulders

black bill

black back

MALE

long black-and-white wings

white underparts

black tail with white outer tail feathers

• **SONG** Series of bold repetitive high trilling musical notes. Sings only on breeding grounds, usually in fluttering display flight and from the ground. Call is whistling *teu*.

• **BEHAVIOR** In pairs on breeding grounds. Fledged young quickly form foraging flocks when independent of parental care. Gregarious after breeding, often roosting, traveling, and feeding in large flocks. Frequently bathes in snow. Forages on ground for seeds, insects, and caterpillars. Coastal birds also feed on small crustaceans and mollusks. Joins other open-landscape bird species in winter, including Lapland Longspurs and Horned Larks.

long black-and-white wings

gray-black upperparts tinged with brown

brownish streaking on white head

white underparts

FEMALE

JUVENILE

WINTER PLUMAGE

Similar Birds

McKAY'S BUNTING
Alaska range
• breeding male completely white except for fine black streaking on forecrown; black tips to central tail feathers; black distal half of primaries and tertials; heavy black bill
• breeding female is similar but shows black chevrons on shoulders; black spot on nape; more black on central tail feathers • winter plumage similar to breeding plumage but with cinnamon crown, washes of cinnamon on upperparts, and yellow-orange bill.

• **BREEDING** Monogamous. Pairs.

• **NESTING** Incubation 10–16 days by female. Young altricial; brooded by female; stay in nest 10–17 days, fed by both sexes. 1 brood per year; birds in the southern limits of range occasionally have 2 broods.

• **POPULATION** Fairly common in summer on arctic rocky shores, dry tundra, cliffs, and talus slopes; winters in stubble fields, grassy fields, and on coastal beaches and around sand dunes.

• **BIRDHOUSES** Will build nest in birdhouses.

Flight Pattern

Swift flight on rapidly beating wings alternating with brief periods of wings pulled to sides.

Nest Identification

Shape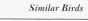

Location

Grass and moss with lining of grasses, mammal hair, and feathers • under grassy tussock or in crevice of rock or cliff; in nest boxes, buildings, empty oil barrels, and other artificial structures • built by female • 4–7 whitish to light blue-green eggs with brown and black markings; subelliptical. 2.3 x 1.8 cm.

Plumage Sexes differ	Habitat	Migration Migratory	Weight 43 g

DATE _____ TIME_____ LOCATION _____

| Family EMBERIZIDAE | Species *Plectrophenax hyperboreus* | Length 16–18 cm | Wingspan 30–33 cm |

McKay's Bunting

Said to be the whitest of all North American songbirds, this bird is closely related to the Snow Bunting, and some consider it to be part of the same species. It has a limited breeding range of only a few Bering Sea islands (Hall and St. Matthew and rarely on St. Paul in the Pribilofs or on St. Lawrence). It winters on the western and southeastern coasts of Alaska. Winter-plumaged birds have yellow-orange bills with black tips and cinnamon-washed crowns, napes, auriculars, and upperparts.

- **SONG** A loud trilled flutelike warbling, similar to the Snow Bunting's song. Call is abrasive *tew*.
- **BEHAVIOR** In pairs during breeding season. Gregarious at other times. Male performs courtship flights, skylarking in circles over female. Also sings from perches or from ground. Forages on ground. Eats seeds, spiders, flowers, leaflets, and insects. Breeds on shores of tundra pools, rocky ground, and beaches.
- **BREEDING** Monogamous and solitary.
- **NESTING** Incubation 10–16 days by female. Young altricial; brooded by female; stay in nest 10–17 days, fed by both sexes. 2 broods per year.
- **POPULATION** Uncommon to fairly common on breeding islands. Uncommon in winter in coastal Alaska. Accidental south along coast to Oregon.
- **BIRDHOUSES** Nest boxes.
- **CONSERVATION** Seriously threatened by native and introduced predators on its nesting islands.

bright white overall

black tertials

black distal half of primaries

black tips to central tail feathers

large black bill

black legs and feet

MALE

bill has blackish upper mandible and paler dusky lower mandible

fine black streaking on crown and nape

black chevron streaking on back and shoulders

black alula

primaries have white base

FEMALE

more extensive black in central tail feathers

WINTER MALE

WINTER FEMALE

Similar Birds

SNOW BUNTING Breeding adults have black or smoky gray back; more black on wings and tail • winter plumage shows more black on wings and tail; more black streaking on upperparts; more extensive cinnamon wash on underparts; cinnamon on crown, auriculars, nape, and back • basic-plumaged female also shows cinnamon rump.

Flight Pattern

Swift flight with series of rapid wing beats alternating with brief periods of wings pulled to sides.

Nest Identification

Shape

Location

Grass with lining of finer grasses • in rock crevice, building, nest box, or on ground under grass tussock or moss hummock • built by female • 3–5 pale green eggs with spots of pale brown; oval to subelliptical, 2.3 x 1.8 cm.

| Plumage Sexes differ | Habitat | Migration Migratory | Weight 54 g |

DATE _____ TIME_____ LOCATION _____

Family CARDINALIDAE	Species *Cardinalis cardinalis*	Length 19–23 cm	Wingspan 25–30 cm

NORTHERN CARDINAL

The official bird of seven US states sings a variety of cheerful melodies year-round. The male fights other birds to defend his territory and sometimes tries to attack his own reflection in windows, automobile mirrors, chrome, and hubcaps. Having adapted to suburban areas, these birds visit backyard feeders regularly and sometimes take food from the hand. Juveniles resemble the adult female but have a blackish instead of reddish bill.

black mask through eyes

cone-shaped reddish bill

black patch at base of bill extends onto throat

accentuated crest

red overall

MALE

• **SONG** Variable. Variety of gurgling and clear whistled melodies. More than 25 different songs. Best-known phrases include *whoit cheer, whoit cheer, cheer-cheer-cheer; cheer, whoit-whoit-whoit-whoit; wheat-wheat-wheat-wheat;* and *bir-dy, bir-dy, bir-dy, bir-dy.* Female in courtship duets with male after territory is established and prior to nesting. Call is abrasive metallic *chip* or *pik.*

red tip

dusky lores and patch at base of bill

buffy golden brown head and underparts

buffy olive upperparts

FEMALE

buff-brown underparts

JUVENILE

• **BEHAVIOR** Solitary or in pairs during breeding season. Gregarious at other times, forming flocks in winter or joining mixed-species foraging flocks. Forages in trees, bushes, and on ground. Eats insects, seeds, grains, fruits, and snails. Drinks sap from holes drilled by sapsuckers. Hops rather than walks on ground.

red wash on wings and tail

• **BREEDING** Monogamous. Solitary. Male feeds female during courtship and while incubating.

• **NESTING** Incubation 12–13 days, mostly by female. Young altricial; brooded by female; stay in nest 9–11 days, fed by both sexes. Male may continue to tend fledglings while female begins incubating new set of eggs. 2–4 broods per year.

• **POPULATION** Abundant and widespread in woodland edges, undergrowth, thickets, and residential areas. Range has expanded north in the last century, partly due to increase of feeding stations. Casual in West.

• **FEEDERS** Cracked corn, sunflower seeds, birdseed. Will bathe in birdbaths.

• **CONSERVATION** Common cowbird host, especially in the central portion of its range.

Similar Birds
PYRRHULOXIA ♀ Resembles female and juvenile Northern Cardinal; stubby sharply curved yellowish bill; red eye ring; red tip to long gray crest; grayish upperparts; red edging to primaries; reddish wash on throat and underparts.

Flight Pattern
Short flight just above vegetation or below canopy; rapidly beating wings alternate with brief periods of wings pulled to sides. |

Nest Identification	Twigs, weeds, grass, bark strips, and leaves • lined with hair and grass • in fork of low tree or bush or set in tangled twigs or vines • usually less than 1.5 m above ground (but up to 4.5 m) • built by female • 3–4 pale greenish, bluish, or grayish eggs with dots and flecks of gray, purple, and brown; oval, 2.5 x 1.8 cm.
Shape 🥄 Location 🌳 🌿 🏡	

Plumage Sexes differ	Habitat 🌳 🔺 🌿	Migration Nonmigratory	Weight 45 g

DATE _____ TIME_____ LOCATION _____

Family CARDINALIDAE	Species *Pheucticus ludovicianus*	Length 18–22 cm	Wingspan 30–33 cm

ROSE-BREASTED GROSBEAK

This bird's clear notes are delivered in robinlike phrases, but the song is sweet. Males sing constantly, even while sparring to win a female. In flight the male shows rosy red wing linings, a white rump, and black-tipped white uppertail coverts; females flash yellow wing linings. First fall males have less streaking on underparts than females, buffy wash across the breast, and rose-red wing linings. First spring males are similar to adult males but with brown edges to the black plumage.

black head and back

white or buff-colored bill

white shoulder patch

white wing patch

black throat

white underparts with rosy red triangular patch on breast

- **SONG** Rich warbled melodious phrases interspersed with call notes. Squeaky abrasive call, *eek*.
- **BEHAVIOR** Solitary or in pairs in breeding season. Flocks in migration and winter. Forages in trees, shrubs, and on ground. Eats seeds, insects, caterpillars, tree flowers, fruits, and berries. Hover gleans high in trees at branch tips; females more often than males.

black tail with white inner webs to outer tail feathers

JUVENILE MALE

MALE

white eyebrow

brownish upperparts with dark streaking

2 broad white wing bars

white mustache and throat

FEMALE

whitish to buff underparts with brownish streaking

FIRST SPRING MALE

Similar Birds

BLACK-HEADED GROSBEAK ♀ Buff to white supercilium; pale cinnamon chest with fine streaking on sides and flanks; upperparts have buffy mottling and streaking; lemon-yellow underwing coverts.

- **BREEDING** Monogamous. Solitary. Male and female rub bills to display affection during courtship.
- **NESTING** Incubation 13–14 days by both sexes. Altricial young brooded by both sexes, more by female; stay in nest 9–12 days, fed by both sexes. Male may tend while female begins second nesting. 1–2 broods per year.
- **POPULATION** Common to fairly common in deciduous forest, woodland, and second growth. Rare migrant in West. Rare to accidental in winter on southern California coast.
- **FEEDERS** Use increases during migration.
- **CONSERVATION** Neotropical migrant. Common cowbird host. Vulnerable to habitat loss due to logging.

Flight Pattern
Swift flight on rapidly beating wings with brief periods of wings pulled to sides.

Nest Identification	
Shape	Location	Twigs, weeds, and leaves • lined with fine twigs, rootlets, and mammal hair • in vines, low tree, or shrub, 1.5–4.5 m above ground (but up to 15 m) • built mostly by female, but male helps • 3–5 light greenish or bluish eggs marked with reddish brown; oval, 2.5 x 1.8 cm.

Plumage Sexes differ	Habitat	Migration Migratory	Weight 45 g

DATE _____ TIME_____ LOCATION _____

Family CARDINALIDAE	Species *Pheucticus melanocephalus*	Length 18–22 cm	Wingspan 30–33 cm

BLACK-HEADED GROSBEAK

Easily observed in western woodlands, this tame bird attends feeders and sometimes takes food from the hand. Both sexes aggressively defend their territory from other grosbeaks. Lemon wing linings are conspicuous in flight. First fall males have rich cinnamon-buff underparts, blackish brown cheek patches, white eyebrow and mustache, and white tips to tertials.

• **SONG** Rich back-and-forth series of warbled phrases, robinlike. Similar to Rose-breasted Grosbeak but lower pitched. Female sings less with more variations. Call is high squeaky *plik*.

• **BEHAVIOR** Solitary or in pairs in breeding season. Gregarious in migration and winter; may form flocks. Forages in trees, bushes, and on ground. Eats seeds, insects, caterpillars, berries, and fruits. Some hybridize with Rose-breasted Grosbeak where ranges overlap in Great Plains. Both sexes may sing "whisper" songs while incubating and brooding.

• **BREEDING** Monogamous. Solitary.

• **NESTING** Incubation 12–14 days by both sexes. Altricial young brooded by both sexes, more by female; stay in nest 11–12 days, fed by both sexes. 1 brood per year.

• **POPULATION** Common to fairly common in open woodlands, especially pine-oak and oak, forest edge, and riparian woodlands. This bird is casual in migration and winter to the Midwest and the East.

• **FEEDERS** Various seeds.

• **CONSERVATION** Neotropical migrant. Uncommon cowbird host. Vulnerable to habitat loss due to logging and fires.

black head

cinnamon-orange hind collar and postocular stripe

large dark conical bill

black upperparts with brown edging to feathers

MALE

2 white wing bars

white patch at base of primaries

cinnamon rump

cinnamon underparts

black tail with white inner webs to outer tail feathers

brown head and upperparts with dark streaking

white median crown stripe

white supercilium and mustache

2 white wing bars

pale cinnamon throat and underparts

JUVENILE MALE

lemon wash on belly

fine brown streaks on sides and flanks

white undertail coverts

FEMALE

Similar Birds

ROSE-BREASTED GROSBEAK ♀ Heavier streaked white to buffy underparts; darker upperparts; brown edging to feathers on back; gray to pale creamy pink bill; paler upper mandible.

Flight Pattern

Short flights with rapid wing beats alternating with brief periods of wings pulled to sides.

Nest Identification

Shape	Location	Sticks, weeds, rootlets, and pine needles, lined with finer materials • in dense part of tree or shrub, usually near water, about 1–7.5 m above ground • built by female • 3–4 light greenish or bluish eggs dotted with reddish brown; oval, 2.5 x 1.8 cm.

Plumage Sexes differ	Habitat	Migration Migratory	Weight 43 g

DATE _____ TIME_____ LOCATION _____

Family CARDINALIDAE	Species *Passerina amoena*	Length 13–15 cm	Wingspan 20–23 cm

LAZULI BUNTING

This small turquoise bird is the western counterpart to the Indigo Bunting of eastern North America. Seen in open forests, riparian thickets, chaparral, and arid brushy canyons, the male sings to claim his territory and spreads and flutters his wings to show off his plumage and attract females. The winter plumage of the male shows the blue on its head and upperparts heavily washed with brown.

- **SONG** Various phrases, some paired and somewhat buzzy, *see-see-sweet, sweet-zee-see-zeer.* Call is "wet" *plik.*
- **BEHAVIOR** Solitary or in pairs during breeding season. Gregarious at other times, in flocks and mixed-species foraging flocks with other buntings and sparrows. Forages on ground and low in trees and bushes. Eats mainly seeds; also insects and caterpillars, especially in summer. At end of breeding season many join flocks and move to higher elevations. Hybrids occur where range overlaps with Indigo Bunting. Aggressively defends territory.
- **BREEDING** Mostly monogamous; some males polygamous.
- **NESTING** Incubation 12 days by female. Young altricial; brooded by female; stay in nest 10–12 days, fed by both sexes, but female does more. 2–3 broods per year.
- **POPULATION** Fairly common. Logging and agricultural change in 20th century promoted range and population expansion. Casual throughout the East.
- **FEEDERS** Comes for small seeds and grains.
- **CONSERVATION** Neotropical migrant. Uncommon host to parasitism by cowbirds. Disappearing due to development.

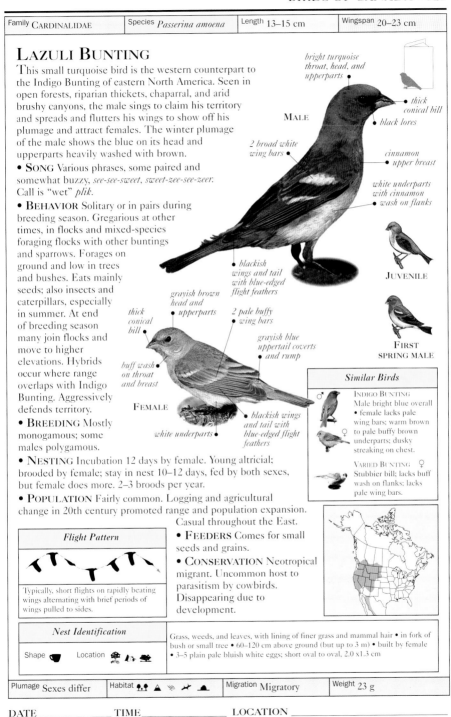

bright turquoise throat, head, and upperparts

MALE

thick conical bill

black lores

2 broad white wing bars

cinnamon upper breast

white underparts with cinnamon wash on flanks

JUVENILE

blackish wings and tail with blue-edged flight feathers

grayish brown head and upperparts

thick conical bill

2 pale buffy wing bars

grayish blue uppertail coverts and rump

FIRST SPRING MALE

buff wash on throat and breast

FEMALE

blackish wings and tail with blue-edged flight feathers

white underparts

Similar Birds

♂ INDIGO BUNTING
Male bright blue overall; female lacks pale wing bars; warm brown to pale buffy brown underparts; dusky streaking on chest. ♀

VARIED BUNTING ♀
Stubbier bill; lacks buff wash on flanks; lacks pale wing bars.

Flight Pattern

Typically, short flights on rapidly beating wings alternating with brief periods of wings pulled to sides.

Nest Identification

Shape 🍵 Location 🪹 🌿 🌳

Grass, weeds, and leaves, with lining of finer grass and mammal hair • in fork of bush or small tree • 60–120 cm above ground (but up to 3 m) • built by female • 3–5 plain pale bluish white eggs; short oval to oval, 2.0 x1.3 cm

Plumage Sexes differ	Habitat 🐾 ▲ 🌾 ✈ 🏔	Migration Migratory	Weight 23 g

DATE _____ TIME_____ LOCATION _____

Family CARDINALIDAE	Species *Passerina cyanea*	Length 13–15 cm	Wingspan 20–23 cm

INDIGO BUNTING

The male's distinctive plumage looks blue in sunlight and almost black in shade or backlighting. Populations are expanding with the creation of disturbed habitat after logging, highway and power line construction, and farmland abandonment. Its breeding range now includes much of the US Southwest.

• **SONG** Series of varied measured strident phrases, usually paired, *sweet-sweet, sweeter-sweeter, here-here,* often with an added trilled ending. Call is a "wet" *spit* or *plik.*

• **BEHAVIOR** Solitary or in pairs during breeding season. Gregarious at other times; in flocks in winter, often with other buntings, sparrows, and finches. Forages in trees, shrubs, and on ground. Eats variety of insects and larvae, especially in summer; also dandelion seeds, weed seeds, grass seeds, small grains, and wild berries. Males defensive of territory; often engage in colorful chases with other males.

• **BREEDING** Monogamous. Solitary. Some males polygynous when outnumbered by females.

• **NESTING** Incubation 12–14 days by female. Young altricial; brooded by female; leave nest at 9–12 days, fed mostly by female; some males bring food. 2 broods per year.

• **POPULATION** Fairly common to common. Abundant in some deciduous forest edges, old fields, clearings, and agricultural areas. Expanding.

• **FEEDERS** Comes for small seeds and grains.

• **CONSERVATION** Neotropical migrant. Common host to cowbird parasitism. Some habitat loss due to maturation of cut-over forests.

blue-purple sheen to head

deep-colored bright blue overall

dark blue to black lores

MALE

blue edging to blackish wings and tail

JUVENILE

WINTER MALE

brown head and upperparts

2 tawny buff wing bars

whitish throat and underparts

buffy brown-washed chest and flanks with dusky streaks

tertials edged with contrasting buff

FEMALE

darker brown wings and tail with blue-edged feathers

Similar Birds

♂ **BLUE GROSBEAK** Larger; large triangular bill; tan wing bars.

VARIED BUNTING ♀ Olive-brown to tawny-brown overall; brown rump; bill with more decurved culmen; narrower tertial edges with less buffy contrast; lacks streaking on underparts; lacks brown wing bars.

Flight Pattern

Short flight low over vegetation with rapid wing beats alternating with brief periods of wings pulled to sides.

Nest Identification

Shape 🍵   Location 🌿 🌳 🌲

Weeds, bark, and fine materials, lined with grass and leaves • in weed clump, dense shrub, or low tree • 30 cm–4.5 m above ground • built by female • 3–4 pale bluish white to white eggs, sometimes with brown or purple spotting; short oval to short subelliptical, 2.0 x 1.3 cm.

Plumage Sexes differ	Habitat 🌳 🌿 🌲 🌱 ✈	Migration Migratory	Weight 14 g

DATE _____ TIME _____ LOCATION _____

Family CARDINALIDAE	Species *Spiza americana*	Length 15–18 cm	Wingspan 23–28 cm

DICKCISSEL

This bird is named for its song of *dick-dick-dick-cissel*. Often flying in flocks over grassy prairies, the Dickcissel, with its black bib and yellow breast, looks like a small meadowlark. Females are similar to males but lack the black bib and have duller chestnut wing patches.

• **SONG** Staccato *dick-dick-dick-cissel*. Has an insectlike call of *bzzrrrt*.

• **BEHAVIOR** Solitary or in pairs during breeding season. Gregarious at other times, forming wintering flocks numbering thousands of birds. Joins communal roosts after breeding season. Male sings from exposed perches and in flight. Forages on ground. Eats grains, seeds, and insects.

• **BREEDING** Polygamous, although some birds are monogamous.

• **NESTING** Incubation 12–13 days by female. Altricial young brooded by female; stay in nest 7–10 days, fed by female. 1–2 broods per year.

• **POPULATION** Common to abundant in grasslands, meadows, savannas, and fields. Local and irregular east of Appalachians. Rare in migration on Atlantic and Pacific Coasts. Casual in winter in the East.

• **FEEDERS** Birds in northern part of range come to feeders.

yellowish eyebrow becomes whitish behind eye
thick stout bill with blackish upper mandible
white chin
brown auricular patch and crown
thin blackish malar stripe
brown upperparts
black chin
black streaking on back
black bib
bold yellow breast
chestnut wing coverts
dusky white underparts

JUVENILE

WINTER MALE

MALE

WINTER FEMALE

yellowish eyebrow becomes whitish behind eye
grayish-brown auricular patch
grayish-brown upperparts
blackish streaking on back
thin dark brown malar stripe
chestnut wing coverts
white throat, chin, and mustache
dusky white underparts
yellow breast

FEMALE

Similar Birds

HOUSE SPARROW ♀ Similar to female Dickcissel • stubbier yellowish bill; buffy supercilium; brown postocular stripe; single white wing bar; lacks pale throat with dark malar stripe; lacks streaking on flanks.

• **CONSERVATION** Neotropical migrant. Frequent host to cowbird parasitism. Nests and young lost annually to the mowing of fields for hay. Thousands are killed annually on wintering grounds for the protection of rice plantations.

Flight Pattern

Series of rapid wing beats alternating with brief periods of wings pulled to sides. Often flies in large flocks in compact undulating formation.

Nest Identification

Shape ▽   Location 🌿 🌳 ▬

Grasses, stems, and leaves, with lining of soft rootlets, grasses, and hair • low in tree or bush, sometimes atop grassy tussock or on ground in field • 0–2 m above ground • built by female • 3–5 plain pale blue eggs; oval to long oval, 2.0 x 1.5 cm.

Plumage Sexes differ	Habitat _ ▲	Migration Migratory	Weight 28 g

Family ICTERIDAE	Species *Dolichonyx oryzivorus*	Length 16–20 cm	Wingspan 26–32 cm

BOBOLINK

In northern meadows and farmland, this bird is known for its cheerful bubbling *bob-o-link* song and handsome plumage. It is said the male wears his breeding plumage upside down, as he has black underparts with a buff nape and hindneck and white scapulars and rump. In all plumages, birds are adorned with sharply pointed tail feathers, unusual for songbirds. All fall-plumaged birds and juveniles are similar to the female but have brighter yellow-buff underparts with less streaking.

• **SONG** Lively bubbling cascade of notes, starting with low reedy notes and rollicking upward, *bob-o-link, bob-o-link, pink, pink, pank, pink*. Call is clear *pink*.

• **BEHAVIOR** Gregarious; in flocks numbering up to thousands. Males sing from perch or in flight display, circling low over fields. In summer eats insects and caterpillars, grass and weed seeds, and grains; eats seeds and grains in migration and winter.

• **BREEDING** Strongly polygynous.

• **NESTING** Incubation 13 days by female. Altricial young brooded by female; stay in nest 10–14 days, fed by both sexes. 1 brood per year.

• **POPULATION** Fairly common to common in tall grass, wet meadows, prairie, hay fields, and grain fields. Decline in the East during 20th century. Rare in the fall on West Coast.

• **CONSERVATION** Neotropical migrant. Rare cowbird host. Vulnerable to destruction of nests and young by mowing of hayfields. Has declined in the Southeast from former 19th-century market hunting for food and from continued destruction to protect rice plantations. Similar killing currently exists on expanding rice plantations on wintering grounds in South America.

buff-colored hindneck

black face and crown

black back

narrow buff stripe in center of back

white scapulars

white rump

MALE

black underparts and wings

buff-edged tertials and wing coverts

black tail

blackish brown crown with buff central crown stripe

pinkish bill

black streaking on back, rump, sides, and flanks

golden buff overall

WINTER MALE

FEMALE

Similar Birds

LARK BUNTING ♂ Entirely black except for large white shoulder patches, white edging to tertials and inner secondaries, and white tips to outer tail feathers.

Flight Pattern

Strong undeviating and slightly undulating flight on rapidly beating wings. Male has display flight with shallow wing strokes on rapidly fluttering wings.

Nest Identification

Shape ⬳   Location ▬ ∗∗∗

Coarse grasses and weed stalks, lined with finer grasses • in slight depression on ground in tall grass, weeds, or clover, sometimes in rut made by tractors and combines • female digs scrape and then builds nest • 4–7 eggs, irregularly blotched with browns, purple, and lavender; oval to short oval, 2.1 x 1.6 cm.

Plumage Sexes differ	Habitat ▬ ▴ ⍦	Migration Migratory	Weight 48 g

Family ICTERIDAE	Species *Agelaius phoeniceus*	Length 19–24 cm	Wingspan 30–37 cm

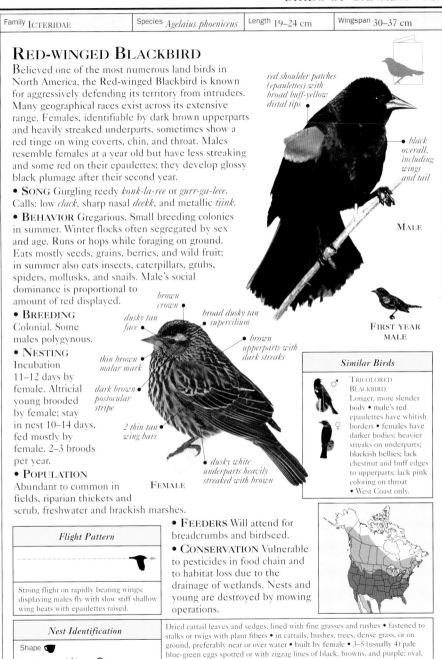

RED-WINGED BLACKBIRD

Believed one of the most numerous land birds in North America, the Red-winged Blackbird is known for aggressively defending its territory from intruders. Many geographical races exist across its extensive range. Females, identifiable by dark brown upperparts and heavily streaked underparts, sometimes show a red tinge on wing coverts, chin, and throat. Males resemble females at a year old but have less streaking and some red on their epaulettes; they develop glossy black plumage after their second year.

- **SONG** Gurgling reedy *konk-la-ree* or *gurr-ga-leee*. Calls: low *clack*, sharp nasal *deekk*, and metallic *tiink*.
- **BEHAVIOR** Gregarious. Small breeding colonies in summer. Winter flocks often segregated by sex and age. Runs or hops while foraging on ground. Eats mostly seeds, grains, berries, and wild fruit; in summer also eats insects, caterpillars, grubs, spiders, mollusks, and snails. Male's social dominance is proportional to amount of red displayed.
- **BREEDING** Colonial. Some males polygynous.
- **NESTING** Incubation 11–12 days by female. Altricial young brooded by female; stay in nest 10–14 days, fed mostly by female. 2–3 broods per year.
- **POPULATION** Abundant to common in fields, riparian thickets and scrub, freshwater and brackish marshes.

red shoulder patches (epaulettes) with broad buff-yellow distal tips

black overall, including wings and tail

MALE

brown crown

dusky tan face

broad dusky tan supercilium

brown upperparts with dark streaks

thin brown malar mark

dark brown postocular stripe

2 thin tan wing bars

dusky white underparts heavily streaked with brown

FEMALE

FIRST YEAR MALE

Similar Birds

TRICOLORED BLACKBIRD
Longer, more slender body • male's red epaulettes have whitish borders • females have darker bodies; heavier streaks on underparts; blackish bellies; lack chestnut and buff edges to upperparts; lack pink coloring on throat • West Coast only.

- **FEEDERS** Will attend for breadcrumbs and birdseed.
- **CONSERVATION** Vulnerable to pesticides in food chain and to habitat loss due to the drainage of wetlands. Nests and young are destroyed by mowing operations.

Flight Pattern
Strong flight on rapidly beating wings; displaying males fly with slow stiff shallow wing beats with epaulettes raised.

Nest Identification	
Shape	Dried cattail leaves and sedges, lined with fine grasses and rushes • fastened to stalks or twigs with plant fibers • in cattails, bushes, trees, dense grass, or on ground, preferably near or over water • built by female • 3–5 (usually 4) pale blue-green eggs spotted or with zigzag lines of black, browns, and purple; oval, 2.5 x 1.9 cm.
Location	

Plumage Sexes differ	Habitat	Migration Migratory	Weight 65 g

DATE _____ TIME_____ LOCATION _____

Family ICTERIDAE	Species *Sturnella magna*	Length 23–28 cm	Wingspan 34–43 cm

EASTERN MEADOWLARK

A common inhabitant of fields and meadows, the Eastern Meadowlark often is observed flicking its tail open and shut while walking through grass and weeds and along roadsides. Clearing of forests in eastern North America has led to the expansion of its breeding range. Fall-plumaged birds show narrow buffy mottling in the black breast band and a buffy wash on the face, supercilium, flanks, and undertail coverts. Juveniles have black spotting on the chest, sides, and flanks.

black-and-white-striped crown

brown upperparts streaked with buff and black

chunky body

white face with black postocular stripe

yellow breast and belly with broad black V on chest

white sides and flanks with black spots and streaks

white outer tail feathers

white undertail coverts with dusky streaking

• **SONG** A plaintive *tee-you, tee-airrr*, or *spring-o'the-year*. Call given on ground or in flight is high buzzy *zzzzrrt*, and a nasal *sweeink* also is given in flight.

• **BEHAVIOR** Solitary or in pairs during summer. Gregarious during other seasons, forming small flocks in winter. Eats mostly insects, especially in summer. Also eats grains, weed and grass seeds, and tender sprouts of spring plants.

• **BREEDING** Monogamous. Solitary. Some males polygynous.

• **NESTING** Incubation 13–14 days by both sexes. Young altricial; brooded by female; stay in nest 11–12 days, fed by both sexes, but female does more. Male may take over brood while female starts second nest. 2 broods per year.

• **POPULATION** Common in meadows, fields, grasslands, and savanna. Decline reported in the East during last quarter of the 20th century.

• **CONSERVATION** Common host to cowbird parasitism. Nests and young destroyed by mowing operations. Vulnerable to habitat loss due to natural succession of abandoned fields, as well as from overgrazing, development, and grassland habitat fragmentation.

Similar Birds

WESTERN MEADOWLARK
Paler upperparts lack dark centers in most feathers; yellow of throat, especially that of breeding males, extends into submustachial region; sides of crown and postocular stripe usually brownish; most have less white in outer tail feathers.

Flight Pattern

Several rapid shallow stiff wing beats followed by short glides close to landscape.

Nest Identification

Shape ✿   Location ▲▲▲

Lined with grass, plant stems, and pine needles • domed or partially domed • often next to dense clump of grass or weeds on damp or wet ground • built by female • 3–7 white eggs, suffused with pink, with brown and lavender spots and speckles; oval to short or long oval, 2.8 x 2.0 cm.

Plumage Sexes similar	Habitat ⬤	Migration Northern birds migrate	Weight 102 g

DATE _____ TIME_____ LOCATION _____

Family ICTERIDAE	Species *Sturnella neglecta*	Length 23–28 cm	Wingspan 34–43 cm

WESTERN MEADOWLARK

Its distinctive song often is the only way to
distinguish this bird from the Eastern
Meadowlark, which is strikingly similar
in appearance. Both birds are known
to be interspecifically territorial and
nest in the same area, interbreeding
in regions where their ranges
overlap. Under such circumstances
some males sing the songs of both
species, creating a tricky
identification challenge for the
observer. Breeding adults show
bright yellow plumage from throat
to belly, with a black V on the
chest. Fall-plumaged birds show a
pale buffy wash on the face, sides,
and flanks, and the yellow in
submustachial regions is much
reduced or veiled, as is the black breast
band. Juveniles are paler and instead of
the black V show a streaked necklace.

dark brown stripes on crown

dark brown postocular stripe

yellow of throat extends well into submustachial area

chunky body

black V on chest

black spots and streaks on sides and flanks

short wide tail with white outer feathers

• **SONG** Repeated bubbling flutelike notes,
varying in length, *shee-oo-e-lee shee-ee le-ee*, accelerating
toward the end. Call is a low *chuk*. Flight note is a nasal *whew*.

• **BEHAVIOR** Solitary or in pairs during breeding season.
Gregarious at other times, forming small to large flocks in
winter, which forage and roost together on the ground. Walks on
ground. Sings from ground or exposed perches, including fence
posts, shrubs, trees, and utility wires. Forages primarily in
vegetation on ground. Eats mostly insects and larvae, spiders,
and some snails; also seeds of grains, grasses, and weeds. Winter
birds often forage in shorter grasses along roadsides.

• **BREEDING** Monogamous. Solitary. Some males polygynous.

• **NESTING** Incubation 13–15 days by female. Young altricial;
brooded by female; stay in nest 11–12 days, fed by both sexes
but more by female. 2 broods per year.

• **POPULATION** Fairly common to common in cultivated fields,
pastures, grasslands, and
savanna. Range expanding in
the Northeast.

• **CONSERVATION** Neotropical
migrant. Uncommon cowbird
host. Nest and young destroyed
by mowing operations.

Similar Birds

EASTERN MEADOWLARK
Darker body; dark
centers to feathers on
upperparts; yellow of
throat generally does
not reach
submustachial area,
barely does so on
males; more extensive
white on outer tail
feathers; black crown
and postocular stripes;
voice differs.

Flight Pattern

Flies low over landscape, with series of
rapid shallow stiff wing beats followed by
short glide.

Nest Identification	
Shape · Location	Dried grass and plant stems; domed or partially domed • lined with grasses and pine needles • against clump of grass or weeds • built by female • 3–7 white eggs, suffused with pink, with brown and lavender spots and speckles; oval or short to long oval, 2.8 x 2.0 cm.

Plumage Sexes similar	Habitat	Migration Northern birds migrate	Weight 113 g

DATE _____ TIME_____ LOCATION _____

Family ICTERIDAE	Species *Xanthocephalus xanthocephalus*	Length 22–28 cm	Wingspan 36–43 cm

YELLOW-HEADED BLACKBIRD

Brilliant yellow plumage and white wing patches contrasting with its all-black body make this robin-sized marsh bird easy to identify. Often nesting in colonies, it is highly aggressive in defending its grounds and will attack other birds and even human intruders, especially if young are in the nest. The song of the male is considered by many to be the poorest vocalization of any North American songbird. Males are larger than females, and the white wing patch is conspicuous in flight. Juveniles show dark brown upperparts with cinnamon-buff edging to the body feathers, pale buff underparts with a cinnamon wash on the flanks, an ocherous buff head and breast, a whitish throat, and dusky brown auriculars.

yellow head, throat, and breast

black body

black loreal mask

white wing patch

MALE

• **SONG** High-pitched raspy honking gurgle, ending with a descending buzz, *klee-klee-klee-ko-kow-w-w-w,w,w,w*. Call is hoarse *ka-aack*.

• **BEHAVIOR** Gregarious; forms breeding colonies and flocks outside breeding season. Flocks forage and roost together and range from small to enormous, containing millions in winter. Males often segregate from females and juveniles in separate winter flocks. Conspicuous. Forages in mud near water and in fields. Walks on ground. Eats insects, larvae, snails, grains, and seeds.

dusky brown crown and cheeks

yellowish eyebrow

dusky brown upperparts

yellowish lower cheek, throat, and breast

dusky brown belly with white streaking

dusky brown crissum

FEMALE

• **BREEDING** Polygynous. Colonial.

• **NESTING** Incubation 11–13 days by female. Young altricial; brooded by female; stay in nest 9–12 days, fed by both sexes, but mostly by female. 2 broods per year.

• **POPULATION** Common in freshwater marshes, reedy lakes and irrigation ditches, and open farmlands. Rare to casual in migration and in winter to the East Coast. Casual spring migrant to southeastern Alaska.

• **CONSERVATION** Neotropical migrant. Rare host to cowbird parasitism. Vulnerable to loss of habitat due to draining of wetlands and freshwater marshes.

Flight Pattern
Strong direct flight with rapid wing beats.

Nest Identification	
Shape ● Location ⱲⱲ	Grasses, reeds, cattails, and bulrushes, with partial canopy that shrinks into tight basket when dry • over water in marsh vegetation • 15–90 cm above surface • built by female • 3–5 light gray or green eggs with brownish or grayish markings; oval to long oval, 2.5 x 2.0 cm.

Plumage Sexes differ	Habitat	Migration Migratory	Weight 79 g

DATE _____ TIME_____ LOCATION _____

Family ICTERIDAE	Species *Euphagus carolinus*	Length 21–25 cm	Wingspan 33–38 cm

RUSTY BLACKBIRD

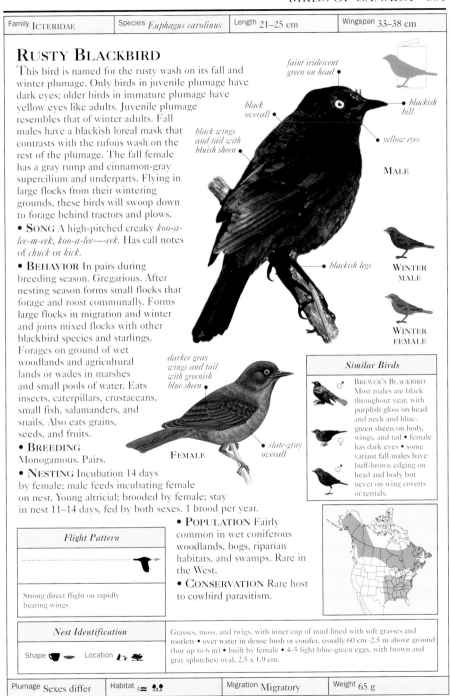

This bird is named for the rusty wash on its fall and winter plumage. Only birds in juvenile plumage have dark eyes; older birds in immature plumage have yellow eyes like adults. Juvenile plumage resembles that of winter adults. Fall males have a blackish loreal mask that contrasts with the rufous wash on the rest of the plumage. The fall female has a gray rump and cinnamon-gray supercilium and underparts. Flying in large flocks from their wintering grounds, these birds will swoop down to forage behind tractors and plows.

• **SONG** A high-pitched creaky *koo-a-lee-m-eek, koo-a-lee—-eek*. Has call notes of *chuck* or *kick*.

• **BEHAVIOR** In pairs during breeding season. Gregarious. After nesting season forms small flocks that forage and roost communally. Forms large flocks in migration and winter and joins mixed flocks with other blackbird species and starlings. Forages on ground of wet woodlands and agricultural lands or wades in marshes and small pools of water. Eats insects, caterpillars, crustaceans, small fish, salamanders, and snails. Also eats grains, seeds, and fruits.

• **BREEDING** Monogamous. Pairs.

• **NESTING** Incubation 14 days by female; male feeds incubating female on nest. Young altricial; brooded by female; stay in nest 11–14 days, fed by both sexes. 1 brood per year.

• **POPULATION** Fairly common in wet coniferous woodlands, bogs, riparian habitats, and swamps. Rare in the West.

• **CONSERVATION** Rare host to cowbird parasitism.

Labels on illustration:
faint iridescent green on head
black overall
black wings and tail with bluish sheen
blackish bill
yellow eyes
MALE
blackish legs
WINTER MALE
WINTER FEMALE
darker gray wings and tail with greenish blue sheen
FEMALE
slate-gray overall

Similar Birds

BREWER'S BLACKBIRD Most males are black throughout year, with purplish gloss on head and neck and blue-green sheen on body, wings, and tail • female has dark eyes • some variant fall males have buff-brown edging on head and body but never on wing coverts or tertials.

Flight Pattern
Strong direct flight on rapidly beating wings.

Nest Identification	
Shape ⬤ ⬢ Location 🌿 🌲	Grasses, moss, and twigs, with inner cup of mud lined with soft grasses and rootlets • over water in dense bush or conifer, usually 60 cm–2.5 m above ground (but up to 6 m) • built by female • 4–5 light blue-green eggs, with brown and gray splotches; oval, 2.5 x 1.9 cm.

Plumage Sexes differ	Habitat 〰 🏔	Migration Migratory	Weight 65 g

DATE _____ TIME_____ LOCATION _____

Family ICTERIDAE	Species *Euphagus cyanocephalus*	Length 22–26 cm	Wingspan 36–41 cm

BREWER'S BLACKBIRD

Huge flocks can be seen flying over farm fields during plowing season, and the species has expanded its range and abundance with the spread of agriculture. One of the most common blackbirds, the male's plumage remains glossy black year-round. In fall, some males acquire buffy edging on the head and body feathers but never on the wing coverts or tertials. Juveniles resemble females but lack the green sheen on wings and tail.

purplish sheen on head and neck

yellow eyes

MALE

greenish blue sheen on body and wings

FALL MALE

black overall

• **SONG** Breathy, creaky *ke-see*. Call is gruff *check*.

• **BEHAVIOR** In pairs during breeding season. Gregarious. Forms large foraging and roosting flocks in migration and winter.

dark brown eyes

dark gray-brown overall

green sheen on wings and tail

FEMALE

Often joins mixed-species foraging flocks with other blackbirds in winter. Nests in small to large colonies. Head bobs forward while walking. Follows farm tractors and plows. Forages on ground. Eats insects; caterpillars; and some fruits, seeds, and grains.

• **BREEDING** Monogamous. Some males polygynous. Can be loosely colonial.

• **NESTING** Incubation 12–14 days by female, guarded by male. Altricial young brooded by female; stay in nest 13–14 days, fed by both sexes. 1–2 broods per year.

• **POPULATION** Common in open habitats, shrub/scrub, riparian woodlands, farms, and around human habitation. Extending range north and east.

• **CONSERVATION** Neotropical migrant. Common cowbird host.

Similar Birds

BROWN-HEADED COWBIRD ♀
Smaller; slimmer; pale face pattern; shorter, deeper-based bill; shorter tail.

RUSTY BLACKBIRD
Faint greenish sheen on head; longer bill
• female slate-gray overall with yellow eyes
• in winter, rusty edging to feathers on back, wing coverts, and tertials • winter male has black loral mask; shows cinnamon edging to head, throat, breast, supercilium, and mustache • winter female has buff eyebrow; gray rump; buffy gray underparts.

Flight Pattern

Strong swift direct flight on rapidly beating wings.

Nest Identification

Shape

Location

Conifer needles, grasses, and sticks, with inside cup of mud or cow manure, lined with hair and rootlets • on ground in meadow or field or in marshes or trees, up to 46 m above ground • built by female • 3–7 light green or grayish green eggs, with blotches of grayish brown; oval, 2.5 x 1.9 cm.

Plumage Sexes differ	Habitat	Migration Northern birds migrate	Weight 68 g

DATE _____ TIME_____ LOCATION _____

Family ICTERIDAE	Species *Quiscalus quiscula*	Length 28–34 cm	Wingspan 43–47 cm

COMMON GRACKLE

This gregarious bird has expanded its range by adapting to suburban areas. Outside the nesting season, noisy groups roost together at night, often with other species. Juveniles are sooty brown with dark brown eyes.

- **SONG** Grating squeaky *coguba-leek*, like a creaking rusty hinge. Call is a bold *chuk*.
- **BEHAVIOR** Conspicuous. Nests, forages, and roosts in groups or flocks all year. Large postnesting season flocks can damage crops, and winter flocks may number in the hundreds of thousands. Walks on ground. Forages in trees, shrubs, grass, and croplands; may wade into water. Eats insects, worms, caterpillars, fruits, grains, seeds, small rodents, small fish, salamanders, and eggs and nestlings of other birds. Male displays by fluffing out shoulder feathers to make a ruffled collar, drooping his wings, and singing.
- **BREEDING** Monogamous. Some males polygynous. Colonial.
- **NESTING** Incubation 13–14 days by female. Young altricial; brooded by female; stay in nest 16–20 days, fed by both sexes. 1–2 broods per year.
- **POPULATION** Abundant and widespread in open areas with scattered trees, open woodlands, agricultural areas, parks, and around human habitation. Casual in southern Alaska and in the Pacific states.
- **FEEDERS** Will come for small grains and seeds.
- **CONSERVATION** Rare host to cowbird parasitism. Birds feeding on crops and making a nuisance in large winter roosts sometimes are destroyed.

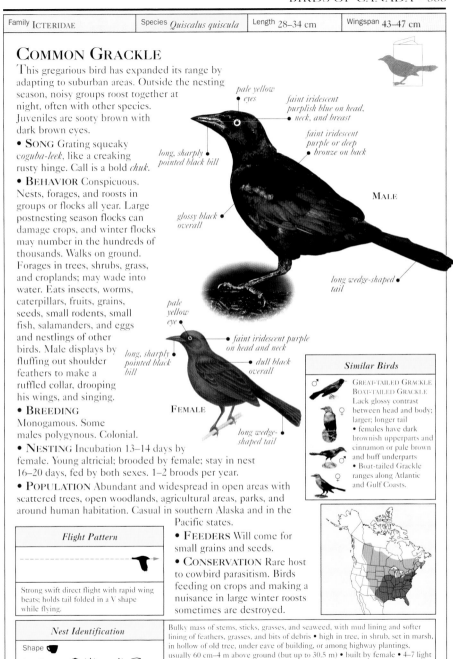

pale yellow eyes

faint iridescent purplish blue on head, neck, and breast

faint iridescent purple or deep bronze on back

long, sharply pointed black bill

glossy black overall

MALE

long wedge-shaped tail

pale yellow eye

faint iridescent purple on head and neck

long, sharply pointed black bill

dull black overall

FEMALE

long wedge-shaped tail

Similar Birds

♂ GREAT-TAILED GRACKLE
BOAT-TAILED GRACKLE
Lack glossy contrast between head and body; larger; longer tail
♀ • females have dark brownish upperparts and cinnamon or pale brown and buff underparts
• Boat-tailed Grackle ranges along Atlantic and Gulf Coasts.
♀

Flight Pattern

Strong swift direct flight with rapid wing beats; holds tail folded in a V shape while flying.

Nest Identification

Shape

Location

Bulky mass of stems, sticks, grasses, and seaweed, with mud lining and softer lining of feathers, grasses, and bits of debris • high in tree, in shrub, set in marsh, in hollow of old tree, under eave of building, or among highway plantings, usually 60 cm–4 m above ground (but up to 30.5 m) • built by female • 4–7 light brown or light green eggs, with brown and lilac markings; oval, 3.0 x 2.1 cm.

Plumage Sexes differ	Habitat	Migration Migratory	Weight 128 g

DATE _____ TIME_____ LOCATION _____

Family ICTERIDAE	Species *Molothrus ater*	Length 18–21 cm	Wingspan 30–35 cm

BROWN-HEADED COWBIRD

This common cowbird travels and roosts in large flocks with other blackbirds after breeding season; winter mixed-species flocks can number in the millions. Originally of the Great Plains, where it associated with bison, this species has expanded its range east and west, with the fragmentation of the eastern forest and the increase in range cattle and ranching. Like all cowbirds it is a brood parasite and lays its eggs in the nests of other birds. Juveniles resemble females but are paler overall; upperparts have pale edging, giving a scaly effect; underparts are streaky and throats gray-white.

black overall with faint green sheen

brown head

short conical bill

MALE

grayish brown upperparts

faint dusky malar mark

FEMALE

pale grayish brown underparts with faint streaking

JUVENILE

• **SONG** Gurgling liquid *glug-glug-glee*, with tail spread, wings drooped, and a forward bow. Female's call is harsh rattle. Male in flight has high slurred *ts-eeeu!*

• **BEHAVIOR** Solitary, in pairs, or small groups during breeding season; otherwise gregarious, foraging and roosting in flocks. Calls and displays from the ground or high exposed perches. Walks on ground to forage. Holds tail cocked over back. Eats insects, caterpillars, spiders, and various grains, seeds, and fruits.

• **BREEDING** Promiscuous.

• **NESTING** Incubation 10–13 days by host. Altricial young usually hatch before host's young and often outcompete them; tended by host. Female usually lays 1 egg in each nest; 10–36 eggs per year.

• **POPULATION** Common in woodlands, forest edge, agricultural areas, and around human habitation.

Similar Birds

BRONZED COWBIRD
Slightly larger; much longer, larger bill; red eyes; ruff on nape • male has bronze-green sheen on head and upper body • female is dull blackish brown overall.

SHINY COWBIRD
Male glossy black overall with purplish sheen on head, back, and breast • female has gray-brown upperparts; faint gray eyebrow; pale gray-brown underparts; paler gray throat.

• **FEEDERS** Attends for small seeds and grains.

• **CONSERVATION** Neotropical migrant. Numbers reduced in Michigan by trapping to protect endangered Kirtland's Warbler in jack pine barrens nesting grounds.

Flight Pattern
Swift somewhat swooping direct flight on rapidly beating wings.

Nest Identification	
Shape Brood parasite Location Active nests of other birds	Lays eggs in nests of other species • usually 1 egg per nest • up to 36 eggs laid per female per nesting season • light blue eggs, often with brown flecks; oval, 2.1 x 1.6 cm.

Plumage Sexes differ	Habitat	Migration Northern birds migrate	Weight 48 g

DATE _____ TIME_____ LOCATION _____

Family ICTERIDAE	Species *Icterus spurius*	Length 15–20 cm	Wingspan 23–26 cm

ORCHARD ORIOLE

This small oriole with its burnt-orange underparts is found in most of eastern North America in summer. It spends most of its time in trees in suburban and rural open stands and is often unwary when approached. Juveniles resemble females, and first spring males are similar to females but have a black chin and throat. Leaves breeding grounds in early fall.

• **SONG** Loud rich varied whistled notes, accelerating into a jumbled ending with a slurred *wheer!*, sounding like *look here, what cheer, wee yo, what cheer, whip yo, what wheer!* Calls sharp musical *chuk* and a dry chattering *chuh-huh-huh-huh.*

• **BEHAVIOR** Solitary or in pairs during breeding season. In small family groups after nesting. Vocal and often conspicuous. Relatively approachable. Forages at middle to high levels in trees and shrubs, often at tips of branches; hops from branch to branch. Eats insects; also berries, flower parts, nectar, and fruits.

• **BREEDING** Monogamous. Solitary and loose colonies.

• **NESTING** Incubation 12–14 days by female. Altricial young brooded by female, some by male; stay in nest 11–14 days, fed by both sexes. Mates often divide fledglings and care for them separately, but family group remains intact until fall migration. 1 brood per year.

• **POPULATION** Common to fairly common in open woodland, farmlands, scrub/mesquite, shade trees, and orchards. Species declining in parts of its western range.

• **FEEDERS** Fruit and nectar.

• **CONSERVATION** Neotropical migrant. Common host to cowbird parasitism.

black hood, back, and wings

single white wing bar

white-edged flight feathers on wings

chestnut rump and shoulders

black tail with narrow white tips

MALE

slightly curved bill with black upper mandible and blue-gray lower mandible

chestnut underparts

olive upperparts

dusky wings with 2 white wing bars

yellowish underparts

FIRST SPRING MALE

FEMALE

Similar Birds

MALE: No other North American songbird is extensively black above and chestnut below.

HOODED ORIOLE ♀ Female and juvenile are larger; longer tail; longer bill; thinner lower wing bar; undertail coverts often washed yellow-orange • juvenile male has more extensive black bib.

Flight Pattern	

Swift slightly swooping direct flight on rapidly beating wings.

Nest Identification	
Shape Location	Intricately woven pouch of grasses with lining of plant down • hanging from fork of tree or bush, often hidden in cluster of leaves, 2–6 m above ground (but up to 15 m) • 3–7 light blue or gray eggs, splotched with gray, purple, or brown; oval, 2.0 x 1.4 cm.

Plumage Sexes differ	Habitat	Migration Migratory	Weight 20 g

DATE _____ TIME_____ LOCATION _____

Family ICTERIDAE	Species *Icterus galbula*	Length 18–21 cm	Wingspan 29–32 cm

BALTIMORE ORIOLE

The eastern counterpart to Bullock's Oriole was once thought conspecific with it and called the Northern Oriole. It is the state bird of Maryland. The male is the only bright orange-and-black oriole north of Florida. Some winter along the southeast Atlantic Coast and may find food in backyard feeders and gardens. Juveniles are similar to females but show a yellow-orange wash on the head and breast and grayish to whitish underparts. Juvenile males have more orange.

• **SONG** Disjointed measured 2-note whistled melodic phrases, some with long pauses, *hue-lee, hue-lee, hue-lee.* Call is rich *hue-lee.* Also a series of rattling chatter, *caw-caw-caw-caw-caw.*

• **BEHAVIOR** Solitary or in pairs in breeding season. In family groups after nesting, although some males remain solitary. May join mixed foraging flocks in winter and migration. Forages in bushes and trees, often high in canopy. Eats insects, caterpillars, berries, and fruits. Sips nectar.

• **BREEDING** Monogamous. Solitary. Displaying male spreads tail and wings, bows to female.

• **NESTING** Incubation 12–14 days by female. Altricial young brooded by female; stay in nest 12–14 days, fed by both sexes. 1 brood per year.

• **POPULATION** Common in deciduous woodlots, riparian woodlands, woodland edges and clearings, and around human habitation. Uncommon in winter in the Southeast. Rare in the West in migration.

• **FEEDERS** Oranges, peanut butter and suet, or nectar.

• **CONSERVATION** Neotropical migrant. Infrequent cowbird host (may eject eggs).

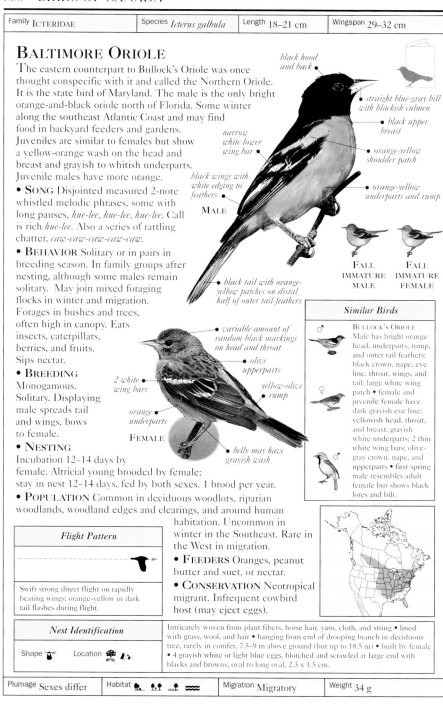

black hood and back

straight blue-gray bill with blackish culmen

black upper breast

orange-yellow shoulder patch

orange-yellow underparts and rump

narrow white lower wing bar

black wings with white edging to feathers

MALE

black tail with orange-yellow patches on distal half of outer tail feathers

FALL IMMATURE MALE

FALL IMMATURE FEMALE

variable amount of random black markings on head and throat

olive upperparts

yellow-olive rump

2 white wing bars

orange underparts

FEMALE

belly may have grayish wash

Similar Birds

♂ BULLOCK'S ORIOLE Male has bright orange head, underparts, rump, and outer tail feathers; black crown, nape, eye line, throat, wings, and tail; large white wing patch • female and juvenile female have dark grayish eye line; yellowish head, throat, and breast; grayish white underparts; 2 thin white wing bars; olive-gray crown, nape, and upperparts • first spring male resembles adult female but shows black lores and bib.

Flight Pattern

Swift strong direct flight on rapidly beating wings; orange-yellow in dark tail flashes during flight.

Nest Identification

Shape   Location

Intricately woven from plant fibers, horse hair, yarn, cloth, and string • lined with grass, wool, and hair • hanging from end of drooping branch in deciduous tree, rarely in conifer, 7.5–9 m above ground (but up to 18.5 m) • built by female • 4 grayish white or light blue eggs, blotched and scrawled at large end with blacks and browns; oval to long oval, 2.3 x 1.5 cm.

Plumage Sexes differ	Habitat	Migration Migratory	Weight 34 g

Family ICTERIDAE	Species *Icterus bullockii*	Length 18–21 cm	Wingspan 29–32 cm

BULLOCK'S ORIOLE

Once considered the same species as the Baltimore Oriole, with which it hybridizes in the Great Plains, this bird was formerly called the Northern Oriole. The bright orange male differs from other orioles in its face pattern and in its large white wing patches that flash in flight.

• **SONG** Measured clear whistled single and double notes with some gruff or scratchy notes. Has rough nasal call of *cheah*, given singly or in series. Also has a loud rattle.

• **BEHAVIOR** Solitary or in pairs during breeding season. In small family groups after nesting. Pairs spend much time together and both will attack predators. Noisy and conspicuous. Frequents river valley and agricultural areas. Forages in trees and bushes. Sips nectar. Eats insects, caterpillars, berries, and fruit.

• **BREEDING** Monogamous; also solitary.

• **NESTING** Incubation 12–14 days by female. Young altricial; brooded by female; stay in nest 12–4 days, fed by both sexes. 1 brood per year.

• **POPULATION** Common in open areas with shade trees and in foothill oak forests. Uncommon in winter in southern California; casual vagrant to the East in migration and winter.

• **FEEDERS** Suet, sliced orange, and nectar water.

• **CONSERVATION** Neotropical migrant. Frequent host to cowbird parasitism. Range increasing near man-made watercourses planted with shrubs and trees.

black cap, nape, bib, and eye stripe

black back

straight blue-gray bill with blackish culmen

black tail with orange outer tail feathers

MALE

orange face

orange rump

orange underparts

black wings with large white patch and edging to feathers

gray legs and feet

FIRST SPRING MALE

olive-brown crown and nape

dusky eye line

yellow face, throat, and breast

olive-brown back and wings

olive tail

blackish brown wings with 2 white wing bars

FEMALE

buffy gray belly and rump, sometimes washed yellow-orange

Similar Birds

♂ **BALTIMORE ORIOLE**
Male has hooded appearance due to more extensive black on head and throat; orange upper wing bar; white lower wing bar; orange distal half to outer tail feathers • female shows various degrees of black, olive, and orange on head; lacks eye stripe; orange or orange-washed underparts.

Flight Pattern
Swift strong direct flight with rapid wing beats.

Nest Identification	
Shape Location	Plant fiber, horse hair, string, and bark, with lining of moss, plant down, wool, and hair • hanging from end of branch, often in cottonwood or willow, or in clump of mistletoe, 2–4.5 m above ground • built by female, with some help from male • 4–5 light blue or pale gray eggs with dots of brown, gray, or black, scrawled with purplish black line; oval to long oval, 2.4 x 1.6 cm.

Plumage Sexes differ	Habitat	Migration Migratory	Weight 34 g

DATE _____ TIME_____ LOCATION _____

Family FRINGILLIDAE	Species *Fringilla coelebs*	Length 15 cm	Wingspan 24 cm

COMMON CHAFFINCH

A sparrow-sized Palearctic species commonly seen in parts of Asia, and perhaps the most common finch in Europe, this bird occasionally visits the northeastern United States and the Maritimes. It is widely scattered as far as North Africa, western Asia, southern Russia, and western Siberia. Outside the breeding season, the male's pinkish back, face, and underparts become more brownish. In flight the white bar at the base of the primaries and secondaries and the white lesser coverts contrast with the blackish wings and the blackish tail with its conspicuously flashing white outer tail feathers. Juveniles resemble adult females but are paler overall.

blue-gray crown and nape

pinkish brown upperparts

white bases to primaries and broad wing bar

gray-green rump

pinkish face, throat, breast, and sides

white shoulder patch

MALE

blackish gray tail with white outer tail feathers

white belly, flanks, and undertail coverts

- **SONG** A bold warbling *fyeet, fyeet, lya-lya-vee, chee-yew-keak*. Call is *pink-pink*; has flight call of *cheup*.

- **BEHAVIOR** Solitary or in pairs during nesting season. In groups and small flocks after breeding. Gregarious in winter; often joins mixed-species foraging flocks. Forages for food in trees and bushes. Eats mainly seeds and insects. Found almost anywhere with scattered shrubs and trees, orchards, farmlands, parks, gardens, and suburbs.

brown eye line

gray-brown upperparts

gray-brown tail with white outer tail feathers

gray-tan supercilium

gray head

white shoulder patch

white wing bar and base to primaries

gray underparts

FEMALE

- **BREEDING** Monogamous. Solitary.

- **NESTING** Incubation 10–16 days by female; male sometimes feeds female on nest. Altricial young brooded by female; remain in nest 11–18 days, tended by both sexes, but female does more. 1–2 broods per year.

Similar Birds

None in North America.

- **FEEDERS** Will come to feeders for seed.

- **POPULATION** Accidental in the Maritimes and in the US in Massachusetts and Maine. Other reports are thought to be of escaped cage birds.

Flight Pattern

Somewhat bounding flight with rapid wing beats alternating with brief periods of wings pulled to sides.

Nest Identification

Shape 🥣   Location 🌲 🌳

Grasses, lichen, moss, rootlets, and feathers, held together by spiders' webbing and lined with finer materials • decorated with bits of lichen • in fork of tree or shrub • built by both sexes, but female does more • 3–6 light pink or pale gray eggs, with various brownish red markings; oval to short oval, 2.0 x 1.5 cm.

Plumage Sexes differ	Habitat 🌿 🔺 🐦 🌾	Migration Migratory	Weight 23 g

Family FRINGILLIDAE	Species *Fringilla montifringilla*	Length 14–16 cm	Wingspan 22–25 cm

BRAMBLING

This Eurasian native occasionally makes visits during migration to the western islands of Alaska. It is casual in the fall and winter across coastal and southern Canada and the northern US to California. Females are similar to males in fresh fall plumage but are duller in color with an olive-brown head and back. Winter males have orange-buff shoulders and chests, a white shoulder bar, and black spotting on the flanks. In flight the long white wing stripe and white rump are distinctive. Juveniles are similar to adult females but are paler with heavier streaking on the back.

- **SONG** Bold grating *dzhweeeeee*. Flight call is nasal *check-check-check*. Call is harsh *tweerk*.
- **BEHAVIOR** Solitary or in pairs while nesting, but in flocks for rest of year; joins mixed foraging flocks in winter. Forages in trees, bushes, and on ground. Eats seeds and insects in summer; seeds in winter. Nests in northern forests with birch trees. Winters in woodlands and weedy fields.
- **BREEDING** Monogamous. Stays in pairs.
- **NESTING** Incubation 11–12 days by female. Young altricial; brooded by female; stay in nest 11–13 days, fed by both sexes. 1–2 broods per year.
- **POPULATION** Rare to casual except western islands in Bering Sea, where it is fairly common in spring migration; has nested at least once on Attu Island. Scattered fall and winter records exist from coast to coast in southern Canada and in the northern US to California.
- **FEEDERS** Will come to feeders for sunflower seeds.

black head and back

orange shoulder patches, throat, and breast

black median coverts bordered white above and tawny orange below

buff-white flanks with black spotting

white belly and undertail coverts

white rump

MALE

olive-brown head and back

tawny orange lower wing bar and white upper wing bar

black-streaked crown

deeply notched black tail

brownish orange shoulder patches, throat, and breast

blackish streaking on flanks

FEMALE

FALL MALE

Flight Pattern
Somewhat bounding flight with rapid wing beats alternating with brief periods of wings pulled to sides.

Nest Identification		
Shape 🔲	Location 🌲 🐦	Grass, hair, birch bark, and moss, held together with spiders' webbing and lined with hair, wool, down, and feathers • adorned with bits of lichen • low in tree and near trunk • built by female • 5–7 pale blue eggs, with pink and reddish markings; subelliptical to oval, 1.9 x 1.4 cm.

Plumage Sexes differ	Habitat 🌾 🌿 🌲 🌱	Migration Migratory	Weight 23 g

DATE _____ TIME_____ LOCATION _____

Family FRINGILLIDAE	Species *Leucosticte tephrocotis*	Length 15 cm	Wingspan 23–24 cm

GRAY-CROWNED ROSY-FINCH

Flying in large flocks, these birds sometimes migrate as far as the Great Plains during the winter months. Like all Rosy-Finches, during nesting season these birds develop a gular pouch in the upper throat with an opening to the floor of the mouth, which helps them carry large amounts of seeds to their young. These birds inhabit barren rocky places nestled among glaciers or above timberline in montane subalpine tundra. Populations living on the Pribilof and Aleutian islands are larger, darker, and show more gray on their faces than continental forms. Females are similar but not as pink on the wings and body as males. The black bills of adults become yellow in winter. Juveniles are gray-brown.

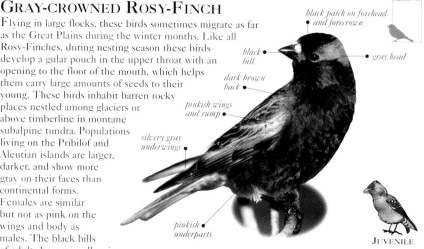

black patch on forehead and forecrown
gray head
black bill
dark brown back
pinkish wings and rump
silvery gray underwings
pinkish underparts

JUVENILE

• **SONG** Long series of high chirps, similar to that of a House Sparrow chorus. Has calls of high lisping *chew*, an abrasive *pert*, and a high-pitched *peent*.

• **BEHAVIOR** Gregarious. Lives in flocks and loose colonies all year. Males weakly territorial. Forages in shrubs, grasses, and on ground, hunting in crevices, among rocks, around tundra and snow pools, and along glaciers. Walks rather than hops. Eats mostly seeds but actively takes insects, sometimes hawking them in flight. In many populations, males greatly outnumber females, and competition during courtship can be vigorous. Mountain populations descend to lower elevations in winter.

• **BREEDING** Monogamous. Colonial. Female chooses territory while male follows and defends her from other birds.

• **NESTING** Incubation 12–14 days by female. Young altricial; brooded by female; stay in nest 16–22 days, fed by both sexes. 1 brood in the mountains; 2 broods elsewhere.

Similar Birds
BLACK ROSY-FINCH Dark blackish brown back, head, throat, and breast; rosy pink rump, wing patch, and underparts; black forehead and forecrown; gray head band • only in the West.
BROWN-CAPPED ROSY-FINCH Dark brown cap; rich brown back, nape, face, throat, and chest; reddish pink underparts, wing patch, rump and uppertail coverts • western range.

• **POPULATION** Common and widespread in Alaska and northwestern Canada. Locally common on alpine tundra over remaining range. Casual in winter to the Midwest and southern California; accidental to Ontario, Quebec, and Maine.

Flight Pattern

Somewhat bounding flight with several rapid wing beats alternating with brief period of wings pulled to sides.

Nest Identification

Shape 🐦   Location 🌿 🏚 ⌂

Grass, rootlets, lichen, and moss, lined with fine grass, plant down, and occasionally feathers • in ridges of rocks and cliffs, sometimes in cave or eave of building • built by female • 4–5 white eggs, occasionally dotted with reddish brown; short pyriform, 2.3 x 1.5 cm.

Plumage Sexes differ	Habitat	Migration Some migrate	Weight Undetermined

DATE _____ TIME _____ LOCATION _____

Family FRINGILLIDAE	Species *Pinicola enucleator*	Length 23–25 cm	Wingspan 35–38 cm

PINE GROSBEAK

The largest of the grosbeaks makes its home in coniferous forests with an abundance of fruiting shrubs and trees. This stout, tame bird is easily approached and may allow itself to be touched by human hands. Like many in the finch family, the male and female develop gular pouches during nesting season to transport food to nestlings. Except for populations in the mountains of several western states and some in New England forests, most of its range is north of the US-Canada border. Irruptive flights in some winters bring birds into the northeastern states. Juveniles resemble adult females but are duller, with washes of dull yellow on the head, back, and rump instead of the female's yellowish or reddish coloring.

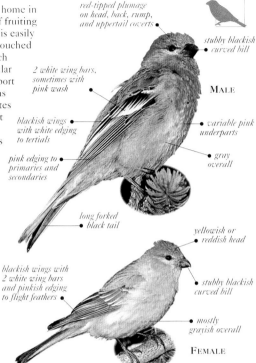

red-tipped plumage on head, back, rump, and uppertail coverts

stubby blackish curved bill

2 white wing bars, sometimes with pink wash

MALE

blackish wings with white edging to tertials

variable pink underparts

pink edging to primaries and secondaries

gray overall

long forked black tail

yellowish or reddish head

blackish wings with 2 white wing bars and pinkish edging to flight feathers

stubby blackish curved bill

mostly grayish overall

FEMALE

• **SONG** Brief clear musical warble, similar to that of the Purple Finch. Call is whistled *pewi, pewi, pewi.* Alarm note is *chee-uli.*

• **BEHAVIOR** Solitary or in pairs during nesting season. Tame. Gregarious. Forms large flocks soon after juveniles become independent. Forages on ground and in trees. Eats mainly seeds; also takes buds, some fruits, and insects. Male feeds female as part of courtship ritual. Mostly sedentary, not often moving south of southernmost breeding ranges in winter.

• **BREEDING** Monogamous. Solitary.

• **NESTING** Incubation 13–15 days by female. Young altricial; brooded by female; stay in nest 13–20 days, fed by both sexes. 1 brood per year.

• **POPULATION** Fairly common in open coniferous forests and along edge of forest. Winters in mixed coniferous-deciduous woodlands, deciduous forests, second growth, and in shade trees in villages and in suburbs.

RUSSET VARIANT

• **FEEDERS** Seeds.

• **CONSERVATION** Vulnerable to loss of habitat due to logging operations.

Flight Pattern
Shallow undulations with series of rapid wing beats alternating with brief periods of wings drawn to sides.

Nest Identification	Twigs, weeds, and rootlets, with lining of soft grass, rootlets, moss, and lichen • on limb of tree or bush, usually 60 cm–7.5 m above ground • built by female • 2–5 blue-green eggs with dots of black, purple, and brown; oval to long oval, 2.5 x 1.8 cm.
Shape Location	

Plumage Sexes differ	Habitat	Migration Northern birds migrate	Weight 57 g

| Family FRINGILLIDAE | Species *Carpodacus purpureus* | Length 14–16 cm | Wingspan 23–27 cm |

PURPLE FINCH

The male is easy to identify by its raspberry-colored plumage, brightest on the head, rump, and chest. Foraging in winter flocks, these birds depend on feeders when food supplies are scarce. Juveniles are similar to adult females; both have two white wing bars.

bright rosy red head

rosy supercilium

MALE

rosy red plumage with brown streaking on back and crown

brown loreal mask extending onto auriculars

pinkish edging to wings and 2 pinkish white wing bars

bright rosy red rump

white belly and undertail coverts

• **SONG** Rapid high-pitched rising and falling warble. Late winter/early spring males may sing in chorus. Call is *chur-lee*. Flight notes are sharp *tuck* or *pit*.

brown loreal mask extending onto auriculars

whitish eye line

brown-gray upperparts with whitish streaks

• **BEHAVIOR** Solitary or in pairs in nesting season. Male sings from exposed perch. Gregarious, tame. In flocks after breeding; joins mixed-species foraging flocks in winter with siskins and goldfinches. Forages in trees and hopping on ground. Eats seeds; some fruits, insects, and caterpillars in summer.

brown malar mark

grayish white underparts with brown streaking

deeply notched tail

FEMALE

Similar Birds

CASSIN'S FINCH ♂
Longer bill with straighter culmen; nape often slightly crested; gray-brown back; wings edged with pale pink; long primary projection; streaked undertail coverts; distinct streaks on sides and flanks • western range.

HOUSE FINCH ♂
Slender not chunky; less pointed bill with decurved culmen; indistinct facial pattern; brighter red on crown, rump, throat, and breast; dusky streaked underparts; squared tail.

• **BREEDING** Monogamous. Male displays by dancing around female and vigorously flapping his wings until he ascends to a foot above the ground.

• **NESTING** Incubation about 13 days by female. Altricial young brooded by female; stay in nest 14 days, fed by both sexes. 1–2 broods per year.

• **POPULATION** Fairly common in open coniferous and mixed coniferous-deciduous forests, in forest edge, and in suburbs; in Pacific states, in oak canyons and lower mountain slopes. Declining in the East.

• **FEEDERS** Millet and sunflower seeds.

• **CONSERVATION** Uncommon cowbird host. Vulnerable to habitat loss due to logging. Decrease in New England due to competition with House Sparrow; recent declines in East suggest same with House Finch.

Flight Pattern
Swift bounding flight with rapid wing beats alternating with brief periods of wings pulled to body.

Nest Identification	
Shape 🥣 Location 🪶 🌿	Twigs, weeds, rootlets, strips of bark, and string, with lining of moss, soft grasses, moss, and hair • on branch or in fork of tree, 2–12 m above ground • built by female • 3–5 pale green-blue eggs, marked with black and brown; oval to short oval, 2.0 x 1.4 cm.

| Plumage Sexes differ | Habitat 🌳 🪴 ⛰ 🏔 | Migration Northern birds migrate | Weight 34 g |

DATE _____ TIME _____ LOCATION _____

Family FRINGILLIDAE	Species *Carpodacus cassinii*	Length 15 cm	Wingspan 25 cm

CASSIN'S FINCH

Inhabiting the coniferous mountain forests of the West, these birds move in autumn with their young to lower elevations for the winter. Females have pale coloring and streaked undertail coverts that help distinguish them from other similar finches. In summer, this bird occurs at higher elevations than the Purple and House Finches. Juveniles closely resemble adult females

• **SONG** Long rich warbling, variable in pattern and length. Calls are clear *cheep, cheep, cheep* and *kee-up*, and a 3-syllabled flight note of *tee-dee-yip*.

• **BEHAVIOR** Solitary or in pairs during nesting season; forms family groups after breeding. Gregarious and tame. Forages on ground and high in trees; eats conifer seeds and buds, some insects in summer. Frequents salt licks and gathers at salted roadsides in winter. Nests in different sites each year.

• **BREEDING** Monogamous. Semicolonial.

• **NESTING** Incubation 12–14 days by female. Young altricial; brooded by female; stay in nest 14 days, fed by both sexes. 2 broods per year.

• **POPULATION** Fairly common in high montane open coniferous forests. In winter in deciduous woodlands, brushy scrublands, and second growth. Casual in winter to the West Coast and east to Minnesota, Oklahoma, and central Texas.

• **FEEDERS** Seeds.

• **CONSERVATION** Neotropical migrant. Rare cowbird host. Vulnerable to loss of habitat due to logging.

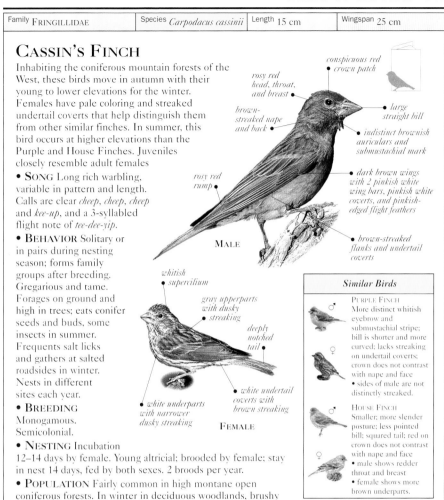

conspicuous red crown patch

rosy red head, throat, and breast

brown-streaked nape and back

large straight bill

indistinct brownish auriculars and submustachial mark

dark brown wings with 2 pinkish white wing bars, pinkish white coverts, and pinkish-edged flight feathers

rosy red rump

brown-streaked flanks and undertail coverts

MALE

whitish supercilium

gray upperparts with dusky streaking

deeply notched tail

white undertail coverts with brown streaking

white underparts with narrower dusky streaking

FEMALE

Similar Birds

PURPLE FINCH
More distinct whitish eyebrow and submustachial stripe; bill is shorter and more curved; lacks streaking on undertail coverts; crown does not contrast with nape and face
• sides of male are not distinctly streaked.

HOUSE FINCH
Smaller; more slender posture; less pointed bill; squared tail; red on crown does not contrast with nape and face
• male shows redder throat and breast
• female shows more brown underparts.

Flight Pattern

Swift bounding flight with rapid wing beats alternating with brief periods of wings pulled to sides.

Nest Identification

Shape

Location

Twigs, weeds, rootlets, and strips of bark, with lining of fibers, soft grass, and hair • sometimes decorated with lichen • on branch of tree, 3–24.5 m above ground • built by female • 4–6 blue-green eggs, dotted with brown and black, concentrated on larger end; subelliptical to long subelliptical, 2.0 x 1.4 cm.

Plumage Sexes differ	Habitat	Migration Northern birds migrate	Weight 26 g

DATE _____ TIME _____ LOCATION _____

| Family FRINGILLIDAE | Species *Carpodacus mexicanus* | Length 15 cm | Wingspan 25 cm |

HOUSE FINCH

- brown cap
- brown upperparts with paler brown streaking
- 2 narrow white wing bars
- squared tail
- bright red to orange bib and front of head

MALE

- brown-streaked underparts

Originally confined to the West, this finch was called a Linnet and introduced as a cage bird on Long Island, New York, in the 1940s. It became abundant in the East, surpassing the House Sparrow. Today, it is among the most widely distributed songbird species in North America. It often feeds with the Purple Finch, especially in winter. Some male variants are orange or yellow instead of red. Juveniles resemble adult females.

- **SONG** Varied rich high-pitched scratchy warble composed chiefly of 3-note phrases; many end with rising inflections. Both sexes sing, but male's song is longer, more complex, and more frequent. Call is nasal *chee* or *chee-wheet;* in flight a sharp nasal *nyee-ah.*

- grayish brown-streaked upperparts
- 2 narrow whitish buff wing bars
- brown-streaked whitish buff underparts

FEMALE

ORANGE VARIANT MALE

- **BEHAVIOR** Solitary or in pairs during nesting season. Gregarious. Forms small family groups when young become independent. Larger foraging flocks in winter may join with other finches. Actively forages on ground, in fields, and in suburban areas. Eats mostly seeds but in summer takes insects and fruits. Drinks maple sap. Males are conspicuous and sing often. Studies indicate that the redder the male's plumage, the more desirable he is to females.

- **BREEDING** Monogamous. Solitary.

- **NESTING** Incubation 12–14 days by female. Altricial young brooded by female; stay in nest 11–19 days, fed by both sexes. 1–3 broods per year.

- **POPULATION** Abundant over much of North America in a wide variety of habitats, from arid scrub, wooded canyons, cultivated fields, and open woodlands to suburban yards and urban areas.

- **FEEDERS** Thistle, millet, sunflower, and other seeds.

- **CONSERVATION** Rare cowbird host in the West; fairly common host in the East.

Similar Birds

PURPLE FINCH ♂ Chunkier; notched tail; distinct rosy eyebrow and submustachial stripe; white crissum lacks streaking; crown does not contrast with face and nape • male shows raspberry-red on head, breast, and rump.

CASSIN'S FINCH ♂ Larger; notched tail; long straight bill; nape often slightly crested; bright red crown; pale pink-edged wings; streaked undertail coverts; distinct streaking on sides and flanks • western range.

Flight Pattern

Swift somewhat bounding flight with rapid wing beats alternating with brief periods of wings pulled to sides.

Nest Identification

Shape

Location

Twigs, grass, leaves, rootlets, bits of debris, and feathers • in tree hollow, cactus, on ground, under eaves of building, in bird boxes, abandoned nests, shrub, tree, etc. • built by female • 2–6 light blue eggs, spotted with lilac and black, often concentrated at larger end; oval to long oval, 2.0 x 1.4 cm.

| Plumage Sexes differ | Habitat | Migration Some migrate | Weight 20 g |

Family FRINGILLIDAE	Species *Loxia curvirostra*	Length 14–17 cm	Wingspan 25–27 cm

RED CROSSBILL

Crossbills take their name from the overlapping tips of the upper and lower mandibles. A resident of evergreen forests, they insert the crossed mandibles into conifer cones, forcing the scales apart while the tongue scoops the seed into the mouth. Nestlings have straight mandibles that cross gradually about three weeks out of the nest. Having abundant food year-round, this species begins nesting as early as January. Juveniles have weakly crossed mandibles, gray-olive upperparts heavily streaked dark brown, dark brown-streaked whitish underparts with yellowish wash, and buff-yellow rump. Subspecies of this bird vary in size, bill size, and vocalizations and may represent up to nine separate species.

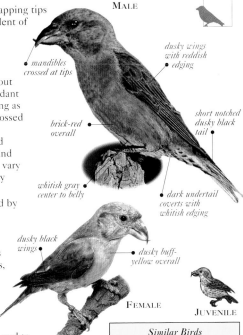

MALE

- *mandibles crossed at tips*
- *dusky wings with reddish edging*
- *brick-red overall*
- *short notched dusky black tail*
- *whitish gray center to belly*
- *dark undertail coverts with whitish edging*

- **SONG** Series of 2-note phrases followed by trilled warble, *jitt, jitt, jitt, jitt, jiiaa-jiiaa-jiiaaaaa*. Calls vary among subspecies.

- **BEHAVIOR** In pairs during breeding season. Gregarious in small to large flocks most of year. Forages primarily in conifers, some on ground. Eats mostly seeds; also insects and caterpillars. Clings under branches and cones chickadee-like or crawls across limbs and cones like a small parrot, using bill and feet. Eats bits of mortar and is attracted to salt licks and to winter salt on the sides of roadways. Individuals and flocks fly high and are generally detected by their flight calls.

- *dusky black wings*
- *dusky buff-yellow overall*

FEMALE

JUVENILE

- **BREEDING** Monogamous. Solitary. Displaying male flies above female, vibrating wings and delivering flight song as he soars in circles overhead.

- **NESTING** Incubation 12–18 days by female. Altricial young brooded by female; stay in nest 15–20 days, fed by both sexes. 1–2 broods per year.

- **POPULATION** Fairly common in conifers and mixed forests. Wanderers, often depend on cone crop. Irruptive flights to Gulf states some winters.

- **FEEDERS** Sunflower seeds.

- **CONSERVATION** Vulnerable to habitat loss caused by logging operations.

Similar Birds

WHITE-WINGED CROSSBILL
White wing bars in all seasons • male pinkish red overall • female has dusky mottled olive-yellow upperparts; yellow rump; grayish underparts with yellowish wash.

Flight Pattern
Swift bounding flights, sometimes high above ground, on rapidly beating wings with brief periods of wings pulled to sides.

Nest Identification	Twigs, pieces of bark, grass, and rootlets, with lining of finer grasses, feathers, fur, hair, and moss • on tree branch far out from trunk, 2–12 m above ground • built by female • 3–4 light green or blue eggs spotted with browns and lilacs; oval to long oval, 2.0 x 1.5 cm.
Shape ◗ Location 🐾	

Plumage Sexes differ	Habitat 🌲🌿	Migration Nonmigratory	Weight 40 g

DATE _____ TIME_____ LOCATION _____

Family FRINGILLIDAE	Species *Loxia leucoptera*	Length 15–17 cm	Wingspan 24–27 cm

WHITE-WINGED CROSSBILL

Frequenting a northern range, White-winged Crossbills rarely are observed in large numbers in the US, except during food shortages and periods of overpopulation. Males are bright pink with a dusky band on the lower back, but plumage pales during winter months. Juveniles resemble adult females but are buffy tan overall with heavy brown streaking.

bright pink overall

2 bold broad white wing bars

black wings and tail

MALE

whitish center to belly

white undertail coverts

- **SONG** Vigorous musical warbles and chatters, *sweet, sweet, sweet,* on different pitches and often issued during display flight on hovering wings. Call is rapid harsh repetitive series of *chif-chif-chif* notes and plaintive *peet.*

yellowish wash on head, nape, back, and breast

black wings with 2 broad white wing bars

grayish olive overall

FEMALE

dusky streaks and mottling

JUVENILE

- **BEHAVIOR** Gregarious. Tame. In pairs during nesting season from early winter to spring. Forages in small flocks most of year. Principal diet is conifer seeds; also eats seeds from other trees, weeds, grasses, and sunflowers. Takes some insects. Attracted to salt licks and salt on surfaces of winter highways. Like Red Crossbill, uses mandible tips to spread cone scales while removing seed with tongue. Climbs over branches parrotlike using feet and bill.

notched black tail

- **BREEDING** Monogamous. Solitary.
- **NESTING** Breeding biology poorly known. Incubation 12–14 days by female. Altricial young brooded by female; stay in nest estimated 15–20 days. Both sexes regurgitate milky seed pulp mixture to nestlings. 1 brood per year.
- **POPULATION** Fairly common but erratic in conifer and mixed coniferous-deciduous forests. Irregular wanderer; irruptive southward migration dependent on cone seed crops.

Similar Birds

RED CROSSBILL
Male brick-red overall; dark brownish black wings without wing bars • female has dusky yellow upperparts with dusky mottling; yellow rump; brownish black wings lack wing bars; dull yellow underparts lack streaking or mottling.

Western populations expanding range southward.
- **FEEDERS** Sunflower seeds.
- **CONSERVATION** Vulnerable to habitat loss due to logging operations. Heavy mortality in winter due to automobile traffic on salted roadways.

Flight Pattern

Swift bounding flight with rapidly beating wings alternating with brief periods of wings pulled to sides.

Nest Identification	
Shape 🥄 Location 🌿	Grass, bark, lichen, moss, and hair • lined with twigs and weeds • on horizontal tree limb far out from trunk, 1–21.5 m above ground • built by female • 3–5 whitish to pale blue-green eggs with brown and lavender spotting at larger end; oval to long oval, 2.2 x 1.6 cm.

Plumage Sexes differ	Habitat 🌳 🌲 🏔	Migration Nonmigratory	Weight 28 g

DATE _____ TIME_____ LOCATION _____

Family FRINGILLIDAE	Species *Carduelis flammea*	Length 13–14 cm	Wingspan 21–23 cm

COMMON REDPOLL

This finch is most commonly observed in the tundra, but during some winters, foraging flocks migrate to southern Canada and the northern US. It is a tame bird that allows close approach and does not fight over territory. The best field mark is the red to orange cap and black chin combined with the streaked rump, uppertail coverts, sides, and crissum. Although primarily nonmigratory, the northern populations do migrate.

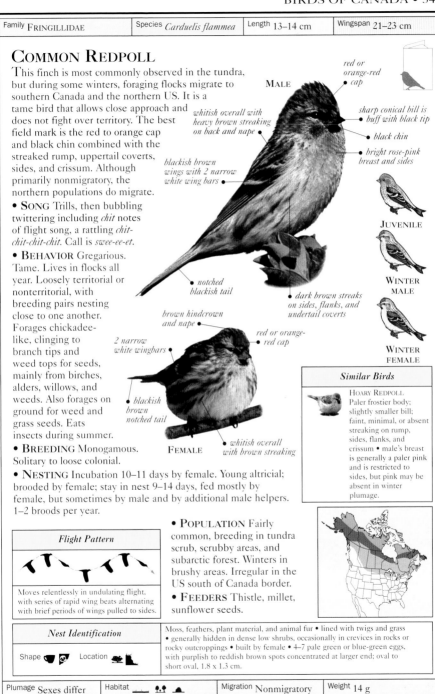

MALE

red or orange-red cap

whitish overall with heavy brown streaking on back and nape

sharp conical bill is buff with black tip

black chin

bright rose-pink breast and sides

blackish brown wings with 2 narrow white wing bars

notched blackish tail

dark brown streaks on sides, flanks, and undertail coverts

brown hindcrown and nape

2 narrow white wingbars

red or orange-red cap

blackish brown notched tail

whitish overall with brown streaking

FEMALE

JUVENILE

WINTER MALE

WINTER FEMALE

- **SONG** Trills, then bubbling twittering including *chit* notes of flight song, a rattling *chit-chit-chit-chit*. Call is *swee-ee-et*.

- **BEHAVIOR** Gregarious. Tame. Lives in flocks all year. Loosely territorial or nonterritorial, with breeding pairs nesting close to one another. Forages chickadee-like, clinging to branch tips and weed tops for seeds, mainly from birches, alders, willows, and weeds. Also forages on ground for weed and grass seeds. Eats insects during summer.

- **BREEDING** Monogamous. Solitary to loose colonial.

- **NESTING** Incubation 10–11 days by female. Young altricial; brooded by female; stay in nest 9–14 days, fed mostly by female, but sometimes by male and by additional male helpers. 1–2 broods per year.

Similar Birds

HOARY REDPOLL Paler frostier body; slightly smaller bill; faint, minimal, or absent streaking on rump, sides, flanks, and crissum • male's breast is generally a paler pink and is restricted to sides, but pink may be absent in winter plumage.

- **POPULATION** Fairly common, breeding in tundra scrub, scrubby areas, and subarctic forest. Winters in brushy areas. Irregular in the US south of Canada border.

- **FEEDERS** Thistle, millet, sunflower seeds.

Flight Pattern

Moves relentlessly in undulating flight, with series of rapid wing beats alternating with brief periods of wings pulled to sides.

Nest Identification	Moss, feathers, plant material, and animal fur • lined with twigs and grass • generally hidden in dense low shrubs, occasionally in crevices in rocks or rocky outcroppings • built by female • 4–7 pale green or blue-green eggs, with purplish to reddish brown spots concentrated at larger end; oval to short oval, 1.8 x 1.3 cm.
Shape 〜 📷 Location 🌿 🪨	

Plumage Sexes differ	Habitat ___ 🐾 ⛰	Migration Nonmigratory	Weight 14 g

DATE _____ TIME _____ LOCATION _____

Family FRINGILLIDAE	Species *Carduelis hornemanni*	Length 13–15 cm	Wingspan 22–23 cm

HOARY REDPOLL

Breeding along the Arctic Coast, this bird closely resembles its cousin, the Common Redpoll, but has little or no streaking on its rump and crissum and has silvery white plumage, presenting a more frosted appearance. Not wary of humans in the manner of many high arctic species, it will sometimes land on a shoulder or come to the hand for food. During the winter, this bird is almost always in the company of Common Redpolls. The female is similar to the male but lacks the pink wash on the breast and the faint streaking on the sides. Juveniles resemble females but lack the black chin and red cap and show more streaking on the underparts.

light brown streaking on back

pale buff-grayish to whitish upperparts

notched black tail

red cap

stubby bill

white crissum and rump with little or no streaking

black chin patch

whitish underparts with pinkish wash on breast

• **SONG** A trill followed by a slow twitter, *zzzzzz-chee-chee-chee-chee*. Call is a plaintive *tweet*.

• **BEHAVIOR** Tame. Gregarious year-round. Nests in loose colonies with pairs close together and males apparently not defending territories. Forms foraging flocks after breeding when young become independent. Joins mixed-species flocks with other finch species in winter. Forages for food on ground and in bushes and trees. Eats seeds and insects. Regurgitates milky mix of seeds and insects to nestlings. Forages in brushy and weedy habitats in winter.

• **BREEDING** Monogamous. Semicolonial.

• **NESTING** Incubation 9–12 days by female. Young altricial; brooded by female; stay in nest 9–14 days, fed by both sexes. 1–2 broods per year.

• **POPULATION** Fairly common on scrubby tundra. This bird is irregular in winter south of Canada.

• **FEEDERS** Will come to feeders for thistle, millet, sunflower, and other seeds.

Similar Birds

♂ COMMON REDPOLL Conspicuous streaking on rump, flanks, and undertail coverts; heavier brown streaking on nape and upperparts; slightly larger bill
• male shows rosy pink on breast and sides extending onto cheeks.

Flight Pattern

Swift bounding flight on rapidly beating wings alternating with brief periods of wings pulled to sides.

Nest Identification

Shape ◖ Location

Twigs, grass, and rootlets, with lining of soft grass, feathers, and hair • in middle of low bush or on ground sheltered by rocks or vegetation • built by female • 4–6 light green to bluish green eggs, dotted with reddish brown, usually concentrated at larger end; oval to short oval, 1.8 x 1.3 cm.

Plumage Sexes differ	Habitat	Migration Northern birds migrate	Weight 14 g

DATE _____ TIME_____ LOCATION _____

Family FRINGILLIDAE	Species *Carduelis pinus*	Length 11–13 cm	Wingspan 22–23 cm

PINE SISKIN

In fall and winter this is a common visitor to northern forests, where it forages in flocks that may include several thousand birds. When food is scarce these daytime migrants may travel as far south as Florida and central Mexico, flying in tightly formed flocks. In flight the yellow wing stripe at the base of the flight feathers and the yellow base to the outer tail feathers are conspicuous. Females are similar to males but with more washed-out yellow plumage. Juveniles resemble females but show a yellowish wash overall.

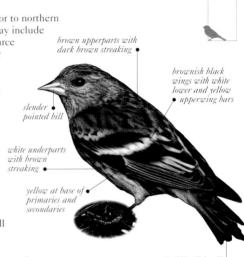

brown upperparts with dark brown streaking

brownish black wings with white lower and yellow upperwing bars

slender pointed bill

white underparts with brown streaking

yellow at base of primaries and secondaries

notched blackish tail with yellow base to outer tail feathers

• **SONG** Husky canary-like twittering warble, rising and falling in pitch and interspersed with a rapid ascending *ZZZzzzzzzzzzrree!*, sounding like the equivalent of a bird with a chainsaw. Call is rising *tee-ee*. Flight note is hoarse descending *chee*.

• **BEHAVIOR** Tame, may allow close approach. Gregarious. In small groups or flocks year-round. Weakly territorial or not at all, with pairs nesting close to one another, often in the same tree. Forages on ground and in trees for seeds from alders, birches, spruce, and other trees. Also eats thistle seeds and weeds, some insects in summer. Nomadic in fall and winter. Attracted to salt licks and salt-treated winter highways. Feeds on sap at drill wells created by sapsuckers. Mountain populations descent to lower elevations prior to winter onset.

• **BREEDING** Monogamous. Semicolonial.

• **NESTING** Incubation 13 days by female. Young altricial; brooded by female; stay in nest 14–15 days, fed by both sexes. 2 broods per year.

• **POPULATION** Widespread and abundant in coniferous and mixed conifer-deciduous forests, in woodlands, parks, weedy fields, and near human habitation. Erratic irruptions in some winters bring large numbers far south of normal wintering range.

Similar Birds

HOUSE FINCH ♀ Stubbier thicker bill; longer tail with squarish tip; 2 narrow white wing bars; lacks yellow at base of tail, primaries, and secondaries.

COMMON REDPOLL ♀ Red cap; black chin; 2 narrow white wing bars; lacks yellow plumage on wings and tail.

• **FEEDERS** Mixed seed, thistle, and black oil sunflower seed. Also will bathe and drink in birdbaths.

• **CONSERVATION** Fatalities high in winter; birds attracted to salt on roads become reluctant to fly.

Flight Pattern
Flight is high and swift in compact flocks with long undulating sweeps.

Nest Identification	Bark, moss, feathers, and animal fur • lined with grass and twigs • usually hidden in conifer, placed far out from trunk • 3–15 m above ground • built by female • 3–5 pale greenish blue eggs, with brown and black spots concentrated on larger end; short oval to short subelliptical, 1.8 x 1.3 cm.
Shape ⬤ ◥ Location 🌲	

Plumage Sexes similar	Habitat 🌳 🔺	Migration Migratory	Weight 14 g

DATE _____ TIME_____ LOCATION _____

Family FRINGILLIDAE	Species *Carduelis tristis*	Length 13 cm	Wingspan 22–23 cm

AMERICAN GOLDFINCH

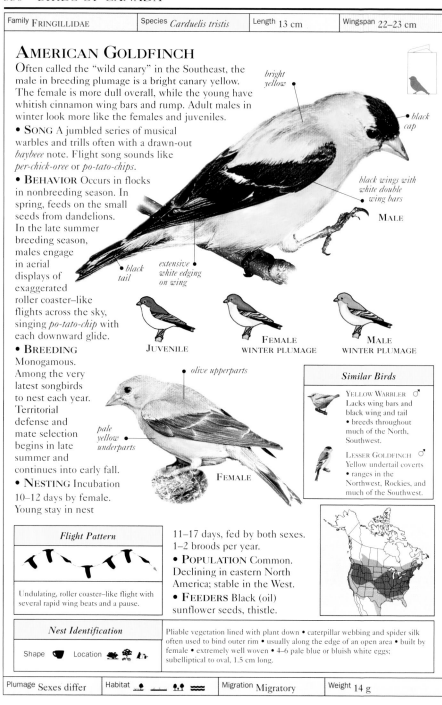

Often called the "wild canary" in the Southeast, the male in breeding plumage is a bright canary yellow. The female is more dull overall, while the young have whitish cinnamon wing bars and rump. Adult males in winter look more like the females and juveniles.

• **SONG** A jumbled series of musical warbles and trills often with a drawn-out *baybee* note. Flight song sounds like *per-chick-oree* or *po-tato-chips*.

• **BEHAVIOR** Occurs in flocks in nonbreeding season. In spring, feeds on the small seeds from dandelions. In the late summer breeding season, males engage in aerial displays of exaggerated roller coaster–like flights across the sky, singing *po-tato-chip* with each downward glide.

• **BREEDING** Monogamous. Among the very latest songbirds to nest each year. Territorial defense and mate selection begins in late summer and continues into early fall.

• **NESTING** Incubation 10–12 days by female. Young stay in nest

bright yellow

black cap

black wings with white double wing bars

MALE

black tail

extensive white edging on wing

JUVENILE

FEMALE WINTER PLUMAGE

MALE WINTER PLUMAGE

olive upperparts

pale yellow underparts

FEMALE

Similar Birds

YELLOW WARBLER ♂
Lacks wing bars and black wing and tail • breeds throughout much of the North, Southwest.

LESSER GOLDFINCH ♂
Yellow undertail coverts • ranges in the Northwest, Rockies, and much of the Southwest.

Flight Pattern

Undulating, roller coaster–like flight with several rapid wing beats and a pause.

11–17 days, fed by both sexes. 1–2 broods per year.
• **POPULATION** Common. Declining in eastern North America; stable in the West.
• **FEEDERS** Black (oil) sunflower seeds, thistle.

Nest Identification

Shape 〰 Location 🌳🌿🌱

Pliable vegetation lined with plant down • caterpillar webbing and spider silk often used to bind outer rim • usually along the edge of an open area • built by female • extremely well woven • 4–6 pale blue or bluish white eggs; subelliptical to oval, 1.5 cm long.

Plumage Sexes differ	Habitat	Migration Migratory	Weight 14 g

DATE _____ TIME_____ LOCATION _____

| Family FRINGILLIDAE | Species *Coccothraustes vespertinus* | Length 20–22 cm | Wingspan 33–35 cm |

EVENING GROSBEAK

Since the late nineteenth century the breeding range of this chunky bird has expanded eastward, supported by seed from new trees and by increased feeding stations. Fall migratory patterns are erratic; birds only leave breeding ranges when food supplies fail or populations become sizeable. Flocks may arrive in a region one winter and not return the next. In flight the short notched tail and large wing patches are distinctive.

• **SONG** Series of clipped warbled phrases, ending in shrill whistled note. Calls are loud piercing *clee-ip*, *peeer* and *chirp*. Flocks sound like chorus of amplified House Sparrows.

• **BEHAVIOR** Gregarious. Tame. Noisy. In groups and flocks during breeding season; pairs nest closely. Eats insects, including spruce budworm, while nesting; also eats buds, sap, and seeds from trees and shrubs; fruits and berries. In winter looks for salt and drinks water from melting snow.

• **BREEDING** Monogamous. Semicolonial.

• **NESTING** Incubation 11–14 days by female; male feeds incubating female on nest. Young altricial; brooded by female; stay in nest 13–14 days, fed by both sexes. 1–2 broods per year.

• **POPULATION** Fairly common in breeding season in conifers and mixed woodlots; in mountains in West. Irregular in winter in woodlots, parks, second growth, suburban areas.

• **FEEDERS** Sunflower seeds; frequents birdbaths.

• **CONSERVATION** Rare cowbird host. Many killed on salt-treated highways in winter.

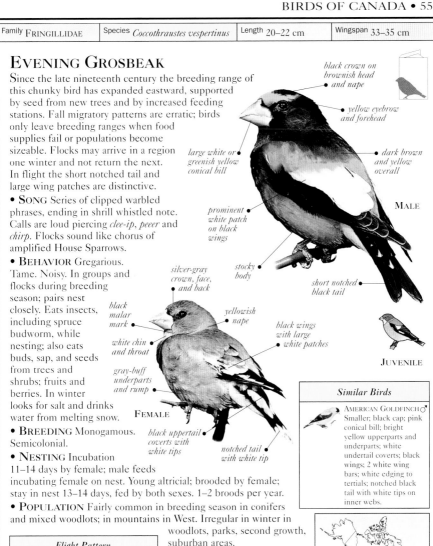

black crown on brownish head and nape

yellow eyebrow and forehead

large white or greenish yellow conical bill

dark brown and yellow overall

MALE

prominent white patch on black wings

silver-gray crown, face, and back

stocky body

short notched black tail

black malar mark

yellowish nape

white chin and throat

black wings with large white patches

JUVENILE

gray-buff underparts and rump

FEMALE

black uppertail coverts with white tips

notched tail with white tip

Similar Birds

AMERICAN GOLDFINCH ♂ Smaller; black cap; pink conical bill; bright yellow upperparts and underparts; white undertail coverts; black wings; 2 white wing bars; white edging to tertials; notched black tail with white tips on inner webs.

Flight Pattern

Swift shallow bounding flight with rapid wing beats alternating with brief periods of wings pulled to sides.

| Nest Identification | Frail structure of twigs, grass, moss, roots, and pine needles • lined with fine materials • built on horizontal branch of tree far out from trunk • usually 6–18.5 m above ground (but up to 30.5 m) • built by female • 3–5 pale blue to bluish green eggs, with brown, gray, and purple spotting; oval to short oval, 2.5 x 2.0 cm. |
| Shape | Location |

| Plumage Sexes differ | Habitat | Migration Some migrate | Weight 60 g |

Family PASSERIDAE	Species *Passer domesticus*	Length 14–17 cm	Wingspan 24–25 cm

HOUSE SPARROW

This bird was introduced in New York City from Europe in the 1850s. By the early 20th century it was established over most of the continent. With the popularity of cars it began to decline; fewer horses meant less undigested grain to be gleaned from horse manure. Sometimes called the English Sparrow, it is the world's most widespread songbird. Juveniles resemble females but have browner upperparts, buffier underparts, and a pinkish bill.

gray crown and cheeks

chestnut nape joins postocular stripe

black bill

buff-brown back and wings with black streaking

black bib and lores

white submustache joins white half-collar

MALE

white wing bar

gray rump and tail

pale gray underparts

• **SONG** Twittering series of chirps. Call is monotonous repeated *cheep-cheep-cheep*.

• **BEHAVIOR** Aggressive and noisy. In pairs during nesting season; family groups and flocks after breeding. Feeds and roosts in huge flocks. Hops. Forages on ground, in trees and shrubs, in urban and rural areas. Eats insects, caterpillars, seeds, grains, and fruits. Inspects car grilles for insects. Usurps nesting cavities from other species.

dusky postocular stripe below buff eyebrow

blackish-streaked buff-brown upperparts

dusky bill with yellowish base to lower mandible

FEMALE

WINTER MALE

white wing bar

brownish gray underparts

• **BREEDING** Monogamous. Some promiscuous. Males form circle around female and aggressively battle with each other.

• **NESTING** Incubation 10–14 days by both sexes, mostly by female. Altricial young brooded by female; stay in nest 14–17 days; both sexes feed by regurgitation. 2–3 broods per year.

• **POPULATION** Abundant and widespread in urban and cultivated areas and around human habitation; gradually declining.

Similar Birds

EURASIAN TREE SPARROW
Reddish brown crown; white cheek with black patch; black loral mask and chin; black-streaked brownish upperparts; white wing bar has black upper border; dusky brown underparts • locally common only in and around St. Louis, Missouri, and Illinois.

• **FEEDERS AND BIRDHOUSES** Will come to feeders for small seeds and grains; nests in bird boxes.

• **CONSERVATION** Rare cowbird host. Out-competes other secondary-cavity nesters but loses to European Starlings.

Flight Pattern
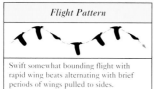
Swift somewhat bounding flight with rapid wing beats alternating with brief periods of wings pulled to sides.

Nest Identification	
Shape Location	Grass, straw, weeds, cotton, bits of debris, twigs, and feathers • in tree hollow, under eaves of building or other sheltered areas, or in bird boxes; abandoned nests of other birds • on the backs of highway signs and billboards in the West • built by both sexes • 3–7 light green or blue eggs, dotted with grays and browns, concentrated toward larger end; oval to long oval, 2.3 x 1.8 cm.

Plumage Sexes differ	Habitat	Migration Nonmigratory	Weight 28 g

DATE _____ TIME_____ LOCATION _____

GLOSSARY

• **AERIE**
A nest located on a cliff or high place, usually built by a raptor, a bird of prey.

• **AGAVE**
A desert plant with a spikelike flower, similar to a Yucca plant.

• **AIR SAC**
A series of thin-walled sacs, typically eight or nine (but ranging from six to fourteen, depending on the species) that in conjunction with the paired lungs comprise the bird's respiratory system.

• **ALAR BAR**
A contrasting line (bar) of plumage beginning in the alar region of the wing (where the wing bends at the wrist and on the leading edge) and running from that point at an angle toward the bird's body, stopping where the back of the wing joins the body. The effect is a patch or line of feathers that differ from the color of the wing feathers around it, thus producing a visible bar on the top of the wing. Sometimes the bar runs from the alula to the base of the wing on the front side (leading edge).

• **ALTERNATE PLUMAGE**
See Breeding Plumage.

• **ALTITUDINAL MOVEMENTS**
(Vertical migrations) A bird's regular seasonal vertical movement, often from the mountaintops in summer to lower regions or valleys during winter, with a return to higher elevations the following spring.

• **ALTRICIAL**
Term for young birds that hatch in a helpless state, usually naked with eyes closed, and are totally dependent on the parents.

• **ALULA**
A small group of feathers that protrude from the outermost joint of the wing. It has its own group of muscles and moves independently from the flight feathers. By adjusting the angle of the alula, the bird is able to regulate the air flow over the top of the wing, allowing it to alight or land at slower speeds without stalling.

• **ANHEDRAL**
The downward curve of a bird's wings when in flight.

• **ARBOREAL**
A tree-dwelling bird.

• **AURICULARS**
Feathers along the sides of the ears, often called ear coverts or ear patches.

• **AXILLARIES**
Rigid feathers along the underside of the wings where they connect to the body, corresponding to the underarm area in a human.

• **BASIC PLUMAGE**
See Winter Plumage.

• **BREEDING PLUMAGE**
(Alternate plumage) Seasonal alterations in appearance to attract birds of the opposite sex, such as changes in color or the addition of ornamental ruffs. This is accomplished by a feather molt from the basic, or winter, plumage.

• **CAMBIUM**
Plant tissue near the inner bark of a tree that produces lateral growth.

• **CATKIN**
A spike of flowers such as those found on a willow or birch tree.

- **CERE**
The fleshy area on top of the base of the upper bill that contains the nostrils. Present on the bills of some bird species, particularly among birds of prey.

- **CLUTCH**
The total number of eggs laid during a single nesting period; some birds lay several clutches in a nesting season.

- **COLONIAL**
The pattern of nesting close together with birds of the same species. Sometimes only a few nests packed close together constitute a colony, but some may hold hundreds or thousands of nesting pairs.

- **CONGENERS**
Distinct bird species that are related to one another by being in the same genus.

- **CONSPECIFIC**
Birds that are members of the same species.

- **COVERTS**
A covering of feathers overlaying the upper and lower part of the wings, covering the bases of the flight feathers (wing coverts); also on top of the tail feathers (uppertail coverts and undertail coverts).

- **CRECHE**
An aggregation of hatchlings of a nesting colony, living together while they are in a dependent state and fed and tended by the adult birds.

- **CREPUSCULAR**
Birds that feed and are active during twilight hours.

- **CRISSUM**
Feathers covering the base of the undertail, usually a different color from the rest of the underparts. Also called undertail coverts.

- **CROP**
Where food is stored in the esophagus for later digestion, or to be regurgitated and fed to hatchlings. Some birds, such as pigeons and doves, have a two-chambered crop that produces special milk to nourish their young.

- **CROWN**
Top of the head between the forehead and the back of the head or occiput.

- **CULMEN**
Top ridge of the upper mandible, darker on some birds than the side of the bill.

- **DABBLING**
Method of surface feeding by a relatively short-necked short-legged duck. It tips up the tail and body, then dips its bill and neck into water. These ducks are called dabblers. See Tipping-up.

- **DECURVED**
Sloped downward, usually referring to the bill.

- **DETRITUS**
Small particles of dead organic matter.

- **DIHEDRAL**
Wings held in a shallow V while bird is in flight.

- **DISTAL BAND**
A strip of color near the end of the tail, end of wing, or on the lower part of the leg.

- **DIURNAL**
Birds that feed and are active during the day.

- **ECLIPSE PLUMAGE**
Dull-colored plumage, similar to that of the female, into which many male ducks briefly molt in summer.

- **EXTIRPATED**
Exterminated or destroyed from a part of a species range.

- **EYE RING**
A circle around the eye, usually of a contrasting color.

- **EYE STRIPE OR EYEBROW**
See Supercilium.

- **FIELD MARKS**
Plumage or anatomical features of a bird that help to distinguish it from other similar species.

- **FLASHMARK**
Color or marking on plumage that is visible only when the bird is in flight.

- **FLEDGE**
The act of a young bird (nestling) leaving the nest. Also fledging.

- **FLEDGLING**
A young bird that has feathers and is old enough to have left the nest but is still dependent on adult birds for care and feeding.

- **GONYS**
A ridge on the lower mandible of a gull that causes the midline to appear angled. Sometimes shows a red patch during breeding season.

- **GORGET**
A small iridescent patch on the throat of a hummingbird.

- **GULAR SAC**
A large or small pouch in the upper throat that helps a bird regulate body temperature and sometimes holds undigested food. In a few species, such as the Magnificent Frigatebird, the pouch greatly expands for courtship display.

- **HAWKING**
The act of catching prey, usually insects, in flight. Generally done with the bill. Typical of flycatchers.

- **HERONRY**
(Rookery) The colonial nesting site for herons, egrets, and ibises.

- **HINDNECK**
The bird's nape or back of the neck.

- **HUMERAL**
The patch of feathers overlying the bone near the upperwing or shoulder area.

- **JIZZ**
The abstract combination of a bird's posture, plumage pattern, shape, size, and behavior that allows an experienced birder to recognize a species instantly without further examination.

- **LAMELLAE**
Miniature ridges inside the bill of a duck or water bird that resemble the teeth of a comb and serve as a strainer during feeding.

- **LARDER**
A place where a shrike impales and stores its prey on sharp branches or wire.

- **LEK**
A communal gathering place during breeding season where males of some species of birds display to attract the females. It contains numerous territories, each guarded by a different male.

- **LORES**
Space between the eyes and the base of the upper part of the bill on the side of the bird's face.

- **MALAR**
Refers to the cheek area along the side of the face. Field mark here is called malar mark or malar stripe.

- **MANDIBLE**
The lower half of the bill. Maxilla is the upper half; both halves collectively are called mandibles.

• **MANTLE**
The feathers covering the back and upperwing coverts; feathers of the back and folded wings.

• **MANUS**
The portion of a bird's wing that corresponds to the hand of a human. The fused bones of the palm and reduced digits bear the primary feathers and the alula.

• **MELANISTIC**
A bird that has a surplus of dark pigment in its plumage.

• **MIMIC THRUSH**
A member of the family Mimidae, which includes thrashers, catbirds, and mockingbirds.

• **MORPH**
When birds of the same species have two or more different colored plumages, that are independent of season, sex, age, or breeding. Color phases may or may not be related to range and climate.

• **NEOTROPICAL**
The New World tropical region that encompasses the northern portion of the Mexican rain forest and the Caribbean islands, and extends to the nontropical regions of South America.

• **NEW WORLD**
Earth's Western Hemisphere; includes North, South, and Central America.

• **NOCTURNAL**
Birds that feed and are active at night.

• **NON-PASSERINE**
Any of the birds that are not Passerines, which are the songbirds or perching birds. Includes loons, waterfowl, owls, shorebirds, hawks, woodpeckers, and doves.

• **NUCHAL PATCH**
A patch of contrasting color located on the back of the bird's neck or nape.

• **OCCIPITAL PATCH**
A patch of color located high on the back of the head. Higher on the head than the nuchal patch.

• **OCCIPUT**
The area on the back of a bird's head between the nape and the crown.

• **OCOTILLO**
A spiny desert shrub with red flower clusters at the tips of its branches.

• **OLD WORLD**
Earth's Eastern Hemisphere: Europe, Asia, and Africa.

• **ORBITAL RING**
See Eye Ring.

• **PALEARCTIC**
Faunal region surrounded by the Atlantic, Arctic, and Pacific Oceans; encompasses Asia north of the Himalayas, Europe, and Africa north of the Sahara desert.

• **PASSERINES**
Any of the birds belonging to the order Passeriformes, which comprise more than fifty percent of the world's birds. Highly evolved, these birds are able to sing and have three forward-pointing toes adapted for perching.

• **PEEP**
Birder's name for a group of small, similar-looking sandpipers; may have been derived from their high-pitched calls.

• **PELAGIC**
Birds that spend most of their time at sea and rarely are seen from shore.

• **PIEBALD**
Plumage that shows two contrasting colors.

• **PISHING**
Sound produced by birders to attract birds; made by clinching the teeth together and

forcing air out through the teeth and lips to create a noise that sounds like *pish-pish-pish*.

• POLYANDROUS
When female bird has two or more mates; female often larger, has brighter plumage, and defends her territory. Male of the species usually incubates and tends young.

• POLYGAMOUS
When both male and female of a species may take two or more mates.

• POLYGYNOUS
When a male bird takes two or more mates.

• POSTOCULAR STRIPE
A line that leads from behind the bird's eye to the auricular or ear patch.

• PRECOCIAL
Term for young birds that hatch with their eyes open, are down-covered, and are able to leave the nest within two days of hatching. These hatchlings may be either partially or not at all dependent on the parents for care and feeding.

• PRIMARIES
One of two sets of flight feathers, or remiges, located distally to the secondaries and joined to the manus of the wing.

• PROMISCUOUS
Birds, male or female, that come together solely for mating purposes and leave within a few hours to mate with other birds.

• PYRIFORM
Pear-shaped; often used to describe shape of egg.

• RAPTORS
A name applied to birds of prey – the hawks, falcons, eagles, kites, and owls.

• RECTRICES
The principal feathers that make up the tail. They range in number from eight to twenty-four, but the average in songbirds is twelve.

• REMIGES
Refers to flight feathers – primaries, secondaries, and tertials.

• RIPARIAN
Located on or near a river bank, stream bank, or other body of water.

• SCAPULARS
Feathers joined to the shoulder area of the bird and covering the top of the folded wing.

• SECONDARIES
One of two sets of flight feathers located between the body and the primaries and joined to the part of the wing that corresponds to the forearm of a human.

• SEMIALTRICIAL
Term for young birds that hatch with eyes either open or closed, are down-covered, and are incapable of leaving the nest; fed by parents.

• SEMICOLONIAL
Nesting pattern in which several birds of the same species nest close to one another, often within sight of each other's nests and do not behave aggressively toward one another.

• SEMIPRECOCIAL
Term for young birds that hatch with eyes open, are down-covered, and able to leave the nest soon after hatching, but remain in nest and are fed by parents.

• SKYLARKING
Elaborate territorial display flight given by a male songbird. It sings and often flutters in circles before swooping back to earth.

• SPATULATE
A long rounded spoonlike shape; sometimes used to describe bill or tail.

- **SPECULUM**
A small area of contrasting iridescent feathers located on the secondary feathers of the wings. Often seen in ducks.

- **SQUEAKING**
Sound produced by birders to attract birds; made by pursing the lips tightly together and sucking air in to make a high-pitched sound. This can be amplified by placing the lips on the back of the hand and sucking in a kissing fashion.

- **SUPERCILIUM**
Line above each eye; an eyebrow. Also called a superciliary stripe.

- **SUPERSPECIES**
Closely related species that are often separated from each other by geographic barriers. Without these barriers the two species probably would interbreed and become one.

- **SYMPATRIC**
Birds that inhabit the same range but remain distinct and separate species.

- **TAIGA**
Subarctic coniferous forests.

- **TARSUS**
The top of the foot behind the toes, often called the shank. Usually either bare or covered with scales, plates, or sometimes feathers.

- **TERTIALS**
The group of secondary feathers that are closest to the body; often a contrasting color.

- **TIPPING-UP**
Method of surface feeding by a duck, goose, or swan in which it raises its tail and dips its bill, head, and neck into the water. See Dabbling.

- **TOTIPALMATE**
All four toes joined together by webbing.

- **TYMPANI**
(Tympaniform membranes) Valves in the vocal organ of a bird that produce sound.

- **UNDERPARTS**
The plumage and coloring on the breast, belly, sides, flanks, and undertail coverts.

- **UPPERPARTS**
The plumage and coloring on the nape, back, shoulders, rump, and upper part of tail.

- **VANE**
Contoured flight feather that acts as a propeller. It consists of a central shaft surrounded by an inner and outer web.

- **VENT**
The opening of the cloaca, or anus; sometimes refers to a contrasting patch of feathers in this area.

- **WATTLE**
Fleshy piece of brightly colored skin that hangs from the lower bill; associated with turkeys and some chickens.

- **WILDTYPE**
A biological term based in genetics that describes the form that most individuals in a wild population take; description includes shape, color, patterns, and size.

- **WINGSTRIP**
A distinct line on the wing, usually of a contrasting color.

- **WINTER PLUMAGE**
(Basic plumage) Seasonal alteration in a bird's appearance produced by the fall molt.

INDEX

ACKNOWLEDGMENTS

The author would like to dedicate this book: *In memory of my father, Fred J. Alsop, Jr., who first took me to the woods and opened my eyes to the wonders of nature. Many thanks to my wife, Cathi Alsop, for her support during the writing of this book and for editing the final proofs of the range maps.*

The publishers would like to thank: Ron Austing for photo coordination; Kristi Tipton for research on species profiles and range maps; Sandra Porter, Kristy Cuccini, Kelly Buford, and Anne Esquivel for species profile research; Jenny Cromie and Nina Costopoulos for editorial assistance; Holly Cross and R. Clay White for copyediting; Denise McIntyre and Rebecca Benton for proofreading; Marianne Thomas, Melissa Givens, George Griswold III, Jim Larussa, Will McCalley, Rick Tucker, and Christana Laycock for graphic assistance; Catherine O'Hare, Michelle Boylan, Taylor Rogers, Brad Reisinger, and Beth Brown for administrative support; and Charles (Chuck) Hunter of the US Fish and Wildlife Service, John C. Sterling, and Joseph DiCostanzo of the American Museum of Natural History for manuscript review and commentary.

PICTURE CREDITS

Abbreviations: b = bottom, t = top, c = center, l = left, r = right, m = male, f = female.

Plumage illustrations: Simone End, Carl Salter.

Silhouettes: Terence Clark/Housewren 18–19

Profile illustrations: Svetlana Belotserkovskaya 428, 444f, 516f, 531f, 533f.

Penny Costopoulos 45.

Ernie Eldredge 10c, 11c,46, 47, 48, 56, 57, 61, 203, 204.

Alice Pederson 12, 13, 47, 283, 320, 519f & m.

Inside photographs: Fred J. Alsop III 23tr, 71m, 159, 239m, 429f, 549.

Ron Austing 20lr, 22, 23cl, 24t, 26c. 27t & c, 37, 72, 73f & m, 74, 75, 77, 79, 80, 82, 85, 90, 92, 98f & m, 100f & m, 101m, 102f & m, 104m, 105m, 107m, 109m, 111f & m, 112f & m, 113m, 114f & m, 116m, 117f & m, 118m, 124f & m, 125f & m, 126f & m, 127f & m, 128f & m, 129f & m, 130f, 131f & m, 132, 134f & m, 135, 137, 138, 141, 143, 146f & m, 147f & m, 150, 153f & m, 156m, 162f & m, 164f, 168, 169, 170, 172, 173,178, 181f & m, 183, 185, 190, 195, 196, 198, 200, 201, 205, 210, 221, 230, 236, 245, 252, 254, 263, 282, 288, 291, 292, 293, 297, 298, 299, 302, 303, 304m, 305, 307, 308, 309, 310, 311, 313, 314, 315, 317, 319, 323f & m, 324m, 325f, 326f, 328f & m, 329f & m, 331, 332f & m, 334, 337, 338, 342, 343f & m, 344, 346, 348, 350, 351, 359, 365, 366, 367, 368, 371, 373, 375, 378, 382, 386, 388, 390, 393, 399, 401f & m, 402, 407, 409, 411, 412, 415f & m, 416m, 419f, 423, 426, 428, 432f & m, 434, 435, 437, 438, 446, 448, 449, 450, 452, 453, 454, 455f & m, 456f & m, 457m, 458m, 459f & m, 460f & m, 462m, 464m, 465, 466, 467, 468m, 471, 473f & m, 474, 475, 477, 478, 479f & m, 481f & m, 482f & m, 484f & m, 486f &

m, 489f & m, 490, 491, 492, 494, 495, 496, 498, 499, 501, 504, 506, 507, 509, 510, 512f & m, 514f & m, 515m, 520f, 521f & m, 524m, 525m, 526f, 527f & m, 528, 532m, 534f & m, 535f & m, 536m, 542f & m, 544f & m, 546f & m, 550f & m, 551f & m, 552f.

Rick & Nora Bowers 42, 53, 88, 96, 109f, 123m, 156f, 241, 286, 300, 301, 322, 347, 348f, 392, 397, 500, 520m.

Cornell Laboratory of Ornithology L. Page Brown 139; Lang Elliott 547f.

Mike Danzenbaker 40, 49, 50, 51, 52, 60, 64, 69, 94, 130m, 166, 176, 180f & m, 182, 187, 194, 199, 206, 217, 218, 219, 222, 229, 234, 248, 258, 259, 266, 284, 290, 294, 295, 306, 318, 325m, 330, 336, 345, 353, 381, 383, 385, 389, 395, 413, 450, 433m, 442, 443, 464f, 485, 517m, 531f, 538f & m, 548.

DK Picture Library 24b, 26t & b, 151, 545f; Dennis Avon 198m, 296, 439; Simon Battersby 10b; Peter Chadwick 23cr, 25t & c; Mike Dunning 133; Frank Greenaway 144, 149; Cyril Laubscher 81, 86, 89, 163m, 189, 429m, 552m; Karl & Steve Maslowski 357, 362, 394, 404, 414f, 419m, 421f, 508, 526m; Jane Miller 171; Kim Taylor 103f & m; Jerry Young 145f, 304f.

Frank Lane Picture Agency/ Hans Dieter Brandl 174; Richard Brooks 539f; S. C. Brown 30; H. Hautala 340; John Hawkins 59; Steve McCutcheon 478f; Mark Newman 175; P. Reynolds 281; Roger Tidman 87; John Tinning 108m; R. Van Nostrand; Roger Wilmshurst 108f, 152f & m, 193, 431; Martin Withers.

Kevin T. Karlson 35, 63, 71f, 83, 95, 97, 99m, 104f, 105f, 106f & m, 110f & m, 113f, 115f & m, 118f, 122f, 123f, 136, 158f & m, 160f, 167, 188, 191, 192, 232, 239f, 242, 256, 265, 271, 275, 363, 374, 414m, 445, 451f & m, 457f, 458f, 476, 497f, 502, 505, 516f.

Naturescape Images/Julian R. Hough 255.

Brian E. Small 53, 54, 58, 68, 70, 76, 78, 84, 91, 99f, 101f, 107f, 116f, 119m,

140, 142, 148, 155m, 160m, 161, 163f, 165, 177, 184, 186, 197, 209, 211, 212, 214, 215, 216, 220, 224, 227, 228, 237f & m, 246, 257, 268, 273, 287, 312, 324f, 327f & m, 333f & m, 335, 339, 341, 352, 354, 355, 356, 358, 360, 369, 370, 372, 376, 379, 380, 384, 387f & m, 391, 396, 400, 403, 415, 416f, 420f & m, 421m, 422, 429, 433f, 436, 440, 444m, 447, 461f & m, 462f, 463f & m, 468f, 469f & m, 470f & m, 472f & m, 480f & m, 483m, 487f & m, 488f, 493, 497m, 503, 511, 513f & m, 515f, 516m, 518f, 522f & m, 523f & m, 524f, 533m, 536f, 537f & m, 540, 541f & m, 543f & m, 545m.

Tom Vezo 29, 31, 32, 34, 36, 38, 39, 41, 45, 65, 66, 67, 93, 119f, 120f & m, 121f & m, 122m, 145m, 155f, 157f & m, 179f & m, 207, 213, 225, 226, 233, 238f & m, 243, 244, 247, 249, 250, 251, 253, 260, 261, 262, 264, 266, 269, 272, 278, 279, 280, 361, 376, 408, 410, 417f & m, 418f & m, 427, 441, 483f, 488m, 518m, 529, 530f & m.

Vireo/ R. & N. Bowers 11tc; 406; R. J. Chandler 231f; H. Clarke 321; Rob Curtis 478m; R. & S. Day 525f; B. de Lange 235; H. & J. Eriksen 547m; W. Greene 154; C. H. Greenewalt 276; T. Laman 62, 506; A. Morris 270, 531m; J. P. Myers 223; R. L. Pitman 203, 285, 289; D. Roby & K. Brink 277; K. Schafer 44, 240; D. Tipling 55, 231m, 398, 539m; F. Truslow 349; Tom Vezo 208; Doug Wechsler 274, 364f & m.

Richard Wagner 326m.

Kenny Walters 23b, 25b.